LEGAL FOUNDATIONS OF
INTERNATIONAL MONETARY STABILITY

LEGAL FOUNDATIONS OF INTERNATIONAL MONETARY STABILITY

Rosa María Lastra

Senior Lecturer in International Financial and Monetary Law
Centre for Commercial Law Studies
Queen Mary, University of London

OXFORD

UNIVERSITY PRESS

OXFORD

UNIVERSITY PRESS

Great Clarendon Street, Oxford OX2 6DP

Oxford University Press is a department of the University of Oxford.
It furthers the University's objective of excellence in research, scholarship,
and education by publishing worldwide in

Oxford New York

Auckland Cape Town Dar es Salaam Hong Kong Karachi
Kuala Lumpur Madrid Melbourne Mexico City Nairobi
New Delhi Shanghai Taipei Toronto

With offices in

Argentina Austria Brazil Chile Czech Republic France Greece
Guatemala Hungary Italy Japan Poland Portugal Singapore
South Korea Switzerland Thailand Turkey Ukraine Vietnam

Oxford is a registered trade mark of Oxford University Press
in the UK and in certain other countries

Published in the United States
by Oxford University Press Inc., New York

British Library Cataloguing in Publication Data

Data available

Library of Congress Cataloging-in-Publication Data

Lastra, Rosa María.
Legal foundations of international monetary stability / Rosa María Lastra.
p. cm.
Includes bibliographical references and index.
1. Money—Law and legislation. 2. Banks and banking, Central—Law and legislation.
3. Foreign exchange—Law and legislation. 4. Money—Law and legislation—
European Union countries. 5. Banks and banking, Central—Law and legislation—
European Union countries. 6. Foreign exchange—Law and legislation—European
Union countries. I. Title.
K4431.L37 2006
343'.032—dc22   2006010327

Typeset by RefineCatch Limited, Bungay, Suffolk
Printed in Great Britain
on acid-free paper by
Biddles Ltd, King's Lynn

ISBN 0–19–926934–3   978–0–19–926934–1

1 3 5 7 9 10 8 6 4 2

For Mats, Alejandro, Eric, Roberto, and Anna

FOREWORD

Some fifty or so years ago, say around 1960, the structure of our financial systems was much simpler than it is today. Financial institutions within each country were mainly constrained and segmented in the functions that they could undertake, eg specializing in insurance, mortgage lending, retail banking, fund management, and so on. These intermediaries were, almost invariably, owned by residents of the same country. Within each country, what was important was the institutional history and legal status within that same single country.

There were, of course, large-scale international transactions, even though capital account transfers then remained mainly under official control. The international monetary system, of pegged but adjustable exchange rates, colloquially known as Bretton Woods, was then beginning to creak, but the central role of the US dollar as reserve currency and of the international financial institutions, such as the International Monetary Fund, the Bank for International Settlements and the World Bank, as the guardians of that system, remained central.

Over the past fifty years this simpler structure has dissolved and been reformulated in a much fuzzier and more complicated fashion. Within the main developed countries, the functional divisions between kinds of intermediaries have become blurred. Any financial intermediary can enter any of these various business lines. In some European countries universal banking had been the norm for decades; now this has spread more widely, it has even become common in the USA where the Glass-Steagall Act was superseded by the Gramm-Leach-Bliley Act. Meanwhile the correspondence between national banks and national ownership of these same banks fell away (though more or less depending on local protectionist tendencies), in the face of growing cross-border competition.

Much financial intermediation has become global in operation, particularly as nation states removed exchange controls on capital flows, one facet of the shift back from control-and-command economic systems to market-driven economies. As a result, capital flows over the foreign exchanges came to outweigh current account transactions. In the process the Bretton Woods system was blown away.

The resulting non-system of floating exchange rates was, however, far more volatile than had been expected, nor it was comfortable for many nations trying to harmonize their economic systems. This was among the reasons why the countries in the European Community sought to move towards, and then to attain, a single currency, to form an island of monetary harmony in an otherwise choppy sea of floating rates.

But this has brought yet another level of complexity to the monetary scene. Rather than two levels of institutional, operational, legal and structural detail, we now have three—national, regional (in effect European), and international. It is not only complex to understand and to analyse, but it also remains subject to constant change. A dramatic example is to be found in the outcome of the proposed European Constitution. This was perceived as likely to have a significant influence on the EU when Rosa Lastra began writing; when she finished it appeared mortally wounded by the 'No' votes in the French and Dutch referenda.

In order to make sense of this complicated, evolving, multi-layered system, an observer now needs many interrelated skills. These include a knowledge of the historical and political pressures that have shaped, and continue to shape, current institutions, of the economic factors that help to determine how, and why, the various systems and institutions function as they do, and of the legal processes, both formal and informal, that fix the rules of the game. It is not possible to explain the international financial system from the standpoint of a single discipline, or from a single viewpoint.

Although Rosa Lastra writes primarily as a legal scholar, her understanding of the financial system has been greatly informed by her thorough understanding of the economic issues involved. She has worked in the IMF, has a close and intimate knowledge of many countries, notably Spain, Sweden, the UK, and the US, and is a committed European, serving, for example, on the European Shadow Financial Regulatory Committee. She combines in full the interdisciplinary skills and multi-country viewpoint that is essential to give a comprehensive and lively explanation of the *Legal Foundations of International Monetary Stability*.

This is, as its title indicates, first of all a legal book—and my colleague Geoffrey Miller, in his companion Foreword, will focus on this—but it is much, much more than just a legal text. This book places the legal framework within the context of the economic, historical, and political developments that have helped to bring about that same framework—and of course the causality runs simultaneously in all directions, since the rules of the game help to determine the subsequent economic evolution of the system.

So the book can be read, and enjoyed, at many levels simultaneously, as history, analysis, public policy, and reference point. It is truly a major work of serious scholarship. If anyone wants to know how the legal structures of the world's various overlapping monetary systems are set up (and how and why) in the first decade of the twenty-first century, this book is the place to turn.

Charles Goodhart
London
December 2005

FOREWORD

In recent years the architecture of financial institutions has undergone profound, even wrenching change. Financial markets have evolved at a dizzying pace. The derivatives market, which hardly existed twenty years ago, is now a key part of the infrastructure of modern finance. Organized securities exchanges have blossomed into significant competitors to financial intermediaries in the formation and distribution of capital around the world. In one key economy, the United States, the banking industry has been transformed by massive consolidations and a wide-ranging expansion in the types of business they are permitted to undertake. Europe appears poised to undergo a similar wave of bank mergers and consolidations. Much of Europe today operates with a common currency—a development that would have been virtually inconceivable a few decades ago.

Mirroring these changes in markets has been the development of a new regulatory infrastructure. At the national level, regulatory authorities have undergone reorganizations in response to marketplace developments or perceived institutional failings. The financial regulatory systems in Japan, the United Kingdom and the United States—among many others—are fundamentally different today than they were only a few years ago. Central banks, once the de facto captives of political authorities in many countries, have gained significant independence and today operate as centres of autonomy in the management of domestic financial systems. The European Central Bank takes this autonomy to yet a new level. Equally remarkable has been the development of regulation at the transnational and international levels. The IMF exercises an increasingly important influence on financial institutions worldwide. And the Basel Capital Adequacy Guidelines, although lacking the force of positive law, have been perhaps the most successful international regulatory initiative in history.

These developments in financial markets and legal regulatory structures are so closely connected as to be part of a single phenomenon. The marketplace changes would not have occurred—at least would not have taken the shape they did assume—without the regulatory developments; and the changes in regulation are themselves the product of marketplace innovation and expansion. The apparent success of the system in offering efficient financial services in an environment characterized by robust institutions and monetary stability is surely due to the influence of both markets and law working in tandem.

To date, legal commentators have focused only on parts of the process, and have often undertaken their analyses from a doctrinal perspective that fails to provide an economic context for the phenomena they seek to explain. In this volume, Rosa Lastra provides a much-needed, comprehensive, timely, and economically sophisticated overview of international financial regulation. The book is remarkable for the breadth of perspective it offers and for its seamless melding of historical, economic, and legal ideas. It represents a significant contribution to the theoretical literature on financial architecture and regulation. It is destined to be an essential reference for lawmakers, central bankers, bank regulators, and legal and policy planning staff in internationally active financial institutions. The coming years will no doubt witness changes in financial markets even more dramatic than those we have seen heretofore. This book provides both a resource for understanding the changes as they occur and an invaluable guide for coping with the challenges that lie ahead.

Geoffrey Miller
New York
January 2006

PREFACE

The genesis of this book can be traced back to the early 1990s. At the time, I was working at the Legal Department of the International Monetary Fund in Washington DC. The break-up of the Soviet Union in December 1991 and the collapse of communism gave rise to a wave of monetary legal reforms, with the establishment of central banks, new currencies, and a commercial banking system based upon the principles of a market economy. The Maastricht Treaty on European Union, signed in 1992, laid out the legal framework for the creation of a single currency and of a European Central Bank. These momentous historical events rekindled the interest in the study of the legal framework of money and finance, and encouraged me to analyse this rather novel legal field.

Monetary law is characterized by the existence of overlapping jurisdictions. This is particularly clear in the European Union, where national developments in monetary and financial law overlap with developments at the EU level and with international developments and obligations imposed by membership of international organizations. A recurrent topic in my study is the juxtaposition of areas of jurisdiction: national supervision versus supranational monetary policy, national supervision versus international markets.

This book analyses in a systematic and comprehensive manner how national, European, and international developments in monetary law and related aspects of financial regulation have dramatically changed this dynamic field of law over the past decades. At the national level (Part I of the book), the central bank is typically the key monetary institution in a country. At the European level (Part II of the book), the European System of Central Banks is the central monetary institution for the member states that have adopted the euro as their single currency. At the international level (Part III), the International Monetary Fund is the central international monetary institution. There is a certain symmetry among the three parts of the book, each one of them commencing with a historical chapter, then analysing the institutional framework, and ending up with a consideration of the 'financial architecture' (financial supervision, regulation, and crisis management).

In examining the legal foundations of international monetary stability, it is important to emphasize that the law typically reflects a notion of monetary stability that focuses primarily on its internal dimension (ie, price stability, keeping inflation under control), while it tends to refer to the external dimension of monetary stability (ie, the stability of the currency vis-à-vis other currencies, which is, in turn, influenced by the choice of exchange regime) in rather ambiguous terms. Article 111 of the EC Treaty exemplifies the ambiguity that surrounds the conduct of exchange rate policy in the Community, a task which is divided between the Council and the ECB under a notoriously unclear set of provisions.

The 'stability culture' is itself a modern phenomenon. Indeed, as I explain in Chapter 2, the emphasis on price stability is a development that needs to be understood in a historical context; that provided by the country experiences, economic policies, and economic thinking that prevailed in the second half of the twentieth century.

The pursuit of financial stability is increasingly seen as a public good; however, one which is difficult to define in 'positive' terms. It is only by references to crises, that a consensus emerges with regard to the understanding of its 'negative' definition (presence of instability or absence of stability).

From a methodological point of view, my approach is mainly public international law (regulatory rather than transactional) as well as law and economics. As acknowledged, public international law provides rules that govern relationships between states. My reference to 'law and economics' indicates a joint substantial consideration (legal and economic) of monetary and financial issues. It is therefore different from the traditional 'economic analysis of law' literature, which applies micro-economic tools, such as cost-benefit analysis, to the study of the law. I believe that the legal approach provides order, clarity, and rationalization to the study of money and finance. Stigler wrote in his *Memoirs of an Unregulated Economist*: 'One cannot communicate effectively with other people unless one uses the language to which they are accustomed.' The challenge remains, in my opinion, to establish such an effective interdisciplinary communication in the field of social sciences.

Two main developments affecting the legal framework of central banks are analysed in depth in the first part of the book: the issue of independence and corresponding accountability on the one hand and the transfer of prudential supervisory responsibilities from the central bank to a separate agency on the other hand. My study aims to provide a source of reference for national developments in monetary law. Though there are frequent references to the legal and regulatory solutions adopted in the US and other jurisdictions in the developed world, I also take into account the experience in developing countries.

The European Central Bank is the institution at the centre of the European System of Central Banks in charge of the management of the single currency.

It is an independent institution enshrined in the framework of Community law. Despite the oneness of monetary policy in the European Union, this exclusive competence is geographically limited to a part of the Community: the Member States that have adopted the euro. These Member States have surrendered the key component of monetary sovereignty: *ius cudendae monetae*, the prerogative of issuing money (with the exception of coins).

The differentiated integration and the bewildering complexity that characterize the EMU structure are the subject of Part II of the book. The asymmetries between monetary policy and fiscal policy and between monetary policy and financial regulation and supervision are an inherent source of tension in the system. The combination of centralized and decentralized competences generates points of friction, which become particularly evident in times of crisis. The European Court of Justice will continue to be called upon to clarify legal issues (as it has already done in the OLAF case and its judgment of 14 July 2004 concerning the 'non-application' of the excessive deficit procedure to France and Germany) though judicial activism should not be expected to sort out the problems of economic policy coordination.

The European project of integration was born out of hopes and fears: the fear of France for Germany and the fear of Germany for itself, the fears of wars and divisions, and the hopes of peace and prosperity, bringing forces together to build a better future. And those hopes and fears remain at the heart of any further integration.

The Treaty establishing a Constitution for Europe signed in Rome on 29 October 2004 was thrown into a legal limbo following the negative results of the referenda in France and the Netherlands in 2005. The suspension of the ratification process (the decision of the European Council Brussels Summit on 16–17 June 2005 to extend the ratification period and allow a time of reflection) and the resulting loss of momentum towards unification do not equate, however, to the total abandonment of the proposed Constitution. The text of the Constitutional Treaty remains a legal instrument of value to refer to, also with a view to its possible entry into force or the taking over of parts of it in other Treaty texts later on, even though it does not propose any fundamental changes in the functioning of EMU. My study provides 'dual referencing' (to both EC Treaty and the proposed EU Constitution) with regard to the primary law applicable to EMU.

The third part of this book analyses the law governing international monetary relations. The challenges that the international monetary and financial system faces in the twenty-first century are very different from the challenges the Bretton Woods institutions—the International Monetary Fund and the World Bank—confronted when they started operations in Washington DC in 1946.

These challenges, particularly the ones encountered by the International Monetary Fund, are examined in Chapters 13 and 14.

The unique nature of the responsibilities of the Fund, the economic character of most of its functions and operations, the idiosyncratic and rather opaque terminology that applies to its activities and financial structure (derided by Keynes as 'Cherokee' language), and the specific knowledge required to understand the legal aspects of those activities (a knowledge that is traditionally the reserve of Fund lawyers and of a few academics who venture into its study) explain the relatively thin body of doctrine dealing with the complex issues of public international monetary law.

The worldwide change from fixed to floating exchange rates, following the collapse of the par value regime, also signified a more profound change in the nature of the IMF. There was a shift in emphasis from being primarily an international monetary institution focusing on issues such as exchange rate stability and convertibility, to becoming an international financial institution with a broader array of responsibilities, encompassing not only monetary issues, but also other financial issues, such as the regulation and supervision of banking and capital markets, financial reform, debt restructuring, and others. The evolution of the role of the Fund over the past three decades has affected the practice of conditionality and the exercise of surveillance.

An analogy can be made between the role of the central bank at the national level and the role of the IMF at the international level. A central bank is typically entrusted by national law to maintain monetary stability in the domestic jurisdiction. The IMF is the international institution entrusted by an international treaty (the IMF Articles of Agreement) to promote stability in the international monetary order. The evolution of national central banks in recent years has been characterized by the increasing importance and attention given to the goal of financial stability, as part of the mandate of the central bank (with or without supervisory responsibilities). By analogy, the interpretation of the mandate of the IMF (according to the broad enumeration of goals in Article I of the Articles of Agreement) has been expanded over the last years and the pursuit of international financial stability has become an important objective in the international financial architecture.

The IMF is not only the international monetary institution par excellence; it is also at the centre of the international financial system. This central role is key to understanding the legal framework for the prevention and resolution of international financial crises and the singular position of the Fund in sovereign debt negotiations.

The process of international financial standard setting (the growth of soft law) that I critically examine in the last chapter of the book is a key feature of the evolving 'international financial architecture'. The IMF, however, is not the only international financial standard setter, nor is it the most relevant one. This regulatory function is shared by a number of formal international organizations, informal groupings and fora of an international character (with the Basel Committee on Banking Supervision and other Committees that have grown under the auspices of the Bank for International Settlements, playing a significant role), professional associations, and other entities. However, the IMF is uniquely placed to monitor the compliance with standards through its function of surveillance and through its assessment of the health of the financial sector (via the Financial Sector Assessment Programme, FSAP, and the Reports on the Observance of Standards and Codes, ROSCs), and to provide countries with the incentive to observe those standards through the design of conditionality.

The final revisions of this manuscript were completed on 6 December 2005, though it has been possible to take account of a few subsequent developments.

The process of writing a book is characterized by a certain solitude. Hence, it is with great gratitude that I acknowledge the feedback, advice, and support received from colleagues and friends in the course of its preparation. I must thank, first and foremost, Charles Goodhart and René Smits for their exceptionally close readings of the manuscript and for their insightful suggestions and criticisms. Harald Benink, Lee Buchheit, Forrest Capie, Sam Cross, François Gianviti, Sean Hagan, Karel Lannoo, María Nieto, Pierre Panchaud, Charles Proctor, Antonio Sainz de Vicuña, Dirk Schoenmaker, Geoffrey Wood, and Chiara Zilioli read parts of the manuscript or earlier drafts and provided valuable comments. I am especially grateful to Geoffrey Miller, with whom I developed some of the ideas that I present in Chapter 2. Apostolos Gkoutzinis and Rodrigo Olivares Caminal were competent and efficient research assistants. My editors and publishers at Oxford University Press encouraged my writing with courtesy and patience. Three anonymous referees, Charles Proctor, and Charles Goodhart reviewed the original book proposal at the request of Oxford University Press. My own limited knowledge of these fascinating issues has been nurtured and challenged by discussions with colleagues in the European Shadow Financial Regulatory Committee, the London Financial Regulation Seminar, the Monetary Committee of the International Law Association, IESE Business School (in particular, Jordi Canals), and the Centre for Commercial Law Studies, Queen Mary, University of London (in particular, Joseph Norton). To all of them I express my gratitude. Errors and limitations are, of course, mine alone.

Over the years, my students in Columbia University in the City of New York and in the University of London have been a constant source of inspiration. And so have been my mentors. Here again, I must show my deepest appreciation to

Charles Goodhart, truly an intellectual father. His teachings were unique, as are his writings and his persona. I also thank and remember with great fondness Gaspar Ariño (who encouraged me to explore new legal horizons), Stephen Breyer, Howell Jackson, and Hal Scott.

My stint at the Legal Department of the International Monetary Fund under the direction of François Gianviti gave me the opportunity to acquire a practical perspective with regard to the functioning of the international monetary system, getting to know lawyers and economists specializing in this field. A special tribute goes to the memories of Sir Joseph Gold and Manuel Guitián, since the conversations I held with them sparked off lines of thought and contributed in no small way to clarifying my own ideas. Working with the legal team of the Federal Reserve Bank of New York under the direction of Tom Baxter in an international case involving monetary issues was also a most formative experience.

A debt is always owed to one's parents and here I must thank my own for their dedication to me and to my siblings throughout the years. And last, but not least, very special thanks to my husband, Mats Kummelstedt, and to our four children, Alejandro, Eric, Roberto, and Anna, since this book would never have been completed without their unfailing support, their generosity, their wit, and their joy. To them I dedicate my work.

Rosa María Lastra
London
8 December 2005

CONTENTS—SUMMARY

CONTENTS

Contents

TABLE OF CASES

TABLE OF LEGISLATION

EU LEGISLATION

RULES, STATUTES, DECISIONS, AND RESOLUTIONS OF INTERNATIONAL ORGANIZATIONS AND OTHER INTERNATIONAL FORA

LIST OF ABBREVIATIONS

AML/CFT	Anti-Money Laundering and Countering the Financing of Terrorism
BCCI	Bank of Credit and Commerce International
BIS	Bank for International Settlements
CAC	Counterfeit Analysis Centre
CACs	Collective Action Clauses
CAMEL	Capital adequacy, Asset quality, Management, Earnings and Liquidity
CAP	Common Agricultural Policy
CCF	Compensatory Financing Facility
CCFF	Compensatory and Contingency Financing Facility
CCL	Contingent Credit Line
CCT	Common Customs Tariff
CEBS	Committee of European Banking Supervisors
CEIOPS	Committee of European Insurance and Occupational Pensions Supervisors
CESR	Committee of European Securities Regulators
CFF	Compensatory Financing Facility
CFP	Pacific Financial Community
CFR	Code of Federal Regulations
CHIPS	Clearing House Inter-bank Payments System
CSF	Currency Stabilisation Fund
CPSS	Committee on Payment and Settlement Systems
DDSR	Debt and Debt Service Reduction
DVP	Delivery Versus Payment
DWL	Discount Window Lending
EAGGF	European Agricultural Guidance and Guarantee Fund
EBRD	European Bank of Reconstruction and Development
EC	European Community
ECA	Economic Cooperation Administration
ECB	European Central Bank
ECOFIN	Economic and Financial Affairs Council
ECOWAS	Economic Community of West African States
ECU	European Currency Unit
EEC	European Economic Community
EFC	Economic and Financial Committee
EFF	Extended Fund Facility
EFSA	European Financial Services Authority
EMAC	Committee on Economic and Monetary Affairs

EMCF	European Monetary Cooperation Fund
EMI	European Monetary Institute
EMS	European Monetary System
EMU	European Monetary Union
EPU	European Payments Union
ERDF	European Regional Development Fund
ERISA	Employee Retirement Income Security Act
ERM	European Exchange Rate Mechanism
ESAF	Enhanced Structural Adjustment Facility
ESC	European Securities Committee
ESCB	European System of Central Banks
ESF	European Social Fund
ESFRC	European Shadow Financial Regulatory Committee
EU	European Union
FATF	Financial Action Task Force on Money Laundering
FDICIA	Federal Deposit Insurance Corporation Improvement Act
FIFG	Financial Instruments for Fisheries Guidance
FIRREA	Financial Institutions Reform, Recovery and Enforcement Act
FRBNY	Federal Reserve Bank of New York
FOMC	Federal Open Market Committee
FSA	Financial Services Authority
FSAP	Financial Sector Assessment Program
FSAP	Financial Services Action Plan
FSC	Financial Services Committee
FSF	Financial Stability Forum
FSSA	Financial System Stability Assessment
GAB	General Agreement to Borrow
GATT	General Agreement on Tariffs and Trade
GDP	Gross Domestic Product
GDDS	General Data Dissemination System
GRA	General Resources Account
HIPC	Heavily Indebted Poor Countries
HICP	Harmonized Index of Consumer Prices
IAIS	International Association of Insurance Supervisors
IBA	International Bar Association
IBRD	International Bank for Reconstruction and Development
ICC	International Chamber of Commerce
ICJ	International Court of Justice
IDA	International Development Association
IEO	Independent Evaluation Office
ILOLR	International Lender of Last Resort
IMF	International Monetary Fund
IMFC	International Monetary Financial Committee
INSOL	Association of International Insolvency Practitioners
ISD	Investment Services Directive

1

ISDA	International Swaps and Derivatives Association
ISPA	Instrument for Structural Policies for Pre-Accession
IOSCO	International Organization of Securities Commission
ITO	International Trade Organization
LDC	Less Developed Countries
LOI	Letters of Intent
LOLR	Lender of Last Resort
MEFP	Memorandum on Economic and Financial Policies
MiFID	Markets in Financial Instruments Directive
MIGA	Multilateral Investment Guarantee Agency
MIT	Massachusetts Institute of Technology
MOF	Minister of Finance
MoU	Memorandum of Understanding
MPC	Monetary Policy Committee
NAB	New Arrangement to Borrow
NASD	National Association of Securities Dealers
NASDAQ	National Association of Securities Dealers Automated Quotation System
NCB	National Central Bank
OCA	Optimum Currency Area
OEEC	Organisation for European Economic Cooperation
OECD	Organisation for Economic Cooperation and Development
OJ	Official Journal of the European Communities
OLAF	European Anti-Fraud Office
OPEC	Organization of Petroleum Exporting Countries
OTC	Over-the-Counter
OTS	Office of Thrift Supervision
PBC	People's Bank of China
PCA	Prompt Corrective Action
PIN	Public Information Notice
PRC	People's Republic of China
PRGF	Poverty Reduction and Growth Facility
ROSCs	Reports on Observance of Standards and Codes
RTC	Resolution Trust Corporation
SAF	Structural Adjustment Facility
SDDS	Special Data Dissemination System
SDR	Special Drawing Rights
SDRM	Sovereign Debt Restructuring Mechanism
SEA	Single European Act
SEC	Securities and Exchange Commission
SEIR	Structured Early Intervention and Resolution
SGP	Stability and Growth Pact
SRF	Supplemental Reserve Facility
SRO	Self-Regulatory Organization
STF	Systemic Transformation Facility

TARGET	Trans-European Automated Real-time Gross-settlement Express Transfer
TIM	Trade Integration Mechanism
TMU	Technical Memorandum of Understanding
UN	United Nations
UNECE	United Nations Economic Commission for Europe
UNCITRAL	United Nations Commission on International Trade Law
UNIDROIT	International Institute for the Unification of Private Law
US	United States
WTO	World Trade Organization

PART I

DEVELOPMENTS AT THE NATIONAL LEVEL

1

MONETARY SOVEREIGNTY AND ITS SURRENDER

The use of words is to express ideas. Perspicuity, therefore, requires not only that the ideas should be distinctly formed, but that they should be expressed by words distinctly and exclusively appropriate to them. But no language is so copious as to supply words and phrases for every complex idea, or so correct as not to include many equivocally denoting different ideas. Hence it must happen that however accurately objects may be discriminated in themselves, and however accurately the discrimination may be considered, the definition of them may be rendered inaccurate by the inaccuracy of the terms in which it is delivered. And this unavoidable inaccuracy must be greater or less, according to the complexity and novelty of the objects defined.

Alexander Hamilton, *The Federalist Papers*, 1788[1]

---

[1] See Alexander Hamilton, James Madison, and John Jay, *The Federalist Papers* (New York: Mentor, New American Library, 1961; a reprint of the original McLean Edition of 1788) 229.

A. Introduction

The power to issue currency is a sovereign power, one of the attributes of sovereignty as classically defined. In this chapter I explore first the notion of sovereignty and its history, a history which is linked to the evolution of the nation state. In this respect, I provide an analysis of the philosophical and political roots of sovereignty, with references to the work of Bodin, Machiavelli, and Hobbes, and of the evolution of this concept over the centuries, with the advent of democracy and the rule of law. While the debate in the eighteenth century and nineteenth century focused upon the evolution of this concept with regard to the *locus* of that supreme power (ie, from the sovereignty of the king—hereditary monarch—to the sovereignty of the people), the debate in recent decades has focused on what is referred to as the 'erosion' of sovereignty. The receding power of the nation state in recent years has been accompanied by a redefinition of the notion of sovereignty. Power today is no longer the exclusive domain of the nation state. Centripetal and centrifugal forces have diffused the power of the nation state, and today a variety of actors, including international organizations, multinational corporations, regions, local communities, and the civil society also exercise power. The process of European integration has redefined the jurisdictional boundaries of the powers of the European states. The advent of European Monetary Union signifies a voluntary surrender of the traditional monopoly power enjoyed by the state—in the case of EMU, the participating Member States—in the issue of currency. The globalization of financial markets and the powers vested upon the International Monetary Fund and other international financial institutions, as well as economic considerations such as the choice of exchange regime, have also limited and altered the powers of the states in the monetary arena. There is nothing sacrosanct about the notion of monetary sovereignty that has traditionally been attributed to the nation state.

B. Definition of Sovereignty

Sovereignty is the supreme authority within a territory. The state is the political institution in which sovereignty is embodied.

Sovereignty in public international law

Sovereignty in the sense of contemporary public international law denotes the basic international legal status of a state that is not subject, within its territorial jurisdiction, to the governmental (executive, legislative, or judicial) jurisdiction of a foreign state or to foreign law other than public international law.[2] It forms part of the fundamental principles of general international law and it is considered to be one of the principal organizing concepts of international relations.[3] It protects the existence and the freedom of action of states, as limited by international law, in their international relations as well as with respect to their internal affairs. In particular, it protects their freedom of self-determination over their political, constitutional, and socio-economic systems and cultural identity,[4] their territorial integrity and exclusive jurisdiction over their territory, and their personal jurisdiction over their citizens and juridical persons established under their jurisdiction as well as over matters with trans-frontier connections which have reasonably close links with or effects upon the state's territory.[5]

Monetary sovereignty

Monetary sovereignty is a particular attribute of the general sovereignty of the state under international law. Some authors argue that the concept of monetary sovereignty predates by thousands of years the concept of political sovereignty that was developed in the Renaissance, since the authority to create money had been proclaimed by the rulers or priesthood of ancient civilizations (Sumer, India, Babylon, Persia, Egypt, Rome and others).[6]

However, the modern understanding of the attributes of sovereignty is rooted in the political thought that was developed in the Renaissance. The history and evolution of sovereignty is intrinsically linked to the history and evolution of the nation state. Both concepts were developed in Western Europe during the end of the fifteenth century and the sixteenth century.

---

[2] See Helmut Steinberger, 'Sovereignty' in *Encyclopedia of Public International Law* (Amsterdam: North Holland, 1987) vol 10, 408.

[3] See Marc Williams, 'Rethinking Sovereignty' in Eleonore Kofman and Gillian Youngs (eds), *Globalization: Theory and Practice* (London: Pinter, 1996) 109. See also Alan James, *Sovereign Statehood* (London: Allen and Unwin, 1986) 267.

[4] See UN General Assembly Res 2625 (XXV) Declaration of Principles of International Law Concerning Friendly Relations and Cooperation among States in Accordance with the Charter of the United Nations, 24.10.1970.

[5] See Steinberger, above note 2, 410. Sovereignty is defined in the *Black's Law Dictionary* as 'the supreme, absolute, and uncontrollable power by which any independent state is governed; supreme political authority; the supreme will; paramount control of the constitution and frame of government and its administration; the self-sufficient source of political power, from which all specified political parties are derived; the international independence of a state, combined with the right and the power of regulating its internal affairs without foreign dictation'.

[6] See Robert A Mundell, 'Money and the Sovereignty of the State' in Axel Leijonhufvud (ed), *Monetary Theory and Policy Experience* (Basingstoke: Palgrave, 2001, in association with the International Economic Association) 298–302.

C. History of Sovereignty

The writings of Machiavelli, Bodin, and Hobbes are of particular relevance to the understanding of the concept of sovereignty. Politics operated without this organizing principle in the Middle Ages. It is generally agreed that the development of a system of sovereign states culminated at the Peace of Westphalia in 1648.[7]

Sovereignty of the monarch

Bodin

Jean Bodin (1520–96) writing soon after the Massacre of the Huguenots on St Bartholomew's Day in 1572 developed in *Les Six Livres de la République* (1576) some of the key ideas that surround the concept of sovereignty. Bodin was concerned with internal order in a time of unrest and introduced his concept of sovereignty to bolster the power of the French king over the rebellious feudal lords and the church: 'It is clear that the principal mark of sovereign majesty . . . is the right to impose laws generally on all subjects regardless of their consent . . . If he is to govern the state well, a sovereign prince must be above the law.'[8]

Bodin's concept of *souveraineté* (sovereignty) is often regarded as the first systematic one in modern European political philosophy and deserves a landmark status.[9]

Machiavelli

In the early sixteenth century, Niccolo Machiavelli (1469–1527) established some of the foundations of modern political philosophy in his work *The Prince*

---

[7] See Williams, above note 3, 111: 'It is difficult to date precisely when sovereignty became accepted and established. The Treaty of Westphalia (1648) is normally taken as the starting point of the European states system, i.e., a system of sovereign states owing allegiance to no superior.' However, it is worth recalling that Spain started operating as a nation state in 1492, following the union between Queen Isabella of Castile and King Ferdinand of Aragon. The latter is thought by some to have inspired the figure of the maverick Prince described in Machiavelli's acclaimed work.

[8] For a translation into English, see Jean Bodin, *The Six Books of the Commonwealth* (Oxford: Basil Blackwell, 1955) Book I (The Final End of the Well-Ordered Commonwealth: Concerning Sovereignty) available at <http://www.constitution.org/bodin/bodin_.htm>.

[9] See <http://plato.stanford.edu/entries/sovereignty>, Stanford Encyclopedia of Philosophy, entry: 'sovereignty'. However, some authors argue that a contemporary of Bodin, François Grimaudet (1520–80), had already printed a book in 1560 that proclaimed the doctrine of sovereignty. See Mundell, above note 6, 302. Mundell also points out that Grimaudet in his treatise on 'The Law of Payment' stated: 'The value of money depends on the State; this is to say, in a monarchy, upon the prince, and in an oligarchy, upon the State, which alone has the right to coin money or to have it coined and stamp a valuation upon it.'

(1513).[10] According to Machiavelli, princes should retain absolute control of their territories and should use any means of expediency to accomplish this end. He relied on his experience of politics and diplomacy in the city states of contemporary Italy and his sound knowledge of history to elaborate on the basic principles of statehood. His aim was to show how to build a strong principality through the use of effective statesmanship rather than the reliance on moral considerations. The thrust of his advice is that the sovereign should have supreme authority within his territory and his authority should lie beyond the reach of the rule of natural law, canon law, Gospel precepts, or any of the norms or authorities relating to the then powerful Christian tradition. The sovereign must demonstrate the readiness to perform evil as a necessary means to the ultimate end which was central to Machiavelli's writings: the strength and well-ordering of the state. He was supreme within the state's territory and responsible for the well-being of this singular, unitary body. Machiavelli did not purport to describe the nature of sovereignty and the content of the relationship between the sovereign and the people. He was primarily concerned with the preservation of that authority, providing advice as to the best model of government for the sake of the government's stability and not for the sake of the people's well-being. And he confined his attention to monarchical regimes rather than republics. Machiavelli is pragmatic rather than ideologist. Force and restraint, cruelty and kindness, must be employed in their turn when necessary to strengthen the authority of the monarch. He considers the creation of strong armies as the only necessary means of holding power and legal authority, leaving no doubt as to the importance of military power as source of sovereignty:

> A Prince, therefore, should have no care or thought but for war, and for the regulations and training it requires, and should apply himself exclusively to this as his peculiar province; for war is the sole art looked for in one who rules, and is of such efficacy that it not merely maintains those who are born Princes, but often enables men to rise to that eminence from a private station; while, on the other hand, we often see that when Princes devote themselves rather to pleasure than to arms, they lose their dominions.[11]

Hobbes

The English philosopher Thomas Hobbes (1588–1679) further developed in *Leviathan* (1651) the notion of sovereignty, which he described as the absolute and unlimited rule or authority over the territory and the peoples in it. Though

---

[10] Niccolo Machiavelli, *The Prince* (New York: Collier and Son, 1909–14, The Harvard Classics) vol 36, pt I, available at <http://www.bartleby.com/36/1/>.

[11] ibid, ch 14, para 1.

there is no direct reference to Bodin's writings in the pertinent paragraphs of *Leviathan*, there is a broad consensus among theorists that there is a sequence and a common understanding of concepts between the French and the English philosophers.[12] Like Bodin (who wrote at a time of civil war in France between Calvinist Huguenots and the Catholic monarchy) Hobbes also wrote at a time of civil war. He believed that absolute sovereignty of the state over the national territory was the only safeguard of a man's preservation: 'For where there is no Commonwealth, there is, as hath been already shown, a perpetual war of every man against his neighbour; and therefore everything is his that getteth it and keepeth it by force; which is neither propriety nor community, but uncertainty.'[13]

The life of human beings was full of dangers and human nature was weak and for that reason they agreed unconditionally to submit themselves to the absolute sovereignty of the state in exchange for guaranteed internal civil order and protection from external threats.[14] Activities and events beyond national borders are not an issue unless other nations threaten to enter the sovereign territory. The Hobbesian concept of sovereignty in *Leviathan* is based upon the theoretical premise that within the sovereign boundaries a state is entitled to regulate the affairs of all individuals being subordinated thereto. Interestingly, Hobbes establishes in rather clear terms the concept of monetary sovereignty.[15] Coinage

---

[12] See, *inter alia*, Joel Feinberg, 'Autonomy, Sovereignty and Privacy: Moral Ideals in the Constitutions?' (1983) 58 Notre Dame Law Review 445, 448; Jean Bethke Elshtain, 'Sovereign God, Sovereign State, Sovereign Self' (1991) 66 Notre Dame Law Review 1355, 1363; Rett R Ludwikowski, 'Supreme Law or Basic Law? The Decline of the Concept of Constitutional Supremacy' (2001) 9 Cardozo Journal of International and Comparative Law 253, 259; David Golove, 'The New Confederalism: Treaty Delegations of Legislative, Executive and Judicial Authority' (2003) 55 Stanford Law Review 1697, 1705; Ronald A Brand, 'Sovereignty: The State, The Individual and the International Legal System in the Twenty First Century' (2002) 25 Hastings International and Comparative Law Review 279, 282–3; Joan Fitzpatrick, 'Sovereignty, Territoriality and the Rule of Law' (2002) 25 Hastings International and Comparative Law Review 303, 308.

[13] Thomas Hobbes, *Leviathan* (New York: Collier, 1962) 174.

[14] ibid, ch 17 (Of the Causes, Generation and Definition of the Commonwealth).

[15] ibid 174–6:

By concoction, I understand the reducing of all commodities which are not presently consumed, but reserved for nourishment in time to come, to something of equal value, and withal so portable as not to hinder the motion of men from place to place; to the end a man may have in what place soever such nourishment as the place affordeth. And this is nothing else but gold, and silver, and money. For gold and silver, being, as it happens, almost in all countries of the world highly valued, is a commodious measure of the value of all things else between nations; and money, of what matter soever coined by the sovereign of a Commonwealth, is a sufficient measure of the value of all things else between the subjects of that Commonwealth. By the means of which measures all commodities, movable and immovable, are made to accompany a man to all places of his resort, within and without the place of his ordinary residence; and the same passeth from man to man within the Commonwealth, and goes round about, nourishing, as it passeth, every part thereof; in so much as this

and the creation of money as a means of exchange and a storage of value must belong to the sovereign. His understanding is rather modern, in the sense that he points out that the value of money is affected by the change of the laws in the country in which the money is created. He notes that there are two methods by which money is made available for public use: the first is the transfer of money to the public coffers by way of taxation and the second is the reverse circulation of money from the government to the citizens by means of public payments. In that, the Leviathan (artificial man) 'maintains his resemblance with the natural; whose veins, receiving the blood from the several parts of the body, carry it to the heart; where, being made vital, the heart by the arteries sends it out again, to enliven and enable for motion all the members of the same.'[16]

Sovereignty of the people

The advent of democracy as a political form of organizing the nation state and the theory of the division of powers signified an important evolution in the understanding of the notion of sovereignty and its roots. The various social contract theories consider that sovereignty resides originally in individuals (the will of the people), who are the principal sovereignty-holders. Rousseau's social contract theory provides a fundamental basis for the modern understanding of the general will of the state, as representative of the will of its citizens. The individuals assemble or aggregate their individual wills into a unity: a general or collective will. The holder or bearer of such collective will (to whom individuals

---

concoction is, as it were, the sanguification of the Commonwealth: for natural blood is in like manner made of the fruits of the earth; and, circulating, nourisheth by the way every member of the body of man. And because silver and gold have their value from the matter itself, they have first this privilege; that the value of them cannot be altered by the power of one nor of a few Commonwealths; as being a common measure of the commodities of all places. But base money may easily be enhanced or abased. Secondly, they have the privilege to make Commonwealths move and stretch out their arms, when need is, into foreign countries; and supply, not only private subjects that travel, but also whole armies with provision. But that coin, which is not considerable for the matter, but for the stamp of the place, being unable to endure change of air, hath its effect at home only; where also it is subject to the change of laws, and thereby to have the value diminished, to the prejudice many times of those that have it.

The conduits and ways by which it is conveyed to the public use are of two sorts: one, that conveyeth it to the public coffers; the other, that issueth the same out again for public payments. Of the first sort are collectors, receivers, and treasurers; of the second are the treasurers again, and the officers appointed for payment of several public or private ministers. And in this also the artificial man maintains his resemblance with the natural; whose veins, receiving the blood from the several parts of the body, carry it to the heart; where, being made vital, the heart by the arteries sends it out again, to enliven and enable for motion all the members of the same.

[16] ibid.

transfer their private will for the conduct of certain affairs) is the state, and its decisions require the agreement of the original sovereignty-holders. This is the basis of democratic legitimacy.

Locke

John Locke (1632–1704), whose work *Two Treatises of Government* (1690) marked a clear departure from the Hobbesian notion of sovereignty, considers that sovereign authority is premised on the individual freedom of every person in the land to place the legislative power into the hands of few with the 'great end' of enjoying their properties in peace and safety. But the power is not absolute, defined merely by geographic sovereignty, but it is limited by the obligation of sovereign authorities to respect the rights of every citizen. This power cannot be exercised arbitrarily over the lives and fortunes of the people.

> For it being but the joint power of every member of the society given up to that person or assembly which is legislator, it can be no more than those persons had in a state of Nature before they entered into society, and gave it up to the community. For nobody can transfer to another more power than he has in himself, and nobody has an absolute arbitrary power over himself, or over any other, to destroy his own life, or take away the life or property of another. A man, as has been proved, cannot subject himself to the arbitrary power of another; and having, in the state of Nature, no arbitrary power over the life, liberty, or possession of another, but only so much as the law of Nature gave him for the preservation of himself and the rest of mankind, this is all he doth, or can give up to the commonwealth, and by it to the legislative power, so that the legislative can have no more than this.[17]

Montesquieu

Charles de Montesquieu (1688–1755) examined extensively the notion of sovereignty, in *L'Esprit des Lois, The Spirit of Laws* (1748).[18] Montesquieu considers three species of government: republican, monarchical, and despotic. A republican government is that in which the body, or only a part of the people, is possessed of the supreme power, sovereignty. When the body of the people is possessed of sovereignty, it is called a democracy. When the supreme power is lodged in the hands of a part of the people, it is then an aristocracy. In a democracy the people are in some respects the sovereign, and in others the subject.

---

[17] John Locke, *Two Treatises of Government* (New York: New American Library, 1965) pt II *Of the Extent of Legislative Power* para 135 at <http://www.swan.ac.uk/poli/texts/locke/locke10.html>.

[18] See Charles de Montesquieu, *The Spirit of Laws* (In two volumes, London: G.Bell & Sons, 1878, 1909) also available at <http://www.constitution.org/cm/sol.txt>.

There can be no exercise of sovereignty in a democracy unless expressed by the will of the people. The people, in whom the supreme power resides, ought to have the management of everything within their reach: that which exceeds their abilities must be conducted by their ministers. Montesquieu established the separation of the legislative, executive, and judicial functions of government in the following terms:

> By virtue of the first, the prince or magistrate enacts temporary or perpetual laws, and amends or abrogates those that have been already enacted. By the second, he makes peace or war, sends or receives embassies; establishes the public security, and provides against invasions. By the third, he punishes criminals, or determines the disputes that arise between individuals. The latter we shall call the judiciary power, and the other simply the executive power of the state.[19]

In the twenty-second book of *The Spirit of Laws, Of Laws in Relation to the Use of Money*, the idea of the sovereign's control over the use and regulation of money is pervasive. He immediately argues in favour of the use of money, particularly among commercial nations: 'When a nation traffics with a great variety of merchandise, money becomes necessary; because a metal easily carried from place to place saves the great expenses which people would be obliged to be at if they always proceeded by exchange.'[20]

On the nature of money, he observes that money represents the value of all merchandise.[21] Metal is used as the sign of money 'because it is consumed little by use; and because, without being destroyed, it is capable of many divisions. A precious metal has been chosen as a sign, as being most portable. A metal is most proper for a common measure, because it can be easily reduced to the same standard.' And he notes the importance of governments almost naturally: 'Every state fixes upon money a particular impression, to the end that the form may correspond with the standard and the weight, and that both may be known by inspection only' (Twenty-second book, *Of Laws in Relation to the Use of Money*, 2nd para). He also provides an account of the exercise of the state prerogative over money throughout history.[22] He states: 'it would be an excellent law for all

---

[19] See Charles de Montesquieu, *The Spirit of Laws* (London: G.Bell & Sons, 1909) vol I, book XI, 162–3.

[20] See Charles de Montesquieu, above note 18, 49. [21] ibid 50.

[22]

Legislators have sometimes had the art not only to make things in their own nature the representative of specie, but to convert them even into specie, like the current coin. Cæsar, when he was dictator, permitted debtors to give their lands in payment to their creditors, at the price they were worth before the civil war (Cæsar, *De Bello Civ*, iii). Tiberius ordered that those who desired specie should have it from the public treasury on binding over their

countries who are desirous of making commerce flourish to ordain that none but real money should be current, and to prevent any methods from being taken to render it ideal.'[23]

Hamilton

The Declaration of Independence of the United States of America and the Constitution of the United States reflected a notion of sovereignty clearly anchored upon the principles of democracy (the holders of sovereign power: We the People . . .) and the rule of law. Alexander Hamilton wrote illuminatingly in *The Federalist Papers* about the nature of sovereign power:

> [T]here is in the nature of sovereign power an impatience of control that disposes those who are invested with the exercise of it to look with an evil eye upon all external attempts to restrain or direct its operations. From this spirit it happens that in every political association which is formed upon the principle of uniting in a common interest a number of lesser sovereignties, there will be found a kind of eccentric tendency in the subordinate or inferior orbs by the operation of which there will be a perpetual effort in each to fly off from the centre. This tendency is not difficult to be accounted for. It has its origins in the love of power. Power controlled or abridged is almost always the rival and enemy of that power by which it is controlled or abridged.[24]

Hamilton and Madison were concerned about the balance between the powers of the states and the powers of the Union (federal government). According to Hamilton, the powers of the Union (ie, the attributes of the sovereign power vested upon the federal Union) were: 'the common defence of the members; the preservation of the public peace, as well against internal convulsions as external attacks; the regulation of commerce with other nations and between the States;

---

land to double the value (Tacitus, *Annals*, vi 17). Under Cæsar the lands were the money which paid all debts; under Tiberius ten thousand sesterces in land became as current money equal to five thousand sesterces in silver. The Magna Charta of England provides against the seizing of the lands or revenues of a debtor, when his movable or personal goods are sufficient to pay, and he is willing to give them up to his creditors; thus all the goods of an Englishman represent money. The laws of the Germans constituted money a satisfaction for the injuries that were committed, and for the sufferings due to guilt. But as there was but very little specie in the country, they again constituted this money to be paid in goods or chattels. This we find appointed in a Saxon law, with certain regulations suitable to the ease and convenience of the several ranks of people. At first the law declared the value of a sou in cattle; the sou of two tremises answered to an ox of twelve months, or to a ewe with her lamb; that of three tremises was worth an ox of sixteen months. With these people money became cattle, goods, and merchandise, and these again became money.

See Charles de Montesquieu, above note 18, 51–2.

[23] ibid 52–3.   [24] See Hamilton, Madison, and Jay, above note 1, 111.

the superintendence of our intercourse, political and commercial with foreign countries'.[25]

Madison

According to Madison, the powers conferred on the government of the Union were:

> 1. Security against foreign danger; 2. Regulation of the intercourse with foreign nations; 3. Maintenance of harmony and proper intercourse among the States; 4. Certain miscellaneous objects of general utility; 5. Restraint of the States from certain injurious acts; 6. Provisions for giving due efficacy to all these powers. The powers falling within the first class are those of declaring war and granting letters of marque; of providing armies and fleets; of regulating and calling forth the militia; of levying and borrowing money.[26]

He includes the issuance of money (coins and paper money) as a prerogative of the Union[27] on the basis that: 'Had every State right to regulate the value of its coin, there might be as many different currencies as States, and thus the intercourse among them would be impeded; retrospective alterations in its value might be made ... and animosities be kindled among the States themselves.'[28]

Alexis de Tocqueville

Alexis de Tocqueville[29] wrote in *Democracy in America*:

> In the United States, the sovereignty of the people is not an isolated doctrine, bearing no relation to the prevailing habits and ideas of the people; it may be regarded as the last link of a chain of opinions which binds the whole Anglo-American world. That Providence has given to every human being the degree of reason necessary to direct himself in the affairs that interest him exclusively is the grand maxim upon which civil and political society rests in the United States. The father of a family applies it to his children, the master to his servants, the township to its officers, the county to its townships, the state to the counties, the Union to the states; and when extended to the nation, it becomes the doctrine of the sovereignty of the people.[30]

According to Tocqueville, 'The very essence of democratic government consists

---

[25] ibid 153.   [26] ibid 256.   [27] ibid 281–2.

[28] ibid 282. The United States has had a common currency since 1863.

[29] Alexis de Tocqueville (1805–59) came to the US in 1831 and later wrote his two-volume study *Democracy in America*. The first volume was published in 1835 and the second one in 1940. I am quoting here from a 1990 edition of this classic book.

[30] See Alexis de Tocqueville, *Democracy in America* (New York: Vintage Classics, 1990) 418.

in the absolute sovereignty of the majority.'[31] And he defined sovereignty as 'the right of making laws'.[32]

This is the basis of modern constitutionalism: the rule of law and the sovereignty of the people, as original holders of such supreme power. The fact that power ultimately resides upon the people explains why such power can be restricted. Indeed, the attributes of sovereignty can also be curtailed if the people who hold such power so decide. The implications of European integration and other developments that have affected monetary sovereignty need to be understood in this light.

D. Money and Monetary Sovereignty under International Law: *Lex monetae*

The concept of money

The concept of money has different meanings in different contexts. Money in this book is primarily analysed as a creature of the law, whose existence must be understood within a legal framework.[33]

The functions of money

The economic definition of money is typically functional, based upon the four basic functions of money: commonly accepted medium of exchange, means of payment, unit of account, and store of value. Of these functions, the defining feature of money is that of being a widely accepted means of exchange, which explains the dynamic character of money throughout history: from the sea salt used in Ancient Rome to pay the soldiers (hence the name salary), to a variety of commodities and precious metals over the centuries (with an intrinsic value), to the notes or paper money of today (with no intrinsic value, *fiat money*), as well as other forms such as electronic money. The current technological and financial innovations will undoubtedly continue to influence the evolution of the concept of money in future.

In common parlance, money is often used as a general term to cover all financial assets. For the purposes of the conduct of monetary policy, only some of those

---

[31] ibid 254.   [32] ibid 123.

[33] For a comprehensive legal study of money (focusing on private law issues), see generally Frederick A Mann, *The Legal Aspect of Money* (5th edn, Oxford: Clarendon Press, 1992) 461. Charles Proctor completed in 2005 an excellent revision of Mann's work, *Mann on the Legal Aspect of Money* (6th edn, Oxford: Oxford University Press, 2005). I sometimes refer to the 5th edition in this chapter (Mann) and sometimes to the 6th edition (Proctor).

assets are included in the monetary aggregates used by the economists and the central banks to define the money supply (M1, M2, M3 . . .). The concept of money supply is, however, different from the concept of money. Only the assets included in narrow definitions of the money supply (M1), namely currency in circulation and demand deposits, come closest to the definition of money as a means of payment.

Money and the law

The law tends to reflect a restrictive notion of money as 'currency' (physical notes and coins), leaving aside other 'monetary assets' such as bank deposits. Since the monetary essence of currency rests upon the power of the issuer, that is, the state (*fiat money*), and since the state typically delegates this power to the central bank, which has the monopoly of note issue, the study of monetary law and the study of central banking law go hand in hand.

Though sometimes the notions of money and currency are used indistinctly, the concept of money is broader than the concept of currency. The state can control the issue of currency within its territory, but the creation of money is not exclusively the monopoly of the state.

Economists tend to have a 'broader' understanding of the notion of money than lawyers do. However, with regard to the functions of money, there is an element of increasing confluence between law and economics and that concerns the attention given in recent decades to the function of money as store of value. The value of money (in terms of purchasing power) has become a concern for lawyers, economists, and policy-makers.[34] The conduct of a price-stability oriented monetary policy by an independent central bank (which I discuss in depth in Chapter 2) is today enshrined in a legal framework, which adds a new dimension—the dimension of monetary stability—to the role of the state in monetary affairs. In this context, the growth of money in circulation, the choice of exchange regime, and other economic and financial issues which have a bearing on the 'value of money' are also relevant for lawyers.

Public international law, as I explain below, focuses on the issue and regulation of money by the state. Private law, on the other hand, focuses on the notion of payment and the function of money as a means of payment,[35] and on the

---

[34] See eg Antonio Sainz de Vicuña, 'The Concept of Money in the XXIst Century', paper presented at the MOCOMILA meeting in Tokyo on 1 April 2004. 'A currency is trusted by society and markets, when there is an institutional framework that ensures preservation of purchasing capacity, ie price stability. Money is then defined as the dematerialised "commodity" produced and managed by central banks that serves the function of store of value.'

[35] Without a means of payment and a unit of account, our system of trade and commerce would have to revert to barter (or counter-trade).

protection of the private rights of contracting parties and the discharge of monetary obligations.[36] If the notion of money is unsettled, so is the notion of payment. Payment has been defined as an act, such as the transfer of money, which discharges the debt.[37] Goode defines payment (settlement) as any act accepted in performance of a monetary obligation.[38] The private law of monetary obligations exceeds, however, the scope of my study.[39]

Monetary sovereignty under public international law

The state sovereignty over the state's currency, that is, the power to issue and regulate money, is traditionally recognized by public international law.[40] In 1929, the Permanent Court of International Justice stated that 'it is indeed a generally accepted principle that a state is entitled to regulate its own currency.'[41]

---

[36] See Proctor, above note 33, for a lucid analysis of these issues in Parts II and III of the book.

[37] See Proctor, ibid 160, n 2.

[38] See Roy Goode, *Commercial Law* (2nd edn, London: Penguin Books, 1995) 501.

[39] See Proctor, above note 33, Parts II and III of the book.

[40] See Mann, above note 33, 461. See also Proctor, above note 33, 500.

[41] *Case Concerning the Payment in Gold of Brazilian Federal Loans Contracted in France* and *Case Concerning the Payment of Various Serbian Loans Issued in France*, Permanent Court of International Justice (PCIJ), Judgments of 12 July 1929, Publications of the Court, Series A, Nos 20–1, 44–5, and 122. The judgments are available at <http://www.worldcourts.com//pcij/eng/decisions/1929.07.12_payment2/> and <http://www.worldcourts.com/pcij/eng/decisions/1929.07.12_payment>. Given the importance attached to this judgment of the PCIJ, I provide in this footnote a summary of the *Case Concerning the Payment of Various Serbian Loans Issued in France*:

A number of loans were made to the Serbian government in the form of bond issues between 1895 and 1913. The loans were denominated in French francs and it had not been denied until 1924 or 1925 that the loans had to be serviced in French francs at their current value. It was from 1924 onwards that the bond holders began to refuse to accept payment of their coupons on that basis and to make protests contending that the loan service should be on a gold basis. When diplomacy failed, the French and Serbian governments decided to refer to the Court's jurisdiction which had to decide whether the loans were repayable and service-able in their gold or current value. An examination of the bonds showed that in each case there was a promise of payment in gold or gold francs. The same provisions applied with regard to the interest coupons. It was clear that the Serbs promised to pay in 'gold francs'. In that respect, the Serbs argued that the 'gold clause' was without legal significance. There was no international gold franc. The reference was to money and not to gold as merchandise and the reference must be taken to be French money. The French monetary unit was silver at that time and there was no gold franc as a monetary unit. It was therefore insisted that despite the terms of the engagement, the promise must be construed as one to pay in French currency at its current value. The Court dismissed the first argument. It confirmed that the concept of 'gold francs' is not superfluous. If the parties wanted to contract in French currency they would have simply said 'francs'. The Court's interim conclusion was that 'it is manifest that the Parties in providing for gold payments were referring not to payment in gold coins but to gold as standard of value. It would be in this way naturally that they would seek to avoid, as was admittedly their intention, the consequences of a fluctuation in the Serbian dinar' (p 33). It was also established that in Brussels, Paris, and Geneva a monetary unit was being

This judgment is cited as authority of the state's sovereignty over its currency.[42]

Treves,[43] however, argues that the interpretation of the notion of sovereignty has changed since 1929, and that the Court's statement 'can only be accepted as a figure of speech' and not as a 'right' of states.

> [S]tate 'sovereignty' belongs to the area of fact and not to the area of law. Sovereignty as the stable and undisturbed exercise of power within a given territory is seen as a factual situation from whose existence international law draws consequences which are the rights and obligations of states, in particular the state's right not to suffer interference from other states in the exercise of the power and the obligation of other states not to interfere with the exercise of the power of the sovereign state.[44]

Burdeau accepts the Court's submission with no further comment,[45] and the same applies for Mann.[46] Mann contends that every country has exclusive authority to replace its currency with a new currency and to fix the conversion of the old currency in relation to the new one.[47]

Monetary sovereignty has a territorial dimension. The law of the currency

---

widely used, the 'gold franc' as a well-known standard of value to which reference could appropriately be made in loan contracts when it was desired to establish a sound and stable basis for repayment. The definition of 'gold franc' was to be found in domestic law. Having established the meaning of the 'gold franc' clause and defeated the main argument of the Serbian government, the Court went on to examine the subsidiary argument of the Serbian government, that if the obligations were subject to French law, a clause for payment in gold or at gold value would have been null and void, in so far as it was to be effected in French money and in France. The Court also dismissed that argument because 'there are no circumstances which make it possible to establish that, either generally or as regards the substance of the debt and the validity of the provisions relating thereto, the obligations entered into were in the intention of the borrowing State or in a manner binding upon the bondholders, made subject to French law.' But the Court continued that although French law is not the law chosen by the parties, nothing precludes the currency in which payment must or may be made in France from being governed by French law for 'it is indeed a generally accepted principle that a State is entitled to regulate its own currency.' Pertinently, however, the Court continued by saying that 'in the present case this situation need not be envisaged' because even if that was the case it is not true that French law prevents the carrying out of the gold stipulation as it matters for the case (p 44). The Court found in favour of the French government.

[42] See Mann, above note 33, 461 and Proctor, above note 33, 500. See also Geneviève Burdeau, 'L'Exercice des Compétences Monétaires par les Etats' (1988) 212 Recueil des Cours 211–368, 236, Dominique Carreau, *Souveraineté et Coopération Monétaire Internationale* (Paris: Cujas, 1970) 52–4, and Milan Robert Shuster, *The Public International Law of Money* (Oxford : Clarendon Press, 1973) 9.

[43] See Tullio Treves, 'Monetary Sovereignty Today' in Mario Giovanoli (ed), *International Monetary Law: Issues for the New Millennium* (Oxford: Oxford University Press, 2000) 111–18.

[44] ibid 112.   [45] See Burdeau, above note 42, 236.

[46] See Mann, above note 33, 461 and Proctor, above note 33, 500.

[47] Mann noted that the right to replace a national currency in many respects flowed from the universal recognition of the principle of nominalism, above note 33, 272. The same point finds voice in the *lex monetae* principle; see Proctor, above note 33, 332–3.

is always confined to a territory. It can only be enforced in that territory.[48] This territoriality does not preclude a voluntary surrender of sovereignty. But it implies that 'limitations to sovereignty cannot be presumed'.[49]

Lex monetae and legal theories of money

The 'state theory of money' holds that it is the jurisdiction of issue of a currency which determines what is to be considered money and what nominal value it has ('only those chattels are money to which such character has been attributed by law'). Money is only what is recognized as such by the laws of a state.

The best known proponent of the theory of *lex monetae* (literally, law of the currency) is Mann, who developed it—as Proctor points out—in the light of the universal acceptance of the principle of 'nominalism', which establishes that the parties contract by reference to a currency, irrespective of any fluctuations that may occur in the value of the currency between the time the debt was incurred and the time of payment.[50] 'The principle of nominalism precludes the argument that a payment of a monetary obligation has become impossible. Monetary obligations are "indestructible". If a currency system become extinct, the amount payable by the debtor will be ascertained to the recurrent link',[51] as indeed happened with advent of the euro in 1999.

The state theory of money—recognized in modern constitutions[52]—has been typically construed as a necessary consequence of the sovereign power over currency. With regard to the acceptance of this theory in US law and doctrine,

---

[48] See Treves, above note 43, 117. '[B]ecause any reference to a monetary unit automatically entails a reference to the rules that define it, the rules on legal tender and those involving the exercise of the powers of public authorities are territorial, in the sense that they can be enforced in the territory of the state of the country.'

[49] ibid 112.   [50] See Proctor, above note 33, 16 and 225–8.   [51] ibid 339–40.

[52] For example, see Art 1 s 8 paras 5 & 6 of the US Constitution (The Congress shall have the power . . . 5. To coin money, regulate the value thereof, and of foreign coin, and fix the standard of weights and measures. 6. To provide for the punishment of counterfeiting the securities and current coin of the United States). Though the power to issue currency has been transferred from the national to the supranational arena in the European Union since the advent of European Monetary Union, it is useful to recall that European constitutions have referred to the state prerogative over monetary affairs in clear terms. Eg, Art 73(4) of the German Constitution, *Grundgesetz* (The Federation has exclusive power to legislate in the following matters: 4. currency, money and coinage, weights and measures, as well as the determination of standards of time); Art 34 (Legislative Powers) of the French Constitution (1) All legislation shall be passed by Parliament. (2) Legislation shall establish the rules concerning: . . . the assessment bases, rates, and methods of collecting taxes of all types; the issuance of currency); Art 117(2)(e) of the Italian Constitution (The state has exclusive legislative power in the following matters . . . e) money, protection of savings, financial markets; protection of competition; currency system; state taxation system and accounting; equalization of regional financial resources; Art 149(1)(11) of the Spanish Constitution (The State—central government—has exclusive power over the monetary system); Art 80(2) of the Greek Constitution (A law shall provide for the minting of issuance of currency).

Wahlig points out that '*lex monetae* is also recognised (even if not under this designation) in the United States, in the guise of the "act of state doctrine" or also the "state theory of money".'[53]

The scope of *lex monetae* has been debated in the legal literature. As I further contend below, I support a broad interpretation of the state theory of money. Strictly speaking, it has been argued that *lex monetae* should be distinguished from *lex contractus* (or *lex causae*) which refers to the substantive law applied to a contract as a result of the parties' choice of law,[54] an issue which was discussed with regard to the continuity of contracts in the context of European Monetary Union, following the substitution of national currencies by the euro. Under the theory of *lex monetae*, judges must recognize the validity of the monetary law of other states. A distinction can be drawn—as Jean Victor Louis points out— between a narrow concept of *lex monetae* limited to the definition of a currency in a given territory and its relationship with the currency it may replace, and a broader concept that covers the provisions adopted by a state with regard to the regulation of its currency.[55]

According to Mann, each sovereign state possesses the exclusive sovereign power to determine what constitutes legal tender within its territory and what the nominal value of that currency is. The definition of legal tender acts as a legal barrier imposed by the authorities against the use of currency substitutes (such as foreign currencies and gold) to settle debts.

Mann considers that money, like tariffs or taxation or the admission of aliens, is one of those matters which prima facie must be considered as falling within the exclusive domestic jurisdiction of States.[56] This means that the state's exclusive right to regulate its money would fall under Article 2 paragraph 7 of the Charter of the United Nations, which states:[57]

> Nothing contained in the present Charter shall authorize the United Nations to intervene in matters which are essentially within the domestic jurisdiction of any state or shall require the Members to submit such matters to settlement under the

---

[53] See Bertold Wahlig, 'European Monetary Law: the Transition to the Euro and the Scope of Lex Monetae' in Mario Giovanoli (ed), *International Monetary Law: Issues for the New Millennium* (Oxford: Oxford University Press, 2000) 123. The act of state doctrine maintains that a nation is sovereign within its own borders, and its domestic actions may not be questioned in the courts of another nation.

[54] See Michael Gruson, 'The Scope of *Lex Monetae* in International Transactions: a United States Perspective' in Mario Giovanoli (ed), above note 43, 434–5.

[55] See Jean Victor Louis, 'The New Monetary Law of the European Union' in Mario Giovanoli (ed), above note 43, 154.

[56] See Mann, above note 33, 462.

[57] Wahlig, above note 53, 123, points out that Hugo Hahn also considers the currency-issuing state's exclusive right to regulate its money as covered by Art 2, para 7 of the Charter of the United Nations.

present Charter; but the application of this principle shall not prejudice the application of enforcement measures under Chapter VII [which refers to 'Action with Respect to Threats to the Peace, Breaches of the Peace and Acts of Aggression']

With regard to the fate of national monetary law outside the boundaries of the state, Mann cites a few cases where it was held that the domestic monetary legislation applies only internally and does not affect contracts denominated in the currency if entered into before the enactment of the legislation. In his view, there cannot be any doubt that attempts to limit the international recognition of monetary changes must today be considered as obsolete and extravagant. Both national and international law recognize the right of the state to depreciate its own currency. Further, a state is within its rights to bring about the external devaluation of its currency.[58] Mann also contends that there is much authority in support of the further right of the state to introduce exchange controls at its discretion with all its incidental ramifications.[59] Essentially, any reference to a monetary unit entails automatically a reference to the municipal laws that define it. But the rules on legal tender and those aspects of the law of the currency involving the exercise of powers by the state may only be enforced within the territorial boundaries of its jurisdiction.

With regard to the question whether the issuer of a currency may prohibit the use of its currency by another country,[60] there is at present no basis in international law to support the view that the issuer may object to the currency being used by other countries. In the UK and in the US, the courts have explicitly recognized the unfettered right of the sovereign (monarch or Congress) to grant legal tender status to specified foreign currencies, without requiring the consent of the issuer.[61]

The 'state theory of money' contrasts with the 'societal theory of money', which considers that the attribution of the character of money derives from the usages of commercial life, and of practices in society in general, irrespective of the intervention of the state.[62]

---

[58] See Mann, above note 33, 464–5. The same point is reflected in the sixth edition by Proctor, above note 33, 505–6.

[59] See Mann, ibid 467, with references to the British, Canadian, and US authorities and the International Claims Commission.

[60] See generally François Gianviti, 'Use of a Foreign Currency under the Fund's Articles of Agreement' (17 May 2002) at <http://www.imf.org/external/np/leg/sem/2002/cdmfl/eng/gianvi. pdf>.

[61] See in the UK the *Wade* case ((1601) 77 ER 232) and in the US the *Tyson v United States* case (285 F 2d 19 (1960)). As Lee Buchheit pointed out to me in private correspondence, Ecuador's surprise announcement in early 2000 that it had dollarized its economy was done without consulting the United States.

[62] See Mann, above note 33, 12–14. See also René Smits, *The European Central Bank. Institutional Aspects* (The Hague: Kluwer Law International, 1997) 194, footnote 186.

Antonio Sainz de Vicuña advocates a third explanation: an 'institutional theory of money', in which money is not limited to 'cash', but encompasses a dematerialized concept (called 'scriptural money', which includes demand deposits with credit institutions). This is based on the small proportion of money physically represented in banknotes and coins, as compared with the generalized use of the banking system for holding money and for payments. The wide acceptance and use by society of scriptural money is based on an institutional framework of two pillars: (i) an independent central bank that ensures the stability of the purchasing capacity of money and its sound use as means of payment, and (ii) a legislative framework that supports such independence, the solvency and liquidity of credit institutions, and the reliability of scriptural money as means of payment.[63] He considers that the concept of legal tender is obsolete in view of the overwhelming use of scriptural money in today's economy, the limitation of the use of cash to the settlement of petty transactions, and the general need for consent by the creditor for the settlement of debts in cash. The concept of legal tender is thus limited to the official standardization of the design and the features of cash. The value of money is dependent, in a world of no absolute anchors, on such an institutional framework only.[64]

Though the societal theory of money and the institutional theory of money provide an important complementary approach to the legal study of money, as long as we have a system in which the state keeps an important role in money creation (with regard to the issue of currency), control of the money supply through monetary policy (a function entrusted to a central bank, usually with independence from political instruction, yet a state function), and a certain degree of control over the banking and financial system through regulation and supervision and oversight of payment systems, the state theory of money—broadly understood as the public legal framework in which the economic institutions of money and central banking operate—remains valid in my opinion.

E. The Attributes of Monetary Sovereignty

The notion of monetary sovereignty is not expressly recognized or defined as such in the Charter of the United Nations, nor in the Articles of Agreement of the International Monetary Fund, nor in other key instruments of international law.[65]

It has been argued in the legal literature that monetary sovereignty includes the

---

[63] See Antonio Sainz de Vicuña, above note 34. [64] ibid.
[65] See Burdeau, above note 42, 236–7.

power to issue the currency, to define the monetary unit and the notes and coins in multiples of that unit, to require that payments in such notes and coins must be accepted as legal tender, to decide whether or not the currency should be based on gold or silver, to depreciate and appreciate the value of the currency, to impose exchange controls, and to take other measures affecting the monetary system or monetary relations.[66]

In the economic literature, Nobel laureate Mundell, bearing in mind the functions of money, argues that monetary sovereignty comprises the right to determine what constitutes the unit of account, the right to determine the means of payment—legal tender for the discharge of debt—and the right to produce money.[67] He argues that the most important dimension of this monetary sovereignty is the right of a state to declare that which counts as legal tender.[68]

In my view, monetary sovereignty includes:

1. The power to issue notes and coins. The prerogative of issuing currency (*ius cudendae monetae*) is a classic attribute of monetary sovereignty. This power is typically a monopoly power, exercised by a country's central bank.[69] A national currency is both a symbol and a tool of national identity. A currency, like a language, like a flag, can stimulate the cohesion among a group of people and build a nation. Indeed, following the break-up of the Soviet Union in 1991, the nascent republics were keen—as a manifestation of their newly gained independence and an assertion of their sovereignty—to issue their own currency and to establish their own central bank. There are other benefits related to the issue of currency, such as the potential for generating seigniorage revenues.
2. The power to regulate money (to dictate laws and regulations that affect the external or internal dimension of money), the banking system (regulation of credit) and the payment system (clearing and settlement).
3. The power to control the money supply and interest rates (monetary policy).

---

[66] See Mann, above note 33, 461–2 and Treves, above note 43, 117. In principle, customary international law does not fetter the legislator's discretion in these matters (Mann 461), whereas international law does not prevent states from devising their own systems of conflict of laws or private international law to decide whether the monetary laws of other states are applicable within its boundaries (Mann 462). The same points are made in the sixth edition by Proctor, above note 33, 501.

[67] See Mundell, above note 6, 303.   [68] ibid 303–4.

[69] There is no compelling case for governments to monopolize the production of shoes, sausages, or steel. The experience of the centrally planned economies showed that monopoly decision-making in economic affairs obstructs the creation of wealth, not just for a few, but for all. Why should monopoly decision-making in money be an exception? I discuss this issue, and the proposals of the so-called 'free banking economists' that advocate competition in currency in Rosa M Lastra, *Central Banking and Banking Regulation* (London: Financial Markets Group, London School of Economics, 1996) 252–7.

This power is typically delegated to a central bank. The instruments of a market oriented monetary policy (open market operations and discount policies) also provide the central bank with a degree of flexibility in dealing with banking problems (including the power to act as lender of last resort, as I further explain in Chapter 4).

4. The power to control the exchange rate and to determine the exchange regime (exchange rate policy). Responsibility for the formulation of exchange rate policy usually rests with the government, though its implementation is often entrusted to the central bank. The central bank often manages the official monetary reserves (both gold reserves and foreign currency reserves), which are generally owned by the government.

5. The power to impose exchange and capital controls. Though this imposition runs counter to the objectives of trade liberalization, it remains a tool of monetary sovereignty,[70] albeit a controversial one, opposed by the advocates of unrestricted capital movements or 'capital account convertibility' as I further discuss in Chapter 13.[71]

Does monetary sovereignty include the power to discriminate against foreign nationals (or in favour of their own nationals)?

This is a thorny issue, because though *de jure* it can be argued that this alleged power runs counter to the principles of international law,[72] *de facto* it remains true that sovereign states do within their territory enact laws that prejudice against foreign nationals, implicitly or explicitly. Freezing orders—of assets—unilaterally imposed are an example of the coercive power of the state within its own territory, when security or political considerations prevail.[73] Other examples of unilateral decisions taken by sovereign states—often in flagrant violation of

---

[70] Treves, above note 43, 115–16, points out that following the imposition of controls on capital movements by Malaysia (one of the states involved in the Asian Crisis in the late 1990s) the International Monetary Fund's directors broadly agreed 'that the regime of capital controls—which was intended by the authorities to be temporary—had produced more positive results than many observers had initially expected'. Monetary sovereignty with regard to the control of capital movements had shown its strength.

[71] With regard to capital account convertibility, see Cynthia Lichtenstein, 'International Jurisdiction over International Capital Flows and the Role of the IMF: Plus ça Change?' in Mario Giovanoli (ed), *International Monetary Law: Issues for the New Millennium* (Oxford: Oxford University Press, 2000).

[72] With regard to the 'non-discrimination obligation in customary international law', John Jackson remarks: 'From time to time it is argued that countries are obliged under customary international law to extend non-discriminatory treatment to other nations. Prior to World War I, there was no such obligation. As summarized by Professor Georg Scharzenberger, customary law of the time recognised that: "Freedom of commerce is a purely optional pattern of international economic law." See John Jackson, William Davey, and Alan Sykes (eds), *Legal Problems of International Economic Relations* (3rd edn, St Paul, Minnesota: West Publishing Co, 1995) 443.

[73] See Treves, above note 43, 118. Treves also refers to freezing orders in implementation of sanctions imposed by the UN Security Council.

their international obligations—include the confiscation of monetary assets (expropriation without compensation) and the repudiation of external debt obligations.

In a case cited by Mann,[74] a Cuban law (1961) rendering all currency outside the territory of the country null and void was considered to amount to confiscation without compensation and appeared to be contrary to international law.[75] The US Foreign Claims Settlement Commission recognized Cuba's undeniable sovereignty over its currency under public international law. It argued, however, that although persons using foreign money may risk market fluctuations in its value, there was no reason why they should be presumed to have agreed to allow their money to be expropriated as the result of foreign exchange control or currency legislation.[76] This cannot happen even if a new state succeeds another state and seeks to cancel all currency issued by the old state. There are also cases where foreign nationals have become the victims of unreasonable and unfair discrimination as prohibited by international law or other forms of discrimination on the basis of religion, race, or gender.[77]

Mann argues that monetary sovereignty needs to be exercised by the state in accordance with the principles of customary international law: 'While normally the State is entitled at its discretion to regulate its monetary affairs, there comes a point when the exercise of such discretion so unreasonably or grossly offends against the alien's right to fair and equitable treatment or so clearly

---

[74] Mann, above note 33, 470.

[75] See Claim of Betty G Boyle, claim CU–3473–Decision No CU–3380 in Foreign Claims Settlement Commission of the United States *Annual Report to the Congress for the Period January 1–December 31, 1968,* 81–4.

[76] ibid 82.

[77] See Mann, above note 33, 474–5. Before the adoption of the single currency, the EC Treaty prohibited the enactment of monetary legislation discriminating against foreign nationals. The Case 55/79, *Commission v Ireland* [1980] ECR 481 is significant in this respect. Irish excise duties legislation provided in favour of producers of sprits, beer, and made wine for deferment of payment of between four and six weeks according to the product, whereas in the case of the same products from other Member States, the duty is payable either at the date of importation or of delivery from the customer's warehouse. In defence, the government of Ireland relies in addition upon the fact that Irish producers, as consideration for the advantage given to them (deferment of payment of excise duties), must accept corresponding disadvantages. Thus in order to obtain deferred payment, they must pay an additional duty and furnish the authorities with security for payment. Moreover, it is necessary to take into account the disadvantage suffered by Irish whisky producers in competition with Scotch whisky owing to the divergent exchange rates between the Irish and the UK 'Green Pounds' (para 6.) The Court dismissed the argument in the following terms: 'The argument based on the difference in the rate of the Irish and United Kingdom "Green Pounds" must be rejected. If the Irish Authorities consider that the exchange rates in question were not fixed appropriately, they should seek the remedy for that situation by the appropriate means. A monetary situation cannot be corrected by means of discriminatory tax provisions.' (para 11).

deviates from customary standards of behaviour that international law will intervene.'[78]

Monetary laws must be in accordance with public international law. As Mann explains, 'monetary laws are fully capable of giving rise to legal disputes concerning international law within the meaning of Article 36(2) of the Statute of the International Court of Justice.'[79] This Article reads as follows:

> The states party to the present Statute may at any time declare that they recognise as compulsory *ipso facto* and without special agreement, in relation to any other state accepting the same obligation, the jurisdiction of the Court in all legal disputes concerning:
>
> (a) the interpretation of a treaty;
> (b) any question of international law;
> (c) the existence of any fact which, if established, would constitute a breach of an international obligation;
> (d) the nature or extent of the reparation to be made for the breach of an international obligation.

In the *Case of Certain Norwegian Loans*,[80] cited by Mann, the Court held that

---

[78] Mann, ibid 472–3. Proctor argues for a distinction between the internal and external aspects of monetary sovereignty, and argues that the external aspects may be more amenable to challenge by other states, above note 33, 501–2.

[79] Mann, ibid 468.

[80] *Case of Certain Norwegian Loans* [1957] ICJ Rep 9. Given the relevance of this case, I provide a summary of it in this footnote. Facts: Between 1896 and 1905, the Norwegian Government floated six public loans on the French market and on other foreign markets. From 1885 to 1909, various loans were floated on foreign markets, including the French market, by the Mortgage Bank of the Kingdom of Norway, an establishment created by the State and whose capital belongs to the State. Finally, in 1904, the Norwegian Small Holding and Workers' Housing Bank floated a loan on the French market and on other foreign markets. The French Government contends that the bonds contain a gold clause which varies in form from bond to bond, but which that Government regards as sufficient in the case of each bond, this being disputed by the Norwegian Government. The Norwegians abolished the gold clause in 1923. In its application to the Court, the French Government requests the Court to adjudge and declare that the international loans issued by the Kingdom of Norway, by the Mortgage Bank of the Kingdom of Norway, and by the Small Holding and Workers' Housing Bank, which are listed in the Application, stipulate in gold the amount of the borrower's obligation for the service of coupons and the redemption of bonds; and that the borrower can only discharge the substance of his debt by the payment of the gold value of the coupons on the date of payment and of the gold value of the redeemed bonds on the date of repayment. Objections: The first preliminary objection of the Norwegians was that the abolition of the gold clause is a matter for national law and not a matter for international law. The Court eventually found that the Court did not have jurisdiction on procedural grounds but it is interesting to read the opinion of one of the judges. A separate opinion was provided by Judge Sir Hersch Lauterpacht (37–8):

> With regard to the first preliminary objection referred to above I am unable to accept the view that the subject-matter of the present dispute is not related to international law but exclusively to the national law of Norway. Undoubtedly, the question of the interpretation of the contracts between the Norwegian State and the bondholders is primarily a question of Norwegian law. It is not disputed that the Norwegian law is the proper law of the contract

'the question of conformity of national legislation with international law is a matter of international law.'[81]

F. The Erosion of Monetary Sovereignty

The monopoly power enjoyed by the state with regard to the issue and regulation of money within its territory has been eroded or limited by a number of considerations in recent years. Some of those limitations are consensual, a voluntary surrender of monetary sovereignty, and some others have not been agreed by the state/s, but are the result of globalization, the information revolution, and of economic and financial developments in the last three decades.

The problem of monetary sovereignty lies at the crossroads of law, politics, and economics.[82] The erosion of monetary sovereignty is related to the erosion of the general sovereignty of the state. Though nation states remain the main actors in the international community, power today is no longer the exclusive domain of the nation state.[83] Centripetal and centrifugal forces have diffused the power of the nation state, and today a variety of actors, including international

---

and that it is for the Norwegian courts to decide what Norway had actually promised to pay. However, the complaint of the French Government is that, having regard to the currency legislation suspending the operation of the gold clause, the Norwegian law which the Norwegian courts are bound to apply in this case is contrary to international law. The Norwegian courts may hold that the gold clause in the bonds is a gold coin clause (as distinguished from a gold value clause), that that gold coin clause has been rendered inoperative as the result of the legislation in question, and that the existing currency is, therefore, a lawful means of payment. In the view of the Norwegian Government this is the proper interpretation of what it has in law promised to pay. However, it is that very legislation, in so far as it affects French bondholders, which may be the cause of violation of international law of which France complains.

It may be admitted, in order to simplify a problem which is not at all simple, that an 'international' contract must be subject to some national law; this was the view of the Permanent Court of International Justice in the case of the Serbian and Brazilian Loans. However, this does not mean that that national law is a matter which is wholly outside the orbit of international law. National legislation—including currency legislation—may be contrary, in its intention or effects, to the international obligations of the State. *The question of conformity of national legislation with international law is a matter of international law.* The notion that if a matter is governed by national law it is for that reason at the same time outside the sphere of international law is both novel and, if accepted, subversive of international law. It is not enough for a State to bring a matter under the protective umbrella of its legislation, possibly of a predatory character, in order to shelter it effectively from any control by international law' (italics added).

[81] See Mann, above note 33, 468–9.

[82] See Burdeau, above note 42, 223.

[83] See Kenichi Ohmae, *The End of the Nation-State* (New York: Simon and Schuster, 1996) and Susan Strange, *The Retreat of the State: The Diffusion of Power in the World Economy* (Cambridge: Cambridge University Press, 1996).

organizations, multinational corporations, regions, local communities, and the civil society also exercise power.

The state no longer monopolizes the supreme and exclusive power to control affairs in a given territory. If we look at the different types of power that the state can hold: political power, military power, economic power, we realize that even if some states still reign supreme within the territory of their jurisdiction in the political and military arena (though in the case of a federal state, political power is shared, and in the case of a military alliance or a defence organization, sovereignty is pooled, as with NATO), in the economic arena few states can claim to be sovereign nowadays. States need to comply with their international economic commitments, regarding trade, investment, finance, and others.

As I have already discussed, a national currency can be an expression, a symbol of national identity and national pride. However, there is nothing sacrosanct about money and not a tear should be shed about the decline of monetary sovereignty. In a way, there is nothing unique about this process. Other symbols of national identity (even if not so closely associated with the notion of sovereignty as money is) have also lost their sparkle in recent years: airlines used to be seen as a matter of symbolic pride for the citizens of a state. No longer: the advent of privatization and the upheaval in the airline industry in recent years have changed that perception.

Voluntary or consensual limitations of monetary sovereignty

The advent of European Monetary Union

At a regional level, the most clear example of consensual limitations of monetary sovereignty is the establishment of European Monetary Union in 1999. The adoption of a single currency, the euro, and the creation of the European System of Central Banks with responsibility to formulate and implement the monetary policy of the Community has been described as 'the most profound limitation to monetary sovereignty ever to be agreed by sovereign states'.[84] Member States participating in EMU have agreed to transfer sovereign rights to the European Community. Of course, the surrender of monetary sovereignty does not imply the erosion of national sovereignty in other respects. It is a limited surrender, a non-exclusive transfer of sovereign powers. The members of the Euro zone retain their national sovereignty in those domains where no other consensual limitation has been agreed.[85]

---

[84] See Treves, above note 43, 116.

[85] The European Court of Justice ruled in the *Costa v Enel* case that 'by creating a Community of unlimited duration, having its own institutions, its own personality, its own legal capacity and capacity of representation on the international stage and, more particularly, real powers stemming

Member States participating in EMU have given up their national currencies. I contend that the bearer, the holder of monetary sovereignty for those Member States whose currency is the euro, is not the ECB, but the European Union.[86] The Union's 'exclusive competence' in monetary policy is exercised by the ESCB as I further explain in Chapter 7.[87]

However, the language of the Treaty with regard to the exchange rate policy and the external aspects of the euro is characterized by a notorious lack of clarity. I elaborate in Chapter 9 upon the contents of Article 111 EC Treaty, which is a cumbersome provision in legal and economic terms, the result of a calculated obfuscation for political purposes. The need to create a 'single voice for the Euro' has been advocated in various political and academic fora.[88]

Other 'attributes of monetary sovereignty' (as spelt out above) remain at the national level, such as the responsibility to supervise the banking system and the power to legislate and regulate in some monetary and banking matters.

Though there is no provision in the EC Treaty which permits the revocation of EMU[89] and though the wording 'irrevocably fixed' adopted by the Maastricht Treaty suggests that EMU is 'a trip with no return', the Member States retain— as a residual attribute of their sovereignty—the possibility of reversing the

---

from a limitation of sovereignty or a transfer of sovereign powers from the States to the Community, the Member States have limited their sovereign rights, albeit within limited fields, and have thus created a body of law which binds their nationals and themselves.' See Case 6/64, *Costa v Enel* [1964] ECR 585, para 9, 593.

[86] This is in line with the established doctrine of monetary sovereignty, where the state, as representative of the will of the people, is the holder of such sovereignty, even if the exercise of some of its prerogatives—such as the monopoly of note issue—is the responsibility of the central bank. Regarding the constitutional position of the European Central Bank, which I further discuss in Ch 7, see *inter alia*, Chiara Zilioli and Martin Selmayr, 'The European Central Bank: an Independent Specialized Organization of Community Law' 37 Common Market Law Review 591 (2000) and René Smits, 'The European Central Bank in the European Constitutional Order' (Inaugural Lecture in the University of Amsterdam, 4 June 2003, subsequently published in Utrecht: Eleven International Publishing, 2003).

[87] See Art I–13 of the proposed EU Constitution. The Treaty establishing a Constitution for Europe, signed in Rome on 29 October 2004, and available in the Official Journal No C 310 of 16 December 2004 was thrown into a legal limbo following the rejection of the Treaty in referenda in France (28 May 2005) and Holland (1 June 2005). The suspension of the ratification process (according to the declaration of the European Council Brussels summit on 16–17 June 2005 to allow for a 'period of reflection') does not equate to the abandonment altogether of the proposed Constitution. The text of the Constitutional Treaty remains a legal document of value to refer to, also with a view to its possible entry into force or the taking over of parts of it in other Treaty texts later on.

[88] See Kathleen McNamara and Sophie Meunier, 'Between National Sovereignty and International Power: what external voice for the Euro?' (2002) 78 International Affairs 849.

[89] However, the proposed EU Constitution introduces in its Art I–60 a procedure for 'voluntary withdrawal from the Union'.

current status quo by unanimous agreement (ie, by signing a new Treaty to that effect).[90]

International obligations: The IMF Articles of Agreement

At the international level, the most relevant example of consensual limitations to the monetary sovereignty of states is the Articles of Agreement of the International Monetary Fund.[91] These limitations were greater with the par value regime under the original Articles of Agreement than they are nowadays. Since the collapse of the Bretton Woods regime (*de facto*), and the Second Amendment to the Articles of Agreement (*de jure*), IMF member states reaffirmed some of the attributes of their monetary sovereignty with regard to the conduct of exchange rate policy.[92] However, IMF members must still comply with the obligations under Article IV and Article VIII of the IMF Articles of Agreement, where the jurisdiction (regulatory powers) of the Fund applies, as I further explain in Chapter 13.[93]

Andreas Lowenfeld[94] suggests that the regime of conditionality of the International Monetary Fund in the use of its resources is changing the traditional boundaries between the domestic jurisdiction of the states and the international community. Lowenfeld points to the ever increasing level of examination of a large variety of domestic policies in the IMF programmes of structural reform: ranging from national budgets, taxes, interest rates, and exchange rates to subsidies, wage policies, competition law, corporate governance, and even accounting practice and legal reform. These domestic policies are subject to scrutiny, negotiation, and commitment. The eagerness to get or maintain the IMF (conditional) financial assistance may lead the legitimate political institutions in the country to design the economic reform programme without a full analysis of its

---

[90] See Treves, above note 43, 116 and Christoph W Herrmann, 'Monetary Sovereignty over the Euro and the External Relations of the Euro Area: Competences, Procedures and Practice' (2002) 7 European Foreign Affairs Review 4. For an opposite view, see Chiara Zilioli and Martin Selmayr, above note 86, 604.

[91] See Treves, above note 43, 113.

[92] Following the de facto abandonment of the par value regime and until the entry into force of the Second Amendment (effective 1 April 1978), this reassertion of sovereignty was done in breach of the rules. See Treves, ibid 114. I further discuss the nature and operations of the International Monetary Fund in Part 3.

[93] From the point of view of the consensual limitations of monetary sovereignty, Charles Proctor mentioned, in his comments to this chapter, the recent dispute between the US and China over the valuation of the renminbi. In his opinion, this dispute emphasizes that—though the issue and management of a currency falls under the domestic jurisdiction of a state—the adoption of an exchange rate policy occurs within a framework of international law which may involve obligations to other states.

[94] See Andreas F Lowenfeld, 'The International Monetary System and the Erosion of Sovereignty. Essay in Honor of Cynthia Lichtenstein' (2002) 25 Boston College International and Comparative Law Review 257.

potentially negative social implications.[95] Lowenfeld suggests that in some cases the 'jurisdictional barrier between the international organization and the sovereign states' has been overstepped or breached, and that a new understanding regarding the relationship between the IMF (and other international agencies) and the countries that need financial assistance is needed.[96]

Other limitations of national monetary sovereignty

The erosion of the traditional notion of sovereignty is also linked to the demise of national frontiers in today's global financial markets.[97] Sovereignty as a supreme power is typically exerted over the territory of the state: principle of territoriality. It is therefore unsurprising that the ongoing process of globalization and the frequency of cross-border movement of persons, capital, goods, or services entail implications for the scope of unfettered sovereignty, which continues to shrink.[98]

Cohen refers to the 'deterritorialization' of money, to express the reality that the circulation of national currencies is no longer confined within the territorial frontiers of nation states.[99]

The growth in cross-border private capital flows (the volume of such flows, for instance in the foreign exchange market, clearly dwarfs what national central banks and even international organizations can do) is an example of a de facto erosion of monetary sovereignty. Arguably, the ability to have a truly independent monetary policy diminishes with the growth of cross-border capital flows.[100]

In the presence of 'transnational money markets', the lack of coercive power of the state beyond its territory means that 'the state does not have the power effectively to regulate credit in its currency by banks outside its territory.'[101] The growth in Eurocurrency markets entails a partial loss of monetary

---

[95] I discuss the issues surrounding the conditionality of the International Monetary Fund in Ch 13. See also Rosa M Lastra, 'IMF Conditionality' (2002) 4(2) Journal of International Banking Regulation 167.

[96] Above note 94.

[97] I borrow the term 'erosion' in this context from Treves, above note 43, 117.

[98] See Helen Stacey 'Relational Sovereignty' (2003) 55 Stanford Law Review 2029, 2040–51.

[99] See Benjamin Cohen, 'Life at the Top: International Currencies in the Twenty-First Century', Essays in International Economics No 221, December 2000, Princeton University, 1–2. 'Currencies may be employed outside their country of origin for either of two purposes: for transactions between nations or for transactions within foreign states. The former purpose is conventionally referred to as "international currency use", or currency "internationalization"; the latter is described as "currency substitution" and can be referred to as "foreign-domestic use". The top international monies are widely used for both purposes.'

[100] See David Llewellyn, *International Financial Integration: The Limits of Sovereignty* (New York: John Wiley and Sons, 1980) 198.

[101] See Treves, above note 43, 117.

sovereignty.[102] However, to the extent that bank transfers in a particular currency involve clearing and settlement in the country of origin of the currency, the mechanisms of control are reasserted and the notion of erosion of sovereignty may be questioned.[103]

As I pointed out above, the government has the monopoly over the issue of currency only—ie, notes and coins in circulation—but not over other assets that individuals might hold instead of currency and that are contributing to the blurring of the definition of money and to a de facto erosion of monetary sovereignty. Commercial banks have an important role in the process of money creation: current accounts (demand deposits) are used as means of payment. Demand deposits constitute the major part of the narrow definition of the money supply (M1).[104] This characteristic of bank liabilities provides the rationale for many monetary and banking laws and regulations.

The role of banks and other private financial institutions in the creation of money cannot be underestimated. There have also been radical proposals, which are not further analysed here, suggesting the reliance on 'private money'. Hayek and other economists in the 'free banking school' have advocated the 'de-nationalization of money', opening up the provision of currency to competition both from the private sector and from foreign issuers of currency.[105]

The power to issue currency is a sovereign prerogative, but one that can become an empty concept if the government is incompetent in the management of its currency. In times of heavy depreciation, for example, citizens will figure out some way of devising a substitute currency. Failing that, the society reverts to barter. A sovereign can punish people who counterfeit the sovereign's own currency, or who use alternative currency without the sovereign's permission, but a sovereign is less able to control the proliferation of faux currencies if society loses faith in the government's declared legal tender. In practice, the other limits of monetary sovereignty are thus defined by monetary incompetence.[106]

---

[102] Initially, Eurocurrency financial instruments (Eurodollar deposits, Eurobonds . . .) were denominated in dollars; the prefix 'euro' is due to the fact that the markets originated in Europe. Eurodollar deposits are deposits denominated in US dollars and held outside the jurisdiction of the United States.

[103] See Mann, above note 33, 199–201, and Treves, above note 43, 117.

[104] As acknowledged, the central bank can influence the banks' reserve position by raising and lowering interest rates (through open market operations and discount policies) and by modifying the reserve requirements.

[105] See Friedrich A von Hayek, *Denationalization of Money* (London: Institute of Economic Affairs, 1976). Hayek's first writing on this subject dates back to 1937, *Monetary Nationalism and International Stability* (reprint, New York: Augustus M Kelly, 1971). For further references on this issue, see Rosa M Lastra, *Central Banking and Banking Regulation* (London: Financial Markets Group, London School of Economics, 1996), 252–7.

[106] I thank Lee Buchheit for this observation.

The experience of inflation can be viewed as an 'abuse of sovereignty'.[107] Infla-tion makes people turn to other forms of payment, for example, foreign curren-cies. The public authorities have various ways of obtaining command over real resources: expropriation, taxes, bond issues, and the issue of currency.[108] In a market economy, taxes and bond issues are preferred. However, the temptation to print money to finance government expenses remains a powerful argument to depoliticize the management of money; hence the support in recent years for central bank independence, analysed in Chapter 2.

The degree to which a currency is a good store of value in international monet-ary relations ('hard currencies' and 'soft currencies') is an economic consider-ation that can also limit in practice the effectiveness of monetary control. Depreciation (the loss in value of a currency vis-à-vis other currencies under a system of flexible exchange rates) and devaluation (the loss in a value of a currency vis-à-vis other currencies by official intervention under a system of managed exchange rates) can lead to a de facto erosion of national monetary sovereignty.

The choice of exchange regime adopted by a state clearly affects the external value of the currency. Under a fixed exchange rate system, a national central bank only enjoys control over monetary policy if it is the central bank which sets monetary policy for the whole area. In the words of Robert Mundell, 'when a country opts for fixed exchange rates . . . it sacrifices policy sovereignty in the field of money.'[109] In the case of a currency board arrangement (discussed in Chapter 2), monetary sovereignty is greatly reduced. In the case of dollarization, there is a surrender of monetary sovereignty.

---

[107] See Robert Mundell, 'Monetary Unions and the Problem of Sovereignty' (2002) 579 The Annals of the American Academy of Political and Social Science 123, 127. Monetary sovereignty is also restricted under a system of fixed but adjustable exchange rates, because countries need to cooperate and engage in supranational decision-making. See entry 'fixed exchange rates' in Peter Newman, Murray Milgate, and John Eatwell (eds), *Palgrave Dictionary of Money and Finance* (London: Macmillan Press Ltd, 1992).

[108] See Charles Goodhart, *Money, Information and Uncertainty* (2nd edn, London and Hampshire: Macmillan, 1989) 44.

[109] See Mundell, above note 6, 292–3. Mundell differentiates between policy sovereignty, which refers to the ability to conduct policy independent of commitments to other countries, and legal sovereignty, which refers to the ability of a state to make its own laws without limitations imposed by any outside authority.

2

INSTITUTIONAL DEVELOPMENTS
TO PROMOTE
MONETARY STABILITY

Out of the realisation of the central bank's power to determine the volume of credit there arose the notion that it should consciously direct monetary policy along 'scientific lines.' The question then arises: What is to be the criterion of this 'scientific' management? The criterion which has so far usually been adopted, that of the stability of the general price level, has been suspect in theory and just as unfortunate in practice . . . We have yet to wait for the formulation of some other criterion in clearly delineated terms to allow of its adoption as a rule of monetary policy.

Vera C. Smith, *The Rationale of Central Banking*, 1936[1]

A. Introduction

In the field of monetary law, economic definitions and theories have often found their way into the law through the adoption or reform of monetary legislation. In this chapter, I study the notion of monetary stability, which has become a fundamental policy objective enshrined in national laws and international treaties, and I discuss the extent to which a legal definition is either possible or desirable. I also explore the main institutional arrangements—independent central banks and currency boards—that have been developed in recent years in the pursuit of that fundamental objective, as well as the limits of such arrangements. In the case of central bank independence, the need to enhance the credibility and long-sightedness of monetary policy must be reconciled with the requirements of democratic legitimacy, accountability, and transparency.

B. Definition of Monetary Stability

The introduction to the Federal Reserve Act of 1913 (the Act that led to the establishment of the US Federal Reserve System) is a most illuminating legal provision for understanding the history of money and central banking, two economic institutions whose histories converged to some extent during the twentieth century. This introduction reads as follows: 'To provide for the establishment of Federal Reserve Banks, *to furnish an elastic currency*, to afford means of rediscounting commercial paper, to establish a more effective supervision of banking in the United States, and for other purposes.' (emphasis added.)

I refer to this introduction to the Federal Reserve Act in other parts of the book, but the focus in this section is the mandate given to the Federal Reserve System (Fed): 'to furnish an elastic currency'. Elastic is not stable; elastic means adaptable, the ability to stretch and then go back to its original form. The 'stability culture' is in itself a modern phenomenon, which has influenced legislative developments in recent decades. Indeed, the US Federal Reserve Act was

---

[1] See Vera C Smith, *The Rationale of Central Banking and the Free Banking Alternative* (Indianapolis: Liberty Press, 1990) 189–90. The book was originally published in 1936.

modified to give due emphasis to the notion of 'stable prices' as an important goal to be pursued by the Board of Governors and the Federal Open Market Committee.[2]

Monetary stability can be defined in positive terms or in negative terms. In positive terms, monetary stability refers to the maintenance of the internal value of money (ie, price stability) as well as of the external value of the currency (ie, the stability of the currency vis-à-vis other currencies, which is, in turn, influenced by the choice of exchange rate regime). In negative terms, monetary stability refers broadly to the absence of instability.

In recent years, it has become generally accepted that the primary objective of monetary policy as an instrument of economic policy should be price stability. Most modern central bank laws refer to this goal as their most important objective. This is based on economic theory (vertical Philips curve in the long run and time inconsistency) and supported by empirical evidence: independent central banks do a better job than politicians at controlling inflation.[3]

The economic literature in the last decades—which has influenced legal and political developments—relies on a notion of monetary stability that focuses primarily on keeping inflation under control. The standard definition of inflation is that it is a fall in the value of money, not just a rise in the consumer price index.[4] Though movements (measured in percentage rate of change) in Consumer Price Indices or Retail Price Indices tend to be used as a measurement of inflation,[5] in recent years there has also been a debate about the importance of other economic indicators to measure inflation. Some economists have expressed concerns about the limitations of using as measures of inflation price indices of currently provided consumer goods and services. Goodhart, for instance, suggests that an analytically correct measure of inflation should take account of asset price changes, in particular of housing prices and of changes in

---

[2] Section 2(a) of the Federal Reserve Act (12 USC 225a), which was added by Act of 16 November 1977 (91 Stat 1387) and amended by Acts of 27 October 1978 (92 Stat 1897) and 23 August 1988 (102 Stat 1375) refers to 'stable prices'.

[3] See Rosa M Lastra, *Central Banking and Banking Regulation* (London: Financial Markets Group, London School of Economics, 1996) 13–24, for a broader explanation of the arguments for and against central bank independence, and Rosa M Lastra, 'The Independence of the European System of Central Banks' (1992) 33 Harvard International Law Journal 475, 476–82. With regard to the economic literature on this issue, see *inter alia* Alex Cukierman, *Central Bank Strategy, Credibility and Independence: Theory and Evidence* (Cambridge MA: MIT Press, 1994).

[4] See definition of 'inflation' in Peter Newman, Murray Milgate, and John Eatwell (eds), *The New Palgrave Dictionary of Money & Finance* (London: Macmillan Press Ltd, 1992). Inflation is a process of continuously rising prices, or equivalently, of a continuously falling value of money.

[5] Monetary stability can be defined in narrow terms or in broad terms. In the UK and New Zealand it is defined in narrow terms.

financial asset prices.[6] At the EU level, Eurostat is investigating how to bring owner occupied housing into its harmonized index of consumer prices (HICP). This is an interesting development, as according to the current EC Regulation No 1688/98, the HICP only covers expenditure in monetary transactions in goods and services that are used for the direct satisfaction of individual needs and wants. Thereby, imputed rents and mortgage interest payments are currently excluded from the HICP coverage.[7]

Monetary stability is the lack of instability in the movement of prices. It refers to the absence of erratic or unanticipated movements in the level of prices through inflation or through deflation. Rapidly falling prices can cause as much 'instability' as rapidly rising prices. However, the studies of deflation as a phenomenon of monetary instability have been less numerous and more recent[8] and, their influence on legal developments in this field is so far limited. Hence, the law tends to reflect a notion of monetary stability as low inflation or keeping inflation under control. However, the law will need to adjust to reflect the fact that monetary instability can be caused both by rapidly rising prices and by rapidly falling prices, particularly when such phenomena are 'unanticipated' or when they occur on a continuous basis. (The economic literature on inflation distinguishes between anticipated and unanticipated inflation, with the latter having a more pernicious effect upon the economy than the former.)

Monetary stability is an important economic goal. However, there are other important economic goals that the government needs to take into account in the design of its economic policies: growth, employment, and so on. The question then arises: what is the best way of achieving several goals? In recent years, the solution adopted by the political authorities in many countries is to pursue growth and employment directly through fiscal policy and other instruments of economic policy—typically under political instruction—and to delegate the mandate of price stability and the conduct of monetary policy to an independent central bank. This model relies upon the pursuit of one goal: monetary stability;

---

[6] See Charles Goodhart, *Time, Inflation and Asset Prices*, Special Paper 117 (London: Financial Markets Group, London School of Economics, 1999). Few economists have contributed as much to the history and understanding of central banking in theory and practice as Charles Goodhart has. For long relegated to the abstruse universe of the specialist, central banking has now come to the front of economic policy debate. This process has been facilitated in no small way by the writings, teachings, and policy advice of Professor Goodhart.

[7] See Carsten Olsson and Jean-Claude Roman, 'A Harmonized Price Index for Owner Occupied Housing. Experiences from the Eurostat Pilot Study' (paper submitted by Eurostat at the joint UNECE/ILO Meeting on Consumer Price Indices in Geneva on 4–5 December 2003), at <http://www.unece.org/stats/documents/ces/ac.49/2003/17.e.pdf> (visited 24 February 2004).

[8] See eg, Paul Krugman, 'Can Deflation be Prevented?' at <http://www.pkarchive.org/economy/deflator.html>, (visited 23 February 2004); Manmohan Singh Kumar et al, *Deflation: Determinants, Risks and Policies*, IMF Occasional Paper No 221 (Washington DC: IMF, June 2003).

using one instrument: monetary policy. In the eyes of many central banking experts, since monetary policy is essentially a single instrument, it cannot simultaneously be assigned to more than one objective. If a monetary tool is assigned two objectives, for example, it is unlikely to achieve both and may end up achieving neither because of the related compromises necessarily involved. According to this line of thought, monetary tools are best suited to achieving price stability, while other policies and mechanisms should be applied to other objectives.

A further twist to the definition of monetary stability is provided by its dual dimension. As I have already indicated, in addition to the internal dimension, there is also an external dimension, which refers to the value of the currency. The stability of exchange rates (the exchange rate being the price of a currency in another currency) and the issue of which is the best exchange rate arrangement for a given country (fixed, floating, or some version of managed float) remain a matter of great controversy in the economic literature. This means that the law tends to refer to the external dimension of monetary stability (the stability of the currency) in rather ambiguous terms.[9]

The US Federal Reserve Act of 1913 is an important example of a central bank whose law includes other objectives such as growth and employment and the stability of the financial system in addition to monetary stability. When the Federal Reserve System was established in 1913, the major concern in the USA was financial fragility in the banking system. At the beginning of the twentieth century, banking crises and panics had caused a great deal of distress in North America. The lender of last resort role of the Fed (discount window lending) was conceived as an instrument to preserve financial stability. Over the years, the Fed has developed a sophisticated system of bank supervision which is also seen by the authorities as an effective instrument to safeguard financial stability, as I further discuss in Chapters 3 and 4. The history of the Fed illustrates the vicissitudes of monetary developments. Another important historical consideration is the experience of deflation in the USA in the 1930s following the Great Depression. At that time, the early 1930s, the emphasis was on growth and employment, not on controlling inflation. Indeed, until the Second World War, during times of peace from 1850 to 1939 inflation was zero. However, for much of the post-war period, policy makers in developed and developing countries have been worried about rising inflation, especially in the late 1970s and early 1980s.

The so-called 'oil shock' of 1973—ie, the quadrupling of oil prices which plunged much of the industrialized world into an era of soaring inflation and low

---

[9] Article 111 of the EC Treaty is an example of the ambiguity that reigns with regard to exchange rate policy. Indeed, such provision can be referred to as a 'calculated obfuscation for political purposes', as I further discuss in Ch 9.

and volatile growth, known in economic jargon as stagflation—is a historical development which marked a turning point in the understanding of the need for price stability. The oil shock destroyed the post-war pattern where governments had tried to buy a little more growth with a little more inflation (Philips curve), instead entrenching price stability as their primary concern.[10] Hence, the emphasis on price stability is a development that needs to be understood in a historical context: that provided by the country experiences, economic policies, and economic thinking which prevailed in the second half of the twentieth century. This development has had important legal implications nationally and internationally, particularly in the 1990s, as a substantial number of domestic laws as well as some international treaties (most notably the Maastricht Treaty on European Union) have made this objective the primary goal of central banks/ monetary agencies and as a number of provisions have been elaborated to hold those institutions accountable for their success (or failure) in pursuing this goal.

The phenomenon of deflation,[11] once considered a ghost of the past, has made its reappearance in economic circles in recent years, and Japan's experience with falling prices is often cited as an example of deflation.[12] In 2003, the European Central Bank also cautioned—for the first time in its short history—against the risks of deflation in the euro-zone.[13]

---

[10] Much has been written about the oil shock (oil shocks) in the context of inflation, the ensuing banking practices where petrodollars were 'recycled' to loans to Latin America and the international debt crisis that exploded in 1982 (Mexico being the first country to default on its international debt). Suffice is to say here (as Chapter 14 further explores these issues) that the oil shock rocked the world's economy, as the *Financial Times* summarizes in two articles published on the 30th anniversary of the oil shock: 17 October 2003, 2.

[11] 'There are different intensities of deflation. Deflation may be relatively mild, with aggregate price indices declining only by a percent or so, and temporary, lasting not more than a few quarters; or it may be mild but persist for several years; or it may be sustained and virulent, with economic stagnation and high unemployment accompanying falling prices and costs, as during the Great Depression of the 1930s, the most severe deflation of the twentieth century.' See Manmohan S Kumar, 'Deflation, the New Threat?', *Finance and Development*, IMF, June 2003, at p. 16, <http://www.imf.org/external/pubs/ft/fandd/2003/06/pdf/kumar.pdf>, (visited 23 February 2004). As Kumar points out in the article, 'if it is unanticipated, deflation leads to a redistribution of income from debtors to creditors.'

[12] See eg, Tim Callen and Jonathan D Ostry (eds), *Japan's Lost Decade. Policies for Economic Revival* (Washington DC: IMF, 2003).

[13] 'Price stability is defined as a year-on-year increase in the Harmonised Index of Consumer Prices (HICP) for the euro area of below 2%. Price stability is to be maintained over the medium term. Today, the Governing Council confirmed this definition (which it announced in 1998). At the same time, the Governing Council agreed that in the pursuit of price stability it will aim to maintain inflation rates close to 2% over the medium term. This clarification underlines the ECB's commitment to provide a sufficient *safety margin to guard against the risks of deflation*. It also addresses the issue of the possible presence of a measurement bias in the HICP and the implications of inflation differentials within the euro area.' See ECB Press Release, 'The ECB's Monetary Policy Strategy' (8 May 2003), <http://www.ecb.int/press/03/pr030508_2en.htm>, (visited 24 February 2004).

In the United States, the Board of Governors of the Federal Reserve System has also warned about the dangers of disinflation and the former chairman of the Board of Governors, Alan Greenspan, noted that it was crucial 'to ensure that any latent deflationary pressures are appropriately addressed well before they become a problem'.[14]

The consensus that has surrounded the need to delegate control over the money supply to an independent central bank is also a recognition of the importance given nowadays to monetary policy. Under the Keynesian policy modalities of the 1950s and 1960s fiscal policy had primacy and demand management policies (goals of growth and employment) were prevalent. With an independent central bank, priority is given to a monetary policy aimed at achieving price stability. In Germany, the pre-1999 Bundesbank stated that price stability was the primary objective. The secondary objective of the Bundesbank was to support the general economic policies of the Government (including growth and employment). German commentators of the Bundesbank law referred to this provision of the law (which is also replicated in the EC Treaty with regard to the ESCB: supporting the general economic policies of the Community, without prejudice to price stability) as the 'squaring of the circle', given that such economic policies could sometimes conflict with the sacrosanct goal of price stability. In the end, the trade-off between objectives is often a political decision.

Perhaps in the twenty-first century we shall witness the emergence of a rebalanced framework of macroeconomic policy (with fiscal policy regaining part of its earlier role) that may lead to a realignment of the goals to be pursued by the monetary authorities, which in turn will lead to a new wave of legal reforms. Though the importance of monetary stability as a foundation of the economic order, nationally and internationally, will remain, it may lose the quasi-sacrosanct nature that it enjoyed during the last quarter of the twentieth century.

C. Institutional Arrangements to Promote Monetary Stability

Though there are other arrangements that can promote monetary stability, such as legislated monetary rules (akin to the ones proposed by Milton Friedman[15]),

---

[14] See Alan Greenspan, 'Issues for Monetary Policy' (speech to the Economic Club of New York, December 2000) at <http://www.federalreserve.gov/boarddocs/speeches/2002/20021219/default.htm> (visited 14 October 2003).

[15] Milton Friedman formally proposed his monetary rule—for a constant growth of the money supply at a rate roughly equal to underlying productivity growth—in Milton Friedman, *Program for Monetary Stability* (New York: Fordham University Press, 1960). Friedman had already advanced some of his ideas in 1948, in Milton Friedman, 'A Monetary and Fiscal Framework for Economic Stability' 38 American Economic Review 245 (1948).

in recent years increasing attention has been given to the institutional aspects of money and consequently to those institutional arrangements that can promote monetary stability, such as independent central banks and currency boards. It is not that the merits of rules regulating the quantity of money are neglected. Indeed the rules versus discretion literature[16] and the quantity theory of money have inspired not only the economic debate and the way monetary economics has been taught since the 1970s but also monetary policy in North America and Europe in the mid 1970s and early 1980s. Monetary targets—ie, targets of growth for some monetary aggregate, typically announced at the beginning of the target period—were adopted in Germany and Italy in 1974, Canada, Switzerland, and the United States in 1975, in Australia, France, and the UK in 1976.[17] However, strict monetary targeting (ie, reliance on rigid monetary rules) was abandoned or modified by the mid-1980s in the USA and the UK.[18]

Nowadays, the UK relies on inflation targeting[19] (ie, a numerical target for the rate of inflation, according to section 12.1 of the Bank of England Act 1998[20]), while in the USA, the Federal Reserve does not have a commitment to a specific, known inflation target. Such a target would arguably limit the Fed's freedom of manoeuvre and, given the fact that the Fed's mandate encompasses other

---

[16] The rules versus discretion economic literature—which interestingly resembles the rules versus discretion debate in administrative law—dates back to Henry C Simons, 'Rules versus Authorities in Monetary Policy' (1936) 44 Journal of Political Economy 1. Most of the recent economic literature on central bank independence has followed the so-called time inconsistency argument, first formulated by Finn E Kydland and Edward C Prescott, 'Rules rather than Discretion: The Inconsistency of Optimal Plans' (1977) 86 Journal of Political Economy 473, and further developed by Robert J Barro and David B Gordon, 'Rules, Discretion, and Reputations in a Model of Monetary Policy' (1983) 12 Journal of Monetary Economics 101.

[17] According to some commentators, the introduction of strict monetary targeting can be regarded as marking a sharp break with the Keynesian macroeconomic policy making of the 1960s and 1970s, which had culminated in the high inflation of the late 1970s. See eg, John S Fforde, 'Setting Monetary Objectives' (1983) 23 Bank of England Quarterly Bulletin 200.

[18] However, from an operational point of view there is a beneficial legacy of monetary targeting, namely the continuing, albeit non-mechanical, concern with the growth of the quantities of a range of financial assets (included in monetary aggregates) and the understanding of the value of publishing and monitoring detailed information about the authorities' actions and intentions. See definition of 'monetary targeting' in Peter Newman, Murray Milgate, and John Eatwell (eds), *The New Palgrave Dictionary of Money & Finance* (London: Macmillan Press Ltd, 1992).

[19] New Zealand was the first country to adopt inflation targeting, according to the Reserve Bank of New Zealand Act 1989. The theoretical work on inflation targeting has been developed by the Swede Lars EO Svensson in the seminal articles Lars EO Svensson, 'Inflation Forecast Targeting: Implementing and Monitoring Inflation Targets' (1997) 41 European Economic Review 1111 and Lars EO Svensson, 'Inflation Targeting as a Monetary Policy Rule', (paper presented at the Sveriges Riksbank–IIES Conference on Monetary Policy Rules in 1998), later published as Lars EO Svensson, 'Inflation Targeting as a Monetary Policy Rule' (1999) 43 Journal of Monetary Economics 607.

[20] Section 12.1 Bank of England Act 1998 reads as follows: 'The Treasury may by notice in writing to the Bank specify for the purposes of Section 11 (a) what price stability is to be taken to consist of, or (b) what the economic policy of Her Majesty's Government is to be taken to be.'

objectives besides price stability, it would complicate the task of holding the Fed accountable for its actions.

In the context of the rules versus discretion monetary debate, it is interesting to observe that the advent of central bank independence grants a substantial degree of discretion (technical, not political) to central bankers within the realm of their legal mandate to strive for monetary stability.

D. Independent Central Banks: Theory and Practice

Introduction: The relations between the central bank and the government

The relations between the central bank and the government have always been the subject of much controversy. These relations involve several aspects: ownership, separate juridical personality, and dependence/independence (which in turn is related to the issue of control).

The issue of public or private ownership is of marginal importance these days, though the ownership of reserves and the allocation of central bank profits can be a source of contention in privately owned central banks, since the interests of private shareholders may conflict with the central bank's public responsibilities.[21] A great number of central banks were nationalized in the twentieth century (eg, the Bank of England was nationalized in 1946), while others that were newly created were established as public agencies, typically endowed with public ownership.

Most central banks these days enjoy separate juridical personality, which means that they can sue or be sued, and are the subject of rights and obligations. The attribution of separate legal personality is different from the granting of independence in the exercise of some delegated government functions. The issue of legal personality becomes more interesting in complex central banking systems, such as the US Federal Reserve System or the European System of Central Banks.

The nature of the Federal Reserve System is intricate. The primary components of the Federal Reserve System are the Board of Governors and the twelve regional Federal Reserve Banks.[22] The Federal Reserve System itself is not an entity; the entities with legal personality are the Board of Governors, which is a

---

[21] 'Central Bank Ownership Issues' was the title of a presentation by Daniel Lefort, General Counsel of the BIS, in Cambridge on 7 September 2005 in the Central Banking Annual Training Course, organized by Central Banking Publications.

[22] The Federal Open Market Committee (FOMC), established in 1933, adds another layer of complexity to the understanding of the System.

federal government agency (ie, a public body) created by Congress and account-able to Congress, and which performs administrative functions[23] (central bank-ing functions), and the twelve Federal Reserve Banks, which are separate legal entities,[24] privately owned,[25] organized as corporate entities and with a different legal personality each. The Federal Reserve Banks perform a duality of func-tions: central banking functions[26] on the one hand (eg, administration of mon-etary and credit policies) and corporate functions proper of a bank on the other (eg, managing depository accounts for other banks).[27]

The European System of Central Banks (ESCB) is composed of the European Central Bank (ECB) and the National Central Banks (NCBs). The ESCB does not have legal personality, and, therefore, is not a carrier of rights and obliga-tions. The entities that do have a legal personality are the ECB (European Central Bank) and the NCBs (National Central Banks).[28] The legal position of the ECB and its independence have been the subject of much debate in recent

---

[23] 12 USC 241.

[24] Section 4 Rules of Organization of the Board of Governors, issued pursuant to 5 USC 552.

[25] 12 USC 282, 323. See also Art 4 of the by-laws of the FRBNY.

[26] The central banking functions are conferred by statute or by express delegation of authority pursuant to 12 USC 248(k).

[27] In 1997–8 I acted as an expert witness in the case *Bank Markazi Iran v Federal Reserve Bank of New York*, Case No 823 presented before the Iran–United States Claims Tribunal at the Hague, the Netherlands (1997–9). The Tribunal reached its decision on 16 November 1999, Award No 595–823–3. At stake in the case were the issues of independence, control, and separate juridical personality. I was asked by the FRBNY to assess the independence of the Federal Reserve Bank of New York and of the Federal Reserve System. To this effect I wrote an expert opinion on the nature, independence, and operations of the Federal Reserve System. In that opinion, I wrote the following:

> The Federal Reserve Bank of New York (FRBNY) undoubtedly performs a major role both within the Federal Reserve System (as a part of the US central banking system) and in the international banking community (as a corporate entity). *In its capacity as a part of the US central banking system*, the FRBNY carries out a variety of functions, in some instances with independence from instruction of the executive branch of the US Government (e.g., in regard to the implementation of monetary policy) and in some others as an agent of the Government (e.g., when it acts as an agent of the Treasury in the carrying out of foreign exchange operations or when it acts as fiscal agent of the US Government (12 USC 391) in matters specified by the US Treasury). In its *corporate capacity*, on the other hand, the FRBNY carries out corporate activities proper of a bank, such as managing depository accounts for foreign central banks, including custodian and investment services; indeed, in these cases, the FRBNY acts as an agent of 'foreign central banks' and not as an agent of the US government.

I was a member of the legal team of the FRBNY in subsequent hearings, held at the Hague on 1–2 December 1998. During the hearing, Judge Gaetano Arangio-Ruiz asked me about the relation between separate legal personality and dependence/independence. I responded by saying that separate legal personality does not mean necessarily independence, nor dependence.

[28] See Art 8 and Art 107(2) EC Treaty and Arts 9 and 14 Protocol on the Statute of the European System of Central Banks and of the European Central Bank, annexed to the Treaty (hereinafter, ESCB Statute). See also Rene Smits, *The European Central Bank, Institutional Aspects* (The Hague: Kluwer Law International, 1997) 92–3.

years. The European Court of Justice has defined the limits of the independence of the ECB in the OLAF case,[29] which I further explore in Chapter 7. The proposed EU Constitution clarifies the legal position of the ECB in its Article I-30 paragraph 3: 'The European Central Bank is an institution. It shall have legal personality. It alone may authorise the issue of the euro. It shall be independent in the exercise of its powers and in the management of its finances. Union institutions, bodies, offices and agencies and governments of the Member States shall respect that independence.'[30]

The NCBs act in a dual capacity.[31] On the one hand they are the operational arms of the ESCB when carrying out operations that form part of the tasks of the ESCB. On the other hand, they are national agencies when performing non-ESCB functions.[32] For these reasons, while the law governing the ECB is solely EC law, the laws governing the status of the NCBs emanate not only from EC sources, but also from their respective national legislation. Furthermore, there are substantial differences between the range of functions and responsibilities assigned to each NCB in the various jurisdictions that comprise the euro area. In terms of its capital structure, it should be noted that the NCBs are the ECB's sole shareholders.

In exercising its responsibilities, the central bank can be dependent on or independent of political instruction. Dependence implies subordination to the dictate of the political authorities. A dependent central bank is 'controlled' by the government. However, the notion of control is not equivalent to the notion of dependence/independence. Independent central banks are still subject to

---

[29] See Case 11/00 *Commission of the European Communities v European Central Bank* [2003] ECR 1–7147, para 92. This case is referred to as 'the OLAF (European Anti-Fraud Office) case'.

[30] The Treaty establishing a Constitution for Europe, signed in Rome on 29 October 2004, is available in the Official Journal No C 310 of 16 December 2004. The proposed EU Constitution was thrown into a legal limbo following the rejection of the Treaty in referenda in France (28 May 2005) and the Netherlands (1 June 2005). The suspension of the ratification process (according to the declaration of the European Council Brussels summit on 16–17 June 2005 to allow for a 'period of reflection') does not equate to the abandonment altogether of the Constitution. The text of the Constitutional Treaty remains a legal document of value to refer to, also with a view to its possible entry into force or the taking over of parts of it in other Treaty texts later on.

[31] See Ch 7.

[32] According to Art 14(4) ESCB Statute. 'National central banks may perform functions other than those specified in this Statute unless the Governing Council finds, by a majority of two thirds of the votes cast, that these interfere with the objectives and tasks of the ESCB. Such functions shall be performed on the *responsibility and liability of national central banks and shall not be regarded as being part of the functions of the ESCB*' (emphasis added). According to Art 12(1) of the ESCB Statute: 'The Executive Board [of the ECB] shall implement monetary policy in accordance with the guidelines and decisions laid down by the Governing Council. In doing so the Executive Board shall give the necessary instructions to the national central banks. . . . [T]he ECB shall have recourse to the national central banks to carry out operations which form part of the tasks of the ESCB.'

some degree of control over their activities by the government. They are also accountable as I further discuss below. Before the advent of central bank independence, the relationship between the Treasury or Minister of Finance and the Central Bank was a principal–agent type of relationship in which the Treasury or MOF instructed the Central Bank what to do, and the latter was subservient to the wishes of the former, whether that meant to finance government deficits, or to use interest rate policy for a variety of government objectives.

The case for central bank independence

Central bank laws in numerous jurisdictions have granted independence or greater operational autonomy to their central banks with an explicit price stability mandate over the last two decades. Central bank independence has become a kind of 'graduation issue' for countries wishing to exhibit or consolidate their credentials in monetary stability and fiscal restraint.

The movement towards enhanced independence for central banks has been supported by a nearly overwhelming consensus among scholars[33] and policy makers that independent central banks are desirable from the standpoint of public policy. The argument for central bank independence is relatively straightforward. Inflation, in the view of most contemporary economists, has no long-range welfare benefits. But it does have significant costs. These costs include distortions in economic activity, the costs of repricing real assets according to a changing nominal price level, the costs of the effort people have to undertake to avoid losing the value of their financial claims, and, in cases of very high inflation, the subtle but pervasive effects of social demoralization.[34] Because inflation is unequivocally bad for a society, everyone would be better off if the political institutions maintained stable prices.

Experience has shown that political institutions often do not maintain stable

---

[33] See eg, Michael Parkin and Robin Bade, *Central Bank Laws and Monetary Policies: A Preliminary Investigation*, Research Report No 7804, (London, Ontario: University of Western Ontario, November 1977); Vittorio Grilli, Donato Mascianddaro, and Guido Tabellini, 'Political and Monetary Institutions and Public Financial Policies in the Industrial Countries' (1991) 13 Economic Policy 341; Alberto Alesina and Laurence Summers, 'Central Bank Independence and Macro-economic Performance: Some Comparative Evidence' (1992) 25(2) Journal of Money, Credit and Banking, 151; Alex Cukierman, Steven Webb, and Bilin Neyapti, 'Measuring the Independence of Central Banks and its Effects on Policy Outcomes' (1992) 6(3) World Bank Economic Review 353. It is interesting to observe that the empirical studies supporting central bank independence have contributed a novel feature to the law and economics literature. Rather than applying economic tools to legal matters (as with cost-benefit analysis applied in the field of torts), those empirical studies apply a legal index (based upon a number of selected legal provisions/indicators) for the purpose of developing economic and statistical tests that show a negative correlation between central bank independence and inflation.

[34] See Geoffrey P Miller, 'An Interest Group Theory of Central Bank Independence' (1998) 17 Journal of Legal Studies 433, 436.

prices. They have several powerful incentives to expand the money supply beyond the rate of real growth in the economy. In non-democratic societies, the control of the money supply is an important instrument of economic policy that can address various political needs, most notoriously the financing of government needs. In a democracy, political parties try to appeal to various constituencies and, in their eagerness to increase economic activity, the incumbent party may engage in inflationary policy in the period immediately before an election in order to raise employment, and create a strong, if temporary, sense of euphoria among voters that translates into votes for the politicians then in office.[35]

It is against this background that independent central banks find their contemporary justification: central bank independence is conceived as a means to achieve the goal of price stability. Central bank independence has been the preferred institutional arrangement to promote monetary stability since the end of the 1980s and beginning of the 1990s. A number of factors have contributed to this development. In the European Union, the Maastricht Treaty on European Union made legal central bank independence a *conditio sine qua non* to participate in European Monetary Union, in addition to the four criteria of economic convergence and the additional requirements regarding fiscal responsibility. In developing countries and emerging economies, governments have been strongly advised and sometimes compelled (eg, via a 'recommendation' of the International Monetary Fund) to grant autonomy or independence to their central banks.[36] Central banks around the world have become by law less subordinate to the dictate of political authorities.

The phenomenon of 'independence' is not, however, unique to central banking. It is a feature inherent in an administrative law tradition in which certain powers are delegated to certain agencies, with regulatory powers, as I further discuss below. This feature of functional decentralization used to be considered more acceptable in those countries which also favoured geographic decentralization (ie, a federal structure, such as the USA or Germany, with power divided between the centre and the states (*länder* in the case of Germany). The skills, expertise, and superior qualifications of technocrats (central bankers, energy regulators, etc) compared with those of politicians with regard to the conduct of their delegated functions, reinforce the case for independence.

---

[35] There is another inflation motivation as well: politicians can disrupt interest group deals by creating unanticipated inflation, which then causes the interest groups to return to the politicians with more campaign contributions. I thank Geoffrey Miller for bringing this point to my attention. For a further elaboration on this issue, see Miller, above note 34, 436–45.

[36] I further discuss the expansion of IMF 'structural conditionality' into areas like legal reform in Ch 13. See also the article I wrote on IMF conditionality in Rosa M Lastra, 'IMF Conditionality' (2002) 4(2) Journal of International Banking Regulation 167.

Despite the economic merits of central bank independence,[37] the actual decision to grant independence is a political one. Relations between central banks and governments have not always been easy. Indeed, quite often they are rather confrontational. The link between economics and politics is a difficult and complex one, which changes across countries and over time. This is true both for developed and for developing countries. Central bank independence, as I have already pointed out, is advocated mainly in the conduct of monetary policy, as a way of accomplishing a partial depoliticization of the money supply process. In this respect, central bank independence provides an intermediate solution between full depoliticization, as advocated in the free-banking proposals, and politicization, in which all economic policy is under governmental control.

Legal guarantees concerning the organization and functions of central banks on the one hand and the integrity and professionalism of central bankers on the other hand are an important measurement of legal central bank independence. The incentive structure of independent central bankers is different from that of elected politicians. Political economy and political science have contributed to the understanding of this 'incentive structure'. However, these incentives need to be enshrined in the law in order to be effective and enforceable.

The legal articulation of central bank independence

I recommend that the following elements be included in a law that truly safeguards independence:[38] (1) declaration of independence; (2) organic guarantees and professional independence; (3) functional or operational guarantees; (4) the 'economic test of independence' (ie, the central bank's ability to withstand government pressure to finance government deficits via central bank credit); (5) financial autonomy; and (6) regulatory powers.

Declaration of independence

A provision declaring that the central bank will be independent or autonomous from the Government and that interest rate decisions will not be politicized.

---

[37] Above note 3.

[38] I have had the opportunity of participating in programmes of legal technical assistance in the field of central banking during my stint at the International Monetary Fund, and more recently, in the summer of 2003, with regard to the People's Republic of China (PRC) in an ADB program of legal technical assistance coordinated by the Washington DC based International Law Institute. The new Law of the People's Republic of China on the People's Bank of China (PBC)—ie, the new Central Bank Law of the PRC—was promulgated on 27 December 2003 and came into force on 1 February 2004. Art 7 of the new Law contains a declaration of independence of the PBC from the State Council with regard to the implementation of monetary policy.

Organic guarantees and professional independence

A number of provisions regulate the organization of the central bank and its institutional relationships with the Government. I call these provisions 'organic guarantees' of independence,[39] though some of the measures I advocate also protect the scope of 'professional' or 'personal' independence. In particular, a law on central bank independence should guarantee security of tenure (typically for period of time longer than that held by legislators) and well defined appointment and removal procedures for central bank board members. The provisions relating to the appointment, dismissal, and term of office of the Governor and other central bank officials will give an indication of the degree of dependence or independence that the government wishes to grant to the central bank. There is an extensive literature on the need to provide for what I call 'pluralistic' appointment procedure, to avoid politicization. Accordingly, membership of the central bank governing bodies can be based upon (a) region, (b) sector and/or (c) expertise. In a geographically decentralized structure of government (such as a federal country), membership on the basis of region is important so as to represent the various interests of various parts of the country (or Union, as in the case of the EU). Membership based upon sector refers to the inclusion of the various sectors of the economy: industry, commerce, agriculture. For instance, in the USA, the Federal Reserve Banks have a Board of Directors with nine members each (and the president of each Federal Reserve Bank must be a person of 'tested banking experience'). Of those nine members, three members are known as Class A Directors, who are required to be representatives of the member banks, and may themselves be bankers. Three others are designated as Class B Directors, and must represent industry, commerce, and agriculture in the district and must not be officers, directors, or employees of any bank. The remaining three comprise the Class C Directors and are appointed by the Board of Governors of the Federal Reserve System. In the UK the main criterion for membership of the Monetary Policy Committee is expertise in either monetary policy, financial markets, or the running of the economy in general (at the macro or micro level). The ESCB combines a geographic criterion (because of the composition of the European Central Bank and the national central banks) and criteria based on expertise (the members of the Executive Board must be selected among 'persons of recognized standing and professional experience in monetary or banking matters').

Another recommendation is for 'professional independence', which is enhanced

---

[39] As I have articulated elsewhere, (see eg Rosa M Lastra, 'The Independence of the European System of Central Banks', above note 3, 475–519; and ch 1 of my *Central Banking and Banking Regulation*, above note 3) the legal framework of independence ought to include a number of organic and functional guarantees that range from the appointment and dismissal procedure to the relations between the central bank and the Treasury or Minister of Finance.

by the appointment of qualified candidates, well versed in monetary economics and central banking theory and practice. Professional independence is also safeguarded by the establishment of a list of incompatible or disqualifying activities so as to prevent conflicts of interest. For instance, while in office central bankers should be precluded from simultaneously holding private-sector jobs. Central bank officials should perform their duties on a full-time basis (with the possible exception of academic/university engagements). A central banker should not be simultaneously a financial adviser, an employee or a shareholder of a bank, or a member of parliament, as those occupations would engender conflicts of interests. Central bank officials should also be limited in pursuing private employment in credit and financial institutions for a reasonable period following their term of office. These restrictions are designed to preclude their susceptibility to 'private' incentives while in office. Such provisions are particularly necessary to avoid the 'capture' of the regulator by the regulated institutions.

A further safeguard of professional independence refers to the procedures for dismissal of central bank officials. Grounds for dismissal should be clearly defined in the law, including criminal offence or serious misconduct and permanent incapacity. Grounds for dismissal should not include 'displeasure' with central bank actions, or criticism that the Governor or other members of the governing bodies are not fulfilling their obligations.

Functional or operational guarantees

The central bank law should include what I refer to as 'functional' or 'operational guarantees' of independence, that is provisions that grant the central bank room for manoeuvre with regard to the carrying out of its functions and operations, without government interference.[40] Since monetary policy is the quintessential function of an independent central bank, the law should provide provisions that safeguard the central bank's decisional autonomy in the exercise of this function. A dependent central bank is required to secure prior government approval of its monetary policy decisions. An independent central bank does not require such prior approval. Therefore, clear provisions regarding the instruments of monetary control (monetary operations) available to the independent central bank are needed. Market-related (indirect) instruments of monetary control, such as discount policies and open market operations, are to be preferred over direct instruments of monetary control, such as credit ceilings

---

[40] See OLAF case, above note 29, para 134: 'Article 108 EC seeks, in essence, to shield the ECB from all political pressure in order to enable it effectively to pursue the objectives attributed to its tasks, through the independent exercise of the specific powers conferred on it for that purpose by the EC Treaty and the ESCB Statute.' See also paras 135 and 126.

or interest rate controls. (However, reliance upon market-related instruments needs to be accompanied by the development of the money market). With regard to the proper understanding of 'functional independence', it is important to bear in mind that most countries' central banks do not have 'goal independence' (ie, the ability to choose the goal), but 'instrument independence' (ie, the ability to choose the instruments necessary to achieve the goal).[41] The 'goal constraint' as I further discuss below is an important limitation of central bank independence.

Economic test of independence

The key economic test of independence is the central bank's ability to withstand government pressure to finance government deficits via central bank credit. In this respect, the central bank law should include a provision prohibiting or severely limiting the central bank's lending to the public sector. A truly independent central bank should have complete command over its own credit and, in particular, should be under no obligation to extend credit to the government.[42] This provision and others related to fiscal restraint are further discussed with regard to the European Union in Chapter 8.

Financial autonomy

An independent central bank should be able to adopt its internal budget, in accordance with criteria defined in the law so as to ensure that the bank's expenditures are reasonable. This criterion of financial autonomy has been recently tested at the EU level in the OLAF case. The European Court of Justice clarified that, though the ECB has its own resources and budget (not included in the Community budget),[43] it does not mean that it is exempt 'from every rule of Community law'. Hence, the ECB is not exempt from the anti-fraud investigations conducted by the Commission's anti-fraud office (OLAF). The proposed EU Constitution recognizes that the ECB is 'independent in the management of its finances' in its Article I–30 paragraph 4, as I further discuss in Chapter 7.

Regulatory powers

The power to issue rules and regulations is a measure of the autonomy (ability to give rules to itself) of an agency. However, while in the USA this rule-making power of independent regulatory commissions is consistent with the

---

[41] See Rosa M Lastra, *Central Banking and Banking Regulation*, above note 3, 36–8, & 44–8.
[42] See Latin American Shadow Financial Regulatory Committee, Statement No 4, Montevideo, 18 October 2001, 'Central Bank Independence: the Right Choice for Latin America' available at <http://www.aei.org>.
[43] See OLAF case, above note 29, para 132.

administrative law tradition of the country, the legitimacy of rules and regulations issued by the central bank (or by an independent agency) and not directly
by the government has been a contentious issue in civil law countries. In the USA,
rule-making is the administrative counterpart of what a legislative body does
when it enacts a statute. In the case of the Federal Reserve System (the Fed), the
Federal Reserve Act gives authority to the Fed to issue rules that are binding on
depository institutions and other institutions under its scope of influence (ie,
limited application). Such rules are codified in the Code of Federal Regulations
(CFR) published in the Federal Register by the Executive departments and
agencies of the Federal Government.[44] The EC Treaty gives rule-making powers
to the ESCB. Article 110 of the EC Treaty states that in order to carry out the
tasks entrusted to the ESCB, the ECB shall issue regulations (with general application and binding in their entirety and directly applicable in all Member States),
decisions (binding in their entirety upon those to whom they are addressed), and
recommendation and opinions (the latter two with no binding force).

The limits of central bank independence

The notion of independence that I support in this book is one that I developed
in a paper I wrote with Geoffrey Miller in 1999.[45] By an 'independent' central
bank, we mean a particular kind of institution that is independent in some
respects, but highly constrained in others. In particular, an independent central
bank is relatively free of short-term political pressures: its officers serve for long
periods and may not be removed from office for disagreements over policy with
other government officials, and it does not take orders from any other institution. In this respect it enjoys a high degree of autonomy. At the same time, an
independent central bank is not autonomous in its goals. Rather, a principal
goal of an independent central bank is typically to achieve price stability, either
absolute stability of prices, or prices that change within some range set in
advance and publicly observable.

The goal constraint: The case against 'absolute' independence

Though independent central banks are generally free to formulate and implement monetary policy, they remain constrained by their statutory objective.

---

[44] The Code is divided into 50 titles which represent broad areas subject to Federal regulation.
Each title is divided into chapters which usually bear the name of the issuing agency. Title 12
refers to Banks and Banking and Chapter II of Title 12 refers to rules issued by the Federal Reserve
System.

[45] This paper, which was presented at a joint conference in Stockholm in December 1999,
was subsequently published as a book chapter. See Rosa M Lastra and Geoffrey Miller, 'Central
Bank Independence in Ordinary and Extraordinary Times' in Jan Kleineman (ed), *Central
Bank Independence. The Economic Foundations, the Constitutional Implications and Democratic
Accountability* (The Hague: Kluwer Law International, 2001) 31–50.

Sometimes the objective is defined in narrow terms as a numerical target and some others in broad terms. In some jurisdictions, most notably in the USA, the central bank's mandate may encompass several objectives, rather than a single or primary goal. As I have already mentioned, the Fed is required by law to pay attention to a variety of unranked targets, including stable prices, growth, and employment. Since independent central banks can seldom choose their goals, the discussion about central bank independence mainly focuses on the scope of powers delegated to central banks for the achievement of their statutorily defined objectives.

A central bank that is politically autonomous but goal-constrained in this sense can devote itself to maintaining price stability, without being subject to the political pressures that might otherwise induce inflationary policies. The independent central bank can be seen as a form of pre-commitment by the political system to tie its hands, like Ulysses at the mast, to avoid taking destructive actions when the siren of inflationary temptation appears. If the central bank is truly independent of the political cycle, and is truly committed to the goal of maintaining price stability, it will not be subject to the pressures that tend to generate inflation when monetary policy is in the hands of political actors. There is some evidence that, in fact, this theory has practical merit: in the developed world, at least, independent central banks tend to have a somewhat better record of achieving price stability than their non-independent counterparts.[46]

The case for central bank independence is often presented as a virtual absolute. That is, the theory recognizes no limits on central bank independence, so long as the bank itself is reliably pre-committed to achieving price stability. Taken at face value, the theory would suggest that central banks should be *completely* insulated from politics. But this is not the case in the real world. Even highly independent central banks, such as the Federal Reserve Board, the pre-1999 Bundesbank, or the European Central Bank, do not enjoy this kind of independence. Although they operate with a high degree of protection from political pressures, they are far from isolated from the political process. And while maintaining price stability is typically the primary goal of such institutions, it is rarely—if ever—the sole objective. The charters of these banks often also contain clauses that permit or require them to consider other objectives, such as maintaining the stability of the financial system, enhancing employment, facilitating economic growth, and so on. Moreover, even if the central

---

[46] See eg Alex Cukierman, *Central Bank Strategy, Credibility and Independence: Theory and Evidence* (Cambridge MA: MIT Press, 1994). As I have discussed in my *Central Banking and Banking Regulation*, above note 3, 16–18, the experience in developing countries or emerging economies is different.

bank charters purported to establish absolute independence, they are only pieces of paper. A legislative charter can always be revised by subsequent legislation; and even if the charter is embodied in a national constitution, the constitution can always be amended or ignored. It is obvious that there are limits to central bank independence in the real world, however much the economist's pure theory might question the rationale for such limits. Why do we observe, in fact, considerably less independence than would be suggested by orthodox economic theory? Three answers suggest themselves.[47]

First, it might be that the observed limits on the independence of central banks around the world are the results of political compromise. Politicians may recognize that an independent central bank provides significant benefits. If they are public-spirited, they will understand and support the role of the independent central bank as a form of pre-commitment to price stability even in the face of considerable political temptation. The current cynicism about politics overlooks the fact that some politicians might actually wish to be in office in order to deliver long-lasting prosperity for the country and that, therefore, they will not sacrifice that long-term goal for the short-term benefits of inflationary policies. But even if politicians are purely self-interested, they may find a degree of central bank independence to be in their interests, either because an autonomous bank can be blamed as a scapegoat for failed or unpopular policies, or because the price stability that an independent central bank can ensure allows the politician to milk interest groups for larger financial support in the short run.[48] However, these motivations that a politician may have to favour independent central banks are likely, in the real world, to be counterbalanced by conflicting motivations to acquire, maintain, and exercise power. Control over the price level is one of the most important powers of any government, and politicians are likely to give up that power only reluctantly—especially because politicians themselves tend to be people who like and desire power. Thus, some limits of central bank independence are the result of political compromise.

A second possible explanation for the observed limits on central bank independence is based on simple necessity. While an absolutely independent central bank may be an appealing idea from a policy standpoint, in practice, institutions must be able to operate. For example, the central bank must have officers to direct its operations. These officers must be appointed somehow. One might suppose that to achieve maximum independence from the political process, the

---

[47] In this section of the paper I draw substantially on the paper I wrote with Geoffrey Miller. See above note 45.

[48] On the rent-extraction motivation for central bank independence, see Geoffrey P Miller, above note 34, at 36.

officers could be appointed through some ostensibly non-political process—for example, they might be selected by a panel of experts who are not politicians, or vacancies may be filled by the incumbent officers. Yet it requires little thought to realize that these alternative selection mechanisms are not themselves immune from political influence. Members of the nominating panel must themselves be nominated; and all parties involved in the process are human beings who are subject to the normal pressures of friendship, loyalty, and inducement. And even if politics in the narrow sense does not play a role, the process of insulating the officers of the central bank from political influence also removes an important check on their behaviour, and thus allows the bank's officers greater flexibility to ignore the goal of price stability in the service of other objectives. As a practical matter, politics has to play a role in the activities of central banks: the goal of complete insulation from politics cannot be realized. In an imperfect world, some compromise with the ideal of central bank independence is a practical necessity.

A third possibility is that the ideal of central bank independence is not an absolute *even in theory*, even if we could overcome the political and practical impediments to creating a fully independent central bank. If central bank independence—and the price stability that such independence seeks to achieve—were unambiguously good in all circumstances, it would be good social policy for the central bank to be replaced by a computer that was programmed to achieve price stability in any and all circumstances, set in motion, and equipped with fail-safe mechanisms to deter any future tampering with its operations. If such a machine were to be constructed, as long as prices remain stable, the element of human intervention would seem to be irrelevant. Such a central bank would be both completely autonomous and absolutely goal-constrained. This machine, of course, does not exist in reality, but we can construct it imaginatively in order to investigate the theoretical point.[49]

Most people would not be comfortable with this level of independence in the central bank. Even if we generally accept the economists' view that price level stability is a good and desirable thing, the idea of committing a central governmental function to a mechanical operation appears bizarre and undesirable. Intuitively, it is not an appealing idea. This intuition appears to be supported by observations described above of the structure of central banks around the world. Although most of the world supports the concept of independent central banks, no country has attempted to achieve the level of independence of our hypothetical computer.[50] It may be that these limits to central bank independence reflect genuine concerns of social policy as well as the influence of politics or

---

[49] Above note 45.   [50] ibid.

practicality. The increasing complexities of monetary and financial management imply an expanding two-way flow of consultation and cooperation between the central bank and the government.

While a very high level of central bank independence is highly desirable, complete independence is not, even if it could be achieved.

Democratic legitimacy

There are two principal limits on central bank independence that all democratic societies should maintain. One of these limits of central bank independence principally concerns the limitations of the goal, 'the goal constraint', an issue which I discussed in the first section of this chapter. Important as stable prices are in ordinary times, the commitment to preventing inflation should not impair a nation's ability to respond to fundamental threats or basic changes in its identity. The other limit refers to the issue of democratic legitimacy, an issue which I survey below, and which is related to the debate about central bank accountability. A democratic society always retains the discretion to reinvent itself; and should the people of a country make a considered, deliberate choice to seek some other goal, the institutions of central bank independence should respect that decision.[51]

Ordinary versus extraordinary times

In ordinary times, countries do not face profound threats to, or alterations of, their basic identity. Ordinary times are structured around more limited disputes that do not go to the identity of the nation or to its basic security. In extraordinary times, when a country's basic identity or survival is at stake, as I illustrate below with the example of Germany, the government may need to raise revenues very quickly and efficiently in order to provide the necessary funding for the enterprise. One means of raising revenues quickly is through seigniorage[52] (ie, the margin between the nominal value of the notes and coins issued and the costs of their production), which can be rather substantial in the current system of *fiat* money, paper money inconvertible into gold or other precious metals.

Seigniorage can be conceived of as a form of taxation. Like any tax, seigniorage raises revenues to finance government operations. And like any tax, seigniorage

---

[51] ibid.

[52] Historically, and as applied to money, seigniorage was a levy on metals brought to a mint for coining, to cover the cost of the minting and to provide revenue to the ruler, who claimed it as a prerogative. In recent monetary literature the term has been revived and applied to the revenue derived by a note issuing authority. Eg, see Alex Cukierman, above note 46, at 47: seigniorage revenues are the amount of real resources obtained by the government by means of new base money injections.

introduces distortions into economic activity. The utility of seigniorage increases when the demand for government funds is sudden and unanticipated. There are two crucial differences between seigniorage and ordinary taxes: the timing of their imposition and the fact that seiginiorage does not require parliamentary approval, while ordinary taxes do. Seigniorage taxes can be imposed very quickly. Conventional taxes, however, require a much longer lead time. They often require authorization from the parliament or other legislative body. Such a process can be time-consuming, especially when interest groups enter to seek advantages for themselves in the tax package being drafted. Even after new taxes have been imposed, the collection process requires a substantial lead time, since the entities being taxed must be given notice of their obligations and time to respond. The upshot is that, if the government needs money quickly, seigniorage is likely to be preferable to ordinary taxation as a temporary measure.

The cost of obtaining seigniorage revenues through inflationary finance is, of course, inflation. But some level of inflation may need to be tolerated in order to achieve the government's compelling need to raise money quickly in times of crisis. Yet the government cannot always be relied on to use the power of inflationary finance only when this course is indicated by extraordinary circumstances. Seigniorage is a highly tempting means of raising revenues to finance ordinary government operations, or to subsidize powerful interest groups. Because its effects are pervasive—felt by the public in the form of price increases—the actual interests that benefit from the policies can often be disguised. And because the inflation tax can ordinarily be imposed by the monetary authorities without the need for parliamentary approval or the consent of other government agencies, the inflation tax may be politically easier than conventional taxes. *The problem of institutional design is how to distinguish the ordinary times from the extraordinary ones,* and how to limit the government to imposing inflation taxes only in extraordinary times. Some features of central bank institutional design can be understood as attempting to deal with this problem. For example, many central bank laws contain strict prohibitions against central bank lending to the government (the economic test of independence). These prohibitions are intended to prevent the government from inflating the economy during ordinary times. In extraordinary times, however, these restrictions need to be eased.

Historical example: The limits of the independence of the pre-1999 German Bundesbank

The pre-1999 German Bundesbank has often been regarded by commentators and policy makers as the bastion for price stability in Germany and a symbol of monetary discipline around the world. The anti-inflationary record of the

Bundesbank was typically cited in the literature as the quintessential example of the inverse relationship between inflation and central bank independence. However, even the most independent of central banks has limits, as the history of the Bundesbank over the years proves.

In 1957 the Bank Deutscher Länder that had been set up by the Allies in 1948, as a federally organized, provisional central banking institution in the western occupied zones, was transformed into the Bundesbank through the enactment of the Bundesbank Law.[53] The federal structure of the Bank Deutscher Länder (modelled upon that of the US Federal Reserve System) was maintained in the Bundesbank, and the idea of independence was embedded in the new legislation. This double degree of decentralization of power: geographic (federalism) and functional (independence), satisfied the US occupying authorities that wanted to establish strong institutional mechanisms against a possible totalitarian backlash. However, the aim of stability (*stabilität*), which became enshrined in the 1957 Law, was not new. As David Marsh emphasizes in his excellent book on the Bundesbank, '*Stabilitätspolitik* [in Germany] transcends the boundaries between dictatorship and democracy.'[54] Indeed the German visceral hate for inflation and their unwavering support for monetary stability dates back to the disastrous experience of hyperinflation in 1923 in an economy already overburdened with onerous war debts and reparations.[55] Enormous popular discontent at the time paved the way for the rise of National Socialism, with its dire consequences for the German nation. Adolf Hitler came to power promising currency stability to the German people, though he eventually sacrificed it (as well as the independence of the Reichsbank) because of the needs of the armaments policy first and war thereafter.[56]

---

[53] See *Gesetz über die Deutsche Bundesbank* (Act concerning the *Deutsche Bundesbank*), as last amended by the Seventh Act amending the Bundesbank Act of 23 March 2002 (Federal Law Gazette I, 1159). For an English translation of the Bundesbank Law, see the official website of the Bundesbank at <http://www.bundesbank.de/presse/download/bbkgesetz_lesefassung_20020323_en.pdf> (visited 23 February 2004).

[54] David Marsh, *The Most Powerful Bank: Inside Germany's Bundesbank* (New York: Times Books, 1992) 13.

[55] The heavy burden of reparations imposed on Germany in 1919 in the Versailles Peace Treaty was criticized by John Maynard Keynes in *The Economic Consequences of the Peace* (London: Macmillan, 1919). Keynes argued forcefully that the reparations payments discussed at Versailles were far too high and that the peace was to be Carthaginian. See Arminio Fraga, 'German Reparations and Brazilian Debt: a Comparative Study' (1986) 2 163 Princeton University Essays in International Finance.

[56] Above note 54. The incident is recalled by David Marsh in ch 4 of his book, in particular 99–101. Marsh interestingly points out (75): 'The Reichsbank's profoundly undemocratic nature made it, in a sense, a perfect tool in Hitler's hands. It shared with the Führer the precept that *monetary stability had to be dispensed from above, rather than created by the people themselves.*' (italics added).

The provisions in the 1957 Bundesbank Law that encapsulate the idea of independence for the sake of monetary stability are Articles 3 and 12.[57] According to Article 3: 'The Deutsche Bundesbank regulates the amount of money in circulation and of credit supplied to the economy, using the monetary powers conferred on it by this Act, *with the aim of safeguarding the currency*, and sees to the execution of domestic and external payments.' According to Article 12: 'Without prejudice to the performance of its functions, the Deutsche Bundesbank is required to support the general economic policy of the Federal Cabinet. *In exercising the powers conferred on it by this Act, the Bank is independent of instruction from the Federal Cabinet*' (italics added).[58]

Though the Bundesbank Law entrusted the Bundesbank with 'monetary powers' with the 'aim of safeguarding the currency', those monetary powers were in fact restricted to one instrument: the ability to raise and lower interest rates. The room for manoeuvre for an independent central bank is monetary policy. Exchange rate policy typically remains in the hands of government. Former German Chancellor Helmut Schmidt had written in his memoirs that 'he regarded exchange rate policies . . . as important elements of general foreign and strategic policy.'[59] The exchange rate is not only an anchor of external price stability but an important element in other governmental economic policies, linked to the trade and employment objectives of a country, and with a clear impact upon its external competitiveness. However, the need for coordination between monetary policy—the internal dimension of monetary stability—and exchange rate policy—the external dimension of monetary stability—cannot be ignored by independent central bankers. Disputes over the exchange rate have been a frequent source of discord between the Bundesbank and the Government. In these disputes, the Government typically prevailed, in particular when a greater national objective was at stake as, for instance, in the case of German reunification, when the conversion rate between the Ostmark and the Deutschmark was fixed at one to one for political imperatives, against

---

[57] The wording of these provisions is reproduced in part in Art 105(1) EC Treaty as amended by the Maastricht Treaty on European Union and Art 2 Protocol on the Statute of the European System of Central Banks and the European Central Bank: 'The primary objective of the ESCB shall be to maintain price stability. Without prejudice to the objective of price stability, the ESCB shall support the general economic policies in the Community.'

[58] Art 12 has been referred to by some German authors as the 'squaring of the circle': independent from the government in the conduct of monetary policy, but supporting the general economic policy of it. See eg, Klaus Stern, *Das Staatsrecht der Bundesrepublik Deutschland, vol. II Staatsorgane, Staatsfunktionen, Finanz- und Haushaltsverfassung, Notstandsverfassung* (Munich: CH Beck, 1980) 463–508.

[59] This is recalled by Michele Frattiani and others in 'The Maastricht Way to EMU' (1992) 187 Princeton University Essays in International Finance 35.

the Bundesbank's advice. There have been other instances throughout its history in which the Bundesbank has opposed unsuccessfully exchange rate policies pursued by the Government. For instance, in 1961 the Bundesbank opposed the Deutschmark revaluation, but was forced to change its mind by the economics minister at the time, Ludwig Erhard.[60] Nonetheless, the Government learnt over the years that discord with the Bundesbank could be destabilizing for the political party in power.[61] In 1969, the Deutschmark was revalued after the Bundesbank's proposal was at first rejected by the Bonn Government. The row helped precipitate the defeat of Chancellor Kurt Georg Kiesinger.[62]

The Bundesbank's room for manoeuvre (ie, independence) was seriously curtailed in the last decade through two major historical developments: German unification and European Monetary Union. In the case of German unification, the interest at stake was national identity, not price stability. The ERM (the Exchange Rate Mechanism of the European Monetary System) was sacrificed in order to achieve a greater national objective: the unity of the German people. In the case of European Monetary Union, supranational integration was considered to be more important for the future of the German nation than the maintenance of an independent central bank.

The fall of the Berlin Wall was an event of tremendous symbolic importance in the history of Germany and in the history of Europe. Chancellor Kohl seized the historical opportunity of bringing unity to the German people with courage and decisiveness, as well as improvization. The Chancellor had vision, but lacked a coherent blueprint of how to accomplish unification. This is particularly evident when talking about monetary unification (1 July 1990) which preceded full political reunification (3 October 1990). The timing of it took everybody by surprise, including the Bundesbank. Kohl's political instinct cautioned him against long negotiations that could have dragged for years, and possibly, hampered the prospect of unity. The Bundesbank had expressed its view that the process of monetary unification could not be rushed. However, the decision to go ahead was indeed 'rushed' and on 6 February 1990 Kohl proposed 'immediate' talks on extending the Deutschmark to East Germany. The Bundesbank opposed the conversion rate of one to one, based on sound

---

[60] See *Financial Times*, 1 October 1993, 'Bundesbank's record in standing up to Bonn Government'.

[61] As David Marsh, above note 54, 146, points out: 'Three Chancellors—Ludwig Erhard in 1966, Kurt Georg Kiesinger in 1969, and Helmut Schmidt in 1982—owe their downfall directly or indirectly to the actions of the Bundesbank. All three leaders were ousted not by defeat in general elections, but as a consequence of shifts in coalitions, sparked off by controversies over monetary policy.'

[62] Above note 60.

economic logic.[63] But the government did not listen and went ahead with such parity: 'One for one, or else we will never be one.' In 1991 Bundesbank President Karl Otto Pöhl resigned. In his formal departure speech in August 1991,[64] Pöhl reminded his audience that when he had taken office, he had acknowledged that the Bundesbank, for all its independence was legally required to support the government's overall economic policies. But he criticized the economic consequences of reunification: Germany was suffering a 'homemade' acceleration in price rises resulting from the failure to increase taxes to finance German unity, a development that the Bundesbank had warned against, though unsuccessfully.

Throughout the process of European monetary integration, the Bundesbank's belief that the abandonment of the Deutschmark (or any watering down of its *stabilität* credentials) would lead to a weaker and more inflation-prone European currency, helps explain its lack of enthusiasm, or even reluctance in some instances, towards the advent of monetary union in Europe and, in particular, towards the speed with which politicians proposed to advance to it. In 1978 Chancellor Helmut Schmidt and French President Valéry Giscard d'Estaing reached an accord to form a Franco-German zone of monetary stability, which gave rise to the European Monetary System (EMS). The Bundesbank expressed its misgivings about the setting up of the EMS, fearful that the new system might undermine the pursuit of monetary stability. In November 1978, Helmut Schmidt visited the Bundesbank to persuade its members of the need for greater monetary cooperation in Europe. The Chancellor reflected on the active role that Germany should play in this endeavour and suggested that if the Bundesbank were to oppose the signing of the agreement setting up the EMS, he might ask parliament to reduce the central bank independence through a change to the Bundesbank Law.[65] The goal here was supranational (European) integration not price stability, Schmidt reminded his audience. The fear of Germany for itself and the fear of France for Germany cannot be ignored in any discussion about the history of European integration after the Second World War. Indeed the Treaty of the European Economic Community which was signed in Rome in March 1957 (the very same year in which the Bundesbank Act was passed by the German Parliament) as well as subsequent revisions of the Treaty—in particular

---

[63] See eg David Marsh, above note 54, 178: 'At the beginning of 1990, the rate used for exchanging east marks against D-marks in commercial transactions was 4.5 to 1. On the free exchange market (illegal according to the East German authorities) the rate was 7 to 1.' He further recalls on page 186: 'Too low a level for the east mark against the D-mark would sharply cut East German incomes and encourage more migration to the west. Too high a rate would, on the other hand, spark greater unemployment and this would also spur desperate East Germans to seek the prosperity of the Federal Republic. At the end of March [1990], the Bundesbank suggested that the east-mark assets and payments should be converted into D-marks on the basis of 2 to 1.'

[64] See David Marsh, above note 54, 35.   [65] See David Marsh, above note 54, 168.

the Maastricht Treaty on European Union—have not been alien to these fears. The political agenda in both France and Germany—indeed the political agenda in the construction of Europe—has always been mindful of the need to channel and contain the mighty power of Germany (political and economic) within a context of European integration.

The Bundesbank was mostly concerned about its daily fight against inflation. European integration has been a government's goal, not a central bank goal. The progress towards monetary union was tainted with incidents of discord between the Federal Cabinet and the Bundesbank. In 1987, for instance, there was a discord over the setting up of a Franco-German finance and economic council as part of a bilateral treaty to 'harmonize' economic policies between the two countries. The Bundesbank feared that such a committee might compromise its independence. In the years that preceded the signing and entry into force of the Maastricht Treaty (from 1988 to 1992–3) there were some disagreements with Chancellor Helmut Kohl over European Monetary Union. The Bundesbank, loyal to its tradition of monetary stability, tried to shift the discussion away from the 'political' argument for EMU and towards the 'technical' discussion of what economic conditions needed to precede the advent of monetary union. Those conditions—the criteria of economic convergence—were formulated in onerous terms for German partners (though in the end Germany struggled to qualify as much as other countries from the 'garlic belt') with regard to budget deficits and size of public debt, long term interest rates, inflation rates, and exchange rate stability (within the ERM). Following the events of 1992–3, with the reformation of the Exchange Rate Mechanism of the EMS and the exit from the ERM of the Italian lira and the British pound, there was a growing consensus that the Bundesbank's position as the de facto anchor of the ERM was politically hard to justify with its European partners, who had no voice and no vote in the Bundesbank's decisions. This was particularly evidenced by the high interest rate policy of the Bundesbank in 1992–3, in response to a purely domestic problem: the rise in inflationary pressures due to the costs of German reunification in the light of the government's failure to articulate an appropriate fiscal policy.[66] The tightening of monetary policy in Germany had a very negative impact upon the rest of Europe, which was suffering from an economic slowdown and therefore needed lower interest rates.

As with German monetary unification, European Monetary Union (EMU) was a political decision for the government to take, not for the central bank. The

---

[66] As Karl Blessing, a former Bundesbank president (as well as Reichsbank senior official during the Nazi regime) eloquently put it: 'The less it is supported by fiscal policy, the tougher monetary policy has to be.' See Karl Blessing, speech at Mainz University, 24 February 1966, quoted in David Marsh, above note 54, 161.

Bundesbank succeeded in pressing forward its arguments on some occasions. In the end, it was a pyrrhic victory, as the Bundesbank became an integral part of the European System of Central Banks on 1 January 1999, with the transfer of monetary policy responsibilities from the national to the supranational arena. However, as a small consolation for the Bundesbank, the European Central Bank is located in Frankfurt and modelled functionally upon the Bundesbank.

The independence of the Bundesbank and its corresponding ability to stand up to the government's wishes is also supported by a 'positive record' in which the Bundesbank succeeded in pursuing a tight monetary policy against the government's wishes. It is upon this record that the anti-inflationary reputation of the Bundesbank grew so strong over the years. For instance, in 1966 tight money precipitated the first post-war recession, and contributed to the departure of Ludwig Erhard as Chancellor. In 1972 there was a row over capital controls, that led to the resignation of the economics minister, Karl Schiller, who opposed such controls as running counter to the principles of market economics. In 1981–2 high interest rates discomfited the Bonn Government, helping Chancellor Helmut Schmidt's downfall. In 1992–3 tight Bundesbank policies increased problems for the Exchange Rate Mechanism (ERM) of the European Monetary System and eventually led to the widening of the ERM bands and to the exit from the system of the Italian lira and the British pound. In 1997, the German Government, after strong opposition from the Bundesbank, abandoned its attempt to use profits from revaluing the country's gold reserves in order to meet the criteria of economic convergence required to qualify for European Monetary Union.[67]

In summary, the independence of the Bundesbank has seldom been sacrificed on the grounds that the economy was suffering. Indeed the ghosts of deflation and recession are not as feared in Germany as in other countries. When it comes to price stability, the German public is truly inflation-averse and is ready to accept the anti-inflationary policies proposed by the central bank (through a rise in interest rates for instance). It is when it comes to other goals that compromise the very identity or security of the nation that independence and price stability have been sacrificed.

E. Democratic Legitimacy and Accountability

Functional decentralization and the model of independent agencies

The model of independent agencies or independent regulatory commissions has a long-standing tradition in the United States as a way of dealing with the

---

[67] See *Financial Times*, 4 June 1997, 'Bonn backs down over gold reserve revaluation'.

regulation of complex realities: money, securities, energy, transport, telecommunications, the environment, and others. Agencies have been described as 'miniature governments', typically endowed with executive powers, quasi-legislative (rule-making) and quasi-judicial (adjudication) powers. Since agencies are by definition technocracies (a 'headless fourth branch of government', according to some commentators),[68] a basic problem of political legitimacy arises: how to reconcile their powers with the demands of a democracy. In the United States, independent regulatory commissions have been the subject of extensive debate and criticism.[69] For instance, the 1971 Ash Council Report[70] (the Report of the President's Advisory Council on Executive Organization) on Selected Independent Regulatory Agencies recommended that functions of six agencies, including the Securities and Exchange Commission (SEC), should be transferred to single administrators under the President. In particular the agencies were criticized for their alleged lack of accountability and their excess of independence.

In many European jurisdictions, the advent of central bank independence on the one hand and the establishment of agencies to regulate privatized utilities on the other hand have signified a change in their administrative law tradition, which used to rely on executive departments headed by a cabinet officer. Since important elements of that tradition remain deeply embedded in the legal framework of many European countries, this background is important to understand the debate about the legitimacy and accountability of independent central banks.

---

[68] See Chiara Zilioli, 'Accountability and Independence: Irreconcilable Values or Complementary Instruments for Democracy? The Specific Case of the European Central Bank' in Georges Vandersanden et al (eds), *Mélanges en Hommage à Jean-Victor Louis* (Brussels: ULB, 2003), footnote 18 where she cites Robert Litan and William Nordhaus, *Reforming Federal Regulation* (New Haven: Yale University Press, 1983) 50: '[Independent Commissions] are in reality miniature independent governments set up to deal with the railroad problem, the banking problem or the radio problem. They constitute a headless "fourth branch" of the government, a haphazard deposit of irresponsible agencies and uncoordinated powers. They do violence to the basic theory of the American Constitution that there should be three branches of government and only three.'

[69] There are two kinds of 'independent' agencies in the USA: those whose independence is ostensibly created by statutes which protect officials against dismissal by the President (such as the Fed, the SEC, and others) and those which are given separate status within the government, but which are subject to ostensibly plenary control by the President (such as the Environmental Protection Agency, EPA). Theoretically, this distinction is important, because while there is Supreme Court precedent upholding some independent agencies in the first sense, there is still a constitutional cloud over them because the US Constitution nowhere provides for a 'fourth' branch of government. I thank Geoffrey Miller for his observation on this distinction. See Geoffrey Miller, 'Independent Agencies' (1986) Supreme Court Review 41, 50–8.

[70] The Report is quoted in Kenneth Culp Davis, *Administrative Law and Government*, (2nd edn, St Paul MN: West Publishing Co, 1975) 20–2.

Democratic legitimacy of independent central banks

To begin, it is important to realize that the question of legitimacy pre-exists and is a prerequisite of accountability.[71] Democratic legitimacy is a prerequisite for the establishment of an independent central bank. The creation of such an entity must be the fruit of a democratic act (an act of the legislator, a constitutional decision, or a treaty provision). This first source of legitimization is fundamental in a democratic society. It is then in the continuing life of that entity that accountability becomes necessary: the process of bringing back (by giving account, explaining, justifying, or taking measures of amendment or redress) that independent entity to the procedures and processes of a democratic society. This is, for instance, the basic rationale of judicial review of the central bank's actions or decisions: in a democracy no institution or individual can be above the law. However, accountability also encompasses other 'technical' elements that are not related to the 'political' legitimacy of the institution, such as performance control. Accountability per se does not politicize a central bank.

The legitimacy of independent institutions may be understood by reference to the 'Robinson Crusoe' paradigm. Just as an individual—recognizing his own imperfection in the face of possible temptations—imposes constraints upon himself, 'in order to channel his own expedient behaviour towards rationally selected norms',[72] a government, recognizing its own weakness in the face of temptations, limits itself by allowing or creating autonomous or independent bodies. This willingness to submit itself to restrictions provides a degree of democratic legitimacy.

Central banks are not majoritarian, democratic institutions.[73] Central banks are, instead, technocratic bureaucracies, staffed by career government employees and, typically, a few leaders who have been appointed by the political authorities. It might be said that any bureaucratic agency is non-majoritarian, since decisions are made by appointed officials rather than elected ones. The problem is especially acute when the officers of the agency in question enjoy legal protection against removal during their terms of office.[74] But the problem is greatly

---

[71] This point is made by Chiara Zilioli, above note 68, 403. Zilioli further points out that 'the independent government must be established and the power transferred to it, through a legal act adopted, in accordance with the constitutional framework of the State; by the democratically elected representatives of the people.'

[72] See James Buchanan, *The Limits of Liberty: Between Anarchy and Leviathan* (Chicago: University of Chicago Press, 1975) 93. See also above note 3, 20–1.

[73] Above note 45. See also Giandomenico Majone, *Independence versus Accountability? Non-Majoritarian Institutions and Democratic Government in Europe*, EUI Working Paper, (Florence: European University Institute, 1994).

[74] For discussion in the American context, see eg Gary Lawson, 'The Rise and Rise of the Administrative State' (1994) 107 Harvard Law Review 1231; Geoffrey P Miller, 'Independent

exacerbated in the case of central banks as compared with typical bureaucracies. Central banks do not simply administer a technical regulatory scheme affecting discrete industries or interests. They regulate price levels, which is one of the most fundamental powers of government, and one of the most important practical concerns of the public at large.[75] Though they are accountable for their actions, central banks tend to be more insulated from political control than other independent agencies. This political insulation raises a basic issue of democratic legitimacy.

The case for central bank independence can be reconciled, in general, with the theory of democratic self-determination. An analogy to the independent judiciary may be useful in this respect.[76] Like central banks, the judiciary administers an institution (a nation's laws) that goes to the core of a nation's political identity. And like central bankers, judges, in general, are not popularly elected in liberal democracies.[77] The theory of judicial legitimacy is much better developed than the theory of central bank legitimacy, so it is enlightening to turn to this analogy for instruction. In the United States, the jurist Alexander Bickel advanced an influential justification for the unelected judiciary in his book, *The Least Dangerous Branch*.[78] Bickel here observes that the power of the US Supreme Court to invalidate legislation is nowhere explicitly found in the American Constitution, and argues for a deferential use of that power given the explicit constitutional authorization for Congress to make laws. More fundamentally, Bickel identified the 'counter-majoritarian difficulty' as lying at the root of American constitutional theory: the fact that the fundamental law of a democratic society is defined by an agency that itself is unelected and constitutionally protected against democratic pressures. This issue, which haunts American constitutional law theory, is even more problematic than the parallel issue as pertains to central banks, since, at least in the case of central banks, the authority to control price levels free of political influence is itself set forth in documents adopted through the processes of ordinary law-making. In other respects, however, the issue for central banks is similar to that for judges. What

---

Agencies' (1986) Supreme Court Review 41; Peter L Strauss, 'The Place of Agencies in Government: Separation of Powers and the Fourth Branch' (1984) 84 Columbia Law Review 573; 'Symposium, Administering the Administrative State' (1990) 57 University of Chicago Law Review 331; 'A Symposium on Administrative Law: The Uneasy Constitutional Status of Administrative Agencies' (1987) 36 American University Law Review 277.

[75] Above note 45.

[76] Above note 45. Charles Goodhart and Ellen Meade have also written a paper, 'Central Banks and Supreme Courts' published by *Moneda y Crédito* 218 (2004), 11–59.

[77] Although this is not a universal pattern; some US states, for example, allow popular election of judges. Above note 45.

[78] Alexander M Bickel, *The Least Dangerous Branch, The Supreme Court at the Bar of Politics* (Indianapolis: Bobbs-Merrill, 1962) 16.

justification is there for vesting a fundamental democratic power in an institution that is explicitly protected against democratic control?

Constitutional theorists tend to focus on the unique features of a court to explain the institution of judicial review. The court has a special expertise and legitimacy in interpreting the law that other bodies of government do not have. Moreover, courts are 'less dangerous' than other political institutions. They are less dangerous both because they are largely immunized from the influence of special interests, and because they lack the powers that other governmental agencies enjoy, such as the spending power or the power to exert compulsory force. With regard to central banks, it is possible to devise a similar set of justifications for the conduct of monetary policy by unelected officials who enjoy explicit protections against political influence. First, as already noted, the problems of legitimacy for central banks are less than for a court exercising judicial review because the central bank's powers are explicitly conferred by legislation adopted in the political process. For instance, the possibility of a government override—if allowed by the legislation—actually nullifies independence.[79] Secondly, the central bank, as a bank, can claim a special expertise in the things that banks do, just as a court, as a court, can claim expertise and legitimacy in interpreting the law. Central banks are specialized at managing the money supply and price levels. Thirdly, central banks, like courts, are weak in most respects. They do not enjoy wide-ranging authority to spend money, to execute the law, to bring the coercive power of the state against private citizens. As with the courts, their powers in the area of their activity can be justified by their weakness in other areas.

Technical expertise, for example, is a compelling argument only within a framework of accepted values and institutions. When the fundamental identity, security, or values of a nation are in issue, the matter is no longer one of technical methodology but instead concerns basic democratic choices. Central banks should not be making these kinds of fundamental decisions. Similarly, the fact that a central bank is a bank may justify its conduct of a nation's banking business in ordinary times, but in extraordinary times, the national interest becomes paramount to arguments for legitimacy based on functional role. And the fact that a central bank is relatively powerless over many governmental functions becomes irrelevant when the bank, by virtue of the powers it does have, prevents or impedes much broader and more fundamental processes. If, for example, a central bank refused to allow the government to raise funds

---

[79] See Rosa M Lastra, memorandum submitted to the [UK] House of Commons at the request of the Treasury Select Committee in its inquiry into 'The Accountability of the Bank of England', ordered by the House of Commons to be printed, 23 October 1997, House of Commons, Session 1997–8, HC 282, 28–30.

necessary to defend itself against invasion, the fact that the bank does not enjoy the power to coerce others seems hardly a relevant concern. Or, if the public as a whole made a resolute and considered judgement that price level stability was not a central value for the conduct of economic policy, it hardly seems sensible to deny the public the right to self-determination, even if such a decision is, in the view of contemporary economic theory, not a wise one.

The insulation of the central bank from politics does not pose a serious difficulty for democratic functioning in ordinary times; but in extraordinary times, when the identity, security, or basic values of the nation are at stake, the autonomy of the central bank can, and should, legitimately yield to other concerns. Again, the problem of institutional design becomes that of distinguishing between the ordinary and the extraordinary. Politicians and interest groups will always have the incentive to characterize issues as extraordinary in order to wrest power away from the central bank. It would not be advisable for a nation to allow too easy a recourse to this argument, because of the danger that the value of central bank independence will be lost for very little gain. Usually, the central bank is established, and given its autonomy, by legislation. If the central bank has performed well and enjoys a high degree of public confidence (though confidence is hard to build up and easy to destroy), the authorizing legislation will become deeply embedded in the political fabric of the nation. In some countries, the central bank's autonomy is even more deeply embedded, at least from a legal point of view, by being contained in the political constitution of the country or in a treaty (as in the case of the EU). With regard to the ECB, some commentators have even gone as far as to argue that it can be considered a 'democratic fourth pillar' (after parliament, government, and the courts) of a system of checks and balances.[80] Very few countries, however, have 'constitutionalized' the independence of their central banks (Chile in 1980 is a rare example). Most countries choose to grant independence to their central banks through statute law. Even those countries that choose the 'constitutional path' or the so-called 'contractual path' (as in New Zealand[81]) also proceed through a 'statutory path'. New Zealand and Chile enacted legislation in 1989. The independence of the European System of Central Banks is guaranteed in the EC Treaty and in the yet-to-be-ratified EU Constitution. It is a strong legal commitment to independence, since the amendment of the EC Treaty in this respect (ie, to repeal the independence of the ESCB) would be a very difficult and cumbersome procedure. Yet not an impossible one, since every democratic society retains the right to reinvent itself.

---

[80] See Chiara Zilioli, above note 68, 412.
[81] In New Zealand, the Governor of the Reserve Bank of New Zealand and the Minister of Finance sign a 'policy targets agreement' according to s 9(4) of the Reserve Bank of New Zealand Act 1989. See my *Central Banking and Banking Regulation*, above note 3, 65–8.

The accountability of independent central banks[82]

The consensus that surrounds the case for central bank independence and its legal articulation does not extend to the articulation of accountability. Both the measurement of accountability and the extent to which independent central banks are held accountable for their actions remain a matter of controversy and vary considerably from country to country.

Accountability can be defined as an obligation owed by one person (the accountable) to another (the accountee[83]) according to which the former must give account of, explain, and justify his actions or decisions against criteria of some kind,[84] and take responsibility for any fault or damage.

Four elements are at the core of any understanding of accountability:

- A holder of power (the 'accountable'). Lord Acton's dictum remains true: power corrupts, absolute power corrupts absolutely. Hence, the need for accountability whenever power is exercised. Power cannot be divorced from responsibility.

- An authority to whom accountability is owed (the 'accountee'). Who guards the guardians? Accountability as an obligation must be owed to another party. The latter becomes by virtue of this obligation in a position of authority vis-à-vis the accountable. There are various types of accountability according to the authority that exacts it. We speak of judicial accountability (or accountability to the judiciary) when courts are the authority that enforce accountability. An obvious example is the judicial review of administrative actions or decisions. When parliament is the accountee we speak of parliamentary accountability (or accountability to parliament). We speak of accountability to the public, to refer to the general public as the accountee.

- The content of the obligation. The accountable, the holder of power, is under an obligation (1) to give an account of his decisions or actions, (2) to explain and justify the decision or the course of action taken and, (3) where error is proved or harm inflicted, to own the responsibility and take appropriate measures of amendment or redress. While there is no accountability without a duty to give account and explain, the forms of amends or redress vary from

---

[82] This section draws on previous writings on this subject. In particular: Rosa M Lastra, 'How Much Accountability for Central Banks and Supervisors?' (2001) 12(2) Central Banking 69 and the article I co-wrote with Ms Heba Shams on 'Public Accountability in the Financial Sector' in Eilis Ferran and Charles Goodhart (eds), *Regulating Financial Services and Markets in the Twenty-First Century* (Oxford: Hart Publishing, 2001) 165–88. See also Lastra, above notes 3 and 79; and Lastra and Miller, above note 45.

[83] This usage is borrowed from Dawn Oliver, 'Law, Politics and Public Accountability: The Search for a New Equilibrium' (1994) Public Law, 248.

[84] ibid 246.

one type of accountability to another. With regard to the content of the obligation, a distinction is often made between 'explanatory accountability' where the obligation is to answer questions, to give account of action, and 'amendatory accountability' where there is an obligation to make amends and grant redress. Amendatory accountability presupposes failure, fault, harm, deviation from a given target. While central bank accountability with regard to monetary policy is typically 'explanatory' (unless the law of the central bank is amended or the governor is removed from office, there is very little room for granting redress with regard to monetary policy decisions), the accountability of the central bank or the supervisory agency in the field of prudential supervision and regulation is sometimes 'explanatory' and sometimes 'amendatory'. The liability of financial market supervisors is under discussion in the United Kingdom and in several other EU Member States.[85]

- Criteria of assessment. Any form of accountability presupposes that there are objectives or standards according to which an action or decision might be assessed. In other words, accountability implies an obligation to comply with certain standards in the exercise of power or to achieve specific goals. The more complex the activity, the more difficult it is to establish clear standards of conduct and specific outcomes. In which case accountability becomes ever more evasive. The more specific the goals and standards the more effective the accountability. This might induce the 'accountees' to resort to economic or other measurable criteria of performance (hence the term 'performance accountability'). Though central bank laws often contain a variety of goals, in recent years the primary goal has become price stability. Performance accountability is facilitated when there is one goal, rather than multiple goals, and when that goal is narrowly defined rather than formulated in broad

---

[85] The issue of (state) liability for loss caused by the inadequate supervision of banks has been the subject of extensive debate in the UK in the context of the damages action against the Bank of England for the failure of Bank of Credit and Commerce International (BCCI), *Three Rivers District Council v Governor and Company of the Bank of England (No 3)* [2000] 2 WLR 1220; [2000] 3 All ER 1; [2000] Lloyd's Rep Bank 235, HL. Following the collapse of the BCCI, a licensed deposit-taking commercial bank, in July 1991, the plaintiffs (some 6000 former depositors with BCCI's UK branch) brought an action against the Bank of England, which had principal responsibility for supervising banking activities in the United Kingdom. The Bank of England was protected against claims for damages for negligent supervision by the statutory immunity of s 1(4) of the Banking Act 1984. The plaintiffs however alleged the stronger claim of 'misfeasance in public office' which is not covered by the statutory immunity. After several years of preliminary litigation, the case opened in the High Court of Justice in January 2004 and attracted considerable press publicity. The case was abandoned on 2 November 2005, when BCCI liquidators Deloitte Touche Tohmatsu dropped their claim against the Bank of England, after receiving a legal ruling that it would not be in the best interests of BCCI's creditors to continue with the lawsuit.

terms. If there are multiple goals, a clear and unambiguous ranking is better than no ranking at all.

A further twist to understanding the notion of accountability is the distinction between *ex ante* and *ex post* accountability. Accountability can either be exercised before/during the process of taking the decision/action, or after the decision/action has been taken. It is with reference to this fact, the fact of concluding a decision or action, that we define accountability as either a priori (*ex ante*) or a posteriori (*ex post*). An example of *ex ante* accountability is where the 'accountee' takes part in the process of choosing the holders of power, or where the consent of the 'accountee' is required for the decision of the 'accountable' to be final. For instance, the appointment procedures of central bank officials, when such procedures require parliamentary approval, and the parliamentary debate of inflation targets (if such a parliamentary debate is required) can be regarded as ways of exercising accountability *ex ante* or through scrutiny. The reporting requirements and the appearances of the central bank chairman or governor in front of parliamentary committees are ways of exercising accountability through control or *ex post*.

The lawyers' view and the economists' view

Lawyers and economists tend to give emphasis to different issues when trying to articulate the accountability of independent agencies. Lawyers tend to emphasize the political dimension of accountability, the placing of the institution (the independent central bank) within the existing system of checks and balances, in relation to the three branches of the State—legislative, executive, and judiciary (the question of who regulates the regulators or who guards the guardians). This political dimension is clearly related to the democratic legitimacy of independent central banks. Accountability—from a legal perspective—should be 'diversified' to include parliamentary accountability as well as judicial review of the agency's acts and decisions, and a degree of cooperation with the executive to ensure consistent overall policy making. In a national context, parliament remains sovereign in its legislative decisions, and one statute proclaiming the independence of an agency can always be removed by another one revoking it. Parliamentary accountability should be exercised through a variety of procedures and mechanisms, including annual reports and appearances in front of parliament of public officials on a regular basis, and also in the case of an emergency situation. Judicial review of the agency's actions and decisions (conducted by an independent and non-politicized judiciary) is essential to prevent and control the arbitrary and unreasonable exercise of discretionary powers. This is a fundamental element of the rule of law. The discretion of public officials should never be unfettered but subject to legal control.

Economists, while accepting this 'institutional' articulation of accountability, in

particular parliamentary accountability, tend to put the emphasis on performance accountability on the one hand[86] and on disclosure on the other. Performance control (the question of how accountability is to be achieved) is concerned
with the efficiency of an independent institution and, as I have already pointed
out, it is conditional upon the objectives and targets imposed upon the central
bank. Performance accountability has a 'technical' rather than a 'political'
character. Disclosure can be viewed as a 'market-based' form of accountability,
typically favoured in Anglo-Saxon countries, such as the USA and the United
Kingdom, where competition and transparency are considered to be the two
main pillars of a market economy. For instance, with regard to the transparency
required in the monetary policy decisions taken by an independent central
bank, it is worth noticing that the minutes of the Federal Open Market Committee (in the USA) or of the Monetary Policy Committee of the Bank of
England must be published.

With regard to the measurement of accountability, Fabian Amtenbrink has
developed eight criteria to measure such accountability:[87]

(1) the legal basis of the central bank (typically an act of parliament, but also a
    constitutional or treaty provision in some instances),
(2) the monetary policy objectives (whether price stability is broadly or nar-
    rowly defined and whether this goal coexists with others, such as growth
    and employment),
(3) the relationship with the executive branch of the government (from informal
    discussions to formal consultations),
(4) the appointment and dismissal procedures (which are also a test of
    independence),
(5) the override mechanism (which, if exercised, effectively nullifies
    independence),
(6) the relationship with parliament (the real test of accountability as parliament
    should represent the will of the people),
(7) transparency (ie, disclosure) and
(8) budgetary accountability (the counterpart of financial autonomy).

In some of these categories, it becomes evident that independence and accountability can be seen as opposite ends of a continuum.[88] While too much

---

[86] See eg, Stanley Fischer, 'Modern Central Banking' in Forest Capie et al (eds) *The Future of
Central Banking: The Tercentenary Symposium of the Bank of England* (Cambridge: Cambridge
University Press, 1994).

[87] See Fabian Amtenbrink, *The Democratic Accountability of Central Banks: A Comparative
Study of the European Central Bank* (Oxford: Hart Publishing, 1999) ch 2. See also the review I
wrote of Mr Amtenbrink's book, published in *Public Law*, Spring 2000, 151–3.

[88] Zilioli, above note 68 at 413, points out that accountability and independence are not
incompatible, but complementary.

accountability may threaten the effectiveness of independence, too much independence risks damaging appropriate accountability. A clear illustration of this tension is the liaisons or relations between an independent central bank and the Treasury or Minister of Finance. While too much liaison lessens independence, too little liaison comes at the expense of accountability. The optimal trade-off between independence and accountability varies from country to country, depending upon the political structure of government, the existing system of *Conclusion* checks and balances in a society, and the centralized or decentralized (both geographically and functionally) structure of the State.

The design of the pre-1999 German Bundesbank and of the European System of Central Banks tilt on the side of independence, with relatively weak parliamentary accountability. (Though the public support enjoyed by the Bundesbank is far superior to that enjoyed by the European Central Bank, and the support of public opinion is a form of de facto accountability.) The Reserve Bank of New Zealand tilts on the side of accountability, because of the possibility of government override. In the US, the seven members of the Federal Reserve System Board of Governors are appointed by the President, with the advice and consent of the Senate. The President designates two members to be chairman and vice-chairman and these designations must also receive the Senate's approval. The Board of Governors is required to submit an annual report of its operations to the Speaker of the House of Representatives, 'who shall cause the same to be printed for the information of the Congress', and special reports twice each year on the state of the economy and the system's objectives for the growth of money and credit. The chairman—representing the Board—is responsible for reporting biannually to both houses of Congress on the goals and conduct of monetary policy. These are the so-called 'Humphrey–Hawkings' hearings, under the Full Employment and Balanced Growth Act of 1978. The chairman of the Fed testifies in front of the Senate Committee on Banking, Housing, and Urban Affairs; and the House Committee of Banking, Finance, and Urban Affairs. Furthermore, the chairman and other Board members often testify before the Joint Economic Committee of Congress and other congressional committees.

The Bank of England—according to the Bank of England Act 1998—provides an interesting balance between independence and accountability, though with a lower degree of parliamentary accountability and a higher degree of ministerial control than in the case of the US Federal Reserve System. The Bank of England lacks goal independence, because the objective (inflation target) to be pursued by the Monetary Policy Committee is precisely specified by the Chancellor of the Exchequer in terms of a particular index and quantified, with an obligation imposed on the MPC to report back to the Chancellor if they deviate from the target (by exceeding the bands imposed upon it). The Bank of England Act

1998 imposes a high degree of transparency with regard to the actions and decisions of the MPC, with the obligation to publish the minutes of the meetings of the Monetary Policy Committee.[89] The Bank also needs to produce an annual report of its activities to the Chancellor of the Exchequer, who shall lay copies of every report before Parliament.[90] Other reporting requirements are spelt out in section 18 of the Act (including the publication of the inflation report). The Act also contains a section on 'reserve powers'[91] that the Treasury can exercise in 'extreme economic circumstances'. If this provision were to be applied, it would effectively nullify the independence of the MPC. Indeed, this 'reserve provision' illustrates the trade-off between independence and accountability.

One problem in the design of an 'accountable independence'[92] lies in the possible reversal of the intended objective of 'depoliticizing' the conduct of monetary policy. Indeed, if too much independence may lead to the creation of a democratically unacceptable 'state within the state', too much accountability threatens the effectiveness of independence. *The debate about independence and accountability resembles the philosophical debate about freedom and responsibility: independence without accountability would be like freedom without responsibility.*

The place of transparency in the framework of accountability

Prior to the 1980s, transparency was hardly discussed in academic and policy literature. The 1980s witnessed growing attention to the concept, which was reflected in academic discussions across the disciplines of economics, political economy, information theory, and law. In the 1990s this trend was confirmed. Studies of the concept proliferated, especially in the literature of international organizations, and 'transparency' was established as a term of art in the relevant disciplines. Transparency is an essential feature of governance in a market economy. The emergence of the current concern with transparency coincided with the retreat of the welfare state, which resulted in a wave of privatization in the 1980s and other structural reforms which reinforced the role of markets in the allocation and management of resources. This link between transparency and the market is further illustrated by the increased emphasis on transparency in the 1990s following the collapse of the Soviet Union and the global trend towards a market economy.

The current concern for transparent political and economic structures suggests the need to reach a common understanding of transparency. In this context, two elements are essential: the availability and relevance of the information and the

---

[89] The Bank of England Act 1998, s 15.   [90] ibid s 4.   [91] ibid s 19.
[92] See Lastra, above note 3, 49–59.

time framework in which such information ought to be made available. Typically information is made available through disclosure procedures, reporting requirements, and sometimes by granting the recipient investigative powers or a general right of access to information. For information to be available, some codes of transparency ought to impose on the given organization certain duties regarding the quality of the information and its presentation. The information must be accurate, clear, understandable, complete, and timely. There are two objectives that transparency must achieve: to educate the public and to facilitate financial intermediation. The realization of these two objectives will also contribute to establishing an ongoing dialogue between the central bank and the public.[93] If the public understands and evaluates the performance of the central bank, an important element of political legitimization is introduced. In order to maintain its long-term status of independence, the central bank needs the support of the financial and non-financial community. The public will only lend its support if it is informed.

Any recent discussion of accountability often includes a reference to transparency and vice versa. This poses the question of the relationship between the two concepts. Accountability is an obligation to give account of, explain, and justify one's actions, while transparency is the degree to which information on such actions is available. The provision of information is clearly an element of accountability. But accountability is not merely about giving information. It must involve defending the action, policy, or decision for which the accountable is being held to account. The provision of information (transparency) is hardly ever a neutral account of what happened or of what is happening; hence the need for an explanation or justification of the agency's actions or decisions (ie, accountability).

The provision of information in the context of accountability, whether in an *ex ante* investigation or an *ex post* requirement of disclosure, facilitates transparency. On the other hand, a transparent economic and political environment enhances the effectiveness of accountability. The two concepts are therefore mutually enforcing, and they share the provision of information as a common requirement.

F. Currency Boards

In recent times, currency boards have been adopted as an appropriate means of monetary stabilization in jurisdictions with either a negative past record in

---

[93] See also Zilioli, above note 68, 405.

monetary affairs (eg, hyperinflation in Argentina) or a distrust in the ability of the domestic authorities to maintain currency stability (eg, Hong Kong, Estonia, and Lithuania). A currency board can be construed as a type of 'monetary rule' where the external value of the currency is fixed in terms of the value of another currency, backed by foreign reserves.[94] In this respect, while independent central bankers have a certain degree of discretion in the conduct of monetary policy, as long as they achieve their statutory goal, currency boards enjoy little or no discretion. The discipline and predictability of a currency board (currency boards can only issue notes and coins when there are foreign exchange reserves to back them) need to be weighed, however, against the loss of freedom in the conduct of monetary policy and the ability to tackle banking crises. The record of currency boards is mixed, with some relative successes (eg, Hong Kong) and some failures (eg, Argentina, as the currency board was abandoned in January 2002).

The debate about currency boards needs to be understood in the broader literature about the types of exchange regimes: fixed, floating, or somewhere in between. There is no consensus in the economics profession as to which is the best model. The pendulum has shifted from pegged (Bretton Woods regime[95]) to floating[96] and the issue remains controversial. Assuming that they maintain a currency of their own, countries have three basic choices with regard to their exchange regime:

---

[94] The most enthusiastic academic exponents of currency boards (as well as of dollarization) are Steve Hanke and Kurt Schuler, who have written extensively about the benefits of currency boards (and dollarization) in countries where there is lack of confidence in domestic monetary and other economic policies. See, *inter alia*, Steve H Hanke, 'On Dollarization and Currency Boards: Error and Deception' (2002) 5 Policy Reform 203, and Steve Hanke and Kurt Schuler, 'Currency Boards and Currency Convertibility' (1993) 12(3) Cato Journal 687.

[95] An excellent summary of the history of the Bretton Woods regime is provided by Peter Kenen in Peter Newman, Murray Milgate, and John Eatwell (eds), *The New Palgrave Dictionary of Money and Finance* (London: Macmillan Press Ltd, 1992) entry: 'Bretton Woods system'. In his essay, Kenen recalls the arguments put forth by Ragnar Nurkse writing for the League of Nations (1944) in terms that were widely endorsed at the time. The setting of exchange rates, he concluded, could not be left to market forces:

> Freely fluctuating rates involve three serious disadvantages. In the first place, they create an element of risk which tends to discourage international trade. Secondly, as a means of adjusting the balance of payments, exchange fluctuations involve constant shifts in labour and other resources between production for the home market and production for export. Such shifts may be costly . . . and are obviously wasteful if the exchange market conditions that call for them are temporary. Thirdly, experience has shown that fluctuating exchanges cannot always be relied upon to promote adjustment. Any considerable or continuous movement of the exchange rate is liable to generate anticipations of a further movement in the same direction. (League of Nations 1944: 210.)

[96] In a seminal paper in 1953, Milton Friedman wrote 'The Case for Flexible Exchange Rates' published in *Essays in Positive Economics* (Chicago: Chicago University Press, 1953).

(a) They can let their currency float freely in the exchange markets against all other currencies; (b) They can fix the price of their currency against a specific foreign currency or a basket of foreign currencies; (c) They can pursue intermediate approaches, letting rates float to some extent but intervening to limit those fluctuations either ad hoc (managed floating) or pursuant to some pre-determined parameters (target zones, crawling bands etc).[97]

Currency boards fall within the second category: they are a species of the fixed peg system. The difference between a currency board and a pegged exchange rate is one of degree: 'a currency board can be abandoned just as a pegged exchange rate can' but institutional arrangements render abandoning a currency board considerably more difficult, thus providing extra credibility.[98]

The theory of currency boards

A currency board is a monetary institution or authority that issues domestic currency (notes and coins) subject to (1) an express commitment to exchange domestic currency with the reserve currency at a specified fixed exchange rate and (2) the requirement that its monetary liabilities be backed by reserves of foreign currency (or other foreign assets or gold).[99] The first requirement is the commitment to a fixed exchange regime. The second requirement (the 'backing rule') is the commitment to convertibility, that is, the commitment to hold adequate reserves to ensure that even if all holders of the domestic notes and coins wish to convert them into the reserve currency, the board will be able to do so. The notes and coins are convertible into the reserve currency at a fixed rate and on demand.

A currency board pegs the exchange rate of the domestic currency vis-à-vis some international 'hard' currency ('reserve currency' or 'anchor currency'), such as the US dollar, the euro, and previously the German mark. The currency board thus borrows the 'credibility' of the anchor currency, in the belief that by tying the exchange rate against such foreign currency it will maintain monetary stability and predictability. Interest rates and inflation in the country that adopts a currency board tend to be roughly the same as those of the country of the anchor currency. A currency board effectively hires the monetary policy services

---

[97] See eg, Fred Bergsten (Institute of International Economics) 'Alternative Exchange Rate Systems and Reform of the International Financial Architecture' (Testimony before the Committee on Banking and Financial Services United States House of Representatives Washington DC May 21, 1999) at <http://www.iie.com/publications/papers/bergsten0599.htm>.

[98] See Atish R Ghosh, Anne-Marie Gulde, and Holger C Wolf, *Currency Boards: The Ultimate Fix?* (Washington DC: IMF, 1998) 5.

[99] Veerathai Santiprabhob, *Bank Soundness and Currency Board Arrangements: Issues and Experience*, IMF Working Paper (Washington DC: IMF, 1997) 1.

of a foreign central bank. This has prompted Salzberger and Voigt[100] to declare that from an institutional perspective a currency board is a form of *international delegation,* in the sense that 'monetary policy decisions are delegated internationally and taken over by an organization beyond the immediate reach of domestic actors, namely, the (foreign) central banks that serve as the anchor for the domestic currency.'[101] In contrast of the *international delegation* of domestic sovereign powers, the *domestic delegation* of rule-making and executive powers—which is, of course, a very usual institutional arrangement—occurs when such powers are delegated by the government to an independent administrative body or agency created by the national legislature and which is subject to the national constitution.[102] (This domestic delegation can also be characterized as functional decentralization.)

With regard to the conduct of monetary policy, some form of delegation—domestic or international—is likely to occur as a 'credibility-enhancing' exercise. As Salzberger and Voigt have observed, the delegation is domestic when the conduct of monetary policy is delegated to an independent central bank. The delegation is international when the country adopts a currency board arrangement.

With regard to the operational characteristics of currency board arrangements, one of the main rules is that currency boards should hold 100 per cent reserves or more against the notes and coins in circulation.[103] Effectively, a currency board can only issue notes and coins if they are backed by foreign reserves. The required foreign reserves of the anchor currency typically consist of low-risk, interest-bearing bonds and other assets denominated in the anchor currency. An orthodox currency board would not accept deposits.

The conduct of monetary policy under a currency board arrangement leaves no room for discretion. The currency board increases the monetary base when the private sector wants to sell foreign currency to it and buy the domestic currency at the fixed exchange rate, and it decreases the monetary base when the private sector wants to finance a balance of payment deficit by selling the domestic currency and buying foreign currency.[104] Interest rates adjust automatically. As Colares explains, the establishment of a currency board amounts to

---

[100] See Eli M Salzberger and Stefan Voigt, 'On Constitutional Processes and the Delegation of Power, with Special Emphasis on Israel and Central and Eastern Europe' (2002) 3 Theoretical Inquiries in Law 207.

[101] ibid 247.   [102] ibid 213.   [103] See Hanke and Schuler, above note 94, 690.

[104] See John Williamson, *What Role for Currency Boards?* Policy Analyses in International Economics (Washington DC: Institute of International Economics 1995) 4.

abdication from the sovereign right to set interest rates.[105] Dollarization goes one step further, as a total abdication of monetary sovereignty, since the domestic currency is replaced by the foreign currency (though the name dollarization refers to the US dollar, the domestic currency can be replaced by another currency, such as the euro or the yen).[106]

One of the key implications of the establishment of an orthodox currency board is the fact that governments can no longer finance their budget deficits by printing money. This occurs because the amount of money in circulation is strictly defined by the rules of the currency board—in other words by the availability of foreign reserves which is beyond the political control of the government. The rules of an orthodox currency board also imply that the currency board cannot provide lender of last resort assistance to distraught banks in times of systemic banking crises (unless, of course, it has surplus foreign exchange reserves, as is the case in Hong Kong).[107] As I discuss below, this is the ultimate test of confidence for any currency board: whether or not it can survive a financial crisis.

The history of currency boards

Currency boards were widely used in British colonies in the nineteenth century. Following the establishment of a currency board in Mauritius in 1849, many other British colonies in Africa, Asia, the Middle East and the Caribbean also adopted this institutional arrangement.[108] There were also currency boards in independent countries like Argentina (1902–14 and 1927–9), Iraq (1931–49), Danzig (1922–3), Panama (1904–31), and North Yemen (1964–71).[109] With the end of colonialism central banks replaced most currency boards by the 1970s, with Hong Kong abandoning its currency board in 1974. For a time, currency boards survived only in small territories like the Cayman Islands, Brunei, Bermuda, and Gibraltar. Hong Kong, however, re-established a currency board in 1983.[110]

Modern currency boards are different from the old colonial ones.[111] According

---

[105] See eg, Juscelino F Colares, 'Formal Legal Theory and the Surrender of Political Control over Monetary Policy: What Can Ulysses' Journey to Ithaca Teach Argentina about Appropriate Legal Form?' (2003) 36 Cornell International Law Journal 151, 168–9.

[106] See eg, Michael Gruson, 'Dollarisation and Euroisation' in *Current Developments in Monetary and Financial Law*, vol 2 (Washington DC: IMF, 2003) ch 31.

[107] I am grateful to Charles Goodhart for observations on this point.

[108] See Williamson, above note 104, 5. See also Hanke and Schuler, above note 94, 691–2.

[109] See Williamson, above note 104, 6.   [110] ibid 8.

[111] See generally, Corrinne Ho, *A Survey of the Institutional and Operational Aspects of Modern-Day Currency Boards* (Basel: Bank for International Settlements Monetary and Economic Department, 2002) 2. Corrinne Ho argues that

There are several fundamental reasons why modern currency boards *cannot* be literal replicas of their historical counterparts. First, the function of currency boards has broadened. Earlier

to Williamson, the recent interest in this type of institutional arrangement is partly attributable to the disappointing vulnerability of many central banks, particularly in emerging economies, to political pressure to finance government deficits—which is also an argument in favour of central bank independence— and partly attributable to disquiet about the central bank's use of monetary discretion.[112] A currency board is in the end an arrangement based on the legislative establishment of a certain '*monetary rule*': 'changes in the monetary base will be equal to the country's overall balance of payments surplus or deficit'.[113] It achieves credibility and stability at the expense of monetary sovereignty. However, it still maintains a domestic issue of currency, which can satisfy the local sentiment for keeping a national currency and for keeping the benefits of seigniorage.

Modern currency boards can be divided into two groups. Some countries, like Argentina (1991–2002), Estonia (1992), Lithuania (1994), or Bulgaria (1997), have established a currency board in response to an economic crisis or in support of a stabilization program. Other countries, like Brunei Darussalam, Djibouti, and member countries of the East Caribbean Central Bank—all of them small economies with relative little expertise in monetary management—have adopted a currency board because of its simplicity and predictability.[114]

Currency boards and central banks

Currency boards can and do coexist with central banks. However, central banks that operate in tandem with a currency board are restricted in their operations, because of the lack of an autonomous monetary policy and because of the lack of flexibility in most cases to deal with banking crises (through the provision of emergency liquidity assistance).

According to Ho, the legal frameworks of modern currency boards fall into three categories:[115] (1) The currency boards of the early 1990s (such as Argentina, Estonia, and Lithuania) typically have separate currency board laws in addition

---

currency boards were simply a mechanism to transform a metropolitan currency (mainly sterling) into a form that was convenient for local use, a practical solution to the rather mundane problem of currency issuance, typically in a colony. In the modern, post-colonial context, however, they are an alternative approach to conducting monetary policy. Second, the political and economic landscapes have changed. Modern currency board economies are independent sovereign entities, not colonies. They have no recourse to a parent country and are expected to take responsibility for their own monetary affairs. Furthermore, with the increasing importance of the banking sector and exposure to international capital flows, modern currency board economies must deal with issues that were either non-existent or relatively insignificant in the historical context.

[112] See Williamson, above note 104, 1.   [113] ibid.
[114] See generally, Santiprabhob, above note 99, 2.   [115] See Ho, above note 111, 18.

to central bank laws. (2) The currency boards of the late 1990s (Bulgaria, Bosnia, and Herzegovina) have the relevant details of their currency board operations directly incorporated into their respective central bank laws. (3) Hong Kong is a special case, in part because of its political status (one country, two systems), in part because of its history (a British colony till relatively recently), in part because of its status as a key financial centre in the world.

Ho argues that 'upon the adoption of a currency board regime, the central bank, if one exists, is likely to be *adapted* rather than *abolished*. The monetary policy role is reduced, but the importance of other supporting functions is not diminished.'[116] She also recalls that although several authors with knowledge of the previous historical experience of currency boards were puzzled by the coexistence of a currency board-like arrangement and a central bank, in the modern version of currency board arrangements, this is not surprising. First, the modern version was adopted by independent states rather than colonies and therefore it was wrongly assumed that the central bank would be dismantled as soon as the currency board was introduced. In the author's view 'the policy alternatives in the two eras are not comparable. In the historical case, the alternative to adopting a currency board was not establishing a central bank, but employing some other form of currency issuance and circulation. In the modern context, by contrast, currency boards are adopted as an alternative way of conducting monetary policy, or an alternative exchange rate regime, typically lodged in a central banking framework.'[117] Finally, it should be pointed out that modern central banks perform an array of functions in addition to monetary policy and lender of last resort operations.

The problems with currency boards: Credibility and commitment

The successful introduction of a currency board requires a flexible economy, a strong fiscal position, adequate reserves, and a reasonably well-operated and well-supervised banking system. In addition to these economic prerequisites, the introduction of a currency board is a political decision and hence requires close cooperation among several authorities, including the Ministry of Finance, the central bank (if there is one in the country), and the Ministry of Justice.[118]

In the view of Ho, 'for conceptual purposes, currency boards are usually portrayed using the classic description: 100 per cent reserve backing, conversion of domestic currency into reserve currency (and vice versa) on demand, no lending, no discretion'.[119] Yet, the currency boards established in Argentina, Bosnia,

---

[116] ibid 7.   [117] ibid 6.
[118] See generally, Charles Enoch and Anne-Marie Gulde, *Making a Currency Board Operational* (Washington DC: IMF, 1997) 3.
[119] See Ho, above note 111, 2.

Bulgaria, Estonia, Lithuania, and Hong Kong present 'various non-traditional features'.[120] Ho argues that the discrepancy between the classic definition and modern-day practice has occasionally prompted some debate as to whether the 'currency boards' we see nowadays are truly currency boards or something else. In her view, 'to the extent that a currency board is typically perceived to be an *institution-based* approach to achieving and maintaining monetary stability, deviations from the familiar classic blueprint may indeed appear to be a potential cause for concern.'[121]

The benefits of currency boards in terms of monetary stability need to be weighed against the drawbacks in terms of policy flexibility to tackle problems and crises. Among the benefits the following are typically cited:[122] currency boards remove monetary policy from the political arena; they signal the government's commitment to fiscal restraint and financial rectitude, trying to convince private market actors as well as other governments of a serious intent to maintain discipline;[123] currency boards tend to facilitate trade and investment; the fixed-rate convertibility provides confidence to foreign investors that contracts in the foreign currency will be honoured and therefore currency boards contribute to more inward foreign investment. However, a currency board should not be expected to be a cure-all: in particular, it does not correct investors' short-sightedness.[124] Among the main drawbacks, it is important to point out the following: a self-imposed loss of monetary sovereignty; governments cannot use monetary policy to respond to economic shocks such as a reduction of exports or sharp changes in capital movements; when investors sell the local currency and interest rates rise sharply, local banks are put under pressure; a currency board usually cannot provide lender of last resort (LOLR) assistance to troubled banks in times of banking crises; it sometimes makes exports of goods and services more expensive, hence decreasing the competitiveness of export-oriented industries.[125]

The reputation of currency boards has been tarnished by the experience in Argentina. The ultimate test for a currency board is its ability to withstand a financial crisis: Hong Kong succeeded in this test. Argentina failed.

Argentina passed legislation setting the currency board as its preferred legal form of self-discipline and credibility enhancement in 1991.[126] In addition to the

---

[120] ibid.   [121] ibid.   [122] See Williamson above note 104, 13–19.
[123] See generally, Beth A Simmons, 'Money and the Law: Why Comply with the Public International Law of Money?' (2000) 25 Yale Journal of International Law 323.
[124] See Frank Partnoy, 'Why Markets Crash and What Law Can Do About It' (2000) 61 University of Pittsburgh Law Review 741, 781.
[125] See Williamson, above note 104, 19–29.
[126] Convertibility Law, 'Ley de Convertibilidad del Austral' No 23.928, published on 28 March 1991.

convertibility law, Argentina also passed legislation to grant independence to the Central Bank.[127] For ten years, the country enjoyed the benefits of the currency board.[128] However, some of its drawbacks were creeping in and, after a tumultuous 2001, the country abandoned in January 2002 the convertibility of the peso to the US dollar and moved to a floating exchange regime,[129] in the midst of a profound political and institutional crisis, one of the worst experienced by the country in its eventful political history.[130] Moreover, the Argentine government defaulted on its private creditors' debt repayments.[131]

The Argentine crisis illustrates the limitations of an orthodox currency board to deal with banking crises. The requirement that domestic currency must be backed by the reserve currency or other foreign assets and gold generally limits the scope of LOLR assistance and monetary operations 'to the amount of foreign exchange in excess of that required for backing'.[132] Since this emergency liquidity assistance is often helpful in containing potentially contagious liquidity problems, its absence may have adverse implications for the ability of the domestic banking system to defend itself against a systemic crisis.[133]

As in other monetary and exchange rate regimes, weak banking conditions

---

[127] 'Carta Organica del Banco Central de la Republica Argentina', Law No. 24.244, published on 22 October 1992.

[128] For an analysis on this issue, see eg, Geoffrey Miller, 'Constitutional Moments, Pre-commitment, and Fundamental Reform. The Case of Argentina' (1993) 71 Washington University Law Quarterly 1061, 1083–5.

[129] On 6 January 2002, with the enactment of the Public Emergency and Exchange Regulations Reform Law No 25,561 (as amended by Law No 25,820, the 'Emergency Law'), the fixed peg system between the peso and the US dollar (in force for more than ten years) came to an end.

[130] See Gabriel Gómez Giglio, 'Emergency Law and Financial Entities in Argentina' (2003) 10 Journal of International Banking Law and Regulation 397, note 13.

For the purpose of clarification and for a better understanding, note that President De la Rúa resigned on December 20, 2001, amid nationwide rioting after he decreed a freeze on bank withdrawals on December 3, 2001. The following ten days saw four more presidents, a debt default and a messy devaluation. On December 23, 2001, Congress elected Senator Alfredo Rodriguez Saá to continue the presidential mandate who resigned on December 30, 2001, due to lack of political support. On January 2, 2002, Eduardo Duhalde was elected President by Congress to complete the mandate of former President De la Rúa, namely up to December, 2003. Seeking to assuage popular anger, Mr. Duhalde's interim government then tried to force banks, foreign creditors and investors to shoulder much of the losses from the currency devaluation and the debt default.

[131] ibid. 'Argentina's default was the biggest ever seen by a country. As regards private creditors, the total amount of the debt default—including arrears—reached $76.7bn by the end of 2003. About half of this amount is owed to some 600,000 retail investors, based mainly in Italy, Germany and Japan. To complicate matters further, any restructuring shall have to cover 152 separate issues of bonds issued in 14 different currencies and under eight legal frameworks.'

[132] See Santiprabhob, above note 99, 1.

[133] See generally, Carlos Zarazaga 'Argentina, Mexico and Currency Boards: Another Case of Rules versus Discretion' (1995) Federal Reserve Bank of Dallas Economic Review (4th Quarter) 14–25; See also Ghosh, Gulde, and Wolf, above note 98, 6.

can undermine the credibility of currency boards. Weak, unsound, or poorly managed banks are more likely to take excessive risks and more likely to fail to respond to monetary signals, especially interest rate volatility, in a predictable manner.[134]

A currency board is not 'designed' to address banking problems. A sound and well functioning banking system is typically a precondition for the effective operation of a currency board. Due to the tension between LOLR operations (where a degree of discretion is necessary) and the rules of a currency board arrangement, a country wishing to establish a currency board 'amid a weak banking system' has a difficult choice to make. A banking crisis will certainly put a currency board under strain.[135]

The absence of an exit strategy in Argentina has also been the subject of some debate. It is questionable whether the law must prescribe the circumstances under which the currency board arrangement will be abandoned. It is likely that an explicit 'exit policy' will undermine the credibility of the arrangement which is specifically designed to convince international markets that monetary stability is guaranteed for the foreseeable future. In fact, the country may send an even stronger signal of long-term commitment by incorporating the legal provisions establishing the currency board in the constitution or setting a special majority provision for future modifications of the primary legislation governing its operation.

There is, of course, a clear trade-off between the long-term commitment to a 'monetary rule' (which enhances credibility) and the flexibility that is needed in the management of a financial crisis.

---

[134] See Santiprabhob, above n 99, 6–7 and 12.   [135] ibid.

3

INSTITUTIONAL DESIGN
OF SUPERVISION

A basic continuing responsibility of any central bank—and the principal reason for the establishing of the Federal Reserve—is to assure stable and smoothly functioning financial and payment systems. These are prerequisites for, and complementary to, the central bank's responsibility for conducting monetary policy. . . . Historically, in fact, the 'monetary' functions were largely grafted onto the 'supervisory' functions, not the reverse.

'Federal Reserve Position on Restructuring of Financial Regulation
Responsibilities', December 1983[1]

---

[1] See 'Federal Reserve Position on Restructuring of Financial Regulation Responsibilities', presented to the Bush Commission in December 1983, in Charles Goodhart, *The Evolution of Central Banks* (Cambridge: The MIT Press, 1988) 6–7.

A. Introduction

The debate about the institutional design of supervision, that is, about the optimal allocation of responsibilities with regard to the supervision of financial intermediaries, is a matter of great controversy, both nationally and supra-nationally.[2] From the point of view of monetary law and monetary theory, a major issue at stake in this organizational structure is the role of the central bank—as monetary authority and bankers' bank—and, in particular, whether banking supervision should be inside or outside the central bank. With or without direct supervisory responsibilities, a central bank is typically responsible for financial stability, a concept that cannot be dissociated from monetary stability. (The absence of stable prices harms the stability of the financial system; financial fragility, in turn, negatively affects monetary stability.)

In recent years, another hotly debated issue at the national level has been the optimal number of supervisory authorities, with some jurisdictions adopting the model of a single regulator, while other jurisdictions—most notably the USA—retain a highly fragmented regulatory and supervisory landscape. There are other issues relating to this institutional design: private versus public supervision, independent versus politically directed process, institutional versus functional regulation, and the use of supervisory functions as an organizing principle of supervision, as will be discussed further later in this chapter.

B. Definition of Supervision and Regulation

Many commentators use the terms 'regulation' and 'supervision' interchangeably. However, they are conceptually different.[3] Supervision has to do with monitoring and enforcement, and regulation with rule-making.

Regulation

Banking regulation refers to the establishment of rules, to the process of rule-making, and includes legislative acts and statutory instruments issued by the competent authorities nationally and supranationally, international rules (often 'soft law' in the field of banking and finance), and rules issued by self-regulatory

---

[2] I further explore these issues at the supranational level in Ch 11. Some of the arguments that I expound upon in this chapter have been published in Rosa M Lastra, 'The Governance Structure for Financial Regulation and Supervision in Europe' (2003) 10 Columbia Journal of European Law 49.

[3] See Rosa M Lastra, *Central Banking and Banking Regulation* (London: Financial Markets Group, London School of Economics, 1996) 108.

organizations and private bodies or 'clubs', such as a cooperative bankers' association. Banking regulation draws from national, supranational, and international sources. At a national level the competent authorities are (though this varies from country to country) the government, through the ministry of finance or Treasury, the central bank, and the bank regulatory agency/agencies. At the level of the European Union, Member States must comply with treaty provisions (primary Community Law) and with regulations and directives (secondary Community Law).[4] At an international level, rules that emanate from international organizations suffer from the 'eternal' problem of international law: its effective enforcement. The distinct force and effect of rules is important in order to understand the various sources of banking law and regulation.

Supervision

Rather than adopting a 'monolithic' approach to the notion of supervision, I like to think about supervision in terms of the functions it involves for the supervisory authorities, from the beginning of the business life of a supervised entity (entry into the market through a licence or authorization) to its end, which in banking is less straightforward than in other businesses, since bank failures have relevant public policy implications. Supervision in a broad sense can be understood as a process with four stages or phases: (1) licensing, authorization, or chartering (entry into the business), (2) supervision *stricto sensu,* (3) sanctioning or imposition of penalties in the case of non-compliance with the law, fraud, bad management, or other types of wrongdoing, and (4) crisis management, which comprises lender of last resort, deposit insurance, and bank insolvency proceedings.[5]

Supervision in a narrow sense (ie, supervision *stricto sensu*) refers to the oversight of financial firms' behaviour, in particular risk monitoring and risk control.

Because supervision monitors the degree to which the bank abides by the rules, there is a connection between the two concepts. The very process of supervision is subject to regulation.[6] Most supervisory authorities are also endowed with

---

[4] Article I–33 of the proposed Treaty Establishing a Constitution for Europe refers to the legal acts of the Union and talks about European laws, framework laws, European regulations, European decisions, recommendations, and opinions.

[5] See Lastra, above note 3, 108–44.

[6] Regulators set the rules and supervisors implement and enforce such rules. This point is made by Bryan Quinn, 'Rules v Discretion: The Case for Banking Supervision in the Light of the Debate on Monetary Policy' in Charles AE Goodhart (ed), *The Emerging Framework of Financial Regulation* (London: Central Banking Publications, 1998) 119–32.

regulatory responsibilities.[7] The interaction between supervision and regulation is evidenced in each supervisory stage. For instance, with regard to licensing, the law determines the requirements that a bank needs to fulfil in order to be granted a licence (minimum capital, management competence and integrity, etc). The adequacy of capital—a key element that supervisors assess to determine the health of the bank—is described in detailed rules. Penalties for wrong doing—civil or criminal—are clearly spelt out in the law. In the crisis management stage, most of the tools available to the supervisory authorities are governed by law; this is the case with deposit insurance and with the bankruptcy procedures that apply in the case of liquidation. However, banking law extends beyond the supervisory process and deals with other issues, such as the legal form of the corporation and the bank–customer relationship.

Licensing, authorization, chartering

Licensing is a key first step in the supervisory process. It acts as a catalyst or filter for a safe and sound banking system. However, while entry barriers should not be too lax, neither should they be so restrictive that they lead to inadequate competition. The law ought to consider the following issues in the licensing process: the conditions to obtain a licence (minimum capital, competence and integrity of management and others); the list of activities that banks can do (an important issue with regard to the development of capital markets, as securities firms may find it hard to compete with banks, particularly if the latter are 'protected' by the government); the entry of foreign banks; the authority to revoke a licence, and the relations between banks and industry/commerce.

The role of banks in controlling corporations is a fundamental issue. Broadly speaking, there are two main models of bank–corporate relations: the Anglo-Saxon model, in which the bank maintains a purely commercial relationship with its corporate clients, without direct ownership connections, and the German-Japanese model of closer and continuing relationships, often with direct equity involvement (cross-shareholdings) and participation in corporate decisions. The Anglo-Saxon model is concerned about current performance and equity prices (short-termism), while under the traditional German-Japanese model long-term strategies are encouraged and, in case of trouble, reorganization is favoured over liquidation. The Anglo-Saxon model fosters transparency and market discipline, rather than confidential flows of information. In recent years, there has been a convergence towards some of the features of the Anglo-Saxon model.

---

[7] These considerations are particularly relevant in the debate about the governance structure for financial regulation and supervision in the EU which I discuss in Chs 10 and 11.

Banking laws often require that the authorities give their approval (a licence in some cases, a registration procedure in some other cases) to various forms of bank expansion: via branches (legally dependent units), subsidiaries (legally independent units), joint ventures, and takeovers or mergers. Bank expansion overseas needs to take into account the rules that the Basel Committee has designed over the years for the supervision of cross-border establishments.

Supervision stricto sensu

Although banks in a market economy are operated by their management to generate profits (and thereby take risks), and their shareholders expect a reasonable return on their investment, it is widely recognized that banks are different from other profit-seeking businesses because of their role in the payment system, in the financial system at large, and in the national economy and that, therefore, they require a higher degree of supervision (and regulation) than other types of businesses.

Supervision refers to the on-going monitoring of the health of the banks and the banking system, in particular asset quality, capital adequacy, liquidity, management, internal controls, and earnings. Supervision is exercised through an array of instruments or techniques that range from off-site and on-site examinations (or inspections) to reporting, auditing (internal unpublished audit and external published audits), statistical requirements, and internal controls.[8]

Both the elements of supervision (ie, capital adequacy, asset quality, and the others) and the techniques of supervision are subject to regulation, that is, they are spelt out and described in the law.

Capital regulation has become of such paramount importance in recent years that some economists tend to equate capital regulation with banking regulation. The linkage between the intensity of supervision and the level of capitalization is an interesting example of the interaction between supervision and regulation.[9] However, capital is not per se a panacea for regulation. Considerations of asset loss pervade the concept of capital adequacy; the quality of the asset portfolio was and is the key to 'sound banking'. Capital requirements do not take into

---

[8] For a detailed description of each of these supervisory techniques, see Lastra, above note 3, 111–22.

[9] This approach, with better capitalized banks receiving less attention—a regulatory incentive that favours greater capitalization—and undercapitalized banks being subject to intense scrutiny, and possibly prompt corrective action, PCA, or structured early intervention and resolution, SEIR, has been adopted by law in the USA, and has gained much support amongst academics in recent years. Some of the statements issued by the US and the European Shadow Financial Regulatory Committees, available at <http://www.aei.org> are evidence of this support.

account the competence, depth, and integrity of management, which also plays a crucial role in sound banking.

Because the quality and riskiness of the bank's asset portfolio is difficult to assess at any given time (despite supervisors' best efforts to develop systems of loan classification according to their credit risk: good, substandard, problem, doubtful, non-performing, loss), lending restrictions are often applied. The regulation of lending limits is another interesting example of the interaction between supervision and regulation, since supervisors use some of these limits—defined in banking laws or regulations—as a proxy for excessive risk concentration. For example, large credit exposures to a single party or group of connected counter-parties are limited by law.[10] Other restrictions refer to loans to subsidiaries; the rationale being that if the subsidiary runs into difficulties, that may affect the soundness of the whole bank (as happened in Barings).[11] Lending limits to non-bank subsidiaries are an important issue when talking about financial groups/financial conglomerates. Connected lending (loans to insiders) is a major problem in many countries in Latin America. In order to prevent corruptive practices and abuse of position for personal interests or benefit, it is important to restrict lending to directors, officers, and employees, as well as their families and friends. Finally, lending to shareholders is also subject to limitations in some jurisdictions, though the practice on this issue differs greatly across countries, depending on the role that banks play in controlling corporations, an issue which I briefly discussed with regard to the licensing process.

Another example of the interaction between regulation and supervision refers to the treatment of loan loss reserves. Though there are wide variations from country to country, as a general principle, the authorities should encourage banks to provide for loan losses (loan loss reserves) as that constitutes a big step forward in the resolution of the problems of entities that have a substantial amount of 'bad' loans.[12] Absent adequate provisioning for loan losses, a bank's

---

[10] The aim of these restrictions is to prevent excessive risk concentration (too many eggs in the same basket). The Basel Committee recommends the target of 25% of total capital as a limit for single exposures. In the EU, an EC Directive of 1992 rules that a credit institution may not incur an exposure to a client or group of connected clients of more than 25% of its own funds. See Directive 92/121/EEC on the monitoring and control of large exposures of credit institutions. This Directive also forbids banks from incurring large exposures which in total exceed 800% of their own funds.

[11] In the USA, according to ss 23(a) and 23(b) Federal Reserve Act, the capital limit for banks on unsecured lending to one affiliate is 10% and to all affiliates is 20%.

[12] Loan loss reserves are a form of capital that are not included in core capital, but can be included in Tier II capital to a limited extent. The reason for the special treatment of loss reserves is that these funds play an especially important role in ensuring that the bank is taking account regularly—through deductions from current earnings—of future losses that are statistically predictable on the basis of its past experience. With proper loss reserving, the bank's reported net income should be a reasonably accurate indication of the bank's basic earning power.

earnings are likely to be overstated and could mislead both stockholders and the markets as to the bank's underlying strength.

Sanctioning

The success of banking regulation is always dependent upon its effective enforcement. Penalties for wrongdoing should be clearly spelt out in the law, their severity varying depending on the nature of the wrongdoing (civil versus criminal penalties). However, penalties should not be applied for political considerations or because of displeasure with bank management policies. Courts of justice need to be independent in order to assess cases without political pressures.

Sanctions or penalties can be broadly classified into two types: those that affect the bank and those that affect bank management. 'Institutional sanctions' (such as monetary fines, cease and desist orders, closer supervision, restrictions in activities, prompt corrective action, revocation of a licence, and closure) affect the institution, and thereby, shareholders. 'Personal sanctions' (such as temporary or permanent inability to be a banker, fines, loss of job, call of attention, management overhaul, and imprisonment) penalize management directly.

In recent years, and as a response to some of the corporate and financial scandals such as Enron in the USA, there is a trend to give increasing attention and emphasis to personal sanctions in the light of the fiduciary duties of directors, managers, and officers.

The issue of the legal liability of the supervisory authorities for loss caused by the inadequate supervision of banks is of contemporaneous interest in the UK, where it has been discussed in the context of the damages action against the Bank of England for the failure of Bank of Credit and Commerce International.[13]

Crisis management

Crisis management in banking involves an array of instruments that extend beyond the insolvency proceedings that are the only tool typically available to deal with corporate bankruptcy in other industries. Such an array of instruments includes the lender of last resort role of the central bank, deposit insurance schemes, and bank insolvency proceedings (judicial or extra-judicial).

---

[13] Above Ch 2, note 85. See also Mads Andenas, 'Liability for supervisors and depositors' rights: the BCCI and the House of Lords' (2001) 22 The Company Lawyer 226.

There are other instruments that the authorities use to deal with banking crises such as the government's implicit protection of depositors, banks (the so-called 'too-big-to-fail' doctrine), and the payment system. Reliance on the official safety net is the subject of much criticism in the literature and much controversy in policy-making circles. I further discuss banking crises and crisis management in Chapter 4.

C. Separation between Monetary and Supervisory Functions

The separation between the monetary and the supervisory functions of a central bank is a most contentious issue in the institutional design of supervision. The central bank has a fundamental role with regard to monetary stability and financial stability. The pursuit of price stability has become the primary object-ive of monetary policy as I explained in Chapter 2. Central bankers' duties towards the maintenance of 'financial stability' typically refer to maintenance of the safety and soundness of the banking system.[14] Sound banking is related to three basic central bank functions: central banks as bankers' banks (including their role in the payments system), central banks as supervisory agencies (when they are entrusted with supervisory functions), and central banks as lender of last resort.

Arguments for separation

Banking supervision is not a necessary or exclusive function of a central bank.[15] It is evidently not necessary because there are central banks not directly entrusted with this task; neither is it exclusive, as responsibility for supervision can be shared, and actually often is, with other regulatory agencies. Goodhart and Schoenmaker[16] claim that the main arguments for separating monetary and supervisory functions are the potential conflicts of interests and the likely pref-erability of a single financial regulator (in a context of blurring frontiers between different types of financial intermediaries). The danger of reputational damage should also be considered, given that supervision is a thankless task, criticized by

---

[14] As Christos Hadjiemmanuil and Mads Andenas point out, '. . . the concepts of "financial stability" and "bank safety and soundness", which guide prudential supervision, are broad and imprecise. They do not provide operational criteria for administrative action, but require applica-tion of discretion on an individual basis'. See Christos Hadjiemmanuil and Mads Andenas, 'Banking Supervision and European Monetary Union' (1999) 1(2) Journal of International Banking Regulation 84, 96.

[15] Supervision can be separated from the central bank and yet the central bank always keeps a regulatory role.

[16] See Charles Goodhart and Dirk Schoenmaker, 'Should the Functions of Monetary Policy and Banking Supervision be Separated?' (1995) 47 Oxford University Papers 539.

many, appreciated by very few.[17] Furthermore, since managerial time is limited, and since supervisory issues—particularly in times of crisis—are very time consuming, a case can be made for the central bank to focus its attention on the important and demanding task of conducting monetary policy.[18] Conflicts of interest are possible when the prime concern of the monetary authorities is to keep an external objective, such as a fixed exchange rate. This was the case with the crisis of the Exchange Rate Mechanism (ERM) of the European Monetary System in 1992–3,[19] when the interest rate deemed necessary to keep participating in the ERM endangered financial stability.

Arguments against separation

According to Goodhart and Schoenmaker,[20] the main arguments against separation are the central bank's lender of last resort role (especially in the case of systemic failure) and its oversight function in the payment system (whether or not the central bank participates in the operation of that system). The safeguard of systemic stability might be adversely affected if supervision is transferred from the central bank to a specialized agency, since the ethos, culture, and priorities of the separate supervisory agency may come to focus on conduct of business and consumer protection issues, leaving aside systemic considerations.[21] Another argument against separation is the need for consistency between monetary policy and banking supervision. Those formulating monetary policy must have a comprehensive and intimate understanding of the workings of the banking system, and bank supervisors must understand the policy environment within which they operate. There are also advantages of synergy in placing banking supervision under the central bank, because of the knowledge central banks have about the health of individual credit institutions and the financial system as a whole. Owing to its lender of last resort role, the central bank has a keen interest in monitoring the solvency of the institutions to which it may eventually have to lend.

In emerging economies, the case for keeping supervision under the wing of the central bank is strengthened because of the scarcity of qualified staff and adequate funding. Central banks tend to have greater independence from government officials, better funding, greater knowledge and expertise (and a certain pride in

---

[17] Monetary authorities are respected if they succeed in keeping inflation under control; their actions and decisions find echo in the press. So do their mistakes or failures. But there is a certain equilibrium, a balance between positive and negative press. Supervisors who succeed in their task are typically ignored or merely receive a neutral approval by the public and the press. However, supervisors that fail in their actions are the subject of intense criticism, scrutiny, and, as evidenced by some recent developments, even legal liability.

[18] See Charles Goodhart, *The Organizational Structure of Banking Supervision*, Special Paper 127 (London: Financial Markets Group, London School of Economics, 2000) 29–30.

[19] ibid 33–4.   [20] Above note 16.   [21] Above note 18, 1.

doing their job well) than other government agencies. Frequently, the research department of the central bank is the only serious economic research group in the country. However, some big emerging economies, such as the People's Republic of China, have also transferred supervision away from the central bank (in the case of the PRC, to the new Chinese Banking Regulatory Commission).

The debate about the supervisory responsibilities of central banks (and about central bank independence in banking supervision, which I further discuss below) is linked to the discussion of the goals and history of central banks. The Federal Reserve System was set up in 1913 'to establish a more effective supervision of banking',[22] following the banking crises of the nineteenth and early twentieth centuries (attributable to the inability of banks to convert their demand deposits into cash). The Fed conceives of its monetary policy role as having been largely grafted onto its supervisory functions, and regards its supervisory and regulatory functions as a prerequisite and complement to its monetary policy responsibilities.

The European Central Bank has a clear mandate with regard to monetary policy but no corresponding mandate with regard to financial supervision (which remains decentralized). The implications of this institutional arrangement at the EU level are further discussed below in Chapters 10 and 11.

D. Financial Stability

In this section, I provide first a definition of financial stability and, then, I discuss the relationship between financial stability and prudential supervision when the central bank is not directly and formally in charge of supervision, and the consequences of this organizational arrangement with regard to the conduct of lender of last resort operations.

Definition of financial stability

Financial stability is a broad and discretionary concept that generally refers to the safety and soundness of the financial system and to the stability of the payment and settlement systems.[23] It is only by reference to times of crises, when the central bank has a 'real role' as lender of last resort, that the responsibility for financial stability becomes truly meaningful in the current institutional setup.

---

[22] See Introduction to the Federal Reserve Act of 23 December 1913.

[23] Most central banks, with or without supervisory responsibilities, regard this responsibility for financial stability as one of their key duties. However, many central bank laws do not explicitly refer to this mandate. In the case of the European Central Bank, the EC Treaty includes a specific reference to financial stability in Art 105(4).

Financial stability is an evolving concept. In 'negative terms' it is the absence of instability. In 'positive terms' the achievement of this objective encompasses a variety of elements (many of which are typically the subject of oversight by the supervisory authorities) such as good licensing policies, good supervisory techniques, adequate capital and liquidity, competent and honest management, internal controls, early warning systems, transparency, and accountability. It also refers to the smooth operation of the payment systems.[24]

Acknowledging the lack of a clearly established analytical and operational framework for the understanding of financial stability, Tommaso Padoa-Schioppa refers to it as a 'land in between' monetary policy and supervision.[25] While in the past monetary policy, prudential supervision, and financial stability formed a single composite, those three functions have been unbundled.[26] According to Padoa-Schioppa, financial stability can be defined 'as a condition in which the financial system would be able to withstand shocks, without giving way to cumulative processes, which impair the allocation of savings to investment opportunities and the processing of payments in the economy. In the jargon of my early years in central banking, this function used to be labelled as maintaining "orderly conditions" in the financial system.'[27]

Notwithstanding this definition, he indicates that 'although a number of central banks publish financial stability reports regularly, they tend either to avoid the question of how to define financial stability entirely (e.g., Bank of England) or to explicitly acknowledge the elusiveness of a consistent definition (e.g., the Austrian National Bank.'[28] Padoa-Schioppa uses a broad notion of 'financial system' (for the purposes of defining financial stability), one that encompasses 'all financial intermediaries and markets, as well as market infrastructures and the regulatory system governing it'.[29]

---

[24] In a recently published book on the subject of financial stability (one of the few developments I have been able to take into account after 6 December 2005), Garry Schinassi, *Safeguarding Financial Stability. Theory and Practice* (Washington DC: IMF, 2006) 77, provides the following definition: 'Financial stability is defined as the ability of the financial system to facilitate and enhance economic processes, manage risks and absorb shocks. Moreover, financial stability is considered a continuum, changeable over time and consistent with multiple combinations of finance's constituent elements.'

[25] See Tommasso Padoa-Schioppa, 'Central Banks and Financial Stability. Exploring a Land in Between', (Speech delivered in the European Central Bank's Second Central Banking Conference 'The Transformation of the European Financial System', 24–5 October 2002), available at <http://www.ecb.int/home/conf/cbc2/tps.pdf>. This speech has been published as ch 8 in his book, *Regulating Finance* (Oxford: Oxford University Press, 2004).

[26] ibid.

[27] ibid. Padoa-Schioppa also argues that price stability is a necessary but not sufficient condition for financial stability. Furthermore, he points out: 'In the long-term, price stability is a powerful facilitator of financial stability, but is, in turn, not sustainable without financial stability.'

[28] ibid.   [29] ibid.

The involvement of central banks in financial stability originates in their role as monopolist suppliers of *fiat* money[30] and in their role as bankers' bank. Only the ultimate supplier of money can provide the necessary stabilizing function in a nationwide scramble for liquidity.[31]

Financial stability and prudential supervision

It is more difficult to keep financial stability as a key central banking goal once supervision is transferred to a separate agency. If a central bank wishes to have or retain a real role in financial stability, then it often 'needs' to have supervisory powers. Without these powers, the central bank effectively becomes a 'monetary agency' (with lender of last resort responsibilities as I further elaborate below), limited in its 'positive' reinforcement of such stability to monitor, analyse, and disseminate information about developments in the financial system, to contribute to international standard-setting, and to influence legislative developments in this field and other research and advisory functions.

The transfer of prudential supervision away from the central bank effectively deprives the central bank of a major instrument to deal with financial stability. In the UK, the Bank of England no longer has the supervisory 'tools' to assess the safety and soundness of individual banks. It has a broad mandate with regard to financial stability. However, it is interesting to observe that the legislation in the UK contains no provisions regarding the composition and functions of the financial stability committee. In the words of a former member of the Bank of England, the financial stability committee is a 'glorified briefing committee'. It has no real decision-making powers. Its composition varies. For instance, when Eddie George was Governor of the Bank of England, he chaired this committee. Currently, the committee, which is composed of the Deputy Governors, the Head of Banking Operations, the Head of Central Banking Studies, and the people in the financial stability 'wing' of the Bank, is chaired by the Deputy Governor with responsibility for financial stability, Andrew Large. The safeguard of financial stability in positive terms does not include any real power. Indeed, none of the following responsibilities of the financial stability 'wing' of the Bank of England (mentioned in its website, but not in the Bank of England Act 1998) can be described as a decisive competency: to monitor developments in the financial system both at home and abroad, including the links between individual institutions and between financial markets; to analyse the health of the domestic and international economy; to maintain cooperation with financial supervisors both domestically and internationally; and to promote sound financial infrastructure including efficient payment and settlement arrangements.

---

[30] ibid.   [31] See Lastra, above note 3, 267.

Financial stability and lender of last resort

If prudential supervision is transferred away from the central bank, while the latter retains a role with regard to the safeguard of financial stability, then the main organizational challenge[32] is to establish adequate mechanisms of close and continuous communication and flow of information between the central bank and the supervisory agency/agencies, particularly in times of crisis.[33] The responsibility for financial stability needs to be shared with the central bank when prudential supervision is transferred to a separate agency.

In the UK, following the transfer of supervision to the FSA, the 'real' role left to the Bank of England with regard to financial stability comes in times of crises, through its lender of last resort role and through its participation in the Standing Committee, whose composition and workings are spelt out in the Memorandum of Understanding of 1997.[34] This tripartite committee provides an example of cooperation between HM Treasury, the Bank of England, and the Financial Services Authority in times of crisis. The Committee meets on a monthly basis and also at the request of any of the participating institutions in emergency circumstances. Each institution has nominated representatives which can be contacted, and meet, at short notice. If a financial institution gets into trouble, the first port of call will be the FSA. If either the FSA or the Bank of England spots a problem where liquidity support (ie, LOLR) might be necessary, they will consult each other immediately. If the problem is related to the scope of responsibilities of the FSA, then the FSA will lead the support operation, though the funds will still come from the Bank. If the problem originates in the payment system or other area of responsibility of the Bank of England, then the Bank will lead the support operation and provide the emergency loan. In all cases, the FSA and the Bank are supposed to work together very closely and to inform the Treasury, in order to give the Chancellor of the Exchequer the option of refusing the support operation. Indeed, if fiscal resources—ie, tax-payers' money—are to be committed, then the Chancellor should have a say in deciding whether or not to provide support to the troubled institution.

---

[32] In the case of the transfer of supervisory responsibilities from the Bank of England to the FSA, such transfer has been accompanied by a 'transfer of personnel', ie, the same people doing supervision at the Bank of England are now doing supervision at the FSA (though the latter has a larger staff).

[33] See above note 18, 6. 'Those in charge of banking supervision and those in the central bank most concerned with financial stability, are, perforce, going to have to work together.'

[34] This MoU between HM Treasury, the Bank of England, and the FSA was released on 28 October 1997. See 'Memorandum of Understanding Between HM Treasury, the Bank of England and the FSA', available at <http://www.bankofengland.co.uk/legislation/mou.pdf>.

In my opinion, the UK Standing Committee is a good institutional arrangement to deal with lender of last resort operations, when supervision is not
exercised by the central bank. Indeed, I think such an arrangement ought to
be formally established in those countries that choose to transfer supervision
away from the central bank.[35] Such a high-level standing committee ought to
include representatives from the central bank, the Treasury/Ministry of Finance,
and the supervisory agency/agencies. The standing committee would deal with
threats to the stability of the financial system, in particular in cases where
emergency liquidity assistance is needed. It is important that the responsibilities
of each member of the standing committee be defined clearly according to
the principles of regular and speedy information exchange, efficiency (avoiding
duplication), accountability, and transparency.

At the EU level, I recommend in Chapter 10 the setting up of a European
Standing Committee for Crisis Management, whose composition should balance efficiency (time is of the essence in any support operation) with adequate
representation. The ability to provide sufficient resources means that, in addition to the central banking representation (ECB and NCBs), there should be a
mechanism for incorporating into the decision-making process the national
fiscal authorities as well as the EU Commissioner in charge of competition
policy, given that any assistance to an insolvent institution would bring into play
the EU rules on state aid.

E. The Optimal Number of Supervisory Authorities

The optimal number of supervisory authorities, one for the whole financial
system as in the UK, one for each sector of the financial industry as in Spain,[36]
or multiple authorities in each sector of the financial industry as in the USA, has
become a controversial subject in recent times. However, to my knowledge,
there is no empirical evidence that justifies the superior wisdom of any given
model of organizing financial supervision.

The model that each country adopts is often rooted in historical and political
considerations. Nevertheless, a trend towards consolidation can be identified
since the establishment of the Financial Services Authority in 1997 in the UK.
Despite the fact that the UK is not the first country to adopt this supervisory

---

[35] Indeed, this was my advice to the People's Republic of China (PRC) when I was asked to act
as a legal consultant on the reform of the PRC banking and central banking laws in 2003.
[36] In Spain, banks are supervised by the Banco de España, securities firms by the Comisión
Nacional del Mercado de Valores and insurance companies and pension funds by the Dirección
General de Seguros y de Fondos de Pensiones.

model—Norway and Denmark have had a single authority for the entire financial sector for some time—the significance of the UK development is threefold.
First, it represents the adoption of this model by a country that is not 'bank-
dominated', but where capital markets are well developed. Secondly, it has
triggered a wave of change in other European countries, such as Germany,[37]
which adopted a single supervisor in 2002, and France, which has recently
consolidated supervisory responsibilities.[38] Thirdly, the trend towards unification of supervisory responsibilities in some European countries has wider implications at the EU level, as it could pave the way towards the creation of a single
European Financial Services Authority, a controversial issue which I further
discuss in Chapter 11.

In the eyes of many, the unification of financial market supervision is considered
to be an appropriate response to the rise in financial conglomerates and complex
financial groups. Abrams and Taylor contend that 'the structure of the regulatory system needs to reflect the structure of the markets that are regulated.'[39] In
Germany the establishment of a single authority for integrated financial services
supervision appears to be well suited to the needs of a universal banking system.
In the view of the BaFin, the integration of three supervisory authorities into a
single financial services supervisor has been a necessary response to the deep

---

[37] Following the adoption on 22 April 2002 of the Law on Integrated Financial Services
Supervision (Gesetz über die integrierte Finanzaufsicht, FinDAG), the Federal Financial Supervisory Authority (Bundesanstalt für Finanzdienstleistungsaufsicht, BaFin) was established on
1 May 2002. The functions of the former offices for banking supervision (Bundesaufsichtsamt für
das Kreditwesen, BAKred), insurance supervision (Bundesaufsichtsamt für das Versicherung-
swesen, BAV) and securities supervision (Bundesaufsichtsamt für den Wertpapierhandel, BAWe)
have been combined in a single state regulator, the BaFin. The BaFin is a federal institution
governed by public law that belongs to the portfolio of the Federal Ministry of Finance. See the
website of the Federal Financial Supervisory Authority, BaFin, <http://www.bafin.de>.
[38] In France, recent legislation (Loi no 2003–706 du 1er août 2003 de Sécurité Financière) has
reformed the regulatory and supervisory landscape. Specifically, the first section of this legislative
Act, which is entitled 'Modernisation des Autorites de Controle' (Modernisation of Supervisory
Authorities, Articles 1–38) establishes the so-called Financial Markets Authority, (L'Autorité des
marchés financiers, AMF) which has taken over the responsibilities of the COB (Commission des
Operations de Bourse, Committee for Stock Exchange Operations), CMF (Conseil des Marches
Financiers, Council for Financial Markets) and CDGF (Conseil de Discipline et de Gestion
Financier, Council for Financial Discipline and Management). The Financial Markets Authority
is responsible for the protection of investment in financial instruments, the orderly raising of
capital from the public, the information available to investors, and the well-functioning of securities markets. Within its scope of competence, the Authority has been endowed with rule-making,
licensing, supervisory, and enforcement powers. See generally Autorité des Marchés Financiers,
'Les Missions de l'Autorité des Marchés Financiers', available at <http://www.amf-france.org>.
The changes are not too far-reaching. Banking regulation remains the responsibility of the Bank
of France. The new Financial Markets Authority is the sole regulator for securities markets and in
this respect the new regime consolidates in one entity the fragmentary character of securities
regulation in France.
[39] See Richard K Abrams and Michael W Taylor, *Issues in the Unification of Financial Sector
Supervision*, Working Paper 213 (Washington DC: IMF, 2000) 3.

changes in German capital markets, the gradual disappearance of the former distinctions between banking and financial services on the one hand and the insurance business on the other, and the creation of financial conglomerates whereby new lines of similar or identical integrated products are developed and promoted by banks and insurance companies alike. Against those market developments, the model of three separate authorities, each one responsible for different types of financial institutions, was largely outdated.[40]

The case for a single supervisor is also supported by other arguments. The number of people employed by a single authority is likely to be lower than the combined staff numbers of multiple authorities. Firms may find it expensive, confusing, and time-consuming to answer similar questions to various supervisors; instead of their having to deal with a multiplicity of authorities, a single supervisor enables 'one stop-shopping' for financial institutions.[41]

However, the wisdom of having a single supervisor—particularly in large countries—is still doubted by many commentators and policy-makers alike. Some argue that the central bank is best suited to conduct banking supervision. Some others—including myself—fear that the concentration of power in a single authority can lead to a situation of lack of accountability and problems of institutional legitimacy. If the FSA in the UK has sometimes been criticized as a 'regulatory Leviathan' and accountability remains a major concern, an European FSA would be far too powerful to be acceptable to politicians across Europe, in particular in countries where there is 'reverence' for the decisions of the authorities.[42]

---

[40] See generally Bundesanstalt für Finanzdienstleistungsaufsicht, 'Gründe für eine integrierte Finanzmarktaufsicht' available at <http://www.bafin.de/bafin/aufgabenundziele.htm#p3>.

[41] An excellent summary of the pros and cons of the two models (integrated financial supervisor versus specialist supervisor) is found in Karel Lanno, *Supervising the European Financial System*, Policy Brief No 21 (Brussels: Centre for European Policy Studies, 2002). See also Howard Davies, 'Euro-regulation' (1999) 1(2) Journal of International Banking Regulation 114–15.

[42] I once asked Howard Davies, FSA Chairman, what his response would be to allegations that the FSA would concentrate too much regulatory power in the same hands. And he said:

> The culture in this country as well as in the City is quite open. We have had a great deal of self-regulation and have created an environment in which people do debate regulation and regulatory decisions in a very open way, probably more so than in many other countries, perhaps not more than in the US, but more than in most European countries. *Here, there is no automatic reverence for the decisions of the regulators, there is a common culture of criticising.* . . . I don't feel as if we are the kind of organisation which is going to sit in its ivory tower, handing its decisions to the financial markets; that is not our culture. . . . Our environment . . . is much less directly and rigidly regulated than anywhere else you can think of, be it the US, Japan or many European countries. . . . If other countries would move in the direction of financial supermarkets then I think the pressure for change in the regulatory structure will match the changes in the market. (Italics added)

See Rosa M Lastra, 'The City's Troubleshooter: Interview with Howard Davies' (1998) 5(3) Parliamentary Brief 28, 34.

A single market in financial services does not require a single supervisor.[43] In the US, the creation of such a monopoly supervisory authority is extremely unlikely and, according to Greenspan, 'highly undesirable on both political and economic grounds'.[44] Talks have been going on with regard to the reduction of the number of supervisory agencies within the banking sector; that alone generates much controversy. The US is an interesting example of a single monetary area with a single currency, combined with an extremely fragmented supervisory landscape and a complex regulatory system based upon federal law (financial laws enacted by Congress), state law (laws enacted by state legislatures, particularly relevant in terms of insurance companies), regulation by agencies (the Federal Reserve System (Fed) and the Securities and Exchange Commission (SEC) have rule-making powers), and self-regulation (in the field of securities, the rules of the self-regulatory organizations (SROs)).

As acknowledged, the US model of financial regulation and supervision is characterized by its complexity, the multiplicity of regulators, and the demands of federalism. Banking in the USA is subject both to federal law and to state law. There are several supervisory authorities at the federal level.[45] the Federal Reserve System, the Office of the Comptroller of the Currency, and the Federal Deposit Insurance Corporation (in addition to the federal regulators for thrifts, such as the OTS, Office of Thrift Supervision). There are also supervisory authorities at the state level. The securities industry is subject to a combination of federal law and self-regulation (with some elements of state law). The Securities and Exchange Commission is a federal agency which oversees the exchanges and the National Association of Securities Dealers (NASD) and which administers the federal system for the registration of new issues of securities. The exchanges (such as the New York Stock Exchange) are self-regulatory organizations with powers to promulgate rules for their member firms and listed companies. The NASD is a self-regulatory organization with powers—under the supervision of the SEC—to promulgate rules governing voluntary membership broker-dealers in the over-the-counter securities markets, such as the NASDAQ (National Association of Securities Dealers Automated Quotation

---

[43] See also Ch 10.

[44] See Alan Greenspan, 'Financial Innovations and the Supervision of Financial Institutions' (Paper presented in Proceedings of the 31st Annual Conference on Bank Structure and Competition, Federal Reserve Bank of Chicago, May 1995), 4.

[45] The Gramm–Leach–Bliley Act of 1999 represented the breakdown of the Glass–Steagall wall between commercial and investment banking. This 1999 Act expanded the activities permissible for affiliates of banks and created a new category of bank holding company, the 'financial holding company'. However, despite the blurring of the distinctions among financial institutions, the regulatory systems for different types of institutions remain separate. See eg, Jonathan R Macey, Geoffrey P Miller, and Richard S Carnell, *Banking Law and Regulation* (New York: Aspen Law & Business, 2001) 33–6 and 443–9.

System).[46] Through this two-tiered structure, as Jackson and Symons point out, 'the US Congress intended to strike a balance between the protection of the integrity of the markets and the flexibility necessary to maintain an economically vigorous capital market. The structure was also intended to balance the need for the participation of the market professionals, achieved through SRO self-regulation and the need for an independent watchdog, the SEC.'[47] The Sarbanes–Oxley Act of 2002—which introduces sweeping reforms with regard to corporate governance—does not change much the regulatory structure of US securities markets. Investment companies (mutual funds) are regulated almost exclusively at the federal level by the SEC since the enactment of the 1940 Investment Company Act and the 1940 Investment Advisers Act.[48] Insurance in the USA remains a matter of state law since the McCarran–Ferguson Act of 1945,[49] though pension funds are subject to federal law since the enactment of ERISA (Employee Retirement Income Security Act) in 1974.[50]

F. Public versus Private Supervision

Public supervision, that is, supervision exercised by the public authorities, presents several possible options: (i) the government can exercise these tasks directly through a government department or cabinet office; (ii) the government can carry out this function indirectly by delegating it to a supervisory agency under political instruction; (iii) the government can delegate these responsibilities to an independent agency (eg, independent central bank or independent securities regulator). In practice, the government often delegates certain supervisory functions and retains responsibility for others such as licensing and crisis management. The government can also share the supervisory responsibilities with a self-regulatory organization.

---

[46] The Securities Act of 1933 established a federal system for the registration of new issues of securities, and the Securities Exchange Act of 1934, created a new federal agency, the Securities and Exchange Commission. Following the stock market crash of 1929, these pieces of legislation were enacted to promote stability and confidence in capital markets and to protect investors in view of the shortcomings and inadequacies of the state 'blue sky' laws. The reason why state securities statutes were known as 'blue sky' laws is because some lawmakers believed that 'if securities legislation was not passed, *financial pirates would sell citizens everything in the state but the blue sky.*' See Howell E Jackson and Edward L Symons, *Regulation of Financial Institutions* (St. Paul, Minn: West Group, 1999), 655–62 and 751–755.

[47] ibid 753.

[48] ibid 812–50. Open-end investment companies are otherwise known as mutual funds.

[49] ibid 431–42 and 588–90. The US financial regulatory landscape also comprises other regulators, such as the Commodities Future Trading Commission for financial derivatives (commodity futures and options).

[50] ibid 611–17.

Market supervision, that is, supervision exercised by market institutions, should never be underestimated as either a complement to or a substitute for public supervision. Financial firms are subject to continuous monitoring by their competitors, institutional investors, customers, counter-parties, rating agencies, and other private agents. Indeed, a mix of private and public supervision is increasingly regarded as the most efficient way of monitoring the activities of financial firms. For instance, with regard to risk capital supervision, the Basel II proposals (and the proposed EU framework on capital requirements for banks and investment firms) include elements of private supervision through the internal ratings system and through disclosure requirements. Indeed, a current trend in modern finance is the constant reinforcement of market supervision and regulation.

This is a welcome trend, but it is not without pitfalls. In particular, the dangers of regulatory capture cannot be ignored. In some instances, there is a fine line between being 'market friendly' and being 'market captive'.[51]

Exclusive reliance on private supervision (market discipline) and private regulation (rules or standards set by self-regulatory organizations) would imply the absence of any official involvement by a public authority in the financial system. However, a system based only on private supervision and regulation would be both unfeasible and unacceptable as long as the government keeps an implicit or explicit role in the resolution of a crisis. Official protection justifies public supervision and regulation; the greater the protection, the greater the degree of justifiable public involvement in supervision.

Any shift from public to private supervision or self-regulation also implies a shift in the onus of responsibility. While reliance on private supervision places the onus of responsibility on management, reliance on public supervision places it on the authorities. Such a shift should be welcomed by supervisors, since as Goodhart points out:

> [T]he conduct of supervision is a thankless task, which is all too likely to tarnish the reputation of the supervisor. . . . The best that a supervisor can expect is that nothing untoward happens. A supervisor is only noticed when he/she angers the regulated by some restrictive or intrusive action, or when supervision fails in the sense that a financial institution collapses or a customer gets ripped off. One can talk oneself blue in the face of the desirability of allowing some freedom for banks

---

[51] The economic literature on 'regulatory capture' is well known: any given industry would try to influence the outcome of the regulatory process for its own benefit, rather than the public interest. Industry lobbies can exert undue influence, as shown by the Enron debacle. See Tommaso Padoa-Schioppa, *Regulating Finance* (Oxford: Oxford University Press, 2004) 48–51.

or other financial institutions to fail, etc., but supervisors will always tend to get a bad press when that does happen.[52]

G. Independence versus Politically Directed Process

The debate about central bank independence—which I discussed in Chapter 2 —focuses on the monetary responsibilities of a central bank, leaving aside other central bank functions. However, I have argued in my writings since 1992 that independence to pursue stable money should be accompanied by independence to pursue a sound financial system, and complemented by appropriate mechanisms of accountability. The need for independence from political instruction of the supervisory authority is recognized in the 'Core Principles of Effective Banking Supervision', issued by the Basel Committee of Banking Supervision in 1997. According to principle 1, supervisory authorities 'should possess operational independence and adequate resources'.[53]

Notwithstanding the need to free supervisors from political pressure, monetary independence and supervisory independence are not the same.[54] To begin, the relative simplicity of 'monetary policy independence' contrasts with the complexity of 'supervisory independence'. The one goal, one instrument, one agency of the former (the goal price stability, the instrument monetary policy, and the agency the independent central bank) contrasts with the several goals, several instruments and, often, several agencies of the latter (the goals: financial stability, investor protection, conduct of business, and others; the instruments: licensing requirements, prudential supervision, financial stability reviews, lender of last resort operations, and others; the agencies: the central bank, the ministry of finance or treasury, the supervisory agency or agencies).[55] Central bank independence is limited by the 'goal constraint', namely price stability, and by

---

[52] See Goodhart, above note 18, 30–1.

[53] See Basel Committee for Banking Supervision, 'Core Principles for Effective Banking Supervision' (Basel: Bank for International Settlements, 1997) 4, available at <http://www.bis.org/publ/bcbs30a.pdf>.

[54] For a different opinion, see Marc Quintyn and Michael W Taylor, 'Regulatory and Supervisory Independence and Financial Stability' (2003) 49 CESifo Economic Studies 259, available at <http://www.cesifo.de/pls/guestci/download/CESifo+Economic+Studies+2003./CESifo+Economic+Studies+2/2003./econstudies-2-03-S259.pdf>. Quintyn and Taylor argue that regulatory and supervisory independence is important for financial stability for the same reasons that central bank independence is important for monetary stability.

[55] The main message in the design of appropriate accountability mechanisms in financial supervision is: keep it simple and have clear goals, if possible just one for one agency. This is an important consideration behind the recent reform of the Dutch model of financial supervision, where there is one goal for the prudential supervisor and one goal for the conduct of business supervisor. See Annet Jonk, Jeroen Kremers, and Dirk Schoenmaker, 'A New Dutch Model', Financial Regulator, vol 6, no 3, December 2001, 35–8.

the demands of democratic legitimacy and accountability. The 'goal constraint' in supervision is not as easily identifiable as in the case of the monetary authority.

While central bank accountability with regard to monetary policy is typically 'explanatory' (unless the law of the central bank is amended or the governor is removed from office, there is very little room for granting redress with regard to monetary policy decisions), the accountability of the central bank or the supervisory agency in the field of prudential supervision and regulation is sometimes 'explanatory' and sometimes 'amendatory'. The liability of financial market supervisors is under discussion in several EU Member States. Several legal scholars have recently explored the issue of (state) liability for loss caused by the inadequate supervision of banks,[56] in the context of the damages action against the Bank of England for the failure of Bank of Credit and Commerce International (BCCI).[57]

The design of a proper legal framework for supervisory independence needs to take into account the multi-faceted nature of supervision. Supervision in a broad sense is a process with four stages which entail different functions with a rather 'decentralized' approach. Supervision *stricto sensu* typically relies on a large number of staff to perform examinations and other tasks. In contrast, decisions on interest rate policy are generally taken by relatively few people (the governor/chairman and the members of the executive board/monetary policy committee).[58] The appointment procedures of independent central bankers and other guarantees enshrined in the law to protect 'monetary policy independence' cannot be easily replicated, in my opinion, with regard to the exercise of supervision, since it would be impractical (too expensive and time consuming) to demand the same standards and to apply the same procedures to the cohort of supervisors.[59]

---

[56] See Andrews, above note 13. See also M Andenas and Duncan Fairgrieve, 'To Supervise or to Compensate? A Comparative Study of State Liability for Negligent Banking Supervision' in Mads Andenas and Duncan Fairgrieve (eds) *Judicial Review in International Perspective*, Libor Americorum in Honour of Lord Slynn of Hadley (The Hague, Boston: Kluwer Law International, 2000) 333–60.

[57] As I explained in Ch 2 (note 85), the case against the Bank of England (*Three Rivers District Council v Governor and Company of the Bank of England (No. 3)* [2000] 2 WLR 1220; [2000] 3 All ER 1; [2000] Lloyd's Rep Bank 235, HL) was abandoned on 2 November 2005, when BCCI liquidators Deloitte Touche Tohmatsu dropped their claim (against the Bank of England), after receiving a legal ruling that it would not be in the best interests of BCCI's creditors to continue with the lawsuit.

[58] Though the central bank also needs a team of economists to do the forecasting, to study the transmission mechanisms of monetary policy, etc.

[59] An analogy can be made between the courts of justice and the conduct of supervision and regulation. Supervision is akin to a 'court of first instance', while monetary policy is akin to a 'court of appeals' or 'supreme court'. The qualifications typically required (or expected) of supreme court justices (or justices in courts of appeals) are typically higher than the qualifications of judges in courts of first instance.

This notwithstanding, the need to distance banking from politics is of paramount importance in many developing countries, where banks and their supervisors are more likely to be subject to the whims of politicians. Certain supervisory decisions (such as the closure or non-closure of a bank)[60] need to be 'depoliticized'. A certain degree of independence is needed to protect supervisors and regulators (as well as competition authorities) from political pressures and from the dangers associated with corruption, connected lending, and nepotism.[61] Ruth de Krivoy—on the basis of her experience as Central Bank Governor in Venezuela during the country's banking crisis in the 1990s—makes a strong case for keeping supervision within an independent central bank:

> Giving supervisory powers to an independent central bank is especially advantageous if public institutions are weak, coordination between different public sector agencies is troublesome, or skilled human resources are scarce. Central banks [in emerging economies, such as Venezuela] are usually a country's most prestigious and well-equipped institutions, and are in a good position to hire, motivate and keep skilled staff.[62]

H. Institution versus Business Function

Supervision has traditionally been organized by institution, irrespective of the business function or range of functions that the institution undertakes. However, as banks engage into the securities and insurance business (and as insurance companies engage in securities and new lines of business), the case for supervision/regulation by institution becomes weaker. Inter-industry affiliation and inter-industry competition in the financial sector call for enhanced consolidated supervision and—according to some commentators—this suggests the need for increased reliance on regulation by business function rather than by institution. Under a system of supervision by business function, supervisors focus on the type of business undertaken, regardless of which institutions are involved in that particular business. This means that one institution could be subject to several supervisors if it carries out different types of businesses (for instance banking, securities, and insurance).

As defined by Greenspan:[63]

> Functional regulation is thought of as a system in which each separate 'function'—

---

[60] Other 'banking decisions' that deal with issues of competition, such as the approval or rejection of a banking merger, also need to be freed from political interference, whether they are taken by competition authorities or by bank supervisory authorities.

[61] See Ruth de Krivoy, *Collapse. The Venezuelan Banking Crisis of 1994* (Washington DC: The Group of Thirty, 2000).

[62] ibid 203–4.   [63] Above note 43, 4.

such as commercial banking, investment banking or mortgage banking—is supervised by the same regulatory body, regardless of the function's location within a particular financial institution. Practically, this means that a single financial organisation would have several functional regulators, and that different functions would be somehow separated, most likely through the creation of legally separate subsidiaries, within the broad financial organisation.

To some extent, there are some elements of supervision by business function in the USA following the adoption of the Gramm–Leach–Bliley Act of 1999 (the Financial Services Modernization Act), where, under the umbrella of the financial services holding companies (which are supervised by the Federal Reserve System), the bank subsidiaries—which are engaged in commercial banking activities—are supervised by bank regulators (OCC, Fed, state bank regulators) and non-bank affiliates are supervised by specialist regulators according to the type of business undertaken.[64]

The new organizational structure of the German Federal Authority for the Supervision of Financial Services (BaFin) consists of three supervisory directorates for banking supervision, insurance supervision, and securities supervision/asset management and three cross-sectoral departments dealing with cross-sectoral issues.[65] However, the change in structure has not signified a change in the substantive laws underlying supervision, such as the German Banking Act (Gesetz über das Kreditwesen, KWG), the Insurance Supervision Law (Versicherungsaufsichtsgesetz, VAG) and the German Securities Trading Act (Gesetz über den Wertpapierhandel, WpHG). The justification for keeping these laws is that 'although financial services supervision has been organised in a single body, this does not mean that existing sectoral differences between the banking and insurance businesses will be disregarded. These differences have led to the development of specific supervisory methods and rules for banks and insurance companies which have proved to be successful.'[66]

Another alternative to the cross-sector organization of financial supervision is provided by the new Dutch supervisory model, introduced in the second half of 2002.[67] It can be characterized as a functional model based on the objectives of

---

[64] See Richard Dale and Simon Wolfe, 'The UK Financial Services Authority: Unified Regulation in the New Market Environment', (2003) 4 (3) Journal of International Banking Regulation 209.

[65] The first of these cross-sectoral departments deals with financial conglomerates, and the BaFin's participation in international supervisory forums. The second cross-sectoral department deals with consumer protection issues as well as cross-sectoral legal issues. The third cross-sectoral department focuses on money laundering. See <http://www.bafin.de>.

[66] ibid.

[67] The Dutch model became operational in September 2002, following the entry into force of the necessary Ministerial and Royal decrees and after all the necessary steps had been finalized (such as the change of name of the former securities regulator 'Stichting Toezicht effectenverkeer'

supervision. The Dutch central bank (*De Nederlandsche Bank*, DNB) is the institution responsible for prudential supervision in the pursuit of financial stability. The Authority for Financial Markets (AFM) is the authority responsible for conduct of business supervision. Both supervisory authorities cover the full cross-sector width of financial markets (all institutions in banking, securities, insurance, and pensions).[68]

I. Institution versus Supervisory Function

The Financial Services Authority in the UK, which was launched in 1997, and which is governed by the Financial Services and Markets Act of 2000,[69] was initially organized by regulatory/supervisory functions, rather than by institution. According to the FSA Chairman, Howard Davies,[70] the UK adopted a system based upon what he referred to as 'regulatory functions': authorization, supervision, enforcement, in addition to support functions. This approach was preferred at the time over the other three models/approaches considered. These other three approaches were (1) the establishment of one regulator based upon a federation of regulators with matching business strings of the previous regime; (2) the wholesale–retail split as the dividing organizing principle; and (3) the so-called 'twin-peaks' approach,[71] whereby system concerns and prudential consideration would be kept separate from investor protection and conduct of business rules (ie, a system of regulation by objective or finality, as adopted in the Netherlands).[72]

Significant changes to the FSA structure were made in 2001, 'reflecting the view

---

into the 'Autoriteit Financiële Markten' or Authority on Financial Markets, AFM). The merger between DNB (the Dutch central bank, with responsibility for the prudential supervision of banks and securities firms) and the PVK (the authority responsible for the prudential supervision of insurance companies and pension funds) was established by law, which got into force on 1 November 2004. A new Act for financial supervision (Wet op het Financieel Toezicht), implementing the split between prudential supervision and conduct of business, is expected to enter into force in 2006. I am grateful to Geert Moelker of the Dutch Ministry of Finance for observations on this issue. Dutch legislation is available at <http://www.overheid.nl>.

[68] See 'Financial Supervision in the Netherlands' published by the Dutch Ministry of Finance, March 2004, <http://www.minfin.nl>. See also Jeroen Kremers, Dirk Schoenmaker, and Peter Wierts, 'Cross Border Supervision: Which Model?' in Richard Herring and Robert Litan (eds), Brookings–Wharton Papers on Financial Services, Brookings Institution, Washington DC, 2003, 225–44.

[69] The Bank of England Act 1998 transferred responsibility for banking supervision from the Bank of England to the FSA.

[70] See Rosa M Lastra, above note 41.

[71] The 'twin-peaks' approach was advocated by Michael Taylor, *Twin Peaks: A Regulatory Structure for the New Century* (London: Centre for the Study of Financial Innovation, 1995).

[72] See above note 67.

that the supervision function was too large to be undertaken within a single directorate'.[73] According to the new organization chart of the FSA, insurance, pensions, and investment services are being supervised in one directorate, and banking and markets/exchanges as well as complex groups in another.[74] A third directorate on 'Regulatory Processes and Risk' now comprises a division on Regulatory Strategy and Risk, in addition to the divisions on authorization and enforcement.

Hence, the final structure of the FSA is a combination of a model of supervisory/regulatory function, combined with some elements of regulation by objective and some elements of the previous regime, as deposit taking institutions are treated separately from investment and insurance firms. Issues of systemic stability remain the responsibility of the Bank of England. However, if a crisis arises, the Bank of England consults with the FSA and the Treasury according to the rules set up in a Memorandum of Understanding (MoU).[75]

As I have already pointed at the beginning of this chapter, rather than adopting a monolithic approach to supervision, it is better to break it down into its components (stages or supervisory functions). This approach facilitates the analysis of the possible centralization of some supervisory functions at the supranational level, an important issue which is further discussed in Chapter 10 and Chapter 11.

---

[73] See Dale and Wolfe, above note 63, 216.
[74] See Financial Services Authority, 'Inside the FSA', available at <http://www.fsa.gov.uk/media_centre/pdf/inside_the_fsa.pdf>.
[75] Above note 34.

4

BANKING CRISES AND STABILITY OF THE FINANCIAL SYSTEM

I want to talk for a few minutes with the people of the United States about banking. I want to tell you what has been done in the last few days, why it was done, and what the next steps are going to be.... We had a bad banking situation. Some of our bankers had shown themselves either incompetent or dishonest in their handling of the people's funds. They had used the money entrusted to them in speculations and unwise loans. This was of course not true in the vast majority of our banks but it was true in enough of them to shock the people for a time into a sense of insecurity and to put them into a frame of mind where they did not differentiate but seemed to assume that the acts of a comparative few had tainted them all. It was the Government's job to straighten out this situation—and do it as quickly as possible—and the job is being performed.

Franklin D. Roosevelt, Radio Address, 12 March 1933

A. Introduction

The fragility of the banking industry is a permanent feature in financial history. In his authoritative record on the recurrent nature of crises, Charles Kindleberger describes how displacement, euphoria, distress, panic, and crisis have occurred decade after decade, century after century.[1]

A sound banking system is essential for maintaining monetary and financial stability. However, since the banking industry is inherently unstable, the authorities always need to be prepared to confront the possibility of crises or problems. Over the years, a number of preventive and remedial instruments have been devised to strengthen the banking system and to defend it against any negative contingencies. *Ex ante* measures comprise better banking regulation and supervision, transparency, and disclosure. *Ex post* mechanisms, designed to 'steer the boat through a rowing sea',[2] include the suspension of convertibility of deposits into cash, the lender of last resort role of the central bank, deposit insurance schemes, bank insolvency proceedings, and government policies of implicit protection of depositors (both insured or uninsured) or banks (the 'too-big-to-fail doctrine').[3] Given that the suspension of convertibility of deposits into cash is seldom used nowadays (and, if used, it often fails to restore confidence in the system[4]) and given that the implicit protection of depositors and banks is typically a de facto policy not defined in the law, in the ensuing paragraphs I analyse what I regard as the three main institutional arrangements to deal with a banking

---

[1] See Charles P Kindleberger, *Manias, Panics and Crashes. A History of Financial Crises*, 3rd edn (New York: John Wiley & Sons, 1996). The book was originally published in 1978.

[2] The use of this 'transportation analogy' is borrowed from Joseph Stiglitz, who wrote an article on 'Boats, planes and capital flows' published by the *Financial Times*, 25 March 1998. In that article he eloquently stated: 'Although one cannot predict when it [a crisis] might happen, the chances of their [the boats] being broadsided by a wave are significant, no matter how well they are steered. Bad steering, though, increases the chances of disaster and a leaky boat makes it inevitable.'

[3] I have discussed these issues elsewhere. See eg Rosa M Lastra, *Central Banking and Banking Regulation* (London: Financial Markets Group, London School of Economics, 1996), 124–56; ead, 'Lender of Last Resort. An International Perspective' (1999) 48(2) International and Comparative Law Quarterly 339; ead, 'Cross-Border Bank Insolvency: Legal Implications in the Case of Banks Operating in Different Jurisdictions in Latin America' (2003) 6(1) Journal of International Economic Law 79; and a co-authored paper with Douglas W Arner on 'Comparative Aspects of Depositor Protection Schemes: Comparative' in Douglas W Arner and Jan-Juy Lin (eds), *Financial Regulation, A Guide to Structural Reform* (Hong Kong: Sweet and Maxwell Asia, 2003) 463–78. I draw on all these previous writings in this chapter.

[4] Tommaso Padoa-Schioppa points out that the suspension of convertibility has been sometimes used by public authorities 'as a tool to buy time (most recently in Argentina)'. However, he thinks it has more drawbacks than advantages. 'Not only are its legal foundations unclear, but its effectiveness as a real solution has been shown to be limited. Ultimately, confidence is unlikely to be supported by the statutory possibility, and the actual use, of the suspension of such a crucial obligation as the repayment of what is, for good reason, called a demand deposit'. See Tommasso

crisis, namely lender of last resort, deposit insurance, and bank insolvency proceedings. Bearing in mind that monetary law is the focus of this book, special emphasis is given to the lender of last resort role of the central bank.

I also study in this chapter the notion of systemic risk, that is, the possibility that the default of one bank or financial institution can spread to other financial intermediaries, creating a disruption in the monetary and payment systems. Though the very existence of systemic risk is questioned by some commentators, there is ample evidence, in my opinion, to suggest that the risk is real. The transmission mechanisms of a crisis domestically and internationally, the linkages and interconnections between institutions and markets cannot be ignored. No chain is stronger than its weakest link.

B. The 'Anatomy of a Crisis'

The best description of the 'anatomy of a crisis' is provided, in my opinion, by Kindleberger,[5] drawing on Minsky.[6] The first stage in the build-up to a crisis is a 'displacement', some sudden event that changes investor behaviour, expectations, and profit opportunities, such as the beginning or end of a war, an invention or new technology, surprising financial success, or some other political or economic development.[7] If the opportunities for profit brought about by the displacement dominate, a 'boom' is considered to be under way, leading in some cases to investor 'euphoria'.

Throughout history, a number of assets and commodities have been the object of speculation.[8] As firms or individuals see others making profits from 'speculative' transactions, they tend to follow (a pattern that has been characterized as 'herd behaviour') in the expectation that gains can be made rather easily.[9] 'When the number of firms and households indulging in these

---

Padoa-Schioppa, 'Central Banks and Financial Stability. Exploring a Land in Between,' (Speech delivered in the European Central Bank's Second Central Banking Conference 'The Transformation of the European Financial System', 24–5 October 2002), available at <http://www.ecb.int/home/conf/cbc2/tps.pdf> (visited 1 October 2003) 9–10.

[5] This section draws heavily on ch 2 of Kindleberger's book, above note 1, 11–19. The expression 'anatomy of a crisis' is also borrowed from Kindleberger.

[6] See Hyman P Minsky, *John Maynard Keynes* (New York: Columbia University Press, 1975) and Hyman P Minsky, 'The Financial Stability Hypothesis: Capitalistic Processes and Behaviour of the Economy' in Charles Kindleberger and Jean Pierre Laffargue (eds) *Financial Crises: Theory, History and Policy* (Cambridge: Cambridge University Press, 1982) 13–29.

[7] Kindleberger, above note 1, 12 and 34–8.

[8] For a list of 'objects of speculation' see Kindleberger, ibid 38–9.

[9] ibid 13. 'Pure speculation . . . involves buying for resale rather than use in the case of commodities, or for resale rather than income in the case of financial assets.'

[speculative] practices grows large, bringing in segments of the population that are normally aloof from such ventures, speculation for profit leads away from normal, rational behaviour to what has been described as "manias" or "bubbles". The word *mania* emphasizes the irrationality; *bubble* foreshadows the bursting.'[10]

Speculative excesses propagate quickly through the monetary system.[11] Prices increase. At the peak of the market, some investors decide 'to take their profits and sell out'.[12] This sends a signal to other investors, prompting them to exit the market, too. Prices begin to decline, leading to a situation of 'financial distress', which may or may not be followed by a crash or panic.[13] Sometimes, market developments, policy responses, or regulatory solutions prevent the financial distress from turning into a panic. In many other occasions, however, 'the race out of real or long-term financial assets and into money may turn into a stampede'[14] leading to a 'crash' or a 'panic'.[15]

Kindleberger's style of narrative captures the dynamics of the unfolding of a crisis as much as the eloquence of his argument. His brilliant diagnosis of a crisis provides a durable template against which to measure any financial crisis. However, Kindleberger himself acknowledges that his interest in *Manias, Panics and Crashes* 'is more in [crisis] diagnosis than in therapy and prognosis'.[16]

With regard to crisis prevention and management, I analyse in the following

---

[10] ibid. The impact of psychology in a crisis is an element that Kindleberger emphasizes throughout his book. At 23 he clearly states: 'Manias and panics, I contend, are associated on occasion with general irrationality or mob psychology . . . or hysteria.'

[11] ibid 2 and 44–65 (ch 4, 'Fuelling the Flames: Monetary Expansion'). Kindleberger recalls (22) the hyperbolic language used to describe this phenomenon: 'manias . . . insane land speculation . . . blind passion . . . financial orgies . . . frenzies . . . feverish speculation . . . epidemic desire to become rich quick . . . wishful thinking . . . intoxicated investors . . . turning a blind eye . . . people without ears to hear or eyes to see . . . investors living in a fool's paradise . . . easy credibility . . . overconfidence . . . over-speculation . . . overtrading . . . a raging appetite . . . a craze . . . a mad rush to expand'.

[12] ibid 14.

[13] ibid 86. 'Meteorological metaphors are especially called into play . . . the oppressive atmosphere that precedes a storm.'

[14] ibid 15. 'Liquidation is sometimes orderly, but more frequently degenerates into panic.'

[15] ibid 97–8.

A *crash* is a collapse of the price of assets, or perhaps the failure of an important firm or bank. A *panic*, 'a sudden fright without cause' from the god Pan, may occur in asset markets or involve a rush from less to more liquid assets. Financial crisis may involve one or both, and in any order. . . . The system is one of positive feedback. A fall in prices reduces the value of collateral and induces banks to call loans or refuse new ones, causing . . . prices to fall still further. Further decline in collateral leads to more liquidation. If firms fail, bank loans go bad, and then banks fail. As banks fail, depositors withdraw their money. . . . Prices, solvency, liquidity and the demand for cash . . . are interrelated. Not only banking institutions . . ., but households, firms and banks are very similar to a row of bricks, the fall of one endangering the stability of the rest.

[16] ibid 202.

paragraphs what I regard as the main legal and institutional arrangements to protect safe and sound banking.

C. Lender of Last Resort

The name 'lender of last resort' owes its origins to Sir Francis Barings, who in 1797 referred to the Bank of England as the *'dernier resort'* from which all banks could obtain liquidity in times of crisis.[17] The lender of last resort role (LOLR) of the central bank remains a major rationale for most central banks around the world, both in developed and developing countries.[18] While other central bank functions have recently come under fire (eg, banking supervision, as I discussed in Chapter 3), the importance of having the LOLR under the umbrella of the central bank is seldom contested.[19] It is the immediacy of the availability of central bank credit (the central bank being the ultimate supplier of high-powered money) that makes the LOLR particularly suitable to confront emergency situations. At the international level, the role of the International Monetary Fund as international lender of last resort has been much debated in recent years, as I further discuss in Chapter 14.

---

[17] See Thomas M Humphrey and Robert E Keleher, 'The Lender of Last Resort: A Historical Perspective' (1984) 4 (1) Cato Journal 275. How unfitting that the heirs of the man who named the function—Sir Francis Barings—lived to see the Bank of England failing to rescue Barings in 1995!

[18] I draw in this section on an article I wrote on 'Lender of Last Resort. An International Perspective', (1999) 48(2) International and Comparative Law Quarterly 339, above note 3. From a central bank's point of view, the nature of its lender of last resort role involves three different aspects: (1) The discount rate at which the central bank lends, acting in its capacity as lender of last resort, is an instrument of *monetary policy*. In the United States, the Federal Reserve System has made use of the discount window lending in monetary policy. However, it is argued that 'for the sake of economic stability, it is important that the Fed distinguish at all times between its monetary policy and its LOLR function. The lender of last resort should replace liquidity lost as a result of a customer demands; it should not force additional liquidity into the system.' (See George Benston and others, *Perspectives on Safe and Sound Banking: Past Present and Future* (Cambridge, Mass.: MIT Press, 1986), 113.) Regulation A, which governs the extension of credit by Federal Reserve Banks, states that: 'While open market operations are the primary means of affecting the overall supply of reserves, the lending function of the Federal Reserve Banks is an effective method of supplying reserves to meet the particular credit needs of individual depository institutions. The lending functions of the Federal Reserve System are conducted with regard to the basic objectives of monetary policy and the maintenance of a sound and orderly financial system.' (2) The lender of last resort is an instrument of *banking supervision* in a 'crisis situation' stage. As part of its micro-prudential functions, the central bank acting as lender of last resort provides assistance to a bank (or banks) suffering from a liquidity crisis. (3) The lender of last resort is a service provided by the central bank in its capacity as *bankers' bank*.

[19] Under a currency board arrangement, however, the lender of last resort role of the central bank becomes limited (in the case of a mixed central bank–currency board system) or disappears altogether. For an interesting discussion on this issue, see Gerard Caprio and others, *The Lender of Last Resort Function under a Currency Board. The Case of Argentina* World Bank Policy Research Working Paper No. 1648 (Washington DC: World Bank, 1996).

General principles

Though the operation of LOLR is often surrounded by a degree of ambiguity, there are a few principles that are generally applied, according to the classic understanding of the LOLR doctrine.[20] To begin, the central bank—acting as lender of last resort—should prevent temporarily illiquid but solvent banks from failing. (This type of lending is by nature short-term.) Secondly, the central bank should be able to lend as much as is necessary (only the ultimate supplier of high-powered money has this ability), but charge a high rate of interest (a penalty rate as interpreted by some commentators).[21] Thirdly, the central bank should accommodate anyone with good collateral, valued at pre-panic prices. Finally, the central bank should make its readiness to lend clear in advance.

The central bank's LOLR role is discretionary, not mandatory. The central bank assesses not only whether the situation is of illiquidity or insolvency, but also whether the failure of an institution can trigger by contagion the failure of other institutions. The risk of contagion is not easy to assess, as I further discuss below when I analyse the notion of systemic risk. It is difficult to calculate *ex ante* how far a crisis can extend. Market sentiment is often hard to predict and, sometimes, irrational, which renders any rational prediction meaningless. The dynamic of a panic is typically self-fulfilling. Indeed, it is the consideration of market sentiment that prompted Thornton back in 1802 to suggest that providing liquidity to the market (lending on security) was the best way of containing a panic. Bagehot and Thornton contend that the LOLR responsibility is to the market, to the entire financial system and not to specific institutions. The LOLR aims to restore confidence, thereby re-establishing credibility in a bank or banks; therefore the central bank generally chooses to act as LOLR when it fears that the loss of confidence in the system could prompt even solvent institutions to fail. If the central bank deems that the crisis is isolated or can easily be contained, it may choose not to provide emergency assistance.[22]

---

[20] The theoretical foundations of the lender of last resort doctrine were first set by Thornton in 1802 and then by Bagehot in 1873, who further elaborated and refined them. See Henry Thornton, *An Enquiry into the Nature and Effects of the Paper Credit of Great Britain* (Fairfield, NJ: AM Kelley, 1991, originally published in 1802); Walter Bagehot, *Lombard Street. A Description of the Money Market* (New York: Wiley, 1999, originally published in 1873). Recent studies of the work of Thornton and Bagehot on the LOLR are found in Thomas M Humphrey, 'The Classical Concept of the Lender of Last Resort' (1975) 61(1) Federal Reserve Bank of Richmond Economic Review 2; Michael D Bordo, 'Alternative Views and Historical Experience' (1990) 76(1) Federal Reserve Bank of Richmond Economic Review 18.

[21] Charles Goodhard contends that Bagehot's proposal that LOLR lending be at 'high' rates is incorrectly translated into 'penalty' rates. See Charles Goodhart, 'Myths about the Lender of Last Resort' (1999) 2(3) International Finance 339.

[22] The central bank, in order to determine whether contagion risk is present or not, typically considers a number of elements, including *inter alia*: the size and inter-bank exposure of the institution. In my opinion, no institution is too big to fail. However, size combined with inter-bank

Lender of last resort in central banks' statutes

Central banks' laws tend to provide scarce guidance with regard to their lender of last resort operations. One exception is the US legislation on this topic, which happens to be very detailed and rather extensive.[23] There are rules that specify the short-term nature of the lending (60 days, 120 days . . .) as well as the penalty rate applicable and the type of instruments that can be used as collateral. [24] However, most other countries do not have such detailed operational rules.

The problem of moral hazard

The existence of a public 'safety net' creates a moral hazard, that is, a set of incentives for the protected to behave differently—irresponsibly, carelessly, or less conservatively—simply because of the existence of protection. Lending to insolvent institutions increases the potential for moral hazard, because of the perceived relaxation in the exercise of the principles of the LOLR. Therefore, the risk of contagion in the case of non-assistance to an insolvent institution needs to be weighed against the moral hazard incentives that the bailout of such an institution would create. At the end of the day, the central bank's funds come from the public and the risk of loss to the central bank is ultimately a risk of loss to the public (ie, taxpayers). Lending over an extended period also increases the potential for moral hazard as well as the risk of loss to the central bank. In addition, any extended lending becomes a fiscal issue—as taxpayers' money is committed—and, therefore, requires the agreement of the fiscal authority.

To minimize the risk of moral hazard, it is important to demarcate clearly what the central bank can do and what the central bank cannot do—or should not

---

exposure may justify emergency liquidity assistance. This was, arguably, the case with the failure of Continental Illinois in 1984; the danger to a particular market. For example, Johnson Matthey Bankers—a significant player in the gold market—was assisted in 1984, because of the perceived threat to the gold market; the reputation of a financial centre. When a crisis occurs in a major financial centre, such as London, New York, or Tokyo, the authorities will weigh this factor carefully, as confidence and reputation are hard to build and easy to destroy. If however the individual crisis is rooted in excessive or irresponsible risk-taking or in inadequate regulatory discipline— such as non-compliance or poor compliance with regulatory and supervisory requirements—the central bank may choose not to provide assistance so as to prevent moral hazard.

[23] In the USA, the discount window lending (DWL) operates according to rules set up in ss 10a and 10b of the Federal Reserve Act and in the implementing Regulation A. See 12 CFR Chapter II, Part 201, 'Extension of Credit by Federal Reserve Banks'.

[24] Section 12 CFR 201(5) specifies: 'Satisfactory collateral generally includes United States government and federal agency securities, and, if of acceptable quality, mortgage notes, covering 1–4 family residences, State and local government securities, and business, consumer and other customer notes.' Section 201(109) further specifies the conditions applicable for the 'eligibility for discount of mortgage company notes'.

do—through its LOLR. The central bank can provide emergency liquidity—quick cash upfront—over a short period, when no other sources of funding are readily available. What the central bank cannot do is to lend over an extended period—committing taxpayers' money—without the explicit approval of the fiscal authority. Any extended lending becomes the responsibility of the fiscal authority. Neither should the central bank use its LOLR to bailout bank owners; the ultimate responsibility of the LOLR remains to the market, to the entire financial sector and not to any particular institution.

The central bank, before exercising its discretion to act or not to act as LOLR, should conduct a cost-benefit analysis of the results of its intervention. The costs are typically the risk of loss to the central bank and the creation of moral hazard incentives. The benefits accrue from the speed, flexibility, and decisiveness with which the central bank can cope with an emergency crisis.[25] In this cost-benefit analysis due consideration should be given to the interests of depositors, other creditors, shareholders, and taxpayers.

Accountability

The central bank should be held accountable for the use of its discretionary LOLR powers. Such accountability needs to be articulated carefully, particularly in cases where the central bank has no direct role in bank supervision; due consideration should also be given to the degree of central bank independence from the Treasury or Minister of Finance with regard to the exercise of the LOLR function.

Theory and practice

Developments in the marketplace and in the way central banks operate have altered what I refer to as the 'conventional wisdom' on LOLR. In most developed countries and, increasingly, in many developing countries and transitional economies, the LOLR's first principle—lending to illiquid but solvent institutions—is seldom applied, because with developed money and inter-bank markets the central bank is typically called upon to assist an institution when other sources of financing have dried up, that is, when there is a perception in the market that such institution is already suffering from insolvency problems, and because the immediacy of the need for assistance often makes it difficult to

---

[25] In theory, some argue that if an institution goes bust, there will always be another institution to pick up the pieces; in practice, however, some central bankers contend that in a condition of panic, the central bank needs to keep things going until a market is found for the assets of the assisted institution.

assess at that moment whether the institution is illiquid or insolvent.[26] A situation of bank illiquidity (lack of liquid funds) can be an indication of technical insolvency (value of liabilities exceeds market value of assets) or can quickly turn into insolvency if assets are sold at a loss value or 'fire-sale' price. Goodhart suggests that it is a 'myth' to suggest that it is possible to distinguish between illiquidity and insolvency.[27]

The theory that the lender of last resort role of the central bank is applied to cases of temporary illiquidity, whereas deposit insurance is applicable to situations of insolvency, is challenged by the practice. Today, central banks often provide support to insolvent rather than illiquid institutions. In these circumstances, the short-term nature of the LOLR assistance is likely to be insufficient to solve the troubles of such institutions. Therefore, in practice, the LOLR will be the first step in a chain or process that is likely to include a bank insolvency proceeding.

Lender of last resort and the Federal Reserve System

Anna Schwartz claims[28] that the Federal Reserve System has misused its discount window facility throughout the years, lending to insolvent rather than to illiquid institutions. She cites statistics of the 1920s and of the late 1980s to support her argument. In both cases a great percentage of the failing banks had

---

[26] While the test of illiquidity is rather straightforward (ie, lack of liquid funds), the test of insolvency is often more complicated. As H Schiffman explains in the paper he presented to the October 1997 EBRD Seminar on 'Bank Failures and Bank Insolvency Law in Economies in Transition': 'In commercial bankruptcy there are two traditional definitions of insolvency: failure to pay obligations as they fall due (equitable insolvency); and the condition when liabilities exceed assets (balance sheet insolvency).' Economists usually refer to insolvency following the balance sheet insolvency test, ie, when net worth is negative. (An institution may be liquid but insolvent, so long as its cash flow is positive.) However, an economically insolvent bank need not be declared legally insolvent by the responsible agency and may be offered instead financial assistance. A bank is considered to have failed when the competent authorities order the cessation of its operations and activities. If the bank is declared legally insolvent at the exact moment the market value of its net worth reaches zero, direct losses are only suffered by shareholders. If that declaration occurs when the market value of its net worth is already negative, losses will accrue not only to shareholders but also to uninsured creditors and/or to the insurance fund. See Henry N Schiffman, 'Legal Measures to Manage Bank Insolvency in Economies in Transition' in Rosa M Lastra and Henry N Schiffman (eds), *Bank Failures and Bank Insolvency Law in Economies in Transition* (The Hague: Kluwer Law International, 1999) 135.

[27] See Goodhart, above note 21. Back in 1993, Goodhart and Schoenmaker argued that 'with an efficient money and inter-bank market, a commercial bank that is generally believed to be solvent, can, almost always, obtain sufficient additional money to meet its liquidity difficulties,' and therefore, the central bank will generally act as LOLR 'in circumstances where the solvency of the borrower is subject to doubt'. See Charles Goodhart and Dirk Schoenmaker, *Institutional Separation between Supervisory and Monetary Agencies*, Special Paper No 52 (London: Financial Markets Group, London School of Economics, 1993) 18.

[28] See Anna Schwartz, 'The Misuse of the Fed's Discount Window' (1992) 75(4) Federal Reserve Bank of St Louis Review 58.

been 'habitual borrowers' of the discount window lending (DWL) prior to their failure. However, as Schwartz claims, the assessment of bank performance in the 1980s is easier than in the 1920s because of the existence of CAMEL ratings.[29] She recalls that of the 530 DWL borrowers from 1985 to 1991 that failed within three years of the onset of the borrowings, 437 were classified as most problem ridden with a CAMEL rating of 5 (ie, the poorest rating). These institutions were allowed to continue operations for an average period of one year. At the time of failure, 60 per cent of the borrowers had outstanding discount window loans. The lessons to be learnt from these episodes are two-fold. First, LOLR loans over an extended period have been losing propositions for the Fed, that is, the Fed has lost money on its DWL. Secondly, any delay in closing an insolvent institution shifts the risk and the cost from depositors— insured and uninsured—to taxpayers. (If the central bank does not lend to bankrupt institutions, early closure prevents withdrawals of uninsured deposits. If it lends, LOLR loans merely replace withdrawals of uninsured deposits.) Schwartz more radically concludes that the discount window should be elimin- ated and that the Fed can be an effective LOLR if restricted to open market operations; if the concern is with systematic liquidity, then a general injection of high-powered money will do. With regard to this last point, I would claim, however, that LOLR operations, by providing liquidity where it is needed (micro support), can in fact be more effective than open market operations (macro support).

In recent years, the Fed has provided LOLR loans to insolvent institutions in many highly publicized cases, such as Franklin National Bank in 1974,[30] First Pennsylvania in 1979, Continental Illinois in 1984, as well as during the Savings and Loan Associations (S&L) crisis. There are also examples of this kind of lending in the UK (eg, Johnson Matthey Bankers in 1985) and in other countries.

Arguably, if a solvent bank can nearly always get liquidity from a source other than the central bank, then the concern about inter-bank exposure and contagion as a justification for LOLR would be less cogent: as long as the failure of Bank A does not cause Bank B to become insolvent because of inter-bank exposure, then Bank B can get liquidity financing in the market. Unfortunately, the failure of an insolvent institution (or the troubles of an institution which is

---

[29] As acknowledged, CAMEL is the rating system that US regulatory agencies use to assess bank soundness. CAMEL is an acronym which stands for Capital adequacy, Asset quality, Man- agement, Earnings, and Liquidity.

[30] As Schwartz, above note 28, 64 recalls: 'The bank was insolvent when its borrowing began and insolvent when its borrowing ended. The loans merely replaced funds that depositors with- drew, the inflow from the Reserve Bank matching withdrawals.'

about to become insolvent) can still bring difficulties to solvent ones, because of information deficiencies and other market imperfections.[31]

In recognition of the changes that affect the LOLR practice, particularly with regard to the bailout of insolvent institutions that would cause losses to the deposit insurance fund (and ultimately to taxpayers), some interesting legislative changes have taken place in the US. These changes encourage Federal Reserve banks to lend only to *viable* institutions, and introduce penalties in the case of extended lending to undercapitalized institutions. The new rules introduce an important element of accountability and, in some cases, shift the financial burden from the Federal Deposit Insurance Corporation to the Federal Reserve System, when the latter chooses to lend via its DWL to insolvent or critically undercapitalized institutions.

In order to understand these changes it is important to remember that, according to its original mandate, the Federal Reserve System was to act as lender of last resort to the banking system through its discount window (ss 10(a) and 10(b) of the Federal Reserve Act).[32] Access to the discount window is governed by Regulation A (the first regulation adopted by the Federal Reserve Board at its creation), which refers to the extension of credit—through advances or discounts—in both ordinary and extraordinary circumstances, and which has been periodically revised over time.

The Federal Deposit Insurance Corporation Improvement Act (FDICIA) in 1991[33] amended ss 10(a) and 10(b) of the Federal Reserve Act, by adding a paragraph on 'Limitations on Advances' which states that 'no advances to any undercapitalized[34] institution by any Federal Reserve bank . . . may be outstanding for more than 60 days in any 120-day period,' unless 'the head of the appropriate Federal banking agency certifies in advance in writing to the Federal Reserve bank that any depository institution is *viable*, or the Board [of Governors] conducts an examination of any depository institution and the Chairman of the Board certifies in writing to the Federal Reserve bank that the institution is viable.'[35] The meaning of this new provision is clear: LOLR loans are by nature short-term loans to illiquid but solvent institutions. Any extended lending is an indication of insolvency rather than of mere illiquidity and any

---

[31] The names of the banks that receive LOLR loans but do not fail are not likely to be publicized. Indeed, any publicity might erode frail confidence, possibly causing a run on the institution (the very effect the central bank is trying to prevent through its LOLR assistance).

[32] 12 USC 221 et seq.

[33] FDICIA was enacted on 19 December 1991, Public Law 102–242 (105 Stat 2236–2393).

[34] According to s 38 of the Federal Deposit Insurance Act as amended by FDICIA, an institution is 'undercapitalized' if 'it fails to meet the required minimum level for any relevant capital measure'.

[35] In this case, the 60-day period may be extended for an additional 60-day period.

delay in closing an insolvent institution increases the cost to the insurance fund, thus shifting the risk from depositors to taxpayers. LOLR loans to insolvent institutions are in effect a partial substitute for deposit insurance. What is less clear about the new provision is the 'certification of viability' procedure, as a discretionary element appears to be introduced in its determination.[36]

FDICIA links the intensity of supervision to the level of capitalization and thus reserves especially severe treatment for critically undercapitalized depository institutions[37] as opposed to depository institutions that are merely undercapitalized:

> Federal Reserve banks may have outstanding advances to such institutions only during the 5-day period beginning on the date the institution became critically undercapitalised or after consultations with the Board. After the end of this 5-day period, the Board [of Governors] shall be liable to the Federal Deposit Insurance Corporation for the *excess loss* (i.e., for the loss that exceeds the loss that the FDIC would have incurred if it had liquidated the institution as of the end of that 5-day period), without regard to the terms of advance or any collateral pledged to secure the advance.

Again, this provision tries to prevent the granting of LOLR loans to insolvent institutions by shifting the financial burden of keeping alive insolvent institutions from the FDIC to the Fed. Federal Reserve credit should not be used as a substitute for capital. Finally, FDICIA's amendment to s 10(b) of the Federal Reserve Act also stresses the discretionary nature of the LOLR: 'A Federal Reserve bank shall have no obligation to make, increase, renew, or extend any advance or discount under this Act to any depository institution.' Such a discretionary component is an important safeguard against moral hazard incentives.

Implications for competition

Though I further discuss the role of the ESCB with regard to lender of last resort operations in the EU in Chapter 10, it is important to point out that competition law also plays a part in the discussions about lender of last resort operations. Because an inherent subsidy exists whenever the central bank lends to an insolvent institution, under the EC rules on state aid, the granting of emergency aid to banking institutions can be considered illegal in some cases. The Luxembourg

---

[36] For the purposes of FDICIA, 'A depository institution is *viable* if the Board or the appropriate Federal Banking Agency determines, giving due regard to the economic conditions and circumstances in the market in which the institution operates, that the institution:

(i) is not critically undercapitalized; (ii) is not expected to become critically undercapitalized; and (iii) is not expected to be placed in conservatorship or receivership.'

[37] An institution is critically undercapitalized, according to s 38 of the Federal Deposit Insurance Act as amended by FDICIA, when 'it fails to meet any level specified under subsection c(3)(a)' (ie, when the leverage ratio of tangible equity is less than 2% of total assets).

Court of Justice recognized in a ground-breaking decision, the *Züchner* case, that EC competition rules are also applicable to the banking sector.[38] The state aid policy of the EC runs parallel to the antitrust or competition policy. The state aid policy is built upon the general premiss that aid granted by a Member State which distorts competition or affects trade is incompatible with the common market, and is thus prohibited.[39] The granting of illegal aid[40] may confer an unfair economic advantage to a recipient undertaking, discriminating against those undertakings which do comply with the rules.[41] These considerations have

---

[38] See Case 172/80 *Züchner v Bayerische Vereinsbank* [1981] ECR 2021. The Court's decision made it clear that the banking sector is only exempted from the competition rules to the extent that any anti-competitive conduct by banks is imposed on them by the monetary authorities.

[39] Art 92 of the EC Treaty. See generally Ileana Simplicean-Stroia, 'Study of the State Aid Policy in the European Community: The "Illegal" State Aid Problem' (1997) 3 Journal of International Legal Studies 87.

[40] Member State non-compliance with the procedural rules of Art 93(3) of the EC Treaty.

[41] The notion of state aid to the banking sector has been clarified to some extent in two cases regarding WestLB. See Joined Cases T–228/99 and T–233/99 *Westdeutsche Landesbank Girozentrale v Commission of the European Communities* [2004] 1 CMLR 17. The suspicious transaction involved the integration of WfA—a state-owned financial institution devoted exclusively to the promotion of housing by granting low-interest housing loans—into the WestLB group, the third largest financial services group in Germany by the measure of the balance sheet. WestLB became the sole successor in the assets and liabilities of WfA. Hence, it received the capital injection needed to comply with the stringent capital adequacy requirements imposed by the then recently implemented Own Funds Directive (89/299/EEC). At the complaint of the German Bankers' Association, the Commission ruled in 1999 that the transaction in question infringed the Community rules on state aid. WestLB and the local authorities of the 'Land' sought to annul the decision. In addition to procedural complains, they raised three substantive issues. *First*, they claimed that the transaction did not constitute aid granted through State resources within the meaning of Art 87(1) EC. In their view, State resources are not involved where the State, without going beyond its role as owner or entrepreneur, introduces capital into an undertaking which is permanently in profit, solely for entrepreneurial purposes. The Court dismissed the argument by stating that the prohibition of state aid 'does not distinguish between State interventions by reference to their causes or their objectives but defines them by reference to their effects . . . It follows that the concept of aid is an objective one, the sole test being whether a State measure confers an advantage on one or more particular undertakings'. See para 180. *Secondly*, WestLB and the German authorities argued that by virtue of Art 295 EC—which states that the EC Treaty shall in no way prejudice the rules in Member States governing the system of property ownership—the rules on state aid cannot be interpreted so widely as to practically preclude Member States from having latitude in the operation of public undertakings or in the retention of the shareholdings which they possess in them. The Court also dismissed this argument by stating that although systems of property ownership continue to be a matter for Member States, Art 295 EC does not have the effect of exempting the Member States' systems of property ownership from the fundamental rules of the Treaty, including the rules on competition and state aid. See paras 185–93. *Finally*, the Court confirmed that the aim of state aid rules is to prevent trade between Member States from being affected by advantages granted by public authorities which, in various forms, distort or threaten to distort competition by favouring certain undertakings or the production of certain goods. In the view of the Court, in order to determine whether a State measure constitutes aid, it is therefore necessary to establish whether the recipient undertaking receives an economic advantage which it would not have obtained under normal market conditions. Hence, the profitability or unprofitability of the recipient institution (WestLB) was not in itself decisive in the decision as to whether such an advantage exists and therefore the applicants' argument that

been present with regard to the phasing out of the state guarantees that public sector banks in Germany (*Sparkassen* and *Landesbanken*) have traditionally enjoyed. By virtue of an informal undertaking (of July 2001) between the EU Commissioner and the German Secretary of State, these state guarantees were to be abolished during a transitional period finishing in July 2005.[42]

---

the rules on state aid were not infringed because WestLB was a profitable undertaking were dismissed. Crucially, the Court established that in order to determine whether such action is in the nature of State aid, it is necessary to assess whether, in similar circumstances, a private investor operating in normal conditions of a market economy of a comparable size to that of the bodies operating in the public sector could have been prompted to make the capital contribution in question. In particular, the relevant question is whether a private investor would have entered into the transaction in question on the same terms and, if not, on which terms he might have done so. The Court accepted that the actual rate of return on the invested capital is an effective analytical tool in determining whether in similar circumstances a private investor would have entered into the same transaction. The Commission used the criterion of the rate of return and the Court was satisfied that this was one of the criteria that the Commission could validly have used. See paras 244–74. The Court however annulled the Decision as requested by WestLB and the German authorities because the Court was satisfied that the Commission failed to set out the reasons as regards two of the factors used to calculate the appropriate return for the transaction at issue. The lack of statement of reasons infringes Art 253 EC which states that Decisions must state the reasons on which they are based. The Court considered that those two factors were of essential importance in the general scheme of the contested decision and, consequently, that decision had to be annulled.

[42] Public sector banks in Germany have operated under the protection of the so-called *Anstaltslast* (institutional obligation) and *Gewährträgerhaftung* (guarantee obligation). The *Anstaltslast* dictates that the owners of a public law institution (in this case a *Landesbank* or *Sparkasse*) have a legal obligation to keep that institution financially viable—that is in a position where it can at all times pay its debts as they fall due. Nevertheless, the creditors have no direct claim against the owners of the bank. Under the *Gewährträgerhaftung*, the bank's guarantors (usually, but not necessarily, the owners) have an unlimited, joint and several liability to the creditors. The effect of these guarantees is that the *Landesbanks'* long-term debt has been largely AAA rated, irrespective of their individual financial strength. It is argued that this rating is not only higher than the big four private German banks but is enjoyed by only a handful of banks worldwide and is higher than that of the majority of sovereign states. It therefore enables the *Landesbanks* to borrow at very low rates on the international markets. See generally Patrick Gloyens, 'The Landesbanks: How Long Can They Retain Competitive Advantage' (2002) 17(3) Journal of International Banking Law 53, 55. In July 2001, the European Commission and the German authorities reached agreement on the measures to be taken by Germany to resolve the long-standing state aid issues in connection with the foregoing guarantees existing for the German public financial institutions. The solution is based on the following principles: *Gewährträgerhaftung* were to be be abolished and *Anstaltslast* were to be replaced by a normal owner relationship between the owner and the public financial institution concerned. Liabilities existing at 18 July 2001, the date of acceptance by the German authorities of the Commission's recommendation of 8 May 2001, were to be covered by *Gewährträgerhaftung* until their maturity ran out. During the transitional period (to finish on 18 July 2005) *Anstaltslast* and *Gewährträgerhaftung* could be maintained. See Commission of the European Communities, 'Press statement after the meeting of Commissioner Monti and State Secretary Koch-Weser on 17 July 2001', Press Release IP/01/1007, at <http://europa.e-u.int/rapid/start/cgi/guesten.ksh?p_action .gettxt=gt&doc=IP/01/1007/0/RAPID&lg=EN>. The history of the disagreement and the final terms of the compromise were later consolidated in an internal memorandum prepared by Commissioner Monti for the European Commission. See internal document C (2002) 1286/1 of 22 March 2002, available at <http://www.europa.eu.int/comm/secretariat_general/regdoc/rep/3/2002/EN/3–2002–1286-EN-1–0.Pdf>.

Lender of last resort and securities markets

Another significant development which has affected the LOLR in practice is the blurring of frontiers between the banking and the securities business, which could lead to an undesirable extension of the safety net.[43] The central bank may be called upon to assist—through its LOLR—a bank that gets into trouble because of its securities business, or even a securities firm. The example is not merely theoretical. On Monday, 19 October 1987, the Dow Jones Industrial Average lost twenty-three per cent if its value. On Tuesday, 20 October, before the market opened, Alan Greenspan announced the Fed's readiness to provide liquidity in support of the economic and financial system. In addition, the Fed encouraged banks to lend to securities firms and made it clear that it would extend discount credit to banks so that they could make those loans. Though the central bank typically bails out domestic commercial banks, it can also stand ready to provide emergency liquidity assistance to securities firms and other financial institutions. Regulation A of the Federal Reserve System allows the Federal Reserve banks to extend emergency credit to 'individuals, partnerships and corporations that are not depository institutions if, in the judgment of the Federal Reserve Bank, credit is not available from other sources and failure to obtain such credit would adversely affect the economy'.[44]

Support of foreign institutions

The central bank can also agree to supply emergency liquidity to foreign institutions operating in the country. This issue was debated in the US in 1995 in connection with the Japanese banks operating in New York, in the aftermath of the Daiwa affair. Regulation A also provides that: 'Except as may be otherwise provided, this part [ie, the extension of credit by Federal Reserve banks] shall be applicable to United States branches and agencies of foreign banks subject to reserve requirements under Regulation D in the same manner and to the same extent as [domestic] depositary institutions.'[45]

---

[43] See Geoffrey E Wood, 'The Lender of Last Resort Reconsidered' Journal of Financial Services Research, vol 18, nos 2/3, December 2000, 203–8. Wood contends that attempts to broaden the central bank's responsibilities to encompass supporting not just the banking system, but the financial system more generally are misplaced. According to Wood, the central bank acting as LOLR should continue to be responsible for money stock stability, but not for financial market stability.

[44] 12 CFR 201(3)(d). However, 'the rate applicable to such credit will be above the highest rate in effect for advances to depository institutions. Where the collateral used to secure such credit consists of assets other than obligations of, or fully guaranteed as to principal or interest by, the United States or an agency thereof, an affirmative vote of five or more members of the Board of Governors is required before credit may be extended.'

[45] 12 CFR 201(7) (CFR revised as of 1 January 1996).

The question of ambiguity

A final word on 'constructive ambiguity', a term often used to refer to lender of last resort operations. In my opinion, ambiguity is seldom (if ever at all) constructive, as I further discuss in Chapter 10 at the EU level. There is a need to be clear about the responsibility for lender of last resort before any crisis arises. There is also a need to be clear about the procedures, about the way things will work out. Then, of course, the very provision of assistance should remain at the discretion of the authorities. It is this discretionary element—this uncertainty about whether or not the emergency liquidity assistance will be provided—that reduces the moral hazard incentives inherent in any support operation. But there should not be any doubt about who is in charge and how the assistance will be provided. The law ought to be clear about these issues.

D. Deposit Insurance

Deposit insurance has been the subject of much debate in the literature.[46] In 1959 Milton Friedman expressed a widely held view when he asserted that the introduction of US federal deposit insurance after the bank crisis of 1929–33, as part of the New Deal legislation under President Franklin D Roosevelt, was 'the most important structural change in our monetary system in the direction of greater stability since the post-Civil War tax on state bank notes'.[47]

Though deposit insurance has been adopted by law in many jurisdictions around the world, particularly in the last two decades, its very existence remains a matter of controversy.[48] Indeed, the Basel Committee does not include deposit insurance as a key principle in its 1997 Core Principles of Effective Banking Supervision.[49] Instead, it refers to deposit insurance in an appendix at the end

---

[46] I draw in this section on a paper I wrote with Douglas W Arner, above note 3, 463–78.

[47] Milton Friedman, *The Control of Money. A Program for Monetary Stability.* (New York: Fordham University Press, 1959) 21.

[48] Asli Demirgüç-Kunt and Enrica Detragiache conducted a study of banking crises around the world, covering the period 1980–94 and concluded that 'the presence of an explicit deposit insurance scheme tends to increase the probability of systemic banking problems.' See Asli Demirgüç-Kunt and Enrica Detragiache, 'The Determinants of Bank Crisis in Developing and Developed Countries' (1998) 45(1) IMF Staff Papers 104. In a more recent publication, Asli Demirgüç-Kunt and Edward Kane have come to a similar conclusion: '[c]ross-country empirical research on deposit insurance strongly supports the hypothesis that in institutionally weak environments, poorly designed deposit-insurance arrangements tend to increase the probability of future banking crises.' See Asli Demirgüç-Kunt and Edward Kane, *Deposit Insurance Around the Globe, Where Does it Work?* World Bank Paper No. 2679 (Washington DC: World Bank, 2001) 24.

[49] Basel Committee on Banking Supervision, *Core Principles for Effective Banking Supervision,* Basel Core Principles, (Basel: BIS, 1997) available at <http://www.bis.org/publ/bcbsc102.pdf> (visited 10 December 2003).

of this document. In such appendix, the benefits and drawbacks of deposit insurance are briefly spelt out.

Structure of deposit insurance

The structure of deposit guarantee schemes varies greatly from country to country, with differences with regard to their funding, coverage, and administration.[50] In this chapter, I do not analyse the specific policy and structural features of deposit insurance, but rather some of the legal issues that are most relevant from the point of institutional design. The first issue is the difference between explicit and implicit deposit insurance, the second issue is the status of preferred creditors that insured depositors have under an explicit deposit guarantee scheme. The third issue is the mandatory nature of deposit insurance, as opposed to the contingent nature of the lender of last resort role of the central bank.

Explicit versus implicit deposit insurance

Explicit deposit insurance is the formal creation of a deposit guarantee scheme by law, with specific rules concerning the extent of the 'insurance' or protection, the operation of the scheme, and the type of deposits/depositors protected. Explicit deposit insurance can be useful as an instrument of protective bank regulation. Explicit deposit insurance has traditionally served two purposes: consumer protection and the prevention of bank runs. The rationale behind the first objective is the presumed inability of ordinary depositors to monitor the riskiness of banks in which they place their funds as well as the potentially severe cost of deposit losses to individual savers. The rationale behind the second objective is the inherent fragility of the banking system. Because of the first come, first served nature of bank liabilities, and because bank main assets (loans) are highly illiquid, and worth less at liquidation than on a going concern basis, depositors have a rational propensity 'to run' at the first sign of trouble. Bank failures become highly contagious, thereby exposing the financial system to the risk of depositor panics. I argue that a third rationale of explicit deposit insurance (in addition to consumer protection and prevention of bank runs) is that it allows the public authorities to close banks more easily, as it becomes politically acceptable to liquidate insolvent institutions, in the knowledge that unsophisticated depositors are protected.

Under an explicit deposit guarantee scheme, depositors are only paid once the

---

[50] For a study of these issues, see *inter alia*, Richard Dale, 'Deposit Insurance in Theory and Practice' (2000) 8(1) Journal of Financial Regulation and Compliance 36; Gillian Garcia, *Deposit Insurance: A Survey of Actual and Best Practices*, Occasional Paper No. 197 (Washington DC: IMF, 2001).

bank is closed, liquidated. Thus, there can be no deposit insurance if the bank remains open. Therefore, explicit deposit insurance presupposes that a bank has failed and, hence, it is not compatible with the 'too-big-to-fail' doctrine.

The European Shadow Financial Regulatory Committee (of which I am a member) took the view in 1999 that explicit deposit insurance can and should play a key role primarily in facilitating the liquidation of insolvent banks without the need for implicit deposit protection.[51] The ESFRC argued that the practice of bailing out insolvent institutions (implicit protection) creates expectations of official support beyond deposit insurance limits, thereby distorting market incentives and undermining financial discipline (the so-called moral hazard problem). It is the strongly held view of the ESFRC that deposit insurance should be designed and operated in a way that allows, and indeed requires, national authorities to liquidate insolvent banks, thereby exposing uninsured depositors and other creditors to default risk. Such an approach ensures that high-risk institutions pay a market penalty in terms of higher funding costs. In this way, those institutions that adopt a less prudent investment on lending strategy than is the norm within the industry would have both the costs and benefits inherent in that strategy appropriately internalized.

Implicit deposit insurance, as opposed to explicit deposit insurance, is a 'blanket guarantee' for all sorts of depositors (insured and uninsured), other creditors, shareholders, and even managers. Implicit deposit insurance often presupposes that the bank remains in business (either because it is 'too-big-to-fail' or because it is politically difficult to close the bank) thus creating pervasive moral hazard incentives. While explicit deposit insurance is applied *ex post* (following the closure of a bank), implicit deposit insurance is often applied while a bank is still in operation.

Explicit deposit insurance inflicts only very limited damage upon taxpayers, and, depending on the funding of the scheme, there may no damage at all. However, implicit deposit insurance has the potential of shifting the burden onto taxpayers, since rescue packages tend to be financed by the government. The use of rescue packages results not only in moral hazard considerations but may also affect competition, especially if a too-big-to-fail doctrine is applied.

Preferred creditors

Explicit deposit insurance is a guarantee limited to one type of 'preferred creditors,' that is, insured depositors. Under explicit deposit insurance uninsured

---

[51] See ESFRC Statement No 5 of 18 October 1999. The statements of the ESFRC are available at <http://www.ceps.be> and <http://www.aei.org>.

depositors, other creditors, shareholders, and managers are not protected. Therefore, explicit deposit insurance is more compatible with market discipline, as uninsured depositors and other creditors have an interest in monitoring the solvency of the bank while it is still in operation.

Explicit deposit insurance, by limiting the protection to 'insured depositors', exposes uninsured depositors, general creditors, subordinated debt-holders, shareholders, and management to increased risk exposure, thereby encouraging them to monitor and limit the riskiness of the bank.[52] These incentives are very important, particularly in the case of shareholders, whose limited liability renders them more prone to lend on a high risk–high return basis.[53] In the absence of open bank assistance, management will also be more inclined to run the institution in a prudent manner, or risk being removed from office.

In its statement of October 1999, the ESFRC recommended that uninsured deposits and other liabilities should be 'credibly uninsured', meaning that holders of such claims have no expectation of official support in the event of a bank insolvency. Explicit deposit insurance must be set at a level that enables national authorities to accept the political consequences of bank liquidations.

Mandatory versus contingent guarantee

Deposit insurance provides a guarantee on certain deposits that is non-contingent. It provides legal certainty as to the way the depositors will be protected and the amount covered, should a bank be closed. Lender of last resort, on the other hand, is contingent. The injection of liquidity in times of crisis is not mandatory, but discretionary, that is, subject to the discretion of the central bank authority. There is always a degree of uncertainty regarding the provision of emergency liquidity assistance by the central bank.

While explicit deposit insurance protects mainly the depositors, lender of last resort protects mainly the financial system (systemic considerations).

To minimize the risk of moral hazard, it is important to demarcate what each institutional arrangement can do and what it cannot do or should not do (an issue which I have already discussed in my analysis of lender of last resort operations). Explicit deposit insurance can protect insured depositors, but it cannot—nor should—protect other depositors or creditors, nor shareholders, nor managers. Explicit deposit insurance cannot protect the banks, because it can only be activated once a bank is closed.

---

[52] See Lastra, *Central Banking and Banking Regulation*, above note 3, 130.
[53] See generally Richard S Dale, 'Deposit Insurance, Policy Clash over EC and US Reforms' in Frederick C Shadrack and Leon Korobow (eds), *The Basic Elements of Bank Supervision* (New York: Federal Reserve Bank of New York, 1993).

In my opinion, deposit guarantee schemes should be mandatory and explicit in nature, credible and limited in the amount covered. The latter issue is important to understand the critique often made of the system applied in the USA, where a 'maximalist approach' (with a coverage by the FDIC of $100,000 per account) has contributed to enhanced moral hazard. The system I favour could be described as 'minimalist' with regard to the amount covered. In this respect, The EC Directive on Deposit Guarantee Schemes (94/19/EC)[54] with its harmonized minimum coverage of €20,000 does offer a 'minimalist approach' to deposit insurance.[55] However, the level at which explicit deposit insurance is set should not be so low that it makes it impossible (non-credible) for the authorities to liquidate insolvent institutions.

E. Bank Insolvency Proceedings

General versus special bank insolvency proceedings

Bank insolvency laws differ greatly from country to country. In the USA, for instance, bank failures are not subject to general corporate bankruptcy procedures (such as Chapter 11 of the US bankruptcy code) but to special bank insolvency proceedings that take into account the nature of bank deposits and the possible systemic implications of bank failures. In the UK, on the other hand, bank insolvencies are treated under the same rules as other companies. The result of the US approach, according to some commentators, is that the objectives of general corporate bankruptcy law are somewhat different from the objectives of special bank insolvency law.[56]

In some jurisdictions bank insolvency procedures are operated by courts (judicial procedure), while in other jurisdictions they are operated on an

---

[54] See Directive 94/19/EC of the European Parliament and of the Council of 30 May 1994 on Deposit-Guarantee Schemes OJ 1994 L 135/5, available at <http://europa.eu.int/smartapi/cgi/sga_doc?smartapi!celexapi!prod!CELEXnumdoc&lg=EN&numdoc=31994L0019&model=guichett> (Visited 24 March 2004).

[55] See Art 7(1) of the Directive, which reads as follows: 'Deposit-guarantee schemes shall stipulate that the aggregate deposits of each depositor must be covered up to [euros] 20 000 in the event of deposits' being unavailable. Until 31 December 1999 Member States in which, when this Directive is adopted, deposits are not covered up to [euros] 20 000 may retain the maximum amount laid down in their guarantee schemes, provided that this amount is not less than [euros] 15 000.'

[56] See eg Gerald N Olson, 'The Inadequacy of Bank Insolvency Resolution', in Lastra and Schiffman (eds), above note 26, 112–13. According to Olson, while the primary objective of bank insolvency law is to maintain public confidence in the banking system, bankruptcy laws seek to achieve three objectives: (1) protect creditors from each other; (2) protect creditors from dishonest debtors; (3) protect honest debtors from creditors by discharge.

agency or administrative basis (extra-judicial procedure), without any formal court involvement.

The United States has relied on an extra-judicial bank resolution procedure since 1933. The Federal Deposit Insurance Corporation (FDIC) acts not only as insurer of deposits and administrator of the deposit insurance system (as well as a Federal Bank supervisor), but also as 'receiver' when a bank fails. In some cases, the FDIC may also be appointed as 'conservator'. (A receiver is typically appointed for the purpose of liquidation, while a conservator is appointed to conserve assets and to try to put the institution back in order.)

The Basel Committee recommends that the supervisory authority be responsible for or assist in the orderly exit of problem banks in order to ensure that depositors are repaid to the fullest extent possible from the resources of the bank (supplemented by any applicable deposit insurance) and ahead of shareholders, subordinated debt holders, and other connected parties.[57]

Objectives of bank insolvency laws

Insolvency laws should seek to fulfil two principal objectives:[58] fair and predictable treatment of creditors and maximization of assets of the debtor in the interests of creditors. I would add another objective that is specific to banking: the bank should be closed as soon as the market value of its net worth reaches zero, because at this moment, direct losses are only suffered by shareholders. If the bank is declared legally insolvent when the market value of its net worth is already negative, losses will accrue not only to shareholders, but also to uninsured creditors and/or to the insurance fund/the government. This third objective is reflected in the legislative changes that have taken place in the USA since FDICIA (Federal Deposit Insurance Corporation Improvement Act), with the possibility of adopting 'prompt corrective action' (PCA) if the level of bank capitalization falls below thresholds specified in the statute. PCA provisions allow the authorities to take supervisory action—including the possibility of structure early intervention and resolution, SEIR, before the capital reaches zero.

---

[57] See Basel Committee on Banking Supervision, Basel Core Principles, above note 54, s II 'Preconditions for Effective Bank Supervision', 12. According to the Basel Committee, banking supervision is only part of wider arrangements that are needed to promote stability in the financial markets. One of these arrangements should include precisely procedures for efficient resolution of problems in banks. When problems are not remediable, the prompt and orderly exit of institutions that are no longer able to meet supervisory requirements is a necessary part of an efficient financial system.

[58] See Schiffman, in 'Legal Measures to Manage Bank Insolvency in Economies in Transition', above note 26, 89–90.

In banking, the definition of insolvency is sometimes a matter of controversy,[59] and the line of demarcation between illiquidity (lack of liquid funds) and insolvency is not always clear as I have already pointed out. An economically insolvent bank is not always declared legally insolvent by the responsible authorities and may instead be offered financial assistance. A bank is considered to have failed when the competent authorities order the cessation of its operations and activities. However, the authorities are often wary of liquidating a bank (in part because an 'orderly liquidation of assets' is not always easy, owing to the possible contagion effect on other institutions) and therefore choose instead to rehabilitate the bank.

Indeed, though a clear policy that banks that have failed ought to exit the banking system might appear desirable in some cases, the social cost of closing a bank is significant, as banks are often—particularly in emerging economies—the main repository of the savings of the public and a major source of credit to the economy. That is why failed banks are often not liquidated, but subject to reorganization or rehabilitation.

The Basel Committee on Banking Supervision acknowledges that, in a market economy, failures are part of risk-taking[60] and that a prompt and orderly liquidation of institutions that are no longer able to meet supervisory requirements is a necessary part of an efficient financial system, as forbearance normally leads to worsening problems and higher resolution costs.[61] However, the Committee explicitly states that 'in some cases the best interests of depositors may be served by some form of restructuring, possibly takeover by a stronger institution or injection of new capital or shareholder. Supervisors may be able to facilitate such outcomes. It is essential that the end result fully meets all supervisory requirements, that it is realistically achievable in a short and determinate timeframe and, that, in the interim, depositors are protected.'[62]

Resolution procedures

Though liquidation is the simplest resolution procedure, it is not necessarily the least costly; as a valuable depositor base gets dissipated, vital banking services in a community may be disrupted, and confidence in the banking system may be seriously damaged.[63] Occasionally, the liquidation of one institution may trigger

---

[59] As acknowledged, there are two traditional definitions of insolvency in commercial bankruptcy laws: failure to pay obligations as they fall due (equitable insolvency) and the condition when liabilities exceed assets (balance sheet insolvency). See eg Schiffmann, ibid, 96–7.

[60] See Basel Committee on Banking Supervision, above note 49, 10.   [61] ibid 12.

[62] ibid.

[63] See Jonathan Macey and Geoffrey Miller, *Banking Law and Regulation* (Boston: Little Brown and Company, 1992) 644–5 and generally ch 8.

runs on other institutions. However, in the presence of massive frauds, such as the BCCI affair, liquidation is the only solution appropriate.

In banking, liquidation typically entails a system of depositor preference, that is, depositors' claims are typically paid before those of general creditors. If the country has a deposit guarantee scheme, the insured depositors are paid off up to the insurance limit; uninsured depositors and other creditors are likely to suffer losses in their claims.

In the case of bank rehabilitation, reorganization, or restructuring, the laws vary widely from country to country. Indeed, as Schiffmann points out, 'Under some bankruptcy laws there is still an opportunity for bank reorganisation or rehabilitation as part of bank insolvency proceedings, while in others the only measure contemplated is the liquidation of bank's assets, payment of liabilities and dissolution of the bank.'[64]

When an institution is offered a programme of open bank assistance (also referred to as a 'rescue package'), the institution is not closed but is rescued on an 'open bank' basis through the infusion of new funds. 'Rescue packages' can take a variety of forms including new loans, soft loans, deposits, asset or securities purchases, assumption of liabilities, and capital injections. In many cases the management of the institution is revamped in a programme of open bank assistance.[65]

The granting of 'state aid' (ie, funding coming directly or indirectly from the government) in a 'rescue package' is controversial. A delicate balance between the interests of taxpayers on the one hand and the interests of depositors as well as other bank creditors and bank shareholders on the other hand needs to be reached. Ruth de Krivoy, former central bank governor in Venezuela, points out that crisis management can be more effective if an early decision is made as to how the cost of the crisis is to be shared between shareholders, depositors, and taxpayers. She argues that improvization as the crisis unfolds often leads to the most damaging result for the taxpayers, as illustrated by the Venezuelan case.[66]

In some cases an implicit or explicit 'too-big-to-fail' policy is applied. That was

---

[64] See Schiffman, above note 26, 81.

[65] It is important to differentiate—at least in theory—between rescue packages that imply bank recapitalization and the provision of emergency liquidity assistance or (lender of last resort) to an illiquid but solvent institution. I have dealt with this issue in Lastra, 'Lender of Last Resort. An International Perspective', above note 3.

[66] See Ruth de Krivoy, 'An Agenda for Banking Crises Avoidance in Latin America' (paper presented at the Inter-American Development Bank Group of Thirty Conference on Banking Crises in Latin America, Washington DC, October 1995).

the case in Continental Illinois in the USA and in Credit Lyonnais in France. Government-led rescue packages may not only induce moral hazard behaviour, but may also pose questions of fair competition, particularly when the too-big-to-fail doctrine is applied, as other smaller or less troubled institutions may have to navigate through crises or problems on their own. In the US, FDICIA (1991) requires the resolution of bank failures on a 'least cost basis' to the insurance fund, unless it threatens to trigger a payment system breakdown, in which case FDIC and Fed may recommend a more costly solution.[67] The abandonment of a too-big-to-fail policy tries to encourage market discipline in the resolution of bank failures and to reduce moral hazard incentives.

Another action that may be taken by the authorities in dealing with a financially distressed bank is a takeover or merger (also called purchase and assumption, that is, the purchase of assets and assumption of liabilities). Because the cooperation of other market participants is typically required, this regulatory option has a 'private' flavour, as opposed to the typical 'public' character of most rescue packages. A takeover generally preserves the going-concern value of an institution, as the acquirer succeeds both to a deposit base and to a base of loan customers. As opposed to a straight liquidation, it eliminates the danger that vital banking services in a community will be disrupted. A merger can be 'unassisted' when the acquirer assumes all assets and liabilities (also called 'whole bank's acquisition'), and 'assisted', when all the liabilities but only the good assets go to the acquirer (also referred to as 'clean bank's acquisition'). In an assisted transaction, the bad assets are subject to special administration (see above note 63).

Sometimes, failed banks may be placed under special administration, in the form of bridge banks, new banks, special funds, or other arrangements. This is often meant to be a temporary solution in order to take over the operations of a failed bank and preserve its going-concern value until a more permanent solution to the problems is found.

Cross-border bank insolvency

The growth in cross-border banking activities presents a number of challenges for regulators around the world. These challenges become particularly evident in the field of cross-border insolvency.[68] Though the markets have grown international, regulation remains nationally based, constrained by the domain of

---

[67] See US Federal Deposit Insurance Corporation Improvement Act (FDICIA), 12 USC 1823(c)(4).

[68] I draw in this sub-section on the paper I wrote on 'Cross-Border Bank Insolvency: Legal Implications in the Case of Banks Operating in Different Jurisdictions in Latin America,' (2003) 6(1) Journal of International Economic Law 79, above note 3.

domestic jurisdictions. In the absence of an international insolvency legal regime, the solution to the liquidation of a bank with branches and subsidiaries in several countries needs to be based on national legal regimes and on the voluntary cooperation between different national authorities.

Though there is no international treaty on insolvency law, there have, however, been some attempts at reaching some commonly agreed international rules. In particular, it is important to mention the Model Law on Cross-Border Insolvency that the United Nations Commission on International Trade Law (UNCITRAL) adopted in Vienna in May 1997. However, this model law contains an optional clause whereby special insolvency regimes applicable to banks may be excluded from its scope.[69]

Another example of international rules is the International Bar Association's (IBA) Cross-Border Insolvency Concordat, which was approved by the Council of the Section on Business Law of the IBA in September 1995.[70] This Concordat sets out some essential principles that can assist insolvency practitioners faced with concurrent proceedings in relation to the same debtor in two or more jurisdictions.

In Latin America, two multilateral treaties, the Montevideo Treaties of 1889 and 1940, and the Bustamante Code sanctioned by the sixth Panamerican Conference (Havana Conference) of 1928, establish private international law rules concerning bankruptcy.[71] These treaties provide for the recognition and enforcement of foreign bankruptcies.[72]

The difficulty in reaching some common standards in this area of law is illustrated by the hurdles and delays that the EU has faced over the years in trying to agree on some common principles on bank insolvency. Indeed, only in 2001[73] has the Directive on the Winding Up and Liquidation of Credit Institutions been adopted,[74] though the proposed directive was published in 1988. This

---

[69] Art 1(2) of the Uncitral Model Law. See also Ch 14.

[70] See Erwin Nierop and Mikael Stenström, 'Cross-Border Aspects of Insolvency Proceedings for Credit Institutions—A Legal Perspective' (paper presented at an International Seminar on Legal and Regulatory Aspects of Financial Stability, Basel, January 2002) 7 and 9.

[71] Regarding the Bustamante Code and the Montevideo Treaties, see Juan M Dobson, 'Treaty Developments in Latin America' in Ian Fletcher (ed), *Cross-Border Insolvency: Comparative Dimensions, The Aberystwyth Insolvency Papers* (London: United Kingdom National Committee of Comparative Law, 1990) vol 12, 237–62.

[72] See also Kurt Lipstein, 'Early Treaties for the Recognition and Enforcement of Foreign Bankruptcies' in Fletcher (ed), ibid 228–30.

[73] An analysis of this new regime can be found in Nierop and Stenström, above note 70.

[74] See Directive 2001/24/EC of the European Parliament and of the Council of 4 April 2001 on the Reorganisation and Winding up of Credit Institutions [2001] OJ L125/15, available at <http://europa.eu.int/smartapi/cgi/sga_doc?smartapi!celexapi!prod!CELEXnumdoc&lg=EN&numdoc=32001L0024&model=guichett> (visited 24 March 2004).

Directive does not seek to harmonize national legislation concerning reorganization measures and winding-up proceedings, rather it ensures mutual recognition and coordination of these procedures by the fifteen Member States of the EU, based upon the principle of home-country control. In addition to this Directive, the new EU insolvency regime consists of one regulation on insolvency proceedings[75] and one directive concerning the reorganization and winding-up of insurance undertakings (Directive 2001/17/EC of 19 March 2001).[76]

The EU insolvency regime is binding for all EU Member States, as opposed to the Bustamante and Montevideo Treaties, which are only binding for the Latin American States that have ratified them. As such, the EU regime is the clearest example of binding supranational/regional rules in the field of insolvency law in general and of bank insolvency law in particular. However, the EU rules are mainly of a private international law character. They introduce the principles of unity and universality of bankruptcy (further discussed below), but they do not seek to harmonize in a substantive way national legislation concerning insolvency proceedings, which remain different across the Member States of the EU.

Whenever one surveys the legal issues related to the regulation of cross-border banking, one needs to refer to the work of the Basel Committee on Banking Supervision as the de facto informal 'international bank regulator'. Given the difficulties the EU has faced in reaching any agreement on cross-border bank insolvency, it is small wonder that the Basel Committee has not published any agreed guidelines on this issue (or cross border insolvency) yet.[77] Of course, a number of principles developed by the Basel Committee throughout the years to deal with the cross-border supervision of branches and subsidiaries can be applied when dealing with cases of insolvency of a bank operating in different jurisdictions. In particular, the principle of 'parental responsibility' (or home-country control) in the supervision of branches—as legally dependent units—and the consideration that subsidiaries become independent legal entities under the laws of the country of incorporation (ie, under the laws of the host country) are principles observed generally and often included in Memoranda of Understanding between supervisory authorities in different countries. The principle of consolidated supervision also needs to be taken into account.

---

[75] See Council Regulation (EC) No 1346/2000 of 29 May 2000 on Insolvency Proceedings [2000] OJ L160/1.

[76] See Directive 2001/17/EC of the European Parliament and of the Council of 19 March 2001 on the Reorganisation and Winding-up of Insurance Undertakings [2001] OJ L110/28.

[77] As acknowledged, the recommendations of the Basel Committee are 'soft law' in that they are not legally binding rules, as I further explain in Chapter 14. See generally Mario Giovanoli, 'A New Architecture for the Global Financial Market: Legal Aspects of International Financial Standard Setting' in Mario Giovanoli (ed), *International Monetary Law* (Oxford: Oxford University Press, 2000).

Principles for the supervision of branches and subsidiaries were first developed in 1975 and refined in 1983. Following the collapse in 1974 of the German bank Bankhaus ID Herstatt and of the US bank Franklin National Bank, the Committee issued in September 1975 a paper (subsequently known as the Basel Concordat) outlining some principles—in the form of recommended guidelines of best practice—regarding the supervision of banks operating internationally through branches, subsidiaries, and joint ventures.[78] The Concordat was revised in 1983 following the collapse of the Luxembourg-based Banco Ambrosiano Holdings in 1982, under the title of 'Principles for the Supervision of Banks' Foreign Establishments'.[79]

According to the Basel Committee, there are two basic principles that are fundamental to the supervision of banks' foreign establishments: that no foreign banking establishment should escape supervision; and that the supervision should be adequate.[80] An adequate supervision is one in which the host authorities are responsible for the foreign bank establishments (subsidiaries) operating in their territories as individual institutions, while the parent authorities are responsible for them as parts of larger banking groups.

Parent authorities should be informed immediately by the host authorities of any serious problems which arise in a parent bank's foreign establishment and similarly, parent authorities should inform host authorities when problems arise in a parent bank which are likely to affect the parent bank's foreign establishment.

Thus, the principles related to the management of crisis and bank insolvency of foreign establishments should be analysed within this context of mutual cooperation between supervisory authorities. In some jurisdictions also, supervisory authorities have responsibility for managing pre-insolvency situations,

---

[78] The 1975 'Condordat' was reproduced as an annexe ('Supervision of Banks' Foreign Establishments') to Richard C Williams and GG Johnson, 'International Capital Markets: Recent Developments and Short-Term Prospects', Occasional Paper No 7 (Washington DC: IMF, 1981). See also Lastra, *Central Banking and Banking Regulation*, above note 3, 175.

[79] Basel Committee on Banking Supervision, *Principles for the Supervision of Banks' Foreign Establishments*, the 'Concordat' (Basel: BIS, 1983) available at <http://www.bis.org/publ/bcbsc312.pdf>.

[80] The Committee has published other documents and standards regarding the supervision of cross-border banking. In April 1990 it published a supplement to the 1983 Concordat on 'Information Flows between Banking Supervisory Authorities'. Following the collapse of BCCI in July 1992, the Committee published the 'Minimum Standards for the Supervision of International Banking Groups and Their Cross-border Establishments'. In October 1996 the Committee published a document entitled 'The Supervision of Cross-Border Banking'. In September 1997 the Committee published the 'Core Principles for Effective Banking Supervision' that I refer to below. See also the Compendium of documents produced by the Basel Committee on Banking Supervision, *Volume III: International Supervisory Issues* (Basel: BIS, 2000), ch I: 'The Basel Concordat and Minimum Standards', available at <http://www.bis.org/publ/bcbsc004.htm>.

and when insolvency occurs there is another authority in charge of the actual liquidation of the institution.

In 1997 the Basel Committee published the 'Core Principles for Effective Banking Supervision',[81] which have important implications for the supervision of international banks. Bank supervisors must practice global consolidated supervision adequately monitoring and applying appropriate prudential norms to all aspects of the business conducted by these banking organizations world-wide, primarily at their foreign branches, joint ventures, and subsidiaries.[82] The principle of consolidated supervision[83] means that parent banks and parent supervisory authorities monitor the risk exposure of the banks or banking groups for which they are responsible, as well as the adequacy of their capital, on the basis of the totality of their business wherever conducted.

Consolidated supervision is based on the assumption that financial groups form a single economic entity. However, when one comes to the question of the resolution of a failed multinational bank, or of a complex financial group with activities and business units with different legal entities incorporated in several jurisdictions, the assumption that financial groups form a single economic entity appears to be not always valid in a bankruptcy scenario where the group is split up into its many legal entities and where foreign branches are sometimes liquidated as separate units.[84]

The single entity approach to liquidation goes hand in hand with the principle of unity and universality of bankruptcy, which means that there is only one competent court to decide on the bankruptcy of a bank and that the bankruptcy law of the country in which the insolvency has been initiated is effective in all other countries in which the bank has assets or branches. Thus, this principle assigns extraterritorial effect to the adjudication of bankruptcy. In contrast, the separate entity doctrine goes hand in hand with the principle of plurality of bankruptcy, which means that bankruptcy proceedings are only effective in the country in which they are initiated and that therefore there is a plurality of proceedings, as they need to be initiated in every country in which the insolvent bank holds realizable assets or branches. Thus, this principle assigns territorial effect to the adjudication of bankruptcy. Under a separate entity approach, a

---

[81] See Basel Core Principles, above note 49. The Basel Core Principles for Effective Banking Supervision are intended to serve as a basic reference for supervisory and other public authorities worldwide to apply in the supervision of all banks within their jurisdictions.

[82] ibid 6–7 and 41, principle 23.

[83] Consolidated supervision was first emphasized in the (revised) 1983 Concordat, above note 79.

[84] See Daniel Zuberbuhler (Swiss Federal Banking Commission), 'The Financial Industry in the 21st Century. Introduction' (Speech in the Bank for International Settlements, Basel, 21 September 2000) 2, available at <http://www.bis.org/review/rr000921c.pdf>.

domestic branch of a foreign bank receives a liquidation preference, as local assets are segregated for the benefit of local creditors.

US law applies the single entity approach to the liquidation of a US bank with foreign branches. The Federal Deposit Insurance Corporation as receiver of a failed bank collects and realizes all assets, and responds to all claims of the institution regardless of their *situs*.[85] However, US law applies the separate entity approach to the liquidation of US branches of a foreign bank.[86] The inconsistency of the US legal approach to the liquidation of multinational banks, depending on whether it is dealing with foreign branches in the US or with US branches of a foreign bank, illustrates the difficulties of reaching a common international platform with regard to the liquidation of multinational banks.

The need for a coordinated liquidation of multinational banks would be best served by the adoption of an international convention or regime on cross-border insolvency.[87]

---

[85] See Christopher T Curtis, 'The Status of Foreign Deposits under the Federal Deposit Preference Law' (2000) 21 (2) University of Pennsylvania Journal of International Economic Law 237, 254.

[86] A general principle which has been applied in several jurisdictions is that the home office is ultimately liable for a deposit placed in its foreign branch, rejecting with it the doctrine of separate entity, which implies that the deposit would be legally payable only at the foreign branch. With regard to the liability of the bank's home office for deposits placed in a foreign branch, it is important to mention some legislative developments in the USA. In particular, amendments to the New York Banking Law and to the Federal Reserve Act were introduced in 1994 providing that the home office of a bank located in the USA will not be required to repay a deposit made at a foreign branch if the branch cannot repay the deposit due to an act of war, insurrection, or civil strife, or an action by the foreign government in which the branch is located, unless the bank has expressly agreed in writing to repay the deposit under such circumstances. Both amendments apply only to deposits that cannot be repaid owing to political risk. Traditionally, home offices have been responsible for credit risks of their foreign branches, such as losses due to insolvency, fraud, theft, fire, natural disaster, and so forth. These traditional home office liabilities will not be affected by the amendments. Thus, though the general rule remains that a depositor placing funds in the foreign branch of a US bank is a creditor of the bank as whole and not merely of the branch or office where the deposit was made, and that therefore has recourse—for the repayment of his/her deposit—against the bank at its home office, this general rule has now an exception in the case of political risk. Both amendments (to the NYBL and to the FRA) were legislative responses to two court decisions (*Trinh v Citibank*, 850 F 2d 1164, 6th Cir 1988 and *Wells Fargo Ltd v Citibank*, 936 F 2d 723, 2d Cir 1991), which held that a bank domiciled in New York was responsible to a depositor for funds deposited in a foreign branch when the deposits were expropriated or frozen by the foreign country in which the branches were located. In response to these decisions, some banks began lobbying for legislation that would protect the home office assets of US banks from claims by foreign branch depositors where those deposits could not be repaid as a result of local government action. This practice is sometimes referred to as the 'ring-fencing' of foreign branch deposits.

[87] See Chapter 14, in particular notes 45, 155, and 156 with regard to the development of a set of principles and guidelines on insolvency.

F. Systemic Risk and Systemic Crises

'Systemic risk' ('contagion risk') in a general sense is a phenomenon not confined to economics or to the financial system. For instance, with regard to the area of health, throughout history there have been epidemic diseases (the Great Plague in the Middle Ages, the Spanish flu after the First World War) where widespread contagion and contamination have had devastating effects.

In the economic literature, systemic risk is predominantly analysed as a feature of the financial system. The fear that problems in a few institutions can spread to other institutions and potentially bring the entire financial system to a halt, has prompted much empirical and theoretical economic research. The Great Depression in the 1930s provides a widely cited historical example that this fear is not without foundation. Friedman and Schwartz conclude their excellent study of the Great Contraction, with the following words:

> It is a sound general principle that great events have great origins. . . . Yet it is also true that small events at times have large consequences and that there are such things as chain reactions and cumulative forces. It happens that a liquidity crisis in a fractional reserve banking system is precisely the kind of event that can trigger— and often has triggered—a chain reaction. And economic collapse often has the characteristic of a cumulative process. . . . Because no great strength would be required to hold back the rock that starts a landslide, it does not follow that the landslide will not be of major proportions.[88]

Within the financial system, banks are particularly prone to contagion and panics. The literature on banks runs and 'financial fragility' focusing on the banking system ('domino effect', chain reaction in the case of a liquidity shortage) is extensive.[89] Systemic risk may also occur in other parts of the financial sector, such as securities markets (with simultaneous declines in the prices of a large number of securities in one or more markets in a country or across countries).

Definition of systemic risk

Systemic risk can be defined as the risk that financial difficulties at one or more banks spill over to a large number of other banks or the financial system as a

---

[88] See Milton Friedman and Anna Schwartz, *The Great Contraction 1929–1933* (Princeton: Princeton University Press, 1965) 123. See also Irving Fischer, 'The Debt Deflation Theory of Great Depressions' (1933) 1 Econometrica 337.

[89] See Martin Summer 'Banking Regulation and Systemic Risk' (2003) 14 Open Economies Review 43. See Olivier De Bandt and Philipp Hartmann, *Systemic Risk: A Survey*, Working Paper No 35, (Frankfurt: European Central Bank, 2000), 10–13.

whole.[90] While for some authors this risk can be identified with default or credit risk, in my opinion, any risk (interest rate risk, exchange rate risk, etc) can grow into systemic proportions when its negative impact extends beyond an individual institution and affects or threatens to affect other institutions, often creating a disruption in the monetary and payments systems.

The very existence and the relevance of systemic risk are debated in the literature. While Kaufman concludes in his review of the empirical evidence of bank contagion that concerns about systemic stability are greatly exaggerated,[91] Schoenmaker reaches the opposite conclusion in his empirical study of bank failures in the US from 1880 till 1936.[92] Schoenmaker's findings suggest that there may be a role for the central bank to act as lender of last resort for ailing banks whose failure is expected to have a systemic impact. However, even Kaufmann concedes that systemic risk may exist, and that there may be a role for the central banks in such a case (lender of last resort as 'a political fact of life').[93] Though according to Kaufman, bank instability is more a regulatory than a market phenomenon, since the success of macroeconomic policies to achieve stability is questionable, backup prudential policy is still desirable. Kaufman and Scott suggest that systemic risk, when it does occur, appears to be both rational and confined primarily to 'insolvent' institutions, without randomly affecting solvent banks.[94] They also argue that the evidence in the USA indicates that problems in one bank or a group of banks only spill over to other banks with the same or similar risk exposures and subject to the same shock.

---

[90] Davis defines systemic risk as a 'disturbance in financial markets which entails unanticipated changes in prices and quantities in credit or asset markets, which lead to a danger of failure of financial firms, and which in turn threatens to spread so as to disrupt the payments mechanism and capacity of the financial system to allocate capital'. See Philip Davis, *Debt, Financial Fragility and Systemic Risk* (Oxford: Clarendon Press, 1992) 117.

[91] See George Kaufman, 'Bank Contagion: A Review of the Theory and Evidence', (1994) 8 Journal of Financial Services Research 123. Kaufman further elaborates his views in: 'Bank Failures, Systemic Risk and Bank Regulation' (1996) 6(1) Cato Journal 17, available at <http://www.cato.org/pubs/journal/cj16n1–2.html> (visited 25 March 2004).

[92] See Dirk Schoenmaker, *Contagion Risk in Banking*, Discussion Paper No 239, (London: LSE Financial Markets Group, 1996).

[93] See Kaufmann, 'Bank Failures, Systemic Risk and Bank Regulation', above note 91, 7. Kaufmann also notes: 'Indeed the evidence for countries that do not have explicit government insurance indicates that they generally have implicit 100 percent insurance.' Molyneux in a paper on 'Banking Crises and the Macroeconomic Context', presented at the EBRD Seminar on 'Bank Failures and Bank Insolvency Law in Economies in Transition' in October 1997, says that 'everybody knows' the central bank will provide emergency liquidity assistance to what he calls 'core banks'. See Philip Molyneux, 'Banking Crises and the Macroeconomic Context' in Lastra and Schiffman (eds), above note 26. Caprio and others have found that in all currency board regimes with no explicit LOLR, in instances of crises 'some LOLR appears to have emerged.' See Caprio and others, above note 19, 6.

[94] See George G Kaufman and Kenneth E Scott, 'What is Systemic Risk and Do Bank Regulators Retard or Contribute to It?' (2003) 7 The Independent Review 371, 376.

There is, in their opinion, little if any empirical evidence that the insolvency of an individual bank directly causes the insolvency of other economically solvent banks, either before or after the introduction of federal deposit insurance.[95] Anna Schwartz also questions the relevance of systemic risk, arguing that many episodes that are referred to as financial crises are in fact 'pseudo' crises and not 'real' ones.[96] (Financial markets do not go bankrupt and tend to recover after some time.)

The existence of systemic risk is accepted in Kindleberger's analysis of the propagation of boom and bust domestically and internationally. The literature on bank runs and bank contagion and financial fragility and instability also suggests that this risk is real. The East Asian crises in 1997–8 as well as the Mexican crisis in 1995 (the so-called Tequila effect) provide ample evidence, in my opinion, that systemic risk does exist and that it should not be underestimated.

> Systemic risks are for financial market participants what Nessie, the monster of Loch Ness, is for the Scots (and not only for them): Everyone knows and is aware of the danger. Everyone can accurately describe the threat. Nessie, like systemic risk, is omnipresent, but nobody knows when and where it might strike. There is no proof that anyone has really encountered it, but there is no doubt that it exists.[97]

However, there is a need to reach a better understanding of systemic risk, as Alan Greenspan has emphasized:[98]

> It would be useful to central banks to be able to measure systemic risk accurately, but its very definition is still somewhat unsettled. It is generally agreed that systemic risk represents a propensity for some sort of significant financial system disruption. Nevertheless, after the fact, one observer might use the term 'market failure' to describe what another would deem to have been a market outcome that was natural and healthy, even if harsh. . . . Until we have a common theoretical paradigm for the causes of systemic stress, any consensus of how to measure systemic risk will be difficult to achieve.

Systemic risk refers to the risk or probability of breakdowns in an entire system, as opposed to breakdowns in individual parts or components.[99]

---

[95] ibid.

[96] See Anna J Schwartz, 'Real and Pseudo-Financial Crises' in Forrest Capie and Geoffrey E Wood (eds) *Financial Crises and the World Banking System* (London: Macmillan, 1986).

[97] George Sheldon and Martin Maurer, 'Inter-Bank Lending and Systemic Risk: An Empirical Analysis for Switzerland' (1998) 134 Swiss Journal of Economics and Statistics 685.

[98] See Alan Greenspan, 'Remarks at a Conference on Risk Measurement and Systemic Risk' (Board of Governors of the Federal Reserve System, Washington DC, 1995) cited by Kaufman in 'Bank Failures, Systemic Risk and Bank Regulation', above note 91, 7.

[99] See Adriano Lucatelli, *Finance and World Order—Financial Fragility, Systemic Risk and Transnational Regimes* (Westport Connecticut: Greenwood Press, 1997), 70–4.

Kaufman and Scott have identified 'macro' and 'micro' concepts of systemic risk.[100] A 'macro' concept of systemic risk can be found in the Group of Thirty Report on 'Global Institutions, National Supervision and Systemic Risk',[101] which defines it as 'the risk of a sudden, unanticipated event that would damage the financial system to such an extent that economic activity in the wider economy would suffer. To qualify as systemic shocks must reverberate through and threaten the financial system and not just some small part of it.'[102] Mishkin also favours this 'macro' approach.[103]

A 'micro' definition of systemic risk is provided by Kaufman, who defines systemic risk as the 'probability that cumulative losses will accrue from an event that sets in motion a series of successive losses along a chain of institutions or markets comprising a system . . . That is, systemic risk is the risk of a chain reaction of falling interconnected dominos.'[104] Likewise, the Bank for International Settlements (BIS) defines systemic risk as 'the risk that the failure of a participant to meet its contractual obligations may in turn cause other participants to default with a chain reaction leading to broader financial difficulties.'[105] Former Bank of England Governor George described this 'domino effect' as occurring 'through the direct financial exposures which tie firms together like mountaineers, so that if one falls off the rock face others are pulled off too.'[106]

Transmission mechanisms

The definition and understanding of systemic risk would be incomplete without a reference to the transmission mechanisms, the channels of propagation of a crisis. What makes a crisis of a systemic nature is not so much the trigger event (*causa proxima*) but these transmission mechanisms, domestically and internationally. If the linkages are strong, the potential for systemic instability increases. If the connections are weak, there is less of a threat of systemic risk.

Both the occurrence of 'shocks' and the extent of the subsequent propagation,

---

[100] Above note 94, 2.

[101] See Group of Thirty, *Global Institutions, National Supervision and Systemic Risk, A Study Group Report* (Washington DC: Group of Thirty, 1997).

[102] ibid 3.

[103] Mishkin also defines systemic risk as 'the likelihood of a sudden, usually unexpected, event that disrupts information in financial markets, making them unable to effectively channel funds to those parties with the most productive investment opportunities'. See Frederic Mishkin, 'Comment on Systemic Risk' in George Kaufman (ed), *Research in Financial Services: Banking, Financial Markets and Systemic Risk* (Greenwich Connecticut: JAI Press, 1995) vol 7, 32.

[104] See George Kaufman, 'Comment on Systemic Risk' in Kaufman (ed), ibid 47.

[105] See Bank for International Settlements, *64th Annual Report* (Basel: BIS, 1994) 177.

[106] See Edward AJ George, 'The New Lady of Threadneedle Street' (Governor's Speech, Bank of England, London, 24 February 1998).

however, are difficult to predict. Nobody could have foreseen that that crisis which began in Thailand in August 1997 would unsettle global financial markets to the extend it did. Confidence deteriorated sharply in the course of 1998 and reached its nadir in October 1998. This uncertainty has damaging consequences, since once a crisis strikes the consequences can be very severe both for the financial sector and for the real economy (negatively affecting output and general welfare).

The channels of contagion or transmission mechanisms can be classified into four categories (sometimes the various transmission mechanisms also become interconnected among themselves):[107] (1) the inter-bank channel; (2) the payment systems channel; (3) the information channel; and (4) the psychological channel.

The inter-bank channel

This channel of financial contagion is rooted in the tight network of credit interconnections in the banking system, where problems in one bank can quickly get propagated, affecting other sound institutions.[108] Banks, particularly within a domestic jurisdiction, tend to be closely interconnected through inter-bank deposits and loans and through payment systems.[109] In addition, to the extent that banks operate across national borders, they link the countries in which they operate. Cranston points out that 'exposure in the inter-bank market is less extensive than it was: banks use the inter-bank market for basic funding needs, but derivatives for hedging and position-taking.'[110]

However, the increasing volume of derivatives transactions has also implications for systemic risk. Schinasi and others[111] have identified several factors which magnify systemic risk in derivatives markets. The amounts involved are very large and the counterparty exposures are typically concentrated in few global players; the linkages between institutions, markets, and financial centres in

---

[107] In a research summary on 'Financial Contagion: ABC Channels', published by the International Monetary Fund <http://www.imf.org/external/pubs/ft/irb/2000/eng/02/index.htm>, Haizhou Huang identifies three main channels of financial contagion: the asset market channel, the banking channel, and the currency channel.

[108] See eg Jean-Charles Rochet and Jean Tirole, 'Interbank Lending and Systemic Risk' (1996) 28 Journal of Money, Credit and Banking 733.

[109] See eg Ross Cranston, *Principles of Banking Law* (Oxford: Oxford University Press, 1997) 72.

[110] ibid.

[111] See Garry Schinasi and others, *Modern Banking and OTC Derivatives Markets—The Transformation of Global Finance and its Implications for Systemic Risk*, Occasional Paper (Washington DC: IMF, 2000) 49–58; see also Adam R Waldman, 'OTC Derivatives and Systemic Risk: Innovative Finance or the Dance into the Abyss?' (1994) 43 American University Law Review 1023.

OTC (over-the-counter) derivatives activities can also trigger a chain reaction in the case of a major counterparty's default.[112]

The payments system channel

There is a complex network of exposures among banks and other financial intermediaries through the payment and settlement systems. Systemic risk considerations with regard to clearing and settlement systems have been the subject of extensive analysis by academics and policy makers in recent years.[113]

The fundamental underlying risks in these systems are similar to those encountered by financial institutions in general: operational risk (such as the failure of a computer, as in the case in the Bank of New York in 1985), liquidity risk (reception of final or 'good' funds not being realized at the desired time but at an unspecified time in the future), credit risk (failure of an insolvent participant with a subsequent loss of principal), and legal risk.

The growth of wire transfers or paperless credit transfers (electronic fund transfers) is a concern for regulators nationally and internationally, given the massive amounts involved in such transfers.[114]

The inability of one financial institution to fulfil its payment obligations in a timely fashion results in the inability of other financial institutions to fulfil their obligations in that clearing and settlement system or in other systems, or in the

---

[112] For further conceptual analysis of financial derivative transactions see indicatively, Group of Thirty, *Derivatives: Practices and Principles*, Special Report (Washington DC: Group of Thirty, 1993); Basel Committee on Banking Supervision, *Risk Management Guidelines for Derivatives* (Basel: BIS, 1994); Simon Firth, *Derivatives: Law and Practice* (London: Sweet and Maxwell, 2003).

[113] For a conceptual legal analysis of clearing and settlement systems, including references to systemic risk, see generally, Benjamin Geva, *Bank Collections and Payment Transactions: A Comparative Legal Analysis* (Oxford: Oxford University Press, 2001) chs 1 and 7–8; and Robert C Effros (ed), *Payment Systems of the World* (New York: Oceana Publications, 1994). For an economic analysis of these issues, see David Folkerts-Landau, 'Systemic Financial Risk in Payment Systems' in International Monetary Fund, *Determinants and Systemic Consequences of International Capital Flows*, Occasional Paper No 77 (Washington DC: IMF, 1991) 46–67; David B Humphrey, 'Payments Finality and Risk of Settlement Failure' in Anthony Saunders and Lawrence J White (eds), *Technology and the Regulation of Financial Markets: Securities, Futures, and Banking* (Lexington, MA: Lexington Books, 1986) 97–120; Richard Dale, 'Risk Management and Public Policy in Payment, Clearing and Settlement Systems' (1998) 1(2) International Finance 229. See also Committee on Payment and Settlement Systems, *Delivery versus Payment in Securities Settlement Systems* (Basel: BIS, 1992); Committee on Payment and Settlement Systems, *Settlement Risk in Foreign Exchange Transactions* (Basel: BIS, 1996); Board of Governors of the Federal Reserve System, *Policy Statement on Payments System Risk* (Washington DC.: Board of Governors of the FRS, 30 May 2001).

[114] In the US, for example, the dollar volume of payments made by wire transfers far exceeds the dollar volume of payments made by other means.

failure of that clearing house or other clearing houses.[115] The fear is that the inability to settle payment obligations could then lead to a severe liquidity shortage as healthy and solvent institutions, not having received the payments expected at settlement time, might be unable to settle their own payments obligations.[116]

Banks tend to play a key role in wholesale and retail payment and settlement systems. Banks may be linked to a network providing clearing and settlement facilities or they may use correspondent accounts with other banks.

In *net settlement systems* payments (such as CHIPS in the USA), banks send numerous payment instructions to other banks during a certain period, typically a day, and, at the end of that period, the instructions are netted and settled. However, without additional provisions, net settlement systems are relatively vulnerable to systemic risk, since gross exposures accumulating between settlement times can become very large. Systemic risk considerations have become a factor in the move to real-time gross settlement systems.[117]

In *real-time gross settlement systems* (RTGS), such as FedWire in the USA or TARGET in the EU, payment finality is virtually immediate for every transaction (intra-day settlement), so that the systemic risk from unsettled claims appears to be more limited than in a net settlement system. However, RTGS have also their own problems, because of the incentive to delay outgoing payments, which can lead to a system 'gridlock'[118] and the need for collateral to support intra-day borrowing from central banks.[119]

Correspondent banks provide payment services for groups of usually smaller or foreign banks, which are not linked to the primary domestic net or gross settlement systems. The failure of an important correspondent bank can directly affect a large number of those institutions.

At the international level, and in contrast to national inter-bank systems, foreign exchange and securities transactions involve the settlement of two 'legs'. In the foreign exchange market, the existence of different time zones can create 'Herstatt risk', which occurs because of the need to settle different legs of a single

---

[115] See Charles Freedman and Clyde Goodlet, 'Large-Value Clearing and Settlement Systems and Systemic Risk' (1996) 7(2) North American Journal of Economics & Finance 153.

[116] See David Folkerts-Landau, *Systemic Financial Risk in Payment Systems*, Working Paper No 65, (Washington DC: IMF, 1990) 6–7.

[117] See Cranston, above note 109, 72 and ch 10.

[118] See Olivier De Bandt and Philip Hartmann, *Systemic Risk: A Survey*, Working Paper No 35 (Frankfurt: European Central Bank, 2000), 33.

[119] I am grateful to Charles Goodhart for observations on this point.

transaction in different markets, and in different time zones.[120] An analogous risk to Herstatt risk in securities transactions is that the delivery of the securities might not coincide with payment, that is, the 'payment leg' may have a different timing from the 'delivery leg'. Increased concerns about principal risk in securities settlement have led to major initiatives to achieve 'delivery versus payment' (DVP), the simultaneous settlement of both transaction legs.[121]

There is an ongoing academic debate about whether private payment arrangements (clearing houses, self-regulation) could be more efficient than and equally stable as current regulated banking systems and partly public payment systems in industrial countries. 'Free banking' economists point to the disciplinary effects of market forces[122] and historical episodes of relatively unregulated and publicly unprotected banking systems in various countries that appeared, in the view of these authors, to be at least as stable as their more regulated counterparts.[123]

The information channel

This channel is relevant both in the case of banking markets and in the case of capital markets, where the information concerning asset prices can have systemic implications.

---

[120] The Herstatt risk is named after the failure of Bankhaus Herstatt in 1974. On 26 June 1974, the German *Bundesaufsichtsamt für das Kreditwesen* withdrew the banking licence of Bankhaus Herstatt, a small bank in Cologne active in the foreign exchange market, and ordered it into liquidation during the banking day, but after the close of the interbank payment system in Germany. Prior to the announcement of Herstatt's closure, several of its counterparties had, through branches or correspondents, paid Deutschmark to Herstatt on that day through the German payment system, against anticipated receipts of US dollars later the same day in New York in respect of maturing spot and forward transactions. Upon the termination of Herstatt's business at 10.30 am New York time (3.30 pm in Frankfurt) on 26 June, Herstatt's New York correspondent bank suspended outgoing US dollar payments from the Herstatt account. This action left Herstatt's counterparty banks exposed for the full value of the Deutschmark deliveries made (credit risk and liquidity risk). Moreover, banks which had entered into forward trades with Herstatt not yet due for settlement lost money in replacing the contracts in the market (replacement risk), while others had deposits with Herstatt (traditional counterparty risk).

[121] See Committee on Payment and Settlement Systems, *Delivery versus Payment in Securities Settlement Systems* (Basel: BIS, 1992). See also Cranston, above note 109, 315.

[122] See Charles Calomiris and Charles Kahn, 'The Role of Demandable Debt in Structuring Optimal Banking Arrangements' (1991) 81 American Economic Review 497.

[123] See Lawrence White, *Free Banking in Britain: Theory, Experience, and Debate, 1800–1845* (Cambridge: Cambridge University Press, 1984); Arthur Rolnick and Werner Weber, 'Inherent Instability in Banking: The Free Banking Experience' (1986) 5(3) Cato Journal 877; Kevin Dowd (ed), *The Experience of Free Banking* (London: Routledge, 1992); Kevin Dowd, *Competition and Finance* (London: Macmillan, 1996) ch 7; Charles Calomiris and Charles Kahn, 'The Efficiency of Self-regulated Payments Systems: Learning from the Suffolk System' (1996) 28 Journal of Money, Credit, and Banking 767.

Bank assets, loans, are inherently opaque to outsiders. The non-marketability of loans creates uncertainty, making it difficult to assess the creditworthiness of banks and the risk profile of their strategies. Thus, depositors and other bank creditors have limited information (information asymmetries or deficiencies) about their banks' asset portfolios and are often not able to assess their soundness. Banks have a specialized role in monitoring and screening their borrowers. Typically, this information is not available to the general public.

An adverse piece of news such as the failure of a particular bank will lead depositors at other institutions to re-evaluate the soundness and risk profile of their own bank.[124] Although it is relatively easy to distinguish the solvent from the insolvent *ex post*, that is, after the crisis, it can be difficult in practice to do so before a crisis. *Ex ante* information is frequently not sufficiently available, timely, or reliable to make the distinction with confidence. Banks often fail to disclose relevant information, particularly as they approach insolvency.[125]

A distinction is sometimes made between rational or information-based direct systemic risk and irrational, non-information-based or random systemic risk.[126] Rational or informed contagion assumes that investors (depositors) can differentiate among parties on the basis of their 'fundamentals'. Random contagion, based on actions by uniformed agents, is viewed as more frightening and dangerous since it does not differentiate among parties, affecting solvent as well as insolvent parties, and is therefore likely to be more difficult to contain.[127]

The theory of rational expectations is particularly relevant in the analysis of securities markets contagion. Changes in asset prices in one market may reveal changes in the value of assets in other markets. The few theoretical models dealing with securities market contagion are mostly based on the revision of investors' expectations.[128] Contagion effects among international securities markets are often defined either as changes in securities prices that affect the countries beyond what would be justified by 'fundamentals' or as unexpected volatility during crisis periods.[129]

---

[124] See Varadarajan Chari and Ravi Jagannathan, 'Banking Panics, Information, and Rational Expectations Equilibrium' (1988) 43 Journal of Finance 749, and Charles Jacklin and Sudipto Bhattacharya, 'Distinguishing Panics and Information-based Bank Runs: Welfare and Policy Implications' (1988) 96 Journal of Political Economy 568 and by many commentators thereafter.

[125] See Kaufman and Scott, above note 94.

[126] See Joseph Aharony and Swary Izhak, 'Additional Evidence on the Information-Based Contagion Effects of Bank Failures' (1996) 20 Journal of Banking and Finance 57; Kaufman and Scott, above note 94, 6.

[127] See George, above note 106.

[128] See De Bandt and Hartmann, above note 118, 27. See Mervyn King and Sushil Wadhwani, 'Transmission of Volatility between Stock Markets' (1990) 3 Review of Financial Studies 5.

[129] See De Bandt and Hartmann, ibid.

The psychological channel

'Panics also travel through psychological conduits.'[130] The psychological argument is related to the information channel. Public perception is very important. A failure of one bank may cause the public to believe that other banks will fail. The belief in a panic is self-fulfilling. Market sentiment can shift suddenly and quickly. 'Herd behaviour' is a recurring pattern in 'boom and bust' cycles.

There is an element of irrationality in the way a crisis unfolds. Kindleberger talks about the rationality of individuals and the irrationality of markets.[131] The terms distress, euphoria, mania, panic have a psychological connotation. They express emotions that often get out of control. Of course, these conduits are difficult to quantify. But they are real.

Given that confidence and trust are preconditions of well functioning markets, it is easy to realize that the loss of confidence in an institution or market (whether informed or uninformed, rational or irrational) will undermine the functioning of that institution or market.

The resolution of a crisis also presents, in some cases, a psychological component: the mere belief that the problem has been solved will bring investors back to the market and will operate as a positive incentive to open up again the sources of credit. It is not so much the ability to lend but the willingness to do so that really counts in the resolution of a financial crisis. 'The mere knowledge that one can get money is frequently sufficient to moderate or eliminate the desire.'[132]

Dealing with systemic risk: Prevention and resolution

Following up the analogy drawn by Stiglitz[133] between a small boat in a rowing sea and a crisis, crisis management involves both good steering of the boat through a storm as well as any due diligence as well as preventive measures to strengthen the design of the boat.

The management of a system crisis will vary depending upon the geographical reach of the crisis, the economic development of the country, and the level of involvement of the private sector.

The geographical reach of systemic risk can be regional, national, or international.[134] The recent Argentine crisis—a combination of currency, banking, and debt problems with very negative effects upon the real economy—has been mainly confined to Argentina (though it had damaging spillover effects upon Uruguay, it left relatively unaffected other countries in Latin America). The

---

130 See Kindleberger, above note 1, 109.   131 ibid 23.   132 ibid 16.
133 See above note 2.   134 See De Bandt and Hartmann, above note 118, 10–13.

crises in Thailand, Indonesia, South Korea, Malaysia in 1997–8 constitute an example of regional crisis. The debt crisis of the 1980s constitutes an example of international crisis.

Though crises are costly and difficult to resolve in developed countries, their effects are even more severe in the developing world, where 'economic fundaments' and 'bad policies' can often be blamed as a *causa remota*. A system crisis tends to be a result or a reflection of the deterioration on the economic environment or of poor macroeconomic management. Rojas-Suárez and Weisbrod demonstrate that banking crises in Latin America last longer, are more costly, and hurt the local economies more than banking crises in the industrial countries, because of the fragility of their financial systems. They argue that this fragility is the result of 'frequent periods of destabilizing economic policies and structural problems in the market, which include inexact legal and accounting standards and weak supervision'.[135]

At a 'macroeconomic' level, the observance of a code of good fiscal conduct and the avoidance of excessive and prolonged current account deficits provide *ex ante* defences against systemic crises. The most important contribution any government can make with regard to crisis prevention is the adoption of sound monetary and fiscal policies (monetary stability and fiscal restraint). Nevertheless, the responses of the bank and depositors to poor government policies are likely to exacerbate risk taking, the fragility of financial sector, and the magnitude and damage of 'bad' policies.[136]

Kaufman emphasizes the role that private market incentives play in limiting systemic risk. Governments should always be highly sensitive to whether their actions are undermining or reinforcing the private mechanisms,[137] an issue which I also discuss in Chapter 14. There should be no deposit-insurance cover of inter-bank transactions. A fortiori, there should be no safety-net policy for too-big-to-fail banks, which eliminates entirely the need for counterparties to take even elementary measures to reduce their risk exposure.

A *system crisis* (a generalized banking crisis) is treated by the supervisory authorities differently from an isolated individual bank failure in a sound economy. When confronting a system crisis, the government can choose to deal with each troubled bank on a case-by-case basis, using a mix of strategies: takeovers and

---

[135] See Liliana Rojas-Suárez and Steven R Weisbrod, 'Banking Crises in Latin America: Experience and Issues', (paper presented at the Inter-American Development Bank Group of Thirty Conference on Banking Crises in Latin America, Washington DC, 1995).

[136] See Andrew Crockett 'Marrying the Micro- and Macro-Prudential Dimensions of Financial Stability' (Remarks before the Eleventh International Conference of Banking Supervisors, held in Basel, 20–1 September 2000).

[137] See Kaufman, above note 91.

rescue packages in some cases, liquidation in others; or the government can choose an overall strategy to deal with all the actual or potential troubled institutions. The difficulty of calculating *ex ante* the total amount of the losses and the speed with which a system crisis unfolds add to the complexity of its resolution. At the beginning of a system crisis, the authorities may provide emergency liquidity assistance to banks under stress, hoping for an early restoration of confidence.[138] However, if banks start failing, the government will often be compelled to provide solvency assurances to depositors and to design a coherent policy—with an expeditious decision-making process and a clear voice—to overcome the crisis. The government also faces the delicate and difficult policy choice of whether and when to commit fiscal resources to recapitalize banks. Timing is always important. As Kindleberger suggested, with regard to LOLR: 'As for timing, it is an art. That says nothing and everything.'[139]

There are two extreme solutions available to governments when dealing with a system crisis: the government can inject capital into all troubled institutions and the government can do a large-scale liquidation. Direct government injection of capital into the troubled institutions, as happened in Sweden in 1992 or in Venezuela in 1994, often leads to a de facto nationalization of the assisted banks (or of the whole banking system); it also complicates the conduct of monetary and fiscal policies. Liquidation on a large scale, on the other extreme, is seldom considered a viable option, because of its detrimental effects on the workings of a market economy, because of a potential 'domino effect' on other (sound) financial institutions (the very malaise the government is trying to avoid) and because of the difficulty in judging whether the problems are permanent or merely cyclical or temporary. The banking crisis in Russia in the summer of 1995 illustrates how liquidation of a large number of small institutions can, under certain circumstances, be beneficial for the restoration of confidence in the system.[140]

Between these two radical options, de facto nationalization (saving all institutions) and liquidation (letting all institutions fail), there are a variety of solutions and policies available to governments to confront a system crisis. Debt restructuring techniques (debt-to-debt conversions and debt-to-equity conversions) have been applied in the resolution of the Latin American debt crisis of

---

[138] Furthermore, if the crisis has been magnified because of a weak bank supervisory structure (eg, in Venezuela in 1995) or because of supervisory and regulatory mistakes (eg, the US thrift crisis in the 1980s) those issues also need to be redressed in order to restore confidence in the banking system.

[139] See Kindleberger, above note 1, 163.

[140] See Anders Aslund, 'When a Banking Crisis Is a Good Thing', *Financial Times* (13 September 1995): 'A government-ordered inspection of the banks could not possibly clean up the wild Russian banking sector. Fortunately, the market is doing the cleaning up instead.'

the 1980s and are back in vogue after the mixed experience with the so-called 'bailout packages' that I further discuss in Chapter 14. The government can also ask other private institutions to provide assistance to troubled banks. In the UK, such a mix of government assistance and private assistance was named 'lifeboat' operation and was applied following the secondary banking crisis of 1974. The lifeboat—in the form of loans to the secondary banks—was coordinated by the big four clearing banks and the Scottish clearing banks. A centralized agency can also be created to dispose of the assets of the failed institutions. Such a centralized solution was adopted in the resolution of the US thrift crisis of the 1980s. The Resolution Trust Corporation (RTC) was created by the 1989 Financial Institutions Reform, Recovery and Enforcement Act (FIRREA) to manage the assets of the failed savings and loan associations.

At the international level, I also discuss in Chapter 14 the proposals to create a Sovereign Debt Restructuring Mechanism (SDRM) to be administered by the International Monetary Fund.

5

MONETARY AND FINANCIAL LAW REFORM IN EMERGING ECONOMIES

Commerce and manufactures can seldom flourish long in any state which does not enjoy a regular administration of justice, in which the people do not feel themselves secure in the possession of their property, in which the faith of contracts is not supported by the law, and in which the authority of the state is not supposed to be regularly employed in enforcing the payment of debts from all those who are able to pay. Commerce and manufactures, in short, can seldom flourish in any state in which there is not a certain degree of confidence in the justice of government.

Adam Smith, *An Inquiry into the Nature and Causes of the Wealth of Nations*, first published in 1776

Commercial credit may be defined to be that confidence which subsists among commercial men in respect to their mercantile affairs. . . . In a society in which law and the sense of moral duty are weak, and property is consequently insecure, there will, of course be little confidence or credit, and there will also be little commerce.

Henry Thornton, *An Enquiry into the Nature and Effects of the Paper Credit of Great Britain*, first published in 1802.

A. Introduction

The term 'emerging economies' is rather imprecise. It encompasses both developing countries (also referred to in the past as Third World countries or Less Developed Countries) and transitional economies (formerly communist countries). It is also a dynamic term: the words developing, emerging, or transitional reflect a state of flux in the long march through development. A common feature of these jurisdictions is the emphasis given in recent years to institutional and legal reform, which has become an essential component of 'development'. Indeed, the major new thrust of 'development' economics in the 1990s has been the recognition of the crucial role of institutions in permitting an economy to function effectively.[1]

This chapter focuses primarily on monetary and financial law reform.[2] In many cases, laws creating central banks have been enacted, with the adoption of new currencies and the establishment of a commercial banking system. In other cases reform of the existing systems has implied a great deal of legislative and regulatory activity. While in former communist countries, market-based financial systems have been typically created from scratch, in developing countries in Latin America and other regions of the world, there is already a legal infrastructure, often inefficient, almost always incomplete, but yet a platform which cannot be ignored in the reform process.

With regard to the contents of the reform programmes, the preceding four chapters provide ample analysis as to the major questions that monetary and financial law should consider, namely institutional developments to promote monetary stability (independent central banks and currency boards), the institutional design of prudential supervision, and the management of financial crises. The responses, of course, will vary from country to country.

The law reform process can follow different routes: adoption of a model law or treaty, adoption of standards ('soft law') set by the Basel Committee on Banking Supervision and other 'international standard-setters' (further analysed

---

[1] See generally John Williamson and Pedro-Pablo Kuczynski (eds), *After the Washington Consensus: Restarting Growth and Reform in Latin America* (Washington DC: Institute for International Economics, 2003).

[2] See generally Joseph J Norton, *Financial Sector Law Reform in Emerging Economies* (London: The British Institute of International and Comparative Law and the London Institute of International Banking, Finance, and Development Law, 2000); Rumu Sarkar, *Development Law and International Finance* (The Hague: Kluwer Law International, 1999); Gerard Caprio, David Folkerts-Landau, and Timothy D Lane (eds), *Building Sound Finance in Emerging Economies* (Washington DC: IMF, 1994); Tomás J T Baliño and Carlo Cotarelli (eds), *Frameworks for Monetary Stability. Policy Issues and Country Experiences* (Washington DC: IMF, 1994).

in Chapter 14), adoption of harmonized rules (as in the case of the EC), drafting or revising laws based or inspired upon the laws of another country/countries (or a compromise law), and others.

The law reform process does not only encompass the creation or amendment of laws. It also includes the implementation of rules, the dissemination of legal information, the building of institutions that effectively support the legal environment, such as independent courts, central banks, regulatory agencies, and others. The ownership, sustainability, sequencing, and interconnectedness of the legal reforms are often mentioned as indicators of its potential success.

B. The Importance of the Legal Framework

It was once the practice in economics to pay due respect to the law. The opening paragraphs of this chapter illustrate how Adam Smith (widely regarded as the founding father of economics as an autonomous discipline) and Henry Thornton (who laid down important foundations of financial economics) paid close heed to the legal framework. However, in the course of the twentieth century, economics started gravitating towards mathematics and other 'hard sciences'. This meant that the two social sciences started drifting apart from each other, which contributes to explaining the difficulties in holding an effective interdisciplinary dialogue. However, in recent years, economists have begun to appreciate again the importance of sound legal structures and 'institutions' for the proper functioning of markets and for the success of economic reform. *Nihil novum sub sole!*

These days, when economists write about 'institutions', they mean law.[3] Nobel Laureates Ronald Coase[4] and Douglass North[5] have stressed the important role that legal norms and institutions play in the functioning of markets. Douglass North defines institutions as the formal and informal rules governing human interactions. 'Institutions are the rules of the game in a society or, more formally, are the humanly devised constraints that shape human interaction. . . . That institutions affect the performance of economies is hardly controversial.

---

[3] This point has been often made by John Jackson, the world's leading authority in the field of international trade law.

[4] See Ronald H Coase, *The Firm, the Market and the Law* (Chicago: The University of Chicago Press, 1988). This book is a collection of Coase's main papers, including his two seminal articles: 'The Nature of the Firm' (1937) and 'The Problem of Social Cost' (1960).

[5] See Douglass C North, *Institutions, Institutional Change and Economic Performance* (Cambridge: Cambridge University Press, 1990).

That the differential performance of economies over time is fundamentally influenced by the way institutions evolve is also not controversial.'[6]

Most of the recent work done by economists on institutions has focused on a particular set of them, namely those that protect property rights and ensure that contracts are enforced. Dani Rodrik and Arvind Subramanian refer to them as market-creating institutions, since, without them, markets cannot exist or, if they do exist, they would function very poorly.[7] They also acknowledge, however, the importance of other institutions, which they classify into market regulating, market stabilizing, and market legitimizing. Other definitions focus on the degree of property rights protection, the degree to which laws and regulations are properly applied, and the extent of corruption.[8] Corruption, where it exists, is certainly a major obstacle to any process of legal and institutional reform.[9]

The collapse of the former Soviet Union signified the collapse of an economic model based on collectivism and state planning. The political, economic, and legal implications of the abandonment of communism and the embracement— to a greater or lesser degree—of capitalism have been significant. A market economy cannot be supported in an institutional vacuum. Hence the enthusiasm in recent years for a proper legal and institutional infrastructure.

C. Reform Agenda: Beyond the 'Washington Consensus'

Reform programmes in emerging economies in the 1990s have been influenced by the so-called 'Washington Consensus'. This term was coined by John Williamson in 1989 to summarize the main policy reforms that he argued were needed in Latin America as of that date.[10] The list included ten items: fiscal

---

[6] ibid 3.

[7] See Dani Rodrik and Arvind Subramanian, 'The Primacy of Institutions' (2003) 40 Finance and Development, 32, at <http://www.imf.org/external/pubs/ft/fandd/2003/06/pdf/rodrik.pdf>. This article draws upon Dani Rodrik, Arvind Subramanian, and Francesco Trebbi, *Institutions Rule: The Primacy of Institutions and Integration in Economic Development*, Working Paper No 9305, (Cambridge MA: NBER, 2002).

[8] See eg Hali Edison, 'Testing the Links. How Strong are the Links between Institutional Quality and Economic Performance' (2003) 40 Finance and Development 36, at <http://www.imf.org/external/pubs/ft/fandd/2003/06/pdf/edison.pdf>.

[9] For a definition of corruption, see World Bank Institute 1–64, 1–65 at <http://lnweb18.worldbank.org/ECA/Transport.nsf/ExtECADocByUnid/AEBC8BC811C9581E85256B7A0052E51C/$file/CORRUPT1. pdf>. Corruption in public service can be defined as the abuse of public office for private gain, through bribery, patronage and nepotism, the theft of state assets, or the diversion of state revenues.

[10] See John Williamson, 'What Washington Means by Policy Reform' in John Williamson (ed), *Latin American Adjustment: How Much Has Happened?* (Washington DC: Institute for International Economics, 1990).

discipline, reordering public expenditures priorities to be pro poor and pro growth (ie, switching expenditures to basic health care, education, and infrastructure), tax reform, liberalization of interest rates, a competitive exchange rate, trade liberalization, liberalization of inward foreign direct investment, privatization, deregulation, and property rights.

Though it was never Williamson's intent to define an ideology with this phrase,[11] the reality is, that for better or for worse, it has become associated with the neo-liberal agenda and, hence, often blamed for the ills of globalization by those who opposed reform. In addition to this meaning which equates Washington consensus with neo-liberalism, a second alternative interpretation is that 'the Washington consensus represents the policies collectively pursued by the Washington-based international institutions that dispense advice to developing countries: the Bretton Woods institutions (the IMF and the World Bank), the Inter-American Development Bank, the US Treasury, and perhaps the US Federal Reserve.'[12]

Williamson explains that with the exception of the fifth item (a competitive exchange rate) he did a good reporting job reflecting what was important in Latin America at that time.[13] Nonetheless, he concedes that he omitted a number of reforms that should have been on the agenda, such as institutional reforms (which he and other economists refer to as 'second-generation reform') and income distribution.[14]

The importance of legal and institutional reform for the success of the overall reform process has long been advocated by lawyers.[15] Perhaps economists are slowly coming to the realization that after a long period when economics tended toward other ('hard') sciences in its search for an optimal interdisciplinary

---

[11] See John Williamson, 'From Reform Agenda to Damaged Brand Name' (2003) 40(3) Finance and Development 10–13, at <http://www.imf.org/external/pubs/ft/fandd/2003/09/pdf/williams.pdf>.

[12] ibid 11.

[13] ibid. With regard to item four of his list (liberalization of interest rates), in retrospect Williamson wishes he had formulated this more broadly as financial liberalization accompanied by appropriate financial supervision.

[14] ibid. He points out that the importance of institutional reforms in complementing 'first generation' liberalizing reforms was first emphasized by Moíses Naím, 'Latin America: The Second Stage of Reform' in Larry Diamond and Marc F Plattner (eds), *Economic Reform and Democracy* (Baltimore: Johns Hopkins University Press, 1995).

[15] Indeed, when I was working as a consultant in the Legal Department of the International Monetary Fund in 1992–3, a major thrust of the work in which I participated (technical assistance in the field of monetary and banking law) was the importance of legal and institutional reforms for the success of the overall reform process both in developing countries and in transition economies.

balance (mathematics, statistics, physics), emphasis should now turn toward its institutional and legal linkages.[16]

Though the Washington Consensus as originally proposed by Williamson 'has simply ceased to exist',[17] its legacy remains. It has contributed to the discussion of where economic reform should be heading and has emphasized the importance of maintaining prudent macroeconomic policies (stable money and fiscal restraint).

Salacuse argues[18] that until the 1980s most developing countries adopted a development model (which he refers to as 'Development Model I') based upon public ordering, state planning, reliance on public sector enterprises, pervasive regulation, restrictions on the private sector, and restrictions on foreign influences ('closed economies'). This Development Model I influenced the legal system in many ways, with administrative law rather than commercial law being considered as the basic law of economic and business activity in many countries. By the mid 1980s however, the faith in the power of the State to bring about development had declined. 'The end of communism in Eastern Europe and the Soviet Union in 1989 deprived many developing countries of sources of moral and material support for Development Model I.'[19] The failure of Development Model I and the debate of what constituted good economic reform led to the formulation of a new model of development, 'Development Model II'. According to Salacuse, the four most important elements of Development Model II are: reliance on markets and private ordering, privatization, deregulation, and 'openness' (to the world) with regard to trade and investment. From a legal point of view, the movement from 'plan back to contract'[20] implies a shift from administrative law to a private law system capable of sustaining business and market transactions (commercial law, contracts, and property rights). It also implies a change in approach to regulation (less pervasive and invasive) and a reinforcement of the legal and institutional mechanisms to protect individual rights. Independent courts of justice are essential for the proper functioning of markets.

In my opinion, however, 'fatigue' with the Washington consensus, a realization

---

[16] See Rosa M Lastra, *Central Banking and Banking Regulation* (London: Financial Markets Group of the London School of Economics, 1996) 7.

[17] Williamson, above note 11, 12.

[18] See Jeswald W Salacuse, 'The Legal Architecture of Emerging Markets' in Rosa M Lastra (ed), *The Reform of the International Financial Architecture* (The Hague: Kluwer Law International, 2001) 47–66.

[19] ibid 58. Salacuse identifies the policies advocated by the so-called Washington consensus with the Development Model II.

[20] ibid 63. Salacuse also recalls (ibid 56) that the growth of state economic regulation in the 1950s and 1960s had signified a movement 'from contract to plan' (a phrase coined by Robert Seidman).

that financial crises require effective government regulation and sometimes intervention, and a reassessment of the functions of the State, suggest that we may be witnessing the emergence of a different development model (a 'Development Model III'), in which both public and private sector have a significant role to play. Indeed the emphasis on institutional reform presupposes the existence of a set of public institutions. The importance of the State cannot be underestimated.[21]

D. The Law Reform Process

In this section I discuss the stages, features, issues, and methods of law reform, with emphasis on monetary and financial law reform. References to the 'law reform process' (which, in a broad sense, is a permanent feature in the history of law) are generally circumscribed in this chapter—and in a large portion of the literature that has been developed in recent years—to the process that started with the collapse of communism in Eastern Europe and the former Soviet Union and with the ensuing unprecedented effort to establish a new legal system in the newly independent states in the former Soviet Union and the Eastern European countries.

Legal technical assistance has experienced a dramatic growth in the last fifteen years, with many countries and regions in the world embarking on a process of law making and law reform either at the national level or at a regional level.[22]

---

[21] Trevor A Manuel, Minister of Finance of the Republic of South Africa, points out that 'Most African States need to expand, not contract, their public sector and dramatically improve its efficiency in delivering quality public services. This demands institutional capacity, especially in areas of regulation, service delivery and social spending.' He further argues that 'The Problem in Africa is that most states are weak and limited, not that states try to do everything and account for 50 percent or so of national income, as in other regions.' See Trevor A Manuel, 'Africa and the Washington Consensus. Finding the Right Path' (2003) 40(3) Finance and Development 19–20, at <http://www.imf.org/external/pubs/ft/fandd/2003/09/pdf/manuel.pdf>.

[22] See The World Bank Group, 'Legal and Judicial Reform' at <http://www4.worldbank.org/ legal/leglr/>. For a list of the legal and judicial reform programmes approved by the World Bank see <http://www1.worldbank.org/publicsector/legal/MajorStandAloneJudiciallReformProjects. doc>. Because of the significance of the amount, it is worth pointing out that a loan of $58 million was approved for a Legal Reform Project (8331) for the Russian Federation in June 1996, to focus on: 1) assistance for the legal drafting of economic laws at the federal level and on a pilot basis in the Sverdlovsk and Orel oblasts; 2) development of legal information guidelines and pilot implementation of electronic systems; 3) improvements in legal education and a public education campaign to raise awareness of the role of law in a market economy; and 4) judicial training and a study to analyse the structure and administration of courts, including selection and appointment of judges and court personnel, the creation of judicial districts and budgets, and the management of courts.

Stages of the law reform process

Law reform is not simply about enacting laws. It is a process that encompasses the following stages:

1. Creation of laws or amendment of laws. With regard to law drafting, it is important to establish clear guidelines with regard to the legislative process, the way that laws are proposed, prepared, enacted, and updated.

2. Implementation of laws through rules and regulations. Regulations are sometimes issued by a government department, sometimes by an independent agency with delegated rule-making powers.

3. Dissemination of legal information. This stage deals with how laws, regulations, and court decisions are recorded, authenticated, and disseminated to government bodies, courts of justice, lawyers, academics, the business community, non-governmental organizations, and the general public. It is sometimes referred to as 'regulatory transparency'.

4. Effective enforcement and sanctions in the case of non-compliance with the law.

5. Building of institutions that efficiently support the legal environment, such as independent courts of justice, regulatory agencies, private bar groups or associations, law schools, and other training institutions.

6. Legal education. The letter of the law does not change the minds of the people. Legal education is needed. The introduction of new teaching methodologies in law schools, the training of lawyers and government officials in new laws and legal concepts (with emphasis on commercial law rather than administrative law in the legal studies), the cooperation and exchange of students with law schools in countries firmly anchored in the principles of a market economy, and the information to the general public about the role of law in a market economy are important components of this process of legal education. Though legal and economic structures can be dismantled overnight, the same cannot be said about their construction.

7. Judicial reforms.[23] The aims of these reforms will vary depending upon the specific legal tradition and circumstances in each country. In some cases, such reforms will seek to limit corruption and to safeguard the independence

---

[23] See The World Bank Group, 'Judicial Reform' in 'Legal and Judicial Reform' at <http://www4.worldbank.org/legal/leglr/>.

By consistently enforcing clear rules, an independent and impartial judicial system supports legal reform and promotes economic and social development. An effective judiciary applies and enforces laws and regulations impartially, predictably and efficiently. Economic growth and social development cannot be sustained and promoted in countries where the justice system fails. We assist governments to develop and implement judicial reform programs to achieve sustainable economic growth and social development based on empowerment, opportunity, and security for all citizens.

of the judiciary. In some other cases, the reforms will seek to improve the functioning of the judiciary, through the training of judges and the efficiency in the handling of cases, with rapid and low-cost enforcement of court decisions.

8. Alternative mechanisms of dispute resolution, such as arbitration, conciliation, and mediation, ought to be established or strengthened.

Some features of the law reform process

The law should add clarity, certainty, and predictability to the reform process. In addition, the ownership, sustainability, proper sequencing, and interconnectedness of the law reform process are four indicators of its potential success.[24]

The 'ownership' of legal reforms signifies that countries should make their 'own' decisions about the direction of their legal systems. It refers to the issue of legitimacy, and, in countries with democratic regimes, to the issue of democratic accountability. Countries should be aware of the problems of transplanting laws or of adopting model laws, which may provide useful lessons as a tested system or a reference guide, yet need to be adapted or modified to fit local institutions. I further discuss the issues of ownership (with regard to international soft law) in Chapter 14.

In September 2000, IMF Managing Director Horst Köhler issued an Interim Guidance Note on Streamlining Structural Conditionality to staff, indicating that he viewed streamlining and focusing conditionality as well as 'strengthening national ownership' as a priority. Accordingly, Fund staff embarked on a review of various issues associated with conditionality which culminated in the 2002 Guidelines on Conditionality as I further discuss in Chapter 13.[25] It was recognized in the review that Fund-supported programmes have sometimes 'short-circuited' national decision-making processes and failed to take adequate account of the authorities' ability to muster public support for the policies envisaged, as well as their administrative capacity to implement these policies. Streamlining the contents of conditionality, it was recognized, should proceed hand in hand with strengthening the national ownership of the (IMF) programme.[26]

A proper 'sequencing' of legal reforms is fundamental to guaranteeing that an adequate infrastructure and resources are available to ensure their effective

---

[24] See generally Katerina Mathernová (Legal Department, World Bank), 'The World Bank and Legal Technical Assistance: Initial Lessons', World Bank Research Working Paper No 1414, January 1995 http://ssrn.com/abstract=620591>.

[25] See also Rosa M Lastra, 'IMF Conditionality' (2002) 4 (2) Journal of International Banking Regulation 167.

[26] ibid.

implementation. For instance, banking and securities laws need to be preceded by contract, property, company, secured transactions, registration, and bankruptcy laws as I further explain below. A step-by-step approach is particularly recommended when new institutions (such as central banks) are created from new. The importance of appropriate sequencing with regard to economic reforms (eg, financial markets liberalization ought to be accompanied by adequate regulation and prudential supervision) has also been advocated by many economists.[27]

The law reform process ought to be 'sustainable'. This implies a long-term horizon on the part of national legislators and on those who advise with regard to specific legal reforms. It takes time to design programmes and to establish institutions.[28] Laws must not just be passed, they need to be widely known, applied, and enforced. Changes in public attitude take time to settle. The public and the business community need to be educated about the rule of law in a market economy.

The legal foundations of a market economy are 'interconnected'. They are akin to the pillars of a building: the building can only be sustained if all the pillars are in place. Weakness in one area will affect success in other areas. Reforms cannot be designed or carried out in isolation. A comprehensive and consistent approach is needed. For instance, privatization requires an adequate protection of property rights.

Issues in the law reform process

The legal framework of a market economy consists of a number of substantive and procedural rules with regard to the functioning of the economy. Some of those rules flourish better when the system is democratic, such as the recognition and protection of property rights or the existence of independent courts of justice. However, market-oriented law reforms have also been adopted in

---

[27] Above note 1.

[28] See Charles W Calomiris, 'Statement before the Joint Economic Committee' (United States Congress. Tuesday, 24 February 1998), at <http://www.house.gov/jec/hearings/imf/calomiri.htm> (visited 10 March 2004):

> [R]eal reform in the banking system takes years to accomplish because it entails new ways of measuring and managing risk, new regulations, and new supervisory procedures. These changes are both politically difficult (because the politically powerful must forego subsidies) and technically challenging. The time horizon necessary to implement successful reform is at least five years (judging from the successful examples of Argentina and Chile, which did so very aggressively and without IMF pressure). Building effective financial institutions, and reforming the legal and regulatory environment in which they operate, is a protracted and difficult learning process, even when countries have the political will to do so. The horizon of IMF crisis assistance and conditionality (typically two years or so) is simply not suited to achieve true reform in the banking system.

non-democratic societies. This has been the case, for instance, in the People's Republic of China and its so-called 'gradualist approach' towards market economics.

The financial law reform process is bound to have a 'substantive law' component and a 'procedural and enforcement mechanism' component.[29] The first element relates to the rules which govern activities in financial markets. The second aspect refers to the establishment of supervisory authorities, independent courts of justice, alternative dispute resolution mechanisms, and others. In developing countries and emerging market economies, the reform or the creation of sound mechanisms of enforcement and supervision, both judicial and administrative, is often more difficult than the reform of the substantive rules.[30]

The issues that ought to be included in a programme of monetary and financial law reform are not different from the ones that I have already discussed in the preceding chapters.[31] In this subsection I discuss the *preconditions* for a successful reform programme in this field, that is, the laws that need to be in place for a market economy to function properly. The list that I provide below draws in part on a note that I wrote in 1992 (during my stint at the IMF) with regard to the legal changes that were needed to support a market economy (in the context of the transformation of a socialist economy into a market economy). It also draws on a list proposed by John Walker[32] and on other lists that have been suggested on the core requirements for the institutional framework of market economies.[33]

---

[29] See Howell Jackson, 'The Selective Incorporation of Foreign Legal Systems to Promote Nepal as an International Financial Services Centre' in Christopher McCrudden (ed), *Regulation and Deregulation—Policy and Practice in the Utilities and Financial Services Industries* (Oxford: Oxford University Press, 1998) 372–81.

[30] ibid.

[31] Goodhart and others argue that the general analysis of, rationale for, and principles of financial regulation are not fundamentally different in emerging and developing countries from in developed economies. In their view, the need for regulation is even greater in emerging markets than elsewhere in the light of their vulnerabilities; prophylactic rules based on numerical ratios are more important, since less reliance can be placed in more sophisticated internal mechanisms. See Charles Goodhart et al (eds), *Financial Regulation Why, How and Where Now?* (London: Routledge, 1998) 99.

[32] See John L Walker, 'Building the Legal and Regulatory Framework' (paper presented in the Conference of the Federal Reserve Bank of Boston 'Building an Infrastructure for Financial Stability' June 2000), at <http://www.bos.frb.org/economic/conf/conf44/cf44_3.pdf> (4 March 2004).

[33] See generally Gerhard Pohl et al, *Creating Capital Markets in Central and Eastern Europe* (Washington DC: World Bank, 1995); Robert Pardy, *Institutional Reform in Emerging Securities Markets* (Washington DC: The World Bank, 1992); Joseph J Norton and Hani Sarie-Eldin, 'Securities Law Models in Emerging Economies' in Joseph J Norton and Mads Andenas (eds), *Emerging Financial Markets and the Role of International Financial Organizations* (London: Kluwer Law International, 1996).

The legal infrastructure of a market economy must comprise:

1. Laws that clearly define and protect private property rights. The right to inheritance should also be recognized. Expropriation should be confined to exceptional cases for a public purpose and respecting the principles of non-discrimination, prompt, adequate, and effective compensation, and due process of law/judicial review.

2. Contract laws. The sanctity of contracts, *pacta sunt servanda*, is at the core of commercial transactions. The law ought to protect the rights and enforce the obligations of counterparties, including lenders and borrowers. The availability of credit is also contingent upon the existence of security; hence the need for laws on collateral, on secured transactions.

3. Corporate or company laws with adequate corporate governance standards and fiduciary duties for management and the protection of shareholders' rights.

4. Bankruptcy laws to address defaults and restructurings. The rights of creditors must be adequately defined and protected in an insolvency proceeding. However, bankruptcy laws should not 'penalize' entrepreneurship and private initiative.

5. Laws on registration (land registration and a general system of registration). Registration provides legal certainty and is a complement to the protection of property rights.

6. Administrative laws to prevent the arbitrary exercise of discretion by the public authorities.

7. Competition or antitrust laws to prevent excessive concentration of power, abuse of dominant position, and collusive price setting.

8. Tax laws and an adequate system of tax collection. Taxes ought to provide the government with sufficient financial resources to meet its obligations and to support a minimum social safety net. The level of taxation is a policy decision, which has fundamental consequences for the citizens. Excessive taxes unduly interfere with the system of private incentives and, if there is labour and capital mobility, excessive taxes can drive firms or individuals out of the country.

9. An accounting code.

10. Laws regarding payments and payment systems.

11. Laws for the 'transitional period', such as privatization laws, foreign investment laws, and others.

12. Labour laws that establish a fair balance between the protection of workers (with unemployment benefits and right to collective action) and the protection of employers (allowing them to fire employees on the basis of fair compensation, and creating a favourable environment for private initiative).

These legal reforms are 'preconditions' for successful monetary and financial law reforms in emerging economies.

Monetary and financial law reform also needs to take into account the particular economic and political circumstances of the country seeking such reform. 'Transition economies' exhibit a particular set of problems, because of the 'legacy of the past'. In the field of banking, this legacy comprises the so-called 'debt overhang', (that is, the substantial amount of 'bad loans' inherited from the communist period), the absence or inadequacy of control mechanisms and credit assessment over the state-owned enterprises which receive loans, the shift from a 'mono-bank' to a two-tiered banking system (ie, a central bank on the one hand and a commercial banking system on the other), the need to develop a system of banking supervision, an inefficient payment system, and the lack of accounting, statistics, reporting, and auditing standards.

> The transformation of socialist banking systems was bound to be difficult. While cement companies could still produce and sell cement, the services of socialist banks were of little use in a market economy. These institutions were primarily bookkeepers for the planned allocation of resources, providing 'monetary' accounts for resource flows. However, these accounts differed fundamentally from bank deposits in a market economy. There were tight restrictions on the use of the monetary balances of enterprises and households, and interest rates on these balances were set administratively. Credits were allocated to enterprises on the basis of planned investment priorities, and the repayment of credits was subject to bargaining. Bankruptcy and legal enforcement of creditor rights were non-existent. Moreover, to facilitate their role in the planning process, socialist banking systems were highly concentrated, with little separation of central banking and commercial banking activities. Some banks specialized by activity, particularly in industry, agriculture, foreign trade and household savings.[34]

In the early stages of transition, financial law reform tended to concentrate on setting up a basic infrastructure in banking and capital markets, strengthening financial supervision,[35] and building the appropriate skills in the commercial sector and the administrative authorities.[36] During the first half of the 1990s, most countries adopted new banking laws, including minimum capital and capital adequacy requirements, licensing and exit rules, and overall banking supervision arrangements. Once the basic foundations were in place and skills

---

[34] See Steven Fries and Anita Taci, *Banking Reform and Development in Transition Economies* (London: European Bank for Reconstruction and Development, 2002) 1.

[35] See generally Malcom Knight et al, *Central Bank Reforms in the Baltics, Russia and the other Countries of the Former Soviet Union* (Washington DC: IMF, 1997); Claudia Dziobek and Jan Willem van der Vossen, 'Banking Sector Reform' in Malcolm Knight et al (eds), ibid.

[36] See generally Steven M Fries and Timothy D Lane, 'Financial and Enterprise Restructuring in Emerging Market Economies' in Gerard Caprio, David Folkerts-Landau, and Timothy D Lane (eds), *Building Sound Finance in Emerging Market Economies* (Washington DC.: IMF–World Bank, 1993) 21–42 and 64–8.

have been strengthened,[37] deeper reforms were considered, in particular the recapitalization of insolvent banks and financial restructuring of heavily indebted enterprises. Securities markets were often built from scratch.[38]

Methods of law reform

The law reform process can follow different routes.[39] In this subsection I survey these various approaches, which sometimes can be combined in a reform programme. I discuss in further detail the growth of international soft law in Chapter 14.

Development of a home-grown legal system

This choice entails the development of a domestic legal system, based upon the national regulatory structures and legal tradition. From the point of view of national sovereignty and respect for the local culture, the development of an indigenous legal system has a 'certain romantic appeal' (in the words of Jackson).[40] However, not only is it costly to develop such a system, but also, given that one cannot 'reinvent the wheel' and given the uncertainty about the outcome (which can only be assessed in the long-term), it is not sensible to ignore 'foreign' legal and regulatory examples. Tested and successful solutions

---

[37] See generally Lajos Bokros 'A Perspective on Financial Sector Development in Central and Eastern Europe' in Lajos Bokros et al (eds), *Financial Transition in Europe and Central Asia— Challenges of the New Decade* (Washington DC: The World Bank, 2001).

[38] Black summarizes the institutional and legal preconditions for strong securities markets:

The complex institutions that support strong securities markets can't be built quickly. . . . Some institutions can precede market development. Others will grow only as the securities market grows. . . . Investor protective rules are only part of the framework that supports securities markets, but they can perhaps speed the development of other elements of this framework. . . . Accounting rules are a central part of information disclosure. Here, the International Accounting Standards Committee is not far from completing a workable set of International Accounting Standards that countries can draw on in preparing their own rules, or even adopt wholesale. Another important long-term step . . . is to establish or strengthen business schools (for investment bankers and accountants) and law schools (for securities lawyers and regulators). The payoff from training young people will be measured in decades. But if the investment isn't made, the decades will go by, and the country still won't have the prerequisites it needs. Significant piggybacking is feasible here; a country can establish a program (perhaps with foreign aid funding) to send top students to foreign professional schools. In developed countries, scholars often think of good corporate governance as revolving around subtle variations in director independence, the existence and role of the audit committee, constraints on the corporate control market, and the like. In developing countries, corporate governance is often much more basic. These countries need honest judges and regulators, good disclosure rules, and the beginnings of a culture of honesty before it makes sense to worry whether public company boards have, say, a majority of independent directors.

See Bernard S Black, 'The Legal and Institutional Preconditions for Strong Securities Markets' (2001) 48 UCLA Law Review 781, 847–9.

[39] Above note 29.   [40] Above note 29, 373.

elsewhere—particularly in the field of monetary law and financial regulation—are always worth some consideration.

It is possible, however, to design a system that combines the reception of some foreign laws with the development of some indigenous rules and institutions.

Local adaptation of an existing foreign legal regime

This approach, whereby existing foreign solutions are modified to meet local needs, prevails in many programmes of technical assistance and advice by foreign legal experts.[41] It has the advantage that the chosen legal regime has demonstrated its ability to function in at least one other country.[42]

Jackson refers to it as the 'domestication' of foreign regulatory structures.[43] Though foreign regulatory structures comprise both substantive rules and enforcement mechanisms, many programmes of technical assistance only cover the local adaptation of substantive rules. However, without appropriate enforcement mechanisms, the success and effectiveness of foreign substantive rules can be compromised. Jackson gives the example of the US federal securities law, which comprises not only substantive rules, but an institutional infrastructure (with the Securities and Exchange Commission, the New York Stock Exchange, and other self-regulatory organizations) and enforcement mechanisms: 'A country that adopts US federal securities laws has taken only a relatively small step toward achieving an effective system of securities regulation.'[44]

Reception of foreign law

This approach refers to the reception or importation of foreign law into a domestic legal structure. The importation of a foreign legal regime can proceed through a 'wholesale' approach or through a 'piecemeal' approach. It can encompass the incorporation of both substantive rules and enforcement mechanisms.

Law reform programmes in Eastern Europe and the former Soviet Union in the 1990s often imported legal concepts from commercial legal systems

---

[41] See Marc Gillen and Pittman Potter, 'The Convergence of Securities Laws and Implications for Developing Securities Markets' (1998) 24 North Caroline Journal of International Law and Commercial Regulation 83, 89–90; Andrew T Guzman, 'Capital Market Regulation in Developing Countries: A Proposal' (1999) 39 Virginia Journal of International Law 607, 616–23.

[42] However, this approach is not without drawbacks. Black, above note 37, points out that the country 'needs to understand that if it engages five sets of foreign advisors, they will propose five different laws, which will be inconsistent with each other and with the country's existing laws. Local draftsmen need to be closely involved in the drafting process, to ensure that the rules fit into the existing legal framework and build on existing terminology and practice to the extent possible'.

[43] Above note 29.   [44] Above note 29, 375.

anchored in the principles of a market economy as if they were 'legal transplants' (analogy with surgery) to replace malfunctioning organs.[45] The viability and success of the transplant is contingent *inter alia* on the compatibility between the socio-political structure and the legal culture between the 'donor' state and the 'recipient' state.[46] The 'recipient' or 'importing' country needs to ensure that the legal concepts or rules to be 'transplanted' fit into the existing legal framework.

In order to promote a developing country as an international financial services centre, Jackson[47] proposes—using Nepal as an example—the selective direct incorporation of a foreign (and successful) regulatory system, such as the US system of securities regulation. Jackson's approach is a variant of the method of 'importation' of foreign laws, in which both substantive rules and enforcement mechanisms are directly incorporated into a domestic legal system (as a complete 'substitute' for domestic regulation). A firm conducting business in the relevant developing country (in his example, Nepal) would simply have to comply with the rules of another designated jurisdiction with strong regulatory structures and be supervised by foreign authorities. In essence, the developing country imports financial law and regulation from another country in the same way as another country imports goods or services. Jackson favours this approach, because he believes it would enhance credibility amongst foreign investors and allow the local professionals to benefit from 'advanced rules'.[48] However, he acknowledges some of the potential objections to his proposal, such as the loss of sovereignty, political unacceptability, and delays in the development of efficient domestic institutions and rules.

Adoption of model laws and of model clauses

A model law is a set of legislative provisions that states can adopt by enacting it into domestic law. According to the website of the United Nations Commission on International Trade Law (UNCITRAL) a model law is a suggested pattern for lawmakers in national governments to consider adopting as part of their domestic legislation.[49] A model law serves as a reference point or guide, a checklist for the law reformer. A model law is not intended to serve as detailed legislation for direct incorporation into local legal systems. It should therefore combine carefully worded and relatively detailed legal text with a high degree of

---

[45] See Loukas Mistelis, 'Regulatory Aspects: Globalization, Harmonisation, Legal Transplants and Law Reform—Preliminary Remarks' in Rosa M Lastra (ed), *The Reform of the International Financial Architecture* (London: Kluwer Law International, 2001) 168–70.

[46] ibid. See also Otto Kahn-Freund, 'On Use and Misuse of Comparative Law' (1974) 37 Modern Law Review 1.

[47] See Jackson, above note 29, 373–4.   [48] Above note 29, 387–8.

[49] <http://www.uncitral.org>.

flexibility to be able to adapt to the local needs and circumstances of the country seeking reform. The advantages a model law offers are a substantial degree of harmonization and predictability for investors. This is the case for instance with the UNCITRAL model laws, such as the UNCITRAL Model Law on Electronic Commerce and Electronic Signatures.[50]

A model law can be drawn from a broad range of legal systems. For instance, in Eastern Europe, the text of an EBRD (European Bank for Reconstruction and Development) model law on secured transactions published in 1994[51] is compatible with the civil law concepts which underlie many Central and Eastern European legal systems and, at the same time, draws on common law systems which have developed many useful solutions to accommodate modern financing techniques.

The idea of the model law is advantageous as it sets a standard. However, problems arise if the model law is not adapted to the local needs and legal tradition of the country seeking reform. Model laws can be publicly available, as in the case of the EBRD model law, or limited in their availability to those countries seeking technical assistance from a given organization.

In addition to model laws (legislative instruments), there are model contracts, model clauses, and uniform rules that private contracting parties can adopt voluntarily and incorporate in their transactions. Contractual incorporation of foreign law is also identified by Jackson as a method of incorporation of foreign law into domestic transactions.[52]

The International Chamber of Commerce plays an important role in forging internationally agreed rules and standards that companies adopt voluntarily and that can be incorporated in contracts.[53]

The idea behind model contracts and clauses is to provide a sound legal

---

[50] ibid. UNCITRAL legislative texts, such as conventions, model laws, and legislative guides, may be adopted by States through the enactment of domestic legislation. UNCITRAL non-legislative texts, such as the UNCITRAL Arbitration Rules, can be used by parties to international trade contracts. Since model laws are not international conventions, there are no signatories to them. However, UNCITRAL monitors enactments of UNCITRAL Model Laws into domestic legislation. This information is provided in the 'UNCITRAL Texts and Status' area of the UNCITRAL web site. This list is updated as soon as the Secretariat is informed of changes in status or new enactments.

[51] See <http://www.ebrd.com/country/sector/law/st/modellaw/modlaw0.htm>.

[52] Above note 29, 380–1.

[53] See <http://www.iccwbo.org>. The ICC has several commissions. The Commission on Commercial Law and Practice (CLP) develops ICC model contracts and ICC model clauses which give parties a neutral framework for their contractual relationships. These contracts and clauses are carefully drafted by experts of the CLP Commission without expressing a bias for any one particular legal system.

basis upon which parties to international contracts can quickly establish an even-handed agreement acceptable to both sides.[54]

Harmonization and other techniques of regulatory convergence

Law reform in the Member States of the European Union (actual and prospective) has been a frantic activity. Two techniques of regulatory convergence have been influential in advancing the integration goals of the European Union: mutual recognition and minimum harmonization. Mutual recognition presupposes the equivalence of the objectives of national legislations and the existence of similar public interest goals. Mutual recognition implies and requires mutual trust. Mutual trust in turn is fostered through the adoption of common rules. At the EU level this has been mainly achieved through the technique of minimum harmonization or harmonization of essentials. Mutual recognition and minimum harmonization are accompanied by other pillars: home country control and the single banking licence.

The success of the 'EC banking policy' since the publication of the White Paper on the Internal Market in 1985 and the Single European Act of 1986, however, should not hinder the fact that important challenges remain ahead (as I further discuss in Chapters 10 and 11). The application of the principle of home country control (in which home country supervision of banking and financial transactions is accepted as a 'substitute' for host country supervision)[55] is starting to show 'friction points' with regard to the banking systems of the new EU Member States from Central and Eastern Europe, where a different model of cooperation and sharing of information between home and host authorities is often advocated.[56]

One interesting phenomenon about many of the Eastern European countries which have acceded or are in the course of acceding towards an enlarged European Union is that their otherwise Herculean efforts towards law reform in

---

[54] ibid.   [55] Above note 38, 379.

[56] See 'Challenges to financial regulators in the accession countries', European Shadow Financial Regulatory Committee, Statement No. 18 Budapest, 17 May 2004.

The banking sectors in the CEE countries are predominantly in private hands. Banks also appear to be profitable with healthy capital ratios in most of the countries. A striking result of the transition process is that the banking systems have become dominated by foreign-controlled banks. The share of total bank assets held by foreign-controlled banks exceeds 70 percent in most of these new member states, with one notable exception being Slovenia, where the foreign share in the state dominated banking system is less than 20 percent. The foreign control of the CEE banks, which typically are operated as subsidiaries, as well as the typically high degree of market concentration among them, create challenges for regulators with respect to the supervision of the foreign owned banks, and the development of securities markets.

The statements of the ESFRC are available at <http://www.ceps.be> and <http://www. aei.org>.

general and financial reform in particular have been further complicated by the simultaneous efforts to adopt and implement the *acquis communautaire*.[57] As observed by Padoa-Schioppa,

> While the transition economies are in the process of building political and economic systems based on those in Western Europe, the financial systems in these 'model economies' are evolving rapidly into new models. The financial landscape in Western European countries is experiencing deep economic, institutional and legal changes of its own and—being a standard of reference for transition economies— in fact it represents a rapidly moving target.[58]

It is also important to bear in mind that 'regulatory competition' in the EU implies that Member States will strive to tailor and adapt the applicable legal framework in order to satisfy business preferences and attract investment and tax revenues or even repel undesirable firms.[59] In response, private parties will engage in 'regulatory arbitrage' selecting the best regulatory environment for their activities, which in turn may lead to 'regulatory emulation' by states and regulators.

Adoption of international financial standards ('soft law')

International financial standards are typically 'soft law'. They have contributed to law reform initiatives in both developed and developing countries, as I discuss in greater detail in Chapter 14.

The essential feature of 'soft law' is that it cannot be enforced by formal legal means because it is not legally binding.[60] Hard law is binding in a coercive,

---

[57] There is no single definition of what constitutes the *acquis*: for some purposes, use is made of a very broad definition to include, in addition to the treaties, regulations, directives and decisions, the Case Law of the Court of Justice, and non-binding Acts such as resolutions and recommendations. For this reason, the Commission has recently issued a Communication to the Council, the European Parliament, the European Economic and Social Committee, and the Committee of the Regions in which it advocates a narrower definition, encompassing primary law and binding secondary legislation (ie, regulations, directives, and decisions in the sense of Art 240 of the EC Treaty). See Commission of the European Communities, *Updating and Simplifying the Community Acquis* (Brussels: Commission of the European Communities, 2003), (Communication to the Council, the European Parliament, the European Economic and Social Committee, and the Committee of the Regions of 11 February 2003), COM(2003)71 final. This body of legislation amounted at the end of 2002 to 97,000 pages of the Official Journal.

[58] See Tommaso Padoa-Schioppa, 'Financial Integration in Western Europe: Can the East Catch Up?' in Lajos Bokros et al (eds), above note 36, 7.

[59] See generally Roger Van den Bergh, 'Regulatory Competition or Harmonization of Laws? Guidelines for the European Regulator' in Alain Marciano and Jean-Michel Josselin (eds), *The Economics of Harmonizing European Law* (Cheltenham: Edward Elgar, 2002); Stephen Woolcock, 'Competition among Rules in the Single European Market' in William Bratton et al (eds), *International Regulatory Competition and Coordination: Perspectives on Economic Regulation in Europe and the United States* (Oxford: Clarendon Press, 1996).

[60] See Mario Giovanoli, 'A New Architecture for the Global Financial Markets: Legal Aspects of International Financial Standard Setting' in Mario Giovanoli (ed), *International Monetary Law. Issues for the New Millenium* (Oxford: Oxford University Press, 2000) 35.

externally imposed way. Soft law is observed in a voluntary, self-imposed way. Enforcement is the key element in distinguishing between hard and soft law.

The growth of international financial standards fills a legal vacuum. In the absence of a formal international regulator, international financial soft law standards are agreed among regulators, supervisors, or other national authorities and groups of experts. The Basel Committee on Banking Supervision, the International Organization of Securities Commissions (IOSCO), the International Association of Insurance Supervisors (IAIS), and others have become important 'international financial standard setters'. Their rules are addressed to national authorities who in turn undertake the obligation to implement them in their national jurisdictions.

International financial standards also steer the direction of financial law reform in those emerging economies that include the implementation of a particular set of standards as a 'condition' under an IMF programme of (conditional) financial assistance, an important issue which I further explore in Chapter 13.

PART II

DEVELOPMENTS AT THE EU LEVEL

6

HISTORY OF MONETARY INTEGRATION IN EUROPE

> Europe will not be created at a stroke or emerge fully formed; it will be created by tangible achievements whose first effect is to generate a spirit of solidarity.
>
> Robert Schuman, Paris Conference, 9 May 1950, based on a memorandum prepared by Jean Monnet

A. Introduction

The European Union is often quoted as a paradigm of an integration process. The gradual development of a common market, the progressive liberalization of economic activities, the free movement of goods, persons, services, and capital, the achievement of monetary union, and the further ideals of political integration have often been hailed by other countries and organizations as an interesting development of an 'ever closer union' amongst the citizens of a regional area.

173

According to its own website,[1]

> The European Union (EU) is a family of democratic European countries, committed to working together for peace and prosperity. It is not a State intended to replace existing states, but it is more than any other international organisation. The EU is, in fact, unique. Its Member States have set up common institutions to which they delegate some of their sovereignty so that decisions on specific matters of joint interest can be made democratically at European level. This pooling of sovereignty is also called European integration.

The history of the European Community (EC),[2] as the history of any other organization, is a history of successes and failures. Sometimes, the EC has been praised for its achievements, some other times it has been criticized for its shortcomings or for its excessive ambitions or for its alleged democratic deficit. Overall, the positive aspects of integration outweigh the negative ones, as evidenced by the appeal the Community exerts over prospective members. However, the momentum towards further integration suffered a serious setback in 2005, with the suspension of the ratification process of the Treaty establishing a Constitution for Europe (hereinafter, the proposed EU Constitution), which had been signed in Rome in October 2004.[3]

---

[1] <http://www.europa.eu.int>.

[2] *NOTE*. Though the terms *European Union* (EU) and *European Community* (EC) are not the same, they are sometimes used indistinctly. The term European Union was formally introduced by the 1992 Treaty on European Union (the so-called Maastricht Treaty), whose Art A stated that the Union was founded on the three existing European Communities, supplemented by the policies and forms of intergovernmental cooperation established in the [Maastricht] Treaty (common foreign and security policy and cooperation in the fields of justice and home affairs). Art G of the Maastricht Treaty renamed the European Economic Community as the European Community: 'Throughout the Treaty the term European Economic Community shall be replaced by the term European Community.' (As acknowledged, the EEC was one of the three European Communities established by Germany, France, Italy, Belgium, Luxembourg, and the Netherlands in the 1950s; the other two being the EURATOM, or European Atomic Energy Community, and the European Coal and Steel Community.) The 1997 Treaty of Amsterdam amended both the EC Treaty and the Treaty on European Union and renumbered both. The Treaty of Nice signed on 26 February 2001 further amended the Treaties. The Treaty of Nice entered into force on 1 February 2003. *The consolidated version of the Treaty establishing the European Community (EC Treaty) and of the Treaty on European Union (EU Treaty), incorporating the amendments made by the Treaty of Nice, is to be found in the Official Journal of 14 December 2002 (No C 325).* The complex and intricate structure of the European Union makes it difficult sometimes for legislators and commentators to make the correct distinctions.

[3] The Treaty establishing a Constitution for Europe, signed in Rome on 29 October 2004, is available in the Official Journal No C 310 of 16 December 2004. The proposed EU Constitution was thrown into a legal limbo following the rejection of the Treaty in referenda in France (28 May 2005) and the Netherlands (1 June 2005). The suspension of the ratification process (according to the declaration of the European Council Brussels summit on June 16–17 2005 to allow for a 'period of reflection') does not equate to the abandonment altogether of the Constitution. The text of the Treaty remains a legal document of value to refer to, also with a view to its possible entry into force or the taking over of parts of it in other treaty texts later on. If ever ratified by all EU Member States, the Treaty establishing a Constitution for Europe aims to replace all existing Treaties, except for the Treaty establishing the EURATOM, according to its Art IV–437.

Monetary union is considered to be one of the European Union's greatest successes. Though European Monetary Union (EMU)[4] is often justified on economic grounds, the political will to achieve a single currency in Europe has been the driving force behind integration in this field. There are, however, some clouds on the horizon following the events in 2005 and some doubts about the sustainability of the monetary union in the long run have been revived.[5]

The schedule of changes and the deadlines foreseen for the different stages to be accomplished in the gradual realization of economic, monetary, and political integration have not always been fulfilled. However, the chronological sequence of the steps to be taken in the building up of the Community offers a valuable experience for other regional groupings in the world pursuing similar integration patterns. Even the delays in the accomplishment of some objectives are instructive with regard to the understanding of what works and what does not work in an integration process. The law has been a fundamental instrument in the progressive achievement of the goals of the European Union.

In the ensuing sections, I analyse the history of monetary union, the stages of European integration (customs union, common market/internal market, monetary union, economic union, and political union), the theory of optimum currency areas (OCAs), and the impact of EMU upon other regional groupings.

B. Progress Towards Monetary Union in Europe

The history of European monetary cooperation is linked to the history of international monetary cooperation (the subject of Chapter 12). The Bretton Woods par value regime provided an anchor for international monetary stability until its demise in the early 1970s. It is no coincidence, in my opinion, that the real momentum for monetary integration came after the international anchor ceased to exist (though the Werner Report predated the break-up of Bretton Woods).

In the following paragraphs, I bring together international and European

---

With regard to the use of the terms EC and EU, Art IV–438 paragraph 1 states: 'The European Union established by this Treaty shall be the successor to the European Union established by the Treaty on European Union and to the European Community.' However, the term Community is still used in some other provisions of the proposed EU Constitution, such as Art I–1.

[4] EMU is an acronym that stands both for 'European Monetary Union' (as used in this context) and for 'Economic and Monetary Union', a meaning which is historically and legally correct. See eg, the reference to 'economic and monetary union' in Art 2 EC Treaty.

[5] See eg, Wolfang Munchau, 'Is the Euro forever? As the strains turn to pain, its foundations look far from secure', *Financial Times*, 8 June 2005. See also Daniel Gros, Thomas Mayer, and Angel Ubide, 'EMU at risk', Seventh Annual Report of the CEPS Macroeconomic Policy Group, Centre for European Policy Studies, June 2005, at <http://www.ceps.be>.

developments in order to understand the progress from monetary cooperation towards monetary integration in Europe. Today, EMU is a reality amongst those Member States that have surrendered national monetary sovereignty and that are tied together by unified institutional arrangements: the European Central Bank as the central bank of the Community and the euro as the single currency.

The early years

After the Second World War, and with the formal establishment of the International Monetary Fund (IMF) and the World Bank (International Bank for Reconstruction and Development, IBRD),[6] the emerging system paved the way for a relatively long historical period of international monetary stability. The *par value* regime, often referred to as the Bretton Woods regime, meant that the value of currency was defined in terms of gold or, alternatively, in terms of the US dollar of 1 July 1944, which had a fixed gold value (one ounce of gold was equal to $35).

The IMF mandate was to maintain the good order of this predictable and 'stable' international monetary system, by enforcing rules about adjustment in international monetary relations and by providing temporary resources to deal with short-term balance of payments problems.

The IMF had a much greater influence upon European developments than the IBRD. It was the Marshall Plan rather than the World Bank that played the major role in the reconstruction and recovery of war-torn European economies. US Secretary of State George Marshall unveiled the 'European Recovery Program' (which became known as the Marshall Plan) in his famous Harvard commencement speech in June 1947, where he announced a programme of massive financial assistance to Europe. The Marshall Plan, which was supervised by the US Economic Cooperation Administration (ECA), contributed to the establishment of a multilateral system of European payments: the European Payments Union in 1950. The EPU was a mechanism for settling payments amongst seventeen West European Countries: Austria, Belgium, Denmark, France, West Germany, Greece, Holland, Iceland, Ireland, Italy, Luxembourg, Norway, Portugal, Sweden, Switzerland, Turkey, and the United Kingdom.[7]

---

[6] The IMF and the World Bank were set up in 1944 and started operations in 1946. I have discussed the origins of these institutions in Rosa M Lastra, 'The Bretton Woods Institutions in the XXIst Century' in Rosa M Lastra (ed), *The Reform of the International Financial Architecture* (London: Kluwer Law International, 2001) 67–90.

[7] The European Payments Union was a clearing arrangement to which creditors and debtors in the various countries participating in the arrangement could settle their claims with one another without the use of foreign exchange reserves. A debtor to a foreign creditor was able to pay in his local currency the equivalent of his foreign debt into an account with his national

The EPU was a clearing union which encouraged movement towards full currency convertibility. After the creation of the Organisation for European Economic Cooperation (OEEC), the Bank for International Settlements operated the EPU as an agent for the OEEC.[8] By 1958, member currencies became de facto fully convertible, ie, transferable between each other (*de jure* in 1961 on formal acceptance of Art VIII of the IMF Articles of Agreement).

Against this background of international monetary stability, the drafters of the 1957 Treaty of Rome Establishing the European Economic Community (the EEC Treaty) only included scarce references to the concept of 'money' in the original EEC Treaty.[9] Indeed, the few provisions dealing with coordination of national monetary policies (Arts 104–109 EEC Treaty) are included in a chapter dedicated to 'balance of payments' (Ch 3 EEC Treaty).

The objectives of the Community were to promote a harmonious development of economic activities, a continuous and balanced expansion, an increase in stability, an accelerated raising of the standard of living, and closer relations between the states belonging to it, and these objectives were to be achieved by establishing a common market and progressively approximating the economic policies of Member States.[10]

---

central bank. At the same time, this process would be repeated in the country in which the foreign debt was owed: ie a local debtor paying an amount of local currency that was the equivalent of his foreign debt into an account with his national central bank. The upshot was that the national central banks would then satisfy the debts owed to their respective local creditors, who tender to them their claims denominated in foreign currencies while receiving in satisfaction the equivalent in local currencies. The two central banks maintained accounts on their books in each other's favour. In the EPU, any foreign currency that one member country earned in transactions with another member country could be utilised for payments to another member country. Each central bank had an account with the EPU and debts had to be settled. The United States contributed, through the Marshall plans, capital funds to facilitate the settlement of member country debts to the EPU in gold and dollars.

See Robert Effros, 'The Maastricht Treaty, Independence of the Central Bank and Implementing Legislation' in Tomás Baliño and Carlo Cotarelli (eds), *Frameworks for Monetary Stability. Policy Issues and Country Experiences* (Washington DC: IMF, 1994) 280–1.

[8] The OEEC was formed to distribute Marshall Plan funds. By the end of the 1950s its objectives had been largely achieved. The OEEC was succeeded by the OECD. The convention establishing the OECD (Organisation for Economic Cooperation and Development) was signed on 14 December 1961.

[9] The Treaty of Rome was signed by France, West Germany, Italy, and the three Benelux countries. There was a reference to stable prices in Art 104 EEC and to monetary coordination in Art 105. For a description of the Community monetary coordination during the Bretton Woods monetary order and its reactions to the breakdown of the Bretton Woods system, see René Smits, *The European Central Bank—Institutional Aspects* (The Hague: Kluwer Law International, 1997) 10–14. René Smits emphasizes the reliance on the Bretton Woods regime of the EEC Treaty negotiators and hence the scarce references to the concept of 'money' in the original EEC Treaty.

[10] See Art 2 EEC. Art 3 EEC further specified the activities and policies to be carried out by the Community in the pursuit of its overarching objectives, including 'the abolition, as between

The liberalization of trade in goods, services, and capital requires the liberalization of cross-border payments.[11] However, under the original Treaty of Rome, the liberalization of cross-border payments did not mean that all restrictions on the movements of capital were to be abolished. Capital movements were not fully liberalized.[12] Under Article 67 EEC Treaty, Member States were to 'progressively abolish between themselves all restrictions on the movement of capital belonging to persons resident in the Member States and any discrimination based on the nationality or on the place of residence of the parties or on the place where such capital is invested'.[13] The influence of the Bretton Woods regime in these provisions is clear, since the IMF Articles of Agreement provide for current account convertibility, but not capital account convertibility. The IMF jurisdiction over payments extends only to restrictions on current international transactions; controls on international movements of capital are not subject to approval by the Fund.[14]

Member States of the EEC were required to liberalize capital movements to the extent necessary to ensure the proper functioning of the common market, which was a matter to be assessed by the Council in accordance with Article 69 of the EEC Treaty.[15] Similarly, in relation to cross-border payments, the provisions relating to exchange rate and monetary policy were intended to be a matter of intergovernmental concern among the Member States and were not intended to create rights enforceable by private persons.[16]

Proctor notes that in those early days the provisions of the Treaty of Rome dealing with capital flows and balance of payments 'began life in a relatively rudimentary form' and attributes the lack of further integration by way of

---

Member States, of obstacles to freedom of movement of goods, persons, services and capital' and 'the application of procedures by which the economic policies of Member States could be co-ordinated and disequilibria in their balances of payments remedied'.

[11] According to Art 106 EEC, Member States were under the obligation to grant any foreign exchange or other approvals required to authorize payments in connection with supplies of goods, services, or capital by residents of other Member States.

[12] See Arts 67–73 of the EEC. See generally, Sideek Mohamed, *European Community Law on the Free Movement of Capital and the EMU* (The Hague: Kluwer Law International, 1999) ch 2.

[13] Art 67 EEC. The implementation of Art 67 was to be achieved by the Council acting on a proposal from the Commission and after consultation with the Monetary Committee.

[14] For a legal analysis of these issues, which I further discuss in Chapter 13, see Cynthia Lichtenstein, 'International Jurisdiction over International Capital Flows and the Role of the IMF: plus ça change' in Mario Giovanoli (ed.), *International Monetary Law* (Oxford: Oxford University Press, 2000), 61–80. Art XXX(d) of the IMF Articles of Agreement defines 'payments for current transactions'. However, the distinction between current and capital transactions is 'conceptually and operationally awkward' according to the late Manuel Guitián, 'The Unique Nature of the Responsibilities of the International Monetary Fund', IMF Pamphlet Series No. 46 (Washington DC: IMF, 1993) 31.

[15] See Case 203/80 *Re Casati* [1981] ECR 2595.

[16] See Case 9/73 *Schlüter v HZA Lörrach* [1973] ECR 1135.

judicial intervention from the European Court of Justice to the lack of direct effect of the provisions on capital movements and exchange controls of Articles 67–71.[17]

In 1958, a Monetary Committee with advisory status was established under Article 105(2) EEC. In 1964, the Committee of Governors of the Central Banks of the Member States was established in order to promote cooperation between the Central Banks of the Member States.[18] The seeds of the future institutional arrangements for monetary integration had already been planted.[19]

In February 1968, the Commission proposed that Member States commit themselves to adjusting their exchange rate parities only by common agreement and to considering the elimination of margins on each other's currencies around the established parities.[20] Making use of Article 105 EEC, the Commission and Council began a series of attempts to alleviate monetary crises in particular Member States and to coordinate economic and monetary policy in order to achieve greater stability within the Community.[21] In that context, on 12 February 1969, the 'Barre Report', named after Raymond Barre, then Governor of the central bank of France, called for concerted economic policies for the purpose of ensuring the attainment of agreed medium-term objectives in the field of monetary coordination. The Council agreed with many features of the Barre Report and committed members to prior consultation before a member altered its economic policies in such a way as to have an important impact on other members.[22]

In a related move, the Committee of Governors of Central Banks agreed on 9 February 1970 to provide lines of credit to support Member States in times of monetary crisis.[23]

---

[17] See Charles Proctor, *The Euro and the Financial Markets* (Bristol: Jordans, 1999) 6–7.

[18] See EEC Decision 64/300 of 8 May 1964 (as amended in 1990). The Committee of Governors subsequently assumed responsibility for the operation of the Exchange Rate Mechanism upon the establishment of the European Monetary System in 1979 and on 1 July 1990 became responsible for the coordination of monetary policies of Member States until dissolved at the beginning of the second stage of the EMU, as I explain below.

[19] See Robert A Mundell, 'The European Monetary System 50 Years after Bretton Woods: A Comparison Between Two Systems' (Paper presented at Project Europe 1985–95, the tenth edition of the 'Incontri di Rocca Salimbeni' meetings, in Siena, 25 November 1994) available at <http://www.columbia.edu/~ram15/ABrettwds.htm>; Juan Luis Millán Pereira, 'Economic Restructuring and the European Monetary Union' (2001) 9 University of Miami International and Comparative Law Review 45, 52–3.

[20] See Mundell, above note 19.

[21] See Roger J Goebel, 'European Economic and Monetary Union: Will the EMU Ever Fly?' (1998) 4 Columbia Journal of European Law 249, 249–56.

[22] ibid.   [23] ibid.

The Werner Report: The seeds of the three-stage approach to EMU

The Heads of State and Government of the countries of the EEC meeting at The Hague in December 1969 decided that the Community would have to be transformed progressively into an economic and monetary union.[24] A committee was appointed, under the chairmanship of the then Prime Minister of Luxembourg, Pierre Werner, to study the possibilities of such union. The committee submitted its final report, named after its Chairman, in October 1970.

The Werner Report was the first concrete proposal for monetary integration in Europe.[25] It envisaged the achievement of economic and monetary union within ten years according to a three-stage plan. The ultimate goal was to achieve full liberalization of capital movements, the irrevocable fixing of parities, and even the replacement of national currencies with a single currency. The report also recommended that the coordination of economic policies be strengthened and guidelines for national budgetary policies drawn up.

In the words of the Report, 'the Group has not sought to construct an ideal system in the abstract. It has set out rather to determine the elements that are indispensable to the existence of a complete economic and monetary union. The union as it is described here represents the minimum that must be done, and is a stage in a dynamic evolution which the pressure of events and political will, can model in a different way.'[26] The Report set out the necessary elements of the envisaged monetary union in the following terms:

> A monetary union implies inside its boundaries the total and irreversible convertibility of currencies, the elimination of margins of fluctuation in exchange rates, the irrevocable fixing of parity rates and the complete liberation of movements of capital. It may be accompanied by the maintenance of national monetary symbols or the establishment of a sole Community currency. From the technical point of view, the choice between these two solutions may seem immaterial, but considerations of a psychological and political nature militate in favour of the adoption of sole currency which would confirm the irreversibility of the venture.[27]

The Report required that the essential features of public budgets (including variations in their volume, the size of balances and the methods of financing) would have to be decided at the Community level. It also stated that regional and structural policies should no longer be exclusively within the jurisdiction of the member countries.[28]

---

[24] See Pereira, above note 19.

[25] See Report to the Council and the Commission on the Realisation by Stages of Economic and Monetary Union in the Community, (Luxembourg, 8 October 1970, Supplement to Bulletin 11/1970 of the European Communities), available at <http://aei.pitt.edu/archive/00001002/01/monetary_werner_final.pdf>.

[26] ibid 9.   [27] ibid 10.   [28] ibid 12.

The Werner Report led to adoption of a Resolution by the Council and the representatives of the Governments of the Member States on 22 March 1971.[29] Although unable to agree on some of the key recommendations of the Report, the Six gave their approval in principle to the introduction of EMU in three stages.[30] The first stage, involving the narrowing of currency fluctuation margins, was to be launched on an experimental basis and did not entail any commitment regarding the continuation of the process. As a forerunner to the future Community system for the central banks, a European Fund for monetary cooperation was proposed.

The 'snake'

In March 1972, the Six introduced—through a Council Resolution of March 1972[31]—the so-called 'snake in the tunnel', that is, a mechanism for the managed floating of currencies (the 'snake') within narrow margins of fluctuation against the dollar (the 'tunnel').

In the words of the Resolution,

> as a first step towards the creation of its own monetary zone within the framework of the international system, the Council requests the Central Banks of the Member States, using to the full the margins of fluctuation allowed on a world wide scale by the International Monetary Fund, to reduce by stages the difference which exists at any given time between the highest and the lowest rates of exchange of the currencies of the Member States.[32]

In accordance with the Member States' response to the Werner Report, the long-term objective of the new arrangement remained the elimination of any margin of fluctuation between the currencies of the Community as the first stage of full monetary integration.[33] Member States agreed that exchange rate fluctuations between the national currencies and the dollar were to be kept within 0.75 per cent, which meant that the currencies of the Member States would fluctuate by at most 1.5 per cent around their bilateral central rates.

The maintenance of fluctuation margins was mainly to be safeguarded by intervention in currency markets, which was the responsibility of the Central Banks

---

[29] See Smits, above note 9, 15. A Council Decision adopted also on 22 March 1971 initiated the strengthening of the cooperation between the central banks. See Council Decision 71/142/EEC [1971] OJ L 73/14.

[30] Resolution of the Council and of the Representatives of the Governments of the Member States of 22 March 1971 on the attainment by stages of economic and monetary union in the Community [1971] OJ C28/1. This is often referred to as the '1971 EMU Resolution'.

[31] Resolution of the Council and of the Representatives of the Governments of the Member States of 21 March 1972 on the application of the Resolution of 22 March 1971 on the attainment by stages of economic and monetary union in the Community [1972] OJ C38/3.

[32] ibid.   [33] ibid.

of the Member States.[34] It was argued that the attempt to control intra-Community exchange rate volatility would serve the objective of the EMU by promoting trade in goods and services and facilitating capital movements. It would also reduce the cost of servicing the Common Agricultural Policy, a crucial political concern.

Thrown off course by the oil crises, the weakness of the dollar, and the differences in economic policy, the 'snake' lost most of its members in less than two years and was finally reduced to a 'mark' area comprising West Germany, the Benelux countries, and Denmark.[35]

The 'snake' was a forerunner of the Exchange Rate Mechanism of the European Monetary System, further discussed below.

The European Monetary Cooperation Fund

The European Monetary Cooperation Fund (EMCF) was established in 1973 to promote the narrowing of the margins of fluctuation between the currencies of the Member States.[36] The EMCF facilitated the central bank cooperation required for the functioning of the 'snake'. The EMCF was endowed with separate legal personality and had purely technical functions.[37]

The EMCF provided for the administration and settlement of claims resulting from interventions in the foreign exchange market. The Fund was entrusted with three interrelated tasks: the promotion of the proper functioning of the progressive narrowing of the margins of fluctuation of the Community currencies against each other, the conduct of interventions in Community currencies on the exchange markets, and the carrying out of settlements between central banks leading to a concerted policy on reserves.[38]

The collapse of the Bretton Woods par value system

In the early 1970s and despite the initial acceptance of the Werner Plan by the Member States, the political and economic momentum for further monetary integration was lost. A turning point in this 'loss of momentum' was the announcement by US President Nixon on 15 August 1971 that the US would no longer carry its obligation to deliver gold for US dollars at the parity

---

[34] ibid.

[35] See generally Proctor, above note 17, 10.

[36] See Regulation (EEC) No 907/73 of the Council of 3 April 1973 establishing a European Monetary Cooperation Fund [1973] OJ L89/2.

[37] See Smits, above note 9, 19. Smits recalls (ibid at 12) that Jean Monnet, one of the founding fathers of European integration, proposed a European Reserve Fund in the late 1950s.

[38] Above note 36, Art 2.

which had been established in 1944 and applied since the IMF started operations. According to Mundell,[39] 'the biggest casualty of the breakup of the international monetary system was the plan for European Monetary Union put into motion at the Hague Summit in 1969'.

The abandonment of the par value regime signified a worldwide shift to flexible exchange rates. Within the European Community, the maintenance of narrow fluctuation margins among the currencies participating in the 'currency snake' arrangement became increasingly difficult. The 'snake' began to unravel. The attempts to preserve some elements of the Bretton Woods system in Europe largely failed and the 'snake' became transformed into a Deutschmark zone after the withdrawal of the pound, the lira, the punt, and the French franc.[40]

Inflation, oil crises, instability, and economic slowdown shaped the international economic landscape in the 1970s and, with an uncertain future, countries became more 'inward looking'. When the European Commission proposed the move into stage two as suggested by the Werner Report, there was no agreement at the ECOFIN Council and the project of EMU as envisaged in the Werner Report was abandoned in December 1974.

The European Monetary System

The par value regime had been an external 'anchor' of monetary stability. With its demise, currency instability became a feature of the European and global economic order. The need for an 'anchor' became a matter of serious concern for European policy makers in the late 1970s.

In 1977, Roy Jenkins, President of the European Commission at that time, recommended progress in the monetary area. In 1978, Helmut Schmidt of Germany and Valéry Giscard d'Estaing of France proposed a 'zone of monetary stability in Europe', which became known as the European Monetary System (EMS). The European Council, after meeting in Bremen, issued a communiqué on 7 July 1978 announcing its intention to create the European Monetary System as an institutional arrangement to establish closer monetary cooperation leading to a zone of monetary stability in Europe. A Resolution of the Council on 5 December 1978 established the European Monetary System and an

---

[39] See Robert Mundell, 'Optimum Currency Areas', extended version of a luncheon speech presented at a 'Conference on Optimum Currency Areas,' Tel Aviv University, 5 December 1997, at <http://www.columbia.edu/~ram15/eOCATAviv4.html>.

[40] See Loukas Tsoukalis, *The New European Economy Revisited* (Oxford: Oxford University Press, 1997) 38.

Agreement of 13 March 1979 among the central banks of the EC set forth the operating procedures.[41]

Despite the weak legal value of this Resolution,[42] the EMS became the primary arrangement of monetary cooperation in the EC from its inception to the advent of European Monetary Union. The EMS was a 'creature' of the Franco-German alliance, an alliance which has often been regarded as the 'engine' of European integration.

The EMS had three fundamental objectives: to stabilize the exchange rates in order to rectify the existing instability, to reduce inflation, and to prepare for eventual European monetary unification through cooperation.

The EMS consisted of two main elements. First, the establishment of the European Currency Unit (ECU) as a basket of currencies. The share of each of the participating currencies in the basket was determined by the percentage of their state's contribution to the GNP of the Community. The value of the composite currency derived from the addition of all the currency elements.[43] The ECU was not legal tender but it served as unit of account in Community affairs, as a means of payment between the monetary authorities in the Community, and as a store of value (reserves at the central banks).

The second element of the EMS was the establishment of the exchange rate and intervention mechanism (ERM). The ERM was conceived as a system of fixed but adjustable exchange rates (a successor to the snake). The ERM was a parity grid of bilateral exchange rates, with interventions limiting the swings in currency prices between pre-announced floors and ceilings.[44] The currencies could fluctuate against each other within a maximum band of plus or minus 2.25 per cent (or six per cent for currencies at the beginning of their participation in the exchange rate mechanism). The central banks were committed to intervening in

---

[41] See Joseph Gold, 'Legal Models for the International Regulation of Exchange Rates' (1984) 82 Michigan Law Review 1533, 1546–8.

[42] See Smits, above note 9, 24–5.

The monetary arrangements agreed before the conclusion of the Maastricht Treaty were deliberately left outside the sphere of Community law proper. The basic text of the EMS is a European Council Resolution. Since the European Council had no position [at the time] under Community law, and a resolution has no binding character, the status of the fundamental instrument laying down the EMS is uncertain, to say the least. Some elements of the EMS were only laid in secondary legislation, while others were regulated by central bank agreements.

[43] All Community currencies were represented in the basket until it was frozen on 1 August 1994. This explains why the currencies of the new Member States acceding on 1 January 1995 were not represented. The basket was revised at a five-year interval; the freezing of its composition derives from Art 118 EC Treaty, inserted by the Maastricht Treaty. I am grateful to René Smits for observations on this point.

[44] See Smits, above note 9, 21.

order to attempt to maintain their currencies within the established fluctuation margins. The central bank of each participant had an obligation to deposit with the EMCF 20 per cent of its US dollars and gold holdings in renewable swaps of three months' duration. In return, the EMCF issued ECUs to the participant. The ERM set for each one of the participating currencies a central exchange rate against the ECU. That, in turn, gave them central cross-rates against one another.

An important contemporaneous development at the international level was the Second Amendment of the IMF Articles of Agreement of 1 April 1978, which established the right of members to adopt exchange rate arrangements of their choice, including (i) the maintenance by a member of a value for its currency in terms of the special drawing right or another denominator, other than gold, selected by the member, or (ii) cooperative arrangements by which members maintain the value of their currencies in relation to the value of the currency or currencies of other members, or (iii) other exchange arrangements of a member's choice.[45] This discretion is, of course, without prejudice to the overarching obligations of IMF Members (a) to endeavour to direct their economic and financial policies toward the objective of fostering orderly economic growth with reasonable price stability, with due regard to its circumstances; (b) to seek to promote stability by fostering orderly underlying economic and financial conditions and a monetary system that does not tend to produce erratic disruptions; and, crucially, (c) to avoid manipulating exchange rates or the international monetary system in order to prevent effective balance of payments adjustment or to gain an unfair competitive advantage over other members.[46] I further discuss these obligations in Chapter 13.

In 1987, the EMS rules were strengthened through an agreement reached in Basel and Nyborg on monetary policy cooperation.[47] However, and despite this 'strengthening', speculative attacks in September 1992 led to the exit from the ERM of the British pound and to the temporary suspension of intervention limits for the Italian lira. Further turbulence in the foreign exchange markets in 1993 led the ministers of finance and central bank governors of the Community to adjust the ERM in August 1993, widening the fluctuation margins from plus or minus 2.25 per cent to plus or minus fifteen per cent (although the British pound and the Italian lira remained outside the system).[48]

---

[45] See Articles of Agreement of the IMF, Art IV, s 2.   [46] ibid, Art IV, s 1.

[47] For the press notice of 18 September 1987 with regard to this Basle–Nyborg Agreement see the Bundesbank Annual Report 1987, 68. The Basle–Nyborg agreement is described in pages 67–72. See also Smits, above note 9, 26.

[48] Communiqué of the European Community, 2 August 1993. On 25 November 1996, the lira re-entered the ERM.

The 1992 Maastricht Treaty on European Union included membership of the ERM of the EMS in two of the four criteria of economic convergence that Member States must meet in order to qualify for monetary union.[49]

The ERM has 'survived' in a revised form (called ERM II) as an exchange rate mechanism between the euro and the national currencies of the countries not participating in the euro area. An agreement of 1 September 1998 between the European Central Bank and the National Central Banks of the Member States outside the euro area laid down the operating procedures for the 'exchange rate mechanism in stage three of Economic and Monetary Union'.[50] To join the euro area, the aspiring EU Member States must first join the ERM II for two years before adopting the euro.[51]

Developments in the 1980s: The Single European Act

The Single European Act,[52] which was signed in Luxembourg and The Hague in 1986 and came into force on 1 July 1987, was the first major amendment of the founding treaties of the European Communities. The Single European Act (SEA) was the institutional catalyst for the revival of the internal market project. It also demonstrated that further European integration was not unrealistic.

Once the Community had settled some internal disputes in the early 1980s (budget, UK financial contribution, and others), it was time for new political initiatives to advance the European project. With regard to the monetary aspect of this project, Article 20 of the SEA inserted a new chapter in the EC Treaty on 'Cooperation in Economic and Monetary Policy'. Under a new Article 102A of the EEC Treaty, Member States were required to cooperate in order to ensure the convergence of economic and monetary policies taking into account the experience acquired in cooperation within the framework of the European Monetary System.

The SEA gave fresh impetus to the liberalization of capital movements. A single market in financial services requires free flow of capital, and this liberalization is a precondition to advance to monetary integration.

---

[49] See Art 121 EC Treaty. *References to the EC Treaty are references to the consolidated version of the Treaty establishing the European Community (EC Treaty), OJ C325 of 14 December 2002.* See above note 2.

[50] OJ C 345 of 13 November 1998. This agreement was amended on 14 September 2000 with regard to the adoption of the single currency in Greece from 1 January 2001. See OJ C362 of 16 December 2000. It was further amended with a view to the new accession states in 2004. See the Agreement of 29 April 2004 in OJ C135, 13 May 2004, 3.

[51] See Arts 121(1) EC Treaty and 122 EC Treaty.

[52] Single European Act (1986) [1986] OJ L169/1.

The 'Delors Report'

The establishment of the internal market brought a new stimulus to the objective of further integration. On the one hand, the decision to complete the single market gave renewed impetus to the view that 'one market needs one money'[53] (though in the end the driving force supporting the argument that a single currency was a necessary condition for a successful single market was political rather than economic). On the other hand, the decision to lift exchange controls, through the adoption of the 1988 Directive on the liberalization of capital movements,[54] triggered concerns about the possibility that the ERM's fixed but adjustable exchange rates would generate speculative movements that could lead to exchange rate realignments.[55] This led some economists at the time to warn against the so-called 'inconsistent quartet' of policy objectives: free trade, full capital mobility, pegged (or fixed) exchange rates, and independent national monetary policies.[56] At least one of these objectives had to go. The only long-term solution to this inconsistency—as Padoa-Schioppa suggested—was to complement the internal market with monetary union,[57] thus abandoning national control over domestic monetary policies.

The renewed interest in monetary union (which coincided with an economic upturn in Europe) was given an official seal of approval in June 1988, when the Hanover European Council concluded that 'in adopting the Single Act, the Member States of the Community confirmed the objective of progressive realization of economic and monetary union.'[58] The Heads of State meeting in the Council set up a committee to examine the means of achieving the economic and monetary union, the so-called Delors Committee (named after its Chairman).[59]

---

[53] See Commission of the European Communities (Directorate General for Economic and Financial Affairs), 'One Market, One Money: An Evaluation of the Potential Benefits and Costs of Forming an Economic and Monetary Union' 44 European Economy, October 1990.

[54] This Directive 88/361/EEC of 24 June 1988 adopted the principle of liberalization of capital movements both between Member States and with third countries (*erga omnes* liberalization). Transitional arrangements were introduced for Spain, Portugal, Greece, and Ireland, which were allowed to maintain restrictions until 31 December 1992. (An extension not exceeding three years was granted to Portugal and Greece: the latter availed itself of this possibility up to 16 May 1994.)

[55] See Peter Kenen, *EMU and ESCB after Maastricht* (London: Financial Markets Group of the London School of Economics, 1992) 15.

[56] ibid.

[57] ibid. See generally Tommaso Padoa-Schioppa, *The Road to Monetary Union in Europe: The Emperor, the Kings and the Genies* (Oxford: Oxford University Press, 2000).

[58] Conclusions of the Hanover European Council, DN DOC/88/8, 28 June 1988.

[59] The other members of the 'Delors Committee' were the governors of the national central bank, a second Commissioner, and three outside experts: Niels Thygesen, Alexandre Lamfalussy, and Miguel Boyer.

While Jean Monnet is rightly considered as one of the founding fathers of European integration, Jacques Delors—the then President of the European Commission—can surely be regarded as a founding father of EMU.

The 'Delors Report', the *Report on Economic and Monetary Union in the European Community*, was published in April 1989.[60] It proposed the introduction of economic and monetary union in three stages, including an institutional framework to allow policy to be decided and executed at the Community level in economic areas of direct relevance to the functioning of EMU. The Report proposed the creation of a new monetary institution, namely the European System of Central Banks (ESCB), which would become responsible for formulating and implementing monetary policy as well as managing external exchange rate policy.[61]

Stage One of the development of EMU would involve the increased cooperation between central banks with relation to monetary policy, the removal of obstacles to financial integration, the monitoring of national economic policies, and the coordination of budgetary policy.[62] Stage Two would be the preparatory stage for the final phase of EMU. It would see the establishment of the ESCB, the progressive transfer of monetary policy to European institutions and the narrowing of margins of fluctuations in the currencies within the ERM.[63] Finally, during Stage Three, the fixing of exchange rates between national currencies would occur with their eventual replacement by a single European currency and the transfer of responsibility for the conduct of monetary policy from the national to the supranational arena.[64]

The Delors Report was adopted by the European Council in its Madrid summit in June 1989. The European Council decided to launch the first stage of EMU on 1 July 1990, the date of entry into effect of the 1988 Directive on freedom of capital movements.[65]

C. The Maastricht Treaty on European Union

In December 1989 the Strasbourg European Council called for an intergovernmental conference that would identify what amendments needed to be made to the Treaty in order to attain economic and monetary union. The work of this

---

[60] Committee for the Study of Economic and Monetary Union, *Report on Economic and Monetary Union in the European Community*, 12 April 1989, available at <http://europa.eu.int/comm/economy_finance/euro/origins/delors_en.pdf>.

[61] ibid 21–2.   [62] ibid 30–3.   [63] ibid 33–5.   [64] ibid 35–6.

[65] See Madrid European Council, Presidency Conclusions, DN DOC/89/1, 27 June 1989.

intergovernmental conference and the one on political union (both launched at the Rome European Council in December 1990) led to the Treaty on European Union (the so-called Maastricht Treaty), which was formally adopted by the Heads of State and Government at the Maastricht European Council in December 1991 and signed on 7 February 1992.

While the Single European Act captured the momentum gained in the launching of the 'internal market programme' and prepared the way for further monetary cooperation, the Maastricht Treaty capitalized on the political momentum gained on the road towards EMU (though the economic arguments on the costs and benefits of EMU were finely balanced[66]). The drafting, signature, ratification, and implementation of the Maastricht Treaty provide a good example of the 'ups and downs' of European integration. The Treaty represents a compromise between those who favour a federal Europe and those who oppose it. Its ambiguity in many provisions is rooted in this difficult balance.

The Maastricht Treaty made extensive amendments to the EC Treaty for the purpose of ensuring a gradual movement of the Member States towards full economic and monetary union (EMU).[67] The Maastricht Treaty adopted the proposals of the 'Delors Report' by providing for a 'three-stage' approach to introduce economic and monetary union by the end of the century. The Treaty came into effect on 1 November 1993, following the final ratification by Germany.

The Maastricht Treaty is greatly influenced by the 'monetary stability' culture that I discussed in Chapter 2. This is essential to understand the unyielding commitment of the European Central Bank to keep inflation under control.

Paradoxically, the Treaty gained binding legal force at a time when some European Member States were more preoccupied about their growth prospects and their unemployment problems than they were about the pursuit of price stability. The economic slowdown in many European countries, the currency turmoil triggered by the ERM crisis in September 1992, and the momentous historical events that took place in the European continent at the beginning of the 1990s—namely German reunification, the break-up of the former Soviet Union, the transition in Eastern European and newly created Republics in the former USSR from centrally planned economies to market economies, the

---

[66] See Charles Goodhart, 'The Transition to EMU' in Mads Andenas, Laurence Gormley, Christos Hadjiemmanuil, and Ian Harden (eds.), *European Economic and Monetary Union: The Institutional Framework* (London: Kluwer Law International, 1997) 6.

[67] See Christos Hadjiemmanuil, 'European Monetary Union, the European System of Central Banks and Banking Supervision: A Neglected Aspect of the Maastricht Treaty' (1997) Tulane Journal of International and Comparative Law 105, 106–12.

break-up and war in Yugoslavia (a name which already belongs to history)—signified a change in priorities in Europe.

Despite these geopolitical and economic considerations, the project of economic and monetary union (EMU)[68] was not abandoned nor sidelined.

Stage One of EMU

In accordance with the conclusions of the Madrid European Council on 26 and 27 June 1989, the first stage of economic and monetary union began on 1 July 1990 (and lasted until 31 December 1993). However, the entry into force of the Treaty on European Union on 1 November 1993 marked the genuine starting point of preparations for Economic and Monetary Union.

In Stage One, capital flows were to be liberalized (the principle of freedom of capital movements was incorporated into the Treaty) thus implying the removal of exchange controls. By the end of December 1993 and before the beginning of Stage Two on 1 January 1994, Member States were also required to revise their domestic laws so as to prohibit national central banks from providing overdraft or other credit facilities to their central governments or other public authorities and also to prohibit privileged or favourable access by central governments and other public authorities to facilities from financial institutions.[69]

Member States were further obliged to coordinate their economic policies with the Council[70] and to adopt multi-annual economic programmes designed to secure durable economic convergence necessary to achieve the EMU objective. In addition, Member States were required to regard their exchange rates as matters of concern to the Community as a whole and to seek to avoid undue exchange rate fluctuations.[71]

From an institutional perspective, the Committee of Governors of the Central Banks of the Member States of the European Economic Community was given additional responsibilities. These were laid down in a Council Decision of 12 March 1990 and included holding consultations and promoting the coordination of the monetary policies of the Member States with the aim of achieving price stability. In view of the relatively short time available to advance to monetary union and the complexity of the tasks involved, the preparatory

---

[68] Above note 4.   [69] See Art 101, Art 102, and Art 116 EC Treaty.

[70] See Art 98 and Art 99 EC Treaty. The coordination of the general economic policies of the Member States is the first task of the Council according to Art 202 EC (ex Art 145).

[71] This is the effect of the first indent of Art 124 EC, which read as follows: 'Until the beginning of the third stage, each Member State shall treat its exchange rate policy as a matter of common interest.'

work for Stage Three of Economic and Monetary Union (EMU) was also initiated by this Committee of Governors.

During the negotiations of the Maastricht Treaty, the United Kingdom obtained its famous 'opt-out' clause, exempting it from the third stage of EMU. A protocol annexed to the Treaty stipulated that the UK was not required to introduce the single currency even if it fulfilled the convergence criteria. The protocol was necessary in order to secure the UK ratification of the Treaty. Denmark, which had also secured a monetary opt-out, rejected the Treaty in a referendum held in June 1992,[72] and it subsequently obtained an agreement exempting it from several provisions of the Treaty. Sweden also rejected the euro in a referendum in September 2003. (Sweden has no formal opt-out but availed itself of the possibility of not complying with several of the convergence criteria in order to obtain a semi-permanent status as a derogation State.)

During the process of ratification of the Treaty, the speculation sparked off by the negative result of the first Danish referendum, the uncertainty surrounding the French referendum, and the speculative attacks that led to the widening of the fluctuation margins of the exchange-rate mechanism cast some doubts both on the feasibility of the EMU project and on the timing for its completion. But the project remained on track.

Stage Two of EMU

Stage Two of EMU began on 1 January 1994, in accordance with the EC Treaty, following the Maastricht Treaty revision. The EMCF and the Committee of Central Bank Governors were replaced by the European Monetary Institute, the predecessor of the ESCB. No formal decision was needed for the transition to this second stage, during which Member States were to make significant progress towards economic policy convergence. Precise but non-binding rules on public financing were adopted and a new type of monitoring, this time of public finances, was introduced and carried out by the Commission.

From 1 January 1994, a number of Treaty provisions (Arts 73a to 73g of the EC Treaty as amended by Art G of the Treaty on European Union) introduced arrangements fully to liberalize capital movements within the EU Member States.[73]

---

[72] The Danish monetary opt-out already existed since Maastricht and was merely confirmed in the Edinburgh European Council conclusions, published in [1992] OJ C 348/2. See Smits, above note 9, 137–8.

[73] Article 73a stated that from 1 January 1994, Arts 67 to 73 Treaty of Rome would no longer apply and would be replaced by Arts 73b to 73g EC Treaty as amended by the Maastricht Treaty. Given that this Art 73a was a transitional provision, it was omitted in the 1997

The coordination of monetary policies was institutionalized in Stage Two by the establishment of the European Monetary Institute (EMI).[74] The tasks of the EMI were twofold: (1) strengthening cooperation between the national central banks and the coordination of Member States' monetary policies (during this stage, monetary policy remained in the hands of the national authorities); (2) carrying out the necessary preparatory work for establishment of the European System of Central Banks (ESCB), which was to conduct the single monetary policy.

Member States had to ensure that they would coordinate their economic policies with the Council, endeavour to avoid excessive government deficits, and ensure that their national law was compatible with the Treaty and with the Statute of the ESCB, with special reference to independence of their national central bank. They were also required to make significant progress towards convergence of their economies, since the move to the third stage was conditional on fulfillment of the four convergence criteria laid down in the Treaty.

During the Madrid European Council of 15 and 16 December 1995, Member States expressed their political determination that the third stage of Economic and Monetary Union was to go ahead on 1 January 1999 in accordance with the convergence criteria, the timetable, the protocols, and the procedures laid down in the Treaty.[75] On the basis of the discussions initiated by the Commission's Green Paper, the fifteen Heads of State or Government spelled out the scenario and the timetable for introducing the single currency, which they decided to call the 'euro'.

Rounding off two years of intensive work by all the EU institutions, the Dublin

---

Amsterdam Treaty, which renumbered the EC Treaty provisions and which entered into force on 1 May 1999. *(Articles 73b to 73g became Arts 56–60 of the EC Treaty following the Amsterdam Treaty renumbering.)* Article 73b introduced the principle of full freedom of capital movements and payments, both between Member States and between Member States and third countries. Article 73c introduced the possibility of maintaining certain existing restrictions vis-à-vis third countries. Article 73d set out the fields in which Member States can maintain information, prudential supervision, and taxation requirements without capital movements being hindered. Article 73e provided for the derogations adopted prior to the entry into force of the Treaty on European Union to be maintained for a transitional period. Article 73f provided for the possibility of taking safeguard measures if movements of capital to or from third countries cause serious difficulties for the operation of economic and monetary union. Article 73g allowed the Community or a Member State to take measures on movements of capital to or from third countries for security or foreign policy reasons.

[74] See Rosa M Lastra, 'The Independence of the European System of Central Banks' (1992) 33 Harvard International Law Journal 475, 503–6.

[75] The Treaty provided that the transition to the third stage of EMU was to take place in 1997 if a majority of Member States fulfilled the convergence criteria. If by the end of that year the date for the beginning of the third stage had not been set, the third stage was to start on 1 January 1999 with those Member States which had achieved the degree of convergence stipulated in the Treaty.

European Council of 13 and 14 December 1996 noted that there was political agreement on all the necessary foundations for setting the single currency in place: the legal framework for the use of the euro, the Stability and Growth Pact for ensuring strict budgetary discipline (which was adopted in 1997), and the structure of the new exchange rate mechanism for those Member States not joining the euro zone (the ERM II).

At the same time the EMI presented the designs of the banknotes that would be put into circulation from 1 January 2002. The euro became a tangible reality for the general public.

Throughout 1996 and 1997 the economic upturn, with inflation rates at exceptionally low levels, stable exchange rates,[76] and a general improvement in the state of public finances, paved the way for the majority of Member States to switch to the euro in 1999.

Most of the necessary preparatory work for an orderly transition to the third stage and the smooth operation of EMU was completed by the end of 1997. The first Euro Regulation (which I further examine in Chapter 7) was adopted following the Amsterdam European Council of June 1997.[77] The fifteen Heads of State or Government also adopted the resolutions on the Stability and Growth Pact[78] (which I critically analyse in Chapter 8) and on the new Exchange Rate Mechanism (ERM II) at the Amsterdam summit.

The Luxembourg European Council (December 1997) completed this legislative framework by spelling out the principles and procedures for closer economic coordination during the third stage of EMU.[79]

---

[76] The Finnish markka joined the EMS Exchange Rate Mechanism in October 1996 and the Italian lira returned to the ERM in November 1996.

[77] Council Regulation (EC) No 1103/97 of 17 June 1997 on certain provisions relating to the introduction of the euro [1997] OJ L162/1.

[78] Council Resolution 97/C236/01 on the Stability and Growth Pact, [1997] OJ C236/1; see also Council Regulation 1466/1997 of 7 July 1997 Strengthening of the Surveillance of Budgetary Positions and the Surveillance and Coordination of Economic Policies [1997] OJ L209/1. The Regulation improves the surveillance of the Member States' economic and monetary positions by ensuring the flow of information from Member States to the Commission and Council. Essentially, the Regulation outlines the rules concerning the content, submission, examination, and monitoring of each Member State's 'stability programme'; see also Council Regulation 1467/97 of 7 July 1997 Speeding Up and Clarifying the Implementation of Excessive Deficit Procedure [1997] OJ L209/6. The Regulation provides a clear method for proposing and implementing prompt corrective actions within a year of the reporting of the excessive deficit.

[79] Work on the technical details and practical arrangements for the introduction of the euro also made decisive headway, with the Commission setting up expert working groups to discuss the various practical issues involved, such as bank charges for conversion, dual price displays, and others.

The transition to the third stage was subject to the achievement of a high degree of durable economic convergence measured against four criteria laid down by the Treaty (Art 121 EC Treaty, ex Art 109j), which refer to price stability, sustainability of government financial positions (non-excessive budgetary deficits), stability within the ERM, and low long-term interest-rate levels. These four economic criteria as well as the legal criterion of central bank independence (Art 109 EC Treaty)[80] constitute the necessary requirements to qualify for monetary union.

The weekend of 1–3 May 1998 will go down in history as a milestone on the road to Economic and Monetary Union. On the basis of a recommendation adopted by the Ecofin Council (Economics and Finance Ministers), and having consulted the European Parliament, the Council, meeting at the level of Heads of State or Government, unanimously decided that eleven Member States, namely Belgium, Germany, Spain, France, Ireland, Italy, Luxembourg, the Netherlands, Austria, Portugal, and Finland, fulfilled the necessary conditions for adopting the single currency on 1 January 1999.[81]

The following instruments were also adopted on 3 May 1998: a joint communiqué stating that the bilateral central rates currently in force within the Exchange Rate Mechanism were to be used on 1 January 1999 in determining the irrevocable conversion rates for the euro vis-à-vis the currencies of the participating Member States, and a regulation on the denominations and technical specifications of euro coins.[82] The regulation laying down the conditions in which the currencies of the participating Member States will be replaced by the euro from 1 January 1999 was only adopted on 31 December 1998.[83]

The Heads of State or Government also reached political agreement on the names of the persons to be recommended for appointment to the Presidency, Vice-Presidency, and Executive Board of the European Central Bank. The appointments of Mr Wim Duisenberg as President, Mr Christian Noyer as Vice-President, and Mr Otmar Issing, Mr Tommaso Padoa-Schioppa, Mr Eugenio Domingo Solans, and Mrs Sirkka Hämäläinen as members of the Executive Board were confirmed on 26 May 1998.

The European Central Bank was therefore established on 1 July 1998, succeeding

---

[80] See also Art 116(5) EC Treaty.
[81] Council Regulation (EC) No 974/1998 of 3 May 1998 on the introduction of the euro [1998] OJ L139/1.
[82] Council Regulation (EC) No 975/1998 of 3 May 1998 on denominations and technical specifications of euro coins intended for circulation [1998] OJ L139/6.
[83] Council Regulation (EC) No 2866/98 of 31 December 1998 on the conversion rates between the euro and the currencies of the Member States adopting the euro [1998] OJ L359/1.

the European Monetary Institute, based in Frankfurt. It became operational on 1 January 1999.[84]

Stage Three of EMU

On 1 January 1999, the third stage began. At that point, (a) the ECU (euro) became a currency in its own right (meaning that it ceased to be a composite currency whose value depended on the currencies of which it was composed; most of these were now legally abolished and replaced by the single currency); (b) the Council fixed the irrevocable fixed rates at which participating currencies were to be substituted by the euro; (c) the ECB and the ESCB took up their full powers and assumed responsibility for the single currency from the first day of the third stage; and (d) participating Member States became subject to an absolute obligation to avoid excessive government deficits.

Commentators often divided this third and final stage into Stage 3(a) and Stage 3(b).[85] Stage 3(a) referred to the irrevocable locking of exchange rates that took place on 1 January 1999. Stage 3(b) referred to the actual introduction of euro banknotes and coins that took place on 1 January 2002.

In 2000, Greece asked that its progress towards convergence be reassessed. The Commission issued a favourable opinion and the 'derogation' (under Art 122 of the Treaty) was abrogated by the Council. Greece thus embarked on the third stage of EMU on 1 January 2001.

In September 2001 the first euro notes and coins were distributed to banks and companies. Individuals wishing to acquaint themselves with their new currency could inspect the notes and coins at their bank. Information campaigns explained the new safety measures for protecting the European currency against counterfeiting. As of mid-December individuals could buy mini-kits of euro coins in order to acquaint themselves with the new currency. On 1 January 2002 cash payments could be effected in euros and the European currency quickly replaced the former national currencies in everyday payments. The changeover period during which both the euro and the national currencies were used together—the so-called 'dual circulation'—lasted up to two months in some countries. On 28 February 2002, the former national currencies lost their status as legal tender, with 'old' national notes and coins exchanged at national banks on terms set by each Member State.

---

[84] See Art 123(1) EC Treaty.

[85] See eg Bertold Wahlig, 'European Monetary Law: The Transition to the Euro and the Scope of Lex Monetae' in Mario Giovanoli (ed), *International Monetary Law. Issues for the New Millenium* (Oxford: Oxford University Press, 2000) 126.

Transition to the euro has now been completed. The new Member States that joined the EU on 1 May 2004 hope to join the Euro by 2010. Prospective membership, however, remains a divisive issue in the United Kingdom, Denmark, and Sweden. History will tell.

D. Degrees of Integration

One significant characteristic of the EC integration process has been its changing nature and dynamic character. The EC has been proved adept at evolving in terms of objectives to be achieved, institutions, policies and responsibilities, techniques, mechanisms, and procedures to move forward. The challenge in the late 1950s and in the 1960s was the consolidation of the customs union; the challenge in the 1970s was the consolidation of the EEC institutions and the first enlargement; the challenge in the 1980s was the single market programme and the second enlargement; the challenge in the 1990s was the realization of monetary union and the need for institutional reform. The challenge since the year 2000 has been the enlargement eastwards and the deepening of the union through constitutional reform and the prospect of further political integration.

In this section I examine the various stages or degrees of European integration: customs union, common market/internal market, monetary union, economic union, political union.

Customs union

In international trade relations, a customs union is formed when two or more countries agree to remove all barriers to free trade with each other, while establishing a common external tariff against other nations.

The legal basis for the customs union was the 1957 EEC Treaty. According to its Article 23, 'the Community shall be based upon a customs union which shall cover all trade in goods and which shall involve the prohibition between Member States of customs duties on imports and exports and of all charges having equivalent effect, and the adoption of a common customs tariff in their relations with third countries.' The provision makes it clear that the customs union has both internal and external aspects.

The internal aspect requires the elimination of customs duties and charges having equivalent effect on goods in free circulation within the Community. The external aspect involves the adoption of the common customs tariff. The EC Treaty declares that 'by establishing a customs union between themselves Member States aim to contribute, in the common interest, to the harmonious development of world trade, the progressive abolition of restrictions on international trade, and the lowering of customs barriers.'[86]

The provisions regarding a common commercial policy (Arts 131–134 EC Treaty) relate both to the external needs of a customs union and to the broader needs of a common market.

The customs union was completed on 1 July 1968 (eighteen months earlier than the deadline laid down in the Treaty): all customs duties and restrictions among the six founding Member States of the Community were eliminated and the Common Customs Tariff or CCT (an external tariff which applies to third country goods) was introduced. Customs checkpoints at borders between EU countries disappeared in 1993. The first stage of integration was completed.

Common market/internal market

The second stage of European integration was the creation of a common market amongst the participating Member States. The legal basis of the common market is also to be found in the original 1957 EEC Treaty. The common market was to be progressively established during a transitional period of twelve years ending on 31 December 1969.[87]

However, the creation of a common market proved to be a much more complex and multifaceted process than the rather straightforward establishment of a customs union. The very denomination of this 'one market' has given rise to three different terms over time: 'common market', 'single market', and 'internal market'. Though these three terms express the same integration goal, the EC Treaty refers only to the 'common market' (this term appears thirty-three times in the EC Treaty) and the 'internal market' (this term appears seventeen times in the EC Treaty).[88] The term 'single market' does not appear in the EC Treaty though it is frequently used by the European Court of Justice and by commentators of EC law, often as a synonym of 'internal market'.

The term 'common market' was not defined in the original EEC Treaty. The

---

[86] Article 131 EC Treaty. See also Arts 25 and 26 and Art 135 EC Treaty.

[87] Apart from the free movement of goods, there was to be free movement of services, free movement of workers and self-employed persons, freedom of establishment, and—first limited, later unrestricted—free movement of capital with, as a corollary of the first four freedoms, freedom of payments.

[88] Under Art 3(1)(c) EC Treaty, the internal market is characterized by the abolition, as between Member States, of obstacles to the free movement of goods, persons, services, and capital. Under Art 14(2) the internal market shall comprise an area without internal frontiers in which the free movement of goods, persons, services, and capital is ensured.

so-called Spaak Report,[89] which formed the basis for the EEC Treaty, described the 'common market' in the following terms:

> The objective of a common European market must be to create a vast zone of common economic policy, constituting a powerful unit of production, and making possible continuous growth, an increase in stability, an accelerated raising of the standard of living and the development of harmonious relations between the States which it unites . . . However, these advantages of a common market can only be achieved if time is granted and means are collectively made available to permit necessary adaptations to be made, if practices which distort competition between producers are ended and if co-operation between the States is established in order to ensure monetary stability, economic growth and social progress. This is the basic reason why, where in theory liberalization of trade at a world wide level appears to be desirable, a true common market can in the end only be realized between a limited group of States, which one would wish to be as broad as possible.[90]

In the 1980s it became clear that progress towards one market required new political initiatives and more flexible strategies for integration. This was the context in which a new term, the 'internal market' was coined. A White Paper on the Internal Market (not a legally binding document) was published in 1985, containing a list of almost 300 measures needed to remove physical, technical, and fiscal barriers.[91] This White Paper was followed by the revision of the EC Treaties in 1986 with the Single European Act (SEA), which is the legal basis of the internal market. According to the new Article 8A (currently Art 14(2) EC) introduced in the EEC Treaty by the SEA: 'The internal market shall comprise an area without internal frontiers in which the free movement of goods, persons, services and capital is ensured in accordance with the provisions of this Treaty.'

The internal market programme was a 'revamping' of the original common market objective. The Single European Act introduced a number of 'devices' or procedures (eg, the requirement of qualified majority, the use of Directives, the 1992 'deadline') to speed up its accomplishment.

The notion of the 'common market' is fundamental to the European project ('One Market, One Europe'). In fact, the 'common market' is, together with the

---

[89] See Comité Intergouvernemental Creé par la Conference de Messine, 'Rapport des chefs de delegation aux Ministres des Affaires Etrangeres' (Brussels, 21 April 1956), commonly called the Spaak Report, available at <http://aei.pitt.edu/archive/00000996/01/Spaak_report_french.pdf>.

[90] The translation is from Kamiel Mortelmans, 'The Common Market, the Internal Market and the Single Market, What's in a Market?' (1998) 35 CMLR 101, 102–3.

[91] See Commission of the European Communities, *Completing the Internal Market, White Paper from the Commission to the European Council*, 1985, COM (85) 310. This White Paper is also known as the 'Cockfield Report' as Lord Cockfield was the commissioner responsible for the internal market directorate general at the time. The measures identified in this White Paper gave rise to the adoption of a similar number of EEC Directives.

economic and monetary union, the basic mechanism by which the Community seeks to achieve its overarching tasks.[92]

The common market involves the removal of barriers to trade, direct and indirect, technical and non-technical, between the Member States. It is therefore a form of negative integration because it entails measures which Member States shall abolish and actions which they shall refrain from taking. In *Gaston Schul*,[93] the European Court of Justice ruled that the concept of a common market 'involves the elimination of all obstacles to intra-Community trade in order to merge the national markets into a single market bringing about conditions as close as possible to those of a genuine internal market. It is important that not only commerce as such but also private persons who happen to be conducting an economic transaction across national frontiers should be able to enjoy the benefits of that market.'[94]

The establishment of the common market also requires positive integration, the coordination of Member State policies. The approximation of laws and regulations is considered to be of fundamental importance in this respect.[95] The term 'common market' is associated with competition policy and state aid policies (Arts 81–9 EC Treaty) and with the Common Agricultural Policy (Art 32(4) EC), which involve law-making at the Community level.[96]

Though great advances have been made in the establishment of a single market, the truth of the matter is that this multifaceted and ambitious stage of integration has not been completed yet.

Monetary union

The concept of the monetary union, the focus of Part II of this book, was first introduced in the EEC Treaty by the 1986 Single European Act—through the

---

[92] Article 2 EC Treaty clearly states that the overarching objectives of the Community shall be achieved 'by establishing a common market and an economic and monetary union'.

[93] See Case 15/81 *Gaston Schul Douane Expediteur BV v Inspecteur der Invoerrechten en Accijnzen* [1982] ECR 1409.

[94] ibid, para 33.

[95] Article 3(1)(h) EC Treaty counts among the activities of the Community 'the approximation of the laws of Member States to the extent required for the functioning of the common market'. See also Arts 94–5 EC Treaty.

[96] Whether the term 'common market' is broader than the term 'internal market' is debatable. There are instances in the EC Treaty where the two terms appear to be used interchangeably. For example, Art 94 refers to the approximation of laws (by unanimity) with regard to 'the establishment or functioning of the common market'. Then Art 95 refers to the approximation of laws (by qualified majority) with regard to 'the establishment and functioning of the internal market'. In my opinion, there is an important chronological element in this debate. Article 94 (ex Art 100) is one of the original EEC provisions according to the text of the 1957 Treaty of Rome. Article 95 (ex Art 100A) was introduced by the 1986 Single European Act. In many ways, the 'internal market' project was a revamping of the 'common market'.

inclusion of a new Article 102A—and is now firmly anchored in EC law since the entry into force of the 1992 Maastricht Treaty on European Union. Monetary Union has three components: (1) an integrated Community monetary system; (2) an institutional structure, with a European Central Bank at its centre; (3) a single currency, the euro, replacing present national currencies in all the participating Member States.[97]

Monetary Union is a reality: integration in this field has been achieved to its full extent by the transfer of sovereign powers from the national to the supranational arena. The euro as a single currency is a symbol of the Union, as recognized in Article I–8 of the EU Constitution. The monetary policy of the Community (of those Member States whose currency is the euro) is one and indivisible and the European Central Bank is the institution responsible for its formulation.[98] Article I–13 of the EU Constitution clearly states that the Union shall have exclusive competence in the monetary policy for the Member States whose currency is the euro.[99]

Since monetary sovereignty is an attribute of sovereignty (as I discussed in Chapter 1) monetary union can also be seen as a prelude to a potential future political union.

The sequencing of monetary union and economic union that has taken place at the EU is not necessarily a paradigm that other regional groupings in the world may wish to follow. In the run up to EMU it was argued by many that monetary union could only be securely achieved as the culmination of a general process of convergence (the view of German 'Economists'). In the end, the view that early moves toward monetary union would put pressure on members to converge in other economic respects prevailed (the view of French 'Monetarists').[100]

Economic union

While the meaning of monetary union is clear, the term economic union is a bit of a misnomer. In much of Europe today (ie, in the euro-zone) there is one currency, one monetary policy and one central bank. The reality of 'oneness' is conveyed by the term monetary union. There has been a real transfer of sovereign responsibilities from the national to the supranational arena in the

---

[97] See Roger J. Goebel, 'European Economic and Monetary Union: Will the EMU Ever Fly?' (1998) 4 Columbia Journal of European Law 249, 249–56.

[98] See Ch 7 for an in-depth analysis of the institutional framework of monetary union.

[99] Treaty establishing a Constitution for Europe, signed in Rome on 29 October 2004. See Official Journal C310 of 16 December 2004.

[100] For an excellent analysis of the political economy of monetary union (including an examination of this debate between 'Monetarists' and 'Economists') see Charles AE Goodhart, *The Central Bank and the Financial System* (Cambridge: MIT Press, 1995) ch 8, 156–202.

monetary field. Economic union is, in fact, economic policy coordination, since Member States—participating or not in monetary union—are still in charge of their fiscal policies (subject to Community rules) and retain other important national prerogatives with regard to their 'economic policies', as I further discuss in Chapter 8.

The advent of monetary union took place without a corresponding transfer of fiscal powers to a supranational authority. German 'Economists' had argued that monetary union could not easily survive without greater fiscal and political integration. This view contrasted with the view of the 'Monetarists', who thought that monetary union could proceed ahead without any such transfer. Goodhart notes that 'most of the Monetarists also hope[d], however, that monetary unification would accelerate the transfer of fiscal powers.'[101] A compromise was finally reached, since the German view that a convergence of macroeconomic policies and performances was needed for monetary union determined the choice of criteria of economic convergence and the Stability and Growth Pact.

There is no doubt that greater coordination of economic policy, a degree of harmony and consistency between the economic developments and policies in the various Member States, is an important stage of integration.

The first clear legal basis of 'economic union' was Article 102A of the EC Treaty as revised by the Single European Act (SEA). This provision (which was also the first clear legal basis for monetary union) was the only article in a new Chapter I, entitled 'Co-operation in Economic and Monetary Policy (Economic and Monetary Union)' which was inserted by the SEA in Part Three, Title II of the EEC Treaty. Because of its historical significance, I reproduce below the full text of this Article 102A:

1. In order to ensure the convergence of economic and monetary policies which is necessary for the further development of the Community, Member States shall cooperate in accordance with the objectives of Article 104 [balance of payments]. In so doing, they shall take account of the experience acquired in cooperation with the framework of the European Monetary System (EMS) and in developing the ECU, and shall respect existing powers in this field.
2. Insofar as further development in the field of economic and monetary policy necessitates institutional changes, the provisions of Article 236 [procedure to amend the treaty] shall be applicable. The Monetary Committee and the Committee of Governors of the Central Banks shall be consulted regarding institutional changes in the monetary area.

The Maastricht Treaty on European Union introduced important provisions

---

[101] ibid 181.

regarding economic policy coordination (with the aim of achieving 'economic union') in Articles 98–104, as I further discuss in Chapter 8. Accordingly, the EC Treaty imposes a permanent obligation upon the Member States to avoid excessive deficits, so as to prevent fiscal irresponsibility (through the excessive deficit procedure), and provides for further macro and micro-economic coordination, multilateral surveillance, and regional adjustment. The need for economic and social cohesion is of great relevance for economic coordination, in particular in the light of the enlargement of the EU eastwards, with the accession of ten new Member States in May 2004. In this respect, the need for a regional policy to reduce structural differences between the various regions of Europe and the backwardness of the less developed regions is clear.

Political union

A political union, the establishment of a true federal state, with transfer of sovereign powers from the national to the supranational arena with regard to defence policy, security, justice, and other affairs, would be the final stage of European integration. Whether or not it will ever be achieved depends upon the political will of the Member States. Within the EU there are those who passionately believe in an ever closer union and those who with equal passion argue that no more integration (and certainly no more political integration) is needed.

The EU is indeed a complex reality. According to Article I–8 of the proposed EU Constitution,[102] the motto of the Union is: 'United in Diversity'. The proposed EU Constitution would signify a step forward in the building up of a common foreign and security policy, with the creation of a Union Minister for Foreign Affairs (Art I–28) assisted by a European diplomatic service (the European External Action Service),[103] and the establishment of a full-time president of the European Council (Art I–22).

Peter Norman states in the conclusions of his book, *The Accidental Constitution. The Story of the European Convention*:

> The draft produced by the Convention [on the future of Europe] recognises that the Union is rooted in dualities and sets out to reconcile these. It is a Union of states and citizens; a Union of the federal and intergovernmental where states both pool sovereignty and co-operate on policies. It is a union that has emerged in a bewildering and often accidental manner into something that is less than perfect, often infuriating and capable of great improvement. But capable of improvement it is, and the constitutional treaty produced by the Convention is, both in terms of process and product, evidence of that.[104]

---

[102] See above note 3.   [103] ibid, Art III–296 of the proposed EU Consitution.
[104] See Peter Norman, *The Accidental Constitution. The Story of the European Convention* (Brussels: EuroComment, 2003) 339. In this paragraph he is referring to the Convention on the

The European project of integration was born out of hopes and fears: the fear of France for Germany and the fear of Germany for itself,[105] the fears of wars and divisions, and the hopes of peace and prosperity, bringing forces together to build a better future. And those hopes and fears remain at the heart of any further integration.

E. Optimum Currency Areas

An optimum currency area (OCA) refers to the 'optimum' geographic domain within which the general means of payments is either a single common currency or several currencies whose exchange values are pegged to one another with unlimited convertibility for both current and capital transactions, but whose exchange rates fluctuate in unison against the currencies of the rest of the world.[106] The concept of OCAs was developed in the context of debates over the relative merits of fixed versus flexible exchange rates. The pioneering work in this field was done by Nobel laureate Robert Mundell (1961),[107] though Ronald McKinnon (1963)[108] and Peter Kenen (1969)[109] were also influential in the development of the OCA theory. In particular, the realization that in addition to the fixity of exchange rates (within the OCA), the complete freedom of capital movements is another precondition for an optimal currency area.

The OCA doctrine has been influential in the development of a theoretical economic justification for European Monetary Union (though controversy remains regarding the relevance of the OCA criteria for deciding to form a monetary union on economic grounds).[110] Interestingly, both those who

---

future of Europe (whose chairman was Valéry Giscard D'Estaing) and the Draft Constitutional Treaty that was handed to the Italian presidency on 18 July 2003. See [2003] OJ C169.

[105] See Smits, above note 9, 29, who quotes a speech by Chancellor Helmut Kohl referring to Thomas Mann when stating the policy of keeping Germany firmly anchored in the Community structure, striving for a 'European Germany' and not for a 'German Europe'.

[106] See entry 'optimum currency areas' in Peter Newman, Murray Milgate, and John Eatwell (eds), the *New Palgrave Dictionary of Money and Finance* (London: Macmillan Press Ltd, 1992). The properties of an optimum currency area are: price and wage flexibility, financial market integration, factor market integration, good market integration, and macroeconomic policy coordination.

[107] See Robert A Mundell, 'A Theory of Optimum Currency Areas' (1961) 51 American Economic Review 657.

[108] See Ronald McKinnon, 'Optimum Currency Areas' (1963) 53 American Economic Review 717.

[109] See Peter Kenen, 'The Theory of Optimum Currency Areas: an Eclectic View' in Robert Mundell and Alexander Swoboda (eds), *Monetary Problems of the International Economy* (Chicago: Chicago University Press, 1969).

[110] See Charles Goodhart, above note 100, 168. The three main criteria that define an OCA are: (1) the openness of the economies involved to trade amongst themselves, an issue emphasized by McKinnon; (2) the susceptibility of the participating members to asymmetric shocks, an issue

favoured EMU and those who opposed EMU used arguments drawn from Mundell's own work. As McKinnon explains, this paradox, where Mundell appears to be on both sides of the debate over monetary unification in Europe, is resolved by noting that there are two Mundell models: the earlier Mundell of 1961 and the later Mundell of 1969–70.[111]

Mundell himself acknowledges an evolution in his ideas, by pointing out that while his 1961 article presented a qualification to the case for flexible exchange rates,[112] by 1966 he had reached 'the conclusion that a movement to generalized flexible exchange rates would be a step backward for the international monetary system' thus distancing himself in this issue from his mentors James Meade and Milton Friedman.[113]

The interpretation of the 'earlier Mundell'—which reflects a post-war Keynesian mindset—considers that 'an independent national monetary policy with exchange rate flexibility is the most efficient way to deal with asymmetric

---

emphasized by Kenen; and (3) the flexibility to adjust to such shocks, an issue emphasized by Mundell.

[111] See Ronald McKinnon, 'Mundell, the Euro and Optimum Currency Areas' 22 May 2000 available at <http://www-econ.stanford.edu/faculty/works/swp00009pdf> (visited 17 May 2004).

[112] See Mundell, above note 107, 657–63. Mundell argues that if the world can be divided into regions within each of which there is factor mobility and between which there is factor immobility, then each of these regions should have a separate currency which fluctuates relative to all other currencies. Mundell's argument is based on the concept of 'region' which does not necessarily coincide with sovereign nations. A region may include geographic areas cutting across more than one sovereign nation using as pertinent criterion the similarities in the economic characteristics. After dismissing the case for a global currency because the world is not a region and can never be an optimum currency area, Mundell uses the following example: two countries, Canada and the United States each have separate currencies. Suppose however that this particular continent is divided into two regions which do not correspond to national boundaries: the East (comprising east US and Canada) and the West (comprising the west coast of the US and Canada). The East produces goods like cars and the West produces goods like timber. Let us suppose that a shift in consumer tastes leads to increased demand for timber from the West and reduced demand and excess supply of cars from the East. This will result in inflation in the West and unemployment in the East. Mundell argues that the central banks of the two countries may relieve the unemployment in the eastern regions by expanding the national money supplies in the US and Canada. Or to prevent inflation in the West, they may decide to contract the money supply in the two countries. Thus, unemployment can be prevented in both countries' eastern regions, but only at the expense of inflation in the western's regions. Or inflation can be restrained in both countries' western regions but at the expense of unemployment elsewhere. Or the burden of economic adjustment can be shared between East and West, with some unemployment in the East and some inflation in the West. 'But both employment and inflation cannot be escaped.' He concludes that a flexible exchange rate system does not serve to correct the balance of payments situation between the two regions (which is the essential problem). Flexible exchange rates shall be based on regional currencies, not on national currencies. Mundell argues that if regions cut across national boundaries or if countries are multiregional then the argument for flexible exchange rates is only valid if currencies are reorganized on a regional basis.

[113] See Mundell, above note 39, 4.

shocks.'[114] On the basis of this interpretation much of the British press and many economists still argue that 'a one-size-fits-all monetary policy run from Frankfurt' can't be optimal for Britain.[115]

In 1969 Mundell presented a paper in New York called 'The Case for a European Currency'. A revised version of this paper, entitled 'A Plan for a European Currency' was then presented at a Conference on Optimum Currency Areas in Madrid in March 1970.[116] (He also presented a paper entitled 'Uncommon Arguments for Common Currencies'.) These papers constitute, according to McKinnon, 'the later Mundell', the one whose arguments are considered to provide a theoretical endorsement of European monetary integration.[117] In 1970, Mundell's work explains how having a common currency across countries can mitigate asymmetric shocks by better reserve pooling and portfolio diversification.[118] In his paper 'A Plan for a European Currency' Mundell suggests that 'the exchange rate should be taken out of both national and international politics within Europe. Rather than moving towards more flexibility in exchange rates within Europe, the economic arguments suggest less flexibility and a closer integration of capital markets.'[119]

F. Impact of EMU upon Other Regional Groupings

The arrival of EMU has ignited interest in cooperative monetary arrangements in other parts of the world: Latin America (Mercosur), Asia, and Africa. However, it would be a misconception to apply a particular model of integration to any other group of countries. Though there are some common principles and techniques that can be extrapolated from the EU experience and applied to other regional groupings pursuing further economic and monetary integration (eg, the need for binding fiscal rules and the fact that a monetary union can be successfully implemented without first forming a political union),[120] there are many elements that can only be understood and adequately solved *in situ*, that is, taking into account the particular historical, political, economic, geographic, and other circumstances of the countries that want to achieve greater integration.

Ortega y Gasset, renowned Spanish writer and philosopher of the twentieth century, once stated that 'a nation is a unity forged in history with a common

---

[114] See Mc Kinnon above note 111, 3.   [115] ibid 4.
[116] See Mundell, above note 39, 14.   [117] See Mc Kinnon, above note 111, 4–6.
[118] ibid.   [119] ibid.
[120] See Eduard H Hochreiter and Pierre L Siklos (eds), 'From Floating to Monetary Union: The Economic Distance between Exchange Rate Regimes', SUERF Studies, Vienna, 2004.

destiny.' Though he had in mind the nation state, the idea of a 'common destiny' is a useful motto to approach to integration. Of course, such 'common destiny' can be brought about by a variety of circumstances: geographic proximity, sharing natural resources, and others. The process of achieving integration is a complex one. In developing countries, the difficulties are further compounded by the lack of adequate institutions to support legal and economic reform.[121] The remnants of colonialism also need to be taken into account.

Honohan and Lane have examined the impact of European Monetary Union on Africa.[122] They consider *inter alia* the advantages that regional monetary integration could have as an external source of restraint upon the fiscal and monetary behaviour of governments, 'given the record of macroeconomic mismanagement in many African countries'.[123]

Cohen examines the wider economic implications of EMU for the developing world.[124]

Economic considerations (as well as political stability) are indeed important. However, the single most important obstacle that developing countries face in their pursuit of effective integration is the lack of the necessary institutional and legal mechanisms to achieve the objectives of regional economic and monetary integration. The making of integration is founded upon an institutional and legal structure. This is a fundamental feature of the European integration process. The European Community is a Community of Law, as Gunter Hirsch eloquently stated: 'The Community derives its legitimacy, its political standing and its claim to continuity from its capacity as a community of law, in fact, it is but a community of law. Created as it were by the law, the law is what it brings forth.'[125]

---

[121] See Iwa Akinrinsola, 'Monetery Integration in West Africa' (2003) 5 Journal of International Banking Regulation 21.

[122] See Patrick Honohan and Philip Lane, 'Will the Euro Trigger More Monetary Unions in Africa?' in Charles Wyplosz (ed), *The Impact of EMU on Europe and the Developing Countries* (Oxford: OUP, 2001).

[123] ibid 324.

[124] See generally Benjamin J Cohen, 'EMU and the Developing Countries' in Charles Wyplosz (ed), *The Impact of EMU on Europe and the Developing Countries* (Oxford: OUP, 2001).

[125] See Smits, above note 9, 37, quoting Günter Hirsch.

7

THE INSTITUTIONS OF
MONETARY UNION

At midnight tonight, the twelve national currencies of the euro area will cease to be legal tender. . . . [T]he citizens of the euro area have been . . . the key actors in this major step in the history of European integration. The euro area economy will undoubtedly build on this achievement in the months and years to come.

Willem F. Duisenberg, ECB President, Press Release 28 February 2002[1]

A. Introduction

The institutional foundations of monetary union are the euro and the European Central Bank. The latter, together with the National Central Banks of the EU Member States, forms the European System of Central Banks. According to its own website, 'The ECB is the central bank for Europe's single currency, the euro.'[2]

In this chapter I explore first the law applicable to the European System of Central Banks (ESCB) and the division of responsibilities between the European Central Bank (ECB) and the National Central Banks (NCBs). Secondly, I survey the objectives and tasks of the ESCB. Then, I examine the constitutional position of the European Central Bank, its independence and accountability. Finally, I analyse the legal provisions regulating the euro.

B. The European System of Central Banks

The ESCB is the central banking system of the European Union. The ESCB has a dual structure with the European Central Bank (ECB) at the centre, headquartered in Frankfurt, and the National Central Banks (NCBs) at the periphery. Since not all Member States have adopted the euro as their single currency, a distinction is made between the 'ins' and the 'outs'. The 'dualities' inherent in the functioning of the ESCB are examined in this section.

The complex structure of the ESCB is left unchanged by the proposed EU Constitution,[3] whose Article I–30 states: 'The European Central Bank, together with the national central banks, shall constitute the European System of Central Banks. The European Central Bank, together with the national central banks of

---

[1] See ECB Press Release of 28 February 2002, <http://www.ecb.int>.

[2] See <http://www.ecb.int>.

[3] The proposed EU Constitution (ie, the Treaty establishing a Constitution for Europe, signed in Rome on 29 October 2004, and available in the Official Journal C310 of 16 December 2004) was thrown into a legal limbo following the rejection of the Treaty in referenda in France (28 May 2005) and Holland (1 June 2005). The suspension of the ratification process (according to the declaration of the European Council Brussels summit on 16–17 June 2005 to allow for a 'period of reflection') does not equate to the abandonment altogether of the proposed Constitution. The text of the Constitutional Treaty remains a legal document of value to refer to, also with a view to its possible entry into force or the taking over of parts of it in other Treaty texts later on.

the Member States whose currency is the euro, which constitute the Eurosystem, shall conduct the monetary policy of the Union.'

Primary and secondary community law

The primary community law applicable to the ESCB (the ECB and the NCBs) comprises Articles 105 to 124 of the EC Treaty as amended by the Treaty on European Union, and the protocol on the Statute of the European System of Central Banks and the European Central Bank (ESCB Statute), which is annexed to the EC Treaty.[4]

The proposed EU Constitution specifically deals with the European Central Bank in Article I–30 and in Article III–382. A major novelty in Article I–30 of the proposed EU Constitution is that it enshrines into EC law the term 'Eurosystem' (which is not included in the EC Treaty) to refer to the ECB and the NCBs of the Member States whose currency is the euro. Articles III–185 to III–202 of the proposed EU Constitution are the legal equivalent of Articles 105–124 EC Treaty.

The Protocol on the Statute of the European System of Central Banks and of the European Central Bank is annexed to the proposed EU Constitution (Protocol 4) with some—minor—changes, such as the amendment of Article 10 of the ESCB Statute adopted by the Treaty of Nice regarding voting in the ECB Governing Council.[5]

Wherever appropriate, I point out the differences between the provisions in the EC Treaty and those of the proposed EU Constitution.[6] In the words of René Smits, 'a legal limbo continues for as long as the ratification process or possible amendments of the Constitution are on the agenda.'[7] This 'legal limbo' suggests the need to provide 'dual referencing' (to both the EC Treaty and to the proposed EU Constitution)[8] with regard to the primary law governing EMU.

---

[4] Since the entry into force of the Amsterdam Treaty—which amended and renumbered the EC and the EU Treaties—on 1 May 1999, Arts 105 to 109m became Arts 105 to 124 EC. For the purposes of clarity and legal certainty, treaty references were made—for some time—according to the new enumeration introduced by the consolidated version of the Amsterdam Treaty, followed by the original number of the Article in brackets.

[5] Article IV–442 of the proposed EU Constitution states clearly that 'The Protocols and Annexes to this Treaty shall form an integral part thereof.'

[6] Above note 3.

[7] See René Smits, 'The European Constitution and EMU: an Appraisal' (2005) 42 Common Market Law Review 425, 463.

[8] References to the consolidated version of the Treaty establishing the European Community, OJ C325 of 14 December 2002 and references to the Treaty establishing a Constitution for Europe, OJ C310 of 16 December 2004, whose ratification process has been suspended (interrupted), as I have already pointed out.

This notwithstanding, the ECB's legal position would not be significantly affected if the proposed EU Constitution were to be abandoned altogether.

The secondary community legislation applicable to the ESCB comprises a range of legal acts of the ECB (ECB regulations, decisions, recommendations, and opinions)[9] and intra-ESCB agreements on internal matters (guidelines and instructions) between the ECB and the NCBs.[10] There is also secondary Community legislation[11] regarding the ESCB, such as the European Council regulations on minimum reserves, statistical information gathering, and others. The secondary law regarding the euro is surveyed in the last section of this chapter.

The proposed EU Constitution refers to the European Regulations, European Decisions, recommendations, and opinions of the European Central Bank in Article III–190. Article III–191 further states: 'Without prejudice to the powers of the European Central Bank, European laws or framework laws shall lay down the measures necessary for use of the euro as a single currency. Such laws or framework laws shall be adopted after consultation with the European Central Bank.'

The division of responsibilities between the ECB and the NCBs

The European System of Central Banks is a complex central banking system.[12] This complexity is multi-layered. First, there is the structural complexity, which is a permanent feature of the system. The ESCB is composed of the ECB and the NCBs. The complex duality of the ESCB is further compounded—for a transitional period of unknown duration—by the division between the 'ins' (ie, Member States whose currency is the euro) and the 'outs' (ie, Member States not participating in the single currency or 'Member States with a deroga-tion' according to the language of the Treaty).[13] The NCBs of the 'ins' and the ECB constitute the Eurosystem. The proposed EU Constitution sought to establish a detailed distinction in the provisions applicable to the 'ins' and to the 'outs', with Articles III–194 to III–196 dealing with Member States whose

---

[9] See Art 110 EC Treaty and Art 34 of the ESCB Statute.

[10] Article 14(3) of that ESCB statute refers to 'guidelines and instructions' of the ECB to the NCBs.

[11] Article I–33 of the proposed EU Constitution defines the legal acts of the Union: European laws (Regulations according to the EC Treaty), European framework laws (Directives according to the EC Treaty), European regulations, European decisions, recommendations, and opinions.

[12] This section draws on an article I wrote on 'The Division of Responsibilities between the European Central Bank and the National Central Banks within the European System of Central Banks' (2000) 6 Columbia Journal of European Law 2, 167–80.

[13] See generally Chiara Zilioli and Martin Selmayr, *The Law of the European Central Bank* (Oxford: Hart Publishing, 2001) ch 4.

currency is the euro and Articles III–197 to III–202 dealing with Member States with a derogation.

The NCBs, in turn, are also characterized by a duality. On the one hand they are an integral part of the ESCB (operational arms of the ESCB), when carrying out operations that form part of the tasks of the ESCB.[14] On the other hand, they are also national agencies when performing non-ESCB functions.[15] For these reasons, while the law governing the ECB is solely EC law, the laws governing the status of the NCBs emanate not only from EC sources, but also from their respective national legislation (though such legislation needs to be compatible with Community law before the adoption of the euro).[16]

Furthermore, there are substantial differences between the range of functions and responsibilities assigned to each NCB in the various jurisdictions that comprise the euro zone. For instance, some central banks have exclusive responsibility for banking supervision (eg, in Spain or Italy), while others either share supervisory responsibilities with other bodies (eg, in France)[17] or have limited supervisory responsibilities (eg, in Germany, where the BaFin is formally in charge of supervision).

In terms of the ECB's internal organizational structure, the Eurosystem is governed by the Governing Council and the Executive Board, the two main decision-making bodies of the ECB, by which the ESCB is governed.[18] Only the NCBs of the Member States whose currency is the euro are represented in these two decision-making bodies. The NCBs of those countries that do not participate in EMU ('Member States with a derogation') either because they have opted out (the UK and Denmark), rejected membership through a referendum (Sweden),[19] or have not qualified yet (the ten new Member States that joined the EU in May 2004) still participate in the third governing body of the ESCB, the General Council, entrusted mostly with advisory functions (Art III–199

---

[14] ESCB Statute, Arts 12(1) and 14(3).

[15] ESCB Statute, Art 14(4). The ECB can 'test' whether an NCB task is compatible with its ESCB functions.

[16] See Art 109 EC Treaty and Art III–189 of the proposed EU Constitution.

[17] Although the Banque de France does not have formal supervisory authority, it does function as the secretariat of the three banking supervision committees that are formally responsible.

[18] See Art 107(4) EC and Art III–187(1) of the proposed EU Constitution.

[19] Under Community law the Swedish position is that of a Member State with a derogation; Sweden does not fulfil two of the convergence criteria, ie on CB independence and on participation of the krona in ERM-II. That Sweden itself considers that it requires a positive outcome of a referendum and can stay aloof from EMU is irrelevant, strictly speaking, from a Community legal perspective as *tertium non datur*. States have either an opt-out or the derogation status. I am grateful to René Smits for observations on this point.

of the proposed EU Constitution).[20] The tasks of the General Council can be classified into coordinating functions (between the monetary policies of the 'outs' and that of the Eurozone) and preparatory functions (helping the 'outs' prepare for eventual Eurozone membership).

It is worth recalling that the ESCB as such does not have legal personality, and that, therefore, it is not a carrier of rights and obligations. The entities that do have legal personality are the ECB[21] and the NCBs. Only the ECB and the NCBs, but not the ESCB, have the powers to sue and to be sued.[22]

A claim against an NCB is not a claim against the ECB and certainly not against the ESCB, since the latter does not have legal personality. A claim against an NCB is not necessarily a claim against the Member State of that NCB nor against the Community. Article 35(6) of the ESCB Statute allows the ECB to bring a suit before the European Court of Justice against an NCB if the latter does not comply with its obligations under this Statute (though, interestingly, there is no corresponding provision allowing the NCB to sue the ECB).[23]

The division of responsibilities between the ECB and the NCBs within the ESCB resembles to some extent the structure of the US Federal Reserve System (the 'Fed'). Indeed, while the ESCB functionally is reminiscent of the pre-1999 Bundesbank, geographically it resembles the Federal Reserve System. It is interesting to observe that in the congressional debates that led to the establishment of the Federal Reserve System in 1913, there was a considerable discussion as to the use of the name 'central bank' and that is why the name Federal Reserve System was adopted, to reflect the federal structure of the US, the balance of power between the Federal Government and the States.

The Federal Reserve System does not have legal personality. The entities with legal personality are the Board of Governors and the Federal Open Market Committee (which are both federal agencies and, as such, public legal persons) on the one hand, and the twelve Federal Reserve Banks on the other. However, in contrast to the NCBs, which are typically public legal persons (publicly

---

[20] See Art 123(3) EC and Art III–199 of the proposed EU Constitution, which refer to the General Council as the 'third decision making body of the ECB'. See ESCB Statute Arts 45–7. In the Protocol annexed to the proposed EU Constitution, the articles governing the General Council have become Arts 44–6.

[21] As recognized in Art 107(2) EC and Art I–30 para 3 of the proposed EU Constitution.

[22] Article 9(1) of the ESCB Statute states that the ECB 'shall enjoy in each Member State the most extensive legal capacity accorded to legal persons under its law. It may, in particular, acquire or dispose of movable or immovable property and may be a party to legal proceedings'.

[23] In his comments on this chapter, René Smits points out that this is the equivalent of Art 226 EC, under which the Commission can sue a State before the ECJ for neglecting Community obligations, and a token of the independence of the NCBs since their actions as ESCB members are no longer imputed to their State, but may come up for scrutiny before the ECJ directly.

managed and, for the most part, publicly owned), the Federal Reserve Banks have private legal personality, with private ownership (wholly owned by the member banks in each district) and private management.[24] Nonetheless, the analogy between the Federal Reserve System and the ESCB is useful in understanding the duality of functions of the NCBs. In some instances, the NCBs act as a part of the ESCB, and in other instances on their own, that is, separately and independently from the ECB. In terms of its capital structure, it should be noted that the NCBs are the ECB's sole shareholders.

The analogy between the Fed and the ESCB is helpful in casting some light on potential developments within the Eurosystem. For instance, the influential role played by the Federal Reserve Bank of New York (FRBNY) within the Federal Reserve System is an interesting 'precedent' that suggests the possibility of one (or a few) of the NCBs playing a predominant role within the ESCB in future. Because of its location in New York City, the world's leading financial centre, the FRBNY undoubtedly performs a major role within the Federal Reserve System (as a part of the US central banking system) and in the international banking community (as a corporate entity). In its capacity as a part of the US central banking system, the FRBNY carries out a variety of functions, in some instances independently of the Executive Branch of the US Government (eg, in regard to the implementation of monetary policy) and in some others as an agent of the Government (eg, when it acts as an agent of the Treasury in the carrying out of foreign exchange operations or when it acts as a fiscal agent of the US Government in matters specified by the US Treasury). In its corporate capacity, on the other hand, the FRBNY carries out corporate activities, such as managing depository accounts for foreign central banks, including custodian and investment services.[25]

---

[24] Not all NCBs are public legal persons: the Banque Nationale de Belgique, the Banca d'Italia, the Bank of Greece, and De Nederlandsche Bank NV are public limited companies, ie, firms with private legal personality.

[25] As mentioned in Ch 2, note 27, in 1997–8 I participated in a very interesting case brought against the FRBNY by Bank Markazi Iran, Case 823, *Bank Markazi Iran v Federal Reserve Bank of New York*, presented before the Iran–United States Claims Tribunal at The Hague, the Netherlands. Bank Markazi (BM) claimed an amount of principal as well as 'unpaid interest' on the grounds that the FRBNY had breached the contractual obligations that it had with respect to the investment of BM's funds during the period of the freezing of the Iranian assets (1979–81). BM also claimed that the FRBNY was 'an agency, instrumentality or entity controlled by the Government of the United States'. This was 'the jurisdictional issue of the case' and it is with regard to this issue that I was asked by the FRBNY to assess the independence of the Federal Reserve Bank of New York and of the Federal Reserve System. I wrote an expert opinion on the nature, legal personality, independence, and operations of the Federal Reserve System, including a comparison with other central banks. The Tribunal reached its decision on 16 November 1999, Award No 595–823–3. The award of the chamber (Chamber 3) dismissed the claim on its merits (concluding that the New York Fed acted honourably and appropriately) but did not decide on the jurisdictional issue. Judge Arangio-Ruiz wrote in the decision (para 34): 'The issue of whether or

The analogy with the Fed is also useful in understanding the process of central-ization that the Fed has experienced over the years in the field of monetary policy, as illustrated by the fact that the discount rate, originally set by each Federal Reserve Bank, has become centralized.[26] However, centralization of one function does not imply centralization of all functions, as the example of the Federal Reserve Banks within the Federal Reserve System clearly manifests. The Federal Reserve Banks are organically independent from the Board of Governors in Washington DC and from the US Government (each has its own Board of Directors, a distinct legal personality, and private ownership) while, function-ally, they sometimes act in conjunction with the other components of the Federal Reserve System in the implementation of monetary policy, at other times as agents of the US Government (eg, when they act as fiscal agent or as an agent of the Treasury and the Federal Open Market Committee in the conduct of foreign exchange interventions), and in further instances as a corporate entity, performing corporate functions. The complexity of the tasks assigned to the Federal Reserve Banks is a useful reference in understanding the tasks assigned to the NCBs within the ESCB.

A general principle applicable to the division of responsibilities between the ECB and the NCBs is Article 12(1) paragraph 3 of the ESCB Statute, which sets out that '[t]o the extent deemed possible and without prejudice to the provisions of this Article, the ECB shall have recourse to the national central banks.'

C. Objectives and Tasks of the ESCB

The objectives and tasks of the ESCB are laid down in the EC Treaty (most notably in Art 105) and in the Statute of the European System of Central Banks

---

not it [the FRBNY] is an agency, instrumentality or entity controlled by the Government of the United States is a complex one. Even the law in the United States as to the status of the Federal Reserve Banks is arguably not consistent.' Judge Richard Mosk concurred with Judge Gaetano Arangio-Ruiz as to the merits, but thought that a decision on the jurisdictional issue of 'control' would have been appropriate, since he argued that the FRBNY is not an agency or instrumentality of the United States under the Claims Settlement Declaration. (The Algiers Accords, an agree-ment to settle financial matters between the USA and the Islamic Republic of Iran in the wake of the hostage-taking of diplomatic personal at the American Embassy in Tehran during 444 days after the Islamic Revolution.)

[26] Journalists and commentators have often discussed the process of centralization of power within the Federal Reserve System. However, it should be pointed out that this process of central-ization refers to the monetary policy functions entrusted to the Fed, and not necessarily to other functions. For instance, when the Federal Reserve Banks act in their private or commercial capacity, such as when they enter into depository agreements with the banks in their respective districts, or when they manage investment accounts for foreign central banks, they act as separate legal persons from the Board of Governors, zealously guarding their independence from the 'centre'.

and of the European Central Bank, which was introduced by a Protocol annexed to the Maastricht Treaty (the ESCB Statute).

The provisions of the EC Treaty regarding objectives and tasks are reproduced— largely untouched—in the proposed EU Constitution.

Objectives of the ESCB

The objectives of the ESCB are spelt out in Article 105(1) EC Treaty, whose text is reproduced in Article III–185(1) of the proposed EU Constitution. The primary objective of the European Central Bank is price stability, that is, the control of inflation. The ECB is heir to the stability culture of the Bundesbank and a creature of its time: economic theory and evidence have supported the case for a price-stability oriented independent central bank since 1989, when the Reserve Bank of New Zealand Act establishing such a system was introduced. The primary objective—the pursuit of the internal aspect of monetary stability—is to be pursued without prejudice to the secondary objective, the support of the general economic policies in the Community. The wording of this provision is heavily influenced by Article 12 of the 1957 Bundesbank Law, which was the subject of academic controversy in Germany, with one author referring to it as the 'squaring of the circle'[27] (for hundreds of years it was attempted to find a square of the same area as a circle, until in 1882 it was proved impossible).

Price stability is not only the primary objective of the ESCB. It is also one of the objectives of the Community, according to Article 2 EC Treaty which makes 'sustainable and non-inflationary growth' one of the EC's objectives, and to Article 4(3) which states that stable prices shall be one of the 'guiding principles' of EMU, as well as of the Union, according to Article I–3(3) of the proposed EU Constitution.

In addition to price stability and support of the general economic policies of the Community, I think it is also important to add financial stability (mentioned in Art 105(5) EC Treaty and Art III–185(5) of the proposed EU Constitution) to the enumeration of objectives, since modern central banks have two core objectives: monetary stability and financial stability.[28]

---

[27] See Klaus Stern, *Das Staatsrecht der Bundesrepublik Deutschland* (Munich: CH Beck'sche Verlagsbuchhandlung, 1980) 463–508.

[28] As I have explained in Ch 2, monetary stability refers both to the internal value of money (ie, price stability or control of inflation) and to the external value of the currency (ie, the stability of the currency vis-à-vis other currencies). For the ESCB, the internal value of the currency, ie, price stability, is the primary objective to be achieved (See Art 4 EC Treaty and Art III–177 of the proposed EU Constitution). Financial stability (as I discussed in Ch 3, is a broad and discretionary concept that generally refers to the safety and soundness of the financial system and to the avoidance of systemic risk (all of them also discretionary concepts). The lender of last resort role of the central bank and banking supervision are both instruments to preserve financial stability.

The other condition mentioned in Article 105(1) EC Treaty and in Article III–185 of the proposed EU Constitution, namely to act in accordance with the principles of an open market economy with free competition and favouring an efficient allocation of resources, and in compliance with the principles set out in Article 4 EC Treaty (Art III–177 of the proposed EU Constitution), is a generic statement of respect for market economics in the workings of the ESCB.[29] Because of this 'generic' nature it is difficult to hold the ECB accountable for its performance in the pursuit of this goal.

With regard to Article 4(2) EC Treaty (Art III–177) it is interesting to observe that its second paragraph refers to the primary objective of price stability as being the primary objective both for the 'single monetary policy' and for 'exchange rate policy'.

Tasks of the ESCB

The functions of the ESCB are divided into 'basic tasks', which are defined in Article 105(2) EC Treaty and Article III–185 of the proposed EU Constitution and reproduced in Article 3(1) of the ESCB Statute, and other functions (non-basic tasks) that are scattered throughout other provisions. Though this distinction is not always clear in my opinion (eg, why is the issue of banknotes not included in the enumeration of basic tasks?), it is enshrined in the Treaty and, therefore, has legal consequences.

While the language applicable in Article 105(2) refers to the 'basic tasks to be carried out through the ESCB' (the ESCB being construed as the compound of its constituent parts, ie, both the ECB and the NCBs), the language applicable to the other tasks typically mentions the ECB and the NCBs separately (with the one significant exception of Art 105(5) EC Treaty, which refers to the ESCB).

Basic tasks

The basic tasks 'to be carried out through the ESCB' are four: (1) to define and implement the monetary policy of the Community, (2) to conduct foreign exchange operations consistent with the provisions of Article 111 EC Treaty, (3) to hold and manage the official foreign reserves of the Member States, and (4) to promote the smooth operation of payment systems.[30]

Monetary policy   The formulation and implementation of monetary policy is the first and most important basic function to be 'carried out through' the

---

[29] As it is for the Community and the Member States under Arts 3(1) and 98 EC Treaty.

[30] Art 105(2) EC Treaty, Art III–185(2) of the proposed EU Constitution, and Art 3(1) ESCB Statute.

ESCB. Responsibility for monetary policy has been clearly transferred from the national arena to the supranational arena. In this sense, it is both accurate and entirely appropriate to talk about a 'single monetary policy' (for the Member States whose currency is the euro). Indeed, while the single market has not been fully realized, the idea of a single currency has indeed been fully achieved through the introduction of the euro on 1 January 1999. The transfer of monetary policy powers from the national to the supranational arena signifies the surrender of one of the classic attributes of sovereignty of the nation state.

Though the EC Treaty and the ESCB Statute refer to the 'monetary policy of the Community' in certain Articles (Art 105(2) EC Treaty and Arts 3(1), 12(1), and 31(2) of the ESCB Statute),[31] in such instances 'the Community' refers to the Member States that have adopted the single currency. This view has been clarified by the proposed EU Constitution, which refers to the 'monetary policy for the Member States whose currency is the euro' in Article I–13 (an article which enumerates the areas of exclusive competence of the Union) and to 'the Union's monetary policy' in Article III–185(2) (which enumerates the ESCB's basic tasks) and in Article I–30. The Union's monetary policy is also the monetary policy of the Member States whose currency is the euro. Article I–30 states: 'The European Central Bank, together with the national central banks of the Member States whose currency is the euro, which constitute the Eurosystem, shall conduct the monetary policy of the Union.'

Though monetary policy in the Eurosystem is 'one and indivisible', there still remains an operational distinction between the ECB and the NCBs in the sense that while the decision-making stage of monetary policy is fully centralized at the ECB, the implementation stage is decentralized. It is the responsibility of the twelve NCBs to conduct the monetary policy operations according to instructions set out by the Executive Board.[32] Article 14(3) clearly states that '[t]he NCBs are an integral part of the ESCB and shall act in accordance with

---

[31] ESCB Statute Arts 3(1), 12(1), and 31(2).

[32] See Tommaso Padoa-Schioppa, 'EMU and the Launch of the Euro' (Speech given at the Academy of Social Sciences, Beijing, 2 March 1999) available at <http://www.ecb.de/key/sp990302.htm> (visited 10 June 2004). In October 1998, the ECB's Governing Council agreed on a monetary policy strategy consisting of three elements. First, price stability was defined as an annual rise in the Harmonized Indices of Consumer Prices (HICP) below 2 per cent, to be achieved in a medium-term context. Secondly, a prominent role was given to money, signalled by a quantitative 'reference' value for the growth of a broad aggregate, derived in a manner consistent with price stability. Thirdly, in parallel with an analysis of monetary growth, a broadly based assessment of the outlook for future price developments is to be made using a range of economic and financial indicators. In December 1998, the ECB announced that the reference value for broad money growth would be 4.5 per cent. This reference value does not apply to a specific time-frame, but is to be reviewed on a regular basis.

the guidelines and instructions of the ECB.'[33] Accordingly, in the implementation of their ESCB tasks, that is, monetary policy and other responsibilities resulting from the EC Treaty and the ESCB Statute, the NCBs act in their capacity as a constituent part of the ESCB, and not as national agencies.

An important issue with regard to the interpretation of this basic task, which I further explore in Chapter 9, concerns the scope of monetary policy responsibilities, that is, whether monetary policy should be narrowly construed (ie, strict monetary policy operations) or whether it should be widely construed, encompassing the internal as well as the external dimension of monetary stability.[34]

Foreign exchange policy   The second basic task of the ESCB according to Article 105(2) EC Treaty and Article III–185(2) of the proposed EU Constitution is 'to conduct foreign-exchange operations consistent with Article 111' (Art III–326 of the proposed EU Constitution). The conduct of foreign exchange policy involves the determination of the exchange rate and the exchange regime and the management of the official foreign reserves (both gold reserves and foreign currency reserves). While the ECB has sole responsibility for monetary policy in the euro area, the responsibility for exchange rate policy is divided between the Council (primary role) and the ECB under a notoriously unclear set of Treaty provisions.

The proposed EU Constitution does not alter the complex 'institutional structure' with regard to the conduct of foreign exchange policy in the EU. The 'actors' in this field remain the same, as I further explain in Chapter 9.[35] The proposed EU Constitution introduces a new Article III–196 (which replaces paragraph 4 of Art 111 EC Treaty) with regard to the 'need to secure the euro's place in the international monetary system'. Paragraph 2 of this new Article specifically refers to the need to ensure 'unified representation within the international financial institutions and conferences'.

---

[33] ESCB Statute Art 14(3).

[34] See also Jean-Victor Louis, 'Monetary Policy and Central Banking in the Constitution', *Legal Aspects of the European System of Central Banks, Liber Amicorum Paolo Zamboni Garavelli* (Frankfurt: European Central Bank, 2005), 29–30.

[35] The proposed EU Constitution also recognizes the 'Euro Group' in a Protocol annexed to the Treaty (Protocol 12). According to its Art 1, 'The Ministers of the Member States whose currency is the euro shall meet informally. Such meetings will take place when necessary to discuss questions related to the specific responsibilities they share with regard to the single currency. The Commission shall take part in the meetings. The European Central Bank shall be invited to such meetings, which shall be prepared by the representatives of the Member States whose currency is the euro and by the Commission.' With regard to the president of the Euro Group, Art 2 of the Protocol states that 'The Ministers of the Member States whose currency is the euro shall elect a president for two and a half years, by a majority of those Member States.'

Article 111 EC Treaty is a cumbersome provision in legal and economic terms, the result of a calculated obfuscation for political purposes. There is a degree of inconsistency, or conflict, between giving the ESCB independence of political control in the conduct of a price-stability oriented monetary policy on the one hand, and leaving the choice of exchange regime (fixed, floating, or managed float) to the political authorities on the other. As René Smits, quoting the German commentator Stadler, emphasizes, '[t]he compromise finally arrived at in the monstrous arrangements laid down in Article 111 EC Treaty, with their attributions of competence and the participation in procedures in the area of external monetary policy, unmistakably expresses the labour pains which accompanied the creation of the provision.'[36]

Article 4 EC Treaty and Article III–177 of the proposed EU Constitution state that price stability is the primary objective both for 'a single monetary policy' and for 'exchange rate policy'.

The room for manoeuvre in the field of exchange rate policy—traditionally the domain of the Treasury or Minister of Finance—varies from country to country, with some central banks deciding on the exchange rate (eg, the Swedish Riksbank) and others with freedom only to implement the foreign exchange policy formulated by the government.[37] Article 111 EC Treaty does allow a degree of 'political meddling' because of the intergovernmental nature of the Council. Before the advent of EMU, governments or Ministers of Finance in the Member States (with the exception of Sweden) had the last word on exchange rate matters. Therefore, the agreement reached in Article 111 EC Treaty reflected the status quo, that is, political responsibility for the external aspects of exchange rate policy.

As acknowledged, the exchange rate has a dual dimension. On the one hand, it is the external anchor of monetary stability (and in this respect the ESCB has a vested interest in safeguarding it) and—on the other—it is an instrument of the general economy policy of a country, closely linked to its trade and employment objectives.[38] For this reason, independent central bankers committed to price-stability oriented monetary policy, but deprived of parallel powers in the

---

[36] See René Smits, *The European Central Bank: Institutional Aspects* (The Hague: Kluwer Law International, 1997) 375, footnote 40.

[37] According to the Swedish Central Bank Law of 1991 Art 4 (SFS 1988: 1385), the Riksbank is responsible for Sweden's foreign exchange and credit policies.

[38] See Rosa M Lastra, *Central Banking and Banking Regulation* (London: Financial Markets Group, London School of Economics, 1996) 276, footnote 454, for a quote of former German Chancellor Helmut Schmidt who had stated in his memoirs, that he 'regarded exchange rate policies . . . as an important part of general foreign and strategic policy'.

field of exchange rate policy, are likely to clash with politicians who have other objectives to pursue besides price stability.[39]

Management of official foreign reserves   The management and holding of the official foreign reserves of the Member States is one of the basic tasks to be 'carried out' through the ESCB according to Article 105(2) EC Treaty and Article III–185 of the proposed EU Constitution. However, only part of the reserves have been transferred to the ECB (according to Art 30 of the ESCB Statute), while part of the reserves are held by the NCBs (according to Art 31 of the ESCB Statute). Further complexity is added by the fact that Member States must comply with their international obligations and hold reserves with such organizations. In particular, EU States are members of the International Monetary Fund, and, as part of their membership responsibilities, they hold reserve positions with the IMF. Though Article 30(5) of the ESCB Statute states that 'The ECB *may* hold and manage IMF reserve positions and special drawing rights and provide for the pooling of such assets,' it is worth recalling that the IMF—according to the Articles of Agreement—is country-oriented and member-oriented. Therefore, only if the EU were to become a political union or if the IMF Articles of Agreement were revised, could the IMF 'deal' directly with the ECB/EU, in terms of representation (Art IV consultations and other obligations of IMF membership) and pooling of reserves.[40]

Promotion of the smooth operation of payment systems   According to Article 105(2) EC Treaty and Article III–185 of the proposed EU Constitution, the ESCB is entrusted with the 'smooth operation of payment systems'. However, Article 22 of the ESCB Statute refers to the constituent parts of the ESCB, that is, to both the ECB and the NCBs, when it states that '[t]he ECB and national central banks may provide facilities, and the ECB may make regulations, to ensure efficient and sound clearing and payment systems within the Community and with other countries.' The ECB and the NCBs are both competent to offer facilities for Community-wide payment systems (typically through Trans-European Automated Real-time Gross-settlement Express

---

[39] See Stanley Fischer, 'Modern Central Banking' (a paper presented at the Bank of England's Tercentenary Celebration) 4 (1994), in which Fischer contends that in today's world, interest rate and exchange rate policies are increasingly interrelated. Fischer also contends that the very effectiveness of central bank independence will depend on the government's choice of exchange regime. Under floating rates, monetary policy affects the exchange rate, whereas a system of fixed exchange rates greatly curtails an independent central bank's room for manoeuvre in the conduct of monetary policy.

[40] The proposed Art III–196 (which I further discuss in Ch 9) states that the Council shall adopt 'European decisions establishing common positions on matters of particular interest for economic and monetary union within the competent international financial institutions' (para 1). Article III–196 further states that the Council may 'adopt appropriate measures to ensure unified representation within the international financial institutions' (para 2).

Transfer, TARGET), but only the ECB—not the NCBs—is given regulatory powers in this area.

Because payment systems are largely conducted—though not necessarily nor exclusively—through the banking system, it is often difficult to dissociate payment system supervision (a basic ESCB task) from banking supervision (a 'non-basic ESCB task'), which for the most part remains a national competence, not a Community competence. However, the Treaty and the Statute do establish that dissociation and, as anything that is enshrined in a legal text, it has legal consequences. For instance, in the case of an explicit payment system gridlock, the ECB has competence to act as lender of last resort (LOLR).[41] This point is actually borne out by the fact that the Bank of England had to put up substantial collateral with the ECB to take part in TARGET, whereas this was not the case for the NCBs of the 'in' Member States participating in TARGET in their capacity as agents of the ECB.

Non-basic tasks

There are four other 'non-basic' tasks (ie, not included under the umbrella of 'basic tasks'): (1) issue of banknotes, (2) prudential supervision and stability of the financial system, (3) advisory functions and collection of statistical information, and (4) international cooperation and 'external operations'.

Issue of banknotes   According to Article 106(1) EC Treaty and Article III–186 of the proposed EU Constitution, 'the ECB shall have the exclusive right to authorize the issue of banknotes within the Community. The ECB and the NCBs may issue such notes. The banknotes issued by the ECB and the national central banks shall be the only such notes to have the status of legal tender in the Community.' Article 106(2) EC Treaty further adds that 'Member States may issue coins subject to approval by the ECB of the volume of the issue.' Article 16 of the ESCB Statute is the relevant provision in the ESCB Statute with regard to the issue of banknotes.

Prudential supervision and stability of the financial system   The Draft Statute of the ESCB—released by the Committee of Governors of the EC Central Banks in November 1990—included prudential supervision amongst the basic tasks of the ESCB. However, the opposition of some countries (notably Germany) to such an inclusion means that the final version of the ESCB Statute and of the EC Treaty (as revised by the Maastricht Treaty) only referred to supervision in a limited way, as a non-basic task, according to the language of Article 105(4)–105(6) EC Treaty (Art III–185(4)–185(6) of the proposed EU Constitution) and Article 25 of the ESCB Statute. However, Article 105(6)

---

[41] Article 105(2) EC.

EC Treaty leaves the door open for a possible expansion of supervisory responsibilities following a simplified procedure (simplified in the sense that it does not require the formal amendment of the Treaty, but not likely to be exercised lightly owing to the requirement of unanimity in the Council plus, currently, the assent by the European Parliament).[42] I further discuss the ECB's responsibility in supervision and with regard to financial stability in Chapters 10 and 11.

For the time being, I would just like to criticize the fact that the proposed EU Constitution did not attempt to introduce substantial changes to this provision, even though it is an anachronism to refer—as Article 105(6) EC Treaty and Article III–185(6) of the proposed EU Constitution do—to 'prudential supervision of credit institutions and other financial institutions with the exception of insurance undertakings'. Financial developments in the last decades have rendered this exception meaningless, since nowadays financial conglomerates encompass banking, securities, and insurance undertakings.

Advisory functions and collection of statistical information   According to Article 105(4) EC Treaty (Art III–185 of the proposed EU Constitution), other Community institutions, bodies, and Member State authorities are to consult with the ECB regarding any Community act or draft national legislative provision within its field of competence. In addition, the ECB may ex officio submit opinions to EU or national authorities on matters within its field of competence (Arts 4 and 34 ESCB Statute). Article 5 of the ESCB Statute refers to the collection of statistical information by both the ECB and the NCBs

International cooperation and 'external operations'   International cooperation is recognized by the EC Treaty in Article 111 and by the proposed EU Constitution in Article III–326 and in Article III–196. Articles 6 and 23 of the ESCB Statute are also relevant. A number of problems arise over the tasks entrusted to the ESCB in this field and over the external representation of the EU in EMU matters. These problems, resulting in a multiplicity of competent economic authorities in various international forums and in friction points with regard to international obligations, are further examined in Chapter 9.

D. The Constitutional Position of the European Central Bank

The structural and functional duality of the ESCB, its organizational complexity and the novelty of a truly 'independent institution' within the Community's

---

[42] In his comments on this chapter, René Smits rightly points out that the European Parliament (EP) assent nowadays required for the kissing awake of the Sleeping Beauty provision has been abolished in the Constitution which permits the Council by a law of the Council, after *merely consulting* the EP, to confer specific tasks upon the ECB.

institutional structure, have triggered a heated legal debate with regard to the constitutional position of the European Central Bank.[43]

The OLAF case clarified the legal position of the European Central Bank. '[T]he ECB, pursuant to the EC Treaty, falls squarely within the Community framework.'[44] The proposed EU Constitution considers that the European Central Bank is an institution (Art I–30, para 3) endowed with legal personality, but not included within the EU's main 'institutional framework'. Such core 'institutional framework' comprises (according to Art I–19 of the Constitution) the European Parliament, the European Council, the Council of Ministers, the European Commission, and the Court of Justice.

The ECB is therefore a 'special' EU institution. This will no doubt trigger jurisprudence to clarify such specialty, since the ECB is in charge of a major 'area of exclusive competence' of the Union (namely, 'the monetary policy for the Member States whose currency is the euro' according to Art I–13 of the proposed EU Constitution) and yet 'somehow outside' the core EU institutional framework.

The ESCB is the central banking system of the European Union (in the same way as it can be rightly stated that the Federal Reserve System is the central banking system of the US) and the European Central Bank is the institution at the heart of the ESCB in charge of the formulation of the monetary policy of the Union. The legal personality of the ECB as a central bank is 'derivative'.[45]

---

[43] Chiara Zilioli and Martin Selmayr regarded the ECB as 'an independent specialised organisation of community law'. They first elaborated this theory in an article on 'The External Relations of the Euro area: Legal Aspects' (1999) 36 Common Market Law Review 286 drawing on the previous work done by Selmayr. They further polished their views in 'The European Central Bank: an Independent Specialized Organization of Community Law' (2000) 37 Common Market Law Review 591–644 and in *The Law of the European Central Bank* (Oxford: Hart Publishing, 2001) 29. Ramon Torrent argued that the ECB is the central bank of the European Community. See Ramon Torrent, 'Whom is the European Central Bank the Central Bank of? Reaction to Zilioli and Selmayr' (1991) 36 Common Market Law Review 1231. Smits suggests that the ECB is an organ of the European Community, 'not an organ in the same sense as the EC's institutions but as an independent agency of the performance of the monetary policy attributed to the Community level of government and for the execution of several other tasks within the overall price-stability objective'. See René Smits, 'The European Central Bank in the European Constitutional Order', Eleven International Publishing, The Netherlands (2003) 24–5. This was his inaugural address on accepting the Jean Monnet Chair of the Law of the Economic and Monetary Union at the Faculty of Law of the University of Amsterdam on 4 June 2003. See <http://europa.eu.int/futurm/documents/speech/sp040603_2_en.pdf>.

[44] See Case 11/00 *Commission of the European Communities v European Central Bank* [2003] ECR 1–07147, para 92. This case is referred to as 'the OLAF (European Anti-Fraud Office) case'.

[45] See Chiara Zilioli and Martin Selmayr, above note 43, (1999) 277. They argue that central banks, unlike States, but similar to international organizations, never have an originary, but only a derivative international legal personality, the existence of which always depends on the intention of their respective States or on recognition by other subjects of public international law.

And the theory of independent agencies that I explored in Chapter 2 helps us to understand the status of the ECB as an independent institution.

Independence

The independence from governmental direction of the ECB and the independence of the National Central Banks constitute a key feature of the ESCB. Heir to the stability culture of the Bundesbank and a child of the economic theories of its time, the ECB is a highly independent institution. On the one hand, it is independent from the other institutions and bodies of the EU and, on the other hand, it is independent from the national authorities. This 'dual independence' is another expression of the duality that characterizes the ESCB.

The independence of the NCBs is a criterion of 'legal convergence' for any prospective member of the euro area. As specified in the EC Treaty (Art 109), the ESCB Statute (Art 14(1)) and in the proposed EU Constitution (Art III–189 and Art III–198 para 1), any country wishing to join the euro area needs to ensure that its national legislation including the statutes of its national central bank is compatible with the EC Treaty and the ESCB Statute.

The independence of the ECB is enshrined in the EC Treaty (Art 108), as well as in the proposed EU Constitution (Art III–188). The ECB and the NCBs are independent in the exercise of their powers and in the carrying out of their tasks and duties. Article 108 prohibits the ECB, the NCBs, and the members of their decision-making bodies from seeking or taking any instruction from the Community institutions or bodies, from any government of a Member State, or from any other body, and also prohibits those Community institutions or bodies and the national governments from seeking to influence the members of the decision-making bodies of the ECB and the NCBs in the performance of their tasks.

The European Court of Justice has clarified the extent of the independence of the ECB in the OLAF case.[46] The Court advocates that the ECB 'should be in a position to carry out independently the tasks conferred upon it by the Treaty'.[47] The Court further states that 'Article 108 [EC] seeks, in essence, to shield the ECB from all political pressure in order to enable it effectively to pursue the objectives attributed to its tasks, through the independent exercise of the specific powers conferred on it for that purpose by the EC Treaty and the ESCB statute.'[48] The Court is clearly in favour of a limited notion of independence,

---

[46] OLAF case, above note 44, paras 130–5.   [47] ibid, para 130.   [48] ibid, para 134.

limited by the functions, by the tasks and powers specifically conferred upon the ECB. The Court upholds a concept of 'independence within the Community structure' (not independence from the Community) that is reminiscent of the notion of 'independence within government'.[49] The 'recognition that the ECB has such independence does not have the consequence of separating it entirely from the European Community and exempting it from every rule of Community law'.[50]

Article I–30 paragraph 3 of the proposed EU Constitution states that the ECB 'shall be independent in the exercise of its powers and in the management of its finances. Union institutions, bodies, offices and agencies and the governments of the Member States shall respect that independence'. It is interesting to observe that the Constitution introduces the notion of financial autonomy (independent in the management of its finances) in this provision. Accordingly, the ECB is independent both in the exercise of its powers and in the management of its finances.[51]

The ECB is independent 'organically', 'functionally', and 'financially'.[52] The 'organic independence' is evidenced by a number of safeguards or guarantees such as the appointment and removal procedures of the members of its governing bodies (eg, Arts 11(2) and 11(4) of the ESCB Statute with regard to the Executive Board and Art 10 ESCB Statute with regard to the Governing Council). The 'functional' independence is enshrined in Article 108 EC Treaty and Article III–188 of the proposed EU Constitution (as recognized by the Court of Justice in the OLAF case) and is also safeguarded by other provisions, such as those dealing with the prohibition to finance public sector deficits via central bank credit (eg, Art 21(1) of the ESCB Statute) or those dealing with the regulatory powers of the ECB. The 'financial autonomy' is recognized in Chapter 6 of the ESCB Statute ('Financial Provisions of the ESCB') and in Article I–30 paragraph 3 of the proposed EU Constitution.

The ECB is independent within the limits of the powers expressly conferred upon it by the Treaty and the ESCB Statute. The 'controls' to which the ECB is subject constitute another limit. The European Court of Justice in the OLAF case specifically mentions the review by the Court of Justice and the

---

[49] See Board of Governors of the Federal Reserve System, 'The Federal Reserve System Purposes and Functions' Washington DC (1984) 2.

[50] OLAF case, above note 44, para 135.

[51] Smits, above note 7, makes the following comment in this regard: 'The special wording of the Constitution devoted to the recognition of financial independence . . . is a welcome sweetener after the OLAF debacle.'

[52] See Ch 2 for further elaboration on the various guarantees of independence. See also above note 38, Ch 1.

control by the Court of Auditors.[53] These are, in fact, important mechanisms of accountability.

Accountability

Since 1992 I have advocated the need for 'accountable independence'.[54] As explained in Chapter 2 above, the notion of independence that I support is the one which Geoffrey Miller and I have developed.[55] An independent central bank is a particular kind of institution that is independent in some respects, but highly constrained in others, constrained by the goal, by the statutory objective, and by the demands of democratic legitimacy and accountability.

Though a consensus has been reached on the definition and adequate quantum of independence, a debate is still going on regarding the definition and the adequate quantum of accountability. The ECB has often been criticized for its alleged lack of accountability and transparency. But what do we mean by accountability and transparency? There are several paradigms and forms of accountability.[56] And depending on which paradigm one judges the institution (the ECB), one reaches different results. Amtenbrink[57] argues that the existing democratic deficit of the European Central Bank is an expression of the democratic deficit of the European Community at large, rather than a particular deficiency of the institution. Zilioli[58] argues that the ECB is accountable if we use a new 'economic paradigm of accountability' rather than the traditional 'formalistic' notion of accountability based on the theory of the division of powers and the existing system of checks and balances. The economic notion of accountability (performance accountability)[59] is based on the assessment of the results achieved in relation to the specified statutory objective, namely

---

[53] OLAF case, above note 44, para 135.

[54] Rosa M Lastra, 'The Independence of the European System of Central Banks' (1992) 33 Harvard International Law Journal 475, 476–82.

[55] See Rosa M Lastra and Geoffrey Miller, 'Central Bank Independence in Ordinary and Extraordinary Times' in Jan Kleineman (ed), *Central Bank Independence. The Economic Foundations, the Constitutional Implications and Democratic Accountability* (The Hague: Kluwer Law International, 2001) 31–50.

[56] See Ch 2. See also Rosa M. Lastra, 'How Much Accountability for Central Banks and Supervisors?' (2001) 12 (2) Central Banking 69 and the article I co-wrote with Ms Heba Shams on 'Public Accountability in the Financial Sector' in Eilis Ferran and Charles Goodhart (eds), *Regulating Financial Services and Markets in the Twenty First Century* (Oxford: Hart Publishing, 2001) 165–88.

[57] See Fabian Amtenbrink, *The Democratic Accountability of Central Banks: A Comparative Study of the European Central Bank* (Oxford: Hart Publishing, 1999) 9.

[58] See See Chiara Zilioli, 'Accountability and Independence: Irreconcilable Values or Complementary Instruments for Democracy? The Specific Case of the European Central Bank' in Georges Vandersanden et al (eds), *Mélanges en Hommage à Jean-Victor Louis* (Brussels: ULB, 2003) 402–5.

[59] See above note 56.

price stability. I would further suggest that the new paradigm is also based on participation (consultation) and transparency (disclosure).

Zilioli argues that the ECB is highly transparent.[60] Even though it does not publish the minutes of the deliberations of the meeting of the ECB Executive Council, the ECB publicly announces a quantitative definition of price stability (despite the fact that the Treaty does not set an obligation in this regard). Zilioli also explains that the ECB has developed both an inter-institutional dialogue and a dialogue with financial markets,[61] thus facilitating the disclosure of information with regard to its activities and modus operandi.

My own view of the accountability of the ECB reconciles some of the arguments made by Amtenbrink with some of arugments made by Zilioli. When it was created, the ECB was influenced by the Bundesbank model of stability and independence. The Bundesbank Law contained scarce provisions regarding the accountability of the central bank, relying instead on the support of public opinion and the statutory objective to legitimize its existence in a democratic society. This contributes to explain, in my opinion, why accountability only played a 'subsidiary role' in the negotiations that led to the establishment of the ECB (a point emphasized by Amtenbrink).[62] But accountability can only be judged through the life of the institution. Accountability cannot be guaranteed by the fact that the initial stage of its creation is legitimate democratically. It is in its continuing operations and policies that the institution must be subject to appropriate mechanisms of accountability. And if the ECB gives 'proper account', explains and justifies the actions or decisions taken (or omitted) in the exercise of its responsibilities, is subject to judicial review and to audit control, and responds to Parliament through reports and testimonies, then it can be judged to be sufficiently accountable. The jury is out.

E. Legal Provisions Regulating the Euro

The euro is the currency that unifies Europe (even though it is not the currency of all EU Member States). From the point of view of monetary law, the introduction of the euro is a major historical development. Its symbolic value as a unifying force in the project of European integration cannot be underestimated either. Article I–8 of the proposed Constitution includes the euro (as 'the currency of the Union') amongst the 'symbols of the Union'. The abandonment of the national currencies and the embracement of the euro took place without

---

[60] See above note 58, 408–9. [61] ibid 409. [62] See above note 57, 359–63.

any major problems or delays. The euro is truly one of the Union's greatest successes.

The changeover to a single currency

As I examined in Chapter 6, the birth of the single European currency was scheduled to take place at the starting date of the third stage of EMU. The language of Article 123(4) EC Treaty is clear in its mandate:

> At the starting date of the third stage, the Council shall acting with the unanimity of the Member States without a derogation, on a proposal from the Commission and after consulting the ECB, adopt the conversion rates at which their currencies shall be irrevocably fixed [*inter se*] and at which irrevocably fixed rate the ecu [euro] shall be substituted for these currencies, and the ecu [euro] will become a currency in its own right. This measure shall by itself not modify the external value of the ecu [euro]. The Council, acting by a qualified majority of the said Member States [Member States without a derogation], on a proposal from the Commission and after consulting the ECB, shall take the other measures necessary for the rapid introduction of the ecu [euro] as the single currency of those Member States.

Crucially for the introduction of the new currency unit, under Article 123(4) EC Treaty, the Council was empowered to take the other measures necessary for the rapid introduction of the ecu (euro) as the single currency of those Member States participating in the monetary union (with qualified majority this time).[63]

The EC Treaty also provides for the introduction of the single currency in those 'states with a derogation', following of course a due abrogation of the derogation. In accordance with Article 123(5) EC Treaty, if it is decided to abrogate a derogation,[64] the Council shall adopt the rate at which the ecu (euro) shall be substituted for the currency of the Member State concerned, and take the other measures necessary for the introduction of the ecu (euro) as the single currency in the Member State concerned.[65]

---

[63] At that time, it was envisaged that those measures would relate to the status of the euro in the participating Member States eg, on the redenomination of claims, assets, thresholds previously denominated in national currencies, on the transition from national currencies to the euro in payment systems, and so on. It was also thought that the confirmation of the continuity of contracts denominated in national currencies and henceforth expressed in euro could be regulated on the basis of that Treaty competence. See Smits, above note 36, 129–33.

[64] The procedure is set out in Art 122(2) EC.

At least once every two years, or at the request of a Member State with a derogation, the Commission and the ECB shall report to the Council in accordance with the procedure laid down in Art 121(1). After consulting the European Parliament and after discussion in the Council, meeting in the composition of the Heads of State or Government, the Council shall, acting by a qualified majority on a proposal from the Commission, decide which Member States with a derogation fulfil the necessary conditions on the basis of the criteria set out in Art 121(1), and abrogate the derogations of the Member States concerned.

[65] Article 123(5) EC.

However, the EC Treaty did not set out detailed rules for the introduction of the single currency.[66] Those rules were elaborated in the EC Regulations that I analyse below.

The first concrete step towards the introduction of the single currency was taken by the Commission in a green paper, 'One Currency for Europe', on the practical arrangements for the introduction of the single currency.[67]

At its meeting in Cannes in June 1995, the European Council requested the Ecofin Council to define, in consultation with the Commission and the European Monetary Institute (EMI), a reference scenario for the changeover to the single currency and to report back to the European Council at its meeting in December 1995 in Madrid with a view to its adoption. The Presidency Conclusions following the European Council held at Madrid in December 1995 included a detailed framework for the changeover to the euro under the title 'The Scenario for the Changeover to the Single Currency' as Annexe 1 to those Presidency Conclusions.[68]

The financial markets wanted legislative certainty on key issues—such as the continuity of contracts or the treatment of ecu denominated obligations—at an early stage. It was decided in Madrid that a Council regulation entering into force on 1 January 1999 would provide the legal framework for the use of the euro. As Proctor contends, this was intended 'to reassure financial markets that a complete legal framework would be put in place well in advance of the birth of the single currency'.[69]

The naming of the single currency as 'euro' instead of 'ecu' (the name given to

---

[66] Proctor argues that any change in currency, whether purely domestic or involving a cross-border monetary union, requires a strong legal framework to support it. The legal framework must at least confirm the identity and status of the currency and that the physical representations of the currency are intended to constitute legal tender for the settlement of debts within the monetary area concerned, and provide the foundations for the conversion of debts expressed in the old currency to be converted into and discharged by payment in the substituted currency. See Charles Proctor, *The Euro and the Financial Markets, The Legal Impact of EMU* (Bristol: Jordans, 1999) 87. Bertold Wahlig argues that the introduction of the a new currency essentially involves four basic steps: (1) the adoption of a new currency unit in a given recurrent link to the former currency unit; (2) the introduction of monetary tokens denominated in the new currency as legal tender; (3) the renaming of existing references to the former currency unit in the legal system in the new currency unit; and (4) the redenomination of claims and liabilities denominated in the former currency unit in the new currency unit at a specific conversion rate on a given reference date. See Bertold Wahlig, 'European Monetary Law: The Transition to the Euro and the Scope of *Lex Monetae*' in Mario Giovanoli (ed), *International Monetary Law-Issues for the New Millennium* (Oxford: OUP, 2000) 125.

[67] 31 May 1995, COM (95) 333.

[68] See Madrid European Council, 15–16 December, Presidency Conclusions available at <http://ue.eu.int/ueDocs/cms_Data/docs/pressData/en/ec/00400-C.EN5.htm>.

[69] Proctor, above note 66, 90.

the single currency in the current EC Treaty) was also agreed at the Madrid summit.[70] It was decided then that no Treaty amendment was necessary to change the name, since ecu should be regarded as a 'generic term' standing for European Currency Unit, while 'euro' was the 'specific name' for the generic term European currency unit.[71] In the proposed EU Constitution, the name 'euro' is the only name given to the single currency.

As I have already pointed out, the proposed EU Constitution provides distinct rules for members whose currency is the euro (Arts III–194 to III–196) and for Member States with a derogation or 'transitional provisions' (Arts III–197 to III–202). Article III–198 (one of these 'transitional provisions') specifies the procedure to follow when a Member State wishes to abrogate such derogation and to adopt the euro.

Issue of banknotes and coins

Following the establishment of the single European currency and in accordance with Article 106(1) of the EC Treaty and Article III–186(1) of the proposed EU Constitution, the European Central Bank has the exclusive right to authorize the issue of banknotes within the Community, though both the European Central Bank and the national central banks may physically issue such notes. Article 16 of the ESCB Statute allocates the exclusive right to authorize the issue of banknotes to the Governing Council of the European Central Bank. The prerogative of issuing currency (*ius cudendae monetae*), which is a classic attribute of monetary sovereignty, has been transferred to the supranational arena.

And the legal tender status is also clear according to Article 106(1) EC Treaty. 'The banknotes issued by the ECB and the national central banks

---

[70] In para 2 of the Presidency Conclusions, the European Council stated:

The name of the new currency is an important element in the preparation of the transition to the single currency, since it partly determines the public acceptability of Economic and Monetary Union. The European Council considers that the name of the single currency must be the same in all the official languages of the European Union, taking into account the existence of different alphabets; it must be simple and symbolize Europe. The European Council therefore decides that, as of the start of Stage 3, the name given to the European currency shall be Euro. This name is meant as a full name, not as a prefix to be attached to the national currency names.

See Madrid European Council, 15–16 December, Presidency Conclusions available at <http://ue.eu.int/ueDocs/cms_Data/docs/pressData/en/ec/00400-C.EN5.htm>.

[71] This decision of the European Council is reflected in the preamble to Regulation (EC) No. 1103/97 of 17 June 1997 on certain provisions relating to the introduction of the euro, [1997] OJ L162/1 and Regulation (EC) No. 974/1998 of 3 May 1998 on the introduction of the euro, [1998] OJ L139/1.

shall be the only such notes to have the status of legal tender within the Community.'[72]

According to Article 106(2) and Article III–186(2) of the proposed EU Constitution, Member States retain the right to issue coins subject to the approval by the ECB of the volume of the issue. The Council may also adopt 'measures' ('European regulations' according to the text of Art III–186(2)) to harmonize the denominations and technical specifications of all coins intended for circulation within the Community.[73]

With regard to the definition of the term 'issue', Smits[74] argues that it includes several acts relating to circulation of banknotes in addition to the initial introduction of new banknotes. Those acts encompass 'all instances of bringing into circulation the physical expression of the single currency'.[75] He mentions in particular the withdrawal of banknotes, the decisions on the number of notes put into circulation, the standards applying to the re-issue of used notes, the cancellation and compensation for loss.[76]

Weenink argues that 'in line with established doctrine' the issue of banknotes

> means the creation for legal or accounting purposes of a liability by giving value to pieces of paper that (a) act as a store of value, (b) represent the official unit of account and (c) serve as a means for discharging debts. Such a liability cannot be created without a corresponding asset having the face value of the issued banknotes having been received by the issuing central bank. It is this act of creating money out of mere pieces of paper backed by assets that constitutes the legal concept of issue of banknotes.[77]

The actual issue of euro notes is a competence shared by the ECB and the NCBs.[78] Hence, notes can be printed and put into circulation by the ECB, the NCBs, or both the ECB and the NCBs at the discretion of the Governing Council. Exercising this discretion, the ECB has decided that both the ECB and the NCBs shall issue euro banknotes according to a structured process for the

---

[72] Regulation 974/1998 awards the same legal tender status to euro coins in Arts 10 and 11.

[73] See Council Regulation (EC) No 975/98 of 3 May 1998 on Denominations and Technical Specifications of Euro Coins Intended for Circulation, [1998] OJ L139/6, as amended by Council Regulation (EC) No 423/1999 of 22 February 1999, [1999] OJ L52/2.

[74] See above note 36, 206

[75] ibid. See also the Decision of the European Central Bank of 20 March 2003 on the denominations, specifications, reproduction, exchange and withdrawal of euro banknotes [2003] OJ L78/16, recital 4, which I examine below.

[76] ibid

[77] See Hans Weenik 'The Legal Nature of Euro Banknotes' (2003) 18 Journal of International Banking Law and Regulation 433, 433–4. See also the public procurement Guideline of the ECB of 16 September 2004 (ECB/2004/18; 2004/703/EC), OJ L320, 21.10.2004, 21.

[78] Article 16 ESCB Statute further specifies that the ECB 'shall respect as far as possible existing practices regarding the issue and design of banknotes'.

even allocation of the total value of euro banknotes in circulation to the ECB and NCBs.[79]

The legal instruments regulating the euro

The law of the euro is mainly secondary law. The Treaty only provided a blueprint for the introduction of the euro, but not the detailed rules that were needed for the substitution of the national currencies by the single currency. A comprehensive legal framework for the euro is spelt out in several EU regulations. The legal bases in the EC Treaty for enacting these euro regulations were Article 123(4) (ex Art 109l(4)) Article 308 (ex Art 235), and Article 95 (ex Art 100a).

The proposed EU Constitution introduces a clear legislative competence with regard to the euro in Article III–191: 'European laws or framework laws shall lay down the measures necessary for the use of the euro as a single currency.'[80]

Regulation 1103/97 on certain provisions relating to the introduction of the euro (the Article 308 Regulation)

Regulation 1103/97 was the first and most significant regulation governing the introduction of the euro.[81] It was adopted on 20 June 1997 and applied to all Member States. It is often referred to as the Article 308 Regulation (or Art 235 Regulation).

The choice of Article 308 EC Treaty (ex Art 235) as the legal basis for enacting this Regulation indicates that the Maastricht Treaty had not specifically provided the necessary powers for the adoption of all the measures needed for

---

[79] See Decision of the European Central Bank of 6 December 2001 on the Issue of Euro Banknotes [2001] OJ L337/52, as amended by the Decision ECB/2003/23 of the European Central Bank of 18 December 2003. A Decision of the ECB of 22 April 2004 (amending Decision ECB/2001/15 of 6 December 2001 on the issue of euro banknotes) specifies the banknote allocation key as well as the obligations of the ECB and NCBs as issuers of notes. The banknote allocation key means the percentages that result from taking into account the ECB's share in the total euro banknote issue and applying the individual NCB's shares in the ECB's subscribed capital in accordance with the weightings in the key referred to in Art 29.1 of the ESCB Statute. As acknowledged, each of the members of the European System of Central Banks is assigned a weighting in the key for subscription to the ECB's capital which is based on the population and gross domestic product of each Member State.

[80] According to Smits, above note 7, this development is welcome, since 'it will no longer be necessary to make use of either Article III–172 (the equivalent in the Constitution of Article 95 EC) or Article I–18 (the equivalent of the current Art 308 EC) in order to adopt the necessary legislation on, eg, payments in euro.'

[81] Council Regulation (EC) No 1103/97 of 17 June 1997 on Certain Provisions Relating to the Introduction of the Euro [1997] OJ L162/1, as amended by Council Regulation (EC) No 2595/2000 of 27 November 2000, [2000] OJ L300/1.

the changeover to the single currency.[82] Article 308 empowers the Council, acting unanimously, to take the necessary measures only if 'action by the Community should prove necessary to attain, in the course of the operation of the common market, one of the objectives of the Community, and this Treaty has not provided the necessary powers'.

The key issues in this 'Article 308 Regulation' were the continuity of contracts, the treatment of ecu-denominated obligation and the issues of conversion and rounding. The Regulation was based on the firm conviction that[83]

- 'it is a generally accepted principle of law that the continuity of contracts and other legal instruments is not affected by the introduction of a new currency';

- 'the principle of freedom of contract has to be respected';

- 'the principle of continuity should be compatible with anything which parties might have agreed with reference to the introduction of the euro';

- 'in order to reinforce legal certainty and clarity, it is appropriate explicitly to confirm that the principle of continuity of contracts and other legal instruments shall apply between the former national currencies and the euro and between the ECU; this implies, in particular, that in the case of fixed interest rate instruments the introduction of the euro does not alter the nominal interest rate payable by the debtor, whereas the provisions on continuity can fulfil their objective to provide legal certainty and transparency to economic agents, in particular for consumers, only if they enter into force as soon as possible';

- 'the introduction of the euro constitutes a change in the monetary law of each participating Member State';

- 'the recognition of the monetary law of a State is a universally accepted principle'; and

- 'the explicit confirmation of the principle of continuity should lead to the recognition of continuity of contracts and other legal instruments in the jurisdictions of third countries'.

---

[82] Though it was originally thought that Art 123(4) EC—ex Art 109l(4)—would have been the legal basis for the secondary law of the euro, the procedure established under such Article required that 'the participating Member States' were to vote on legislation. However, since in 1997 the Council had not voted yet on which Member States were eligible to participate in EMU and since a Regulation under this Art would not have been effective in the UK if it exercised the opt-out clause, it was decided to base the first of the two euro regulations on Art 308 (formerly Art 235) EC Treaty, the so-called flexibility clause which is retained in the Constitution in Art I–18. See Clifford Chance, 'European Monetary Union: the Legal Framework', October 1997, 5–6. See also Art III–198(3) of the proposed EU Constitution.

[83] Recital 8, Regulation 1103/97, [1997] OJ L162.

Regulation 974/1998 on the introduction of the euro (the Article 123(4) Regulation)[84]

Regulation 974/1998,[85] the second euro regulation, purports to define the 'monetary law provisions of the Member States which have adopted the euro'.[86] While the Article 308 Regulation applied to all Member States, this Article 123(4) Regulation applied only to the Member States participating in EMU.[87]

The main issues covered are the replacement over a transitional period of the national currencies by the euro, the gradual introduction of euro banknotes and coins, and the full substitution of euro for national currency units at the end of the transitional period.

A transitional period was needed to prepare a smooth changeover, to allow for the production and distribution of sufficient banknotes and coins, and to 'educate' the public and the financial markets about the new currency. During this transitional period the national currency units were defined as sub-divisions of the euro and thereby a 'legal equivalence' was established between the euro unit and the national currency units.[88] It became clear that despite the lack of euro notes and coins during the transitional period, the euro unit and the national currency units were in all effects units of the same currency.[89] Hence, in transactions which did not involve the physical exchange of notes and coins there was no reason why the euro unit could not be used. In the same spirit, the Regulation prescribed in the preamble that payments inside a participating Member State by crediting an account could be made either in the euro unit or the respective national currency unit and the same could apply to those cross-border payments which were denominated in the euro unit or the national currency unit of the account of the creditor.[90]

Article 2 of the Regulation 974/1998 (as amended by Regulation 2595/2000) articulated what is probably the most important historical development in the

---

[84] Council Regulation (EC) No 974/1998 of 3 May 1998 on the Introduction of the Euro [1998] OJ L 139/1 as amended by Council Regulation (EC) No 2595/2000 of 27 November 2000, [2000] OJ L300/1.

[85] As I proceed to complete the revisions of this chapter, a new Regulation amending Regulation 974/1998 has been adopted: Council Regulation (EC) 2169/2005 of 21 December 2005, OJ [2005] L 346/1, to prepare for the further enlargement of the euro zone, taking into account the fact that the euro is now an established currency. Estonia, Lithuania, and Slovenia are expected to adopt the euro on 1 January 2007; Cyprus, Latvia, and Malta in 2008; Slovakia in 2009; and the Czech Republic and Hungary in 2010.

[86] Recital 1.

[87] Article 123(4) EC Treaty (ex Art 109l.4) stipulates that the Council, acting by a qualified majority of the Member States without a derogation on a proposal from the Commission and after consulting the ECB, shall take the other measures necessary for the rapid introduction of the ecu (euro) as the single currency of those Member States.

[88] ibid, recital 8.   [89] ibid, recital 13.   [90] ibid.

European monetary field for centuries: 'As from 1 January 1999 the currency of the participating Member States except Greece shall be the euro. As from 1 January 2001 the currency of Greece shall be the euro. The currency unit shall be one euro. One euro shall be divided into one hundred cents.'

Article 3 of the Regulation complemented the changeover. The euro was to be substituted for the currency of each participating Member State at the 'conversion rate', defined as the irrevocably fixed conversion rate adopted for the currency of each participating Member State by the Council.

Pursuant to Article 4 of the Regulation, the euro became the unit of account of the European Central Bank (ECB) and of the central banks of the participating Member States.

A contract expressed in the former currency of a participating Member State would continue to create a valid and binding obligation of a monetary character. It was clear under Article 7 of the Regulation that the substitution of the euro for the currency of each participating Member State did not in itself have the effect of altering the denomination of legal instruments in existence on the date of substitution. Acts to be performed under legal instruments stipulating the use of or denominated in a national currency unit had to be performed in that national currency unit; acts to be performed under legal instruments stipulating the use of or denominated in the euro unit had to be performed in that unit,[91] without prejudice to anything which the parties might have agreed.[92]

Any amount denominated either in the euro unit or in the national currency unit of a given participating Member State and payable within that Member State by crediting an account of the creditor, could be paid by the debtor either in the euro unit or in that national currency unit. The amount had to be credited to the account of the creditor in the denomination of his account, with any conversion being effected at the conversion rates.[93]

The Regulation contained further provisions which enabled participating countries to re-denominate in the euro unit outstanding debt issued by that Member State's general government, denominated in its national currency unit and issued under its own law.[94]

Article 10 of the Regulation established the time-frame for the introduction of euro notes and coins. From 1 January 2002, the ECB and the central banks of the participating Member States were instructed to put into circulation banknotes denominated in euro. These banknotes denominated in euro were to be the only banknotes which have the status of legal tender in all these Member

---

[91] ibid, Art 8(1).   [92] ibid, Art 8(2).   [93] ibid, Art 8(3).   [94] ibid, Art 8(4).

States. Similarly for euro coins, as from 1 January 2002, the participating Member States were empowered to issue coins denominated in euro or in cents and complying with the denominations and technical specifications which the Council may lay down in accordance with the Treaty.[95] Again, these coins were to be the only coins which have the status of legal tender in all these Member States.[96] Article 12 imposed on participating Member States the responsibility to ensure adequate sanctions against counterfeiting and falsification of euro banknotes and coins.

Banknotes and coins denominated in a national currency unit could remain legal tender within their territorial limits until six months after the end of the transitional period at the latest.[97] This period could be shortened (but not extended) by national law.[98] Each participating Member State could for a period of up to six months after the end of the transitional period, lay down rules for the use of the banknotes and coins denominated in its national currency unit and take any measures necessary to facilitate their withdrawal.[99] Finally, in accordance with the laws or practices of participating Member States, the respective issuers of banknotes and coins would continue to accept, against euro at the conversion rate, the banknotes and coins previously issued by them.[100]

During the transition period, national central banks were authorized by the ECB to continue to issue national banknotes with the obligation to inform the ECB by the end of February of each year of the amount of national banknotes issued during the preceding year.[101] This specific authorization was given in fulfilment of the requirements of the EC Treaty which grants the ECB the exclusive right to authorize the issue of banknotes within the Community from the beginning of Stage Three.[102]

Other instruments of secondary law relating to the euro

In addition to the two Regulations which I have just surveyed, the Council has adopted other instruments of secondary law relating to the euro, which I briefly survey below.

Technical specification of euro coins The Regulation 975/98 on Denominations and Technical Specifications of Euro Coins Intended for Circulation[103]

---

[95] ibid, Art 11.   [96] ibid.   [97] ibid, Art 15(1).   [98] ibid.
[99] ibid, Art 15(2).   [100] ibid, Art 16.
[101] See Art 1 of the Guideline of the European Central Bank of 22 April 1999 on the authorisation to issue national banknotes during the transitional period, [2001] OJ L55/71.
[102] Article 106(1) EC Treaty.
[103] Council Regulation (EC) No 975/98 of 3 May 1998 on Denominations and Technical Specifications of Euro Coins Intended for Circulation, [1998] OJ L139/6, as amended by Council Regulation (EC) No 423/1999 of 22 February 1999, [1999] OJ L52/2.

set out the denominations and technical specifications of euro coins, such as diameter, weight, shape, colour, composition, and so on, fulfilling the mandate given by the EC Treaty to the Council to adopt measures in order to harmonize the denominations and technical specifications of all coins intended for circulation to the extent necessary to permit their smooth circulation within the Community.[104] It was envisaged that the new European single coinage system should induce public confidence and entail technological innovations that would establish it as a secure, reliable, and efficient system.[105] Other practical matters were also considered in the design. For example, giving the coins one European and one national side is an appropriate expression of the idea of European monetary union between Member States and could significantly increase the degree of acceptance of the coins by European citizens.[106]

Conversion rates The Regulation 2866/98 on the Conversion Rates Between the Euro and the Currencies of the Member States Adopting the Euro[107] adopted the conversion rates at which the currencies of the 'Member States without derogation' were irrevocably fixed *inter se* and also the irrevocably fixed conversion rates at which the ecu (euro) was substituted for those currencies.

Counterfeiting Article 12 of the Regulation No 974/1998 on the Introduction of the Euro[108] imposed on participating Member States the responsibility to ensure adequate sanctions against counterfeiting and falsification of euro banknotes and coins.

In its framework Decision of 29 May 2000 on increasing protection by criminal penalties and other sanctions against counterfeiting in connection with the introduction of the euro,[109] the Council adopted provisions to ensure that the euro is protected in an appropriate way by effective measures under criminal law. In June 2001, the Council adopted the Regulation 1338/2001 of 28 June 2001 laying down measures necessary for the protection of the euro against counterfeiting.[110]

The purpose of this Regulation 1338/2001 is to lay down measures necessary with a view to uttering euro notes and coins in such a manner as to protect them against counterfeiting.[111] The Council regards the competence to adopt harmonized measures to protect the euro against counterfeiting as part of its

---

[104] ibid.   [105] ibid, recital 5.   [106] ibid, recital 10.
[107] Regulation (EC) No 2866/98 of 31 December 1998 on the Conversion Rates Between the Euro and the Currencies of the Member States Adopting the Euro [1998] OJ L359/1, as amended by Council Regulation (EC) No 1478/2000 of 19 June 2000, [2000] OJ L 167/1.
[108] [1998] OJ L139/1.   [109] OJ L140, 14 June 2000.   [110] [2001] OJ L181/6.
[111] ibid, Art 1(1).

responsibility in respect of the single currency.[112] The Regulation is based on the assumption that the legal protection of the euro cannot be satisfactorily ensured by the individual Member States alone, since euro notes and coins will circulate beyond the territories of the participating Member States.[113]

For the purpose of applying this Regulation, 'counterfeiting' included the following activities:[114] (a) any fraudulent making or altering of euro notes or euro coins, whatever means are employed; (b) the fraudulent uttering of counterfeit euro notes or counterfeit euro coins; (c) the import, export, transport, receiving, or obtaining of counterfeit euro notes or counterfeit euro coins with a view to uttering the same and with knowledge that they are counterfeit; (d) the fraudulent making, receiving, obtaining, or possession of instruments, articles, computer programs, and any other means peculiarly adapted for the fraudulent making or altering of euro notes or coins, or holograms or other components which serve to protect euro notes and coins against fraudulent making or alteration. 'Counterfeit notes' and 'counterfeit coins' shall mean notes and coins denominated in euro or which have the appearance of euro notes or coins and which have been fraudulently made or altered.[115]

Under Regulation 1338/2001, national authorities are obliged to gather and index technical and statistical data relating to counterfeit notes and counterfeit coins discovered in the Member States and to communicate such data to the European Central Bank for storage and processing.[116] The competent national authorities and, within its areas of responsibility, the Commission, shall have access to the technical and statistical data held by the European Central Bank. Europol shall have access to such data under an agreement between it and the European Central Bank in accordance with the relevant provisions of the Europol Convention and the provisions adopted on the basis of the latter.[117]

Regarding the role and contribution of the banking system, the Regulation prescribes[118] that credit institutions, and any other institutions engaged in the sorting and distribution to the public of notes and coins as a professional activity, including establishments whose activity consists in exchanging notes and coins of different currencies, such as bureaux de change, are obliged to withdraw from circulation all euro notes and coins received by them which they

---

[112] According to JAE Vervaele 'Counterfeiting the Single European Currency (Euro): Towards the Federalization of Enforcement in the European Union?' (2002) 8 Columbia Journal of European Law 151, 162. 'The ECB has the exclusive right to authorise the issue of banknotes within the euro area. It does not follow automatically, however, that imposing sanctions on the counterfeiting of such banknotes would be a Community competence. Counterfeiting provisions form part of criminal law, not monetary law. There is no general competence of the Community in the field of criminal law, which is an area falling within the competence of the Member States.'
[113] See above note 110, recital 4.   [114] ibid, Art 1(2).   [115] ibid, Art 2(a).
[116] ibid, Art 3(1).   [117] ibid, Art 3(3).   [118] ibid, Art 6.

know or have sufficient reason to believe to be counterfeit. They shall immediately hand them over to the competent national authorities. Further, Member States shall take the necessary measures to ensure that those undertakings which fail to discharge their obligations under the said paragraph are subject to effective, proportionate, and deterrent sanctions.

The copyright on the designs of the euro bank notes was received by the European Central Bank (ECB) from the European Monetary Institute (EMI).[119] The European Central Bank has concluded that such copyright is administered and enforced by all participating Member States according to their individual national legal systems.[120] The ECB has established a Counterfeit Analysis Centre (CAC) in Frankfurt to centralize the technical analysis and data relating to the counterfeiting of euro banknotes issued by the ECB and the NCBs.[121]

Reproduction, exchange, and withdrawal of euro banknotes An ECB decision of 20 March 2003 deals with the issues of withdrawal, reproduction, and exchange of damaged or mutilated euro banknotes.[122] According to this decision, the right of the ECB and of the NCBs to issue euro banknotes includes the competence to take all necessary legal measures to protect the integrity of the euro banknotes as a means of payment,[123] such as rules on reproduction (to provide for a minimum level of protection in all participating Member States in order to ensure that the general public can distinguish genuine euro banknotes from reproductions), rules regarding the exchange of damaged or mutilated banknotes,[124] and rules with regard to the withdrawal of euro banknotes.[125]

The legal status of the euro in non-EU Member States

The euro is not only the common currency of the twelve Member States of the European Monetary Union, but has also been accorded legal tender status in

---

[119] As successor to the EMI, the ECB emphasizes that it holds the copyright on the designs of the euro banknotes originally held by the EMI. See Decision of the European Central Bank of 20 March 2003 on the denominations, specifications, reproduction, exchange and withdrawal of euro banknotes [2003] OJ L78/16, recital 3.

[120] Guideline of the ECB of 7 July 1998 on certain provisions regarding euro banknotes, as amended on 26 August 1999, recital 1.

[121] ibid, recital 2.

[122] See Decision of the European Central Bank of 20 March 2003 on the denominations, specifications, reproduction, exchange and withdrawal of euro banknotes, [2003] OJ L78/16. This Decision replaced previous decisions of 1998 and 2001.

[123] ibid, recital 4.   [124] ibid, Art 3.

[125] ibid, recital 12. The withdrawal of bank notes, according to Art 5 of this Decision shall be regulated by a decision of the Governing Council published for general information in the Official Journal of the European Union and other media. This Decision shall cover, as a minimum, the euro banknote type or series to be withdrawn from circulation, the duration of the exchange period, the date on which the euro banknote type or series will lose its legal tender status, and the treatment of the euro banknotes presented once the withdrawal period is over and/ or they have lost their legal tender status.

certain States and territories outside the European Union such as St Pierre et Miquelon and Mayotte, the French overseas territories, San Marino, the Vatican City, and Monaco.[126] This is a consequence of various monetary relations which had been entertained traditionally by certain Member States, such as France, Italy, Portugal, and Spain, with other States and territories.

Following the introduction of the euro, the French franc ceased to be legal tender in St Pierre et Miquelon and Mayotte. However, the respective European regulations on the common currency did not automatically apply in those territories, as the institutions of the European Union did not (and still do not) have any jurisdiction over these territories. Thus, the Council authorized France to introduce the euro to St Pierre et Miquelon and to Mayotte in 1999.[127]

The French overseas territories use the franc of the Pacific Financial Community (CFP) as legal currency. As the CFP franc is not identical with the French franc, it was not automatically replaced by the euro. In the past France has guaranteed a parity of 1 CFP franc against 0.005 French francs. This strict parity between the CFP franc and the French franc had to be replaced by a corresponding parity between the CFP franc and the euro. Although such parity between the euro and foreign currencies is normally a matter for the EU, under Protocol No 13 annexed to the Treaty of Maastricht, France has explicitly reserved her right to monetary emissions in her overseas territories and her right to determine the parity of the CFP franc. Hence, France was able to retain an exclusive residual competence with respect to the CFP franc. The monetary relations between France and her overseas territories have therefore been left unaffected by the introduction of the euro.

The Republic of San Marino and the Italian Republic concluded a Monetary Agreement in 2001.[128] Under this agreement San Marino is entitled to use the euro as official currency and legal tender status shall be accorded to euro banknotes and coins in San Marino as from 1 January 2001. San Marino further undertakes to implement Community rules on euro banknotes and coins in the territory and had to follow Italy's timetable for the withdrawal of San Marinese lira coins. Crucially, San Marino cannot issue any banknotes, coins, or monetary surrogates denominated in euro unless the conditions for such issuance have been agreed upon with the European Community.

---

[126] See generally Christoph A Stumpf, 'The Introduction of the Euro to States and Territories outside the European Union' (2003) 28 European Law Review 283.

[127] Council Decision 1999/95/EC of 31 December 1998 concerning the monetary arrangements in the French territorial communities of Saint-Pierre-et-Miquelon and Mayotte [1999] OJ L30/29; cf also Opinion of the European Central Bank 1999/06 [1999] OJ C127/5, and the original proposal for the Council Decision, COM 1999/10 [1999] OJ C36/19.

[128] Monetary Agreement between the Italian Republic, on behalf of the European Community, and the Republic of San Marino [2001] OJ C209/1.

Following a Council Decision of 1998[129] Italy, on behalf of the European Community, concluded with the State of the Vatican City, which was represented by the Holy See, a Monetary Agreement on 29 December 2000 on terms nearly identical to the respective Agreement concluded with San Marino.[130] The same terms were also applied in the Monetary Agreement between France on behalf of the EU and the Principality of Monaco.[131]

Interestingly there are more States or territories in which the euro has now obtained official tender status without a clear legal basis. It is argued for example that the Principality of Andorra does not have any currency of its own, but has traditionally used Spanish pesetas and French francs as legal tender up to 31 December 2001. In the course of 2002 the euro was factually introduced in Andorra.[132] Also the euro has replaced the German mark as the currency in circulation in Kosovo as of the beginning of 2002 without an express approval or authorization by the ECB or the ESCB.[133]

F. The Future of the Euro

The ten new Member States which joined the EU in May 2004 will eventually adopt the single currency, following the procedure set out in Article 121 EC Treaty. (They entered the Union as 'States with a derogation' according to Art 4 of the 2003 Act of Accession). The timetable proposed in some of those jurisdictions for EMU membership can be considered somehow optimistic, although Cyprus, Estonia, Latvia, Lithuania, Malta, and Slovenia have already linked their currencies to the euro in the ERM–II exchange rate mechanism. But optimism is what has characterized the founders of the European integration project.

However, the Cassandras of the project could still have their omens realized. Article I–60 of the proposed EU Constitution foresees the possibility of a

---

[129] Council Decision 1999/98/EC of 31 December 1998 on the position to be taken by the Community regarding an agreement concerning the monetary relations with Vatican City [1999] OJ L30/35.

[130] Monetary Agreement between the State of the Vatican City, represented by the Holy See, and the Italian Republic on behalf of the European Community [2001] OJ C299/1.

[131] Monetary Agreement between the Government of the French Republic, on behalf of the European Community, and the Government of His Serene Highness the Prince of Monaco [2002] OJ L142/59.

[132] Stumpf, above note 126, 284. See also the ECB Opinion on Andorra, CON/2004/32, OJ C256 16.10.2004, 9 on <http://www.ecb.int/ecb/legal/pdf/c_25620041016en00090009.pdf> and on the Council decision on opening negotiations on an agreement concerning monetary relations with Andorra on <http://www.ecb.int/ecb/legal/pdf/com2004_0548en01.pdf>.

[133] ibid.

'voluntarily withdraw from the Union'. A withdrawal (or simply the threat to withdraw) might affect the stability and credibility of the single currency. However, if this hypothetical possibility would ever be exercised, theoretically, the Member State wishing to withdraw—assuming it is a country that has adopted the euro—could try to negotiate an agreement in which it would still keep the euro as its currency.[134]

The prospect that European monetary union might fall apart or that one country might wish to exit from the euro-zone and recreate its own national currency has been raised in some circles.[135]

As I explained in Chapter 1, though there is no provision in the EC Treaty which permits the revocation of EMU (no 'exit-clause') and though the wording 'irrevocably fixed' adopted by the Maastricht Treaty indicates that, from a legal point of view, the adoption of the euro is 'a trip with no return' (irreversible),[136] the Member States retain—as a residual attribute of their sovereignty—the possibility of reversing the current status quo by unanimous agreement (ie, by signing a new Treaty to that effect).[137]

We should not forget that laws, treaties, and constitutions can change and do change, and that they need 'societal legitimacy' for their long term survival.

---

[134] For an extensive discussion of the legal consequences of such a theoretical possibility, see Charles Proctor, *Mann on The Legal Aspect of Money*, 6th edn (Oxford: Oxford University Press, 2005), ch 32. See also Jean-Victor Louis, above note 34, 29.

[135] See Daniel Gros, Thomas Mayer, and Angel Ubide, 'EMU at risk', Seventh Annual Report of the CEPS Macroeconomic Policy Group, Centre for European Policy Studies, June 2005, <http://www.ceps.be>. See also Martin Wolf, 'The Crushing Reality of Making the Eurozone Work', *Financial Times*, 8 June 2005.

[136] The Protocol (nowadays numbered No 24) attached to the EC Treaty on the irreversible character of the Community's movement to the third stage of economic and monetary union, is a document that the authors of the proposed EU Constitution did not include among the texts adopted. I thank René Smits for observations on this point.

[137] See Tullio Treves, 'Monetary Sovereignty Today' in Mario Giovanoli (ed), *International Monetary Law: Issues for the New Millennium* (Oxford: Oxford University Press, 2000) 116, cited in ch 1. See also René Smits, 'The European Constitution and EMU: an Appraisal', (2005) 42 Common Market Law Review 444, 465.

8

ECONOMIC POLICY COORDINATION ('ECONOMIC UNION')

The concern of the Bundestag to oppose any relaxation of the stability criteria derives support from the Protocol on the Convergence Criteria. Without German agreement, the convergence criteria cannot be relaxed.

Extract from the Judgment of the German Federal Constitutional Court, 18 October 1993, recital 86[1]

---

[1] See Judgment of the German Federal Constitutional Court (Bundesverfassungsgericht) of 12 October 1993 in the case of *Brunner v The European Union Treaty*, published in Recht der Internationalen Wirtschaft 1993, Supplement No 5 to Issue No 12. An English translation was published in (1994) 1 Common Market Law Review 57.

> We must not apply the treaty provisions on imposing [fiscal] mandatory requirements and sanctions too mechanically. . . . More respect should be given to the EU members' primary competence over economic and fiscal policy.
>
> Gerhard Schröder, former German Chancellor writing in the *Financial Times*, 17 January 2005, on the reform of the Stability and Growth Pact ('A Framework for a Stable Europe')

A. Introduction

I start this chapter with two different quotations. The first represents the 'official' German view at the time when the Maastricht Treaty was ratified. As Samuel Brittan lucidly put it: 'Fiscal criteria are the German price for EMU'.[2] The second quote represents the more recent German view, characterized by a desire to relax the Stability and Growth Pact. The costs of German reunification have proven to be more onerous and long-lasting than originally anticipated; structural reforms in tax, pensions, and the labour market are still needed; the 'stability culture' that I referred in Chapter 2 appears to have been replaced by a pragmatic approach focused on business cycles and current economic needs.

This is an interesting turn of events. In the negotiations that led to the Maastricht Treaty, Germany was adamant that fiscal sustainability was to be a key foundation for monetary stability and, accordingly, the Community's primary and secondary law enshrined numerical and quantitative criteria with regard to the prohibition of 'excessive' deficits and the size of the public debt and established procedures to enforce such rules. Germany was the main 'architect' of the Stability and Growth Pact as introduced in 1997 to ensure that the prohibition of excessive deficits could be enforced through strict rules and sanctions and to introduce an EU-wide medium-term objective of budgetary balance for the Member States.

These rules and sanctions, which constitute the framework underpinning fiscal policy in the European Union, and which were hailed by many as a guarantee of restraint and a condition for the success of the euro, have been the subject of intense debate. In particular, the automatic nature of the excessive deficit procedure has been much criticized in recent years (the words of the former President of the EU Commission, Romano Prodi, still resonate: 'stupid' rules). According to Mario Monti,

---

[2] See Samuel Brittan, 'EMU in Perspective' in Mads Andenas et al (eds), *European Economic and Monetary Union: The Institutional Framework* (The Hague: Kluwer Law International, 1997) 118.

[I]t would have been far preferable for the EU to have adopted a more rational pact from the start, or to have modified it only after the completion of a full first round of enforcement. Instead, the imperfect pact was applied rigorously to two small member states—Ireland and Portugal—then suspended and changed when France and Germany, the same countries that originally opposed the adoption of a lax pact, ran into difficulty. In the process, the fundamental principle of equality of treatment has been violated and the EU's credibility damaged.[3]

The breach of the budgetary rules by Germany and France (as I explain below) has seriously damaged the credibility of the SGP. The judgment of the Court of Justice of 13 July 2004,[4] which I also discuss below, has shown that judicial involvement cannot sort out the problems of economic policy coordination (the Court, in this case, limited its judgment to the clarification of the powers of the Council and the Commission relating to the excessive deficit procedure but did not rule on the wisdom of the fiscal rules). Judicial activism that occurs in other areas of EC law (particularly competition law and the area of the internal market) may not be expected in this field.

This chapter examines the rules on economic policy coordination according to the EU's primary and secondary law. Though the SGP (secondary law) has been reformed in 2005, the EC Treaty (primary law) imposes a permanent obligation upon the Member States to avoid excessive deficits and provides for further macro- and micro-economic coordination, multilateral surveillance, and regional adjustment.

The need for economic and social cohesion is of great relevance for the success of economic coordination, in particular in the light of the enlargement of the EU eastwards, an issue which I briefly discuss at the end of this chapter.

B. The Area of Jurisdiction of Fiscal Policy

There is no common fiscal policy in Europe. As I mentioned in Chapter 6, the term 'economic union' is a misnomer, because while the term monetary union conveys the reality of 'oneness', there is no 'oneness' with regard to the Member States' primary competence over economic and fiscal policy. The singleness of

---

[3] See Mario Monti, 'Toughen Up the Reform Agenda and Make it Count', *Financial Times*, 22 March 2005.

[4] See Case C–27/04 *Commission of the European Communities v Council of the European Union* 13 July 2004, in OJ C228/16, 11 September 2004, <http://europa.eu.int/eur-lex/lex/LexUriServ/site/en/oj/2004/c_228/c_22820040911en00160017.pdf>, concerning the action of the Commission and the conclusions of the Council with regard to the excessive deficits of France and Germany. See also the European Court of Justice Press Release No 57/04 of 13 July 2004 concerning Case C–27/04.

monetary policy contrasts with the multiplicity of fiscal policies. The area of jurisdiction of fiscal policy is national. The area of jurisdiction of monetary policy (for those countries which have adopted the euro) is supranational.

According to Alexandre Lamfalussy, 'the greatest weakness of EMU is the E. The M Part is institutionally well organised. We have a solid framework. We don't have that for economic policy.'[5]

The term 'economic' is a broad concept that in other contexts also encompasses exchange rate and monetary policies, trade policy, and others. In the EU context, however, the term 'economic union' refers mostly to the budgetary position and fiscal policies of the Member States.

It should be noted that the EU budget is small and financed wholly from 'own resources'.[6] According to Begg, 'it amounts to just over 1% of Community Gross National Income, with nearly half of the spending going on the Common Agricultural Policy (CAP).'[7] The EU budget is a 'curious hybrid', since it is much more than the budget assigned to international organizations such as the IMF, but not comparable to the budget of 'an autonomous political entity which . . . has some direct link with a local electorate in relation to fund-raising'.[8]

The advent of monetary union took place without a corresponding transfer of fiscal powers to a supranational authority. A centralized monetary policy now coexists with decentralized fiscal policies, albeit subject to significant procedural and substantive supranational constraints, in particular the permanent obligation imposed upon Member States to avoid excessive deficits.[9]

> EMU essentially rests on an asymmetric two-pillar structure, splitting competences between the Community and the Member States. The competence for the execution and, to a considerable extent, also for the formulation of economic policy has been left with the Member States. Arguably, at the time of the drafting of the

---

[5] See Alexandre Lamfalussy, interview published in *The Guardian*, 16 August 2003.

[6] See Art 269 EC Treaty.

[7] Iain Begg, 'Future Fiscal Arrangements in the European Union', (2004) 41 Common Market Law Review 776.

[8] ibid 781.

[9] A somewhat contrary view is expressed by the President of the Dutch Central Bank, who in the President's introduction to the 2004 Annual Report of the Dutch Central Bank, available at <http://www.dnb.nl/dnb/bin.doc.ar03_tcm13–39878.pdf> mentions that

> Where national monetary sovereignty in Europe has been transferred to the European Central Bank, the pendant—in order to avoid conflicts between monetary and fiscal policies—is the limitation of national budget deficits and the agreement, measured over the cycle, to reduce the deficit close to zero or to realise a surplus. In essence, this comes down to a partial transfer of national fiscal sovereignty. The partial nature of the transfer should be stressed; the transfer of sovereignty relates solely to the balance of revenues and expenditures, and not to their level or composition.

I thank René Smits for bringing this report to my attention.

provisions on EMU this not only reflected the diversity between the Member States' economic structures and economic developments and the different beliefs of what economic policy can and cannot achieve, but also the political conviction of the Member States at large that fiscal policy should essentially remain a national competence.[10]

'Economic union' is, in fact, economic policy coordination, which can be defined as 'supranational rules or norms which are agreed by all Member States, which leave primary responsibility for the policy area with national authorities, but set limits on their discretion. The EC Treaty mentions various forms of economic policy co-ordination: the broad economic policy guidelines, multilateral surveillance and the excessive deficit procedure'.[11]

Below I present an analysis of the legal provisions regulating economic policy in the EU, differentiating between primary law and secondary law, since it is far easier to amend the latter than the former.

C. Primary Law Regarding 'Economic Union'

The establishment of economic and monetary union is, alongside the establishment of the common market, a key component of the Community strategy towards the high aims of Article 2 EC Treaty. Article 4(1) EC Treaty defines the economic component of EMU as 'the adoption of an economic policy which is based on the close coordination of Member States' economic policies, on the internal market and on the definition of common objectives, and conducted in accordance with the principle of an open market economy with free competition'.

I pointed out in Chapter 6 that the first clear legal basis of 'economic union' was Article 102A EC Treaty as revised by the Single European Act. This provision was the only article in a new Chapter I, entitled 'Co-operation in Economic and Monetary Policy (Economic and Monetary Union)' which was inserted by the SEA in Part Three, Title II of the EEC Treaty.

The Maastricht Treaty on European Union introduced important provisions regarding economic policy coordination in a new Title VI (Economic and Monetary Policy), Chapter 1 (Economic Policy). The Maastricht rules are largely a taking over into primary law of what previously was regulated under secondary law. Articles 98–104 of the EC Treaty set out the core principles and

---

[10] See Fabian Amtenbrink and Jakob De Haan, 'Economic Governance in the European Union: Fiscal Policy Discipline versus Flexibility' (2003) 40 Common Market Law Review 1078.

[11] ibid 1075, quoting Begg, Hodson, and Maher, 'Economic Policy Coordination in the European Union', National Institute Economic Review, No 183, (Jan. 2003) 66.

standards which define the scope and scale of common economic policies in the context of EMU.

The key primary law provisions regarding economic policy are Article 99 EC[12] regarding broad guidelines and multilateral surveillance and Article 104 EC[13] regarding excessive deficits and the excessive deficit procedure. These two provisions have been further elaborated in two regulations (key components of the SGP) as explained below.

Article 99 EC is an element of 'positive integration'.[14] Positive integration requires the coordination of Member State policies, as well as the approximation of laws and regulations. A fundamental principle of the 'economic' component of EMU is that public finances in individual Member States are a matter for common concern at the European level and the subject of 'positive integration' with the adoption of common rules and procedures.

Article 104 EC is an element of 'negative integration', which entails measures which Member States shall abolish and actions which they shall refrain from taking (ie, excessive deficits). There are other forms of negative integration besides the avoidance of excessive deficits, such as the prohibition to finance government deficits via central bank credit, which I further discuss below.

According to Amtenbrink and de Haan, while multilateral surveillance is a form of open coordination, the excessive deficit procedure is a form of closed coordination.

> The open method relies on self-commitment by the Member States, peer review and benchmarking, placing emphasis on policy learning and consensus building, while the closed method tends to have top-down policy formulation and provides for binding rules and severe sanctions. Also in terms of the distinction between hard and soft law, where hard law lies at one end of a continuum and soft law at the other, the multilateral surveillance and the excessive deficit procedures are different, the latter being 'harder'.[15]

---

[12] See also Art III–179 of the proposed EU Constitution.

[13] See also Art III–184 of the proposed EU Constitution.

[14] See René Smits, *The European Central Bank. Institutional Aspects* (The Hague: Kluwer Law International, 1997) 55. In the view of Smits, 'this positive integration does not entail material norm-setting as in the area of competition policy or in the harmonization of legislation for the full exercise of market freedoms or the proper supervision of market participants . . . Yet . . . the economic policies in the Community are to be geared towards objectives specified in the Treaty and embedded in the framework of an open market with free competition. In this respect, economic policy coordination is norm-bound.'

[15] Above note 11, 1076. See also Hodson and Maher, 'Hard, Soft and Open Methods of Policy Coordination and the Reform of the Stability and Growth Pact', Paper prepared for the Conference Building EU Economic Government: Revising the Rules?, organized by NYU in London and UACES, London, 25–6 April, 2003.

The proposed EU Constitution[16] does not alter substantially the contents of the EC Treaty. The provisions on economic policy coordination are inserted in Section 1 (Economic Policy) of Chapter II (Economic and Monetary Policy), comprising Article III–178 to Article III–184.

Economic policy coordination is not included in the 'areas of shared competences' defined in Article I–14 of the proposed Constitution. Instead the Constitution introduces a specific provision, Article I–15 to deal with 'the co-ordination of economic and employment policies', which reads as follows:

1. The Member States shall coordinate their economic policies within the Union. To this end, the Council of Ministers shall adopt measures, in particular broad guidelines for these policies.

   Specific provisions shall apply to those Member States whose currency is the euro.
2. The Union shall take measures to ensure coordination of the employment policies of the Member States, in particular by defining guidelines for these policies.
3. The Union may take initiatives to ensure coordination of Member States' social policies.

Article I–12, which is a provision dealing with 'categories of competence', refers to the coordination of economic policies in its paragraph 3 (while paragraph 1 deals with exclusive competences and paragraph 2 with shared competences). This has prompted some commentators to argue that economic policy coordination is a 'specific competence'.[17] René Smits claims, however, that it is a 'shared competence'.[18] Jean Victor Louis maintains that the 'compromise formula' adopted tries to satisfy the viewpoint of those who favoured a formula expressing that it was up to the Member States to coordinate their economic policy within the Union and the standpoint of those who favoured

---

[16] As I have already pointed out in other chapters, the proposed Constitution (ie, the Treaty establishing a Constitution for Europe, available in the Official Journal No C310 of 16 December 2004) was thrown into a legal limbo following the rejection of the Treaty in referenda in France (28 May 2005) and Holland (1 June 2005). The suspension of the ratification process (according to the declaration of the European Council Brussels summit on 16–17 June 2005 to allow for a 'period of reflection') does not equate to the abandonment altogether of the proposed Constitution. The text of the Constitutional Treaty remains a legal document of value to refer to, also with a view to its possible entry into force or the taking over of parts of it in other Treaty texts later on.

[17] See Dominique Servais and Rodolphe Ruggeri, 'The EU Constitution: its Impact on Economic and Monetary Union and Economic Governance' in *Legal Aspects of the European System of Central Banks, Liber Amicorum Paolo Zamboni Garavelli* (Frankfurt: European Central Bank, 2005) 50.

[18] See René Smits, 'The European Constitution and EMU: an Appraisal' (2005) 42 Common Market Law Review 444. Smits argues that the coordination of economic policies is a shared competence (through a joint interpretation of Arts I–13, which defines the 'areas of exclusive competence', I–14(1), and I–17 of the proposed EU Constitution).

that it was up to the Union to coordinate the economic policies of the Member States.[19]

The doctrinal debate concerning what sort of category of competence economic policy coordination is, reflects the uneasy cohabitation in the Treaty and in the proposed Constitution of a centralized monetary policy and an essentially decentralized (albeit coordinated) fiscal policy.

Coordination ('positive integration')

'A co-ordinated economic policy is not a luxury for a monetary union. It may be essential to its long-term survival.'[20]

According to Article 99(1) of the EC Treaty (and Art III–179(1) of the proposed EU Constitution) Member States shall regard their economic policies as a matter of common concern and shall coordinate them with the Council. The main instruments to achieve coordination are the setting out of broad guidelines—Article 99(2)—and a mechanism for peer review—Article 99(3)—which is referred to as 'multilateral surveillance' (a term reminiscent of the IMF surveillance function that I further discuss in Chapter 13).

The procedure for the adoption of these 'broad economic guidelines' is as follows: The Council, acting by a qualified majority on a recommendation from the Commission, formulates a draft for these guidelines and reports its findings to the European Council. In turn, the European Council, acting on the basis of the report from the Council, discusses a conclusion on these broad guidelines of the economic policies of the Member States and of the Community. On the basis of this conclusion, the Council, acting by a qualified majority, adopts a recommendation setting out these broad guidelines and informs the European Parliament of this recommendation.[21]

---

[19] Jean Victor Louis, 'The Economic and Monetary Union: Law and Institutions' (2004) 41 Common Market Law Review 582

[20] Wolfang Munchau, 'Eurozone faces risks if inflation rates stay out of line', *Financial Times*, 31 May 2004. Wolfang Munchau argues that 'the eurozone's failure to achieve convergence of inflation rates is puzzling.' He cites a paper written by two economists from the European Central Bank, Ignazio Angeloni and Michael Ehrmann, claiming that the main reason for inflation differentials in the eurozone is 'inflation persistence' in some EC countries, ie, the inherent tendency to produce inflation as a result of structural economic factors, such as systems of wage bargaining or price-setting mechanisms. According to these economists, persistent differences in inflation rates among countries in a monetary union can have a dramatic effect on competitiveness. Munchau reflects on this destabilizing effect and suggests that 'the trouble with the eurozone is that the ECB is the only genuine "pan-European player" in the entire game. Fiscal policy is determined by national governments, labour markets are organised on national lines and people and companies still form their price expectations on a national basis. The idea that you can run autonomous national policies in a monetary union seems increasingly unrealistic.'

[21] Article 99(2) EC Treaty.

The recommendations often resemble reports and economic surveys prepared by the IMF or the OECD. For example, the Council Recommendation of 26 June 2003 on the broad guidelines of the economic policies of the Member States and the Community (for the 2003–5 period) urges the Member States 'to reach or maintain budgetary positions of close to balance or in surplus throughout the economic cycle; countries with deficits exceeding the close to balance or in surplus stability and growth pact requirement must improve their cyclically-adjusted position; countries with excessive deficits need to correct them in line with the stability and growth pact'.[22]

Multilateral surveillance, according to Article 99(3) EC Treaty, refers to the assessment of the economic policies of the Member States to ensure convergence and consistency with the broad guidelines defined above. The Member States provide the relevant information, the basis for the assessment, to the Commission. The Commission then prepares the reports that it submits to the Council for the purposes of 'multilateral surveillance'.

If the assessment concludes, according to Article 99(4) EC Treaty, that the economic policies of the Member States are not consistent with the broad guidelines or that they risk jeopardizing the proper functioning of economic and monetary union, the Council may make the necessary recommendations to the Member State concerned, acting by a qualified majority on a recommendation from the Commission. It may also decide to make its recommendations public, acting by a qualified majority on a proposal from the Commission. The President of the Council and the Commission shall report to the European Parliament on the results of multilateral surveillance.

Prohibitions ('negative integration')

There are strong reasons to restrict the fiscal behaviour of governments in the Member States which have adopted the euro, even though the experience of fiscal decentralization in a monetary union is novel. Borrowing and spending decisions by the government in one Member State may have negative influences

---

[22] Council Recommendation of 26 June 2003 on the broad guidelines of the economic policies of the Member States and the Community (for the 2003–2005 period) OJ 2003 L195/1. There is also a section with guidelines addressed to individual Member States. For example, Greece is recommended *inter alia* to (1) ensure that the government debt ratio is kept on a sustained declining trend at a satisfactory pace by maintaining high primary surpluses, (2) ensure effective control of government current primary spending by addressing resolutely the problem of the inelastic elements of expenditures such as the wage bill, (3) use public resources more effectively with the aim of improving labour productivity and enhancing working capacity of the unemployed and (4) continue reforms of the social security system, and in particular the pension system, in order to avoid budgetary strains in the future due to the problem of the ageing population.

in the whole euro-zone, driving up interest rates (inflation) and crowding out private investment.[23] The EC Treaty contains a number of prohibitions which are intended to reinforce market discipline and to impose an official level of fiscal restraint.[24]

Prohibition of monetization of government debt

In accordance with the provisions of Article 101(1) of the EC Treaty (and Art III–181 of the proposed EU Constitution), overdraft facilities or any other type of credit facility with the ECB or with the central banks of the Member States in favour of Community institutions or bodies, central governments, regional, local, or other public authorities, other bodies governed by public law, or public undertakings of Member States are prohibited. The same applies for the purchase directly from these public organizations by the ECB or national central banks of debt instruments. The prohibition does not apply to publicly owned credit institutions which, in the context of the supply of reserves by central banks, are given the same treatment by national central banks and the ECB as private credit institutions.[25]

The rule prohibiting government financing is repeated in Article 21 of the ESCB Statute which concerns operations of the ESCB with public entities. While Article 21 allows the ECB and NCBs to perform functions as fiscal agents for governments, it prohibits the financing of governments.

Prohibition of privileged access to financial institutions

In accordance with Article 102 EC Treaty (and Art III–182 of the proposed EU Constitution), any measure, not based on prudential considerations, establishing privileged access by Community institutions or bodies, central governments, regional, local, or other public authorities, other bodies governed by public law, or public undertakings of Member States to financial institutions is prohibited.

Prohibition of 'bailouts' of governments

In accordance with the provisions of Article 103 EC Treaty (and Art III–183 of the proposed EU Constitution), the Community is not liable for and does not assume the commitments and liabilities of central governments, regional, local, or other public authorities, other bodies governed by public law, or public undertakings of any Member State (with the exception of mutual financial guarantees for the joint execution of a specific project). Similarly, a Member

---

[23] Above note 14, 74.
[24] ibid 74–9. Smits provides an insightful discussion of these prohibitions.
[25] Article 101(2) EC.

State is not liable for and does not assume the commitments and liabilities of central governments, regional, local, or other public authorities, other bodies governed by public law, or public undertakings of another Member State (with the exception of mutual financial guarantees for the joint execution of a specific project).

As Smits points out, 'financial markets are hereby warned that each Member State is "on its own" and not backed by implicit guarantees from the Community or from fellow Member States.'[26] Governments whose behaviour is financially irresponsible are therefore not allowed to 'free ride' on the creditworthiness of other Member States and will pay the risk premiums for their own individual circumstances. The 'no bailout' clause is clear and precise.

In respect of risk premiums, Member States' government bonds have been able to benefit so far from the euro-zone's single interest rate, regardless of the state of their public finances.[27] This is likely to change in future. The financial markets will exert their discipline upon 'weaker governments' (ie, upon members in breach of EU rules on deficits and debt levels) by widening the yield spreads on their government bonds and lowering their credit ratings. The European Central Bank has published minimum credit standards defining the limits on what it will accept as adequate collateral in its credit operations.[28] The ECB President, Jean Claude Trichet, has clarified that the ECB will refuse to accept as collateral government bonds rated below A-, which has been interpreted as a reminder to Member States that serious 'market penalties' await countries that exhibit fiscal indiscipline.[29]

Some economists have argued that a single monetary area would require financial transfers from one region to another to absorb cyclical problems or to deal with other problems.[30] However, the EC Treaty does not include any provision regarding the possibility of fiscal transfers to deal with cyclical problems or to offset regional/national imbalances.

The limited scope for exercising financial solidarity is foreseen in Article 100

---

[26] See Smits, above note 14, 77.

[27] See *Financial Times* editorial, 20 November 2005, 'ECB shows its hand': '[T]here has been little differentiation [so far] in a market that has tended to believe that there is an implicit guarantee of all euro-zone government debt.'

[28] See European Central Bank, 'The Implementation of Monetary Policy in the Euro area', February 2005, Chapter 6, at <http://www.ecb.int/pub/pdf/other/gendoc2005en.pdf> See also <http://www.ecb.int/mopo/implement/assets/coll/html/index.en.html>.

[29] Above note 27. See also Joanna Chung and Ralph Atkins, 'ECB sends powers signal on debt', *Financial Times*, 10 November 2005.

[30] Indeed, this is one of the tenets of fiscal federalism. Above note 7, 779. 'There is plenty of evidence in the literature on the importance of transfers from the federal level in stabilizing economies.'

EC Treaty (Art III–180 of the proposed EU Constitution). Article 100(2) EC Treaty addresses situations in which a Member State 'is in difficulties or is seriously threatened with severe difficulties caused by natural disasters or exceptional occurrences beyond its control'. In these cases, the Council, acting by a qualified majority on a proposal from the Commission, may grant, under certain conditions, Community financial assistance to the Member State concerned. However, this possible assistance is discretionary, not mandatory. The President of the Council shall inform the European Parliament of the decision taken. Article 100(1) EC Treaty establishes that the Council may adopt 'measures appropriate to the economic situation, in particular if severe difficulties arise in the supply of certain products', thus going beyond the mere coordination of States' policies.

Prohibition of excessive deficits

The prohibition in Article 104(1) EC Treaty (and Art III–184 of the proposed EU Constitution) is a firm rule: 'Member States shall avoid excessive government deficits.' This provision entered into force as of Stage Three and replaced the milder provision applicable during Stage Two.[31] (This milder provision still applies to the United Kingdom, according to paragraph 6 of its opt-out protocol.)

It is for the Commission to monitor the budgetary situation in the Member States and for the Council to decide whether an excessive deficit exists and, if necessary, to compel the Member State to reduce the deficit identified.

The reference values   Under Article 104(2) EC Treaty, the Commission examines compliance with budgetary discipline on the basis of the following two criteria:

(a) whether the ratio of the planned or actual government deficit to gross domestic product exceeds a reference value, unless either the ratio has declined substantially and continuously and reached a level that comes close to the reference value, or, alternatively, the excess over the reference value is only exceptional and temporary and the ratio remains close to the reference value;

(b) whether the ratio of government debt to gross domestic product exceeds a reference value, unless the ratio is sufficiently diminishing and approaching the reference value at a satisfactory pace.

The reference values are specified in the Protocol on the excessive deficit

---

[31] 'In the second stage, Member States shall endeavour to avoid excessive government deficits.' See Art 116(4) EC Treaty.

procedure annexed to the EC Treaty.[32] According to Article 1 of the Protocol the reference values referred to in Article 104(2) of the EC Treaty are: (a) three per cent for the ratio of the planned or actual government deficit to gross domestic product at market prices and (b) sixty per cent for the ratio of government debt to gross domestic product at market prices.

The Treaty provides some room for interpretation and a degree of discretion in the application of the reference values. The definition of an excessive deficit according to Article 104 EC entails a judgement. A current deficit, for instance, exceeding the reference value of three per cent does not constitute a lack of budgetary discipline if 'the ratio has declined substantially and continuously and reached a level that comes close to the reference value' or, alternatively, the excess over the reference value is 'only exceptional and temporary and the ratio remains close to the reference value'. Similarly, the total stock of government debt may be in excess of sixty per cent of the GDP without leading to the finding of budgetary imbalance provided that 'the ratio is sufficiently diminishing and approaching the reference value at a satisfactory pace'.

Under the provisions of Article 104(3) EC Treaty, the Commission prepares a report if a Member State does not fulfil the requirements under one or both of these criteria. But the two criteria are not the only ones to be taken into account. The Commission must also take into account 'whether the government deficit exceeds government investment expenditure' (which reflects the golden rule that only investment can be financed through deficits) and 'all other relevant factors, including the medium-term economic and budgetary position' of the Member State in question.

The Protocol on the Excessive Deficit Procedure further defines the technical terms used in Article 104 EC Treaty.[33] Hence, for the purposes of the excessive deficit procedure, 'government' means 'general government', that is, central government, regional or local government, and social security funds, to the exclusion of commercial operations, as defined in the European System of Integrated Economic Accounts; 'deficit' means net borrowing as defined in the European System of Integrated Economic Accounts; 'investment' means gross fixed capital formation as defined in the European System of Integrated Economic Accounts; and 'debt' means total gross debt at nominal value outstanding at the end of the year and consolidated between and within the sectors of general government as defined in the first indent.

Under Article 3 of the Protocol, the governments of the Member States are

---

[32] This protocol is also annexed (as Protocol 10) to the proposed Treaty Establishing a Constitution for Europe.

[33] See Protocol on the Excessive Deficit Procedure annexed to the EC Treaty, Art 2.

deemed responsible for the deficits of general government as defined above. Further, the Member States must ensure that national procedures in the budgetary area enable them to meet their obligations for the purposes of the excessive deficit procedures and must report their planned and actual deficits and the levels of their debt promptly and regularly to the Commission. But crucially, it is the statistical data provided by the Commission and not the statistical data provided by Member States which are decisive for the purposes of the excessive deficit procedure.[34]

The crucial reference values of three per cent and sixty per cent and the remaining provisions of the Protocol can be replaced by appropriate provisions adopted by the Council, acting unanimously on a proposal from the Commission and after consulting the European Parliament and the ECB.[35]

The excessive deficit procedure   The excessive deficit procedure is a procedure in stages. Article 104 EC Treaty (and Art III–184 of the EC Constitution) specifies the manner in which it is carried out and the respective roles and powers of the Commission, the Council, and the Member States. Since these are provisions of primary law, they can only be altered by a revision of the Treaty.

- The Commission monitors the budgetary position of the Member States and the compliance with the reference values of three and sixty per cent of government deficit and total government debt to GDP with a view to identifying gross errors (Art 104(2) EC Treaty).

- According to Article 104(3) EC Treaty, if a Member State does not fulfil the requirements under one or both of the criteria, or if the Commission is of the opinion that there is a risk of an excessive deficit in a Member State, the Commission prepares a report. *The Commission has the right of initiative in the excessive deficit procedure.*[36]

- The Commission Report is discussed in the Economic and Financial Committee, which formulates an opinion (Art 104(4) EC Treaty).

- Should the Commission consider that an excessive deficit in a Member State 'exists' or 'may occur' the Commission addresses an opinion to the Council (Art 104(5) EC Treaty).

- The Council decides after an overall assessment whether an excessive deficit 'exists', acting by a qualified majority on a recommendation from the

---

[34] ibid, Art 4.   [35] See Art 104(14) EC Treaty.

[36] The powers of the Commission and the Council have been clarified by the European Court of Justice in its judgment of 13 July 2004, Case C–27/04 *Commission v Council.* Art III–184 of the proposed EU Constitution establishes that the Council establishes the existence of an excessive deficit on a Commission *proposal* instead of a Commission's recommendation. This point is made by Smits, above note 18.

Commission, and having considered any observations which the Member State concerned may wish to make (Art 104(6) EC Treaty).

- According to Article 104(7) EC Treaty, where the existence of an excessive deficit is decided, the Council may make recommendations to the Member State concerned with a view to bringing the situation to an end within a given period. This first set of recommendations must not be made public.

- The recommendations can only be made public after a separate decision to that effect by the Council, if the Council establishes that there has been no effective action in response to its recommendations within the period laid down (Art 104(8) EC Treaty).

- If, however, a participating Member State persists in failing to put into practice the recommendations of the Council, the Council may decide to give notice to the Member State to take, within a specified time limit, measures for the deficit reduction which is judged necessary by the Council in order to remedy the situation, and to submit reports on its proposed adjustment efforts (Art 104(9) EC Treaty). *Responsibility for making the Member States observe budgetary discipline lies essentially with the Council.*

- According to Article 104(11) EC Treaty, as long as a participating Member State fails to comply with the decision of the Council, the Council may decide to apply or, as the case may be, intensify one or more of the following measures: (1) to require the Member State concerned to publish additional information, to be specified by the Council, before issuing bonds and securities, (2) to invite the European Investment Bank to reconsider its lending policy towards the Member State concerned, (3) to require the Member State concerned to make a non-interest-bearing deposit of an appropriate size with the Community until the excessive deficit has, in the view of the Council, been corrected, and (4) to impose fines of an appropriate size. All these measures must be made public, alerting of course investors in financial markets. The President of the European Council must also inform the European Parliament of the decisions taken.

Article 104(9) and Article 104(11) do not apply to Member States with a derogation, according to Article 122(3) EC Treaty and paragraph 5 of the UK opt-out protocol.

It must be noted that the normal provisions of securing a State's compliance with the EC Treaty (Arts 226 and 227 EC Treaty) do not apply in the excessive deficit procedure.[37]

---

[37] See EC Treaty Art 104(10).

Any decision to impose a sanction or not to impose a sanction is, of course, subject to judicial review.[38]

Once an excessive deficit has been corrected, the Council is obliged to make a public statement that an excessive deficit in the Member State concerned no longer exists, if it, the Council, had previously made public recommendations with regard to its existence (Art 104(12) EC).

Regarding the voting arrangements in the Council, the Member State concerned may vote only in the initial assessment of the deficit situation. For any decision taken thereafter, the Council acts on a recommendation from the Commission by a majority of two thirds of the votes of its members weighted in accordance with Article 205(2), excluding the votes of the representative of the Member State concerned.[39] The adjustments introduced by the Treaty of Nice (signed on 26 February 2001 and with effect from 1 February 2003) and the requirements of Article 3 of the Protocol on the Enlargement of the European Union, with regard to voting procedures in the Council, need to be taken into account.[40]

In its judgment of 13 July 2004,[41] the Court clarified the powers of the Council and the Commission relating to the excessive deficit procedure, as I further explain below.

D. Secondary Law: The Stability and Growth Pact

The secondary law concerning economic policy coordination comprises a number of regulations of which the most significant ones are those that form the core of the Stability and Growth Pact, which I analyse in this section.

In the ensuing paragraphs, I briefly present first some of the instruments of secondary law regarding the 'E' component of EMU which were adopted before the SGP.

Following one of the recommendations of the Delors Report, on 12 March 1990 the Council adopted the Council Decision 90/141/EEC on the Attainment of Progressive Convergence of Economic Policies and Performance during Stage One of Economic and Monetary Union.[42] In that decision, the Council

---

[38] Above note 14, 82. Smits discusses the excessive deficit procedure in pp 78–83.

[39] See Art 104(13) EC Treaty.

[40] See Smits, above note 18, 431–4 with regard to the voting procedures under the proposed EU Constitution and implications thereof.

[41] Above note 4.

[42] [1990] OJ L78, 23. This Council Decision repealed the Council Decision 74/120/EEC of 18 February 1974 on the attainment of a high degree of convergence of the economic policies of the Member States of the European Economic Community as well as the Council Directive 74/121/EEC of 18 February 1974 on stability, growth, and full employment in the Community.

officially acknowledged that progress towards economic and monetary union required a high degree of convergence of economic performances between Member States through greater compatibility and closer coordination of economic policies. According to Article 1 of Decision 90/141, the Council was empowered to undertake 'multilateral surveillance' in order to help to achieve sustained non-inflationary growth in the Community, together with a high level of employment and the degree of economic convergence necessary for the success of Stage One of Economic and Monetary Union.[43]

Council Regulation (EC) No 3604/93 of 13 December 1993 elaborates on the application of the prohibition of privileged access referred to in Article 104a of the Treaty[44] and the concept of 'privileged access'.

Council Regulation (EC) No 3603/93 of 13 December 1993 specifies definitions for the application of the prohibitions referred to in Articles 104 and 104(b)(1) of the Treaty regarding the prohibition to finance government deficits via central bank credit.[45] For example, the term 'overdraft facilities' is defined as any provision of funds to the public sector resulting or likely to result in a debit balance.[46] 'Public sector' means Community institutions or bodies, central governments, regional, local, or other public authorities, other bodies governed by public law, or public undertakings of Member States.[47] The power of the Council to adopt Regulations for the purpose of defining these technical concepts is based on Article 103(2) EC Treaty.

The Council laid down detailed rules and definitions for the application of the provisions of the Protocol on the Excessive Deficit Procedure annexed to the EC Treaty in Council Regulation (EC) No 3605/93 of 22 November 1993, as amended.[48]

---

[43] ibid, Art 3.

[44] [1993] OJ L332, 31 December 1993, 4. The Regulation was adopted under the enabling provisions of Art 102(2) EC. Article 1 of the Regulation defines privileged access

as any law, regulation or any other binding legal instrument adopted in the exercise of public authority which:

- Obliges financial institutions to acquire or to hold liabilities of Community institutions or bodies, central governments, regional, local or other public authorities, other bodies governed by public law or public undertakings of Member States (hereinafter referred to as 'public sector'), or

- Confers tax advantages which may benefit only financial institutions or financial advantages which do not comply with the principles of a market economy, in order to encourage the acquiring or the holding by those institutions of such liabilities.

[45] [1993] OJ L332, 1.   [46] Article 1(a).   [47] Article 3.

[48] [1993] OJ L332, 31 December 1993, 7. Under Art 4 of Council Regulation 3605/93, from the beginning of 1994, Member States shall report to the Commission their planned and actual government deficits and levels of government debt twice a year, the first time before 1 March of the current year (year n) and the second time before 1 September of year n. Regulation 3605/93 was last amended by Regulation 351/2002 of 25 February 2002, [2002] OJ L55, 26 February 2002, 23.

The history of the Stability and Growth Pact

In November 1995, Theo Waigel, then German Minister of Finance, put forward the idea of adopting a scheme which would ensure stricter budgetary discipline for the Member States acceding to monetary union. Though the Maastricht Treaty had already been criticized by many for defining fiscal policy sustainability in quantitative terms,[49] Germany felt that more clearly defined rules on prevention and deterrence (of excessive deficits) were needed to strengthen the 'economic' component of EMU and to achieve sustained and lasting convergence of the economies of the Member States belonging to the euro area.

However, the amendment of the Protocol on the Excessive Deficit Procedure would have required unanimity within the Council, and few countries wanted to renegotiate the agreement reached at Maastricht. Instead, the European Council favoured the adoption of rules by way of a Council Resolution.

Following the agreement reached at the Dublin European Council in December 1996, the Resolution on the Stability and Growth Pact was adopted by the Amsterdam European Council in June 1997.[50]

The SGP initially consisted of the Resolution of the European Council of 17 June 1997 (which reflected a political commitment to ensure fiscal discipline) and of two Regulations: the Council Regulation (EC) No 1466/1997 of 7 July 1997 on the strengthening of the surveillance of budgetary positions and the coordination of economic policies[51] and the Council Regulation (EC) No 1467/97 of 7 July 1997 on speeding up and clarifying the excessive deficit procedure.[52] The SGP fully entered into force on 1 January 1999.

In September 2004, the Commission issued a Communication on 'strengthening economic governance and clarifying the implementation of the Stability and Growth Pact'.[53] Following this communication, on 20 March 2005, the Ecofin Council adopted a report on 'Improving the implementation of the

---

[49] See Editorial Comments, 'Whither the Stability and Growth Pact?' (2004) 41 Common Market Law Review 1197.

[50] Council Resolution 97/C236/01 on the Stability and Growth Pact, [1997] OJ C236/1.

[51] See Council Regulation 1466/1997 of 7 July 1997 Strengthening of the Surveillance of Budgetary Positions and the Surveillance and Coordination of Economic Policies, [1997] OJ L209/1.

[52] See Council Regulation 1467/97 of 7 July 1997 Speeding Up and Clarifying the Implementation of Excessive Deficit Procedure [1997] OJ L209/6. The Regulation provides a clear method for proposing and implementing prompt corrective actions within a year of the reporting of the excessive deficit.

[53] Communication from the Commission to the Council and the European Parliament on strengthening economic governance and clarifying the implementation of the Stability and Growth Pact, 3 September 2004, COM (2004) 581 final.

Stability and Growth Pact',[54] which was endorsed by the European Council meeting in Brussels on 22 and 23 March 2005. The ministers of finance agreed to 'rewrite the SGP', with more flexible fiscal rules, thus lending some credence to the allegation that political pressures had prevailed over economic considerations.

The rewriting of the SGP took place through the adoption on 27 June 2005 of two Regulations (Council Regulation 1055/2005 and Regulation 1056/2005) on the basis of the Ecofin Council Report mentioned above, and bearing in mind that the EC Treaty stands, with the main elements of the Excessive Deficit Procedure and the qualitative and quantitative reference values—three per cent and sixty per cent—unaltered. Regulation 1055/2005 amended Regulation 1466/1997 on the strengthening of the surveillance of budgetary positions and the surveillance and coordination of economic policies.[55] Regulation 1056/2005 amended the Regulation 1467/97 on the excessive deficit procedure (Regulation 1467/97).[56]

Some of the changes that were agreed by the European Council did not require amendments to Regulation 1466/1997 and resulted in a Code of Conduct on the Content and Format of the Stability and Convergence Programmes,[57] that was endorsed by the Ecofin Council on 11 October 2005. This code of conduct incorporates the essential elements of Council Regulation 1466/1997 into guidelines to assist the Member States in drawing up their programmes. It also aims at facilitating the examination of the programmes by the Commission, the Economic and Financial Committee, and the Council.[58]

The objectives of the 'Pact': From the 'old SGP' to the 'new SGP'

According to some commentators, the problem with the 1997 Stability and Growth Pact (SGP) is that it was more about stability than growth.[59] Former Chancellor Schröder wrote at the beginning of 2005 that 'the goal of

---

[54] See <http://register.consilium.eu.int/pdf/en/05/st07/st07423.en05.pdf>.

[55] Council Regulation (EC) No 1055/2005 amending Regulation (EC) No 1466/1997 on the strengthening of the surveillance of the budgetary positions and the surveillance and coordination of economic policies, OJ L174, 7 July 2005, 1–4.

[56] Council Regulation (EC) No 1056/2005 amending Regulation (EC) No 1467/97 on speeding up and clarifying the implementation of the excessive deficit procedure, OJ L174, 7 July 2005, 5–9.

[57] See <http://europa.eu.int/comm/economy_finance/about/activities/sgp/codeofconduct_en.pdf>.

[58] See European Commission, Economic and Financial Affairs, 'The Stability and Growth Pact' at <http://www.eu.int/comm/economy_finance/about/activities/sgp/sgp_en.htm>.

[59] See Lorenzo Bini Smaghi, 'What Went Wrong with the Stability and Growth Pact' in Peter Sørensen (ed), *Monetary Union in Europe. Essays in Honour of Niels Thygesen* (Copenhagen: DJØF Publishing Copenhagen, 2004) 169.

consolidating public budgets may well conflict in the short term with the goal of enhancing the potential for economic growth.'[60] Further, Schröder argued that the complexities of fiscal policy cannot be adequately captured by quantitative limits: 'Whether a fiscal policy is "right" and promotes stability and growth equally cannot be measured solely by compliance with the deficit reference value of 3 per cent of gross domestic product. This indicator is inadequate to deal with the complex realities of fiscal policy.'

The term 'pact' is misleading in that the rules (with preventive and corrective elements) are not a separate agreement. They have been adopted in the form of regulations under the provisions of the EC Treaty.[61] The rules apply to all Member States but the strict enforcement of budgetary discipline pursuant to the excessive deficit procedure apply only to the states which have adopted the euro.[62]

One of the major novelties of the SGP as designed in 1997 was the commitment to budgetary balance over time (which goes one step further than 'simply' avoiding excessive deficits). This commitment has been weakened in the 'new SGP'. This is one of the most visible differences between the 1997 SGP and the 2005 SGP.

In the new SGP, the obligation for Member States to adhere to the medium-term objective for their budgetary positions of close to balance or in surplus 'should be differentiated for individual Member States, to take into account the diversity of economic and budgetary positions and developments' in the light of the economic and budgetary heterogeneity in the Union.[63] Furthermore, the new SGP is more 'growth-oriented' than the old one and considers the impact of long-term structural reforms. Structural reforms, such as the introduction of a multi-pillar system for pension fund reform, which can entail a short-term deterioration of public finances during the implementation period, should be taken into account when defining the adjustment path to the medium-term budgetary objective, so as to safeguard the sustainability of public finances in the long run and to avoid imposing excessive burdens on future generations.[64] The term 'national ownership' (an expression which has become 'fashionable' in

---

[60] Gerhard Schröder, 'A Framework for a Stable Europe', *Financial Times*, 17 January 2005.
[61] See Arts 99(5) and 104(14) EC Treaty.
[62] See recital 9 of the preamble to Regulation 1467/97, above note 52. See also Art 122(3) EC Treaty concerning the non application of Arts 104(9) and 104(11) to Member States with a derogation.
[63] See recital 5 and Art 2a of Regulation 1055/2005.
[64] See recitals 2 and 8 of Regulation 1055/2005 and Art 5 as amended. See Art 2 as amended, paras 3–5 of Regulation No 1056/2005.

many contexts: law reform, IMF conditionality, implementation of soft law standards) recurs in the new version of the SGP.[65]

The SGP does not alter the main organizational divide between monetary and fiscal policy: 'Member States remain responsible for their national budgetary policies, subject to the provisions of the Treaty; they will take the necessary measures in order to meet their responsibilities in accordance with those provisions.'[66]

Regulation 1466/1997 as amended by Regulation 1055/2005 on the strengthening of the surveillance of budgetary positions and the coordination of economic policies

For the purposes of the multilateral surveillance foreseen by Article 99 of the Treaty, Member States prepare 'stability' or 'convergence programmes' in conformity with Regulation 1466/1997 as amended by Regulation 1055/2005. The Member States of the euro area have to present annual 'stability programmes' to the Commission and to the Council, while the Member States with a derogation have to present annual 'convergence programmes'.

The Member States must draw the programmes in accordance with the Regulation and along the guidelines set in the Code of Conduct on the content and format of the stability and convergence programmes.[67] These programmes must present a medium-term objective for the budgetary position (though this requirement has been 'weakened' following the 2005 amendment), as well as the main assumptions about expected economic developments (growth, employment, inflation, and others), a description of the budgetary and other economic policy measures being taken or proposed to achieve the objectives of the programme, and an analysis of how changes in the main economic assumptions would affect the budgetary and debt positions, bearing in mind the reference values of three per cent and sixty per cent. Convergence programmes must also present the medium-term policy objectives and the relationship of those objectives to price and exchange rate stability.

---

[65] See Ecofin Council Report of March 2005, above note 54, 4.

The Council, in reviewing the SGP provisions, detected mainly five areas where improvements could be made: (i) enhance the economic rationale of the budgetary rules to improve their credibility and ownership; (ii) improve 'ownership' by national policy makers; (iii) use more effectively periods when economies are growing above trend for budgetary consolidation in order to avoid pro-cyclical policies; (iv) take better account in Council recommendations of periods when economies are growing below trend; (v) give sufficient attention in the surveillance of budgetary positions to debt and sustainability.

[66] Resolution on the Stability and Growth Pact, Amsterdam, 17 June 1997, [1997] OJ C236/1.

[67] See EC Commission, Economic and Financial Affairs, The examination of stability and convergence programmes, at <http://europa.eu.int/comm/economy_finance/about/activities/sgp/scp_en.htm>.

The programmes are assessed by the Council and the European and Financial Committee, through a process of multilateral surveillance, which has a preventative function, since it aims to identify problems early on (checking that budget deficits do not exceed the three per cent reference value).

The Regulation gives specific content to the obligation to forward relevant information to the Commission foreseen in Article 99(3) EC Treaty[68] and introduces a yardstick for the evaluation of such programmes.

Based upon Article 99(4) EC Treaty, the Regulation also foresees the establishment of an 'early warning procedure' in the event of an imminent breach of the rules (ie, before an excessive deficit as defined in the Treaty has actually occurred).[69]

Council Regulation 1467/97 as amended by Regulation 1056/2005 on speeding up and clarifying the excessive deficit procedure

Regulation 1467/97 has been rightly considered as the cornerstone of the original SGP. This regulation defines more precisely and strengthens the Treaty rules relating to the excessive deficit procedure. Its objective is 'to deter excessive general government deficits and, if they occur, to further their prompt correction' (Art 1(1) of the Regulation).

Regulation 1467/97 establishes a system of sanctions to penalize the country if there is a breach of the rules. Sanctions first take the form of a non-interest-bearing deposit with the Commission, which comprises a fixed component equal to 0.2 per cent of GDP, a variable component equal to one tenth of the difference between the deficit as a percentage of GDP in the year in which the deficit was deemed to be excessive and the reference value of three per cent of GDP. Each following year until the decision on the existence of an excessive deficit is abrogated, the Council may decide to intensify the sanctions by requiring an additional deposit. This will be equal to one tenth of the difference between the deficit as a percentage of GDP in the preceding year and the reference value of three per cent of GDP. The annual amount of deposits may not exceed the upper limit of 0.5 per cent of GDP. A deposit is, as a rule, converted into a fine if, in the view of the Council, the excessive deficit has not been corrected after two years.

In the words of Lorenzo Bini Smaghi (now a member of the ECB's Executive Board),

> while the Treaty aimed at achieving budgetary discipline through a *procedure* (the

---

[68] Regulation 1466/1997, Art 3(2).
[69] Regulation 1466/1997, Art 6(2). As of 7 July 2004, there were four ongoing procedures with regard to this 'early warning mechanism' (concerning Portugal, Germany, France, and Italy). See <http://europa.eu.int/comm/economy_finance/about/activities/sgp/proceduresew_en.htm>.

so-called excessive deficit procedure), the SGP is based on a set of specific *rules* for national policies. According to the Treaty, the identification of an excessive deficit should be the result of a judgement . . . The SGP marked a drastic change in philosophy. . . . The drafters of the SGP did not intend the Treaty's Excessive Deficit Procedure as a procedure but as a rule[70] (emphasis added).

Regulation 1056/2005 introduces some changes that 'relax' the rigidity of some of the rules of Regulation 1467/97, in particular with regard to the concept of exceptional excess, the medium-term budgetary position, and the nature of the assessment. The assessment by the Commission (under Art 104(3) EC Treaty) moves towards more 'qualitative terms' according to the amended Article 2(3) of the Regulation, which reads as follows:

> The Commission shall give due consideration to any factors which, in the opinion of the Member State concerned, are relevant in order to comprehensively assess in qualitative terms the excess over the reference value. . . . In that context, special consideration shall be given to budgetary efforts towards increasing or maintaining at a high level financial contributions to fostering international solidarity and to achieving European policy goals, notably the unification of Europe [a veiled reference to the costs of Germany reunification, which have turned Germany from a saint to a sinner in budget management] if it has a detrimental effect on the growth and fiscal burden of a Member State.

Article 5 as amended by Regulation 1055/2005 states that the Council shall also take into account whether a higher adjustment effort is made in 'economic good times', whereas the effort may be more limited in 'economic bad times'. The reference to good and bad economic times allows for a greater degree of discretionary judgement in the assessment of the budgetary position of a Member State than under Regulation 1667/1997.[71]

The practice of the Stability and Growth Pact

As I have already pointed out, the Stability and Growth Pact requires countries participating in the Euro-zone to present updates of the 'stability programmes' annually to the Council and to the Commission. These programmes provide information on how countries intend to meet the budgetary objectives and, in particular, the medium-term goal of a budget close to balance or in surplus.

Unfortunately, the breaches of the SGP have been a recurrent feature in the life of the 'Pact'. The fiscal rules appear to have had little effect in the way many

---

[70] Above note 59, 171.

[71] Gerhard Schröder, former German Chancellor, writing in the *Financial Times*, 17 January 2005, on the reform of the stability and growth pact ('A Framework for a Stable Europe'), referred to 'cyclical incentives'. He complained about 'the mechanistic application of the pact' which had led the EU to recommend further restrictive measures (in a downturn, albeit not a 'severe economic downturn'), which had delayed recovery (in the country affected).

countries behave. Countries in the eurozone with ongoing excessive deficit procedures under the EDP (excessive deficit procedure) in 2005 include: Portugal, Italy, the Netherlands, Greece, France, and Germany.[72] The case in Italy received a lot of attention in the financial press given that the Council's decision declaring the existence of an excessive deficit was taken after the SGP rules had been rewritten.[73]

There are also ongoing procedures for Malta, Cyprus, Czech Republic, Poland, Slovakia, and Hungary. The European Commission also adopted a report (under Art 104(3) EC Treaty) on the United Kingdom's budgetary situation on 21 September 2005, since the UK reported a deficit of 3.2 per cent of its GDP in the financial year 2004–5, which runs in the UK from April to March.[74]

Below I survey the cases of Ireland, Portugal, France, and Germany, because of their historical relevance.[75]

Ireland

Ireland has the 'honour' of being the first Member State against whom a recommendation issued under the provisions of multilateral surveillance (rather than the excessive deficit provisions) was issued. In the fiscal year 2000, Ireland had a budgetary surplus of 4.7 per cent of GDP and public debts of thirty-nine per cent of GDP. Since the EU ceiling on deficits and debts was fixed at three per cent and sixty per cent of GDP respectively, the Commission concluded that Ireland was in full compliance with the SGP obligations, but that the Irish budgetary plans for 2001 were inconsistent with the 2000 Broad Economic Policy Guidelines.[76] Ireland's robust economic activity became a matter

---

[72] A list of ongoing procedures is available in the website of the European Union. See <http://europa.eu.int/comm/economy_finance/about/activities/sgp/procedures_en.htm>.

[73] On 12 July 2005 the Council adopted a decision on the existence of an excessive deficit in Italy and a recommendation on action to be taken to correct it. See <http://www.eu.int/comm/economy_finance/about/activities/sgp/edp/edpit_en.htm>.

[74] The full report is available at <http://europa.eu.int/comm/economy_finance/ about/activities/sgp/edp/edpuk_en.htm>.

[75] I draw on Sideek M Seyad, 'Destabilisation of the European Stability and Growth Pact' (2004) 19 Journal of International Banking Law and Regulation 239, 242–4, with regard to the cases of Ireland, Portugal, France, and Germany presented in this section.

[76]

> CPI inflation averaged 5.6% in 2000 against a prediction of 3.1% in the last stability programme update. In spite of this, budgetary plans for 2001 are expansionary and pro-cyclical and are therefore considered inconsistent with those guidelines. The Commission has therefore recommended to the ECOFIN Council to adopt, on [12 February 2001], a recommendation under Article 99.4 addressed to the Irish government with a view to ending the inconsistency of the expansionary aspects of budgetary plans with the Broad Economic Policy Guidelines, BEPG.

See <http://europa.eu.int/rapid/pressReleasesAction.do?reference=IP/01/105&format=HTML &aged=1&language=EN&guiLanguage=en>.

of concern to the Commission, the Council, and to the European Central Bank, since it could have inflationary consequences. The Council criticized some of the proposals included in the 2001 budget (such as tax cuts) and issued a recommendation to Ireland under Article 99(4) EC to keep fiscal policy tight.[77]

Portugal

In 2001, Portugal became the first participating Member State to incur an excessive deficit.[78] The Commission proposed to the Ecofin Council to initiate an early warning procedure against Portugal. However, since the Portuguese Government committed itself to achieve a balanced budget by 2004, the Council decided not to follow the Commission's proposal.[79] In 2002, the Portuguese Government revised its budgetary deficit to 4.1 per cent of GDP. The Commission prepared a report (as required in Art 104(3) EC) stating that the excessive budget deficit was not the result of a severe economic downturn nor of an unusual event outside the control of the Portuguese Government. The Commission thus proposed to the Council that it should establish the existence of an excessive deficit in Portugal in accordance with Article 104(5) EC Treaty. In November 2002, the Council, acting by a qualified majority, endorsed the Commission's proposal and adopted a decision stating that an excessive deficit had been incurred (Art 104(6) EC Treaty), and a recommendation addressed to the Portuguese Government with a view to bringing the deficit down in 2003 (Art 104(7) EC Treaty).[80] The Portuguese Government adopted austerity measures and reduced the deficit in 2002 and 2003. In April 2004, the Commission recommended to the Council that the decision on the existence of an excessive deficit be abrogated.[81]

---

[77] See Council Recommendation of 12 February 2001 with a view to ending the inconsistency with the broad guidelines of the economic policies in Ireland (2001/191/EC) at <http://europa. eu.int/eur-lex/pri/en/oj/2001/1_069/1_06920010310en00220023.pdf>. An immediate Council decision to publish the recommendation was adopted on the same day.

[78]
> The general government deficit in Portugal rose . . . in 2001. . . . The economic slowdown explains part of this outcome but other factors also contributed to it, notably unexpected tax shortfalls following the 2001 tax reform and overruns in current primary expenditure. . . . With a view to securing close monitoring and the needed reduction in the deficit to create a safety margin to avoid breaching the 3% of GDP deficit laid down in the Treaty, the Commission proposes to the Ecofin Council to give Portugal an early warning on the basis of Regulation 1466/97 of the Stability and Growth Pact.

> See <http://europa.eu.int/rapid/pressReleasesAction.do?reference=IP/02/165&format=HTML &aged=1&language=EN&guiLanguage=en>.

[79] See Seyad, above note 75, 242.

[80] Council Recommendation to Portugal with a view to bringing an end to the situation of an excessive government deficit (Application of Article 104.7 of the EC Treaty), of 5 November 2002. OJ L322, 27/11/2002, 30–1.

[81] See <http://europa.eu.int/comm/economy_finance/about/activities/sgp/procedures_en. htm>.

However, the fiscal position of Portugal deteriorated sharply again in 2005. According to the June 2005 update of the Portuguese stability programme, the planned government deficit is 6.2 per cent of GDP for 2005. On 20 September 2005, the Council adopted a decision under Article 104(6) EC Treaty that an excessive deficit exists in Portugal and a recommendation under Article 104(7) EC Treaty with a view to bringing an end to the excessive deficit by 2008.[82]

Germany

In February 2002, upon examining Germany's proposed stability programme, the Commission proposed to the Ecofin Council to give Germany an early warning on the basis of Regulation 1466/1997 of the Stability and Growth Pact (SGP). The Council, however, did not follow the Commission's recommendation for an early warning.[83] Germany's budget deficit and projected government debt in 2002 exceeded the reference values of three and sixty per cent (reaching 3.7 and 60.9 per cent, respectively). In accordance with Article 104(3) EC, the Commission adopted a report on the budgetary situation in Germany. The report stated that the excessive deficit did not result from an unusual event outside the control of Germany or from a severe economic downturn. The Commission recommended to the Council that it should decide that there was an excessive deficit in Germany.

On 21 January 2003, the Council adopted a decision on the existence of an excessive deficit in Germany according to Article 104(6) EC Treaty[84] and a recommendation on action to be taken to correct it (according to Art 104(7) EC Treaty). The Council informed the German Government that it should bring the excessive deficit situation to an end as rapidly as possible in accordance with Article 3(4) of Regulation 1467/97 (ie, within four months). According to the Commission's forecast of the German finances, the deficit for 2003 was over four per cent of GDP. In view of this budgetary development, the Commission declared that Germany was not in compliance with the Council recommendation issued in January 2003.

The Commission further declared that Germany should put an end to the excessive deficit situation by 2004 as required by the Council. The Commission proposed that the Council should adopt two recommendations in relation to the excessive deficit procedure for Germany (as well as for France, as I explain below). The first recommendation—under Article 104(8) EC—stating that the actions taken by Germany in 2003 had proved inadequate to bring the excessive

---

[82] See <http://europa.eu.int/comm/economy_finance/about/activities/sgp/edp/edppt_en.htm>.

[83] Above note 10, 1090.

[84] Council Decision 2003/89/EC of 21 January 2003 on the existence of a government deficit in Germany—Application of Article 104(6) of the EC Treaty, OJ L034, 11/02/2003, 16–17.

deficit to an end in 2004. The second—under Article 104(9) EC—requesting Germany to bring the government deficit below three per cent by 2005.[85]

However, on 25 November 2003, the Council of Ministers did not adopt the two Commission recommendations (it did not achieve the required majority). Instead, it merely adopted a set of conclusions stating that it had decided to hold the excessive deficit procedure in abeyance with regard to Germany (and also to France) and addressed recommendations to Germany (and to France) for correcting the excessive deficit in the light of the earlier commitments made by each of them.

France

Fiscal problems in France in 2002 prompted the Commission and the Council to take action under the SGP rules. In its assessment of the 2002 stability programme, the Commission concluded that general government finances had deteriorated markedly in 2002, with a significant divergence from the projections of 2001.[86] On 21 January 2003, the Council adopted a recommendation with a view to giving an early warning to France in order to prevent the occurrence of an excessive deficit.[87]

In June 2003 on the basis of a Commission Recommendation, the Council decided in accordance with Article 104(6) EC Treaty that an excessive deficit existed in France,[88] and issued a recommendation based on Article 104(7) EC to bring the excessive deficit situation to an end by 2004 at the latest. The Council also established 3 October 2003 as the deadline for the French Government to take appropriate measures.[89] On 8 and 21 October, the Commission adopted two recommendations on the basis of Articles 104(8) and 104(9) respectively for the Council to decide (1) that no effective action had been taken by France in response to the recommendation of 3 June and (2) to give notice to France to take necessary measures to bring the government deficit below three per cent of GDP in 2005.[90]

At the Ecofin meeting held on 25 November 2003, the Council did not adopt the decisions recommended by the Commission under Articles 104(8) EC and

---

[85] See Seyad, above note 75, 243–4.

[86] <http://europa.eu.int/rapid/pressReleasesAction.do?reference=IP/03/18&format=HTML&aged=0&language=EN&guiLanguage=en>.

[87] See Council Opinion of 21 January 2003 on the updated Stability Programme of France, 2004–2006, OJ C026, 4 February 2003, 5–6.

[88] Council Decision 2003/487/EC on the existence of an excessive deficit in France—Application of Article 104(6) of the EC Treaty, OJ L165, 03/07/2003, 29–30.

[89] Above note 75, 244.

[90] <http://europa.eu.int/comm/economy_finance/about/activities/sgp/year/year20032004_en.htm>.

104(9) EC against France (nor against Germany). It merely adopted, instead, a set of conclusions holding the excessive deficit procedure in abeyance and addressing recommendations to both France and Germany for correcting their excessive deficits in the light of their previous commitments.

In its report assessing the stability programme of France for 2004, the Commission states: 'France is one of the 10 countries currently in the so-called excessive deficit procedure. As analysed in December [2004] and confirmed at last month's Finance Ministers meeting, the country appears to be on track for bringing its deficit below the 3% reference value in the treaty. But the budgetary situation remains vulnerable.'[91]

'Fiscal delinquents' and lessons thereof

Breaches of the SGP have become commonplace. It is not surveillance ('carrots') that deters countries from misbehaving; it is the effective application of sanctions that is the true deterrent ('sticks'). By analogy with the IMF functions of surveillance and conditional financial assistance (which I survey in Chapter 13), it is not IMF surveillance that makes countries comply with their self-imposed reform programmes, but the 'conditionality' that governs the access to and use of IMF resources (conditionality as a 'stick').

Under this test of 'carrots and sticks', it can be said that if the sanctions or penalties foreseen in the excessive deficit procedure when the budgetary rules are breached are not applied, the 'deterrent effect' of the SGP disappears, 'inviting' other Member States to be 'fiscal delinquents' too. The 'non-application' of the excessive deficit procedure in the cases of Germany and France has damaged the credibility of the SGP and distorted the incentives to comply with its rules.

The SGP (as any other rule) cannot survive without societal legitimacy. The widespread breach of the fiscal rules damages the credibility of the commitment of the eurozone Member States to fiscal discipline. Going forward, it is possible to envisage the application of a greater amount of discretion (discretionary judgement) in the assessment of what actually constitutes an excessive deficit. However, the future of the 'pact' is constrained by the demands of primary law. From a legal point of view, only a treaty change could dramatically alter the existing framework for economic policy coordination.[92]

---

[91] <http://europa.eu.int/comm/economy_finance/about/activities/sgp/country/countryfiles/fr/fr20042005_en.pdf>.

[92] Eijffinger has pointed out that 'in the end only a higher degree of fiscal integration would remove the inflexibility inherent in the recourse to predefined budgetary rules.' See Sylvester Eijffinger, 'How can the Stability and Growth Pact be improved to achieve stronger discipline and higher flexibility', European Parliament Briefing Paper, November 2002, 1. See also above note 7, 780: 'Fiscal federalism is predicated on the coherence of the political system where it is practiced,

E. The Judgment of the ECJ

On 27 January 2004, the Commission brought an action before the European Court of Justice challenging (1) the Council's failure to adopt the decisions recommended by the Commission under Articles 104(8) and 104(9) EC which, if adopted, would have ordered France and Germany to put an end to their excessive deficits by 2005 and to achieve a reduction of the deficit in 2004; and (2) the conclusions adopted by the Council.[93] On application by the Commission, the President of the Court ordered on 13 February 2004 that the case be determined in accordance with an expedited procedure.

The Court of Justice did react speedily and on 13 July 2004 its judgment was published.[94] In the words of Lorenzo Bini Smaghi: 'The July 2004 judgment of the European Court of Justice closed the *annus horribilis* of the Stability and Growth Pact.'[95]

The Court found that failure by the Council to adopt the decisions recommended by the Commission 'does not constitute an act challengeable by an action for annulment' and that, therefore the action (for annulment) brought by the Commission against the Council was inadmissible.

The Court also ruled that the conclusions of the Council holding the excessive deficit procedures in abeyance and modifying the recommendations that it had previously adopted were unlawful. The Court clarified that though the Council has a discretion in this field, it cannot depart from the rules laid down by the Treaty or those which it set for itself in Regulation 1467/97. Accordingly, the Court stated that once the Council has adopted recommendations for the correction of the excessive deficit, the Council cannot modify such recommendations without being prompted again by the Commission, which has the right of initiative in the excessive deficit procedure. The Court also found that the recommendations contained in the Council's conclusions were adopted in accordance with the voting rules prescribed for a decision to give notice, which are different from those prescribed for the adoption of the recommendations for correcting the excessive deficit. The Court therefore annulled the Council's conclusions of 25 November 2003.

The ECJ's judgment on 13 July 2004 focused on procedural issues. The nature of the fiscal rules and budgetary policy has been left to politicians to renegotiate.

---

and it is about balancing efficiency and equity in an optimizing fashion. Whether in a federal system or in other polities in which there are substantial budgetary flows between central and sub-national tiers of government, many of the tenets of fiscal federalism can only plausibly apply if there is a sufficient degree of political commitment.'

[93] Above note 4.   [94] ibid.   [95] Above note 59, 167.

The recent amendments in 2005 have not restored credibility to the SGP (breaches of the fiscal rules have continued), which suggests the need for a different set of incentives and rules.

F. Regional Adjustment

Effective economic coordination at the macroeconomic level (through fiscal rules and multilateral surveillance) needs to be accompanied by the economic development of the EU Member States. Regional disparity and regional imbalances have been a permanent feature in the history of the European Community. Hence the importance of microeconomic policies and regional adjustment.

Although the European Union is one of the richest parts of the world, there are striking internal disparities of income and opportunity between its regions. The entry of ten new member countries in May 2004 (with incomes well below the EU average) has widened these gaps. Regional policy[96] transfers resources from affluent to poorer regions. It is both an instrument of financial solidarity and a powerful force to promote economic and social cohesion. The proposed EU Constitution includes in its Article I-3 the promotion of economic, social, and territorial cohesion and solidarity among the Member States as one of the Union's objectives.

Experience has shown that the effects of EU membership, coupled with a vigorous and targeted regional policy, can bring positive results. The gap between the richest and the poorest regions has narrowed over the years. The case of Ireland is a good example. Its GDP, which was sixty-four per cent of the EU average when it joined thirty years ago, is now one of the highest in the Union.[97]

The need to promote balanced development by reducing the gap between the different regions and helping the poorest regions to catch up was recognized in the preamble to the Treaty of Rome in 1957. The EEC Treaty also provided for the establishment of the European Investment Fund.

Articles 2 and 3 of the EC Treaty state that one of its tasks is to 'promote throughout the Community a harmonious, balanced and sustainable development of economic activities, a high level of employment and of social protection, . . . the raising of the standard of living and quality of life, and economic and social cohesion and solidarity among Member States'. More specifically, Articles 158 to 162 EC Treaty, on 'Economic and social cohesion' (Arts III–220 to III–224 in the proposed EU Constitution) explain that the Community aims

---

[96] <http://www.europa.eu.int/pol/reg/overview_en.htm>.   [97] ibid.

to reduce disparities between the development of various regions and the backwardness of the least favoured regions or islands, including rural areas.

The European Union grants financial assistance under multi-annual regional development programmes negotiated between the regions, the Member States, and the Commission, as well as under specific Community initiatives and schemes, through four 'Structural Funds':[98] the European Regional Development Fund (ERDF); the European Social Fund (ESF); the European Agricultural Guidance and Guarantee Fund (EAGGF); and the Financial Instrument for Fisheries Guidance (FIFG) which provides financial support for fishing communities as part of the common fisheries policy (CFP).[99] In addition to these four 'structural funds', a special solidarity fund, the Cohesion Fund, was set up in 1993 to finance transport and environment infrastructure in Member States with a GDP of less than ninety per cent of the Union average at the time (at that time, Greece, Ireland, Spain, and Portugal).[100]

To address the substantial needs of the Member States that joined the EU in May 2004 (with regard to the development of their infrastructure, transport, agriculture, environment, and other areas), two facilities were established: (1) the Instrument for Structural Policies for Pre-Accession (ISPA), to finance transport and environment projects, and (2) the Special Accession Programme for Agriculture and Rural Development (SAPARD), to help the countries prepare for the Common Agricultural Policy.

Economic development in the poorer regions of Europe is necessary for the success of economic policy coordination in the EU. Solidarity and cohesion imply prosperity for all. This is one of the premises upon which the project of European integration rests.

G. Conclusions

Before the advent of monetary union, Member States were in charge of both monetary policy and fiscal policy. Since the introduction of the euro, a centralized monetary policy coexists with decentralized fiscal policies in the countries which have adopted the common currency. The need for economic policy coordination in the light of this asymmetry is evident. The problem is to define

---

[98] See Council Regulation (EC) No 1260/99 of 21 June 1999 laying down general provisions on the Structural Funds.

[99] These funds will pay out about €213 billion, roughly one third of total EU spending, between 2000 and 2006. See <http://www.europa.eu.int/pol/reg/overview_en.htm>.

[100] ibid. A further €18 billion for the period 2000–6 is allocated to the Cohesion Fund.

what such 'coordination' should entail. The thinking on this issue has changed over the course of the last decade. The Maastricht budgetary rules were further strengthened in the Stability and Growth Pact (an instrument of secondary law). However, the rules of the SGP have proven too rigid for many European countries, including Germany (the architect of such rules) and France. This has triggered a legal, economic, and political debate on the wisdom of such rules. Enforcement of the rules on economic policy coordination cannot be achieved through judicial involvement, as the European Court of Justice made clear in its judgment of 14 July 2004. More flexible rules were proposed by the Ecofin council meeting in Brussels in March 2005 and the adoption of two regulations in June 2005. Though the credibility of the SGP has been damaged, any further rewriting of the SGP needs to observe the requirements of primary law, since the key elements of the excessive deficit procedure are defined in the Treaty and the protocol annexed to the Treaty.

'Economic union' is a misnomer. Economic policy coordination has proven to be much less effective in practice than the original drafters of the Maastricht Treaty envisaged. However, the challenge remains. The success of the euro in the long run requires fiscal discipline. One of the tenets of central bank independence is the prohibition to finance government deficits via central bank credit. Fiscal restraint remains a fundamental pillar for the maintenance of monetary stability, the statutory primary objective of the European Central Bank.

9

EXTERNAL ASPECTS OF EMU

The intricate nature of Article 111 [regarding exchange rate policy] and its convoluted language reflect the difficult birth of this provision. The compromise arrived at in the monstrous arrangements laid down in Article 111 EC Treaty . . . unmistakeably expresses the labour pains which accompanied the creation of the provision.

> René Smits, *The European Central Bank. Institutional Aspects* (1997)
> 375, quoting Rainer Stadler, *Der rechtliche Handlungsspielraum des*
> *Europäischen Systems der Zentralbanken* (1996) 172

A. Introduction

The ESCB is entrusted by the EC Treaty with sole responsibility for monetary policy, which is an exclusive Community competence (albeit geographically limited to the Member States that have adopted the euro). Despite the indissoluble link that exists between a single monetary policy (geared towards internal price stability) and external monetary relationships, in the euro area the responsibility for the latter is divided between the Council (primary role) and the European Central Bank under a notoriously unclear set of Treaty provisions.

This EC arrangement reflects, nonetheless, the norm in many countries, where the conduct of external monetary affairs involves an uncomfortable dialogue between the central bank and the Treasury or Ministry of Finance. Politicians are typically involved in tactical decisions concerning the exchange rate regime, while central banks are involved in operational issues. The problem at the European level is that while the voice of the ECB with regard to monetary policy is a 'single voice', the Council represents many voices, the views of all the Member States. This adds an extra layer of complexity to the conduct of exchange rate policy in Europe.

Article 111 EC Treaty is a cumbersome provision in legal and economic terms, the result of a calculated obfuscation for political purposes.[1] There is a degree of inconsistency, and possibly conflict, in giving the ECB independence of political control in the conduct of a price stability oriented monetary policy while leaving the determination of the exchange rate and the exchange regime (pegged, floating, or managed float) in the hands of the political authorities.

The proposed EU constitution does not alter in substance the complex institutional structure that governs the external aspects of EMU. However, it is interesting to observe that, while Article 111 EC is inserted within the EC Treaty's monetary policy provisions (Chapter 2 on Monetary Policy of Title VII on Economic and Monetary Policy of the EC Treaty), Article III–326 is inserted in a chapter on International Agreements, Chapter VI, included in Title V ('The Union's External Action') of the proposed EU Constitution. An important consequence of this repositioning is that, while the relations between the Member States that have adopted the euro and those that have a derogation are considered to be an element of the 'differentiated integration'[2] existent with

---

[1] Article 111 EC Treaty becomes Art III–326 in the proposed EU Constitution (with Art 111(4) being replaced by a new Art III–196). As I have pointed out in previous chapters, the proposed EU Constitution (ie, the Treaty establishing a Constitution for Europe, signed in Rome on 29 October 2004, available in the Official Journal No C310 of 16 December 2004) was thrown into a legal limbo following the rejection of the Treaty in referenda in France (28 May 2005) and Holland (1 June 2005). The suspension of the ratification process (according to the declaration of the European Council Brussels summit on 16–17 June 2005 to allow for a 'period of reflection') does not equate to the abandonment altogether of the proposed Constitution. The text of the Constitutional Treaty remains a legal document of value to refer to, also with a view to its possible entry into force or the taking over of parts of it in other Treaty texts later on.

[2] This term is borrowed from Zilioli. 'Monetary Policy is the most comprehensive and the most successful example of differentiated integration in Community Law. . . . For the first time, the Community has been attributed an exclusive competence, which is geographically limited to a part of it.' See Chiara Zilioli, 'The Constitution for European and its Impact on the Governance

regard to monetary policy, the relations between Member States and third States (non EU) and international organizations are considered to be the true 'external aspects of EMU' in the proposed Constitution.

I dealt in Chapter 7 with the complexities involved in the 'differentiated integration' within the EU with regard to monetary policy, and I referred to the different provisions applicable to the Member States that have adopted the euro and to the 'Member States with a derogation'.[3]

The focus of this chapter is the exchange rate policy of the euro area, the external representation of the euro, and other external aspects of EMU.

B. Exchange Rate Policy

The room for manoeuvre in the field of exchange rate policy—traditionally the domain of the Treasury or Minister of Finance—varies from country to country, with some central banks deciding on the exchange rate (eg, the Swedish Riksbank)[4] and others with freedom only to implement the foreign exchange policy formulated by the government. Before the advent of EMU, governments or Ministers of Finance in the EU Member States (with the exception of Sweden) had the last word on exchange rate matters. Therefore, the agreement reached in Article 111 EC reflected the status quo, that is, political responsibility for the external aspects of exchange rate policy.[5]

The stability of exchange rates (the exchange rate being the price of a currency in another currency) and the issue of which is the best exchange rate arrangement for a given country (fixed, floating, or some version of managed float) remain a matter of great controversy in the economic literature. This means that the law tends to refer to the external dimension of monetary stability (the stability of the currency) in rather ambiguous terms.

---

of the Euro' in Torres, Verdun, and Zimmerman (eds), *EMU and Democracy: Governance in the Eurozone*, forthcoming (to be published by Nomos).

[3] According to Art 124(1) EC and Art III–200 of the proposed EU Constitution, each Member State with a derogation shall treat its exchange rate policy as matter of common interest, taking into account the experience acquired in cooperation within the framework of the exchange rate mechanism (ERM II).

[4] According to the Swedish Central Bank Law of 1991 Art 4 (SFS 1988: 1385), the Riksbank is responsible for Sweden's foreign exchange and credit policies.

[5] Although—as René Smits pointed out to me in his comments on this chapter—it is clear that they can only interfere in specific manners, ie when there is a formal agreement on the exchange rate of the euro, by adopting (non-binding) orientations, or when exchange rate matters are the subject of an international agreement.

There is no reference in the EC Treaty to 'exchange rate stability'.[6] Hence, it can be inferred that exchange rate movements will be the object of 'benign neglect' by the ECB (and the Council) unless they negatively affect or threaten to affect the price stability objective.[7]

As acknowledged, the exchange rate has a dual dimension. On the one hand, it is the external anchor, the external dimension of monetary stability (and, in this respect, the ESCB has a vested interest in safeguarding it). On the other hand, it is an instrument of the general economic policy of a country, closely linked to its trade and employment objectives.[8] For this reason, independent central bankers committed to price stability oriented monetary policy (interest rate policy), but deprived of parallel powers in the field of exchange rate policy, are likely to clash with politicians who have other objectives to pursue besides price stability.[9]

Given the intergovernmental character of the EU Council, as representative of the Member States, one is inclined to think that a degree of 'political meddling' may go into the decision-making. National politicians in the euro area appear to be somehow reluctant to release completely their powers over exchange rate issues. This may help explain the proposals put forward by the former German Minister of Finance, Oskar Lafontaine, with regard to the adoption of target zones for the euro, the US dollar and the yen in order to diminish the volatility of exchange rate movements,[10] or the recent proposals of the Italian Government.[11]

---

[6] 'It is a fact that at the moment the monetary policy of the Community is almost purely looking at the internal price stability and is accused of showing a benign neglect to exchange rate developments as long as they are not excessive. The Constitution has reaffirmed this orientation by making price stability (and not exchange rate stability) a policy objective not only of the ECB but of the constitutionalised Union as such.' Above note 2.

[7] ibid. 'The press has often accused the ECB of remaining inactive in front of a too weak or too strong exchange rate of the euro against the dollar. The ECB, however, is bound by the objective of price stability, and reacts to exchange rate fluctuations only when the latter jeopardise price stability.'

[8] See Rosa M Lastra, *Central Banking and Banking Regulation* (London: Financial Markets Group, London School of Economics, 1996) 276, footnote 454, for a quote of former German Chancellor Helmut Schmidt who had stated in his memoirs that he 'regarded exchange rate policies . . . as an important part of general foreign and strategic policy'.

[9] See Stanley Fischer, 'Modern Central Banking' (a paper presented at the Bank of England's Tercentenary Celebration) 4 (1994), in which Fischer contends that in today's world, interest rate and exchange rate policies are increasingly interrelated. Fischer also contends that the very effectiveness of central bank independence will depend on the government's choice of exchange regime. Under floating rates, monetary policy affects the exchange rate, whereas a system of fixed exchange rates greatly curtails an independent central bank's room for manoeuvre in the conduct of monetary policy.

[10] See Peter Norman, 'Finance Minister in Waiting', *Financial Times*, 4 October, 1998; Wolfgang Munchau, 'Return to Keynes', *Financial Times*, 26 October, 1998. See also, for example, Fred Bergsten, 'How to Target Exchange Rates', *Financial Times*, 20 November 1998, 24, for a more academic explanation with regard to the proposed adoption of target zones.

[11] See *Financial Times*, 11 November 2004, 'Italy raises the prospect of intervention on euro'.

The depolitization of monetary policy (in the hands of an independent central bank) contrasts with the possible politicization of exchange rate policy. However, this is not necessarily a bad thing, since important strategic decisions concerning the exchange rate (such as a hypothetical scenario in which the euro were to be pegged to the US dollar) need to be subject to democratic, that is, political, control, since such decisions should not be taken against the wishes of democratically elected governments.

Who is 'Mr Euro'?

As a result of the sharing of competences between the Council and the ECB in the field of exchange rate policy, the answer to this question is not clear.[12] McNamara and Meunier argue that a single external voice for the euro is needed both to defend its value on international exchange markets and to influence decisions on a wide range of international macroeconomic policy issues, (normally in the G7 or the IMF) such as international policy coordination on fiscal, monetary, and exchange rate policy, the construction of a new international financial architecture, and the management of international financial crises.[13]

The proposed EU Constitution introduces a new Article III–196 (which replaces Art 111(4) EC) with regard to the international role of the euro. It empowers the Council (though only the members of the Council representing the Member States of the euro area) to adopt European decisions 'in order to secure the euro's place in the international monetary system' (para 1) and to adopt 'appropriate measures to ensure unified representation within the international financial institutions and conferences'. In both cases (European decisions and 'appropriate measures') the Commission has the right of initiative and the European Central Bank must be consulted.

Some have spoken of the new President of the Eurogroup (currently Mr Juncker, previously Mr McCreevy) as Mr Euro, while this denomination has also

---

[12] Ziloli, above note 2:

It is not easy for the EU citizens and for third States, to understand who is exercising the power related to governing the currency in the international arena. . . . The sharing between the ECB and the Council of the external representation of the monetary and exchange rate policies of the euro area requires a close internal coordination on these issues. . . . If no amendment to the Treaty is introduced, the ECB cannot be assigned, alone, the responsibility for the problems in this field: if a more active role is wished, then it is the action of the Council that is required.

[13] See Kathleen R McNamara and Sophie Meunier, 'Between National Sovereignty and International Power: What External Voice for the Euro' (2002) 78 International Affairs 849, 851.

been appropriated on some occasions by the President of the ECB (currently Mr Trichet, formerly Mr Duisenberg).[14]

The Eurogroup is formally recognized in Article III–195 of the proposed EU constitution and in the Protocol on the Euro Group as an informal meeting of the ministers of finance of the Member States whose currency is the euro together with the Commission to discuss 'questions related to the specific responsibilities they share with regard to the single currency'. The European Central Bank 'shall be invited' to attend the meetings. The President of the Eurogroup is selected by a majority of the ministers of finance for a period of two and a half years. The Eurogroup is meant to enhance the dialogue and to develop closer coordination of economic policies within the euro area.

Smits points out: 'The Eurogroup president may strive to call himself "Mr Euro"—an epithet that only comes naturally for the ECB President in view of the central competences for the management of the euro with which the central bank is entrusted, certainly in the absence of formal exchange-rate agreements or formal orientations from the Council.'[15]

The press has echoed the uncertainty that surrounds this important issue:

> Who exactly speaks for Europe's single currency? We do, says the European Central Bank, because we run monetary policy and are therefore the guardians of its worth.

---

[14] See eg *Financial Times*, 17 September 2004, 9: 'Jean-Claude Trichet, ECB President said last weekend: 'As far as the currency is concerned, I am evidently Mr Euro.' At the ECB Press Conference of 8 January 2004, one question posed to Mr Trichet was the following: 'Your predecessor said: The euro is me, I am Mr Euro. Hence, your refusal to give us an indication of the exchange rate policy is rather surprising.' At another ECB Press Conference on 4 March 2004 (both press conferences are available at <http://www.ecb.int/pressconf/2004>) Mr Trichet received the following question: 'The European Central Bank is supposed to be the key spokesman for the euro, but over the last few weeks there has been a lot of noise from finance ministers and Heads of State. [Chancellor] Schröder was in Washington and talked to [President] Bush about the euro—does this bother you in any way as Mr Euro?' And this was his answer:

> We have a system which is very clear. The Governing Council of the European Central Bank takes a number of decisions. The President of the ECB is the 'porte parole' or spokesperson of the institution, which has the unique and extraordinary responsibility of having to run a monetary policy, a single monetary policy, for 306 million citizens belonging to 12 different economies and countries. On the side of the executive branches we have an organisation called the 'Eurogroup', which is the college of the 12 ministers of finance of these countries, the members of the euro area, and we have a president of the euro area, which is currently Charlie McCreevy, the Irish finance minister, and we also have the Commission, of course. So the equivalent of the executive branch is the combination of the President of the Eurogroup and the role of Pedro Solbes and the Commission. We have an organised system, and when we were together in the United States for the Boca Raton meeting, I was, if you like, the equivalent of Alan Greenspan and Charlie McCreevy was opposite [Treasury] Secretary Snow. That's the organisation of Europe, and I believe that it is a good organisation.'

[15] See René Smits, 'The European Constitution and EMU: an Appraisal' (2005) 42 Common Market Law Review 425, 455.

We do, say the governments whose countries make up the European Union, because we created the euro, and the unelected people who run the central bank should have a vocal political counterweight. Too many people already speak for it, mutter currency traders. (*The Economist*, 16 September 2000)

Under the EC Treaty, both the ECB and the Council speak for the euro. The former is a single voice, the latter represents the voices of all Member States.

Primary law regarding exchange rate policy

The second basic task of the ESCB according to Article 105(2) EC and Article III–185(2) of the proposed EU Constitution is 'to conduct foreign-exchange operations consistent with Article 111' (Art III–326 of the proposed EU Constitution).

The conduct of foreign exchange policy involves the determination of the exchange rate and the exchange regime and the management of the official foreign reserves (gold reserves, foreign currency reserves, and reserve positions at the IMF, including Special Drawing Rights, SDRs). Article 111 EC deals with the division of responsibilities with regard to the determination of the exchange rate and the exchange regime. The management and holding of the official foreign reserves of the Member States is one of the basic tasks to be 'carried out' through the ESCB according to Article 105(2) EC and Article III–185 of the proposed EU Constitution, as I explained in Chapter 7.[16]

Though the proposed EU Constitution does not include the conduct of exchange rate policy under the areas of exclusive competence (Art I–13 of the proposed EU Constitution), there is no doubt that the area of jurisdiction of the euro is supranational. In an ECB opinion of 4 November 2004, it is clearly stated that 'the euro area's exchange rate policy is an exclusive Community competence.'[17]

The language of the treaty provisions and the provisions in the proposed EU Constitution regarding exchange rate policy remains somewhat confusing. In

---

[16] Only part of the reserves have been transferred to the ECB (according to Art 30 of the ESCB Statute), while part of the reserves are held by the NCBs (according to Art 31 of the ESCB Statute). The distribution among the members of the System is irrelevant for the communal holding and managing of the reserves that no longer are for the Member States to own and decide upon. See the ECB's Opinion CON/2004/6 of 13 February 2004 on cover for exchange losses by the Banque de France, at: <http://www.ecb.int/ecb/legal/pdf/en_con_2004_6_f_sign.pdf>. I am grateful to René Smits for observations on this point.

[17] See para 13 of the ECB's Opinion of 4 November 2004 at the request of the Belgian Ministry of Finance on a draft law introducing a tax on exchange operations involving foreign exchange, banknotes, and currency (CON/2004/34), <http://www.ecb.int/ecb/legal/pdf/en_con_2004_34_f_sign.pdf>.

particular, should the concept of monetary policy be understood *stricto sensu* or *lato sensu*?[18]

Monetary policy 'lato sensu'

Zilioli considers that the term 'monetary policy' as used in Article I–13 refers to monetary policy *lato sensu* (comprising internal and external aspects), as opposed to the term 'monetary policy' as used in Article III–185(2) of the proposed EU Constitution (equivalent to Art 105(2) EC Treaty), which refers to monetary policy *stricto sensu* (interest rate policy).[19] The same view is held by Smits, who considers that exchange rate policy, as an integral part of monetary policy *lato sensu*, is an exclusive Community competence.[20]

Though Article III–326 is included in the chapter on international agreements in the proposed Constitution, Article III–196 remains within the economic and monetary policy chapter. Articles III–185 to III–191 are included in a section entitled 'Monetary Policy' (Section 2), inserted in Chapter II (Economic and Monetary Policy) of Part III, Title III of the proposed Constitution. This is in line with the contents of the current EC Treaty, where Articles 105–111 are included in a chapter entitled 'Monetary Policy' (Chapter 2 of Title VII), thus lending support to a broad interpretation of the term 'monetary policy'. There is one more provision in the proposed Constitution which could add some light (or further darkness, depending on one's viewpoint) to this complex debate. Article I–12 paragraph 6 states that 'The scope and arrangements for exercising the Union's competences shall be determined by the provisions relating to each area in Part III.' Accordingly, it could be inferred that the reference to monetary policy in Article 1–13 paragraph 1(c) should include the competences provided in Articles III–185 to III–191.

Monetary policy 'stricto sensu'

Article III–177 of the proposed EU Constitution (equivalent to Art 4(2) EC Treaty) refers to price stability as the primary objective of 'both' a single monetary policy and exchange rate policy. Article I–13 of the proposed EU Constitution only refers to 'monetary policy' (no mention of exchange rate

---

[18] For a discussion on this issue, see Jean-Victor Louis, 'Monetary Policy and Central Banking in the Constitution', *Legal Aspects of the European System of Central Banks, Liber Amicorum Paolo Zamboni Garavelli* (Frankfurt: European Central Bank, 2005) 29–30.

[19] In private correspondence, Chiara Zilioli suggests that while Art I–13 of the Constitution refers to monetary policy *lato sensu*, in German 'Währungspolitik' (literally currency policy), Art III–185(2) (and Art 105(2) EC) refers to monetary policy in a narrower sense, in German 'Geldpolitik'.

[20] Above note 15.

policy) in its enumeration of the areas where the Union shall have exclusive competence.[21]

Article 105(2) EC and Article III–185(2) of the proposed EU Constitution (in combination with Art 111 EC and Art III–326 of the proposed EU Constitution) differentiate again between monetary policy and foreign exchange operations. The proposed EU Constitution does not place exchange rate policy (III–326, equivalent of 111 EC) within the chapter on economic and monetary policy as the EC Treaty did (Art 111 EC is inserted in Chapter 2 of Title VII on Monetary Policy) but within the chapter on international agreements (Chapter VI of the proposed EU Constitution).

My personal viewpoint is that both the internal and the external competences regarding the management of the euro lie with the EC alone. This notwithstanding, I understand the term 'monetary policy' in a narrow sense as 'interest rate policy', in line with established economic theory. While the ESCB has exclusive responsibility for 'internal' monetary policy (interest rate policy), there is a sharing of responsibilities between the Council (with a primary role) and the ECB (with an important operational role) with regard to exchange rate policy.

The jurisprudence of the ECJ: The doctrine of parallelism

The European Court of Justice, relying upon the theory of implied powers, has developed the doctrine of parallelism between internal and external competences. In the ERTA case,[22] the Court ruled that the authority of the Community to conclude international agreements (external competence) was inferred from the internal attribution. Applying the doctrine of parallelism to EMU, some authors have concluded that the external aspects of monetary management fall within the community competence to protect the *effet utile* of its internal exclusive competence.[23] 'The logic behind the doctrine of parallelism is to avoid internal competences being circumvented by the conflicting exercise of external competences.'[24]

---

[21] Article I–12 of the proposed Constitution states in its first paragraph that 'When the Constitution confers on the Union exclusive competence in a specific area, only the Union may legislate and adopt legally binding acts, the Member States being able to do so themselves only if so empowered by the Union or for the implementation of Union acts.'

[22] Case 22/70, *Commission v Council,* ERTA case [1971] ECR 263.

[23] See Chiara Zilioli and Martin Selmayr, 'The External Relations of the Euro Area: Legal Aspects' (1999) 36 Common Market Law Review 273, and René Smits, *The European Central Bank—Institutional Aspects* (The Hague: Kluwer Law International, 1997) 369.

[24] Zilioli and Selmayr, ibid 292. They further contend, that 'the ECB is the natural bearer of external competences in the field of monetary policy.' As regards the external competence of the Community and the ECB in monetary matters, Zilioli and Selmayr (ibid 294) make the following distinctions: first, the explicit external competences of the Community, exercised normally by the Council, as laid down in Art 111(1),(3), and (4) EC; secondly, the explicit external competences

According to the jurisprudence of the European Court of Justice, the Community's competence to conclude international agreements arises not only from an express conferment by the Treaty but may equally flow from other provisions of the Treaty and from measures adopted, within the framework of those provisions, by the Community institutions. In practice, the Member States lose their right, acting individually or even collectively, to undertake obligations towards non-member countries, from the moment that the Community adopts provisions laying down common rules (whatever form these may take) with a view to implementing a common policy envisaged by the Treaty. As and when such common rules come into being, the Community alone is in a position to assume and carry out contractual obligations towards non-member countries affecting the whole sphere of application of the Community legal system. According to Smits,[25] even in the absence of internal common rules, the Community may be competent to act externally, should the international act be necessary for the attainment of one of the objectives of the Community.[26]

Herrmann observes that the doctrine of implied external competences, which mirror explicit internal competences, can only be applied if no explicit external competences are laid down in the Treaty. The Treaty provisions should be the starting point of any analysis in this field.[27] In this light, it is important to analyse the contents of Article 111 EC.[28]

C. Detailed Analysis of Article 111 EC

Article 111 EC (ex Art 109) governs the exchange rate policy of the euro and other external aspects of EMU. In the proposed EU Constitution, Article 111 is replaced by Article III–326 (with regard to 111(2), 2, 3, and 5) and by Article III–196 (with regard to 111(4)).

---

of the European Central Bank laid down in the provisions of Art 105(2) EC and Art 23 of the ESCB Statute, and, thirdly, the implicit external competences of the ECB which mirror the internal tasks of the ESCB without explicit reference in the legal texts.

[25] Above note 23, 369–70.

[26] Opinion 1/76 (*European Laying-up Fund for Inland Waterway Vessels*) [1977] ECR 741, para 4.

[27] See generally Christoph W Herrmann, 'Monetary Sovereignty over the Euro and External Relations of the Euro Area: Competences, Procedures and Practice' (2002) 7 European Foreign Affairs Review 1, 6–7. Herrmann also points out that though economic theory suggests that there is a link between internal monetary policy and exchange rate policy, 'it does not follow that it is not possible to pursue both policies separately' (ibid 5).

[28] My analysis in this chapter focuses on the external aspects of monetary policy, leaving aside external aspects of other elements of EMU (payments and capital and economic union).

Formal exchange rate agreements

Formal exchange rate agreements between the euro and one or more currencies of third States are the responsibility of the Council in accordance with the first indent of Article 111(1) EC (and Art III–326(1) of the proposed EU Constitution).[29] The Council, acting by unanimity, on a recommendation from the ECB or the Commission, and after consulting the European Parliament, in an endeavour to reach a consensus consistent with the objective of price stability, may conclude formal agreements on an exchange rate system for the euro in relation to currencies of third States.

This means that any formal agreement related to the choice of exchange regime vis-à-vis the dollar or other currencies is the responsibility of the Council. The language, however, is convoluted and the reference to the procedure in paragraph 3, further analyzed before, complicates an already cumbersome provision.

The Annexed Declaration on Article 111 (ex Art 109) clarified that the word 'formal agreements' as used in Article 111(1) was not intended to create a new type of international agreement in Community law.[30] Smits observes that only 'Bretton Woods-type arrangements' were intended in paragraph 1, while less formal exchange rate arrangements, such as those which emanated from the so-called Plaza and Louvre accords, would only give rise to the 'general orientations' that are mentioned in Article 111(2).[31]

While Smits argues that the difference between Article 111(1) which provides for 'formal agreements establishing exchange rate systems' and Article 111(3) which provides for 'agreements concerning monetary and foreign exchange regime matters' is one of procedure,[32] Zilioli and Selmayr consider that Article 111(3) EC includes not only procedural aspects by also the Community's explicit external competence to enter into public international law agreements on monetary and exchange regime matters.[33]

In my opinion, the real difference between Article 111(1) and Article 111(3) is substantive. Article 111(1) is the provision applicable to 'formal' exchange rate arrangements (ie, formal arrangements concerning the exchange rate regime between the euro and other currency or currencies) and Article 111(3) is the provision applicable to 'informal' exchange rate arrangements and other

---

[29] The second indent of Art 111(1) and Art III–326(1) deals with the adoption, adjustment, or abandonment by the Council of the central rates of the euro within the exchange rate system, following a procedure similar to the one the Council must comply with in the case of the adoption of formal exchange rate arrangements.

[30] Declaration on Art 109 of the Treaty Establishing the European Community [1992] OJ C191/99.

[31] See Smits, above note 23, 380.   [32] ibid 377.   [33] Above note 23, 296.

agreements concerning monetary or foreign exchange regime matters that the Community negotiates with third States or international organizations.

Floating exchange rates

The provisions of Article 111(1) have yet to be used. The euro floats freely in international financial and money markets in conformity with current obligations under the IMF's Articles of Agreement, which no longer prescribe fixed exchange rate arrangements, as I further explain in Chapter 12. In the present situation, the provisions of Article 111(2) (and Art III–326(2) of the proposed EU Constitution) are of major practical importance. In a situation where no formal exchange rate agreements have been concluded in relation to one or more non-Community currencies, the Council may 'formulate general orientations for exchange-rate policy in relation to these currencies'.

As to the legal nature of these 'general orientations' for exchange rate policy, the term 'orientations' does not refer to any established legal instruments and, according to Smits, lacks legal binding force.[34] During its Luxembourg summit on 12–13 December 1997, the European Council adopted a Resolution[35] in which it stated that 'in general, exchange rates should be seen as the outcome of all other economic policies'. General orientations may be adopted by the Council only 'in exceptional circumstances, for example in the case of a clear misalignment'. Even in this case, 'such general orientations should always respect the independence of the ECB and be consistent with the primary objective of the ESCB to maintain price stability.'[36]

As I mentioned above, the ESCB is responsible for the conduct of foreign exchange operations (according to Art 105(2) EC consistent with Art 111) and for the management of the Community's foreign reserves. That is, under the present regime, the ESCB is operationally responsible for exchange rate policy, even though the Council could at any time issue 'general orientations'.

International agreements on monetary matters

Article 111(3) EC (and Art III–326(3) of the proposed EU Constitution) contains an explicit external competence of the Community with regard to the negotiation of international agreements concerning monetary matters and foreign exchange regime matters, which constitutes a derogation from the normal treaty-making procedures between the Community/Union and third countries or international organizations.[37]

---

[34] Smits, above note 23, 399.   [35] [1998] OJ C35/1.   [36] ibid.
[37] Art 300 EC and Art III–325 of the EU Constitution.

Article 111(3) EC states:

> Where agreements concerning monetary or foreign exchange regime matters need to be negotiated by the Community with one or more States or international organizations, the Council, acting by a qualified majority on a recommendation from the Commission and after consulting the ECB, shall decide the arrangements for the negotiation and for the conclusion of such agreements. These arrangements shall ensure that the Community expresses a single position. The Commission shall be fully associated with the negotiations. Agreements concluded in accordance with this paragraph shall be binding on the institutions of the Community, on the ECB and on Member States.

The texts of Article 111(3) and Article III–326(3) are confusingly dissimilar,[38] since Article III–326 refers to 'matters relating to the monetary or exchange rate system' instead of the broader formulation of 'monetary or foreign exchange matters' of Article 111(3) EC.[39]

'Monetary matters' under Article 111(3) refer to situations in which the monetary regime of the euro is extended to a third country, for example, if a third country wants to use the euro as its currency under a currency board arrangement, or as parallel legal tender on its territory and is allowed to do so by the Community.[40] 'Foreign exchange regime matters' under Article 111(3) EC (exchange rate system matters according to Art III–326 of the proposed EU Constitution) cover issues not included in Article 111(1) EC (Art III–326(1) of the proposed EU Constitution), such as informal—or less formal—public international law agreements regarding the exchange rate regime of the euro. In terms of procedure, the one described in paragraph 3 also applies to the conclusion of the 'formal exchange rate arrangements' referred to in paragraph 1 of Article 111.

The use of the verbs 'need' and 'shall' in Article 111(3) is more forceful than the use of 'may' in Article 111(1) EC. According to Zilioli and Selmayr,[41] the explicit external competence attributed to the Community (treaty-making powers) by Article 111(3) is limited by two restrictions: by the residual competence of the Member States to negotiate and conclude international agreements regarding economic and monetary union under Article 111(5) EC, and by the external competence of the ECB in monetary matters.

---

[38] I am grateful to René Smits for observations on this point.

[39] The last sentence of Art 111(3) EC (ie, 'Agreements concluded in accordance with this paragraph shall be binding on the institutions of the Community, on the ECB and on Member States') is omitted from Art III–326(3) of the EU Constitution.

[40] The agreements with the principality of Monaco, the Republic of San Marino, the principality of Andorra, and Vatican City with regard to the use of the euro in their territories are included under this category of 'monetary matters'. See eg Manuel López Escudero, *El Euro en el Sistema Monetario Internacional* (Madrid: Tecnos, 2004) 57.

[41] Above note 23, 297–303.

The international role of the euro

As I have already pointed out above, Article III–196 of the proposed EU Constitution, which would replace Article 111(4) EC if it ever enters into force, deals with the need to 'secure the euro's place in the international monetary system'.[42] While Article 111(4) refers in a rather generic sense to international cooperation in economic and monetary matters (making an explicit reference to the allocation of powers in the areas of economic versus monetary union by referring to Art 99 regarding economic policy coordination and Art 105 regarding the ESCB tasks and objectives), the contents of Article 196 are more clearly circumscribed around the international role of the euro in international financial institutions and conferences, even though there is a specific reference to 'economic and monetary union' in paragraph 1.

The residual role of the Member States

Article 111(5) EC (and Art III–326(4) of the proposed EU Constitution) refers to the residual role of the Member States to negotiate in international bodies (international organizations and other groupings) and to conclude agreements as regards economic and monetary union. It states: 'Without prejudice to Community competence and Community agreements regarding economic and monetary union, Member States may negotiate in international bodies and conclude international agreements.'

I further discuss below the obligations of IMF membership for the individual Member States of the euro area.

D. International Relations

An entity needs legal personality in order to act in international relations, to create rights and obligations under international law.[43] Neither the European System of Central Banks, nor the Eurosystem have legal personality.[44] Therefore they do not have the capacity to enter into international legal relations. The entities with legal personality are the ECB and the NCBs, the Community/Union, and the Member States.[45]

---

[42] Article III–196 states that the Council shall adopt 'European decisions establishing common positions on matters of particular interest for economic and monetary union within the competent international financial institutions' (paragraph 1). Article III–196 further states that the Council may 'adopt appropriate measures to ensure unified representation within the international financial institutions' (paragraph 2).

[43] See Zilioli and Selmayr, above note 23, 274.   [44] ibid 275–6.

[45] Ibid 276–86. Zilioli and Selmayr provide an analysis of the actors in the external relations of the euro area (the Member States, the national central banks, the Community, and the European Central Bank).

The Community/the Union

The European Union has been awarded legal personality by Article 281 of the EC Treaty, which states that 'the Community shall have legal personality.' According to Article I–7 of the proposed EU Constitution, the Union has legal personality.[46] The legal power of the Community to act internationally with regard to monetary matters is governed by Article 111 EC (Arts III–196 and III–326 of the proposed EU Constitution).

The Community/Union is typically represented externally by its institutions (notably by the Council and the Commission), which themselves are not endowed with legal personality.[47] The procedures for the conclusion of international agreement foreseen in Article 300 EC[48] do not apply in the case of external monetary relations, which are governed by Article 111 EC. This provision (Article 111) gives the Council a prominent role with regard to the negotiation and conclusion of formal and informal arrangements in monetary and foreign exchange regime matters.

Since the euro area as such has no legal personality,[49] Article III–196(3) of the proposed EU Constitution clarifies that voting within the Council with regard to external euro matters is restricted to the Ministers of the Member States whose currency is the euro.

Herrmann contends that all the fundamental decisions a monetary sovereign can take from the perspective of international law are to be taken by the Council (entering into formal exchange rate systems like Bretton Woods, restricting the flow of capital and payments, or entering into monetary or foreign exchange regime agreements) not by the ECB.[50] Slot also considers that the Council is in the driver's seat.[51]

---

[46] See eg Case 22/70 *Commission Council* (the ERTA case) [1971] ECR 263 paras 13–14.

[47] See Zilioli and Selmayr, above note 23, 281–2 and note 42. See also Joined Cases 7/56 and 3/57 to 7/57 *Algera and others v Common Assembly of the European Coal and Steel Community* [1957] ECR 81, 57. According to Art I–19 of the EU Constitution, the Union's institutions are the European Parliament, the European Council, the Council of Ministers, the European Commission, and the Court of Justice. The European Central Bank does have legal personality as I have already pointed out. Its legal personality is recognized in Art I–30 of the proposed EU Constitution, a provision which is included in Chapter II on 'The Other Union Institutions and Advisory Bodies'.

[48] Article 300 EC and Art III–325 of the proposed EU Constitution refer to the procedure for the conclusion of international agreements between the Union and third countries or international organizations. The proposed Constitution also introduces—Art I–28—the figure of the Union Minister for Foreign Affairs, who will have an important role in the international relations of the EU.

[49] This point is made by Zilioli and Selmayr, above note 23, 274–5.

[50] Above note 27, 6.

[51] P Slot, 'The Institutional Provisions of the EMU' in Curtin and Heukels (eds), *Institutional Dynamics of European Integration. Essays in honour of Henry G. Schemers, Vol II* (Boston/London: Dordrecht 1994) 241.

The European Central Bank

In the field of international monetary cooperation the European Central Bank is entrusted with competences by the EC Treaty and the ESCB Statute. It is important to bear in mind that though the ECB is an institution endowed with separate legal personality, it is enshrined in the Community framework (as the Court of Justice recognized in the OLAF case that I examined in Chapter 7), and in the conduct of its monetary policy responsibilities it exercises an exclusive Union competence.

The European Central Bank governs the ESCB through its decision-making bodies (Art 107(3) EC Treaty). In particular, the decision on external representation of the ESCB is centralized in the hands of the Governing Council of the ECB.[52] According to Article 6(1) of the ESCB Statute, 'in the field of international cooperation involving the tasks entrusted to the ESCB, the ECB shall decide how the ESCB shall be represented.' Moreover, under Article 6(2), 'the ECB and, subject to its approval, the national central banks may participate in international monetary institutions.' For instance, the ECB has participated in the Bank for International Settlements since 1999.

The international legal personality of the ECB is limited to the specific fields of tasks entrusted to the ECB by the Treaty, essentially monetary policy and related matters. It should be noted that, in the absence of formal exchange rate arrangements or general orientations, the operational management of the exchange rate is the responsibility of the European Central Bank.

Article 23 of the ESCB Statute lists the 'external operations' (explicit external competences) which the ECB and the national central banks may conduct:

- establish relations with central banks and financial institutions in other countries and, where appropriate, with international organizations;
- acquire and sell spot and forward all types of foreign exchange assets and precious metals; the term 'foreign exchange asset' shall include securities and all other assets in the currency of any country or units of account and in whatever form held;
- hold and manage the assets referred to in this Article;
- conduct all types of banking transactions in relations with third countries and international organizations, including borrowing and lending operations.

In addition to Article 23, there are other provisions in the ESCB Statute that also refer to 'external operations'. According to Article 22 of the ESCB Statute, the role of the ECB in the promotion of the smooth operation of payment systems also includes an external aspect. The ECB is competent to 'make

---

[52] See Art 6 and 12(5) ESCB Statute.

regulations, to ensure efficient and sound clearing and payment systems within the Community and with other countries'. This regulatory competence implies a parallel external competence to negotiate and conclude, if necessary, international agreements on payment systems.[53] For technical reasons, some of these agreements ought to involve also national central banks in the case where the ECB relies on the payment facilities and infrastructure of national central banks. This is what happened with the Agreement on a Trans-European Automated Real Time Gross-Settlement Express Transfer System, concluded by both the ECB and the euro-NCBs with the NCBs outside the euro area.

The ECB also has the powers to conclude international administrative agreements, particularly with the country of its seat (Art 24 ESCB Statute).

The national central banks

The NCBs of the Member States that have adopted the euro are an integral part of the ESCB (operational arms of the ESCB) when carrying out operations that form part of the tasks of the ESCB.[54] They are also national agencies when performing non-ESCB functions.[55]

According to Article 6(2) of the ESCB Statute, the national central banks may continue to participate in international monetary institutions, such as the Bank for International Settlements, BIS. (Though the ECB has been a member of the BIS since 1999, the individual NCBs retain their participation as members.[56]) Article 31(1) of the ESCB Statute further enables the NCBs to perform transactions in fulfilment of their obligations towards international organizations in accordance with Article 23.

According to Article 43(2) of the ESCB Statute, the national central banks of the Member States with a derogation shall retain their powers in the field of monetary policy according to national law, despite their participation in the ESCB.[57]

The EU Member States: IMF membership

The transfer of monetary powers from the national to the Community level has reduced the legal capacity of the Member States to act on the international

---

[53] Zilioli and Selmayr, above note 23, 312–13.
[54] ESCB Statute, Arts 12(1) and 14(3).
[55] ESCB Statute, Art 14(4).   [56] Above note 40, 121.
[57] This provision has become Art 42(2) in the Protocol annexed to the EU Constitution (since Art 37 regarding the seat of the ECB has been removed).

level.[58] The external competences of the Members States of the euro area have a residual character,[59] as recognized in Article 111(5) of the EC Treaty (and Art III–326(4) of the proposed EU Constitution).

However, EU Member States must still comply with their international obligations. In the following paragraphs I examine briefly the consequences of IMF membership for the Member States in the euro area.

IMF membership

Under the Fund's Articles of Agreement (Art II, Section 2), only 'countries' are allowed membership. Member States that have adopted the euro remain individual members of the IMF, despite the fact that the area of jurisdiction of the euro is clearly supranational. The membership of the Community/Union (or of the ECB) would need an amendment to the Articles.[60]

The euro area as such is not able to appoint a Governor or appoint or elect Executive Directors in the IMF, even though, in December 1998, the ECB was granted observer status at selected Executive Board meetings.[61]

The national–supranational dichotomy presents a challenge for the Member States of the euro area. The differentiated integration with regard to monetary

---

[58] Member States, as a rule, remain externally competent in the field of economic (fiscal) policy provided (1) that they regard their economic policies as a matter of common concern and (2) any international agreements do not circumvent the prohibitions laid down in the Treaty regarding economic policy. Eg, Member States shall not enter into international agreements which would require them to grant public authorities privileged access to financial institutions. See Zilioli and Selmayr, above note 23, 290. In his comments on this chapter, René Smits contends that Member States' obligations extend further than this: they may not, via G8 or G10 arrangements, preclude the internal coordination of economic policies and should at the very least consult their counterparts on possible positions in these contexts, as well as in IMF affairs.

[59] See generally Zilioli and Selmayr, ibid 317–32. According to Art 105(3) the competence of the ECB to hold and manage the official foreign reserves of the Member States 'shall be without prejudice to the holding and management by the governments of Member States of foreign-exchange working balances'. There is also a rather limited external competence of Member States for international agreements with regard to coins, which remain largely a national competence. There are also a number of Protocols and Declarations attached to the Treaty which reserve external competences to specific Member States and thus enable them to continue their public international law relationship with specific countries and territories such as the Republic of San Marino, Vatican City, and the Principality of Monaco. René Smits observes (in private correspondence) that even though France or Italy may act, it is the Community which enters into international relations with these 'mini-States'.

[60] The alternative reading, namely that the Articles of Agreement should be interpreted in conformity with a new legal reality, not foreseen at the time of their conclusion when only 'countries' had currencies and currency unions were always between sovereign States, and that for the purposes of the IMF Articles of Agreement, the Community (Union) is a 'country' has been advocated by René Smits, as he pointed out in his comments on this chapter.

[61] See 'The IMF & the European Economic and Monetary Union', International Monetary Fund, March 1999, available at <http://www.imf.org/external/np/exr/facts/emu.htm>.

policy and to exchange rate policy, the asymmetries between monetary and fiscal policy, and between monetary policy and financial supervision and regulation further complicate the obligations of IMF membership.

Implications for IMF surveillance[62]   Article IV consultations (analysed in Chapter 13) continue to be held with each individual Member State. However, these consultations also require the involvement of representatives of the relevant EU institutions, given the Community competence with regard monetary and exchange rate policies.[63] 'These discussions, and consideration by the IMF's Executive Board of the monetary and exchange rate policies of the euro area, are, as a practical matter, held separately from those with individual euro-area countries, but are considered an integral part of the Article IV process for each member.'[64] The consultations also need to take into account the 'regional perspective' with regard to fiscal policy and other economic policies.[65]

Implications for the SDR   Since the advent of EMU, the euro has replaced the Deutschmark and the French franc in the SDR valuation basket. The value of the SDR is now determined daily on the basis of four currencies: the US dollar, the yen, the euro, and the pound sterling.[66]

Implications for the holding and management of foreign reserves   As part of their membership responsibilities, Member States hold reserve positions with the IMF. Article 31 of the ESCB Statute allows Member States of the euro area to hold some reserves so that they can fulfil their obligations towards international organizations. However, the discretion that a Member State of the euro area retains in managing its foreign reserve assets is limited since part of the assets have been transferred to the ECB (according to Art 30 of the ESCB Statute), and 'transactions above certain limits involving foreign assets that are retained by a country are subject to ECB approval'.[67]

According to Article 30(5) of the ESCB Statute, 'The ECB may hold and manage IMF reserve positions and special drawing rights and provide for the pooling of such assets.'

Only if the EU were to become a political union, or if the IMF Articles of Agreement were revised, could the IMF 'deal' directly with the EU in terms of representation and the obligations of IMF membership (Art IV consultations and others).

---

[62] ibid.
[63] See eg International Monetary Fund, PIN (Public Information Notice) No 04/79, 3 August 2004, 'IMF Executive Board Discusses Euro Area Policies'.
[64] Above note 61.   [65] ibid.   [66] ibid.   [67] ibid.

The problems of relying upon multiple external actors under a multi-layered system of representation

The Community is competent to speak and act in international fora whenever the external competences of the Community are involved.[68] The ECB is competent to speak and act in international fora whenever the tasks entrusted to the ESCB are involved. The Member States of the euro area (the 'ins') have a residual competence and also have the responsibilities of their 'individual' membership in international monetary organizations. The national central banks of the Member States that have adopted the euro remain competent to act in the field of financial supervision and in the exercise of the other responsibilities assigned to them by national law as national agencies, that is, when performing non-ESCB tasks.[69] They also continue to participate in international organizations, such as the BIS. The Member States with a derogation (the 'outs') retain their monetary sovereignty, internally and externally, and their competence to speak and act in international fora, though they need to comply with a number of treaty provisions.[70] The national central banks of the Member States with a derogation retain the competences attributed to them by national law. They act as national agencies, not as an integral part of the ESCB, as opposed to the national central banks of the Member States that have adopted the euro.[71]

The problems of relying upon multiple actors[72] and the existence of a multi-layered complex system of representation in the Community with regard to EMU matters present a picture of bewildering complexity. Smits pointedly remarks: 'If unchecked, [the] panoply of uncoordinated provisions on external action, may lead, in the field of EMU, to an hexagonal representation of the Union', comprising the President of the European Council, President of the

---

[68] Zilioli and Selmayr, above note 23, 336–7.

[69] Though subject to the constraints imposed by Art 14(4) of the ESCB Statute, which reads as follows: 'National Central Banks may perform functions other than those specified in this Statute unless the Governing Council finds, by a majority of two thirds of the votes cast, that these interfere with the objectives and tasks of the ESCB. Such functions shall be performed on the responsibility and liability of national central banks and shall not be regarded as being part of the functions of the ESCB.'

[70] See eg Art 124(1) EC and Arts III–199 and III–200 of the EU Constitution.

[71] However these NCBs of the Member States with a derogation participate in the General Council, the third governing body of the ESCB. See Art 123(3) EC and Art 45 ESCB Statute.

[72] 'One may even observe a certain competition between the Community institutions, the Member States, the European Central Bank and some national central banks to assume the role of "spokesman" for the euro area. The danger involved in such a competition is that a situation could arise which is only too familiar from the field of the common foreign and security policy: a situation in which our American counterparts would still be asking whom they should call in Europe.' Zilioli and Selmayr, above note 23, 273–4.

Commission, Ministers of Finance, President of the EU Council, ECB President, and the President of the Eurogroup.[73] This 'spreading of internal and external power'[74] does not augur well for 'unity' with regard to the external representation of the euro.

The current structure is far too complex and should be simplified.

E. Conclusions

Responsibility for the conduct of exchange rate policy in the euro area is a task which is divided between the Council and the ECB under a notoriously unclear set of treaty provisions. Article 111 EC Treaty is cumbersome in legal and economic terms, the result of a calculated obfuscation for political purposes.

Despite the convoluted language of Article 111 EC, it can be inferred from the treaty provisions and from doctrine of parallelism developed by the case law of the ECJ that the conduct of exchange rate policy in the euro area is an exclusive Community competence.

Though the Council has the primary role according to the language of Article 111, in the absence of formal exchange rate arrangements or general orientations, the management of the exchange rate is the operational responsibility of the European Central Bank.

The external representation of the euro is complicated by the existence of multiple actors with external competences and by a multi-layered system of representation at the EU level. The proposed EU Constitution does not alter in substance the complex institutional structure that governs the external aspects of EMU.

From the point of view of monetary law, the relations between the Member States of the euro area and the International Monetary Fund are of particular relevance. Under Article II, section 2 of the current Articles of Agreement, only countries can be members of the IMF. This raises important challenges in terms of international monetary cooperation, since the area of jurisdiction of the euro is clearly supranational, while IMF membership remains nationally based.

---

[73] See René Smits, above note 15, 455–6.

[74] ibid. Smits cites other provisions on external action by the Union that may affect the functioning of EMU, in particular Art I–26, Art I–28, Art I–24(3), and Art I–40(5). He concludes: 'The external representation is badly organized and will lead to confusion and inter-agency debate about who is going to represent the Union, with dual (the ECB and Eurogroup President) triple (including the Commission President), even quadruple or hexagonal presidencies (including the fixed and rotating presidencies of the different Council formations).'

10

BANKING SUPERVISION AND LENDER OF LAST RESORT IN THE EU

The euro-area has inherited the supervisory framework established for the needs of the EU Single Market. However, the unique challenge faced by the ECB lies in the threefold separation between the regulatory body (the European Union), the single currency area (the euro-area) and supervisory jurisdictions (each euro-area country). This threefold separation requires special forms of cooperation between public bodies.

Tommaso Padoa-Schioppa, *Regulating Finance* (2004) 128

A. Introduction

The abandonment of the coincidence between the area of jurisdiction of monetary policy and the area of jurisdiction of banking supervision is a major novelty brought about by the advent of EMU, as Tommasso Padoa-Schioppa has pointed out.[1] Since the launch of the euro in January 1999, the European

---

[1] Tommaso Padoa-Schioppa, 'EMU and Banking Supervision', Lecture at the London School of Economics (24 February 1999), <http://fmg.lse.ac.uk/events/index.html>, also published in Charles Goodhart (ed), *Which Lender of Last Resort For Europe?* (London: Central Banking Publications, 2000) ch 1.

Central Bank has been in charge of the monetary policy of the countries which have adopted the single currency, while responsibility for supervision remains decentralized.

There is an inevitable tension in the current EU structure: a national mandate in prudential supervision, combined with a single European currency and a European mandate in the completion of the single market in financial services.[2] This chapter discusses some of the implications of this institutional arrangement with regard to the allocation of responsibilities for banking supervision, banking regulation, financial stability, crisis management, and lender of last resort operations. The latter issue is further complicated by the fact that though central banks can create liquidity (a point emphasized by Charles Goodhart), only the fiscal authorities can provide for new injections of equity capital (using taxpayers' money).[3] I propose the creation of a European Standing Committee for Crisis Management to alleviate some of the shortcomings of the present system.

B. Banking Supervision in the EU

Prudential supervision is decentralized at the level of the Member States, based upon the principle of home country control, combined with mutual recognition on the basis of prior regulatory harmonization. The reasons why responsibility for banking supervision in the EU remains at the national level are in part historical and, in part, a result of the multi-faceted character of supervision.[4] Though the Draft Statute of the European System of Central Banks included prudential supervision as a fifth basic task of the ESCB, the final version of the Statute (Article 25) and Article 105 EC Treaty only granted the ECB a limited supervisory role owing to opposition from some countries to such an inclusion. Germany, in particular, was reluctant to accept the assignment of a lender of last resort feature to the ESCB for fear that it might conflict with

---

[2] See Niels Thygesen, 'Comments on "The Political Economy of Financial Harmonisation in Europe"' in Jeroen Kremer, Dirk Schoenmaker, and Peter Wierts (eds), *Financial Supervision in Europe* (Cheltenham: Edward Elgar, 2003) 145.

[3] See Charles Goodhart, 'The Political Economy of Financial Harmonisation in Europe' in Jeroen Kremer, Dirk Schoenmaker, and Peter Wierts (eds), *Financial Supervision in Europe* (Cheltenham: Edward Elgar, 2003) 133–6.

[4] As I have explained in Ch 3, supervision in a broad sense can be understood as a process with four stages or phases: (1) licensing, authorization, or chartering (entry into the business), (2) supervision *stricto sensu*, (3) sanctioning or imposition of penalties in the case of non-compliance with the law, fraud, bad management, or other types of wrongdoing, and (4) crisis management, which comprises lender of last resort, deposit insurance, and bank insolvency proceedings. See also Rosa M Lastra, *Central Banking and Banking Regulation* (London: Financial Markets Group, 1996) 108–44.

the sacrosanct goal of price stability. Other countries—following national practices—favoured the inclusion of a clearly defined LOLR feature.

Prudential supervision is a 'non-basic' task of the ESCB according to Article 105(2) EC Treaty, though Article 105(6) EC leaves the door open for a possible future expansion of such supervisory role, following a simplified procedure (simplified in the sense that it does not require the formal amendment of the Treaty, but not likely to be exercised lightly owing to the requirement for unanimity).[5] Article 105(6) of the EC Treaty—which is often referred to as the 'enabling clause'—reads as follows: 'The Council may, acting unanimously on a proposal from the Commission and after consulting the ECB and after receiving the assent of the European Parliament, confer upon the ECB specific tasks concerning the policies relating to the prudential supervision of credit institutions and other financial institutions with the exception of insurance undertakings.'

This clause has not been activated yet and I contend that it is unlikely ever to be activated in the light of the supervisory and market structure that has emerged in the last few years.[6]

With regard to the subject matter of this chapter (banking supervision and lender of last resort in the EU), a significant recent development is the publication in May 2005 of a press release announcing a Memorandum of Understanding (MoU) on cooperation in financial crisis situations.[7] This 2005 MoU is to complement a previous Memorandum of Understanding on high-level principles of cooperation between banking supervisors and central banks of the EU in crisis management, on which a press release was published in March 2003. However, neither MoU is a legally binding instrument.[8]

The proposed EU Constitution[9] leaves the responsibilities for supervision

---

[5] See Rosa M Lastra, 'The Division of Responsibilities Between the European Central Bank and the National Central Banks Within the European System of Central Banks', The Columbia Journal of European Law, Volume 6, No 2, Spring 2000.

[6] See Rosa M Lastra, 'The Governance Structure for Financial Regulation and Supervision in Europe', The Columbia Journal of European Law, Volume 10, No 1, Fall 2003.

[7] See press release concerning a Memorandum of Understanding on Co-operation between the Banking Supervisors, Central Banks and Finance Ministries of the European Union in Financial Crisis Situations <http://www.eu2005.lu/en/actualites/documents_travail/2005/05/14ecofin_mou/index.html> 14 May 2005. On 18 May, the ECB published a press release concerning this MoU on its website, <http://www.ecb.int>.

[8] See ECB Press Release <http://www.ecb.int/press/pr/date/2003/html/pr030310_3.en.html> regarding the 'Memorandum of Understanding on high-level principles of cooperation between the banking supervisors and central banks of the European Union in crisis management situations', 10 March 2003.

[9] The Treaty establishing a Constitution for Europe was signed in Rome on 29 October 2004 and is available in the Official Journal No C310 of 16 December 2004. The proposed EU Constitution was thrown into a legal limbo following the rejection of the Treaty in referenda in

placed at the national level.[10] Even the obsolete reference of Article 105(6) EC to the exclusion of insurance undertaking, which reflects an outdated notion of financial supervision, is kept intact in Article III–185(6) of the proposed EU Constitution.

Table 10.1 provides a brief summary of the level of centralization or decentralization with regard to the various prudential supervisory functions in the EU. It is clear that, with the exception of lender of last resort (an issue which I explore below) and as long as Article 105(6) EC is not activated, the competence

Table 10.1 Centralization or decentralization in prudential supervision in the EU?

Stage	Principle
1. Licensing	Decentralization with regulatory harmonization[11]
2. Prudential supervision	Decentralization with regulatory harmonization[12] and consultation—ECB and Lamfalussy
3. Sanctioning	Decentralization
4. Lender of last resort	Mix of centralization and decentralization
5. Deposit Insurance	Decentralization with regulatory harmonization[13]
6. Insolvency proceedings	Decentralization with regulatory harmonization[14]

Centralization—Community competence
Decentralization—National competence

France (28 May 2005) and the Netherlands (1 June 2005). The suspension of the ratification process (according to the declaration of the European Council Brussels summit on 16–17 June 2005 to allow for a 'period of reflection') does not equate to the abandonment of the Constitution altogether. The text remains a legal document of value to refer to, also with a view to its possible entry into force or the taking over of parts of it in other Treaty texts later on. The Treaty establishing a Constitution for Europe, if ever ratified by all EU Member States, aims to replace all existing Treaties, except for the Treaty establishing the Euratom.

[10] Elmar Brok, contributed in 2003 a discussion paper with amendments to the then draft constitutional text in which he suggested that the prudential supervision of credit institutions and the stability of the financial system should be a shared community competence. See Elmar Brok, Discussion Paper 111, CONV 325/2/02 REV 2, 27.01.2003 available at <http://register. consilium.eu.int/pdf/en/02/cv00/cv00325-re02en02.pdf>. Article 71(1)(p) of his proposed revision read as follows: 'The Union shall have shared competences with the Member States with regard to . . . (p) prudential supervision of credit institutions and the stability of the financial system, in particular by taking into account the contribution of the ECB and, under its governance, the ESCB.'

[11] See Directive 2000/12/EC of the European Parliament and of the Council of 20 March 2000 relating the taking up and pursuit of the business of credit institutions. [2000] OJ L126.

[12] See Directive 2000/12/EC of the European Parliament and of the Council of 20 March 2000 relating the taking up and pursuit of the business of credit institutions. [2000] OJ L126.

[13] See Directive 94/19/EC of the European Parliament and of the Council of 30 May 1994 on deposit guarantee schemes. [1994] OJ L135.

[14] See Directive 2001/24/EC of the European Parliament and of the Council of 4 April on the reorganization and winding-up of credit institutions. [2001] OJ L125.

is national. The prevailing principle with regard to the various stages of the supervisory process is decentralization.[15]

C. Banking Regulation in the EU

A large number of EU directives and regulations constitute a true body of European banking regulation, binding upon the Member States, which has been extensively studied in the literature. In this section, I only discuss briefly the allocation of responsibilities for banking regulation. As I explained in Chapter 3, while supervision has to do with monitoring and enforcement, banking regulation refers to the establishment of rules, to the process of rule-making.[16]

Rules on prudential standards are largely harmonized and rules on payment systems are actually centralized (the ECB has responsibility for rules in this area). As a result of regulatory harmonization (which does not equate to centralization), the EU banking policy presents a rather unified picture. For this reason, Padoa-Schioppa refers to the current approach as one based on 'European regulation with national supervision'.[17]

The ECB regulatory role is rather extensive (though supervision can be separated from the central bank, an independent central bank always keeps a regulatory role). The legal acts of the ECB comprise ECB regulations, decisions, recommendations, and opinions.[18] There are also intra-ESCB agreements on internal matters (guidelines and instructions) between the ECB and the NCBs.[19] The proposed EU Constitution refers to the European Regulations, European Decisions, recommendations, and opinions of the European Central Bank in Article III–190.

Article III–191 of the proposed EU Constitution further states: 'Without prejudice to the powers of the European Central Bank, European laws or framework laws shall lay down the measures necessary for use of the euro as a single currency. Such laws or framework laws shall be adopted after consultation with the European Central Bank.'

There is also the requirement to consult the ECB (according to Art 105(4) EC Treaty and Art III–185(4) of the proposed EU Constitution) on any proposed

---

[15] For a description of each supervisory stage, see Ch 3.   [16] Above note 4.

[17] See Tommasso Padoa-Schioppa, *Regulating Finance* (Oxford: Oxford University Press, 2004) ch 8 on 'Central Banks and Financial Stability', 121.

[18] See Art 110 EC Treaty and Art 34 of the ESCB Statute.

[19] Article 14(3) of that ESCB statute refers to 'guidelines and instructions' of the ECB to the NCBs.

Community act in its fields of competence and on any draft legislative provision in its fields of competence. The ECB may submit opinions to the appropriate Community institutions or bodies or to national authorities on matters in its fields of competence. The extension of the Lamfalussy framework to banking, with the creation of the Committee of European Banking Supervisors (CEBS) and the level 2 European Banking Committee, adds a new layer of consultation and participation to the rule-making responsibilities of the EU Commission.[20]

D. Financial Stability in the EU

Financial stability is a common objective for both central banks and supervisory authorities that generally refers to the safety and soundness of the financial system and to the stability of the payment and settlement systems.[21] As I discussed in Chapter 3, financial stability is an elusive and evolving concept. There is no commonly accepted analytical framework to define what financial stability means in 'positive terms'. There is only consensus regarding its definition in 'negative terms', as the absence of instability, by reference to times of crisis.

With or without supervisory powers, a central bank has responsibility for financial stability. Tommaso Padoa-Schioppa refers to financial stability as a 'land in between' monetary policy and supervision.[22] The unbundling of monetary policy, prudential supervision, and financial stability (the central bank used to be in charge of these tasks, which formed a single composite) has contributed to the current debate about what exactly financial stability implies when one institution is in charge of monetary policy and one or many other institutions are in charge of supervision.

The mandate to achieve financial stability is both national and European. At the national level, the Member States which have adopted the euro rely both on the European Central Bank and on their own supervisory authorities for the pursuit of this objective; the Member States with a derogation or an opt-out, on the other hand, rely on their own national central banks and on their supervisory authorities (if supervision is conducted by a separate agency). At the European level, the picture is also complex, since the ECB's role in financial stability (recognized in Arts 105(5) EC and III–185(5) of the proposed EU Constitution)

---

[20] Above note 6.

[21] Most central banks, with or without supervisory responsibilities, regard this responsibility for financial stability as one of their key duties. However, many central bank laws do not explicitly refer to this mandate. In the case of the European Central Bank, the EC Treaty includes a specific reference to financial stability in Art 105(5).

[22] See Tommasso Padoa-Schioppa, above note 17, 92 and 109.

is shared with a number of Committees that have been established in recent years (the European Economic and Financial Committee, the Banking Supervision Committee of the European Central Bank, the Financial Services Committee, and the Level 2 and Level 3 Lamfalussy committees, that I discuss in Chapter 11). This suggests a diffused responsibility with regard to financial stability, which does not augur well for the objective of creating a single market in financial services.[23]

One of the main economic arguments in favour of European Monetary Union was the need to solve the 'inconsistent quartet' of policy objectives: free trade, full capital mobility, pegged (or fixed) exchange rates, and independent national monetary policies.[24] The only long-term solution to this inconsistency was to complement the internal market with monetary union,[25] thus abandoning national control over domestic monetary policies. A similar argument is now being made with regard to financial supervision. As Thygesen has pointed out, it is difficult to achieve simultaneously a single financial market and financial stability while preserving a high degree of nationally based supervision.[26] Schoenmaker refers to these inconsistent objectives as the 'trilemma in financial supervision': a stable financial system, an integrated financial market, and national financial supervision.[27]

E. The Role of the ESCB with Regard to Lender of Last Resort (LOLR) Operations

The general principle for crisis management in the European Union is national competence, that is, decentralization. This means that the instruments to deal with a crisis are national (albeit combined with mechanisms for European cooperation)[28] and that the costs of the crisis are typically borne at the national

---

[23] We have a saying in Spain: 'unos por otros y la casa sin barrer' (which means that if you rely on others to sweep the house, no one would end up sweeping it).

[24] Others refer to the 'trilemma' in macroeconomic policy of three desirable yet contradictory or inconsistent policy objectives: fixed exchange rates, capital mobility, and independent monetary policy. See eg Andrew Rose, 'Explaining Exchange-Rate Volatility: An Empirical analysis of the "Holy Trinity" of Monetary Independence, Fixed Exchange Rates and Capital Mobility' (2003) 15 Journal of International Money and Finance, 925–45.

[25] See generally Tommaso Padoa-Schioppa, *The Road to Monetary Union in Europe: The Emperor, the Kings and the Genies* (Oxford: Oxford University Press, 2000).

[26] See Niels Thygesen, above note 2.

[27] See Dirk Schoenmaker, 'Financial Supervision: from National to European?' Financial and Monetary Studies (NIBE–SVV), Amsterdam, 2003.

[28] Xavier Freixas refers to the current system as one of improvized cooperation.

The term 'improvised cooperation' has been coined to convey the view of an efficient, although adaptative exchange of information and decision-taking. The existence of joint

level. However, as the process of financial integration in Europe advances, the likelihood of a pan-European crisis increases, and with it the need for a European solution.

The relevant provisions in the EC Treaty and the ESCB Statute concerning emergency liquidity assistance are ambiguous and provide scope for different interpretations.[29] Nonetheless, a few elements of 'centralization' are already apparent with regard to the LOLR function.

It is important to design and publicize *ex ante* the procedures and mechanisms available at the European level to deal with a 'banking Tsunami'. The surprise element, the unpredictability and uncertainty about the effects that surround such natural catastrophe, are also attributes that could be predicated of a potential European banking crisis.

Different types of crisis

There are three types of crises where the provision of emergency liquidity assistance could be critical: (1) crisis in the payment system; (2) general liquidity crisis, and (3) the classic liquidity crisis.

Crisis in the payments system

If a crisis originates in the payments system, the ECB has competence to act as lender of last resort according to Art 105(2) EC Treaty (and Art III–185(2) of the proposed EU Constitution), which states that the ESCB is entrusted with the 'smooth operation of payment systems'. This point is actually borne out by the fact that the Bank of England had to put up substantial collateral with the ECB to take part in TARGET (Trans-European Automated Real-time Gross-settlement Express Transfer) whereas this was not the case for the NCBs of the Eurosystem participating in TARGET.

---

committees should help to improve the efficiency of information exchange. Padoa–Schioppa argues that the lack of transparency 'on the procedural and practical details of emergency action' is in line with the idea of 'constructive ambiguity'. But this is open to debate, since constructive ambiguity does not need to state the procedural arrangements to solve financial crises on a case-by-case basis. Developing on this point, Favero et al (2000) argue that 'reserving financial stability' is also a matter of reacting swiftly and decisively. The lack of a formal structure for intervention is therefore worrisome.

See Freixas, 'Crisis Management in Europe' in Jeroen Kremer, Dirk Schoenmaker, and Peter Wierts (eds), *Financial Supervision in Europe* (Cheltenham: Edward Elgar, 2003) 110.

[29] The debate about crisis management and lender of last resort in Europe has triggered an abundant literature in recent years. See, *inter alia*, Charles Goodhart (ed), *Which Lender of Last Resort for Europe* (London: Central Banking Publications, 2000), Jeroen Kremers, Dirk Schoenmaker, and Peter J Wierts (eds), *Financial Supervision in Europe* (Cleltenham: Edward Elgar Publishing, 2001), chs 4 and 5, and Tommasso Padoa-Schioppa, *Regulating Finance* (Oxford: Oxford University Press, 2004) chs 7 and 8.

Because payments are largely conducted—though not necessarily nor exclusively—through the banking system, it is often difficult to dissociate payment system supervision (a basic ESCB task) from banking supervision which for the most part remains a national competence, not a Community competence. But, the Treaty and the Statute do establish that dissociation and, as anything that is enshrined in a legal text, it has legal consequences, as pointed out in Chapter 7.

General liquidity crisis

In the case of a general liquidity dry up, for example, in the wake of a dramatic fall in stock prices leading to a widespread and generalized questioning of the liquidity of different sorts of financial institutions, the ECB could technically act through what has been called a 'market operations approach' to lending of last resort. This means that the ECB could provide liquidity through open market operations, according to Article 18 of the ESCB Statute.

The 'classic' liquidity crisis

This is the 'traditional' understanding of LOLR assistance,[30] that is, collateralized lines of credit to an individual financial institution which—owing to problems which do not originate in the payment system—becomes illiquid, but not necessarily insolvent, and whose illiquidity threatens to spread to other institutions and to other markets (the problem of contagion). In principle, the LOLR responsibility is understood to remain at the national level, because it has not been specifically transferred.[31] Since prudential supervision remains at the national level, it is logical to assume that the national authorities have adequate expertise and information to assess the problems of banks within their jurisdictions. The national central banks, working together with the supervisory authorities if supervision is separated from the central bank (and also with the

---

[30] See Ch 4. The theoretical foundations of the lender of last resort doctrine were first set by Henry Thornton in 1802, (See Henry Thornton, *An Enquiry into the Nature and Effects of the Paper Credit of Great Britain* (Fairfield, NJ: AM Kelley, 1991, originally published in 1802)) and then by Walter Bagehot in 1873 (See Walter Bagehot, *Lombard Street. A Description of the Money Market* (New York: Wiley, 1999, originally published in 1873)). Such doctrine is based upon four pillars. To begin, the central bank—acting as lender of last resort—should prevent temporarily illiquid but solvent banks from failing. (This type of lending is by nature short-term.) Secondly, the central bank should be able to lend as much as is necessary (only the ultimate supplier of high-powered money has this ability), but charge a high rate of interest. Thirdly, the central bank should accommodate anyone with good collateral, valued at pre-panic prices. Finally, the central bank should make its readiness to lend clear in advance.

[31] René Smits holds a different opinion. He regards this LOLR responsibility as an exclusive EU competence. See René Smits, 'The role of the ESCB in Banking Supervision', *Legal Aspects of the European System of Central Banks, Liber Amicorum Paolo Zamboni Garavelli* (Frankfurt: European Central Bank, 2005) n 32.

fiscal authorities as I explain below), are ultimately responsible for the decision on whether or not to grant collateralized emergency lending.[32]

It remains unclear, in my opinion, whether the national central banks would be considered to be acting as operational arms of the ESCB (according to Arts 14(3) and 12(1) of the ESCB Statute in combination with a creative and generous interpretation of Art 18 regarding discount and credit operations[33] and Art 20 of the ESCB Statute) or as national agencies (according to Art 14(4) of the ESCB Statute). In the first case, the ECB should grant prior authorization; if they are considered to be acting as national agencies, a consultation procedure suffices.

The wording of the principle of subsidiarity leaves the door open for a possible Community/Union competence (which could be exercised either directly by the ECB or by the NCBs in their capacity as operational arms of the ESCB). According to Article 5 EC (and Art I–11(3) of the proposed EU Constitution), which I further explore below, it could be argued in a crisis that action by the ECB would be more effective than action by a national central bank. The reason why such an argument would be persuasive arises from the risk of contagion. In a closely integrated banking and financial market in the EU a liquidity crisis with one institution in one centre could have immediate implications for institutions in other centres. National supervisory authorities do not have the ability, authority, or inclination to deal effectively with externalities with cross-border effects. The ECB will best be able to judge the risk of contagion. Only if the crisis could be easily contained at the national level (though in a single currency area, this judgement is tricky) would there be no need for a European solution.

According to some commentators a degree of 'constructive ambiguity' is desirable in the case of crisis management. And ambiguity is what the EC law provides. Ambiguity provides scope for different—or even contrasting or possibly conflicting—interpretations. The silence on this point is interpreted by some as a positive sign of the desire of the Treaty negotiators to assign responsibility at the ECB level with respect to LOLR operations, and by some others as a negative signal of those same negotiators on the same point. However, in my opinion, ambiguity is never constructive. The only 'ambiguity' that can be constructive in crisis management and LOLR is the discretionary component in

---

[32] Above notes 7 and 8. I further elaborate below on the 2003 and 2005 MoUs. Another problematic issue is the definition and availability of collateral in times of crisis. This point is made by Lorenzo Bini Smaghi, in Charles Goodhart (ed), *Which Lender of Last Resort For Europe?* (London: Central Banking Publications, 2000) ch 7, 247.

[33] The second indent of Art 18(1)—regarding credit operations—of the ESCB Statute leaves the door open for a generous interpretation that could allow for the ECB to intervene in a generalized liquidity crisis. This article provides that the ECB and the NCBs may 'conduct credit operations with credit institutions and other market participants with lending based on adequate collateral'.

the provision of such assistance, in the sense that there is no obligation for the central bank to provide LOLR loans. It is this discretionary nature, this uncertainty, that reduces the moral hazard incentives inherent in any support operation. I am afraid that the ambiguity in many Treaty provisions is the result of a calculated obfuscation for political purposes, which expresses the labour pains that accompanied the drafting of some of these provisions. It will take the first pan-European crisis to bring some light to the current ambiguity.

Against this background of a rather unclear division of responsibilities, commentators have differed on their understanding of the ECB's role in a liquidity crisis. Padoa-Schioppa in the first public statement by an ECB official on this controversial subject dismissed the concerns about the lack of a clearly defined lender of last resort role for the ESCB on three counts: it reflects an outdated notion of LOLR, it underestimates the Eurosystem's capacity to act, and it represents too mechanistic a view of how a crisis is actually managed.[34]

Table 10.2 summarizes the three cases I have just presented and the principle and legal basis that apply in each of them.

Table 10.2 Centralization or decentralization in the allocation of LOLR responsibilities?

Case	Principle	Legal basis
Payment systems gridlock	Centralization	Art 105(2) EC Treaty
General liquidity dry-up	Centralization	Art 18 ESCB Statute
Emergency credit lines	Decentralization Ambiguity	Arts 105(5) and (6) EC, Art 18 ESCB Statute, MoUs, Subsidiarity, Art 5 EC

F. Consideration of the Principles of Conferral, Subsidiarity, and Proportionality

In the EU, the allocation of supervisory responsibilities—including emergency liquidity support—needs to take into account the principles of strict conferment or attribution of powers, subsidiarity, and proportionality. These three principles ('conferral, subsidiarity, and proportionality') are regarded as 'fundamental principles' in the proposed EU Constitution.[35]

---

[34] Above note 1 at 11.
[35] According to Art I–11 of the proposed EU Constitution, 'The Union shall act within the limits of the competences conferred upon it by the Member States in the Constitution to attain the objectives set out in the Constitution. Competences not conferred upon the Union in the Constitution remain with the Member States.'

With regard to the principle of strict attribution of powers, Article 5 EC Treaty states: 'The Community shall act within the limits of the powers conferred upon it by this Treaty and the objectives assigned to it therein.'

Prudential supervision has not been transferred to the supranational level. Responsibility for it remains with the Member States. Neither Article I–13 of the proposed EU Constitution, which refers to areas of exclusive competence of the EU, nor Article I–14, which refers to areas of shared competence, nor any other provision in the constitutional treaty specifically mentions the attribution of prudential supervision to the supranational institutions.[36]

According to the principle of subsidiarity (Art 5 EC Treaty), 'in areas which do not fall within its exclusive competence, the Community shall take action . . ., only in and in so far as the objectives of the proposed action cannot be sufficiently achieved by the Member States and can therefore, by reason of the scale or effects of the proposed action, be better achieved by the Community'. This principle could be used as a legal basis for justifying the involvement of the European Central Bank in emergency liquidity operations, since the externalities and contagion of a banking crisis with cross-border effect give rise to a set of circumstances than can be construed under this subsidiarity principle. The key words in the wording of this provision that capture the contagion risk are: 'by reason of the scale or effects of the proposed action'.

However, action by the Community/Union 'shall not exceed what is necessary to achieve the objectives of this Treaty' under the principle of proportionality (Art 5 EC Treaty). One consequence of this principle—in the case that the ECB were to assume a centralized role in support operations—is that that centralization of one function, such as lender of last resort assistance, does not require nor imply the centralization of other supervisory functions.

The proposed EU Constitution clarifies the application of the principles of subsidiarity and proportionality in a protocol annexed to the Treaty. It is clear from the provisions of the protocol that the Court of Justice will continue to have a key role in the delimitation of the principle of subsidiarity.[37]

Article I–18 of the proposed EU Constitution introduces a 'flexibility clause', which is a modified version of the current Article 308 EC Treaty. According to Article 308 EC Treaty:

> If action by the Community should prove necessary to attain, in the course of the

---

[36] The references in Art III–185 of the proposed EU Constitution are almost identical to the references in Art 105 EC Treaty.

[37] See Art 8 of the Protocol, annexed to the proposed Treaty establishing a Constitution for Europe as Protocol 2.

operation of the common market, one of the objectives of the Community, and this Treaty has not provided the necessary powers, the Council shall, acting unanimously on a proposal from the European Commission and after consulting the European Parliament, take the appropriate measures.

A review of the jurisprudence on Article 308 shows that this provision has been widely interpreted[38] and could therefore be used as a legal basis to assign LOLR responsibilities to the European Central Bank or even to set up the Standing Committee that I propose below. Indeed, Article 308 was used as the legal basis for granting powers to the European Monetary Cooperation Fund with regard to the operation of the European Monetary System[39] and was also used in one of the regulations concerning the introduction of the euro.[40]

G. Fiscal Assistance and State Aid Rules

A most contentious issue is whether the classic LOLR assistance to troubled institutions, that is, a 'central bank money solution' as opposed to a 'taxpayers' money' solution or a 'private money solution' (drawing on the terminology used by Tommasso Padoa-Schioppa),[41] is solely to illiquid, but solvent institutions. I have argued elsewhere that LOLR operations often provide assistance to insolvent institutions.[42] Hence, the distinction between central bank money solution and taxpayers' solution is not always clear.[43]

As Goodhart points out, 'a central bank can create liquidity, but it cannot provide for new injections of equity capital. Only the fiscal authority can do that.'[44] The central bank and the Treasury/Ministry of Finance (MoF) need to work together in the case of a support operation. This can be arranged at the national level relatively easily. The problem at the EU level is that the ECB has no European fiscal counterpart, which means that the relevant fiscal authorities

---

[38] See Gilles Thieffry, 'After the Lamfalussy Report: The First Steps Towards a European Securities Commission' in Mads Andenas and Yannis Avreginos (eds), *Financial Markets in Europe. Towards a Single Regulator?* (The Hague: Kluwer Law International, 2003) 197.

[39] ibid 207.

[40] Council Regulation (EC) No 1103/97 of 17 June 1997 on Certain Provisions Relating to the Introduction of the Euro, [1997] OJ L162/1, as amended by Council Regulation (EC) No 2595/2000 of 27 November 2000, [2000] OJ L300/1.

[41] Above note 1.

[42] See Rosa M Lastra, 'Lender of Last Resort, an International Perspective', (1999) 48 International and Comparative Law Quarterly, 340–61.

[43] In the UK, in the case of a support operation, the FSA and the Bank work closely with the Chancellor of the Exchequer, who has the option of refusing such support operation.

[44] See Charles Goodhart, Foreword to the book by Tommasso Padoa-Schioppa, *Regulating Finance* (Oxford: Oxford University Press, 2004) xvii.

are by definition at the national level. A further twist is provided by the need to comply with the EU rules on state aid.

The use of taxpayers' money (a fiscal solution) in the bailout of an insolvent institution falls under the definition of 'state aid to the banking sector', thus bringing into play the EC law on legal or illegal state aid, according to the Treaty provisions and the jurisprudence of the European Court of Justice. René Smits argues that 'in support operations of central banks, State funds are involved. After all, the central bank's profits are distributed, mainly or wholly to the State. Thus, taxpayers' money is potentially at risk when central bank funds are used to grant credits to a financial institution in difficulties.'[45]

A Draft Commission Communication on Emergency Rescue Aids, released by the (then) Banking Advisory Committee on 8 June 1998, would have requested Member States to notify the Commission of any emergency aid measure to troubled financial institutions, enabling the EU Commissioner in charge of Competition Policy to accept, on behalf of the Commission, such emergency aid in a very short time (taking into account the Commission's powers to vet state aid). The European Shadow Financial Regulatory Committee, of which I am a member, in its statement of October 1998, called for prior ECB authorization before a NCB provides emergency liquidity assistance to troubled banking institutions. Both the ECB and the EU Commissioner in charge of Competition Policy ought to be involved in support operations, as I propose in the following section.

The need to involve the competition policy authorities is explicitly mentioned in paragraph 7 of the press release of May 2005 announcing a Memorandum of Understanding on Cooperation between the Banking Supervisors, Central Banks, and Finance Ministries of the European Union in Financial Crisis situations.[46]

Mauro Grande, Head of the ECB's Prudential Supervision Division, argued in a paper in 1999[47] that state aid rules should not apply to the Eurosystem. In his opinion, the rules governing the Eurosystem (ie, Treaty provisions and ESCB Statute) had the same legal status as state aid rules and therefore constituted a lawful derogation of such state aid rules (in particular of Art 87 EC).

I disagree with his observations. The rules on state aid remain applicable to the

---

[45] See René Smits, *The European Central Bank: Institutional Aspects* (The Hague: Kluwer Law International, 1997) 270–1. Smits further argues: 'In Stage 3 of Economic and Monetary Union, support by the NCBs and the ECB can likewise amount to State aid.'

[46] Above note 7.

[47] Mauro Grande, paper on 'Possible Decentralisation of State Aid Control in the Banking Sector' presented at the EU Competition Workshop on State Aids in Florence in June 1999.

banking sector. This is consistent with the ruling of the European Court of Justice in the OLAF case. '[T]he ECB, pursuant to the EC Treaty, falls squarely within the Community framework.'[48] The 'recognition that the ECB has such independence does not have the consequence of separating it entirely from the European Community and exempting it from every rule of Community law.'[49]

H. The Need for a European Standing Committee for Crisis Management

Following some of the recommendations of the so-called second Brouwer Report,[50] the Banking Supervision Committee of the ECB published on 10 March 2003 a press release concerning a Memorandum of Understanding on high-level principles of cooperation between banking supervisors and central banks of the EU in crisis management[51] to address the issue of coordination in case of a crisis.

In December 2004, the Ecofin Council suggested that the Financial Services Committee (consisting of representatives of EU Finance Ministries) should focus on continuing the improvement of existing arrangements for crisis management, by developing, in cooperation with representatives of the central banks and supervisors, a proposal for a Memorandum of Understanding on crisis management and a crisis simulation exercise.[52] This work has resulted in an agreement concerning a new MoU on cooperation between the banking supervisors, central banks, and finance ministries of the European Union in financial crisis situations, of which a press release was published on 14 May 2005. This MoU, which complements the 2003 MoU, 'shall enter into effect on 1 July 2005'.[53]

---

[48] See Case 11/00 *Commission of the European Communities v European Central Bank* [2003] ECR 1–7147, para 92. This case is referred to as 'the OLAF (European Anti-Fraud Office) case'.

[49] ibid, para 135.

[50] The first Brouwer Report (See European Commission, Report on Financial Stability prepared by the ad-hoc working group of the Economic and Financial Committee, Economic Papers No 143, FC/ECFIN/240/00, DG ECFIN, May 2000, Brussels) dealt with the need for strengthened cooperation. The second Brouwer Report (See European Commission, Report on Financial Crisis Management (2nd Brouwer Report), EFC/ECFIN/251/01, DG ECFIN, Brussels, April 2001) stated the need to coordinate financial crisis management procedures in the EU.

[51] Above note 7.

[52] In January 2005, a meeting of a high-level group comprising representatives from the Treasuries/Ministries of Finance of the EU Member States, the EU Council, the Internal Market Directorate-General of the EU Commission, the Chairs of the Level 3 Lamfalussy Committees (CEBS, CEIOPS, CESR), and the ECB met to discuss this issue.

[53] Above note 7.

Regrettably, these two MoUs are not public documents and, therefore, I cannot comment on the specific provisions they contain. However, their value from a legal point of view is rather weak: being unpublished memoranda of understanding.[54]

> An MoU is a non legally binding instrument for setting forth practical arrangements aimed at promoting co-operation between authorities in crisis or potential crisis situations without overriding their respective institutional responsibilities or restricting their capacity for independent and timely decision-making in their respective fields of competence, notably with regard to the conduct of day-to-day central banking and supervisory tasks, as set out in national and Community legislation.[55]

According to the information provided in the press releases, the main difference between the two MoUs is that the 2003 MoU deals with cooperation between EU banking supervisors and central banks, while the 2005 MoU also involves EU finance ministries. Though both MoUs deal with cross-border (pan-European) systemic crises,[56] the 2003 MoU also deals with early stages of detection and activation of specific supervisory and central banking tools in financial crises.[57]

The parties to the 2005 MoU comprise a total of sixty-six different authorities: national central banks, national banking supervisory authorities, and national finance ministries of the twenty-five EU Member States, and the European Central Bank.[58]

Laudable as the setting of principles and procedures for sharing information in crisis situations is (the objective of both MoUs), it is 'not enough' to deal with a crisis, particularly when so many parties are involved. I argue in this section that an 'institutional solution' is needed.

---

[54] 'This approach [the MoU of 10 March 2003] has limitations. First, it lacks legal enforceability (hence no penalties are envisaged if it is breached); second the lack of full regulatory harmonization (ie accounting rules) leaves room for interpretation about the financial condition of a bank, and third, the MoU is confidential, which seriously limits the accountability of the institutions involved.' See Maria Nieto, comments on a paper presented by Kahn and Santos on 'Allocating Bank Regulatory Powers: Lender of Last Resort, Deposit Insurance and Supervision' at the Bank of Finland Conference on 'The Structure of Financial Regulation', September 2004. The proceedings of the conference are to be published by Routledge in a book edited by David Mayes and Geoffrey Wood (forthcoming, 2006).

[55] Above note 7, para 6 of the press release.

[56] ibid para 7. 'Although certain crises may require international co-operation with authorities whose jurisdiction lies outside the EU, the MoU does not deal with such co-operation at present.'

[57] Above note 8. The 2003 MoU provides principles and procedures regarding the identification of the authorities responsible to deal with a crisis, the required flows of information between all authorities, and practical conditions for sharing information at the cross-border level.

[58] 'The assumption underlying the agreement is that the most likely cause of an economic crisis in Europe would arise from the banking sector, not from a securities crash.' See *Financial Times*, 16 May 2005, 'EU agrees a financial crisis plan', by George Parker. It is also reported in this article that the MoU 'will be tested next year with a full-scale simulation of a financial crisis'.

Multilateral cooperation amongst the supervisory authorities of the EU Member States is carried out through the Banking Supervision Committee of the ECB (whose mandate focuses on financial stability and structural developments in the banking system of the EU) and through the Committee of European Banking Supervisors or CEBS (whose mandate focuses on convergence of supervisory practices and advice to the EU Commission), though other committees and fora also constitute forms of cooperation with regard to banking supervision and banking problems.[59] In particular, the Economic and Financial Committee (Art 114(2) EC and Art III–192 of the proposed EU Constitution), which promotes coordination of economic and financial policies necessary for the functioning of the internal market, and the Financial Services Committee[60] ought to be taken into consideration. National supervisory authorities meet in a multiplicity of supervisory committees, often with overlapping responsibilities and possibly diverging confidentiality restraints.[61]

Despite the plethora of committees and the concern about the need to improve the mechanisms to deal with crisis management at the EU level, there is no specific institutional arrangement to deal with banking crises at the European level.[62]

In this respect, I propose the setting up of a standing committee or high-level group with adequate representation of the interested parties: the ECB and NCBs, supervisory authorities, Ministers of Finance, the EC Commissioner for Competition Policy, and the EC Commissioner for the Internal Market. This Standing Committee could meet at very short notice. Though the meeting would typically take place over the phone (or by video conference), the physical location of the Committee could be in Frankfurt, the headquarters of the ECB. The composition of this Committee could vary depending on the number of countries affected by the crisis. The rule for the composition of the Committee can draw on a proposal by Goodhart, where he suggests that if 'n' countries become involved, 'a committee with (3n + 3) members, where the extra members would be the ECB, a putative EFSA and the EC [Commission]'.[63] In my proposed Standing Committee, there would be a tripartite representation from

---

[59] I further discuss the new European financial architecture in Ch 11.

[60] The Financial Services Committee established by the ECOFIN Council in a decision of 18 February 2003, Council Decision (Doc. 6264/1/03) available at <http://ue.eu.int/pressData/en/ecofin/74571.pdf> replaced the Financial Services Policy Group which had been created in 1999. The Financial Services Committee, which started functioning in March 2003, reports to the EFC in order to prepare advice to the Council (ECOFIN).

[61] With regard to the issue of diverging confidentiality restraints, see René Smits, above note 31, n 68.

[62] The 2003 and 2005 MoUs only provide a set of principles and procedures on cooperation in financial crisis situations. Above notes 8 and 7.

[63] Above note 3, 135.

the national central bank, supervisory authority, and Ministry of Finance for each Member State affected and the other three members would be the EC Commissioner for Competition Policy, the EC Commissioner for the Internal Market, and a representative of the ECB.

Since time and an expedient course of action are of the essence in any support operation and since it difficult to calculate *ex ante* the extent of the crisis, the rules of this Committee should be framed to promote speed, efficiency, and flexibility. So how would it work in practice? Suppose that a bank or group of banks in a Member State got into trouble. The supervisory authority in that country, together with the national central bank (if supervision is separated from the central bank), would take the lead in the procedure, keeping the Treasury/MoF informed.[64] The NCB would immediately inform the European Central Bank, which, in turn, would communicate with the Commissioner in Charge of Competition Policy and the Commissioner for the Internal Market and with the authorities in the country/countries where spillover effects were expected.

In terms of adequate national representation, the UK tripartite Standing Committee offers an interesting model. In the United Kingdom, following the creation of the Financial Services Authority (FSA), an example of cooperation between those in charge of monetary policy and those in charge of banking supervision (though the Bank of England retains general responsibility for financial stability) is provided by the Memorandum of Understanding (MoU) between HM Treasury, the Bank of England, and the Financial Services Authority, which was released on 28 October 1997. Paragraph 10 of this MoU foresees the setting up of a 'Standing Committee' of representatives of the Treasury, the Bank, and the FSA. This Committee will meet on a monthly basis and also at the request of any of the participating institutions in emergency circumstances. Each institution has nominated representatives which can be contacted, and meet, at short notice. If a financial institution gets into trouble, the first port of call is the FSA. If either the FSA or the Bank of England spots a problem where a support operation might be necessary, they will consult each other immediately. If the problem is related to the scope of responsibilities of the FSA, then the FSA will lead the support operation, though the funds will still come from the Bank. If the problem originates in the payment system or other area of

---

[64] ibid. Dirk Schoenmaker, above note 27, 57, has also advocated the need for a mechanism for cooperation between monetary authorities, supervisory authorities, and fiscal authorities, in times of crisis, and finds a precedent in the former European Monetary System, where confidential decisions on realignment took place over the weekend involving Ministers of Finance, Central Bankers, and the European Commission. He suggests that the rules of procedure of that Committee, speedy, confidential decision-making by many (inter)national players, could serve as a starting point for developing an European structure for crisis management.

responsibility of the Bank of England, then the Bank will be the lead institution in the support operation. In all cases, the FSA and the Bank are supposed to work together very closely and to inform the Treasury, in order to give the Chancellor of the Exchequer the option of refusing the support operation. Indeed, if fiscal resources—that is, taxpayers' money—are to be committed, then, the Chancellor should have a say in deciding whether or not to provide support to the troubled institution/s.

As Goodhart explains, though the description in the MoU of 28 October 1997 suggests a 'sequential approach', in practice the procedure is much more likely to be 'short-circuited'. He also points out that the efficiency of 'crisis management by Committee', rather than by the Bank of England as the main central decision maker, has not been tested since the Committee was established in 1997.[65]

A European Standing Committee for Bank Crisis Management, such as the one I propose, would not be exempt from problems, of course. Tom Baxter lucidly points out that there is always a potential for conflict amongst supervisors from different countries, and this potential becomes ominous when a bank weakens, since conflict rather than cooperation often characterizes the resolution process for troubled banks.[66] However, these problems are not insurmountable, since compromise is in the nature of EU politics.

There is nonetheless one area where compromise would be most challenging and that concerns the *ex post* allocation of the fiscal burden of the costs of recapitalization.[67] As Dirk Schoenmaker suggests,

> While a central bank can extend emergency loans for unlimited amounts, its capacity to absorb losses is limited (up to the size of its capital). The deep pockets do therefore not lie with the central bank as sometimes is suggested, but with the government. Moreover any losses, absorbed by the central bank will result in a lower pay-out (on seigniorage) to the government and thus ultimately be borne by the tax-payer.[68]

---

[65] See Charles Goodhart, 'Multiple Regulators and Resolutions', paper presented at the Federal Reserve Bank of Chicago Conference on Systemic Financial Crises: Resolving Large Bank Insolvencies, 30 September–1 October 2004.

[66] See Thomas Baxter, 'Cross-Border Challenges in Resolving Financial Groups', paper presented at the Federal Reserve Bank of Chicago Conference on Systemic Financial Crises: Resolving Large Bank Insolvencies, 30 September–1 October 2004.

[67] Above note 3.

[68] See Dirk Schoenmaker, in Charles Goodhart (ed), *Which Lender of Last Resort For Europe?* (London: Central Banking Publications, 2000) 222. See also Schoenmaker, above note 27, 56–7, where he discusses the fiscal costs of a possible bailout, suggesting that 'a fixed rule to share the costs (eg the key issued in the Statute of the ESCB and the ECB to distribute monetary income; this key is based on an average of the share in total GDP and total population of participating members) may give rise to moral hazard, as countries with a weak financial system may face reduced incentives to prevent potential bail-outs.'

The possibility of losses is recognized in Article 32 (4) of the ESCB Statute: 'The [ECB] Governing Council may decide that national central banks shall be indemnified against losses incurred . . . in exceptional circumstance for specific losses arising from monetary policy operations undertaken by the ESCB.'

A banking crisis might require at the beginning a liquidity injection authorized quickly by the ESCB. However, any LOLR operations would be potentially subject to loss, and any such loss would have to come out of taxpayers' funds, thus requiring the involvement of the national fiscal authorities. The latter would bring into play the EU rules on state aid as I mentioned above. It is because of the consideration that state aid rules may be infringed in a support operation that I advocate the need to include the EU Commissioner in Charge of Competition Policy in the Standing Committee that I propose.[69]

'He who pays the piper calls the tune' should be the motto for the allocation of costs.[70] And since the moneys will come from the national authorities, they can rightly claim to retain a primary role in any bailout operation. The problem, of course, arises in the case of burden sharing, when a crisis extends cross-border into another country or countries. As Goodhart suggests, there is no easy answer to this problem, unless 'proper reconsideration is given of the necessary extent of fiscal federalism that would be appropriate to give proper support to the single euro-area monetary policy'.[71]

Secrecy or transparency?

There is an aura of secrecy that surrounds emergency support operations and which is also present in the European debate. How justifiable is this secrecy or confidentiality? It is justifiable with regard to the publication of the details of the actual institution or institutions that apply for assistance or that receive such support. The very publication of that sensitive information could trigger a bank run; by definition, the belief in a crisis is self-fulfilling. However, it is not justifiable in terms of the processes and procedures to follow in the case of a crisis and in terms of the allocation of specific responsibilities. There needs to be transparency and publicity about such procedures. This will in turn facilitate

---

[69] In private correspondence, Sander Oosterloo of the Dutch Ministry of Finance said that including competition authorities in a Standing Committee could lead to an overly complex set of arrangements, as competition authorities will only be actively involved when approval is needed for an acquisition or participation in a troubled institution by another institution. An alternative he suggested would be to establish some sort of protocol between the members of the Standing Committee and the competition authorities.

[70] On the important issue of 'who pays for banking failures?' see generally David Mayes and Aarno Liuksila (eds), *Who Pays for Bank Insolvency?* (Hampshire and New York: Palgrave, MacMillan, 2004).

[71] Above note 44, xviii.

accountability. Indeed, ambiguity and uncertainty as to the procedures and loci of power are not constructive. What is needed is discretion (in this case, no guarantee as to whether the assistance will be provided, so as to avoid moral hazard). But in the event of a crisis, the procedures to follow should be crystal clear *ex ante* for the institution affected, other market participants, and the public at large. In this respect, the solutions that have been agreed at the EU level are inadequate. The 2003 and 2005 MoUs to which I referred above, are not public documents. This is entirely unjustifiable in my opinion. The UK published and distributed widely its MoU. Why is the same not done at the EU level?

In a culture that increasingly fosters transparency and accountability, there is no room for not providing that information to the markets. Therefore, the rules and procedures of the European Standing Committee for Bank Crisis Management ought to be publicized and known *ex ante*, even though the actual details of the institution or institutions that receive support as well as the information about the level of such assistance ought to remain confidential.

I. Conclusions

The current structure for prudential supervision and crisis management in the EU is based upon the principle of decentralization (national competence) and characterized by a 'piecemeal approach', with a certain degree of ambiguity and diffused responsibility. National authorities meet in a multiplicity of supervisory committees, often with overlapping responsibilities and possibly diverging confidentiality restraints. This does not augur well for the safety of financial stability in Europe, in particular, if a pan-European crisis were to occur. The objective of creating a single market in financial services for a single monetary area requires a rethinking of the current institutional structure for supervision. Despite the plethora of committees, there is no specific institutional arrangement to deal with banking crises at the European level. Bearing in mind that time and an expedient course of action are essential characteristics of emergency liquidity assistance (LOLR), I have proposed in this chapter the creation of a European Standing Committee for Crisis Management (along the lines of the established UK Tripartite Standing Committee) with adequate representation of the interested parties, the ECB and NCBs, the national supervisory authorities and Ministers of Finance, and the EC Commissioner for Competition Policy, and the EC Commissioner for the Internal Market. I have outlined some of the rules of such Committee, though further research is needed on the complex issue of the burden sharing of the fiscal costs (losses) of a potential pan-European banking crisis.

11

EUROPEAN FINANCIAL ARCHITECTURE

We must avoid becoming trapped in a sterile debate of what is better: supra-national institutions or improved co-operation. There might be a need for supra-national institutions in some areas, but not in others. Centralised decision-making might go hand-in-hand with monitoring and implementation by national authorities.

Alexandre Lamfalussy, 'Regulation under Strain', *Financial Times*,
8 February 2000

A. Introduction

The 'architecture' of financial supervision in the EU is characterized by three principles: decentralization, cooperation, and segmentation (with a multiplicity of committees for banking, securities, insurance, and financial conglomerates). However, there are several forces at play that can alter the current institutional design, in particular the trend towards unification or consolidation of supervisory authorities at the level of the Member States (which could pave the way for the creation of an European Financial Services Authority) and the process of supervisory convergence in response to the needs of a single market in financial services.

This chapter examines what I refer to as the 'unfinished agenda' of the governance structure for financial regulation and supervision in Europe. Given the complexity and multifaceted nature of the issues involved and the interplay between national and supranational authorities, from an analytical point of view it is helpful to consider separately supervision, regulation, and crisis management. The focus of this chapter is on financial regulation and financial supervision in the EU generally while the focus of Chapter 10 was banking supervision and crisis management.

As I pointed out in Chapter 10, the proposed EU Constitution does not alter the allocation of responsibilities in this field. This means that the current financial supervisory structure rests upon an institutional framework set up by secondary law (except for the provisions of Art 105 EC reproduced in Art III–185 of the proposed EU Constitution).[1] Both the Lamfalussy report/framework and the Financial Services Action Plan (FSAP) are important initiatives in this field, but they do not set the current structure 'in stone'. The sense of 'permanence' and 'irrevocability' that is associated with monetary union is absent in financial supervision.

Though there is disagreement about the optimal supervisory structure, there is consensus regarding the proposition that a single market in financial services needs common rules. However, the process of adopting common rules does not require per se the existence of a centralized authority. Common financial rules in the EU have been adopted mainly via directives (minimum harmonization), though the Lamfalussy framework suggests that maximum harmonization should be advocated for the regulation of capital markets.

B. The EU Financial Supervisory Structure

The goal of creating an internal market in financial services was given fresh impetus with the 1999 Financial Services Action Plan (FSAP).[2] The FSAP,

---

[1] The Treaty establishing a Constitution for Europe was signed in Rome on 29 October 2004 and is available in the Official Journal No C310 of 16 December 2004. The proposed EU Constitution was thrown into a legal limbo following the rejection of the Treaty in referenda in France (28 May 2005) and the Netherlands (1 June 2005). The suspension of the ratification process does not equate to the abandonment of the Constitution altogether. The text remains a legal document of value to refer to, also with a view to its possible entry into force or the taking over of parts of it in other Treaty texts later on.

[2] The Financial Services Action Plan (FSAP), set a schedule for the adoption of 42 legislative measures (mostly directives) to be adopted by 2005. See Financial Services—Implementing

which was endorsed by the Cologne European Council in 1999 and by the Lisbon European Council in March 2000, contained forty-two legislative measures intended to remove barriers so as to speed the integration of EU financial markets. The main strategic objectives of the FSAP were the creation of a single wholesale market for financial services, an open and more secure financial retail market, and the implementation of prudential rules and supervision. It also aimed at the wider conditions for a functioning single market, including measures on taxation and the creation of an efficient and transparent legal system for corporate governance. Though the FSAP relates to the single market as a whole, and not just to the euro area, there is no doubt that European Monetary Union has been the catalyst for the renewed attention given in recent years to the challenges of financial integration.[3]

While the FSAP responded to the question of 'what to regulate', the issues of 'who and how to regulate', in particular with regard to securities markets, were addressed in the so-called Lamfalussy Report,[4] published in February 2001 and adopted by the European Council in its Resolution of 23 March 2001 in Copenhagen.

Since the publication of the Lamfalussy Report and the subsequent establishment of the Committee of European Securities Regulators (CESR) in 2001 and the European Securities Committee (ESC) in 2002, this dual structure has been referred to as the 'Lamfalussy framework'. The emerging European financial architecture is the result of the extension of the Lamfalussy framework for the regulation of securities markets to banking and insurance. It is interesting to observe that, though the Lamfalussy approach started as a 'regulatory issue' (confined to the workings of the law-making process concerning securities markets regulation in Europe), it soon became a 'supervisory matter', leading to an overhaul of the institutional design of supervision in the EU.

The Ecofin Council in its meeting of 3 December 2002 approved the proposal

---

the Framework for Financial Markets: Action Plan. Commission Communication COM (1999) 232, 11.05.99, <http://www.europa.eu.int/comm/internal_market/en/finances/general/action_en.pdf>. In May 2005, the Commission published a 'Green Paper on Financial Services Policy (2005–2010)', COM (2005) 177, 1–13; see <http://www.europa.eu.int/comm.internal_market/securities/lamfalussy/index_en.htm>.

[3] For a definition of 'financial integration' see Report of the Financial Services Committee to the Economic and Financial Committee/Council on Financial Integration, FSC 4156/04, Brussels 17 May 2004, 7: 'Financial integration can be described as the absence of obstacles to significant cross border activities and to economic agents in their access to or in their ability to supply financial services and products, in particular in respect to their geographic location. The overall objective of the single market is to remove all public policy/regulatory obstacles to the free movement of goods, services, persons and capital.'

[4] See <http://europa.eu.int/comm/internal_market/en/finances/general/lamfalussy.htm>.

of the Economic and Financial Committee to extend this structure to other sectors of the financial industry.[5] Accordingly, 'Lamfalussy level 2 committees'—akin to the European Securities Committee or ESC—have been established for banking and insurance as well as for financial conglomerates,[6] and 'Lamfalussy level 3 committees'—akin to the Committee of European Securities Regulators (CESR)—have been established for banking and insurance.

The Council stated that, while the new level 2 committees should be set up in an advisory capacity initially so as to give the European Parliament the opportunity to assess their responsibilities, the level 3 committees should be set up as soon as possible. The Commission's decisions establishing the new level 2 and level 3 committees in banking and insurance were taken in November 2003 and the directive conferring the regulatory powers to the level 2 committees was adopted by the European Parliament in April and the EU Council in May 2004.[7] The level 2 committees (the European Securities Committee, the European Banking Committee, the European Insurance and Occupational Pensions Committee, and the Financial Conglomerates Committee), chaired by the European Commission and based in Brussels, and the level 3 committees (the Committee of European Securities Regulators, chaired by Arthur Docters van Leeuwen, located in Paris; the Committee of European Securities Supervisors,[8] chaired by Jose María Roldán, located in London; and the Committee of

---

[5] This Council Decision is available at <http://ue.eu.int/pressData/en/ecofin/73473.pdf>. See also the Report of the EU Economic and Financial Committee on 'Financial Regulation, Supervision and Stability', <http://www.europa.eu.int/comm/internal_market/en/finances/cross-sector/consultation/efc-report_en.pdf>, Brussels, 9 October 2002, and the Note of the European Commission (Internal Market DG Financial Institutions) to the Ecofin Council, Brussels, 3 December 2002, <http://www.europa.eu.int/comm/internal_market/en/finances/cross-sector/consultation/ecofin-note_en.pdf>.

[6] The Financial Conglomerates Committee was established by Art 21 of Directive 2002/87/EC of 16 December 2002 regarding the supervision of financial conglomerates. It is interesting to observe that the structure of the recently created BaFin in Germany would fit in well with these new Lamfalussy level 2 committees.

[7] Proposal for a Directive of the European Parliament and of the Council amending Council Directives 73/239/EEC, 85/611/EEC, 91/675/EEC, 93/6/EEC and 94/19/EC and Directives 2000/12/EC, 2002/83/EC and 2002/87/EC of the European Parliament and of the Council, in order to establish a new financial services committee organizational structure, COM/2003/0659 final of 6 November 2003.

[8] The Committee of European Banking Supervisors (CEBS) was established as of 1 January 2004 following the decision of the Commission of 5 November 2003 (2004/5/EC). The CEBS is now functioning as the level 3 committee for the banking sector in the application of the Lamfalussy process. The first meeting of the CEBS took place in London on 31 March 2004. See <http:www.c-ebs.org>. It is unclear in my opinion whether the existence of the CEBS is really necessary, given the role of the ECB Banking Supervision Committee, and given the fact that the European Central Bank already has a mandate in payment systems supervision (according to Art 105(2) of the EC Treaty) and limited responsibilities in prudential supervision and regulation (advice/consultation) according to Arts 105(4) and 105(5) of the EC Treaty, not to mention the possible—albeit unlikely—activation of the enabling clause (Art 105(6) EC).

European Insurance & Occupational Pensions Supervisors, located in Frankfurt and chaired by Henrik Bjerre-Nielsen) are now fully operational.

In addition to the Lamfalussy level 2 and level 3 committees, and the Banking Supervision Committee of the ECB, there are two other committees where financial supervisory issues are discussed at the EU level: the Economic and Financial Committee (EFC) and the Financial Services Committee (FSC). Though the Economic and Financial Committee (Art 114(2) EC Treaty and Art II–192 EU Constitution) remains the main source of advice for the EU Council and the Commission on financial affairs, the Ecofin council established the Financial Services Committee or FSC (replacing the Financial Services Policy Group) in a decision of 18 February 2003, to focus on financial regulatory issues and to coordinate the work of the Lamfalussy committees. The level 3 committees report to the FSC with regard to supervisory convergence. The FSC reports to the EU Economic and Financial Committee (EFC) in order to prepare advice to the Council (Ecofin). The Committee on Economic and Monetary Affairs (EMAC) of the European Parliament also plays a relevant role in issues of EU financial supervision.

As Lannoo and Casey eloquently point out: 'In a few years, the whole [supervisory] structure was re-drawn.'[9]

The 'Lamfalussy framework' does not imply the centralization of supervisory and regulatory responsibilities. There is no transfer of competencies from the national to the supranational arena. The level 2 and level 3 committees are a form of supervisory cooperation. Hence, the extension of the Lamfalussy framework to banking and insurance reconfigures the current framework of cooperation but does not alter the principles upon which it rests: decentralization, cooperation, and segmentation.

Though it is commendable to foster cooperation, in my opinion such cooperation should generally proceed along the lines of the consolidation and streamlining of existing committees, rather than through the creation of new committees, which bring about a duplicity or multiplicity of supervisory fora, often leading to a confusion or to an overlap of lines of responsibility and membership, to a cumbersome and unduly complicated decision-making process, and, possibly, to bureaucratic inefficiency. This notwithstanding, there may be instances when a new committee or institutional arrangement is needed, such as my proposed European Standing Committee for Crisis Management.

---

[9] See Karel Lannoo and Jean Pierre Casey, 'Financial Regulation and Supervision Beyond 2005', CEPS Task Force Report No 54, Brussels, January 2005, 6.

C. Centralization?

As I discussed in Chapter 10, decentralization (national competence) is the principle that applies to financial supervision in Europe. The existence of a multiplicity of committees (Lamfalussy level 2 and 3 committees, EFC, FSC, BSC of the ECB) cannot hide the fact that the locus of decision-making remains at the national level. However, the needs of a single market, the 'trilemma in financial supervision' that I also referred to in Chapter 10 (the inconsistency of pursuing at the same time a stable financial system, an integrated financial market, and national financial supervision)[10] suggest that a degree of supervisory convergence is needed and that the current structure may evolve in the direction of greater integration or even centralization.

Centralization, as an organizing principle for European financial architecture, could proceed through four different routes: centralization according to the model of a 'single supervisor', centralization according to the model of 'multiple supervisors', centralization of some supervisory functions, centralization in one sector of the financial sector.

Centralization according to the model of a 'single supervisor'

This is the maximum degree of centralization: the creation of a European Financial Services Authority. Several Member States of the European Union, such as the UK and Germany, have taken steps towards the creation within their domestic jurisdictions of a single supervisory authority for the whole financial sector, as I explained in Chapter 3. In the eyes of some commentators, this trend could pave the way for the creation of a single European Financial Services Authority. However, the wisdom of establishing a single supervisor—particularly in large countries—is still doubted by many academics and policy makers. Personally, I am against the creation of such an authority at the EU level on the grounds of excessive concentration of power and potential lack of accountability and transparency. In any case, if such an authority were to be created, it would require, in my opinion, a Treaty amendment and an in-depth discussion of the extent of its mandate.

The possibility of establishing a single EU financial supervisory authority has been suggested in various circles, including the 'Committee of Wise Men on the Regulation of European Securities Markets'. Indeed, the Lamfalussy Report

---

[10] See Dirk Schoenmaker, 'Financial Supervision: from National to European?' *Financial and Monetary Studies (NIBE-SVV)*, Amsterdam, 2003. See also Niels Thygesen, 'Comments on "The Political Economy of Financial Harmonisation in Europe" ' in Jeroen Kremer, Dirk Schoenmaker, and Peter Wierts (eds), *Financial Supervision in Europe* (Cheltenham: Edward Elgar, 2003) 145.

stated in a fall back remark: '[I]f the full review were to confirm in 2004 (or earlier as the case may be) that the approach did not appear to have any prospect of success, it might be appropriate to consider a Treaty change, including the creation of a single EU regulatory authority for financial services generally in the Community.'[11]

I had the opportunity of asking Baron Lamfalussy whether the wording of this statement was intentional when he spoke in London on 3 May 2001 and his answer was positive: the choice of words 'single EU regulatory authority for financial services in the Community' was intentional. Hence, this wording indicated a preference for the conceivable creation of a European FSA rather than for the creation of an European SEC.

Centralization according to the model of 'multiple supervisors'

This model of centralization comprises some variants. One could envisage an agency for banking supervision (ESCB or separate agency) and separate pan-European supervisory authorities for insurance and securities (and perhaps financial conglomerates). It is conceivable that the level 3 Lamfalussy committees (CEBS, CESR, and CEIOPS) could evolve into pan-European supervisory agencies, with powers of rule-making and enforcement. However, such a development would run against the national trend towards consolidation or unification of supervisory responsibilities.

Dirk Schoenmaker and Sander Oosterloo[12] have proposed the setting up of a European System of Financial Supervisors, where national supervisors could work together with a decision-making body or agency at the centre (akin to the ESCB structure with the ECB at the centre and the NCBs at the periphery). Within their proposed system, the lead home supervisor would have a European mandate. Hence, their proposal is a combination of a national and a European mandate with regard to EU financial supervision, that is, a mix of centralization and decentralization in the allocation of supervisory responsibilities.

Another variant of this 'model of multiple supervisors' is the possible combination of a pan-European prudential supervisor and a pan-European conduct of business supervisor (or supervisors), akin to the Dutch model of financial supervision adopted in the second part of 2002.[13] This latter variant would probably give a prominent role to the ESCB as prudential supervisor, while the conduct

---

[11] <http://europa.eu.int/comm/internal_market/en/finances/general/lamfalussy/htm>, 41.

[12] See Sanders Oosterloo and Dirk Schoenmaker, 'A Lead Supervisor Model for Europe', The Financial Regulator Vol 9, No 3, December 2004.

[13] The Dutch Central Bank (DNB) is the prudential supervisor, and the 'Autoriteit Financiële Markten' or Authority on Financial Markets (AFM) is the conduct of business supervisor.

of business supervisor could be a reconfiguration of the existing Lamfalussy committees.

Centralization of some supervisory functions

The centralization of some supervisory functions such as 'lender of last resort', while other supervisory functions remain decentralized (eg, authorization or licensing, enforcement). As I explained in Chapter 10, the possible centralization of one function (LOLR) does not imply nor require the centralization of other supervisory functions.[14]

Centralization in one sector of the financial sector

It is possible to centralize the supervision of one sector of the financial industry, for instance through the creation of a European Securities Exchange Commission, while the other sectors (banking, insurance) remain decentralized.

The US model of financial supervision is a mix of centralized and decentralized elements. Banking in the US is supervised by federal and state authorities; the securities industry is mainly subject to the supervision of a federal agency, the Securities and Exchange Commission, SEC (though self-regulation and, to a lesser extent, state law also play a role), and insurance remains a matter of state law.

The possibility of establishing an 'upgraded CESR' (a kind of European SEC) is considered in the preliminary report on 'Which Supervisory Tools for the EU Securities Markets', an analytical paper published by CESR on 25 October 2004 (alias 'Himalaya report').[15] According to this report, the 'upgrading of competences at EU level' ought to be 'publicly debated and politically agreed' with the involvement of the EU Commission, Council, and European Parliament. Part of that process would also require 'upgrading of the legal profile of CESR', with a specification of the way in which EU decisions would be taken (by CESR), of the legal liability of the members of the network, and of how third parties could appeal against such decisions. In my opinion, the granting of any additional powers to CESR would pave the way towards centralization in this field.

One fundamental question that the 'Himalaya report' raises is the potential 'modification of the legal profile of CESR'. Does it need a Treaty change or just

---

[14] For an opposite view, see Gillian Garcia and Maria Nieto, (2005) 6 Journal of Banking Regulation 206, 213.

[15] Ref: CESR/04–333f, available at <http://www.cesr-eu.org>. See press release, Ref: CESR/04–570 of 25 October 2004, <http://www.cesr-eu.org>.

a political decision? In my opinion, such a change is not a simple 'upgrading'. We are talking here about the transfer of competencies from the national to the supranational arena in the field of securities markets regulation and supervision. The preliminary report published by CESR[16] states that a Directive or Regulation adopted by co-decision by the Council and the European Parliament on the proposal of the Commission would be sufficient.

Gilles Thieffry has argued that Article 308 EC Treaty (which grants power to the European Council to take any step whenever measures are necessary to attain the objectives of the Community) could serve as the legal basis for the creation of a possible European Securities Commission, partially modelled upon the US Securities and Exchange Commission.[17] According to Jörg Asmussen, 'the granting of trans-European supervisory or regulatory powers to CESR or any level 3 committees could not be based on Art 308 of the EC Treaty, but would require a change to EU law. This is not "upgrading" from Economy to Business class, this is "taking another flight".'[18]

A review of the jurisprudence on Article 308 EC shows that this article is widely interpreted and could therefore be used as a legal basis to set up a European body concerning financial supervision.[19]

Besides Article 308 other articles could be considered, such as Article 95 EC Treaty, which refers to the measures that the Council can adopt for the approximation of laws which have as their object the establishment and functioning of the internal market.[20]

To my knowledge, there is no empirical evidence that justifies the superior wisdom of any given model of organizing financial supervision, whether that be the model of one authority for the entire financial system, the model of one authority for each sector of the financial industry, or the model of multiple authorities for each sector of the financial industry.

While market developments should inform the supervisory structure, the

---

[16] ibid.

[17] See Gilles Thieffry, 'After the Lamfalussy Report: The First Steps Towards a European Securities Commission' in Mads Andenas and Yannis Avreginos (eds), *Financial Markets in Europe. Towards a Single Regulator?* (The Hague: Kluwer Law International, 2003) 197. Article 308 was Art 235 before the renumbering of the EC Treaty provisions by the Amsterdam Treaty.

[18] Written remarks by Jörg Asmussen, Director General on European Financial Affairs, commenting on a paper I presented on 'Political Accountability of Financial Supervision at the European Level' at a conference organized by the Dutch Ministry of Finance on European Financial Supervision in the Hague in November 2004.

[19] Above note 17.

[20] In the case of creation of the European Aviation Safety Agency, Art 80, para 2 was also taken into account. In the case of the creation of the European Food Safety Authority, Art 37 was also considered.

complexity of the issues involved, the multifaceted nature of supervision, the differences in tax and corporate laws across the EU Member States, and cultural differences suggest that any development involving centralization or transfer of responsibilities from the national to the supranational arena should be publicly debated *ex ante* and clearly circumscribed, respecting the principles of subsidiarity and proportionality.

D. Accountability

The issue of accountability emerges whenever the question of governance is examined. Accountability is a pervasive concept.[21] One encounters it in political, legal, religious, philosophical, business, and other contexts. Each perspective adds a different shade to its meaning. For instance, the recent debate about corporate accountability, following the Enron and WorldCom scandals, casts some light on the elements of individual responsibility that underpin the exercise of corporate power. At the level of the European Union, the questions of institutional legitimacy and accountability have become of paramount importance.

As I have already explained in Chapter 2, legitimacy pre-exists and is a prerequisite of accountability.[22] Legitimacy has two aspects: a formal, normative one which refers to the legality of the political system and a societal or empirical one, which is determined by the acceptance of, or loyalty to, the system.[23] In the European Union, the formal legitimacy of the integration process rested initially on the Member States' ratification of the foundational Treaties (and subsequent amendments), while its social legitimacy—its 'popular appeal'—rested upon the benefits in terms of peace and welfare that it promised to deliver to its citizens.[24] The need to combine efficiency (to avoid a cumbersome and unduly complicated decision-making process and excessive bureaucracy) with democratic legitimacy (the interest of the citizens of the twenty-five EU Member States) is

---

[21] See Rosa M Lastra and Heba Shams, 'Public Accountability in the Financial Sector' published as ch 12 in E Ferran and C Goodhart (eds), *Regulating Financial Services and Markets in the 21st century* (Oxford: Hart Publishing, 2001) 165–88. See also Ch 2.

[22] This point is made by Chiara Zilioli, See Chiara Zilioli, 'Accountability and Independence: Irreconcilable Values or Complementary Instruments for Democracy? The Specific Case of the European Central Bank' in Georges Vandersanden et al (eds) *Mélanges en Hommage à Jean-Victor Louis* (Brussels: ULB, 2003) 403. Zilioli further points out that 'the independent government must be established and the power transferred to it, through a legal act adopted, in accordance with the constitutional framework of the State, by the democratically elected representatives of the people'.

[23] See Amaryllis Verhoeven, *The European Union in Search of a Democratic and Constitutional Theory* (The Hague: Kluwer Law International, 2002) 10–11.

[24] ibid 63–5.

fundamental for the future of Europe. And since democracy is considered the sole legitimate form of government in the EU, legitimacy equates to democratic legitimacy.

The creation of a supervisory agency, a central bank, or any other type of governmental or intergovernmental entity must be the fruit of a democratic act (an act of the legislator, a constitutional decision, or a treaty provision). This first source of legitimization is essential in a democratic society. It is then in the continuing life of that entity (in particular when such entity is 'independent') that accountability becomes necessary: the process of bringing back (by giving account, explaining, justifying, or taking measures of amendment or redress) that entity to the procedures and processes of a democratic society.

Any form of accountability presupposes that there are objectives or standards (criteria of assessment) according to which an action or decision might be assessed. In other words, accountability implies an obligation to comply with certain standards in the exercise of power or to achieve specific goals. The more complex the activity, the more difficult it is to establish clear standards of conduct and specific outcomes. In which case accountability becomes ever more evasive. The more specific the goals and standards the more effective the accountability. This might induce the 'accountees' to resort to economic or other measurable criteria of performance (hence the term 'performance accountability'). Performance accountability is facilitated when

1. there is one goal, rather than multiple goals;
2. that goal is narrowly defined rather than formulated in broad terms; and
3. if there are multiple goals, a clear and unambiguous ranking is better than no ranking at all.

The absence of explicit statutory objectives hinders performance accountability.

In the United Kingdom, the Financial Services and Markets Act 2000 (the Act) introduces several statutory objectives[25] and principles for financial regulation

---

[25] The stipulation of regulatory objectives in the Act was hailed as enhancing the accountability of the FSA at all levels. The FSA has indicated that the existence of such a set of objectives, and the benchmark they set against which others may judge their performance, will act as crucial discipline on the Authority. The statutory objectives apply to the assessment of the FSA's discharge of its general functions of making rules, issuing codes, and giving general guidance; they also apply to the assessment of the FSA's general policy and principles. By contrast, the statutory objectives do not apply to the assessment of the individual decisions or acts of the FSA. This approach was specifically adopted to allow the FSA the flexibility necessary to respond to the circumstances of individual cases. It means, however, that while the statutory objectives could offer a helpful benchmark for the discharge of general political or public accountability, they will not be very useful for the enforcement of judicial accountability or public accountability for specific decisions and actions.

and supervision. These have been particularly relevant since 1 December 2001, when the Financial Services Authority finally became the UK's single financial services regulator, with a wide array of powers and responsibilities. The FSA is bound by a variety of principles, values, standards, and objectives, thus diffusing the criteria of assessment and making performance accountability more evasive.

Section 2(2) of the Act stipulates four regulatory objectives:

(1) maintaining confidence in the market;
(2) promoting public awareness;
(3) protecting the consumer; and
(4) reducing financial crime.

The four objectives are meant to be pursued simultaneously and in a complementary manner. Attempts to prioritize them were rejected by the Government. In the pursuit of its statutory objectives, the FSA is constrained by deference to a number of principles. Section 2(3) stipulates seven considerations that the FSA must bear in mind in the discharge of its general functions. First, the need to use its resources in the most efficient and economic way. Secondly, the need to have regard to senior management responsibility for the performance and compliance of the regulated firms. Thirdly, the need to ensure that the benefits of regulation are proportionate to the costs of compliance. Fourthly, the need to facilitate financial innovation. Fifthly, the desirability of maintaining the competitive position of the UK in the international financial services markets. Sixthly, the need to minimize the adverse effects on competition from anything done in the discharge of its functions. Seventhly, the desirability of facilitating competition between those who are subject to regulation.[26] Section 7 of the Act also states that: 'In managing its affairs, the Authority must have regard to such generally accepted principles of corporate governance as it is reasonable to regard as applicable to it.'

At the European level, concerns about the accountability of the level 3 committees, such as CESR, are still limited, since the powers of these committees are limited and the real actors remain at the national level. However, should supervisory or regulatory competencies be transferred from the national to the supranational arena, the debate about accountability would become of paramount importance.

---

[26] The FSA is also bound by the European Convention on Human Rights, ECHR (adopted in the UK through the Human Rights Act 1998). Article 6 of the ECHR establishes fairness and certainty as two standards that are binding on the FSA in the discharge of its adjudicative function in the context of disciplining those who breach financial regulations. According to the Convention, everyone is entitled to a fair and public hearing in any proceedings whether civil or criminal with additional safeguards in the case of the latter. The Convention also requires that criminal offences should be clearly defined.

Arthur Docters van Leeuwen, Chairman of CESR, has stressed that, by its very nature, a 'network arrangement' such as CESR has limits and that one of those limits refers to the issue of accountability.[27] He says that

> there is truth in the argument that although we are formally accountable to our national political masters, such masters cannot easily intervene if the other twenty-four members agree. Nor is there a formal link of accountability to the European institutions either, as level 3 is about coordination of national activities. The conclusion must be that, yes the network activities should expand, but in synchronicity with enhanced European institutional accountability.

By analogy with the debate about the accountability of the European Central Bank, it is possible to envisage a system in which an upgraded CESR (or a supranational supervisory agency) could be formally accountable to the EU institutions[28] (ie, to the European Parliament—appearances before Parliament, reporting, and auditing requirements—to the Ecofin Council and the Commission—appointment and removal procedures, formal consultations, reporting and independent reviews/enquiries—and to the European Court of Justice) on the one hand, and to the national authorities (to ensure consistency in the overall design of financial supervision and regulation) on the other hand.

In addition to this institutional/formal articulation of accountability, new mechanisms of accountability (such as advisory panels of practitioners and consumers) ought to be established to channel the representation of the interests of financial market participants.

E. Financial Regulation in the EU

In this section I analyse the processes and procedures for adopting financial legislation and regulation in the EU. As I have already pointed out, though the terms regulation and supervision are often used interchangeably, properly speaking, regulation refers to rule making, and supervision refers to the oversight of financial firms' behaviour (in particular risk monitoring). A single market in financial services does not need a single supervisor (though it may need a more logical, coherent, and integrated structure than the one currently in place in Europe) but it does need some common rules. However, the process of adopting common rules does not require per se the existence of a centralized authority.

---

[27] Above note 15. On the basis of this Report, Arthur Docters van Leeuwen, Chairman of CESR, presented a paper at the conference organized by the Dutch Ministry of Finance on European Financial Supervision in the Hague in November 2004.

[28] I thank Dirk Schoenmaker for suggestions on the possible articulation of accountability mechanisms of an upgraded CESR.

Common rules can also be adopted through the adoption of a Treaty or a model law, through the adoption of harmonized principles, through the adoption of standards ('soft law' as in the case of the Basel Committee on Banking Supervision), and through other regulatory techniques. Common rules can (and do) coexist with different national systems of financial legislation.

Even if supervision remains at the national level, it should be based to a large extent on community regulation of the matter. This is already the case in the banking sector, where a substantial degree of market integration has been achieved through the adoption of a series of banking directives, even though there are still significant national differences with regard to tax laws, company laws, and others that create opportunities for regulatory arbitrage.

History of the legislative processes to adopt financial regulation in the EU

A bit of history helps explain the evolution of the legislative processes for adopting financial regulation in the EU.[29] The approximation of legislations in the field of banking and finance as required by Article 100 of the original EEC Treaty had been difficult before 1985. Indeed while the Commission had succeeded in the approximation of laws (mainly through regulations) in the fields of quality, composition, labelling and control of goods, industrial property rights, public procurement, technical or administrative barriers to trade, industrial safety and hygiene, and so on, the Commission had failed to approximate laws in other fields such as banking and financial services, transport, energy, telecommunications, and the like, owing to stark differences across Member States in the structure of their services industry, owing to the political implications of the liberalization of some 'key' services, and owing to the existence of exchange controls.[30] A new strategy was needed, with new political initiatives and more flexible techniques for integration.

The new strategy first envisaged in the 1985 White Paper on the Internal Market and legally enshrined in the 1986 Single European Act was rooted in the generalization of the concept of mutual recognition on the basis of prior minimum harmonization (rather than full or detailed harmonization) and on the principle of home country control.[31] Directives became the preferred

---

[29] See Rosa M Lastra, *Central Banking and Banking Regulation* (London: Financial Markets Group of the London School of Economics, 1996) 215–23.

[30] The Single European Act also gave momentum to the liberalization of capital movements, one of the four freedoms of a true single market and a precondition for the full liberalization of financial services. In his comments to this chapter, René Smits remarked that he counts five freedoms: (i) goods, (ii) services, (iii) workers and self-employed persons, (iv) freedom of establishment, (v) capital, with payments the corollary sixth freedom.

[31] The principle of home country control and the limitations of the divide between home and host country responsibilities have become a matter of concern for financial supervisors in the EU,

legislative instrument for achieving financial integration.[32] The use of directives is consistent with the principles of minimum harmonization and mutual recognition. Regulations, as opposed to directives, are consistent with the principle of full or detailed harmonization. And regulations leave no freedom to Member States with regard to their national transposition.

Despite the relative success of the new strategy in advancing the Community's goal of creating a single market, it has also limitations. These limitations have become apparent in the process of integrating capital markets in Europe, where the legislative process has often been criticized for being too slow and rigid to adapt to market developments.[33] On past experience, the adoption of directives in the field of financial regulation takes two to three years, followed by a one- to two-year period for national implementation. By the time that a directive is finally implemented, it is time to change it again. In the absence of other legislative instruments, directives have often dealt with both broad framework principles on the one hand and very technical issues on the other hand. This has resulted in a mix of ambiguity in some cases (for instance, when the political consensus is lacking) and excessive prescription in some others. The legislative process has also often proven inadequate to deal with the needs and concerns of market participants. Though bank-dominated systems have traditionally prevailed in Europe (with the exception of the UK), the development of capital markets in recent years has required a greater deal of dialogue, consultation, and cooperation between the many parties involved: lawmakers, supervisors, self-regulatory organizations, market intermediaries, issuers, and investors.[34] The techniques needed to regulate securities markets (disclosure requirements, fiduciary rules) have a much larger component of market discipline and consultation than the regulatory techniques typically applied to lending and deposit taking (mandatory rules, capital requirements).

---

particularly in the new members in Central and Eastern Europe. See, eg, Statement No 18 of the European Shadow Financial Regulatory Committee, of 17 May 2004, at <http://www.ceps.be>.

[32] The Single European Act in its Declaration on Article 100a of the EEC Treaty stated that: '[T]he Commission shall give precedence to the use of the instrument of a directive if harmonisation involves the amendment of legislative provisions in one or more Member States.' The Amsterdam protocol also states in its point 6: '[D]irectives should be preferred to regulations.'

[33] See Rosa M Lastra 'Regulating European Securities Markets: Beyond the Lamfalussy Report' in M Andenas and Y Avreginos (eds), *Financial Markets in Europe: Towards a Single Regulator?* (The Hague: Kluwer Law International, 2003) 211.

[34] See 'EU Securities Market Regulation. Adapting to the Needs of a Single Capital Market', Report of a CEPS Task Force, March 2001; Chairman: Alfred Steinherr, Rapporteur: Karel Lannoo.

The Lamfalussy Procedure

In response to these criticisms, in July 2000 the European Council set up the Committee of Wise Men on the Regulation of European Securities Markets under the chairmanship of Alexandre Lamfalussy. The mandate given to the Wise Men was confined to the workings of the law-making process concerning securities markets regulation in Europe, with the aim of speeding it up and making it more flexible in order to respond to market developments. The Wise Men were asked to identify the imperfections of this process and to come up with recommendations for change. The mandate of the Wise Men was not to identify what should be regulated, nor to look at other relevant issues such as international implications or prudential considerations.[35]

The Final Report of the Committee of Wise Men on the Regulation of European Securities Markets (the Lamfalussy Report)[36] was published on 15 February 2001 and the European Council in its Resolution of 23 March 2001 adopted some of the proposals recommended in the Report. The Report focused on the question of 'how' to speed up reform, that is, on the processes and legal procedures needed to reform securities markets regulation, rather than on the question of 'what' needs to be reformed.[37] The latter was dealt with in the Financial Services Action Plan, as I pointed out at the beginning of this chapter.[38] Thus, the Lamfalussy Report has a procedural character.

The major novelty of the Lamfalussy Report is its four-level regulatory approach (namely framework principles, implementing measures, cooperation, and enforcement) whose aim is to speed up the legislative process for the regulation of securities markets.

Of these four levels, the main innovation is the distinction between 'core principles' in level 1 and non-essential 'technical implementing matters' in level 2, which mirrors at the EU level what happens at the national level with the distinction between primary legislation and secondary regulation. According to

---

[35] Sometimes, the process of financial integration has been hindered by issues other than the 'legislative processes', such as political difficulties.

[36] Above note 4.

[37] For an in-depth analysis of EU securities regulation see Niamh Moloney, *EC Securities Regulation* (Oxford: Oxford University Press, 2002) and Eilís Ferran, *Building an EU Securities Market* (Cambridge: Cambridge University Press, 2004). The European Shadow Financial Regulatory Committee (ESFRC), of which I am a member, has published several statements with regard to the 'how' to regulate (Statements No 2 and 10) and the 'what' to regulate (Statements No 8, 12, and 14) with regard to financial markets in Europe. The statements of the ESFRC are available at <http://www.ceps.be>.

[38] Above note 2. Post-FSAP the Commission has published a Green Paper on financial services policy, at <http://www.europa.eu.int/comm/internal_market/finances/docs/actionplan/index/green_en.pdf>.

Baron Lamfalussy, the Report brings about a 'governance change', a bottom-up approach (rather than top-down), which could also be applied to other areas of European integration.[39]

There is an inevitable tension between the quality and the democratic nature of the legislative output and the need for speed and flexibility. At the national level, this tension, this trade-off has been solved through the distinction between primary and secondary law. By definition, primary law—the legislative process—is rigid and slow, but 'democratically accountable', while secondary law—the regulations and rules issued by regulatory agencies—is flexible and quick, but less 'democratically accountable'.

Though the Lamfalussy regulatory approach has been extended to other sectors of the financial sector, my analysis in the following paragraphs focuses on the actual law-making process with regard to securities markets (the original focus of the Committee of Wise Men).

Level 1

Level 1 refers to *EU framework legislation* and involves the EU Commission, Council, and Parliament (see Fig 11.1). This is the regular EU legislative process, albeit with a 'fast track' feature, according to the wording of the (Stockholm) Resolution of the European Council on More Effective Securities Markets Regulation of 23 March 2001. According to this process, legislative broad framework principles are decided following the normal EU co-decision procedures by the Council and the European Parliament. The Parliament and the Council delegate the adoption of technical implementing measures to the Commission, with the assistance of the European Securities Committee, advised by CESR.[40]

The Stockholm Resolution invited the Commission to use regulations instead of directives, whenever this is 'legally possible'. Though the Wise Men's recommendation to use regulations is sensible, because differences in national transposition have often hindered the integration of financial markets, the new approach needs to be reconciled with the status quo in banking and insurance, where directives have been the norm.

Level 2

Level 2 refers to *EU implementation* and it involves, in addition to the EU Commission, the European Securities Committee (ESC) and the Committee

---

[39] See Alexandre Lamfalussy, 'Reflections on the Regulation of European Securities Markets' SUERF Studies, Vienna, 2001, 16–17.

[40] I discuss below the so-called 'sunset clause' which establishes a time limit of four years with regard to the delegation of powers for the adoption of technical rules.

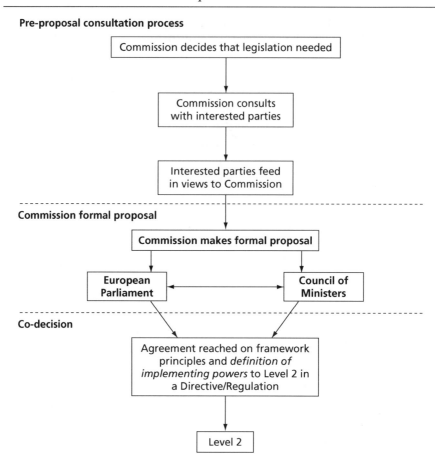

Figure 11.1 Level 1—Framework Principles
Source: Lamfalussy Report

of European Securities Regulators (see Fig 11.2). It is important to understand that the rule-making powers remain with the Commission and not with the ESC. The technical implementing measures are adopted by the Commission with the assistance of a committee. Hence, this level 2 implementation is not comparable to the rule-making powers of the SEC in the US, where the SEC is the one that adopts the rules.

The European Securities Committee functions as a regulatory committee in accordance with the 1999 Decision on 'comitology' to assist the Commission on implementing measures under Article 202 of the EC Treaty.[41] This ESC, acting in an advisory capacity, should be consulted on policy issues by the

---

[41] This 'comitology' procedure is recognized under Arts 202 and 211 of the Treaty. Council Decision 1999/469/EC lays down the procedures for the exercise of implementing powers conferred on the Commission.

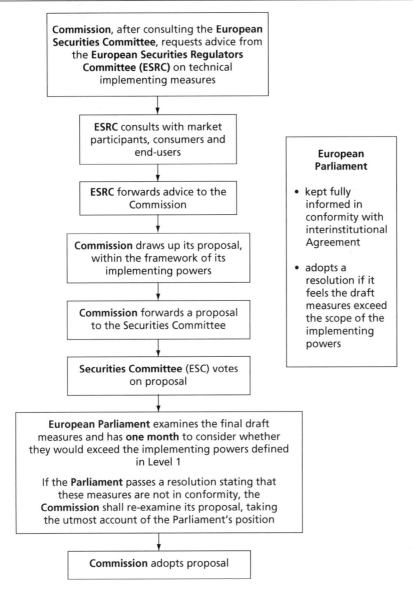

Figure 11.2 Level 2—Decision Making
Source: Lamfalussy Report

Commission. The ESC is composed of high-ranking officials—State Secretaries in the Finance Ministries of the Member States or their personal representatives—and is chaired by the European Commissioner responsible for the Internal Market.

The Committee of European Securities Regulators was formally set up on 11 September 2001 as an independent advisory group to the Commission (outside the comitology process) and is composed of national securities regulators, building on the structure established by FESCO (Forum of European Securities Commissions). While the ESC (and the other level 2 Lamfalussy committees) are often referred to as 'regulatory committees', the CESR (and the other level 3 Lamfalussy committees) are often referred to as 'supervisory committees'.[42]

The CESR makes proposals to the Commission on technical implementing matters. The Commission, on receiving these proposals, adjusts them when it comes to areas where it has a comparative advantage, for instance, with regard to competition law, or on issues which have an international dimension, such as relations with the USA. The Commission then transmits these proposals to the ESC, which votes on them. (The ESC can turn down a proposal only when there is a qualified majority vote against it.)

The European Parliament (EP) is given a period of three months to examine the draft implementing measure and to give its opinion, though in urgent and duly justified cases this period may be shortened. The EP has to consider whether or not the draft measures exceed the scope of the implementing matters. If, within that period, a resolution is passed by the European Parliament, the Commission should re-examine the draft measures (taking the utmost account of the Parliament's resolution).

The discussions in Stockholm in March 2001 and the preparatory discussion of the central features of the Report illustrate the mutual suspicions among national and European institutions (and between the latter) and the struggle of competencies between the Commission, the Council, and the European Parliament, as well as the latter's concerns about accountability and transparency. The European Parliament, through a resolution of 5 February 2002, finally endorsed the Lamfalussy Report, albeit with a number of safeguards. One of those safeguards is the introduction in the basic legislative acts of a so-called *sunset clause*[43] which establishes a time limit of four years with regard to the delegation of powers for the adoption of technical rules. Another safeguard is the requirement to receive from the Commission equivalent treatment to that

---

[42] See European Commission, Financial Services Tenth Report, 'Turning the Corner. Preparing for the Challenges of European Capital Market Integration', Brussels, 2 June 2004, 12.

[43] See point 17 of the 'European Parliament Resolution on the Implementation of Financial Services Legislation' (2001/2247(INI)) of 5 December 2002. The EP passed this resolution on the basis of the solemn declaration made before Parliament the same day by the Commission and the letter of 2 October 2001 addressed by the Internal Market Commissioner to the chairman of Parliament's Committee on Economic and Monetary Affairs, with regard to the safeguards of the European Parliament's role in this process.

given to the Council (the Commission had promised not to go against the predominant views of the Council as regards key implementation issues).[44]

Level 3

Level 3 refers to *national implementation and cooperation* and involves the CESR and the Member States. As stated in the Lamfalussy Report,[45] the CESR is conceived as a committee 'with two hats'. On the one hand, in level 2 it acts as an advisory committee to the European Commission and, on the other hand, in level 3 it acts alone as a fully independent committee of national regulators to ensure more consistent implementation of Community Law. The Lamfalussy Report proposes that the work of CESR (in level 3) should improve the common implementation and uniform interpretation of Community rules and should ensure consistent enforcement of the rules in the Member States.[46]

Level 4

Level 4 refers to *enforcement* and involves the Commission and the Member States. The Commission checks Member State compliance with EU legislation and may bring legal action against a Member State if a breach of Community Law is suspected.[47]

Assessing the Lamfalussy Procedure

The Lamfalussy framework has delivered some positive results, in terms of increased cooperation amongst European supervisory authorities, and greater transparency and consultation in the legislative process. The distinction between level 1 and level 2 principles is sensible, since it mirrors at the EU level what happens at the national level with the distinction between primary legislation and secondary regulation.

However, a simplified legislative procedure involving only one rather than two securities committees or banking committees or insurance committees would have been preferable. In this respect, the level 2 committees could have been dispensed with altogether.[48]

---

[44] EP Resolution of 5 December 2002, point 12.
[45] Lamfalussy Report, above note 4, 31.   [46] ibid 37.
[47] The problem, as Ian Wouters, 'Towards a European Securities Commission? Reflections in an International and Transatlantic Perspective' in Mads Andenas and Yannis Avreginos (eds), *Financial Markets in Europe: Towards a Single Regulator?* (The Hague: Kluwer Law International, 2003) has rightly indicated, is that even with sufficient resources, Commission enforcement procedures are limited due to the nature and cumbersome procedure of infringement proceedings.
[48] In its statement No 10, the ESFRC (of which I am a member) recommended the establishment of one securities committee, instead of two, and predicted that 'whereas the goal of the [Lamfalussy] Report is to speed up EU financial regulation, it appears that level 2 with its five-step procedure may actually slow it.' See <http:www.aei.org>. Regarding 'comitology' see above note 41.

Article I–36 of the proposed EU Constitution, which refers to 'Delegated European Regulations', would render the comitology procedure unnecessary.[49] Article I–36 states that

> European laws and framework laws may delegate to the Commission the power to adopt delegated European regulations to supplement or amend certain non-essential elements of the law or framework law. The objectives, content, scope and duration of the delegation shall be explicitly defined in the European laws and framework laws. The essential elements of an area shall be reserved for the European law or framework law and accordingly shall not be the subject of a delegation of power.

However, the level 2 committees could continue to exist according to Article IV–438 of the proposed EU Constitution on 'Succession and Legal Continuity'.

Whether or not the main aim of the Lamfalussy Report—a faster and more flexible legislative process—is realized remains to be seen. The Lamfalussy approach has been already applied to some recent legislative measures, such as the new Prospectus Directive (2003/71/EC) and the Market Abuse Directive (2003/6/EC). Implementing measures have been adopted for the Market Abuse Directive. The European Securities Committee on 19 April 2004 agreed a second set of implementing measures in the area of Market Abuse using the Lamfalussy process.[50]

The experience so far shows that it is difficult to distinguish in practice between framework principles and implementing measures, between political—level 1— and technical—level 2—measures.[51] For instance, the EP's misgivings about not being involved in the decisions of the Securities Committee resulted in the fact that it (the EP) proposed over 100 amendments to the draft Market Abuse Directive.[52]

The new Investment Services Directive, which has been renamed the Markets in Financial Instruments Directive (MiFID, 2004/39/EC), is one of the centre-pieces of the Financial Services Action Plan. The draft Directive was published in November 2002 following extensive consultations with the interested parties, as required under the Lamfalussy approach. A comparison between the original 1993 Investment Services Directive (ISD I) and the new 2004 Markets in

---

[49] Lannoo and Casey (above note 9, 8) state that the EU Constitution 'strengthens the control of the European Commission over implementing measures, as comitology is formally abolished in Article I–36 meaning that the Commision could, in theory, itself decide on secondary legislation, subject to a "call-back" of the European Parliament and the Council'.

[50] Above note 42, 3.   [51] See Lamfalussy Report, above note 4, 30.

[52] See Karel Lannoo, 'Supervising the European Financial System', CEPS Policy Brief 21, May 2002, 11.

Financial Instruments Directive (MiFID)[53] shows that the number of articles and total word count in MiFID are more than twice those in ISD I. *Plus ça change?*

The Commission has begun a monitoring process, with a wide-ranging consultation, to assess the state of integration of European financial markets and the effectiveness of the FSAP measures.[54] Apart from the subsidiarity and proportionality tests, the Commission also wishes to apply 'regulatory impact assessments' to any further legislative initiative in the field of financial services.[55] Member States meeting in the FSC have also been seeking to develop a collective view on progress on integration of the financial services.[56] These initiatives are welcome. However, the reality is that the process of adopting financial regulation in the EU remains unduly complex and that market participants (to which the rules are ultimately addressed) are showing signs of 'regulatory fatigue'. In May 2005, the Commission adopted a Green Paper on financial services policy for the period 2005–10, focusing on implementing existing rules and enhancing cooperation rather than proposing new laws.[57]

The trend towards 'maximum harmonization' promoted in the Lamfalussy Report is evident in the adoption of some recent legislative initiatives. The Prospectus Directive (2003/71/EC) uses this approach to ensure that a single format for prospectuses applies to securities issues in the EU. However, as Lannoo and Casey point out, reliance on maximum harmonization (via the use of Regulation or very detailed Directives) raises some fundamental problems. 'Under maximum harmonization, member states can only compete in supervisory performance, but not in regulatory standards.'[58]

The wisdom of departing from the previous established techniques of regulatory convergence in the EU (namely, minimum harmonization and regulatory competition through the principle of mutual recognition, combined with the principle of home country control) is a contested matter.

---

[53] Above note 9, 8.

[54] See <http://europa.edu.int/comm/internal_market/en/finances/actionplan/stocktaking. htm>. See also the Commission Staff Working Paper 'Tracking Financial Integration' at <http:// europa/eu/int/comm/internal_market/en/finances/cross-sector/reporting/tracking-financial-integration_en.pdf>.

[55] ibid.   [56] See, eg, Report of the FSC to the EFC, above note 3.

[57] This 'Green Paper on Financial Services Policy (2005–2010)', COM (2005) 177, 1–13, is available at <http://www.europa.eu.int/comm.internal_market/finances/docs/actionplan/index/ green_en.pdf>.

[58] ibid 10.

F. Conclusions

The current European financial architecture rests upon the principle of decentralization (with cooperation) and segmentation. However, it is not a static structure. Forces are already at play that suggest that an integrated financial market requires a more integrated supervisory design (and possibly the centralization of some supervisory function or sector) as well as some degree of consolidation, given the plethora of committees where supervisory issues are currently discussed at the EU level. The 'Lamfalussy framework', however, does not imply the centralization of supervisory and regulatory responsibilities. There is no transfer of competencies from the national to the supranational arena. The level 2 and level 3 committees are a form of supervisory cooperation.

Europe needs efficient capital markets. Efficient capital markets in turn require an appropriate regulatory structure. The jury is still out on the apparent benefits of the Lamfalussy approach to financial regulation in terms of achieving a faster and more flexible legislative procedure. In my opinion, the aim of simplicity and flexibility advocated by the Committee of Wise Men has not been realized yet. The process of adopting financial legislation in the EU remains complex, cumbersome, and time consuming.

Part III

DEVELOPMENTS AT THE INTERNATIONAL LEVEL

12

HISTORY OF INTERNATIONAL MONETARY COOPERATION

Perhaps the most difficult question is how much to decide by rule and how much to leave to discretion.

John Maynard Keynes, 'Proposals for an International Currency (Clearing) Union', 1942

A. Introduction

Central bank cooperation on a bilateral and multilateral basis already existed in the nineteenth and early twentieth centuries.[1] The Bank for International

---

[1] See Gianni Toniolo, *Central Bank Co-operation at the Bank for International Settlements: 1930–1973* (Cambridge: Cambridge University Press, 2005), ch 1. See also Marc Flandreau, 'Central Bank Co-operation in Historical Perspective: a Sceptical View' (1997) 4 Economic History Review 735 for an analysis of the pre-1914 period, and Barry Eichengreen, 'Central Bank Co-operation and Exchange Rate Commitments: the classical and inter-war gold standards compared', (1995) 2 Financial History Review 99.

Settlements (BIS) (the oldest international financial institution) was established in 1930 in the context of the German reparations after the First World War, to act as a centre for central bank cooperation. However, the history of the BIS before and during the Second World War was a troubled one; the Bretton Woods conference even called for its liquidation.

An institutional system of intergovernmental economic relations sanctioned by law was not established until Bretton Woods.[2] The Bretton Woods system foresaw the setting up of three international organizations: the International Monetary Fund (IMF) for the purposes of international monetary cooperation; the International Bank for Reconstruction and Development (IBRD) for the purposes of international development assistance (investment); and an International Trade Organization (ITO) for the purposes of international trade cooperation. However, while the IMF and the IBRD (World Bank) came into existence in the 1940s, the fate of the ITO—which should have played the role of the necessary 'third leg' of the Bretton Woods system—was quite different. Though a charter for the International Trade Organization was concluded in Havana in 1948, the project for its creation died because of the rejection by the US Congress. Instead, the General Agreement on Tariffs and Trade (GATT) was signed in 1947 and entered into force (through a Protocol for Provisional Application) in 1948. Only in 1995 did a 'permanent' international trade organization—the World Trade Organization (WTO)—finally come into existence.[3]

The Bretton Woods system was conceived with the bitter memories of high unemployment, hyperinflation, recession, and fluctuating exchange rates still fresh. The inter-war period had not been properly handled by the international community. In particular, many commentators argue that the harsh reparations

---

[2] There are three dimensions to the economic relations between states: trade, money, and investment. These relations can be cooperative, conflicting, or non-existent. In the latter case, the state retrenches to an inward-looking economic policy of isolationism and protectionism. Conflicts—of any sort—are unavoidable; however, the existence of a rule-based framework for the resolution of international economic conflicts can help promote cooperation. If such a framework does not exist, or if it is not respected, economic conflicts will either lead to the deterioration (or rupture) of economic relations between the States involved or will turn into a political conflict with the possibility of severance of diplomatic ties or, even worse, of a military backlash.

[3] An excellent historical account of the ITO (in the context of the Bretton Woods system), GATT, and WTO is provided by John Jackson in chapter 2 of his book *The World Trade Organization: Constitution and Jurisprudence*, Chatham House Papers (London: Royal Institute of International Affairs, 1998). Despite the provisional character of GATT, it proved to be a rather permanent institution nevertheless, playing a significant role in international trade for almost five decades. Jackson points out (15–16) that the Bretton Woods conference was held under the jurisdiction of ministries of finance, while trade was under the competence of different ministries. However, he also notes that 'the 1944 conference is on record as recognising the need for a comparable institution for trade, to complement the monetary institutions.'

policy towards Germany had proven to be very damaging.[4] Both John Maynard Keynes of the UK and Harry Dexter White of the US referred in their proposals to the need to 'win the peace'.

The challenges that the Bretton Woods institutions face in the twenty-first century are very different from the challenges these two institutions—the Fund and the World Bank—confronted when they started operations in Washington DC in May 1946. These challenges, particularly the ones encountered by the International Monetary Fund are examined here in Part III. Chapter 12 is largely a historical chapter. Chapter 13 focuses on the law of the IMF according to the Articles of Agreement, and Chapter 14 studies the rule-making aspects of the international financial architecture and the framework for the prevention and resolution of international financial crises.

Andreas Lowenfeld points out in his treatise on international economic law that though the International Monetary Fund and the World Bank seemed 'strong' in the 1950s and 1960s, while the agreement on trade issues—the GATT— seemed 'vulnerable', at the beginning of the twenty-first century the situation is the reverse.[5] The GATT has grown into the World Trade Organization, with enforcement powers and an agenda that extends beyond trade in goods to include services and others.

B. The International Gold Standard

Gold, silver, and other metals have been used as money (coins minted by sovereigns) throughout history. However, the term 'international gold standard' has a specific meaning in the economic literature.[6] The international gold standard (sometimes simply referred to as the gold standard), with gold as the principal reserve asset, was a monetary arrangement amongst the major countries in the world during the last part of the nineteenth century and lasted until

---

[4] In *The Economic Consequences of the Peace* (cited by Arminio Fraga, 'German Reparations and Brazilian Debt: a Comparative Study' (1986) 163 Princeton Essays in International Finance 2 Keynes had forcefully argued that the reparations payments discussed in Versailles were far too high. He also argued that post-war prosperity required a lower level of reparations and a cancellation of inter-ally indebtedness incurred during the war.

[5] See Andreas Lowenfeld, *International Economic Law* (Oxford: Oxford University Press, 2002) 18.

[6] See generally Michael Bordo, 'The Gold Standard: the Traditional Approach' in Michael Bordo and Anna Schwartz (eds), *A Retrospective on the Classical Gold Standard 1821–1931* (Chicago: Chicago University Press, 1984). For a brief explanation, see Marcello de Cecco, entry 'gold standard' in Peter Newman, Murray Milgate, and John Eatwell (eds), *Palgrave Dictionary of Money and Finance* (London: Macmillan Press Ltd, 1992).

1914.[7] According to this arrangement, each participating country committed to guaranteeing the free convertibility of its currency into gold at a fixed price. As Paul de Grauwe explains,[8] the fact that each currency was convertible into gold at a fixed price also made it possible that each currency was convertible into all others also at a fixed price.[9]

Gold was the anchor of the system. Countries fixed the value of their currencies against gold and central banks held gold in their reserves to defend that fixed price. The gold standard provided the underlying monetary stability until the beginning of the First World War. However, the gold standard was not based on any formal international agreement and did not impose any international legal obligation upon the countries that adopted it.[10]

From an economic point of view, a key difference between the gold standard and the Bretton Woods regime, discussed in detail below, is the choice of assets into which national currencies could be convertible. As the name indicates, the international gold standard relied on gold, while the Bretton Woods regime was to rely upon a two-tier system of convertibility based upon gold and the fixed US dollar value of gold, that is, a system in which the key currency—the US dollar—would be convertible into gold and the other currencies into the key currency.[11] The reasons for the choice of this two-tier system of convertibility rather than reverting to the gold standard were the following: (1) the distribution of gold after the Second World War was uneven, with the US monetary authorities holding around seventy per cent of the gold reserves, (2) the belief at the time that the existing gold reserves were insufficient to cope with the needs for international liquidity.[12]

---

[7] England was the first country to adopt a de facto gold standard in 1717. By 1870 most countries had abandoned bimetallism and opted for gold. See Michael Bordo, entry 'gold standard: theory' in Peter Newman, Murray Milgate, and John Eatwell (eds), *Palgrave Dictionary of Money and Finance* (London: Macmillan Press Ltd, 1992).

[8] See Paul de Grauwe, *International Money: Post-War Trends and Theories* (Oxford: Oxford University Press, 1990) 11.

[9] De Grauwe (ibid 16) provides an interesting three-stage story of international money and the shift from a metallic currency to paper money. In the first stage (gold standard), the gold was deposited in the vaults of the banks. In the second stage (Bretton Woods regime), the gold was centralized in the central bank, and the private banks replaced the gold convertibility by the convertibility of their liabilities into currency (the liability of the central bank). In the third stage (breakdown of Bretton Woods regime), the central banks abolished the gold convertibility of their national currencies. This leads De Grauwe to conclude: 'the history of international money is to a certain extent a rerun of the history of national moneys.'

[10] Lowenfeld, above note 5, 500. 'No international legal obligation required adherence to the gold standard, and it collapsed almost overnight at the start of World War I.'

[11] De Grauwe, above note 8, 15.

[12] ibid. With regard to the difference between the 'pure' gold standard and the 'gold exchange' standard, Geoffrey Wood explains:

C. The Inter-War Period

The aftermath of the First World War was characterized by acrimony. Though the Paris Peace Conference in 1918, following Germany's unconditional surrender on 11 November 1918, made an attempt to focus on restoring prosperity and peace, a few months later, the Treaty of Versailles of 28 June 1919 imposed a policy of reparations against Germany. However, the Treaty of Versailles was not ratified by the US Congress.[13] The history of the inter-war period is a history of failures. After the First World War there were attempts to reintroduce a system similar to the gold standard (eg, the 1922 Genoa Conference[14]), and some of the features of the gold standard were re-established by some countries (acting unilaterally and sequentially) between 1925 and 1931. The system was ultimately abandoned in 1931 and the inter-war period was to be characterized by rising international tension and great instability.[15]

The disastrous experience of hyperinflation in Germany in 1923, in an economy already overburdened with onerous war debts and reparations as well as high unemployment, created enormous popular discontent. This paved the way for the rise of National Socialism, with its dire consequences for the German nation. Keynes's argument that the reparations policy towards Germany after

---

The gold exchange standard evolved from the gold standard to economise on gold. Some central banks held gold in their reserves, but others held not gold but the currency of countries whose reserves did comprise gold. These central banks which held all or large part of their reserves in the currency of a country whose reserves were comprised entirely of gold were said to be on a gold exchange standard. Before World War I, if a currency was held as a reserve, it was primarily sterling; that system is often described as a sterling–gold exchange system. Under the Bretton Woods system after World War II, the currency held as a reserve was primarily the US dollar and the system was accordingly described as a dollar–gold exchange standard.

See Geoffrey Wood, entry 'gold exchange standard' in Peter Newman, Murray Milgate, and John Eatwell (eds), *Palgrave Dictionary of Money and Finance* (London: Macmillan Press Ltd, 1992).

[13] See Toniolo, above note 1, ch 2. Toniolo's book provides an excellent study of the history of the BIS from its inception until 1973.

[14] ibid 20. With regard to the Genoa conference, Toniolo recalls that Benjamin Strong (of the Fed) opposed the conference knowing that the British intended to discuss the gold standard. A resolution of the Genoa conference declared that the re-establishment of a stable value of money was essential for the economic reconstruction of Europe. The Genoa conference resolutions mark 'the first uncompromising international recognition of the desirability of formal co-operation among central banks'. Toniolo also refers to an economic conference in Brussels in 1920 (ibid 19) where loans for the reconstruction of the European economies and calls for central bank independence were discussed.

[15] See generally Barry Eichengreen, *Golden Fetters: The Gold Standard and the Great Depression, 1919–1939* (New York: Oxford University Press, 1992). With regard to the end of the 'inter-war gold standard', see Toniolo, above note 1, ch 5.

the First World War was not a way of winning the peace[16] was sadly confirmed by history.

The Bank for International Settlements was set up in 1930 in the context of the Young Plan[17] which dealt with the issue of the reparation payments imposed on Germany by the Treaty of Versailles following the First World War. The BIS took over the functions previously performed by the Agent General for Reparations in Berlin: collection, administration, and distribution of the annuities payable as reparations. The BIS was also created to act as a trustee for the Dawes and Young Loans (international loans issued to finance reparations).[18] Although the settlement of the reparations was the *causa proxima* for setting up the BIS (indeed, the Bank's name is derived from this role), the objectives of the BIS were defined more broadly by its statutes,[19] and the BIS was to act as a centre for international central bank cooperation. But by the time the BIS started operations, the world was sliding into depression. The Great Depression, that is, the economic contraction from 1929 to 1933, was the most severe and widely diffused international contraction in modern times and an unprecedented financial catastrophe. 'Though sharper and more prolonged in the United States than in most other countries, it [the Great Contraction] was worldwide in scope'.[20] Between 1929 and 1932 industrial production in the USA contracted by forty-seven per cent. By March 1933 there were at least fourteen million unemployed.[21]

The United States rejected a proposed dollar–franc–pound stabilization plan at the London International and Monetary Conference of 1933, a conference which 'broke up in disarray'.[22] The demise of the gold standard, the end of

---

[16] Above note 4.

[17] See Toniolo, above note 1, 33–4. The Young Plan was named after Owen D Young, an American Banker who presided over a Committee of Experts convened to work out a final settlement on German reparations. I further refer to the BIS in Ch 14.

[18] See <http://www.bis.org>. The BIS was to take over the functions previously performed by the Agent General for Reparations in Berlin: collection, administration, and distribution of the annuities payable as reparations. The Bank's name is derived from this original role. The BIS was also created to act as a trustee for the Dawes and Young Loans (international loans issued to finance reparations) and to promote central bank cooperation in general.

[19] Article 3 of the BIS Statutes (1930) states: 'The objects of the Bank are: to promote the co-operation of central banks and to provide additional facilities for international financial operations, and to act as trustee or agent in regard to international financial settlements entrusted to it under agreements with the parties concerned.' The text of the BIS Statutes is available at <http://www.bis.org/about/statutes-en.pdf>.

[20] See Milton Friedman and Anna Schwartz, *The Great Contraction 1929–1933* (Princeton: Princeton University Press, 1965) 3.

[21] See J. Keith Horsefield, *The International Monetary Fund 1945–1965, Volume I: Chronicle* (Washington DC: IMF, 1969) 5.

[22] Above note 5, 500. See also Toniolo, above note 1, 144–9.

reparations in 1933–4,[23] and the failures in international economic cooperation affected the role and relevance of the BIS.[24]

The political tensions in the 1930s spilt over domestic economic policy considerations. As Harold James explains, 'the depression also acted internally to destroy the stability of democratic regimes. Throughout Europe and Latin America, parliamentary regimes disintegrated in the face of their inability to deal with the economic crisis. At the same time, the collapse of international collaboration reduced the incentive for states to behave responsibly.'[25] Everything that states did in the international economy (trade policy, currency policy, and others) aimed at maximizing their own wealth and power, driven by national considerations. 'The country that excelled in trade and currency manipulation of the international system for its own ends was National Socialist Germany.'[26]

The economic breakdown was a contributing factor to the breakdown of peace.

D. The Keynes and White Plans

Any serious analysis of the origins of the Bretton Woods institutions must trace back to the original proposals of the two men who drafted their foundations: Harry Dexter White and John Maynard Keynes.[27]

Harry Dexter White joined the staff of the US Treasury in 1934 and resigned on 1 May 1946, to take up the post of US Executive Director of the Fund. He died in 1948. John Maynard Keynes (later Baron Keynes of Tilton) combined a multifaceted career with the position, from July 1940 until his death on 21 April 1946, of Honorary Advisor to the British Treasury.

Both men firmly believed that the economic distress of the inter-war period could be avoided after the end of the Second World War only by international economic cooperation. Their proposals were drafted in 1941 and 1942,

---

[23] Toniolo, ibid, ch 5.

[24] Toniolo, ibid 167–75, also refers to the American misgivings towards the BIS, which would turn into outright hostility.

[25] See Harold James, *International Monetary Cooperation since Bretton Woods* (Washington DC and Oxford: IMF and Oxford University Press, 1996) 26.

[26] ibid 32.

[27] This section of the chapter draws on an article I wrote on 'The International Monetary Fund in Historical Perspective' (2000) 3 Journal of International Economic Law 507, 507–23 and a book chapter on 'The Bretton Woods Institutions in the XXIst Century' in Rosa M Lastra (ed), *The Reform of the International Financial Architecture* (London: Kluwer Law International, 2001) 67–90.

negotiated in 1943,[28] and adopted at the International Monetary and Financial Conference of the United and Associated Nations in Bretton Woods, New Hampshire, in July 1944.

White's proposal was greatly influenced by the experience of the Great Depression in the USA, following the stock market crash of 1929. The prime objective of White's proposal was the establishment of a mechanism—'a stabilization fund' in his own words—that would ensure the stability of currencies and avoid the recurrence of competitive devaluations and of the restrictions on payments, as well as the setting up of a 'bank for reconstruction and development'. In the introduction to his plan, entitled 'Preliminary Draft Proposal for a United Nations Stabilization Fund and a Bank for Reconstruction and Development of the United and Associated Nations' and dated April 1942,[29] he stated:

> No matter how long the war lasts nor how it is won, we shall be faced with three inescapable problems: to prevent the disruption of foreign exchanges and the collapse of monetary and credit systems; to assure the restoration of foreign trade; and to supply the huge volume of capital that will be needed virtually throughout the world for reconstruction, for relief, and for economic recovery. If we are to avoid drifting from the peace table into a period of chaotic competition, monetary disorders, depressions, political disruptions, and finally into new wars within as well as among nations, we must be equipped to grapple with these three problems and to make substantial progress toward their solution.

Keynes's proposal was inspired by a different set of events: an analysis of Britain's post-war prospects. Demand for imports would rise with the end of wartime austerity, while Britain's future capacity to export would be cut because of the wartime conversion of industries to military manufacture and the difficulties of reconversion.[30] Keynes proposed the establishment of an international clearing union, aimed at avoiding balance of payments imbalances through a set of rules governing the overdrafts on the Union accumulated by debtors (such as the UK) and the positive balances acquired by creditors (such as the USA). Keynes's plan was entitled: 'Proposals for an International Currency (or Clearing) Union'.[31]

---

[28] Their proposals were presented to the public in April 1944 as 'The Joint Statement of Experts on the Establishment of an International Monetary Fund'. See Toniolo, above note 1, 260.

[29] This proposal is reproduced in J Keith Horsefield, *The International Monetary Fund 1945–1965, Volume III: Documents* (Washington DC: IMF, 1969) 37–82 (though it omits the Articles for the Bank). The final version of Mr White's plan was issued by the US Treasury in printed form on 10 July 1943, and is reproduced in Horsefield, 83–96.

[30] See James, above note 25, 35.

[31] The fourth draft of his proposal (of 1942) is reproduced in J Keith Horsefield, *The International Monetary Fund 1945–1965, Volume III: Documents* (Washington DC: IMF, 1969) 3–18. The final draft which was issued by the British Government in April 1943 as a White Paper (Cmd 6437) is reproduced in pages 19–36 of the same book. The title of the final British draft dropped the word currency and was simply entitled: 'Proposals for an International Clearing Union'.

Keynes spelt out his concerns for the UK economy after the Second World War: 'This [an international clearing union] would give us, and all others, the great assistance of multilateral clearing, whereby (for example) we could offset favourable balances due to the United States or South America or elsewhere. How indeed can we hope to afford to start up trade with Europe (which will be of vast importance to us) during the relief and reconstruction period on any other terms?'[32] Keynes further regarded that an international currency (clearing) union—which in his original plan also included the creation of a new international currency that he named *bancor*—would support other international policies regarding, for example, trade (whose importance was also emphasized by White), investment, and development,[33] though he did not design a specific institutional framework to deal with such other issues.

While the British proposal focused mainly on the work of the International Monetary Fund, which Keynes referred to as the International Currency (or Clearing) Union, the US proposal focused on the establishment of both a stabilization fund and a bank for reconstruction and development. With regard to the stabilization fund, the system would be tied to gold, not to the new international money proposed by Keynes, though by a kinder and gentler tie than the gold standard. With regard to the bank for reconstruction and development, Harry Dexter White was certainly the central figure in the birth of the World Bank,[34] though Keynes and other UK experts eventually became major enthusiasts for the Bank, acknowledging that loans from creditor countries to debtor countries in the early post-war period were essential to avoid economic chaos and that without them no international monetary plan could have a fair start.[35] The World Bank,[36] or more properly speaking, the International Bank for Reconstruction and Development, had—as its name indicated—two main goals, though the 'development' goal would eventually become the primary one. The sequencing of these two goals was summarized by Lord Keynes in his

---

[32] See para 10 of his proposal, repr in Horsefield ibid.

[33] See para 54 of his proposal, repr in Horsefield ibid.

[34] Indeed, as Mason and Asher recall, 'the Bank was essentially a U.S. proposal.' See Edward S Mason and Robert E Asher, *The World Bank since Bretton Woods* (Washington DC: The Brookings Institution, 1973) 13.

[35] See James, above note 25, 52.

[36] Nowadays, the name World Bank is given both to the IBRD and to the World Bank Group. The World Bank Group comprises five institutions: the International Bank for Reconstruction and Development (set up in 1944, the original Bretton Woods institution), the International Development Association (set up in 1960 to deal with the world's poorest countries), the International Finance Corporation (set up in 1956, as the private-based arm of the World Bank Group), the Multilateral Investment Guarantee Agency (set up in 1988 to provide insurance against political risk), and the International Centre for the Settlement of Investment Disputes (set up in 1966 for the resolution of investment conflicts).

opening remarks at the first meeting of the Bretton Woods Commission on the Bank:

> It is likely, in my judgement, that the field of reconstruction from the conse-
> quences of war will mainly occupy the proposed Bank in its early days. But, as
> soon as possible, and with increasing emphasis as time goes on, there is a second
> primary duty laid upon it, namely to develop the resources and productive capacity
> of the world, with special reference to the less developed countries.[37]

E. The Bretton Woods Conference

The International Monetary and Financial Conference of the United and Associated Nations, commonly referred to as the Bretton Woods Conference, was held in Bretton Woods, New Hampshire in July 1944. Delegates from forty-five nations (including the Soviet Union, which, nevertheless, never became a signatory)[38] as well as representatives of international organizations attended the conference. As acknowledged, the world was still at war in July 1944. And yet, the delegates at Bretton Woods were talking about, and indeed were erecting a framework for, future international economic cooperation.

Though the role of the BIS as an existing international institution could have been enhanced in the Bretton Woods Conference, instead, the Conference called for the liquidation of the BIS. This was in part due to US hostility towards the institution, in the light of its 'blunders before and during the war'.[39] (With the start of the Second World War, the BIS had adopted a policy of neutrality in 1939,[40] which was to be questioned by the Allies[41]). The Reso-lution calling for the liquidation of the BIS was included in its Final Act of the

---

[37] See Edward S Mason and Robert E Asher, *The World Bank since Bretton Woods* (Washington DC: The Brookings Institution, 1973).

[38] Harold James, above note 25, 70, recalls the considerations that led the Soviet Union not to sign the Bretton Woods agreements. The decision not to subscribe to the IMF Articles of Agree-ment was first presented by the then Soviet Finance Minister, Molotov, as a postponement. Interestingly, James points out that 'The Soviet postponement of a decision on membership of the Bretton Woods institutions is a useful chronological mark of the beginning of the Cold War.' At a meeting of the General Assembly of the United Nations in 1947, the Soviet representative charged that the Bretton Woods Institutions were merely 'branches of Wall Street' and that the Bank was 'subordinated to political purposes which make it the instrument on one great power'. The incident is recalled by Mason and Asher, above note 37, 29 (n 46).

[39] See Toniolo, above note 1, 259 and 279–80: 'Hostility towards the BIS at Bretton Woods was rooted in a number of factors. One of these was the vague, if pervasive feeling that the Bank was surreptitiously siding with Germany. . . . That aside, there were two political reasons why the US Treasury . . . was opposed to the very existence of the BIS. There seemed to be no place for the BIS in the framework envisaged at Bretton Woods. . . . Domestic political considerations also played a role.'

[40] ibid 215.   [41] ibid 216 and generally ibid, ch 7 ('Wartime').

Conference.[42] However, the institution was not dissolved and today plays an important role as a centre for central bank cooperation and as an 'umbrella organization' for a panoply of committees involved in the process of setting international financial standards, as I further explain in Chapter 14.

The setting up of the International Monetary Fund was the primary focus of the Bretton Woods Conference, while the World Bank was—in the words of some commentators—something of an 'afterthought'.[43]

When the war was over, it was the Marshall Plan rather than the World Bank that played the major role in the reconstruction and recovery of war-torn European economies. As acknowledged, US Secretary of State George Marshall unveiled the 'European Recovery Program' (which became known as the Marshall Plan) in his famous Harvard commencement speech in June 1947, where he announced a programme of massive financial assistance to Europe.[44] As explained in Chapter 6, the Marshall Plan, which was supervised by the US Economic Cooperation Administration (ECA), also created the Organization for European Economic Cooperation (OEEC) and contributed to the establishment of a multilateral system of European payment: the European Payments Union (1949–50).[45]

F. The Bretton Woods Regime

The Bretton Woods regime can be characterized as the first international legal system to govern the monetary relations of states.[46] In contrast to the gold standard, the IMF Articles of Agreement did impose legal obligations upon member states.[47] Though these obligations have changed over time, the

---

[42] ibid 260 and 271.   [43] See Mason and Asher, above note 34, 2.

[44] 'In 1946, the Western European trade deficit with the United States had been $2,356 million, and in 1947 it rose to $4,742 million. In its first year of operation (April 1948–June 1949), the European Recovery Program, ERP, made $6,221 million available, and then $4,060 million in 1949–50 and $2,254 in 1950–51.' See James, above note 25, 74.

[45] The formal proposal for an EPU came in December 1949 from the ECA. It was designed as a provisional measure until it is possible to establish, by other methods, a multilateral system of European payments. See James, above note 25, 76.

[46] See Lowenfeld, above note 5, 500: 'Prior to the close of World War II no international legal regime governed the conduct of states with respect to monetary affairs.' See also James, above note 25, 57: 'The Bretton Woods meeting was the first conference to establish a permanent institutional and legal framework for ensuring cooperation between states, requiring commitments by states to limit their sovereignty for the sake of cooperation and to observe specified rules in economic intercourse.'

[47] 'Bretton Woods constituted the first formal international agreement applicable for economic transactions among the countries that had subscribed to it.' See Manuel Guitián, 'The Unique Nature of the Responsibilities of the International Monetary Fund', IMF Pamphlet Series No 46, Washington DC, 1992, 2.

principles embodied in the IMF Articles of Agreement still provide the legal basis for economic governance in the monetary field at the international level.

The Articles of Agreement of the International Monetary Fund adopted on 22 July 1944 came into force on 27 December 1945.

The par value regime and the original IMF Articles of Agreement

The International Monetary Fund began operations in Washington DC in May 1946. The first meeting of the Governors of the Fund and of the World Bank had taken place in March 1946 at the General Oglethorpe Hotel, Wilmington Island, Savannah, Georgia. At Savannah, the Governors agreed that the headquarters of the new institution should be in Washington. Though the obvious original choice as Managing Director was an American, Harry Dexter White, his reputation was tainted by allegations of involvement with the Soviet cause. In May 1946, Camille Gutt, then Belgian Finance Minister, became the Fund's first Managing Director. 'As a consequence, the President of the World Bank could only be an American, and Eugene Meyer, a distinguished but elderly public servant, was appointed. With these two men began a tradition of non-American (and in practice, at least until the present, European) IMF Managing Directors, and American World Bank Presidents.'[48]

The par value regime, often referred to as the Bretton Woods regime, was a two-tier system of convertibility, also known as the gold–dollar standard. According to this par value regime, the value of currency of each participating member was defined in terms of gold or alternatively in terms of the US dollar of 1 July 1944, which had a fixed gold value (one ounce of gold was equal to $35).[49]

Article IV, section 1(a) of the original Articles of Agreement clearly stated:

> The par value of the currency of each member shall be expressed in terms of gold as a common denominator or in terms of the United States dollar of the weight and fineness [sic] in effect on July 1, 1944.[50]

The US monetary authorities guaranteed the convertibility of the dollar into gold at the fixed price of $35 per ounce of gold. The monetary authorities of the participating countries committed themselves to convert their currency into

---

[48] Above note 25, 72.

[49] 'For original parties to the IMF whose territory had not been under enemy occupation, the par value was required to be based on the exchange rate prevailing on the sixtieth day before the agreement entered into force, which turned to be December 27, 1945, subject to negotiation between the Fund and the member state within 90 days [Original Articles, Art XX(4)(a)]. Other States could set their own par values, but they were required to do so and to notify the Fund.' Above note 5, 524.

[50] The original Articles of Agreement can be found in <http://www.imfsite.org/origins/original1.html>.

dollars at a fixed price, which was called the official exchange rate or the parity rate.[51]

The original Articles of Agreement foresaw the possibility of adjusting the rate of an individual currency if it fell into a 'fundamental disequilibrium', a term which despite its importance was not defined.[52] Article IV, section 5 (a) concerning 'changes in par values' stated:

A member shall not propose a change in the par value of its currency except to correct a fundamental disequilibrium.

The original Articles of Agreement also foresaw the possibility of readjusting all currencies through the 'uniform changes in par values'. For instance, if the world stock of gold at $35 per ounce became too small for a growing world economy. According to Article IV, section 7:

[T]he Fund by a majority of the total voting power may make uniform proportionate changes in the par values of the currencies of all members, provided each such change is approved by every member which has ten percent or more of the total of the quotas.

The IMF's mandate was to maintain the good order of this predictable and relatively 'stable' international monetary system, by enforcing rules about adjustment in international monetary relations and by providing temporary resources to deal with short-term balance of payments problems.

However the faults in the system would soon become apparent. In the following paragraphs I discuss first the economic rationale behind the eventual abandonment of the system and, then, I study the 'life' of the system.

The economic analysis of the collapse of the par value regime

The collapse of the Bretton Woods regime is often explained in economic terms by the so-called Triffin dilemma, developed by Robert Triffin in 1960.[53] Triffin

---

[51] See De Grauwe, above note 8, 15.

[52] Harry Dexter White in an unpublished memorandum of August 1946, reproduced in Joseph Gold, 'The Legal Structure of the Par Value System' (1973) 5 Law and Policy International Business 155, 161, explains why such a term was not defined:

In the drafting of the Articles of Agreement, no attempt was made to define fundamental disequilibrium. This, as we know, was not oversight. It was generally agreed that a satisfactory definition would be difficult to formulate. A too rigid or narrow interpretation would be dangerous; one too loose or general would be useless in providing a criterion for changes in currency parities. It was felt that the matter was so important, and the necessity for crystallization of a harmonious view so essential that it was best left for discussion and formulation by the Fund. Because of the key position of the term and the importance attached to its precise meaning, it would be desirable, if possible, to reach agreement on a tentative formulation before any definitive position to be taken by any of the officials of the Fund.

[53] Robert Triffin, *Gold and the Dollar Crisis* (New Haven: Yale University Press, 1960).

argued that the demands of a growing world economy would imply an increase in the demand for dollar reserves. Though the US could supply these desired dollars by running balance of payment deficits, the problem would arise because the supply of gold is more or less fixed (and guided by new discoveries, technological developments in mining gold, and other factors). In this scenario, if the US accommodated the increased demand for dollar reserves, it condemned the system to its inevitable demise (by undermining confidence in the convertibility of the dollar into gold, leading to a rush to convert dollars into gold and eventually producing the collapse of the system); if it resisted those demands, it condemned the world to deflation. Officials as well as academic economists came to accept Triffin's diagnosis.[54] Concerns about liquidity in the international monetary system led to the establishment of the Special Drawing Right (SDR) as a reserve asset in addition to gold and dollars.

De Grauwe elaborates on the Triffin dilemma.[55] He argues that the move from a gold–dollar standard to a dollar standard can be further explained in economic terms by Gresham's law. The law applies to every monetary system based on the use of two currencies where the monetary authorities fix an official price between the two and where, in addition, they are willing to buy and sell the currencies at that price. If one of the two currencies becomes relatively abundant, its private market price will tend to decline. Economic agents will then buy it cheaply in the private market and sell it in the official market at a higher official price. The scarce currency is taken out of the monetary circuit and used for non-monetary purposes. The opposite occurs with the abundant currency. In the case of the gold–dollar standard, gold ('the good money') was driven out of the international monetary circuit to be used for private purposes (jewellery, art, dentistry, etc), while dollars took the place of gold in the vaults of central banks.[56]

The reason why the Triffin problem was not handled quite simply by revaluing the price of gold, as could have been done under Article IV, section 7 of the Articles of Agreement, was political. The main beneficiaries would have been Russia, South Africa (with gold mines), and the countries which were seeking to destabilize the United States by holding their reserves in gold rather than in US dollars. Politically, it became effectively impossible to revalue gold.[57] According to Joseph Gold: 'An increase in the price of gold, for which the Articles [Art IV, section 7] make provision, was . . . rejected for various reasons, one of which was

---

[54] Geoffrey Wood, above note 12.   [55] De Grauwe, above note 8, 22–6.
[56] De Grauwe, above note 8, 26–30.
[57] I thank Charles Goodhart for observations on this point.

that the direct benefit of the increase would be enjoyed only by those members that held gold.'[58]

De Grauwe points out that the collapse of the Bretton Woods regime has some characteristics that are repeated again and again in the history of the international monetary system. He explains this recurring feature as follows: Central banks commit themselves to defending a given exchange rate. After some time, they realize that it is no longer in their interest to continue their commitment, because the exchange rate has become 'out of touch with reality'.[59] Private speculators often anticipate that policy makers will renege on their commitment, and precipitate its abandonment. By its very definition a system of fixed exchange rates is vulnerable to speculative attacks and the credibility of such a system is eroded when those attacks take place.[60] The crisis in the Exchange Rate Mechanism of the European Monetary System in September 1992 is another example of this recurrent history.

The 'life' of the par value regime

Though the IMF was founded in 1944 and started operations in 1946, the 'proper' Bretton Woods regime did not start functioning till 1959, once European countries achieved convertibility of their currencies.[61] Since the Bretton Woods regime was abandoned at the beginning of the 1970s, the 'life' of the par value regime was short and, as I explain in this subsection, problematic.

Gold, reserves, and liquidity

The gold–dollar two-tier system of convertibility had an inherent flaw in that the United States was willing to convert gold balances of dollars held by the

---

[58] Joseph Gold, 'Law and Reform of the International Monetary System' (1975) 10 The Journal of International Law and Economics 371, 385. Others solutions which were rejected were the general abandonment of par values, and general increases in quotas (ibid 386).

[59] Above note 8, 30.

[60] ibid 53.

[61] After the Second World War, the European countries which had taken part in the war (as well as Japan) were devastated and in desperate need of imports of machinery and essential consumer goods, many of them coming from the United States. If a free market had been allowed, the US dollar would have risen to very high levels. Exchange controls were therefore introduced. But, shortly thereafter, a recovery and continuing fast rate of growth of productivity in continental Europe (and Japan) meant that the currencies in these countries became increasingly competitive against the US dollar, and the balance of trade moved in favour of continental Europe and Japan. I thank Charles Goodhart for observations on this point. As I explained in Ch 6, the European Payments Union was established in 1950 as a mechanism for settling payments amongst European countries. By 1958–9, member currencies became de facto fully convertible, ie, transferable between each other, and *de jure* in 1961, on formal acceptance of the obligations of Art VIII of the IMF Articles of Agreement (which I further discuss in Ch 13). See also De Grauwe, above note 8, 19.

monetary authorities of other members, while private gold markets were permissible and were in operation.[62]

In the beginning of the 1960s, it became clear that the gold reserves were insufficient for the growing demands of the international monetary system. In order to avoid the private price of gold increasing above the official price ($35 per ounce), the central banks of Belgium, France, Germany, Italy, the Netherlands, Switzerland, the United Kingdom, and the United States decided to form in 1961 a 'gold pool' to intervene in the London gold market (the leading gold bullion market) to keep the price of gold at its official level.[63] The gold pool was a cooperative arrangement

> whereby central banks sought to share the cost of maintaining the London price of gold at $35 an ounce rather than depleting US gold reserves. It encouraged collective action by establishing an understanding of how the costs of these operations would be divided, that is, of what share of the gold that needed to be sold in London in order to stabilize the market price would be provided by each participating central bank.[64]

In 1967 and in 1968, the demand for gold became so great that the central banks decided to abolish the 'gold pool'.[65] In March 1968, the authorities announced that the price of gold in the private market would henceforth be determined by supply and demand and that they would no longer intervene in the private gold market. From then on the price of gold started to climb.[66]

Concerns about liquidity and the shortage of reserves led to the creation of the SDR, as a supplementary reserve asset in the late 1960s (the first amendment to the IMF Articles of Agreement).[67]

At the end of the 1960s, the gold–dollar ratio had declined so much that the US was forced to suspend the convertibility of dollars into gold. According to De Grauwe, the gold exchange standard ended de facto in 1968 with the collapse of the gold pool, though it was formally abandoned on 15 August 1971 when US President Nixon ended the American commitment to sell gold at a fixed price to

---

[62] This point is made by Gold. See Joseph Gold, 'Gold in International Monetary Law: Change, Uncertainty and Ambiguity' (1981) 15 The Journal of International Law and Economics 323, 338.

[63] Gold (ibid 338–41) explains the history of the 'gold pool'.

[64] See Barry Eichengreen 'The Dollar and the New Bretton Woods System', text of the Henry Thornton Lecture, delivered at the Cass School of Business, 15 December 2004, 5, available at <http://emlab.berkeley.edu/users/eichengr/policy/cityuniversitylecture2jan3–05.pdf>.

[65] ibid. 'It collapsed in 1968 after French gold purchases became known and was followed by a short-lived Gentleman's Agreement that collapsed in 1970.' See also Norman Humphreys, *Historical Dictionary of the International Monetary Fund*, 2nd edn (Maryland: The Scarecrow Press, 1999), entry 'gold pool'.

[66] Above note 8, 28–9   [67] See Ch 13.

foreign central banks.[68] The major central banks in turn ceased to guarantee the convertibility of their currencies into dollars at a fixed price.

Devaluations, revaluations, and floating rates

Though the possibility of changes in the par value was foreseen in the original Articles of Agreement and the procedure 'to correct a fundamental disequilibrium'—Article IV, section 5—was meant to be an orderly resolution of a problem or crisis,[69] the reality of the international monetary system turned out to be different. Crises are seldom—if ever—orderly and their workout is seldom an orderly process. A sense of urgency prompts countries (or individuals) to forego procedures and rules. Forbearance leads to lack of credibility and lack of credibility may lead to the collapse of the system and/or to a rewriting of the rules.

In the United Kingdom, domestic economic problems in the immediate postwar period led to the adoption of a thirty per cent devaluation of the pound sterling on 19 September 1949. Other continental countries also devalued their currencies.[70]

Germany in the late 1950s and early 1960s presented a different set of circumstances: economic growth and surpluses. This led the German cabinet to vote

---

[68] De Grauwe, above note 8, 29.

[69] Article IV, section 5, (b) to (f) specified the procedure to follow to change the par value in the case of a fundamental disequilibrium. Because of its significance, I reproduce in this note the whole text of Article IV, section 5:

  a. A member shall not propose a change in the par value of its currency except to correct a fundamental disequilibrium.
  b. A change in the par value of a member's currency may be made only on the proposal of the member and only after consultation with the Fund.
  c. When a change is proposed, the Fund shall first take into account the changes, if any, which have already taken place in the initial par value of the member's currency as determined under Article XX, Section 4. If the proposed change, together with all previous changes, whether increases or decreases,
    i. does not exceed ten percent of the initial par value, the Fund shall raise no objection;
    ii. does not exceed a further ten percent of the initial par value, the Fund may either concur or object, but shall declare its attitude within seventy-two hours if the member so requests;
    iii. is not within (i) or (ii) above, the Fund may either concur or object, but shall be entitled to a longer period in which to declare its attitude.
  d. Uniform changes in par values made under Section 7 of this Article shall not be taken into account in determining whether a proposed change falls within (i), (ii), or (iii) of (c) above.
  e. A member may change the par value of its currency without the concurrence of the Fund if the change does not affect the international transactions of members of the Fund.
  f. The Fund shall concur in a proposed change which is within the terms of (c) (ii) or (c) (iii) above if it is satisfied that the change is necessary to correct a fundamental disequilibrium. In particular, provided it is so satisfied, it shall not object to a proposed change because of the domestic social or political policies of the member proposing the change.

[70] Above note 25, 95.

for a small revaluation of the mark by five per cent in February 1961 to correct a disequilibrium in international payments.[71] The revaluation of the mark was followed by a revaluation of the Dutch guilder in March 1961.[72]

Canada adopted a floating rate in 1950. Though the float was seen as a violation of the par value principle, it actually allowed Canada to make the transition to external convertibility at an early stage. In 1952, Canada accepted the obligations of Article VIII (current account convertibility) under the IMF Articles of Agreement.[73]

In the United Kingdom, the second half of the 1960s was a difficult period for the UK economy. Large current account deficits and a drain on British reserves forced the devaluation of the British pound by 14.3 per cent in November 1967.[74]

The economic difficulties in France in 1968, following the student unrest and widespread industrial strikes (eventually settled by large wage rises), led to the devaluation of the French franc by eleven per cent in August 1969.[75] Soon after the French devaluation, in October 1969, a new parity was adopted for the Deutschmark, with a revaluation of 9.3 per cent against the US dollar.[76]

The US dollar

The role of the dollar as the only currency expressly linked to gold succeeded only while the US had a dominant economy and a dominant currency. The immediate post-war period has been described as the period of 'dollar hegemony'.[77] But with the economic recovery in Japan and Germany, the situation of the dollar became untenable. The US position shifted from one of being a creditor country to one of being a debtor country, running persistent deficits in its balance of payments. When the dollar had been perceived as as good as gold, countries had been happy to keep dollar reserves, but when the situation reversed, the US authorities restricted the conversion of dollars into gold.

Amongst the 'manifold and cumulative' causes that put unsustainable pressure on the dollar, Lowenfeld cites the following: the war in Vietnam, which affected the US budget and the payments position; the rise in imports from Japan; the continuing direct foreign investment by corporations based in the United States; and a very different overall economic climate from that of the early post-war period.[78]

---

[71] Above note 25, 114–15.   [72] ibid.   [73] Above note 25, 99.
[74] Above note 25, 188–9.   [75] Above note 25, 193–6.   [76] Above note 25, 197.
[77] Above note 25, 90. See generally Richard Gardner, *Sterling-Dollar Diplomacy: The Origins and Prospects of Our International Economic Order* (New York: McGraw-Hill, 1969).
[78] Above note 5, 526.

In the spring of 1971 the IMF Managing Director suggested the devaluation of the dollar, which the United States rejected. In May 1971 the German Government unilaterally decided to float the mark upwards. Subsequently, the Dutch guilder was also floated upwards against the dollar. 'The German float suddenly transferred the force of global speculative pressures against the dollar to Japan.'[79] The yen was not permitted to float, but the Bank of Japan had to acquire billions of US dollars to maintain the par value of the yen.[80] Sunday, 15 August 1971 marks the day on which the 'gold window' was closed. Moreover, the US would not intervene in exchange markets to defend the par value of the dollar against other currencies. The measures announced by President Nixon in a televised address signified the end of the Bretton Woods par value regime. The faults of the system, though, had been in evidence for some time.

A note on the notion of reserve currency

A national currency can be used as an 'international currency' if there is confidence that it will maintain a stable purchasing power. If a country is a major participant in world trade and a major source of capital, residents and central banks of other countries will find it convenient to hold balances of its currency.[81] With the demise of gold as the main reserve asset of the international monetary system, the notion of 'reserve currency' became more relevant.

The characteristic of becoming a 'reserve currency' is typically associated with the feature of being a 'vehicle currency', that is, a currency used to denominate international trade and capital transactions.[82] Confidence in the value of the currency, convertibility, political stability, and liberalized financial markets are conditions typically associated with vehicle currencies.[83] The dollar emerged as a major international currency at the end of the First World War, and after the Second World War it became the main 'reserve currency' and 'vehicle currency'.[84] Frankel explains why the US dollar is the most important vehicle

---

[79] Above note 25, 216.   [80] Above note 5, 526.

[81] See Jacques J Polak, entry 'reserve currency' in Peter Newman, Murray Milgate, and John Eatwell (eds), *Palgrave Dictionary of Money and Finance* (London: Macmillan Press Ltd, 1992). The IMF Articles of Agreement define a 'freely usable currency' in Article XXX (f):

> A freely usable currency means a member's currency that the Fund determines (i) is, in fact, widely used to make payments for international transactions, and (ii) is widely traded in the principal exchange markets.

[82] See George Tavlas, entry 'vehicle currency' in Peter Newman, Murray Milgate, and John Eatwell (eds), *Palgrave Dictionary of Money and Finance* (London: Macmillan Press Ltd, 1992).

[83] ibid.

[84] See generally Peter Kenen, 'The Role of the Dollar as an International Currency', Occasional Papers No 13, Group of Thirty, New York, 1983.

currency, reserve currency, and all-round international currency.[85] He mentions historical considerations, patterns of trade and finance, well-developed financial markets, and confidence in the value of the currency. The US dollar thus fulfils a dual role: that of being the national currency of the US, and the 'world's currency' of choice. McKinnon had predicted that a move to floating rates would not reduce the private demand for US dollars (only the official demand).[86] This is indeed what happened following the collapse of the Bretton Woods regime.

Being a 'reserve currency' has both advantages and shortcomings. General de Gaulle famously spoke of the 'exorbitant privilege' of the United States of being able to acquire investments abroad with its own currency.[87] However, the position of the pound sterling as a reserve currency became a burden for the UK in the 1960s and 'the instability caused by the sterling balance overhang and the danger of liquidation in fact lay behind each of the major British crises of the second half of the 1960s.'[88]

In recent years, other currencies such as the euro and the Japanese yen have been increasingly used in international transactions and as reserves.

G. The Second Amendment to the IMF Articles of Agreement

In the beginning of the 1970s the par value regime was de facto abandoned. Attempts at repairing the collapsed system, such as the Smithsonian Agreement of 18 December 1971, failed. Speculative pressures in 1972 and 1973 led some members to abandon the fixed exchange rates for their currencies. 'On February 12, 1973, the United States announced that it intended to propose a further devaluation in the par value of the US dollar. This change became effective on October 18, 1973.'[89]

---

[85] See Jeffrey Frankel, entry 'dollar' in edited by Peter Newman, Murray Milgate, and John Eatwell (eds), *Palgrave Dictionary of Money and Finance* (London: Macmillan Press Ltd, 1992).

[86] See Ronald McKinnon, 'Private and Official International Money: The Case for the Dollar', Essays in International Finance, No. 74, Princeton University, Princeton, April 1969.

[87] Polak, above note 81. 'The mythical "advantages" of being a reserve centre are mostly based on a misconception. French President Charles de Gaulle spoke of the "exorbitant privilege of the United States" of being able to acquire investments abroad with its own currency. . . . Both the United Kingdom and the United States have at times felt constrained in the pursuit of domestic monetary policy, by the international "overhang" of foreign holdings of currency that holders might liquidate in their currency markets.'

[88] Above note 25, 186. James also notes (ibid 188) that 'For the Americans the attack on one reserve centre [British sterling] appeared to be a dangerous anticipation of the vulnerability of the other.'

[89] Gold, above note 58, 392.

The worldwide change from fixed to floating exchange rates triggered the second amendment to the IMF's Articles of Agreement, which was adopted on 30 April 1976 and which came into effect on 1 April 1978, allowing members to choose their exchange arrangement and to determine the external value of their currency. Sir Joseph Gold, then General Counsel of the IMF, wrote in 1976:

> On August 15, 1971, the United States, having decided to free itself from certain constraints that had become unacceptable and to exercise greater autonomy for national policies, suspended the convertibility into gold or other reserve assets of balances of US Dollars held by the monetary authorities of the other members of the Fund. This action made it clear that certain fundamental assumptions on which the Articles had been agreed at the Bretton Woods conference in July 1944 were now disputable or even untenable. In due course, the Committee of Board of Governors of the Fund on Reform of the International Monetary System and Related Issues (the Committee of Twenty) . . . was appointed to negotiate reform of the International Monetary System. . . . On March 31, 1976, the Executive Board agreed on the modifications of the Articles that it would recommend, and sent to the Board of Governors a Report entitled 'Proposed Second Amendment to the Articles of Agreement of the International Monetary Fund'. The Board of Governors approved the proposed second amendment on April 30, 1976.[90]

The Second Amendment sanctioned *de jure* what was already the actual behaviour of the IMF member states.

The key amendment was Article IV, concerning the 'obligations regarding exchange arrangements', which I further discuss in Chapter 13. The new Article IV, section 2(b), which allows members freely to choose their exchange arrangement, reads as follows:

> Under an international monetary system of the kind prevailing on January 1, 1976, exchange arrangements may include (i) the maintenance by a member of a value for its currency in terms of the special drawing right or another denominator, other than gold, selected by the member or (ii) cooperative arrangements by which members maintain the value of their currencies in relation to the value of the currency or currencies of other members or (iii) other exchange arrangements of a member's choice.

Since the entry into force of the Second Amendment, the Fund has had no substantive legal rights with respect to the choice of exchange rate arrangements of its members. Members, though, must behave in the manner prescribed by the amended Articles. However, the obligations of Article IV, section 1, are rather generic in their formulation ('endeavour to . . .', 'seek to promote . . .'), with the exception of Article IV, section 1(iii), which specifically requests members to

---

[90] See Joseph Gold, 'A Report on Certain Legal Developments in the International Monetary Fund' published by the World Association of Lawyers, Washington DC (1976) 1–4.

'avoid manipulating exchange rates . . . to gain an unfair competitive advantage over other members'.

Nonetheless, Sweden flouted this 'specific' obligation in 1982, when Prime Minister Olaf Palme announced a devaluation of the Swedish krona by sixteen per cent to improve conditions for Swedish industry. The IMF Executive Board, following the complaints of the other Nordic countries that Sweden was seeking an unfair advantage, met to discuss Sweden's action, but took no specific formal decision nor imposed any sanction against Sweden.[91]

The Second Amendment places the functions of surveillance at the centre of the Fund's activities.[92] From being a virtually self-enforcing arrangement, surveillance now becomes a function in which judgement is of the essence.[93] According to Article IV, section 3(a),

> The Fund shall oversee the international monetary system in order to ensure its effective operation, and shall oversee the compliance of each member with its obligations under Section 1 of this Article.

Article IV, section 3(b) further states:

> [T]he Fund shall exercise firm surveillance over the exchange rate policies of members, and shall adopt specific principles for the guidance of all members with respect to those policies.[94]

The members are obliged to cooperate with the Fund by supplying all the information necessary to allow the Fund to perform effective bilateral surveillance. Apart from the changes inherent in the adoption of flexible exchange rates, surveillance of national policies becomes more complex when countries embark on programmes of trade and financial liberalization, as I further discuss in Chapter 13. The opening up of the economy raises important challenges and sets into motion a process of regulatory reform.

The choice of exchange regime in the absence of an international legal obligation to 'maintain' exchange rate stability[95]

Countries face a wide variety of options regarding the choice of exchange regime, since they are under no international legal obligation to 'maintain' a

---

[91] The incident is recalled by Lowenfeld, above note 5, 536–7.

[92] The function of surveillance is further discussed in Ch 13.

[93] See Manuel Guitián, 'The IMF as a Monetary Institution: The Challenge Ahead', Finance and Development, September 1991, 38.

[94] On 29 April 1977, the Fund adopted a decision entitled Surveillance over Exchange Rate Policies, which I further refer to in Ch 13.

[95] See Charles Proctor, *Mann on the Legal Aspect of Money* (Oxford: Oxford University Press, 2005) 564: 'A clearly defined and self-standing legal duty to maintain stable currencies [stability of exchange rates] does not at present exist'. With regard to the lack of an legal obligation to

given exchange rate or exchange regime. A country can let market forces determine the exchange rate (flexible rates, freely floating according to market discipline) or can control its exchange rate through some form of official rules. Countries can achieve the fixity of rates through the establishment of a common central bank, by adopting a common monetary standard (eg, the gold standard), or through some other monetary arrangement (eg, a currency board). However, according to Sam Cross, 'fixity' is a thing that either you have or you do not. It is a matter of 'yes or no', and not a 'matter of degree'. 'There seems to be a kind of Murphy's law of exchange markets, which says that any exchange rate that can change eventually will change and that there are speculators who will bet that way.'[96]

The reality of exchange markets is that exchange rates do fluctuate. Under a system of flexible exchange rates, such variations (appreciation or depreciation of the currency vis-à-vis other currencies) are triggered by market forces. Under a system of government controlled exchange rates, such variations (devaluation or revaluation) are officially imposed decisions.[97] According to Gold: 'These formal distinctions [pegged or floating currencies] may be misleading. The exchange rate for a floating currency may be managed in order to make it hover more or less around a desired level. The peg for a pegged currency may be changed so often that the exchange rate fluctuates almost as much as one that floats.'[98]

---

maintain exchange rate stability, is is worth considering the following observations by Sir Joseph Gold, 'A Third Report on Some Recent Legal Developments in the International Monetary Fund' published by the World Association of Lawyers, Washington DC (1978) 7–8:

> Under the Second Amendment, the Fund has clear authority to concern itself with the domestic policies of members because only orderly underlying conditions can promote a system of stable exchange rates. *The objective, however, is not exchange stability,* because the accusation is made that it did degenerate into exchange rigidity, *but a stable system of exchange rates. Stability is not incompatible with flexible exchange rate arrangements* provided that a member's policies produce orderly underlying conditions (italics added).

[96] See Sam Cross, 'Thoughts on the International Monetary System and the Future of the IMF', Background paper prepared for the Bretton Woods Commission, 'Bretton Woods: Looking into the Future', Washington DC, April 1994, C–34. Cross also points out that there is an element of contradiction in the phrase 'fixed but adjustable' or any 'fixed-but formula' since they are 'fixed but not fixed' arrangements, and, in terms of market credibility, they become not-fixed.

[97] For a legal interpretation of the notions of 'depreciation' and 'devaluation' see Proctor, above note 95, 504–6. Proctor differentiates between the (nominal) par of exchange and the (real) rate of exchange (ibid 469–75). The former—of virtually no modern significance since the collapse of the Bretton Woods regime—is 'the equation between two money units, each based on a fixed standard'. 'The par of exchange is independent of the rate of exchange of the day' (ibid 470). The (real) rate of exchange refers to the market rate or commercial rate of exchange. The most frequently quoted rate of exchange is the spot rate though more sophisticated contracts often involve a forward exchange rate.

[98] Above note 90, 8.

Pegging is often used as a policy tool of stabilization. The credibility of the 'peg' is conditional upon the rules adopted by the countries under a bilateral or multilateral pegging arrangement. Two historical examples of multilateral pegging are the Bretton Woods regime and the experience of the Exchange Rate Mechanism of the European Monetary System before the advent of EMU. As for bilateral pegging there are multiple examples in Asia and Latin America.[99]

A government can peg its exchange rate to a single currency or to a basket of currencies, let the rate 'crawl', adopt a dual exchange rate (eg, a fixed rate for current account transactions and a floating rate for capital account transactions), or conduct a managed float. Target zones suggest that exchange rates can vary within given bands (narrow or wide, soft or hard).[100] There is a strong body of economic analysis and theory that believes that an intermediate regime, with some kind of peg, is unsustainable under conditions of free capital movements (the 'Walters critique' of all pegged but adjustable exchange rates).[101] Following the experience of the ERM in 1992 and 1993, that viewpoint is widely shared. If one cannot easily maintain a peg, then the alternatives are either a fixed rate system or a relatively free floating one.

Some economists, such as Steve Hanke, differentiate between pegged and fixed exchange rates.[102] Pegged rates (adjustable pegs, bands, crawling pegs, managed floats, etc) require the monetary authority to manage the exchange rate and monetary policy simultaneously. With a fixed rate, a monetary authority sets the exchange rate, but has no monetary policy. The same actually happens with a 'clean' floating, when the monetary authority sets only monetary policy, but leaves the determination of the exchange rate to market forces. Hanke points out that if a country adopts a fixed exchange rate regime such as an orthodox currency board or official dollarization, it must give up its autonomy

---

[99] See Giorgia Giovannetti, entry 'pegged exchange rates' in Peter Newman, Murray Milgate, and John Eatwell (eds), *Palgrave Dictionary of Money and Finance* (London: Macmillan Press Ltd, 1992).

[100] See generally Jacob Frenkel and Morris Goldstein, 'A Guide to Target Zones', IMF Staff Papers No 33, December 1996. The terms 'hard' and 'soft' are used to distinguish bands that must never be breached from bands that may be breached occasionally. Bands may be 'loud' or 'quiet' in that they are known to market participants also or known only to the government involved.

[101] See entry 'Walters' critique' (written by Alan Walters himself) in Peter Newman, Murray Milgate, and John Eatwell (eds), *Palgrave Dictionary of Money and Finance* (London: Macmillan Press Ltd, 1992). See also Alan Walters, *Sterling in Danger: The Economic Consequences of Pegged Exchange Rates* (London: Institute of Economic Affairs, 1986).

[102] See Steve H Hanke, Statement, International Economic and Exchange Rate Policy Hearings, before the Banking, Housing, and Urban Affairs Committee of the United States Senate, 1 May 2002.

in monetary policy. If a country has a pegged exchange rate it must restrict capital mobility to avoid balance of payments and currency crises.[103]

Whether a country should fix the external value of its currency to another currency (or to a basket of currencies) or whether it should let it be freely determined in the foreign exchange market is a hotly debated issue in the economic literature.[104] The case for floating exchange rates was clearly made by Milton Friedman in his seminal paper 'The Case for Flexible Exchange Rates'.[105]

Exchange rate stability remains something to be 'promoted' according to Article I of the IMF Articles of Agreement, but there is no international legal obligation to 'maintain' exchange rate stability.[106]

H. Conclusions

This chapter—bringing together legal, economic, and political considerations—has analysed the history of international monetary cooperation in the twentieth century. The Bretton Woods institutions created in 1944 have survived the passage of time, though the role of the IMF has been substantially altered with the abandonment of the par value regime at the beginning of the 1970s and the worldwide change from fixed to floating exchange rates.

At the international level, there is no central authority with the ability to issue a 'global currency' (Keynes's proposal in this regard was rejected). Since it is highly unlikely that such a world authority will emerge in the near future (or that the IMF will be entrusted with such a role), one has to conclude that the supply of currencies at an international level will remain a competitive business, even though regional currency blocs are likely to emerge. Indeed, this is the case already with the eurozone.

Though the International Monetary Fund was conceived as an international monetary institution (and such a feature remains part of its idiosyncrasy), its role has expanded over the years, as I further discuss in Chapters 13 and 14. The challenges faced by the institution have changed over the years: stabilization in the late 1940s; convertibility in the 1950s; liquidity in the 1960s; flexibility in the 1970s with the abandonment of the par value regime and the new economic

---

[103] ibid.
[104] See generally Peter B Kenen, *Managing Exchange Rates* (London: Routledge, 1988).
[105] Milton Friedman, 'The Case for Flexible Exchange Rates', *Essays in Positive Economics* (Chicago: University of Chicago Press, 1953).
[106] Above note 95.

circumstances; international debt crises in the 1980s; transition to a market economy in the former communist countries in the beginning of the 1990s; financial crises is South-East Asia, Russia, Brazil, and elsewhere in the late 1990s and the beginning of the twenty-first century. The IMF has become an international financial institution (IFI) dealing with a wide variety of financial issues: financial reform, capital markets, financial crises, financial stability.

As we move into the second part of the first decade of the twenty-first century, the words of Henry Morgenthau, in the opening remarks at the 1944 Bretton Woods conference still resonate. Indeed, they seem appropriate to describe the challenges that the IMF and the international community currently face and are likely to face in years to come:

> Prosperity has no fixed limits. It is not a finite substance to be diminished by division. On the contrary the more of it that other nations enjoy, the more each nation will have for itself . . . *Prosperity like peace is indivisible.* We cannot afford to have it scattered here or there among the fortunate or to enjoy it at the expense of others. Poverty, where it exists, is menacing to us all and undermines the well-being of each of us. It can no more be localized than war. (italics added)[107]

---

[107] Address by Henry Morgenthau Jr (US Treasury Secretary and Permanent Secretary of the Conference) at the Inaugural Plenary Session, 1 July 1944, *United Nations Monetary and Financial Conference, Bretton Woods, New Hampshire, July 1 to July 22, 1944: Final Act and Related Documents* (Washington DC: US Government Printing Office, 1944).

THE LAW OF THE INTERNATIONAL
MONETARY FUND

International Monetary Law in a sufficiently comprehensive and systematic form to justify recognition of it as a separate province of public international law came into existence on December 27, 1945.

> Joseph Gold, 'Gold in International Monetary Law: Change, Uncertainty and Ambiguity' (1981) 15 The Journal of International Law and Economics 323.

A. Introduction

It is fitting to start this chapter on the law of the IMF with some words by the late Sir Joseph Gold,[1] since his writings have greatly contributed to the development of the public international law of money and have acted as a source of inspiration for many legal scholars specializing in this field.[2]

The law of the IMF must be analysed in the context of its Articles of Agreement, its By-Laws, Rules, and Regulations and the decisions, interpretations, and resolutions of the Executive Board and the Board of Governors of the International Monetary Fund.[3]

The Articles of Agreement of the IMF were adopted at the United Nations Monetary and Financial Conference, Bretton Woods, New Hampshire, on 22 July 1944 and entered into force on 27 December 1945. They are the constitutional charter of the IMF. They have been amended three times. (An

---

[1] I had the privilege of getting to know Sir Joseph Gold in Washington DC in 1992–3, when I was working as a consultant in the legal department of the IMF. He impressed me as a great thinker, a great lawyer, and a great person. Sir Joseph Gold had joined the Legal Department of the International Monetary Fund in 1946 and served as the Fund's General Counsel from 1960 until 1979 when he retired from active service to become Senior Consultant. He died in the year 2000. Sir Joseph Gold was the main draftsman of the First and Second Amendments to the IMF Articles of Agreement and a prolific writer.

[2] Public international monetary law is still a rather novel legal field. Recent references include: Dominique Carreau and Patrick Juillard, *Droit International Economique* (Paris: Dalloz, 2003) paras 1453–514; Andreas Lowenfeld, *International Economic Law* (Oxford: Oxford University Press, 2002) chs 16–17; Charles Proctor, *Mann on the Legal Aspect of Money*, 6th edn (Oxford: Oxford University Press, 2005) chs 19–23 (in particular, ch 22); and the following contributions by François Gianviti: (i) 'Evolving Role and Challenges for the International Monetary Fund' in Mads Andenas and Joseph Norton (eds), *International Monetary and Financial Law Upon Entering the New Millenium. A Tribute to Sir Joseph and Ruth Gold* (London: The British Institute of International and Comparative Law, 2002), 29–70, (ii) 'The International Monetary Fund and the International Monetary System. Decision Making in the International Monetary Fund' in *Current Developments in Monetary and Financial Law* (Washington DC: IMF, 1999) 31–67, (iii) 'The Reform of the International Monetary Fund (Conditionality and Surveillance)' in Rosa M Lastra (ed), *The Reform of the International Financial Architecture* (London: Kluwer Law International, 2001), 93–106.

[3] A volume on 'Selected Decisions and Selected Documents of the International Monetary Fund' is published annually. The 29th issue, updated as of 30 June 2005, is available at <http://www.imf.org/external/pubs/ft/sd/index.asp>.

amendment, which must be approved by the Board of Governors, becomes effective when it is ratified by three-fifths of the members, having eighty-five per cent of the total voting power).[4] The First Amendment, approved by the Board of Governors in Resolution No 23–5, adopted on 31 May 1968 and effective 28 July 1969, established the Special Drawing Rights (SDRs) account in the Fund, provided for the allocation of SDRs, and improved the characteristics of the 'gold tranche' as a reserve asset. The Second Amendment, approved by the Board of Governors in Resolution No 31–4, adopted on 30 April 1976 and effective 1 April 1978, dealt mostly with the reform of the international monetary system following the worldwide shift from fixed to floating exchange rates. The Second Amendment also modified and expanded the role of the SDR and reduced the role of gold in the international monetary system. The Third Amendment, approved by the Board of Governors in Resolution No 45–3, adopted on 28 June 1990 and effective 11 November 1992, provided for the suspension of voting and related rights of members that do not fulfil their obligations under the Articles of Agreement. There has been a fourth proposed amendment, which was approved by the Board of Governors in 1997 but which has not been ratified yet by the required majority of members, which addresses the allocation of SDRs.[5]

This chapter aims to explain in clear language the workings of the Fund, its organization and functions.[6] It focuses on issues of public international monetary law (where states are the main actors and sovereign relations are to be considered), leaving aside specific questions of private international monetary law (conflict of laws, involving the contractual obligations and relations of private parties—natural or juridical persons—residing in different states).[7] The boundaries between the two are not always clearly defined though. There are 'shades of grey' and areas of intersection. Some issues belong to the private law arena to start with and then turn into public law issues. For example, the problems associated with the insolvency of a bank with cross-border establishments and its default on individual contractual obligations can eventually lead

---

[4] See Art XXVIII, s (a) of the IMF Articles of Agreement.

[5] See Jacques J Polak, 'Streamlining the Financial Architecture of the International Monetary Fund', Princeton Essays in International Finance No 216, September 1999, 24–5.

[6] Regular information on the Fund can be obtained from the IMF's website <http://www.imf.org>, the Annual Report, the bi-weekly survey, fact sheets, pamphlets, and other publications.

[7] For a recent study of such private international law issues and the private law of monetary obligations see Charles Proctor, *Mann on the Legal Aspect of Money*, 6th edn (Oxford: Oxford University Press), in particular chs 4, 13, 15, and 16. Ch 4 considers monetary obligations and the conflict of laws. Chapter 13 further elaborates upon a number of private international law questions and the role of the law of the currency (*lex monetae*). Ch 15 explores in detail the consequences of Art VIII(2)(b) of the IMF Articles of Agreement in proceedings before domestic courts. Ch 16 studies the private international law of exchange control.

to a sovereign debt crisis with external debt and external payments problems. In a way the private–public divide in the legal field resembles the micro–macro divide in the economic field.[8]

B. The Role and Purposes of the IMF

The International Monetary Fund, the international monetary institution par excellence, is a cooperative intergovernmental organization which comprises 184 members (as of 2005). The objectives of the IMF, which are to guide all its policies and decisions, are defined in Article I of its Articles of Agreement:

> (i) To promote international monetary cooperation through a permanent institution which provides the machinery for consultation and collaboration on international monetary problems.
>
> (ii) To facilitate the expansion and balanced growth of international trade, and to contribute thereby to the promotion and maintenance of high levels of employment and real income and to the development of productive resources of all members as primary objectives of economic policy.
>
> (iii) To promote exchange rate stability, to maintain orderly exchange arrangements among members, and to avoid competitive exchange depreciation.
>
> (iv) To assist in the establishment of multilateral system of payments in respect of current transactions between members and in the elimination of foreign exchange restrictions which hamper the growth of world trade.
>
> (v) To give confidence to members by making the Fund's resources available to them under adequate safeguards, thus providing them with the opportunity to correct maladjustments in their balance of payments without resorting to measures destructive of national or international prosperity.
>
> (vi) In accordance with the above, to shorten the duration and lessen the degree of disequilibrium in the international balances of payments of members.

This broad enumeration of goals has allowed the institution to survive over the years, adjusting and readjusting its role in response to diverse economic circumstances. The worldwide change from fixed to floating exchange rates, following the collapse of the par value regime, also signified a more profound change in the nature of the IMF. There has been a shift in emphasis from being primarily an international monetary institution focusing on issues such as exchange rate stability and convertibility, to becoming an international financial institution with a broader array of responsibilities, encompassing not only monetary issues,

---

[8] With regard to the distinction between microeconomics and macroeconomics, Dornbusch and Fischer state: 'The economy in the aggregate is nothing but the sum of its submarkets. The difference between microeconomics and macroeconomics is, therefore, primarily one of emphasis and exposition.' See Rudiger Dornbusch and Stanley Fischer, *Macroeconomics*, 5th edn (Singapore: McGraw-Hill, 1990) 4.

but also other financial issues, such as the regulation and supervision of banking and capital markets, financial reform, debt restructuring and others.

The Fund played a leading role in the sovereign debt restructuring of the less developed countries (LDC) in the 1980s (a financial role), in the transition to market economies of formerly communist countries (a financial and advisory role), and in the financial crises in the 1990s (a financial role).

These changes have undoubtedly influenced the work of the Fund and, in particular, the way it carries out its main functions: surveillance, conditional financial support, and technical assistance. Surveillance these days focuses as much on financial sector policies, including the regulation and supervision of banks and other financial institutions, as it does on macroeconomic policies. Financial assistance to members experiencing balance of payments difficulties is often made conditional upon the fulfilment of some financial sector policy or objective (in addition to macroeconomic considerations). Technical assistance in banking and financial regulation has been one of the areas where the Fund has been most active in recent years. I further discuss below the changing nature of the Fund's responsibilities.

C. Organizational Issues

Membership

Article II of the IMF Articles of Agreement deals with 'Membership'. Section 1 of that Article specifies that the 'original members' were the countries represented at the Bretton Woods conference, whose governments accepted membership before 31 December 1945 (the former Soviet Union was represented at the Bretton Woods conference but declined to become a signatory to the agreements, as I explained in Chapter 12).

Section 2 of Article II specifies that 'membership shall be open to other countries', thus restricting membership to sovereign nation states.[9] I discussed in Chapter 11 the limitation of this approach in terms of the representation of

---

[9] Though the notion of state has no absolute fixed meaning, the IMF has generally considered that a country in formal control of its external relations can be eligible for IMF membership. In this respect, the Republica di San Marino became a member in September 1992. I was working at the IMF Legal Department at the time and wrote a note (earlier that year) on the issue of whether San Marino could be considered a country for the purposes of IMF membership. Based on the documents I examined, such as the agreement of cooperation with the EEC, the statute of the International Court of Justice (whose Art 34(1) says that only states may be parties in cases before the Court) and the Charter of the United Nations, my conclusion was that San Marino was a country, eligible for IMF membership.

the European Central Bank and the interests of the eurozone in the IMF. The IMF accepts members regardless of their political system and human rights record. Democracy is not a requirement to become (or to remain) a member of the Fund.

The Articles of Agreement consider the possibility of 'withdrawal from membership' in Article XXVI. Section 1 deals with the 'right of member of members to withdraw'. There have been three instances of voluntary withdrawal: Poland (1950), Cuba (1964), and Indonesia (1965).[10] Section 2 deals with 'compulsory withdrawal'. If a member fails to fulfil its obligations under the Agreement, the Fund will first declare the member 'ineligible to use its general resources'. If the member persists in its failure then the Fund may (by a seventy per cent majority of the voting power) suspend the voting rights of the member, and, eventually, require the member to withdraw from membership. There has been only one case of compulsory withdrawal: Czechoslovakia (1954).

Management

Article XII of the IMF Articles of Agreement deals with 'organization and management'. The decision-making organs of the International Monetary Fund are the Board of Governors, the Executive Board, and the Managing Director.[11] Gianviti compares this structure to that of a company, with its shareholders' meetings, board of directors, and chairman of the board.[12]

The Board of Governors of the IMF consists of one Governor and one alternate Governor appointed by each member country.[13] The Board of Governors normally meets once a year at the IMF–World Bank Annual Meetings. Resolutions by the Board of Governors may be adopted during meetings of the Board of Governors or by letter.[14]

Article XII, section (2)(j) confers upon the Board of Governors and the Executive Board the power to appoint 'committee as they deem advisable'. On 2 October

---

[10] I thank Sean Hagan for observations on this point.

[11] Article XII, s 2 is about the Board of Governors, s 3 is about the Executive Board, and s 4 is about the IMF Managing Director and staff. Article XII, s 1 foresees the possibility of establishing a Council by a decision of the Board of Governors. However, this Council has never been established. For an excellent legal analysis of the decision-making organs and the decision-making process in the Fund, see François Gianviti, 'The International Monetary Fund and the International Monetary System. Decision Making in the International Monetary Fund', above note 2.

[12] See François Gianviti, 'The International Monetary Fund and the International Monetary System. Decision Making in the International Monetary Fund', above note 2, 39. This is a comprehensive study of the legal framework within which the organs of the Fund must operate. The decision-making process is analysed in depth on pages 50–63.

[13] See <http://www.imf.org/external/np/sec/memdir/members.htm>.

[14] Gianviti, above note 12, 39.

1974, the Board of Governors established the Interim Committee of the Board of Governors on the International Monetary System and the Joint Ministerial Committee of the Board of Governors of the Bank and the Fund on the Transfer of Real Resources to Developing Countries. In September 1999, the Interim Committee was renamed as the International Monetary and Financial Committee or IMFC (made up of twenty-four of the Governors who meet twice a year). The Joint Ministerial Committee of the Board of Governors of the Bank and the Fund on the Transfer of Real Resources to Developing Countries was renamed as the IMF–World Bank Development Committee.

The day-to-day work of the Fund is conducted at its Washington DC headquarters by its Executive Board. The Board of Governors at its first meeting in 1946 made a broad delegation of powers to the Executive Board, in accordance with the possibility foreseen in Article XII, section 2(b). According to the current text of section 15 of the IMF's By-Laws: 'The Executive Board is authorised by the Board of Governors to exercise all the powers of the Board of Governors, except for those conferred directly by the Articles of Agreement on the Board of Governors.'[15] The work of the Executive Board is guided by the IMFC and supported by the Fund's professional staff. The Executive Board usually meets three times a week, in full-day sessions, and more often if needed, at the organization's headquarters in Washington DC.[16] The member countries select the Executive Directors who form the Executive Board (currently twenty-four Directors). The IMF's five largest shareholders—the United States, Japan, Germany, France, and the United Kingdom—along with China, Russia, and Saudi Arabia, appoint their own Executive Directors (ie, each of these countries has its own 'seat' on the Board). The other sixteen Executive Directors are elected for two-year terms by groups of countries, known as 'constituencies'.[17]

The decisions adopted by the Executive Board must be consistent with the provisions of the Articles and the resolutions of the Board of Governors. The members of the Executive Board have a fiduciary duty to the IMF in the discharge of their obligations (which means that they would be in breach of that duty if they disregarded their obligations to the IMF and acted in accordance with instructions received from their countries or constituencies).[18]

The Executive Board selects the Managing Director, who serves as Chairman of

---

[15] ibid 40.

[16] This is in accordance with Art XII, s 3(a) and s 3(g). s 3(g) states that 'The Executive Board shall function in continuous session as the principle office of the Fund and shall meet as often as the business of the Fund may require.'

[17] See Art XII, s 3(b). See also <http://www.imf.org/external/pubs/ft/exrp/what.htm>. With regard to the voting procedures, see Art XII, s 5.

[18] These points are made by Gianviti, above note 12, 47.

the Executive Board and as Head of the staff of the IMF.[19] The Managing Director is assisted by three Deputy Managing Directors (Office of the Managing Director). I explained in Chapter 12 the historical circumstances that led to the appointment of a European, and not an American, as the first Managing Director of the IMF, a 'tradition'—not a written rule—which has been rightly criticized in recent years, since the best person for the post should be considered, regardless of nationality.

Both the Managing Director and the staff in the discharge of their functions shall owe their duty entirely to the Fund, and not to national authorities, according to Article XII, section 4(c).[20]

With regard to the internal organization of the Fund, there are several departments, four institutes, offices in Paris, Geneva, Tokyo, and at the United Nations, and resident representatives located in various member countries.[21] Currently there are five 'area departments' (African, Asia and Pacific, European, Middle East and Central Asia, and Western Hemisphere) in addition to the 'functional and special services departments'.[22] The latter include fiscal affairs, policy development and review, monetary and financial systems (previously monetary and exchange affairs and previous to that denomination simply central banking department),[23] research, finance, statistics, and the legal department. The General Counsel[24] and the Legal Department of the IMF perform an important role in advising the Executive Board on the interpretation of the law

---

[19] See Art XII, s 4(a). The Managing Director cannot be a Governor or an Executive Director.

[20] The employees of the IMF are international civil servants. About two thirds of its professional staff are economists. See <http://www.imf.org/external/pubs/ft/exrp/what.htm>.

[21] The Fund's departments and offices are headed by directors, who report to the Managing Director. Most staff work in Washington DC, although some resident representatives are posted in member countries to help advise on economic policy. The IMF maintains offices in Paris and Tokyo for liaison with other international and regional institutions, and with organizations of civil society, and in New York and Geneva for liaison with other institutions in the UN system. See <http://www.imf.org/external/pubs/ft/exrp/what.htm>.

[22] See <http://www.imf.org/external/np.obp.orgcht.htm>.

[23] As I proceed to complete the revisions of this chapter, one new development must be mentioned. On 1 February 2006, the IMF Managing Director (Rodrigo Rato) announced the creation of a new department in mid-2006 which will merge the functions and staff of the existing Monetary and Financial System Department and the International Capital Markets Department. See IMF Press Release No 06/21, available at <http://www.imf.org/external/np/sec/pr/2006/pr0621.htm>.

[24] In addition to the work of Sir Joseph Gold, above note 1, I should also like to mention the contribution made to the development of the law of the IMF by François Gianviti, who was Director of the Legal Department from January 1986 and General Counsel from 1987, until his retirement from the IMF in December 2004. Gianviti steered the legal work of the institution during the testing times of the late 1980s, through the 1990s, and into the new century. A list of his publications is available at <http://www.imf.org/external/np/bio/eng/fgl.htm>. He has been succeeded as General Counsel by Sean Hagan.

of the Fund.[25] A new 'international capital markets department' was set up in March 2001 to deal with the expanding financial role of the IMF, in particular with regard to crisis prevention and crisis management activities.[26]

With regard to the organizational chart of the IMF,[27] a mention must be made of the Independent Evaluation Office (IEO), which was established by the Executive Board in July 2001.[28] The IEO operates autonomously from IMF management and aims to provide objective and independent assessment of various aspects of the IMF's work.

D. Financial Issues

The various issues related to the finances of the Fund are intricate. They are discussed in part in this section and in part below, when I analyse the financial assistance the Fund provides to its members and the facilities and policies through which financing is made available. These issues are further complicated by the specialized and idiosyncratic terminology that surrounds the Fund's operations.

This section covers subscriptions and quotas (composition, assignment, adjustment), the accounting structure of the Fund (the accounting entities: the General Department, the SDR Department, and the administered accounts), and borrowing by the Fund (powers of the IMF to borrow and the practice in the exercise of those powers).

Quotas and subscriptions

On joining the Fund each member is assigned a quota, which determines its subscription to the capital of the IMF. The quota is an amount calculated by the IMF and expressed in Special Drawing Rights. What the member pays is the

---

[25] See William E Holder, 'On Being a Lawyer in the International Monetary Fund' in Robert Effros (ed), *Current Legal Issues Affecting Central Banks* (Washington DC: IMF, 1998) 14–27. See Art XXIX, s (a) of the IMF Articles of Agreement:

> Any question of interpretation of the provisions of the Agreement arising between any member and the Fund or between any members of the Fund shall be submitted to the Executive Board for its decision.

[26] See IMF News Brief 01/24 of 1 March 2001, at <http://www.imf.org>. See above note 23.

[27] See <http://www.imf.org/external/np.obp.orgcht.htm>.

[28] See <http://www.imf.org/external/np/ieo.index.htm>. At its Spring 2000 Meeting, the International Monetary and Financial Committee (IMFC) endorsed the Executive Board's decision to establish an independent evaluation office (IEO) at the Fund as a means to enhance the learning culture within the Fund, help build the Fund's external credibility, promote a greater understanding of the work of the Fund, and support the Executive Board's institutional governance and oversight responsibilities.

subscription.[29] The subscription has to be equal to the quota, that is, fully paid up before membership becomes effective. Article III, section 1 of the Articles of Agreement states:

> Each member shall be assigned a quota expressed in special drawing rights. . . . The subscription of each member shall be equal to its quota.

Countries pay an amount not exceeding twenty-five per cent of the quota in Special Drawing Rights or currencies specified by the Fund,[30] and the rest in the member's own currency.[31] The first twenty-five per cent segment is the reserve asset portion. The remainder is the non-reserve asset portion. Payment of the non-reserve asset portion of the quota subscription is normally made in the form of promissory notes or by crediting the Fund's account with the member's central bank.[32]

A country that provides reserve assets to the IMF as part of its quota subscription receives a liquid claim on the IMF ('reserve tranche position') which is made instantly available to obtain reserve assets to meet a balance of payments financing need.[33] Reserve tranche positions are on the one hand a part of the Fund's resources (monetary liabilities) and also part of the members' international reserve assets.[34] The 'reserve tranche position' is equivalent to the amount by which the the member's quota exceeds the IMF's holdings of the member's currency.[35] In making the reserve asset portion of their quota payment, members acquire a liquid claim on the IMF.

> The reserve tranche can be considered a 'facility of first resort'. It stands apart from the credit tranches and the various facilities in that a member's reserve tranche position is part of its own foreign exchange reserves. Purchases in the reserve tranche do not therefore constitute use of IMF credit. . . . Reserve tranche

---

[29] See François Gianviti, above note 12, 38. See also Norman Humphreys, *Historical Dictionary of the International Monetary Fund*, 2nd edn (Maryland and London: The Scarecrow Press, 1999), entry 'Subscriptions to the Fund'.

[30] Prior to the Second Amendment the reserve asset portion of the quota was paid in gold.

[31] See Art III, s 3(a). See also Decision No 6266 (79/156) of 10 September 1979, 'Guidelines on Payment of Reserve Assets in Connection with Subscriptions', published in *Selected Decisions of the International Monetary Fund*, 17th issue (Washington DC: IMF, 1992). See also François Gianviti, 'Developments at the International Monetary Fund', in Robert Effros (ed), *Current Legal Issues Affecting Central Banks* (Washington DC: IMF, 1997) 6.

[32] See 'Financial Organization and Operations of the IMF', Pamphlet Series No 45, 6th edn (Washington DC: IMF, 2001), <http://www.imf.org/external/pubs/ft/pam/pa,45/contents.htm>, 19–20.

[33] ibid 21.

[34] IMF, 'Financial Risk in the Fund and the Level of Precautionary Balances', prepared by the Finance Department (in consultation with other departments), approved by Eduard Brau, 3 February, 2004 <http://www.imf.org/external/np/tre/risk/2004/020304.pdf> 7.

[35] See IMF, 'Glossary of Selected Financial Terms' <http://www.imf.org>.

purchases are not subject to conditionality, charges or repurchase expectations and obligations.[36]

A 'freely usable currency' is one that the IMF determines is widely used to make payments for international transactions and is traded in the principal exchange markets.[37] The euro, Japanese yen, pound sterling, and US dollar are classified as freely usable currencies. A freely usable currency serves as a reserve asset, though freely usable currencies are not the only ones regarded as reserve assets.

The sum of all the quotas represents the capital base of the Fund. Quotas are the primary source of IMF resources. The quotas form a pool of money that the Fund can draw from to provide financing to members in balance of payment difficulties, as I explain below. A member's share of general SDR allocations is established in proportion to its quota. Quotas are also the basis for determining how much a country can 'borrow' (draw) from the Fund and they determine their voting rights. Unlike some international organizations that operate under a one-country-one-vote principle (such as the United Nations General Assembly), the IMF has a weighted voting system: the larger a country's quota in the IMF the more votes it has. With regard to the voting procedures, since most decisions of the Fund require seventy per cent or eighty-five per cent of the voting power, these 'super majorities' give a de facto veto to countries with large quotas, such as the USA.

The formula for the determination of the quotas, first introduced by Raymond Mikesell,[38] has been criticized for being a rather 'unscientific exercise', and for

---

[36] Above note 32, 66. Art XXX(c) defines 'reserve tranche purchase' as a 'purchase by a member of special drawing rights or the currency of another member in exchange for its own currency, which does not cause the Fund's holdings of the member's currency in the General Resources Account to exceed its quota'.

[37] Article XXX (f):

A freely usable currency means a member's currency that the Fund determines (i) is, in fact, widely used to make payments for international transactions, and (ii) is widely traded in the principal exchange markets.

The concept of 'freely usable currency' is relevant for some purposes such as the convertibility of amounts purchased by the Fund; the concept of 'usable currency' is relevant for the selection of currencies disbursed or received by the Fund under the Financial Transactions Plan.

[38] See eg, Ariel Buira, 'Reflections on the International Monetary System', *Princeton Essays in International Finance*, No 195, January 1995, 31–3. Buira quotes Mikesell, who had been asked by the US Treasury to estimate the first quotas:

In mid-April 1943, White called me [ie, Mikesell] to his office and asked that I prepare a formula for the quotas that would be based on the members' gold and dollar holdings, national incomes, and foreign trade. He gave no instructions on the weights to be used but I was to give the United States a quota of approximately $2.9 billion, the United Kingdom (including its colonies) about half the US quota; the Soviet Union, an amount just under the United Kingdom; and China somewhat less. He [White] also wanted the total of the quotas to be about $10 billion. White's major concern was that our military allies (President

being influenced by political considerations.[39] A member's quota is broadly based on its relative size in the world economy, determined by various economic factors, including GDP, current account transactions, and official reserves. The richer the country, the higher the quota, with the US being allocated the largest quota. In response to the widespread dissatisfaction with the formulae used to determine the quotas, the IMF established in 1999 an external panel of independent experts, the Quota Formula Review Group, chaired by Professor Richard Cooper.[40] The report of the panel was presented to the Executive Board and published on the IMF's website.[41] However, no formal change was introduced to the way the quotas are determined.

Article III, section 2(a) deals with the 'adjustment' of quotas, a procedure which can take place at intervals of no more than five years, following a 'general review' of quotas by the Board of Governors. There have been twelve 'General Reviews of quotas' in the history of the Fund so far, with the Twelfth General Review taking place in January 2003,[42] with no proposal by the Board of Governors to increase the quota. Any change in quotas (to increase them) requires a majority of eighty-five per cent of the total voting power. There are two main issues addressed in a 'general review': the size of a possible overall increase and the distribution of the increase among the members. There were increases in quotas following reviews in 1958–9, 1965, 1970, 1976, 1978, 1983, and 1998. The Eleventh General Review (in 1998) was the last time that an increase in quotas was proposed. The period of the Thirteenth General Review began after the conclusion of the Twelfth Review and is to be completed by 30 January 2008.[43]

There are also 'ad hoc' adjustments of quotas outside the context of the General

---

Roosevelt's Big Four) should have the largest quotas. . . . Had there been reasonably good official national-income estimates for the major countries in 1943, it might not have been possible for me to approximate White's conditions. . . . I confess to having exercised a certain amount of freedom in making these estimates in order to achieve the predetermined quotas. . . . The final formula for determining the quotas was 2 percent of national income, 5 percent of gold and dollar holdings, 10 percent of average imports, 10 percent of the maximum variation in exports, and these three percentages increased by the percentage ratio of average exports to national income.

[39] Buira (ibid 33) claims: 'It is certainly understandable that the lack of equity and rationality in the quota criteria continue to cause controversy and mistrust among members today, just as it did fifty years ago.'

[40] Above note 32, 63–4.

[41] See <http://www.img.org/external/np/tre/quota/2000/eng/qfrg/report/index.htm>.

[42] See Draft Report of Executive Directors to the Board of Governors on the Twelfth General Review of Quotas <http://www.imf.org/external/np/tre/quota/2002/eng/111820.htm>. ('There is broad agreement that the Fund must have sufficient resources to fulfil its central role in the international monetary system. However differences of view among members remain on the current and prospective adequacy of the Fund's resource base and the possible need for a quota increase.')

[43] See<http://www.imf.org/external/np/exr/facts/quotas.htm>.

Reviews;[44] for instance, in the case of China in 2001 and of Saudi Arabia in 1981.[45]

Total quotas in February 2005 were SDR 213 billion (about $327 billion).[46]

Financial structure

The IMF operates its financial functions through three separate accounting entities: the General Department, the SDR Department, and the Administered Accounts. These accounting entities are not organizational units; the division between the General Department and the SDR Department (Arts XVI and XXI of the Articles of Agreement) is an accounting division. The financial functions of the IMF are discharged by the Finance Department (known as the Treasurer's Department until 2003), which is an organizational unit of the Fund.

The IMF publishes an Annual Report containing audited statements of its accounts. The balance sheet of the General Department shows assets and liabilities of the IMF. The assets held in the General Department comprise currencies of members ('usable' and 'nonusable') and the Fund's own holdings of SDRs and gold. The balance sheet of the SDR Department shows assets and liabilities of its participants and other holders of SDRs. Article XVI, section 2 refers to the separation of assets and property of the two departments.

The General Department has three accounts: the General Resources Account (the principal account of the IMF), the Special Disbursement Account (whose resources have been used in the context of the Poverty Reduction and Growth Facility and the Heavily Indebted Poor Countries Initiative, which I further discuss below), and the Investment Account.[47]

The bulk of transactions between member countries and the Fund take place through the General Resources Account (GRA), which is the principal account of the IMF.

Quota subscriptions are the basic source of financing for the GRA. However, not all the currencies are 'usable', which means that the pool of resources available to the Fund from quota subscriptions is not all used for financing. The IMF may supplement its quota resources by borrowing (as I further discuss below) and through additions to its 'precautionary balances'. These precautionary

---

[44] See Art III, s 2(b).   [45] I thank Sean Hagan for observations on this point.

[46] Above note 43.

[47] Above note 32, 19 and 24. The Special Disbursement Account is the vehicle for receiving and investing profits from the sale of the IMF's gold and for making transfers to other accounts for special purposes authorized in the Articles, in particular for financial assistance to low-income members of the IMF. Though the IMF is authorized to establish an Investment Account in the General Department, to date no decision has been made to this effect.

balances consist of reserves in the GRA as well as resources that have been set aside in the so-called first Special Contingent Account (SCA–1) of the GRA to protect against the risk of overdue financial obligations ('arrears') to the IMF. The main source of these precautionary balances is the 'surcharge income' (ie, the rate above the basic rate of charge applicable to some IMF financial facilities such as the Supplemental Reserve Facility).[48]

The resources of the GRA are used in the IMF's regular financing operations, available to all members in case of balance of payments difficulties. 'The Fund's assistance in the GRA is not provided in the form of loans, but rather in the form of exchanges between the requesting member's currency and an equivalent amount of either another member's currency or SDRs. . . . These swaps, which are called "purchases" by the Articles are often referred to as "drawings" in Fund's parlance.'[49]

The extension of regular Fund financing via standby arrangements is often referred to as access to the 'credit tranches', reflecting the notion that IMF credit is traditionally provided in tranches (segments) equivalent to twenty-five per cent of quota.

The Executive Board adopts a 'Financial Transactions Plan' (previously known as the operational budget) for each forthcoming quarter to specify the amounts of SDRs and selected member currencies to be used in purchases and repurchases expected to be conducted through the GRA during that period.[50] The purchase–repurchase technique explains why, from an accounting perspective, the GRA resources do not vary as a result of the IMF's financial assistance, only the composition of its assets changes.[51]

The GRA does not include resources from the Trust Fund, the ESAF (Enhanced Structural Adjustment Facility) Trust, the PRGF (Poverty Reduction and Growth Facility) Trust, and the PRGF–HIPC (Heavily Indebted Poor Countries initiative) Trust. These 'trusts' are 'administered accounts', used in the IMF's concessional lending, which are further discussed below.[52]

The SDR Department (created through the First Amendment) extends unconditional liquidity to its participants.[53] The Fund has the authority to create

---

[48] See IMF, above note 34, 30 and 25–7. The Fund's policy on arrears is discussed in Ch 14.
[49] See François Gianviti, above note 31, 5.
[50] <http://www.imf.org/external/np/exr/glossary/showTerm.asp?term_id=37>.
[51] Above note 32, 24.
[52] With regard to the law of trust funds in international law, see Joseph Gold, 'Trust Funds in International Law: The Contribution of the International Monetary Fund to a Code of Principles' (1978) 72 The American Journal of International Law 856. Gold explains why the technique of a 'trust fund' was employed.
[53] Above note 32, 88–115.

unconditional liquidity through allocations of SDRs to participants in the SDR Department (participation in this Department is voluntary) in proportion to their quotas (Art XV, s 1). The SDR Department is an accounting entity rather than an organizational unit of the Fund's staff and it records and administers transactions in SDRs.

Article XIX, section 5 provides for a 'designation mechanism' for the use of SDRs. Under this mechanism, the IMF 'designates' certain participants, whose external positions are deemed sufficiently strong, to receive specified amounts of SDRs from other participants and, in exchange, to provide the latter with equivalent amounts of freely usable currencies (ie, US dollars, euros, Japanese yen, and pounds sterling). The designation mechanism aims to ensure that in case of need participants can use SDRs to obtain foreign currency reserves at short notice.

The financial structure of the IMF is complex and the different accounts and departments make the understanding of the transactions of the Fund opaque. In the words of Jacques Polak (who was a delegate at the Bretton Woods conference, a senior official of the staff of the IMF, and an Executive Director of the organization), 'the Fund's financial operations are still shrouded in clouds of specialized terminology',[54] thus hindering the transparency of the Fund's activities. 'The Fund must be the only financial organization in the World for which the balance sheet contains no information whatever on the magnitudes of its outstanding credits or of its liquid liabilities.'[55] He further points out that 'the cumulative weight of the Fund's jerry-built structure of financial provisions has meant that almost nobody outside, and indeed few inside, the Fund understand how the organization works, because relatively simple economic relations are buried under increasingly opaque layers of language.'[56] He suggests that 'a number of esoteric terms' such as 'reserve tranche', 'reserve position in the Fund', and others should disappear.

Polak also proposes that the SDR and General Departments be merged into one and that the Articles of Agreement be amended to reflect this. (The Fund is prevented by Art XVI from consolidating the balance sheets of the General and SDR Department.) Polak's proposal, however, has two major flaws. First, it would change the nature of SDRs. At present, SDRs are allocated, not issued, by the Fund. They are not liabilities of the Fund, as I explain below.[57] Secondly,

---

[54] Above note 5, 1.   [55] ibid 2.   [56] ibid.

[57] SDRs are assets of the participants to whom they are allocated, but they are also their liabilities because of the obligation to return them if they are cancelled. If there were a shortfall, the loss would be on the participants, not on the Fund. Merging the two departments (General Department and SDR Department) would relieve the participants of their liabilities and shift them to the Fund without any corresponding assets to cover them.

from a practical point of view, how would the Fund operate without currencies? How would it pay salaries and other expenditure which cannot be discharged in SDRs? How would the Fund provide currencies to members that hold SDRs but cannot use them in payment? This would require a new system in which the Fund would have to turn to its members to receive currencies needed for its operations and transactions not conducted in SDRs. This would place the Fund at the mercy of members who refuse to cooperate, which is the reason why the Fund has not been made dependent on ad hoc contributions from its members and has thus avoided the problems faced, for instance, by the United Nations.

Though the IMF's external website contains information on all the financial activities of the Fund[58] and though IMF financial statements conform to International Accounting Standards, Polak's critique remains generally valid in my opinion (though I do not support his case for the consolidation of the General and SDR Departments for the reasons mentioned above).

Borrowing by the Fund

The 'capital base' of the Fund, that is, the sum of the quota subscriptions, is by definition limited. Since increases in quotas are difficult to negotiate (and an increase might not be sufficient to cope with the needs of members experiencing difficulties), it has become commonplace that the Fund needs to rely upon borrowed resources to supplement its subscribed resources in order to perform its financial functions effectively.

The Fund has the power to borrow under Article VII of the Articles of Agreement.[59]

The first credit lines established by the Fund to supplement its quota-based resources were the General Arrangements to Borrow or GAB. This was an agreement negotiated by the Fund with eight of the major industrial countries (United States, United Kingdom, France, Japan, Italy, Canada, Netherlands, Belgium) and the central banks of two others (Deutsche Bundesbank and Sveriges Riksbank) in 1962.[60] (As acknowledged the G10 or Group of Ten refers to the group of countries that agreed to participate in the General Arrangements to Borrow.) Under this agreement, the members would consider supplementing

---

[58] See <http://www.imf.org/external/fin.htm>. The IMF's website is excellent in my opinion, both in terms of the information it provides and its accessibility. These attributes cannot be predicated of the websites of other organizations, such as the ECB's.

[59] This power is limited to 'any member's currency', thus excluding gold, SDRs, and non-member's currency. See Joseph Gold, 'Borrowing by the IMF' in *International Financial Policy: Essays in Honour of Jacques J Polak* (Washington: IMF and De Nederlandsche Bank, 1991) 185–6.

[60] See Decision of the Executive Board No 1289–(62/1) of 5 January 1962 with effect from 24 October 1962.

the Fund's resources if further resources were necessary in order to finance the transactions of any of them with the Fund.[61] The GAB have been activated ten times since 1964.

The Swiss National Bank became a participant in the GAB with effect from 10 April 1984. Saudi Arabia provided supplementary resources in association with the GAB with effect from 26 December 1983.[62]

Though the General Arrangements to Borrow were conceived as standby arrangements amongst the participant member states and the IMF, in 1983 they were amended to permit the Fund to make calls under the GAB for 'non participant' member states in 'exceptional situations' in which the 'inadequacy' of the Fund's resources could 'threaten the stability of the international monetary system'.[63] Using this authority, in July 1998 the GAB were activated for an amount of SDR 6.3 billion in connection with the financing of an Extended Arrangement for Russia. Of that amount, SDR 1.4 billion was used.[64]

The New Arrangements to Borrow or NAB were set up in 1997[65] with twenty-five participating countries and institutions because of concerns about the adequacy of the existing resources of the Fund to deal with the financing needs of members experiencing financial crises of the magnitude of that in Mexico in 1994–5. All the participants in the GAB became participants in the NAB, together with Australia, Austria, Denmark, Finland, Korea, Kuwait, Luxembourg, Malaysia, Norway, Singapore, Spain, Thailand, and the Hong Kong Monetary Authority.[66] The NAB came into effect in November 1998.

---

[61] Gold explains the background to the introduction of the GAB: 'On February 6, 1961, President Kennedy sent to Congress a special message on the balance of payments of the United States in the course of which he stated that the United States might use the resources of the Fund. This statement encouraged the Fund to place itself in a position to meet a request by the United States under its large quota without reducing the Fund's ability to meet the requests of other members for balance of payments financing.' See Joseph Gold, 'Symmetry as a Legal Objective of the International Monetary System' (1980) 12 International Law and Politics 424.

[62] See Decision of the Executive Board No 7403–(83/73) of 20 May 1983. The association agreement with Saudi Arabia (like the GAB itself) was of a standby character.

[63] See Decision of the Executive Board No 7337–(83/37) of 24 February 1983. Para 21(b), as amended, reads as follows: 'The Managing Director may initiate the procedure . . . if . . . he considers that the Fund faces an inadequacy of resources to meet actual and expected requests for financing that reflect the existence of an exceptional situation associated with balance of payments problems of members of a character or aggregate size that could threaten the stability of the monetary system.'

[64] The activation of the GAB for Russia was cancelled in March 1999, when the Fund repaid the outstanding amount, following the effectiveness of the Eleventh General Review of Quotas and payment of the bulk of the quota increases. See Lowenfeld, above note 2, 558–9 (and n 94).

[65] See Decision of the Executive Board No 11428–(97/60) of 27 January 1997.

[66] The participants in the NAB are: (i) Australia, SDR 801 million; (ii) Austria, SDR 408 million; (iii) Banco Central de Central de Chile (which became a new participant in February 2003), SDR 340 million; (iv) Belgium, SDR 957 million; (v) Canada, SDR 1,381 million;

The line was first activated in the extended arrangement offered to Brazil in December 1998, when the IMF called on funding of SDR 9.1 billion, of which SDR 2.9 billion was used. The activations for both Russia and Brazil were cancelled in March 1999, when the Fund repaid the outstanding amounts following payments of quota increases under the Eleventh General Review of Quotas.[67] The Banco Central de Chile became a new participant in the NAB in February 2003.

Under the GAB and the NAB, the Fund has currently up to SDR 34 billion available to borrow.[68]

In addition to the GAB and the NAB (which are examples of 'joint lending') the Fund has access to other special programmes in connection with its 'special facilities' as I further discuss below.

The power to borrow under Article V, section 2(b) has been used in the creation of concessional facilities.[69] Concessional operations are conducted under administered accounts ('trusts') with the Fund acting in the capacity of 'trustee' of the resources.[70] For instance, the Enhanced Structural Adjustment Facility (ESAF) was introduced in 1987 in the form of a 'trust' to provide loans on concessional terms, 'trust loans'.[71] The ESAF was replaced by the Poverty Reduction and Growth Facility (PRGF) in 1999 (also in the form of a trust). The PRGF aims at making poverty reduction efforts among low-income

---

(vi) Denmark, SDR 367 million; (vii) Deutsche Bundesbank, SDR 3,519 million; (viii) Finland, SDR 340 million; (ix) France, SDR 2,549 million; (x) Hong Kong Monetary Authority, SDR 340 million; (xi) Italy, SDR 1,753 million; (xii) Japan, SDR 3,519 million; (xiii) Korea, SDR 340 million; (xiv) Kuwait, SDR 341 million; (xv) Luxembourg, SDR 340 million; (xvi) Malaysia, SDR 340 million; (xvii) Netherlands, SDR 1,302 million; (xviii) Norway, SDR 379 million; (xix) Saudi Arabia, SDR 1,761 million; (xx) Singapore, SDR 340 million; (xxi) Spain, SDR 665 million; (xxii) Sveriges Riksbank, SDR 850 million; (xxiii) Swiss National Bank, SDR 1,540 million; (xxiv) Thailand, SDR 340 million; (xxv) United Kingdom, SDR 2,549 million; (xxvi) United States, SDR 6,640 million. In November 2002, the NAB decision was renewed for a further period of five years as of November 2003. See IMF, 'IMF Borrowing Arrangements: GAB and NAB: A Factsheet', September 2004, available at <http://www.imf.org/external/np/exr/facts/gabnab.htm>.

[67] See Lowenfeld, above note 2, 559.

[68] <http://www.imf.org> 'What is the International Monetary Fund?' updated 30 July 2004.

[69] See Gold, above note 59, 221–4. Art V, s 2(b) reads as follows:

If requested, the Fund may decide to perform financial and technical services, including the administration of resources contributed by members, that are consistent with the purposes of the Fund. Operations involved in the performance of such services shall not be on the account of the Fund. Services under this subsection shall not impose any obligation on a member without its consent.

[70] See Gold, above note 52.

[71] See Decision No 8757–(87/176)SAF/ESAF and Decision No 8759–(87/176) ESAF of 18 December 1987.

members a key and more explicit element of a renewed growth-oriented economic strategy.[72]

E. Special Drawing Rights

Since the Fund is responsible for the smooth functioning of the international monetary and payment system, it is also concerned about international liquidity, that is, about the level and composition of reserves available to members to meet their trade and payment obligations.[73] As I discussed in Chapter 12, concerns about liquidity in the international monetary system led to the creation of the Special Drawing Rights (SDR) through the First Amendment to the IMF Articles of Agreement, which became effective on 28 July 1969.[74] Though SDRs were created to supplement existing reserve assets, they were only officially recognized as a reserve asset with the Second Amendment.[75]

The Fund can allocate and cancel SDRs to members that participate in the Special Drawing Rights Department (formerly called Special Drawing Account) 'to meet the need, as and when it arises, for a supplement to existing reserve assets'.[76] Though in the 1960s the Fund considered other solutions to deal with the concerns about inadequate reserves and liquidity in the international monetary system (such as the abandonment of the par value regime, or an increase in the price of gold, or general increases in quotas),[77] in the end the creation of official liquidity by the IMF, through the allocation of SDRs, was considered to

---

[72] The IMF Interim Committee endorsed, on 26 September 1999, the replacement of the Enhanced Structural Adjustment Facility (ESAF) by the new Poverty Reduction and Growth Facility (PRGF). The changes to the ESAF Trust Instrument to rename the facility and redefine its purpose were agreed by the Board on 21 October 1999, and became effective on 22 November 1999. See EBS/99/193 (10/14/99) and Supplement 1 (11/22/99), <http://www.imf.org>.

[73] See 'Financial Organization and Operations of the IMF', IMF Pamphlet Series No 45, 2nd edn (Washington DC: IMF, 1991) 2. However, Art I of the Articles of Agreement does not refer specifically to international liquidity.

[74] 'The SDR was created against a background of perceived potential shortage of reserves. . . . The idea was that a mandatory credit line mechanism backed by a large number of participants, in particular the major reserve countries, and based on objective distribution criteria, such as Fund quotas, might assist in supplying the reserves that a growing world economy would require. It was also thought that such a supply of reserves should provide unconditional liquidity rather than conditional credit.' See Reinhard Munzberg, 'Issues Regarding the Special Drawing Right of the International Monetary Fund' in Robert Effros (ed), *Current Legal Issues Affecting Central Banks*, Vol 4 (Washington DC: IMF, 1997) 26.

[75] See François Gianviti, 'Special Drawing Rights' in Robert Effros (ed), *Current Legal Issues Affecting Central Banks*, Vol 5 (Washington DC: IMF, 1998) 1.

[76] Article XV, s 1 IMF Articles of Agreement.

[77] See Joseph Gold, 'Law and Reform of the International Monetary System' (1975) 10 The Journal of International Law and Economics 371, 385–6.

be the most appropriate response to deal with the problem. Article XVIII, section 1(a) explains the rationale for the 'allocation' and 'cancellation' of SDRs in the following terms:

> In all its decisions with respect to the allocation and cancellation of SDRs, the Fund shall seek to meet the long-term global need, as and when it arises, to supplement existing reserve assets in such manner as will promote the attainment of its purposes and will avoid economic stagnation and deflation as well as excess demand and inflation in the world.

Since 1969, the primary sources of international liquidity have been gold, foreign exchange reserves, and allocations of SDRs by the IMF. 'For increases in global reserves, members need rely no longer on the uncertain production and destination of gold and the unwelcome deficits of the issuers of reserve currencies.'[78]

It can be argued that the introduction of the SDR came too late to be able to save the par value regime and did not go far enough to make a considerable impact in the international monetary system.

The value of this synthetic international reserve asset was first determined in terms of gold or its US dollar equivalent, with one SDR equal to the value of the US dollar at its official rate of $35 per ounce. With the abandonment of the par value regime, a new method of valuation was needed. An interim system of valuation on the basis of a composite basket of sixteen currencies was adopted by the Executive Board in 1974.[79] This interim system was replaced in 1980 by a basket of five currencies[80] that determined the value of the SDR: the US dollar, the Japanese yen, the German mark, the French franc, and the British pound. With the introduction of the euro on 1 January 1999, the IMF replaced currency amounts of the German mark and the French franc with equivalent amounts of euros, based on the fixed conversion rates announced on 31 December 1998. The valuation of the SDR is now determined daily on the basis of four currencies: dollar, yen, euro, and pound.

The SDR is the unit of account of the IMF and the SDR interest rate provides the basis for calculating the interest charged on regular IMF financing. However, the use of the SDR is rather restricted. To begin, holders of SDRs are only prescribed holders, such as multinational central banks and other official entities,

---

[78] ibid 386–7.
[79] See IMF Executive Board Decision No 4233–(74/67)S of 13 June 1974. See Andreas Lowenfeld, *International Economic Law* (Oxford: Oxford University Press, 2002) 522.
[80] See IMF Executive Board Decision No 6631–(80/145)G/S of 17 September 1980, which became effective 1 January 1981.

and some international and regional organizations.[81] In addition, the frequency and size of SDR allocations has been rather limited. SDRs were allocated in the period from 1970 to 1972 and from 1979 to 1981.

In an excellent study on the nature of the SDR, Gianviti explains that a country's reserve assets now include four categories: gold, foreign currencies, reserve positions in the Fund, and SDRs. A reserve position in the Fund gives a member the right to draw all or part of its so-called 'reserve tranche' unconditionally. Gianviti recalls that, in the discussions that led to the eventual creation of the SDR, the search for a name was lacklustre and unimaginative and that 'by analogy with the drawing rights on the Fund and because the new instrument was designed essentially as a credit line among participants, the new instrument was called the special drawing right.'[82] The name SDR would surely have been criticized by Keynes as 'Cherokee language'. (Keynes derided the language used in the American drafts—a language that in many instances was adopted in the final version of the Articles of Agreement—as 'Cherokee', in contrast with the 'Christian English' of his own writings.[83]) In an attempt to explain it in simple terms, Gianviti says:

> The closest analogy to SDRs is Monopoly money. It is distributed at the beginning of the game to all players, because without money there is no game, and it is returned at the end. The difference is that in the SDR department the 'play money' can be used to buy real assets and discharge real liabilities and, at the end, real money must be returned if the allocated SDRs have been spent.[84]

The SDR is not a currency, nor is it a liability of the IMF.[85] It is an official reserve asset. At the international level there has been a conspicuous absence

---

[81] See Art XVII of the IMF Articles of Agreement concerning 'prescribed holders', which must be accepted by the Fund (by decisions of the Executive Board). The following institutions are the prescribed holders of SDRs: African Development Bank, African Development Fund, Arab Monetary Fund, Asian Development Bank, Bank for International Settlements, Bank of Central African States, Central Bank of West African States, East African Development Bank, Eastern Caribbean Central Bank, European Central Bank, International Bank for Reconstruction and Development, International Development Association, International Fund for Agricultural Development, Islamic Development Bank, Latin American Reserve Fund, and Nordic Investment Bank. See also Art XVIII concerning allocation and cancellation of SDRs.

[82] See François Gianviti, above note 75, 3.

[83] See Harold James, *International Monetary Cooperation since Bretton Woods* (Washinton DC: IMF and Oxford University Press, 1996) 54. Keynes also complained about the predominance of lawyers on the American side of the negotiating table. He observed (ibid) that 'lawyers seem to be paid to discover ways of making it impossible to do what may prove sensible in future circumstances.'

[84] See François Gianviti, above note 75, 9. Gianviti also complains about the complexity of the SDR (ibid 4): 'The rules governing the creation, valuation and use of SDRs are extremely complex.'

[85] Above note 32, 11.

of a central authority with the ability to monopolize the issue of currency. Keynes included in his proposals the establishment of an international currency, that he called 'bancor', which would have been a true medium of exchange. White referred in his proposals to a unit of account, that he called 'unitas' which was only a unit of account, not a medium of exchange. In the end no new international unit of account was adopted in Bretton Woods. Instead, the 1944 Bretton Woods agreement stressed the importance of the US dollar, thus satisfying the US negotiators, who privately favoured a post-war world economy centred around the dollar.[86] The IMF took a limited step towards the establishment of an international unit of account with the creation of the Special Drawing Rights. Over the years, several proposals to 'harden' the SDR (so that it could become a medium of exchange) have also been unsuccessful.

In the early 1990s there were discussions with regard to the need for a new allocation of SDRs, either through a general allocation (as foreseen in the Articles of Agreement) or through a targeted allocation to new members, since SDRs can only be allocated to those members that are participants in the SDR department at the time of the allocation on the basis of their quotas. (If a member joins the SDR department after an allocation it will receive SDRs only prospectively in future allocations.) This means that some members have not received allocations at all, while other members have very small quotas at the time the allocations are made.

To remedy these 'inequities' with regard to the allocation of SDRs, there has been a proposed amendment to the Articles of Agreement, which was approved by the Board of Governors in 1997 but which has not been ratified yet by the required majority of members.[87] If ratified, this will become the Fourth Amendment to the Articles of Agreement.

The allocation of SDRs under the proposed fourth amendment would level the distribution of the overall allocation among the membership bringing each member's cumulative allocation of SDRs to the same percentage of its quota as of 17 September 1997. As Polak explains, the new proposed allocation (which would double the amount of SDRs outstanding) requires an amendment because the existing Articles of Agreement stipulate that allocations, and not cumulative allocations, should be proportional to quotas, and because the criterion for an allocation requires a finding that there is a 'long-term global need' to supplement

---

[86] See Harold James, above note 83, 46 and 50.
[87] See Jacques J Polak, 'Streamlining the Financial Architecture of the International Monetary Fund' Princeton Essays in International Finance No 216, September 1999, 25.

reserves, a condition that most industrial country members believed had not been met.[88]

F. Current Account Convertibility and the Control of Capital Movements

The Articles of Agreement impose upon member states a set of obligations of varying nature. The Fund's regulatory powers comprise both Article VIII, section 2 and Article IV. Article IV (as amended in 1976, effective 1978) refers to the 'obligations regarding exchange arrangements', which form the basis of the exercise of surveillance by the Fund as I further explain below. Article VIII (which remains unaltered since its original formulations) imposes some 'general obligations' upon member countries with regard to the absence of restrictions in international transactions.

According to Article VIII, section 2, the jurisdiction of the Fund extends only to payments and transfers for current international transactions, not to capital transactions (the regulation of capital movements is left to the member states). This distinction in the Articles of Agreement between current and capital transactions—largely due to historical considerations—is considered by some experts to be 'conceptually and operationally awkward'.[89] Indeed, in a world where private capital movements have acquired increasing importance, this international code of conduct (freedom of payments and transfers for current international transactions but not for capital transactions) has been often criticized as obsolete. The critique, however, has not resulted yet in any amendment to the Articles of Agreement.

Current account convertibility

Article VIII, section 2 of the IMF Articles of Agreement imposes an obligation upon members to avoid restrictions on current payments and transfers (ie, unrestricted access to foreign exchange to conduct trade in goods and services).

---

[88] ibid. Munzberg, above note 74, 27, recalls that in the 1990s

a proposal was made to cancel all or part of the existing SDRs and to allocate at least the equivalent amount of SDRs on the basis of current quotas. This proposal, however, faced . . . difficulties. . . . While the Fund is entitled to cancel SDRs, it can only do so when there is no longer a need for the SDRs created previously to meet the need for additional liquidity. Therefore, the bases for allocation and cancellation are findings in opposite directions, one for more liquidity and one for less liquidity, and it is not possible to make these findings in good faith at the same time.

[89] See eg Manuel Guitián, 'The Unique Nature of the Responsibilities of the International Monetary Fund', IMF Pamphlet Series No 46 (Washington DC: IMF, 1992) 31.

This obligation is often referred to as an obligation to maintain 'current account convertibility'. Article VIII, section 2 reads as follows:

(a) Subject to the provisions of Article VII Section 3(b) ['scarce currency' provisions] and Article XIV Section 2 [transitional arrangements], no member shall, without the approval of the Fund, impose restrictions on the making of payments and transfers for current international transactions.

(b) Exchange contracts which involve the currency of any member and which are contrary to the exchange control regulations of that member maintained or imposed consistently with this Agreement shall be unenforceable in the territories of any member. In addition, members may, by mutual accord, cooperate in measures for the purpose of making the exchange control regulations of either member more effective, provided that such measures and regulations are consistent with this Agreement.

The Fund has designed policies on approving restrictions that are otherwise subject to Article VIII, section 2(a). One aspect of that policy, which has been widely used by members, refers to the imposition of restrictions for reasons of national or international security.[90] In these cases, the member notifies the Fund prior to the imposition of such restrictions, whenever possible, or as promptly as circumstances permit.

The interpretation of Article VIII, in particular Article VIII, section 2(b), has given rise to an abundant legal literature and to a large body of jurisprudence, where the lack of uniformity of interpretation among the courts of some major countries is noticeable.[91] Since Article VIII, section 2(b) is a rule of private international law/conflict of laws, and since my analysis focuses on public international law, I will not discuss it further in this chapter.[92]

Article XXX(d) explains the meaning of the term 'payments for current transactions'. The definition of 'payments for current transactions' is broader than the statistical definition of 'current transactions' used by economists. Also, it is not limited to transactions in goods, which is used by the GATT. It includes

---

[90] See Decision No 144–(52/51), 14 August 1952, 'Payments Restrictions for Security Reasons: Fund Jurisdiction' above note 3. 'The Fund does not . . . provide a suitable forum for discussion of the political and military considerations leading to actions of this kind.'

[91] See eg Joseph Gold, 'The Fund Agreement in the Courts—XV', IMF Staff Papers, Vol 27, No 3 (September 1980). This fifteenth instalment was preceded by fourteen other articles, all of them dealing with the effect of the IMF Articles of Agreement on litigation. With regard to the interpretation of Art VIII, s 2(b) see also Proctor, above note 2, ch 15, and the contributions by François Gianviti ('The Fund Agreement in the Courts') and Pierre Francote ('Comment') in Robert Effors (ed), *Current Legal Issues Affecting Central Banks*, Vol 1 (Washington DC: IMF, 1992). Gianviti notes that Art VIII, s 2(b) is a substantive rule of private international law (ibid 8).

[92] The IMF provided an interpretation of Art VIII, s 2(b) in Decision No 446–4, 10 June 1949.

transactions in services, now covered by the GATS. It also includes some transfers from capital transactions, such as amortization of loans.[93]

IMF members are to avoid restrictions on payments and transfers for current international transactions, but remain free to impose restrictions or controls on capital transfers. However, members not 'prepared to accept the obligations of Article VIII Sections 2, 3 and 4' are allowed to operate under the transitional arrangements foreseen in Article XIV. (Under Art VIII, section 3, multiple currency practices and discriminatory currency arrangements are prohibited, unless they are approved by the Fund. Art VIII, section 4 refers to the 'convertibility of foreign-held balances'.)

The transitional regime foreseen in Article XIV allows members to maintain and adapt restrictions that were in effect when they joined the Fund. Only about twenty members continue formally to avail themselves of Article XIV status. However, these members have an obligation to consult annually with the IMF concerning the retention of the restrictions on payments and transfers for current international transactions. Article XIV also requires members to withdraw such restrictions as soon as they are satisfied they will be able, without such restrictions, to settle their balance of payments in a manner that will not unduly encumber the Fund's general resources.[94] In addition, if the Fund finds that a member persists in maintaining restrictions which are inconsistent with the purposes of the Fund, the member would be subject to sanctions under Article XXVI, section 2(a), which refers to the ineligibility to use the general resources of the Fund.

From the point of view of restrictions on international transfers and payments, IMF members can be divided into three groups:

(1) members that embrace both current account convertibility (the obligations of Art VIII) and capital account convertibility (no IMF obligation);
(2) members that adopt current account convertibility only (the obligations of Art VIII);

---

[93] Article XXX (d) explains the meaning of the term 'payments for current transactions':

Payments for current transactions means payments which are not for the purpose of transferring capital and includes, without limitation:

(1) all payments in connection with foreign trade, other current business, including services and normal short-term banking and other credit facilities;
(2) payments due as interest on loans and as net income from other investments;
(3) payments of moderate amount for amortization of loans or for depreciation of direct investments; and
(4) moderate remittances for family living expenses.

[94] Countries under the transitional provisions of Art XIV eventually move towards full current account convertibility, even though the transitional period can be a very long one. Eg, India only accepted the obligations of Art VIII in 1994.

(3) members that still operate with restrictions on current account convertibility (operating under the transitional arrangements of Art XIV, or members that maintain restrictions subject to Art VIII, that have either been approved by the Fund, or that are maintained in breach of the Articles, ie, without Fund approval).

Control of capital movements

Under the law of the IMF, member countries can impose restrictions on capital movements, without Fund approval. Article VI, section 3 allows members to exercise 'controls of capital transfers as necessary to regulate international capital movements'. The extension of the Fund's jurisdiction[95] over capital movements would therefore require an amendment of the Articles of Agreement granting the Fund an explicit mandate in this regard.[96]

Both White and Keynes favoured the control of capital movements. Capital movements in the 1920s and 1930s (in particular short-term capital flows) were considered a fundamental ill of the inter-war economy. According to Keynes: 'It is widely held that control of capital movements, both inward and outward, should be a permanent feature of the post-war system. . . . If control is to be effective, it probably involves the machinery of exchange control for all transactions, even though a general open licence is given to all remittances in respect of current trade.'[97] White noted that each member country should 'subscribe to the general policies of permitting foreign exchange trading in an open, free and legal market, and to abandon, as rapidly as conditions permit, all restrictions or controls by which various classes of foreign exchange transactions have been prohibited or interfered with'. However, he also pointed out that, in practice, there are situations 'that make inevitable the adoption of controls' on movements of capital.[98]

A lot has changed since 1944 in terms of volume and composition of capital flows. However, the law of the IMF has not changed in this respect, even though in recent years a number of voices within the Fund, as well as outside it, have

---

[95] 'Jurisdiction' in the context of the Fund's activities is to be understood as the legal authority of the Fund to assess and enforce members' countries compliance with obligations specified in the IMF Articles of Agreement.

[96] See Cynthia Lichtenstein, 'International Jurisdiction over International Capital Flows and the Role of the IMF: Plus ça Change' in Mario Giovanoli (ed), *International Monetary Law* (Oxford: Oxford University Press, 2000).

[97] See para 45 of Keynes's 1942 proposal, repr in J Keith Horsefield (ed), *The International Monetary Fund 1945–1965*, Vol 3: Documents (Washington DC: IMF, 1969) 13.

[98] See White's 1942 proposal, repr in J Keith Horsefield (ed), *The International Monetary Fund 1945–1965*, Vol 3: Documents (Washington DC: IMF, 1969) 47 and 63.

advocated the need to extend convertibility to capital account,[99] since international capital flows have made national boundaries increasingly porous.[100] Private capital flows constitute today a main source of financing for developed as well as developing countries (middle-income developing countries). In the European Community, and in developed countries generally, capital account liberalization is the norm.

In its meeting of 28 April 1997, the Interim Committee of the IMF 'agreed that the Fund's Articles of Agreement should be amended to make the promotion of capital account liberalization a specific purpose of the Fund and to give the Fund appropriate jurisdiction over capital movements'.[101]

However, following the financial crises in East Asia in the late 1990s—crises which arose from disturbances to the capital account—the momentum to push forward such an amendment has been lost and it is unlikely that 'capital account convertibility' will be adopted *de jure* by the Fund in the near future. Some economists have argued that free capital mobility does not lead to an optimal allocation of resources especially when significant domestic distortions exist.[102] Controls on short-term capital inflows, as in Chile, have been appraised on the grounds that countries imposing such controls are subject to less volatility than countries with unrestricted capital mobility; if speculators cannot bring money into the country, then capital will not flow out when market sentiment changes.

There are certainly dangers in liberalizing capital movements in an economy in which the macroeconomic framework and the financial sector are weak. Before adopting such liberalization a country needs to prepare its financial sector, often through the restructuring of the financial industry (adequate sequencing of reforms), the strengthening of the capital base of the financial institutions, and the replacement of capital controls by effective prudential regulation and supervision.[103]

In the absence of a formal mandate to promote open capital accounts, the Fund has not always provided consistent policy advice to its members. This is the finding of a report on the Fund's approach to capital liberalization released in

---

[99] See Stanley Fischer, 'Capital Account Liberalization and the Role of the IMF' in Stanley Fischer, Richard Cooper, Rudiger Dornbusch, Peter Garber, Carlos Massad, Jacques Polak, Danik Rodrik, and Savak Tarapore, 'Should the IMF Pursue Capital Account Convertibility?' Princeton Essays in International Finance No 207, May 1998.

[100] This point is made by the late Manuel Guitián, above note 89, 44.

[101] See Jacques Polak, 'The Articles of Agreement of the IMF and the Liberalization of Capital Movements' in Stanley Fischer et al, 'Should the IMF Pursue Capital Account Convertibility?' Princeton Essays in International Finance No 207, May 1998, 47.

[102] See eg Joseph Stiglitz, 'Capital Market Liberalization, Globalization and the IMF' (2005) 20 Oxford Review of Economic Policy, 57–71.

[103] Stanley Fisher et al, above note 99, 5, 22, and 29.

May 2005 by the Independent Evaluation Office.[104] For instance, Russia was encouraged to open its government bond market to help finance its deficit through foreign borrowing, while the Fund was more cautious in its recommendations to other countries. In China, on the other hand, support for the country's 'gradual' approach to capital account liberalization (given the 'structural weakness' of the financial sector) was reflected in the public information notice (PIN) issued after the conclusion of the 2003 Article IV consultation.[105] The IEO report therefore recommends a clarification by the Executive Board of the elements of agreement on capital controls. However, given the lack of consensus in the academic literature about the wisdom of capital flows (inflows and outflows), and the inconclusive empirical evidence,[106] there is no universal set of criteria against which the IMF's approach to capital account issues can be assessed.

G. IMF Functions

The main functions performed by the IMF in relation to its members are surveillance (Art IV), financial assistance (Art V, s 3) and technical assistance (Art V, s 2(b)).

The Fund uses surveillance, financial assistance, and technical assistance as instruments to accomplish its objectives or purposes as defined in Article I. From the point of view of the member states, they constitute the main 'services' that the Fund provides to them. From the Fund's perspective, its powers can be broken down into three categories: (i) regulatory (jurisdiction), comprising Article VIII, section 2 and Article IV; (ii) financial (Art V, s 3), and (iii) advisory (technical assistance, Art V, s 2(b)).

The authority of the IMF to perform for members specific services that are not mentioned in the Articles but are sufficiently related to the purposes of the institution is made explicit by the Second Amendment, Article V, section 2(b).

While surveillance applies to all members, conditional financial assistance and

---

[104] See IEO Report on the 'Evaluation of the IMF's Approach to Capital Account Liberalization', 25 May 2005, available at <http://www.imf.org/ieo>.

[105] See <http://www.imf.org/external/np/sec/pn/2003/pn03136.htm>.

[106] See Dani Rodrik, 'Who Needs Capital Account Convertibility?' in Stanley Fischer, Richard Cooper, Rudiger Dornbusch, Peter Garber, Carlos Massad, Jacques Polak, Danik Rodrik, and Savak Tarapore, 'Should the IMF Pursue Capital Account Convertibility?' Princeton Essays in International Finance No 207, May 1998, 57: 'Where knowledge is limited, the rule for policymakers should be, first, do no harm. Enshrining capital account convertibility in the IMF's Articles of Agreement is an idea whose time has not yet come. We have no evidence that it will solve our problems, and some reason to think it would make them worse.'

technical assistance apply only to the members that request such assistance. The mandatory nature of surveillance contrasts with the voluntary nature of technical assistance. I explain below the *sui generis* nature of IMF financial assistance.

Article V, section 1 specifies that members will deal with the Fund 'only through its Treasury, central bank, stabilization fund or other similar agency'. Hence the legal study of these activities generally falls within the realm of public international law.

(1) Surveillance

In the words of the late Manuel Guitián, 'The IMF is primarily a surveillance institution',[107] in charge of the oversight of an international financial code of conduct. This code of conduct is a set of obligations that members must comply with according to the Articles of Agreement.

Surveillance is a jurisdictional function, which has traditionally focused on the assessment of the exchange arrangements, the exchange rate, and the balance of payments,[108] and which today focuses upon a wide range of economic policies, encompassing not only exchange rate, monetary, and fiscal policies, but also financial sector issues, structural issues, and institutional developments.[109] Surveillance entails a judgement on the part of the Fund, and as with any judgement, a degree of discretion is always involved. In the case of surveillance, the exercise of this 'judgement' is particularly complex, because of the interconnectedness between domestic and foreign economic policy, the interdependence amongst countries, and the political and social consequences of some sensitive economic decisions.

The legal basis of surveillance

The legal basis of surveillance is Article IV, sections 1 and 3, as amended. Article IV, section 1 imposes a set of obligations upon members, which I further explain below. To make these obligations effective, the Fund is granted powers to oversee, to monitor the compliance of each member with these obligations.

---

[107] See Manuel Guitián, above note 89, 9. During my stint at the Fund I had the opportunity of getting to know Manuel Guitián, a distinguished member of the staff of the IMF for many years, who held *inter alia* the position of Director of the Monetary and Exchange Affairs Department. Guitián made an outstanding contribution to the development of Fund policies through his work and through his writings. He had a fine intellect and an independent mind. He was also a true gentleman.

[108] ibid 11. 'The focus of obligation on the part of members centers on the point and the terms of intersection of their national economies with each other—that is the balance of payments, the exchange rate and the exchange regime.'

[109] See <http://www.imf.org/external/np/exr/facts/surv.htm>.

Article IV, section 3(a) confers upon the IMF a clear role in this regard:

> The Fund shall oversee the international monetary system in order to ensure its effective operation, and shall oversee the compliance of each member with its obligations under Section 1 of this Article.

Article IV, section 3(b) further states:

> [T]he Fund shall exercise firm surveillance over the exchange rate policies of members, and shall adopt specific principles for the guidance of all members with respect to those policies.

The principles of surveillance were set out in further detail in a 1977 decision.[110] Though exchange rate policies and exchange arrangements are at the heart of Article IV and at the heart of this decision (ie, at the heart of surveillance), the decision also refers to a broader scope for the exercise of surveillance in the following terms:

> This appraisal [of a member's exchange rate policies] shall be made within the framework of a comprehensive analysis of the general economic situation and economic policy strategy of the member, and shall recognize that domestic as well as external policies can contribute to timely adjustment of the balance of payments. The appraisal shall take into account the extent to which the policies of the member, including the exchange rate policies, serve the objectives of the continuing development of the orderly underlying conditions that are necessary for financial stability, the promotion of sustained sound economic growth and reasonable levels of employment.[111]

This is in line with the mandate given to the Fund in Article IV, section 3(b), which requires the Fund to 'pay due regard to the circumstances of members' and 'to respect the domestic, social and political policies of members'.

Following the abandonment of the par value regime, the Second Amendment places the function of surveillance at the centre of the Fund's operations, at the core of the international monetary system. From being a virtually self-enforcing arrangement subject to strict rules, surveillance now becomes a function in which judgement is of the essence. Surveillance is no longer a rules-based regime but a 'discretion based regime'.[112]

This broad scope of economic situations and policies has facilitated the evolution of surveillance over the years, the most interesting development in the last

---

[110] See Decision of the Executive Board No 5392–(77/63) of 29 April 1977 as amended. This decision implemented the new Art IV of the IMF Articles of Agreement, which at the time was still in the process of being ratified (The Second Amendment was approved in April 1976 and became effective in April 1978).

[111] ibid.

[112] Above note 89, 6. See also Manuel Guitián, 'The IMF as a Monetary Institution: The Challenge Ahead', Finance and Development, September 1991, 38.

decade being the emphasis given to financial stability and financial sector policies.

Types of surveillance

The Fund carries out surveillance mainly through its so-called 'Article IV consultations' with each individual member country. In addition to this 'bilateral surveillance', there is also 'multilateral surveillance', with the publication by the Fund of a World Economic Outlook Report and a Global Financial Stability Report twice a year. Another form of surveillance is 'regional surveillance', under which the IMF examines developments in regional areas, such as the European Union and the euro area.

The purpose of surveillance is to evaluate the appropriateness of a country's existing policies and at the same time to encourage the country to adopt new policies that enhance the smooth functioning of the international monetary system. IMF surveillance integrates the bilateral aspects of analysing the policies of individual countries with the multilateral aspects of examining the consequences of these policies for the operation of the system as a whole.

The obligations of members

Article IV, section 1 of the IMF Articles of Agreement reads as follows:

> Recognizing that the essential purpose of the international monetary system is to provide a framework that facilitates the exchange of goods, services and capital among countries and that sustains sound economic growth, and that a principal objective is the continuing development of the orderly underlying conditions that are necessary for financial and economic stability, each member undertakes to collaborate with the Fund and other members to assure orderly exchange arrangements and to promote a stable system of exchange rates. In particular, each member shall:
>
> (i)   Endeavor to direct its economic and financial policies toward the objective of fostering orderly economic growth with reasonable price stability, with due regard to its circumstances;
> (ii)   Seek to promote stability by fostering orderly underlying economic and financial conditions and a monetary system that does not produce erratic disruptions;
> (iii) Avoid manipulating exchange rates or the international monetary system in order to prevent effective balance of payments adjustment or to gain an unfair competitive advantage over other members; and
> (iv) Follow exchange policies compatible with the undertakings of this Section.

Article IV, section 1 imposes obligations upon its members that are both positive and negative in character. The positive obligations are the ones described in Article IV, section 1(i), (ii), and (iv). The negative obligation is the one described in Article IV, section 1(iii), which is written in rather forceful terms: 'avoid manipulating exchange rates'.

The first two obligations of Article IV, section 1—(i) and (ii)—are formulated in soft terms. As Proctor points out, 'an obligation to co-operate with a view to achieving a particular objective, does not impose an obligation to achieve that objective'.[113] Gianviti considers that these first two obligations—(i) and (ii)—are 'soft obligations', as opposed to the obligations in (iii) and (iv), which are 'hard obligations', even though the language of section 1(iv) is rather generic.[114] While the obligations in section 1(iii) and (iv) relate to external policies, where the Fund has greater jurisdiction, the obligations in section 1(i) and (ii) relate to domestic policies, where members have greater sovereignty.[115]

The members are obliged to cooperate with the Fund by supplying all the information necessary to allow the Fund to perform effective bilateral surveillance, according to Article IV, section 3(b). The obligation to furnish information to the Fund 'as it deems necessary for its activities', is also recognized in Article VIII, section 5.

Despite the emphasis that Article IV places upon exchange rate policies, in recent years, the practice of surveillance has given greater emphasis to domestic policies (the 'soft obligations' of Art IV, s 1(i) and (ii)), than to exchange rate policies (the 'hard obligations' of Art IV, s 1(iii) and (iv)).[116] I further elaborate below on the change from 'macro-surveillance' to 'micro-surveillance'.

Since Article IV imposes obligations upon members, sanctions can be applied in the case of breach of these obligations. However, 'there has not been a single instance in which sanctions have been applied or a report has been made for breach of obligation under Article IV. This *de facto* transformation of Article IV section 1 into a "soft law provision" is reflected in the description of Article IV consultation with members as "policy advice" . . . or "policy dialogue".'[117]

Gianviti discusses the nature of the obligation of members under Article IV and the ambiguities in Article IV, sections 1 and 3. The focus of the obligation relates to exchange rate policies; other policies (such as trade and investment policies) do not constitute 'an obligation under Article IV' even if they are an important element with which to assess exchange rate policies.[118] However, he acknowledges that the practice of surveillance is expanding beyond the actual

---

[113] Proctor, above note 2, 562.

[114] See Gianviti, 'Evolving Role and Challenges for the International Monetary Fund', above note 2, 46. He defines a 'soft obligation as an obligation that does not require the achievement of a particular objective or even the exercise of best efforts or due diligence, but only a reasonable effort in light of all relevant circumstances. In contrast, soft law means that there is no obligation at all.'

[115] ibid 40–2.   [116] ibid 47–8.   [117] ibid 47.   [118] ibid 42–3.

obligations of Article IV through the conduct of Article IV consultations.[119] He warns against an undue extension in this practice: if surveillance is perceived more as a form of peer pressure than as a means of monitoring compliance with obligations specified in the Articles of Agreement, this may lead to a dilution of its objectives.[120]

The language of Article IV, section 1 reflects the 'labour pains' of the origins of this provision, which came to replace the legal certitude and simplicity of the original par value regime.[121] The choice of verbs (endeavour, seek to promote, fostering, follow), the introduction of a preamble, and what I would describe as a 'hesitant tone' in the new mandate, suggest that the drafters of the provision were unsure about the direction that the new regime would follow and did not want to preclude an eventual return to the regime that they had just abandoned.

Surveillance in practice

In accordance with Article IV of the IMF Articles of Agreement, IMF staff hold annual bilateral meetings with officials from the member country. When an 'Article IV consultation' takes place, a Fund staff team (called an IMF 'mission') visits the country to collect information about macroeconomic policies (fiscal, monetary, and exchange rate), the soundness of the financial system, and other relevant issues such as social, labour, and environmental policies as well as institutional developments. Following the review of these policies, the Fund team holds discussions with the authorities regarding the effectiveness of their economic policies as well as prospective changes for the domestic economy and the member's balance of payments positions. At the conclusion of these discussions, and prior to the preparation of the staff's report to the Executive Board,[122] the IMF mission often provides the authorities with a statement of its preliminary findings. Once the IMF's Executive Board has discussed the staff report,

---

[119] ibid 47. 'In some cases, Article IV consultations offer an opportunity to exercise peer pressure without asserting the existence of an obligation under Article IV.'

[120] ibid 48–9.

[121] ibid 38. 'The new provision was a political compromise with the necessary calculated ambiguities to allow both sides to claim victory. . . . [I]nstead of the former obligation to achieve a certain result, there is now an obligation to cooperate toward common goals.'

[122] Holder, above note 25, 19–20.

The Fund's regulatory jurisdiction focuses especially on each member's exchange rate policies and exchange restrictions, usually in the context of the annual Article IV consultation report to the Executive Board. For each of the Fund's members, therefore, the exchange system of each member must be identified, understood and explained; specifically it is for the 'country lawyer' to identify any restrictions, in order that they may be included in the relevant Article IV consultation report to be considered by the Board, as appropriate, for approval. When a member is considering relinquishing its reliance on the transitional processes of Article XIV, thereby accepting the obligations of Article VIII, the Legal Department undertakes a full and intensive review of the exchange system.

they forward a summary of the discussion to the country's government. The conclusions of the report are only published if the country consents. However, with the increased transparency of the IMF and its work in recent years, the summary of the Executive Board discussions for many Article IV consultations are published in Public Information Notices (PINs), which are available on the IMF website.

The evolving nature of the practice of surveillance has been made possible thanks to the ample room for interpretation granted to the Fund in the exercise of surveillance. Every two years, the IMF reviews the principles and procedures that guide its surveillance, as originally set out in the 1977 Executive Board decision.[123]

From macro-surveillance to micro-surveillance

IMF surveillance has evolved significantly over the last decades, with the increased attention to financial sector issues and policies being the main development in recent years. While surveillance in the past was typically focused on the jurisdiction over the exchange arrangements of members and macroeconomic policies, surveillance nowadays also takes into account other issues, often involving the workings of the private sector ('micro' issues), such as good governance (both political and corporate governance), legal and institutional reform, bank restructuring, financial reform, and so on. There is a widespread recognition that surveillance must be strengthened to increase the Fund's ability to detect incipient financial tensions and vulnerabilities in international capital markets. I further discuss this issue in Chapter 14 with regard to the role of the IMF in the resolution of international financial crises.

The need to provide effective surveillance of the financial system (a need which became pressing following the crises in the late 1990s) has given rise to the Financial System Stability Assessments (FSSAs), which the Fund carries out as part of the Financial Sector Assessment Programme (FSAP), a joint IMF–World Bank initiative which was introduced in May 1999.[124] In an FSSA, IMF staff address issues of relevance to the function of surveillance, including risks to macroeconomic stability stemming from the financial sector and the capacity of the sector to absorb macroeconomic shocks.

The FSAP is characterized by its voluntary nature and its joint Bank–Fund

---

[123] See Decision of the Executive Board No 5392–(77/63) of 29 April 1977, as amended.

[124] See 'Financial Sector Assessment Program (FSAP)' at <http://www.imf.org/external/np/fsap/fsap.asp>. See also 'IMF Executive Board Review of the Experience with the Financial Sector Assessment Program', 6 April 2005 (PIN No 05/47) at <http://www.imf.org/external/np/sec/pn/2005/pn0547.htm>. The reports prepared by the World Bank under the FSAP are called Financial Sector Assessments (FSAs).

character. The voluntary participation—which is a key feature of the programme —results in greater country 'ownership'.[125]

In addition to the FSSAs, a key component of the FSAP are the Reports on Observance of Standards and Codes (ROSCs) which summarize the extent to which countries observe certain internationally recognized standards and codes.[126] The IMF has recognized twelve areas and associated standards as useful for the operational work of the Fund and the World Bank. These comprise accounting, auditing, anti-money laundering and countering the financing of terrorism (AML/ CFT), banking supervision, corporate governance, data dissemination, fiscal transparency, insolvency and creditor rights, insurance supervision, monetary and financial policy transparency, payment systems, and securities regulation.

ROSCs provide a focus to surveillance, and also facilitate performance accountability. ROSCs also provide a direction to programmes of technical assistance by identifying the areas which the country must aim to improve or strengthen.[127] Finally, ROSCs highlight the close relationship between conditionality and surveillance, and contribute to clarifying the obligations inherent in the international code of conduct, which the IMF oversees.

While FSAPs and ROSCs inform Fund surveillance, they are, as a legal matter, performed as technical assistance.[128] Such activities are voluntary for both the member and the Fund. According to Gianviti, 'FSAP reports and ROSCs are not by themselves an exercise of surveillance.'[129] ('The Fund cannot expand the scope of its surveillance beyond the provisions of Article IV. A finding of non compliance with standards and codes would not constitute a breach of obligation under the Articles.')[130] The FSAP reports and ROSCs, however, 'feed into surveillance, ie provide material which deepens the Fund's understandings of the member's circumstances'. He concludes: 'While expanding the sources of information available to the Fund in the exercise of surveillance, FSAP reports and ROSCs illustrate the evolution of surveillance from an assertion of jurisdictional powers as contemplated by the Fund's Articles to a policy dialogue coupled with peer pressure.'[131]

Surveillance of national policies becomes more complex when countries embark

---

[125] ibid.

[126] See 'Reports on Observance of Standard and Codes' at <http://www.imf.org/external/np/ rosc/rosc.asp>.

[127] Gianviti, 'Evolving Role and Challenges for the International Monetary Fund', above note 2, 49, points out that ROSCs 'bridge the gap between technical assistance and surveillance'.

[128] I thank Sean Hagan for observations on this point.

[129] See François Gianviti, 'Legal Aspects of the Financial Sector Assessment Program', paper presented at the IMF Seminar on Current Developments in Monetary and Financial Law in May 2002, available at <http://www.imf.org/external/np/leg/sem/2002cdmfl/eng/gianv2.pdf>.

[130] ibid. [131] ibid.

on programmes of trade and financial liberalization.[132] The opening up of the economy raises important challenges and sets into motion a process of regulatory reform. In the 1970s the emphasis of surveillance was on the traditional macroeconomic policies such as exchange rate, monetary, and fiscal policies. In the 1980s, structural policies became more relevant, particularly in the aftermath of the debt crisis. At the beginning of the 1990s, the transition from centrally planned to market economies in countries in Eastern Europe and the former Soviet Union moved surveillance in the direction of further structural reforms, with emphasis on legal and institutional reform. In the late 1990s the financial crises in South East Asia, Russia, and other emerging economies, suggested that financial reform and financial law reform should be the object of IMF surveillance.

At the beginning of the twenty-first century, concerns about poverty and the response of the international community to the financial needs of countries which are both poor and heavily indebted are among the greatest challenges the institution must confront. The social and economic injustice of impoverished Africa, the troubled Middle East, and the populist policies that can appeal to many in developing countries are a reminder that the economic foundations of peace (with shared prosperity) are a necessary complement of the political foundations of peace. This implies a renewed attention on institutional issues, given that an adequate legal and institutional framework is fundamental for successful economic development.[133] The IMF functions of surveillance, technical assistance, and financial assistance can be used to this end.

(2) Financial Assistance

IMF financial assistance (support to members experiencing temporary balance of payments problems) is generally conditional on the adoption and implementation of adjustment policies. IMF financing is typically available through 'standby arrangements' (or extended arrangements). Though these arrangements are not technically nor legally loans, however, they are the 'functional equivalent' of loans.[134]

---

[132] I refer below, and in note 266, to the Trade Integration Mechanism approved in April 2004.
[133] I refer below to the initiatives the Fund has undertaken with regard to low income developing countries.
[134] Above note 32, 5.

The provision of financial assistance by the IMF is not technically or legally 'lending' as such. Rather, financial assistance is provided via an exchange of monetary assets, similar to a swap. Nevertheless, the purchase and repurchase of currencies from the IMF, with interest charged on outstanding purchases, is functionally equivalent to loan. . . . Accordingly, for ease of reference, the terms 'lending', 'loans' and 'borrowing' are used in this pamphlet to refer to the provision of financial resources by the IMF to its members.

In this section, after a few introductory notions (a bit of 'Cherokee language'), I discuss the nature of standby arrangements and I dissect then the notion of conditionality, taking into account its history and legal basis. In the following section, I survey the various financial facilities and instruments that the Fund has developed over the years to deal with 'special' balance of payments problems and with the needs of developing countries (concessional lending).

The terminology applicable to the Fund's financial operations is cumbersome (a point which I emphasize throughout this chapter) and for those not familiar with Fund jargon it makes understanding the Fund's activities rather difficult.

Some introductory notions[135]

All members are in principle eligible to use the Fund's general resources in proportion to their quota. A member is entitled to 'purchase' the currencies of other members in exchange for an equivalent amount of its own currency, subject to the four conditions established in Article V, section 3(b). These four conditions are: (i) the use must be consistent with the Articles of Agreement; (ii) the member makes a declaration ('representation') of balance of payments need; (iii) the proposed purchase does not raise the Fund's holdings of the member's currency above 200 per cent of the member's quota; and (iv) the member has not been declared ineligible to use those resources. The third and fourth requirements can be waived.[136]

'Purchases' (drawings in Fund's parlance) are the financial transactions foreseen in Article V, section 3(b). 'Outright purchases' are purchases outside an arrangement.

Arrangements are commitments of resources by the Fund under which purchases may be made by a member. There are two types of arrangements: standby arrangements under the credit tranche policies, and extended arrangements under the Extended Fund Facility (EFF).

'Credit tranche policies' are defined in the Glossary of Selected Financial Terms as 'policies under which members make use of IMF credit'.[137] The amount of such use is governed by the member's quota; uniformity of treatment for IMF members does not mean equal access to Fund resources but access in proportion to quotas.

---

[135] With regard to these introductory notions, I draw heavily on François Gianviti, 'The Role of the Fund in the Financing of External Debt', *Recuil des Cours* III (1989), 246–60 and Gianviti, 'Evolving Role and Challenges for the International Monetary Fund', above note 2.

[136] See Art V, s 4.

[137] See <http://www.imf.org/external/np/exr/glossary/showTerm.asp?term_id=21>.

Under the credit tranche policies, both direct requests for purchases (ie, outright purchases) and requests for standby arrangements can be made.

The 'credit tranche policies' are generally for short-term adjustment purposes, 'with a lower conditionality when total outstanding purchases do not exceed 25% of the quota (which, added to a prior use of the reserve tranche,[138] would raise the Fund's holding to 125% of the quota) and a higher conditionality for additional purchases. Hence, the distinction between "first credit tranche conditionality" and "upper credit tranches conditionality".'

The Fund's attitude to drawings in the 'first credit tranche' is rather liberal, provided that members demonstrate reasonable efforts to overcome their balance of payments difficulties. In contrast, requests beyond this 'first credit tranche', that is requests for access to 'upper credit tranches'—normally via standby arrangements—require substantial justification (conditionality).[139]

According to Gianviti:

> Once the reserve tranche has been fully drawn and replaced with the purchasing member's currency, the Fund's holdings of the member's currency stand at 100 percent of quota. Beyond that, the member is using the Fund's financial assistance, and the use of Fund's general resources will continue as long as the Fund's holdings of the member's currency are not reduced to 100 per cent or below. Above 100 percent of quota, the Fund's conditions for the use of its resources gradually tighten, and these conditions may also vary with the type of problem faced by the member.... Between 100 percent and 200 percent of quota, a member is 'entitled' to use the Fund's resources.... [W]hen the Fund's holding of the member's currency reach 200 percent of quota, the entitlement ceases, and, for any additional assistance, a waiver must be obtained by the Fund.[140]

Stand-by arrangements

The history of stand-by arrangements is inextricably linked to the history of conditionality. Conditionality is made 'specific' through a stand-by arrangement (or other 'arrangements'). Conditionality ends when an arrangement ends.

IMF members have always been able to draw on the Fund's pool of resources 'to correct maladjustments in their balance of payments' (Art I). According to

---

[138] See Gianviti, 'The Role of the Fund in the Financing of External Debt', above note 135, 251. As I explained above, the drawing by a member of the 'reserve tranche' (previously 'gold tranche') is automatic (unconditional); it can be drawn at any time by the member, with no charge and no expectation of repayment.

[139] See above note 32, 41. 'The segmentation in terms of first and upper credit tranches underscores the basic principle that the IMF requires stronger justification in terms of policy understandings from the member at higher levels of IMF credit outstanding.'

[140] See François Gianviti, 'Developments at the International Monetary Fund' in Robert Effros (ed), *Current Legal Issues Affecting Central Banks*, Vol 4 (Washington DC: IMF, 1997) 7–8.

Article V of the original Articles of Agreement, a member had the right to purchase the currency of another member in exchange for gold or its own currency.[141]

The stand-by arrangement, the quintessential financial instrument of the Fund, was not foreseen in the original Articles of Agreement. In 1952, the then Managing Director, Ivar Rooth, stated the desirability of a means by which a country would not necessarily make an immediate drawing but would receive from the Fund the *assurance* that it would be able to make a drawing within a prescribed period (originally six months) should the need arise.[142] The Fund, Rooth stated, should help members that need 'temporary help' and the Fund should assess 'whether the policies the members will pursue will be adequate to overcome the problems within such a period'.[143] The new instrument,[144] which was initially named 'stand-by agreement' but would soon thereafter be called 'stand-by arrangement', has been refined and expanded since it was formalized in 1953.[145]

Stand-by arrangements were originally conceived as precautionary arrangements. It was thought that the right to purchase would by itself be sufficient to satisfy the member's requirements without a purchase actually being made.[146] Precautionary arrangements have remained an important instrument over the years even though the 'typical' standby arrangement is one in which members meet their immediate balance of payments needs by actually 'drawing' resources.

---

[141] The concept of 'outright purchases' is still used today (a purchase outside an arrangement), albeit not frequently. Support in the form of outright purchases is provided in the first credit tranche policy, the 'compensatory financing facility', and in the cases of emergency assistance for natural disasters and for post-conflict situations. See IMF, 'Review of Fund Facilities— Preliminary Considerations', prepared by the Policy Development and Review Department in consultation with other Departments, 2 March 2000, 30, <http://www.imf.org/external/np/pdr/fac/2000/faciliti.pdf>.

[142] '[A]t other times discussions between the member and the Fund may cover its general position, not with a view to an immediate drawing, but in order to assure that it would be able to draw if, within a period of 6 to 12 months, the need presented itself. . . . In cases where it would appear appropriate and useful, the Fund might arrange drawings to deal with special short-run situations accompanied by arrangements for repurchase in a period not exceeding 18 months.' The statement of the Managing Director was then accepted by the Executive Board in Decision No 102–(52/11), 13 February 1952, published in *Selected Decisions and Selected Documents of the International Monetary Fund*, 17th issue (Washington DC: IMF, 1992).

[143] ibid.

[144] James, above note 83, 81, recalls: 'In the course of providing aid to Finland in 1952 it was established that in order to secure the principle of revolving access to Fund resources, drawings should not be for more than three years.'

[145] See Decision of the Executive Board on 'Stand-By Arrangements', Decision No 270–(53/95) of 23 December 1953, as amended.

[146] See IMF, 'Review of Fund Facilities—Preliminary Considerations', prepared by the Policy Development and Review Department in consultation with other Departments, 2 March 2000, 5, <http://www.imf.org/external/np/pdr/fac/2000/faciliti.pdf>.

The exercise of the member's 'right to purchase' gradually became subject to 'conditions', thus linking the history of stand-by arrangements to the history of conditionality.

The Second Amendment in 1978 introduced a definition of the standby arrangement in Article XXX(b):

> Stand-by arrangement means a decision of the Fund by which a member is assured that it will be able to make purchases from the General Resources Account in accordance with the terms of the decision during a specified period and up to a specified amount.

Stand-by arrangements are the main instrument or vehicle for disbursing credit tranche resources. According to the IMF Glossary of Selected Financial Terms, a stand-by arrangement is a decision of the IMF by which a member is assured that it will be able to make purchases (drawings) from the General Resources Account (GRA) up to a specified amount and during a specified period of time, usually one to two years, provided that the member observes the terms set out in the supporting arrangement.[147]

A stand-by arrangement is therefore not a contract or an agreement but a decision of the Fund. This is important to understanding its legal nature.[148] The letter of intent (signed by the applicant member and outlining 'its' programme) and the decision of the Executive Board of the IMF announcing that a stand-by arrangement has been approved do not constitute together an international legally binding agreement (hence the name 'arrangement' instead of 'agreement').

> Fund arrangements are not international agreements and therefore language having contractual connotations will be avoided in arrangements and in program documents.[149]

Stand-by arrangements are not technically or legally loans, but purchase and repurchase arrangements. However, they are the functional equivalent of a loan. The 'revolving character' is a basic feature of the standby arrangement. Purchases (drawings) have to be reversed by repurchases (or repayments).

The Fund offers its general resources available to members through standby arrangements (and extended arrangements). Member countries use the general resources of the IMF by making a purchase (drawing) of other members currencies or SDRs with an equivalent amount of their own currencies. The IMF levies charges on these drawings and require that members repurchase (repay)

---

[147] See <http://www.imf.org/external/np/exr/glossary/showTerm.asp?term_id=74>.
[148] See generally Joseph Gold, 'The Legal Character of the Fund's Stand-by Arrangements and Why it Matters', IMF Pamphlet Series No 35, Washington DC, 1980.
[149] Para 9 2002 Guidelines (Decision I).

their own currencies from the IMF with other members currencies or SDRs over a specified time.

On 25 September 2002, the Fund published new guidelines on conditionality. These new guidelines comprise two decisions and a statement to staff with the principles underlying the guidelines on conditionality. Decision No I is entitled 'Guidelines on Conditionality' and Decision No II is entitled 'Stand By Arrangements'.[150] This latter decision, which refers to Article V, section 3(a), (b), and (c), Use of Fund's Resources, Credit Tranche Policies, Stand-By Arrangements, Extended Fund Facility, and Extended Arrangements, states the following:

1. Access to Fund resources in the credit tranches will normally be provided through a stand-by arrangement.
2. A representation of need by a member for a purchase requested under a stand-by arrangement will not be challenged by the Fund.
3. The normal period for a stand-by arrangement will range from 12 to 18 months. If a longer period is requested by a member and is considered necessary by the Fund to enable the member to implement its adjustment program successfully, the stand-by arrangement may extend beyond this range, up to a maximum of three years.
4. Phasing and performance clauses will be omitted in stand-by arrangements within the first credit tranche. They will be included in all other stand-by arrangements but will apply only to purchases outside the first credit tranche. For an arrangement within the first credit tranche, a member may be required to describe the general policies it plans to pursue, including its intention to avoid introducing or intensifying exchange and trade restrictions.

Financial assistance through an arrangement (stand-by arrangement in the credit tranches or extended arrangement under the Extended Fund Facility) is the instrument typically used in the non-concessional facilities the Fund offers to its members to help them remedy their balance of payments difficulties.

Extended arrangements

An extended arrangement (under the Extended Fund Facility, which I discuss below) is similar in nature to a traditional standby arrangement, though the assistance is given for a longer period (typically three years) and in amounts larger in relation to quotas than ordinary standby arrangements, and repayment of the currencies the member draws is to be made within four to ten years of the drawing.

> Extended arrangements are not defined in the Articles but they are regarded as 'similar' to stand-by arrangements for purposes of Article V, Section 3(a). There are certain differences between the two instruments because they are used under

---

[150] <http://www.imf.org/external/pubs/ft/sd/index.asp?decision=12865-(02/102)>.

different policies, but the source and nature of the commitment are the same as for stand-by arrangements. Therefore, the same definition applies to them and their legal nature is identical.[151]

Conditionality

Conditionality refers to the policies and procedures developed by the Fund to govern the access to and the use of its resources by member countries. Since these resources exist for the benefit of the entire membership and are finite, their use needs to be temporary and consistent with the purposes of the Fund.

Conditionality can be defined as the link between the approval or continuation of the Fund's financing and the implementation of specified elements of economic policy by the country receiving the financing, that is, the link between the adjustment effort by the country and the financing by the Fund.[152] Ross Leckow defines conditionality as 'those features of a member country's program of economic reform whose successful implementation is expressly established by the IMF as a condition for the availability of IMF financial assistance'.[153]

The 2002 'Guidelines on Conditionality' which I further discuss below, present some elements for a definition:

> Conditionality—that is program-related conditions—is intended to ensure that Fund resources are provided to members to assist them in resolving their balance of payments problems in a manner that is consistent with the Fund's Articles and that establishes adequate safeguards for the temporary use of the Fund's resources.[154]
>
> Conditionality is one element in a broad strategy for helping members strengthen their economic and financial policies.[155]
>
> Program-related conditions may contemplate the members meeting particular targets or objectives (outcomes-based conditionality) or taking (or refraining from taking) particular actions (actions-based conditionality).[156]

The history of conditionality

The word conditionality did not appear in the original Articles of Agreement. John Maynard Keynes had advocated in his proposals that member states should

---

[151] See Gianviti, 'Evolving Role and Challenges for the International Monetary Fund', above note 2, 57.

[152] 'Conditionality is the framework that assures Fund financing is being used in support of an agreed program.' See IMF, 'Financial Risk in the Fund and the Level of Precautionary Balances', above note 34, 13.

[153] See Ross Leckow, 'Conditionality in the International Monetary Fund' in *Current Developments in Monetary and Financial Law*, Vol 3 (Washington DC: IMF, 2005) 53.

[154] Decision No 12864–(02/102), 25 September 2002, Guidelines on conditionality (Decision I), principle 1. See <http://www.imf.org/external/pubs/ft/sd/index.asp?decision=12864–(02/102)>.

[155] ibid, principle 2.   [156] ibid, principle 7(c).

have 'an automatic entitlement' to draw on the resources of the Fund, while Harry Dexter White had urged that the resources only be made available if the country met the 'conditions' set down by the Fund.[157] In the end, Keynes's case for unconditional access would apply only to the 'gold tranche' (now the 'reserve tranche'), while White's proposals influenced the original text of Article V, section 3 of the Articles of Agreement, which established a set of 'conditions governing the use of the Fund's resources'. However these 'conditions' did not amount to the current notion of 'conditionality'.

The original Articles of Agreement contained no explicit statement that the Fund had to adopt policies on the use of its resources.[158] The First Amendment to the Articles of Agreement introduced clear language that required the Fund to have policies on the use of its resources.

Though the word conditionality was first used in the 1964 IMF Annual Report,[159] two decisions of the Executive Board of 10 March 1948[160] and 13 February 1952[161] already anticipated the concept. The 1952 decision is of particular importance in the Fund's history, since it also set the basis for the creation of the standby arrangement.

The reference to stand-by arrangements in the IMF Articles of Agreement was introduced by the Second Amendment, Article V, section 3(a) and Article XXX(b).

Conditionality evolved through the life and practices of the institution. Sir Joseph Gold[162] once wrote that 'the dynamism of the Fund has been particularly apparent in the development of new policies and practices connected with the use of its resources in order to meet the changing needs of the international monetary system.'[163] It is in this context that conditionality needs to be understood.

---

157 See Lowenfeld, above note 2, 513.

158 See Joseph Gold, 'Conditionality', IMF Pamphlet Series No 31 (Washington DC: IMF, 1979) 3.

159 ibid 2. Gold cites the following extract from the 1964 IMF Annual Report: 'Drawings beyond the gold tranche . . . are conditional, in greater or lesser degree, on the adoption by the drawing countries of policies designed to ensure the temporary character of their payments problem.'

160 Decision No 284–4, 10 March 1948. '[T]he Fund may postpone or reject the request [use of Fund's resources], or accept it subject to conditions.'

161 Decision No 102–(52/11), 13 February 1952. 'The Fund's attitude toward the position of each member should turn on whether the problem to be met is of a temporary nature and whether the policies the member will pursue will be adequate to overcome the problems within such a period.'

162 His article on 'Conditionality', published as IMF Pamphlet No 31 in 1979, remains an authoritative reference for the understanding of the subject.

163 See Gold, above note 158, 24.

In 1968 the Fund published some guidelines on conditionality[164] that were revised and expanded in 1979.[165] Though those guidelines were useful at the time, they became obsolete with the passage of time. In September 2000, the then Managing Director, Horst Köhler, issued an Interim Guidance Note on Streamlining Structural Conditionality to staff, indicating that he viewed streamlining and focusing conditionality as well as 'strengthening national ownership' as a priority. Accordingly, Fund staff embarked on a review of various issues associated with conditionality. This review gave rise to a number of papers,[166] which were then discussed by the Executive Board.[167] The comprehensive review resulted in the adoption of a new set of conditionality guidelines by the Executive Board on 25 September 2002, replacing the 1979 guidelines.

These 2002 guidelines were prepared by the Legal and Policy Development and Review Department in consultation with other departments, and comprise two decisions. Decision No I is entitled 'Guidelines on Conditionality' and Decision No II is entitled 'Stand By Arrangements'.[168] In considering the new guidelines, the Board also discussed and approved a statement to staff, providing additional explanation and context with regard to the principles underlying the guidelines on conditionality.

On 8 May 2003, a note entitled 'Operational Guidance on the New Conditionality Guidelines' was published.[169] This guidance elaborated upon the operational implications of the new guidelines, covering three areas: (i) negotiation and programme design progress; (ii) design of conditionality; and (iii) the presentation of conditionality in Board papers. In March 2005, the Executive Board

---

[164] Decision No 2603–(68/132), 20 September 1968.

[165] Decision No 6056–(79–38), 2 March 1979.

[166] The following papers prepared by IMF staff are available at the IMF's website <http: www.imf.org>: 'Conditionality in Fund-Supported Programs—Overview', 'Conditionality in Fund-Supported Programs—Policy Issues', 'Structural Conditionality in Fund-Supported Programs', 'Trade Policy Conditionality in Fund-Supported Programs', 'Strengthening Country Ownership of Fund-Supported Programs', 'Streamlining Conditionality and Enhancing Ownership', 'Strengthening IMF–World Bank Collaboration on Country Programs and Conditionality', 'Modalities of Conditionality'.

[167] The results of these discussions by the Board are typically published as Public Information Notices (PINs). The following PINs relating to conditionality have been issued at the request of the Board: Public Information Notice (PIN) No 01/28, March 2001; Public Information Notice (PIN) No 01/92, July 2001; Public Information Notice (PIN) No 01/125, December 2001, and Public Information Notice (PIN) No 02/26, March 2002.

[168] The Guidelines on Conditionality are published on the IMF's website at <http://www.imf.org/external/np/pdr/cond/2002/eng/guid/092302.pdf> and in the volume of 'Selected Decisions and Selected Documents of the IMF', as updated of 31 December 2004 (Decision I at <http://www.imf.org/external/pubs/ft/sd/index.asp?decision=12864–(02/102)> and Decision II at <http://www.imf.org/external/pubs/ft/sd/index.asp?decision=12865–(02/102)>.

[169] See <http://www.imf.org/External/np/pdr/cond/2003/eng/050803.htm>.

reviewed the application of the new guidelines, concluding that substantial progress had been made.

The legal basis of conditionality

The word conditionality does not have a precise legal meaning under the IMF Articles of Agreement. This lack of clearly defined legal contours helps explain why conditionality has changed over the years.[170] The interpretation of conditionality is not independent of the international economic regime in place.[171]

In the words of the late Sir Joseph Gold in 1979: '[T]he word conditionality . . . is not a legal term of art. . . . There is no absolute standard on conditionality. The [IMF] Articles [of Agreement] give no express guidance on what policies the Fund should encourage members to follow under its policies of conditionality'.[172]

The word conditionality is currently interpreted by the Fund according to Article V, section 3(a) as amended in 1978, which reads as follows:

> The Fund shall adopt policies on the use of its general resources, including policies on stand-by or similar arrangements, and may adopt special policies for special balance of payment problems, that will assist members to solve their balance of payments problems in a manner consistent with the provisions of this Agreement and that will establish adequate safeguards for the temporary use of the general resources of the Fund.

In addition to Article V, section 3(a), the interpretation of conditionality must also take into account Article I, paragraph (v) which refers to the need for 'adequate safeguards' in the temporary provision of resources by the Fund.[173] As Gianviti points out, 'The broad definition of its purposes in Article I gives the IMF a large degree of latitude in the formulation of policies on the use of its

---

[170] This changing nature of conditionality was stressed by the former Director of the Monetary and Exchange Affairs Department, Manuel Guitián, in three papers: 'Fund Conditionality: Evolution of Principles and Practices', IMF Pamphlet No 38, 1981; 'The Unique Nature of the Fund's Responsibilities', IMF Pamphlet No 46, 1992; and 'Conditionality: Past, Present and Future', 42 IMF Staff Papers, No 4, December 1995.

[171] See 'Fund Conditionality: Evolution of Principles & Practices' and 'Conditionality: Past, Present and Future', ibid.

[172] See Gold, above note 158, 2. Sir Joseph also noted (ibid 1) that 'conditionality cannot be defined by reference to the "conditions" of Article V, Section 3(b).'

[173] According to Principle 1 of the 2002 Guidelines on conditionality: 'Conditions on the use of Fund resources are governed by the Fund's Articles of Agreement and implementing decisions of the Executive Board'. See <http://www.imf.org/external/pubs/ft/sd/index.asp?decision=12864-(02/102)>.

resources, and over the years, has allowed the IMF to adapt its policies and expand the scope of conditionality in the light of experience.'[174]

The guidelines on conditionality are not legally binding principles in the way the Articles of Agreement are. A decision of the Executive Board can be repealed or amended by a subsequent decision. Indeed, the Decision regarding the 1979 guidelines was repealed by the 2002 Decision adopting the new guidelines.

According to Gianviti, conditionality consists of 'three layers of conditions'.[175] He explains that the first layer consists of the Articles of Agreement and the policies adopted by the Fund under the Articles. The second layer consists of the standby or other arrangements, which specify the particular conditions applicable to the assistance provided under that arrangement (in particular, performance criteria and reviews). The third layer of conditionality is based upon the recommendations by the Managing Director and the staff with regard to the approval of an arrangement (prior actions and benchmarks).[176] Four types of 'conditions' are identified: performance criteria, reviews, prior actions, and benchmarks, in addition to the 'conditions' imposed by the IMF Articles of Agreement.

The rationale of conditionality

Conditionality has served a variety of purposes over the years:[177]

1. It is a filter to channel financial assistance. The provision of financial assistance to countries in need is not automatic, but conditional (only the reserve tranche can be accessed unconditionally). IMF financial assistance (support to members experiencing balance of payments problems) is conditional on the adoption and implementation of adjustment policies. The logic behind the conditionality requirements is that a country with external payments problems is spending more than it is taking in. Unless economic reform takes place, it will continue to spend more than it takes in. This filter function is clearly manifested in the 'phasing out' technique of conditionality: successive tranches of financing are delivered only if key objectives remain attainable.

---

[174] See Gianviti, above note 12, 56. For a discussion of the procedural requirements that govern the adoption of decisions by the Executive Board, see Gianviti, ibid 50–6. He points out, *inter alia*, that despite the different semantics, there is no clear distinction between guidelines and decisions (53). The decisions of the organs of the IMF must be (i) consistent with the Articles; (ii) consistent with higher norms; (iii) consistent with the regulations made by that organ (ibid 54). *The IMF may not make retroactive decisions to the detriment of its member countries* (ibid 59).

[175] See François Gianviti, 'Evolving Role and Challenges for the International Monetary Fund' in Mads Andenas and Joseph Norton (eds), *International Monetary and Financial Law Upon Entering the New Millenium. A Tribute to Sir Joseph and Ruth Gold*, above note 2, 57–9.

[176] ibid.

[177] See Rosa M Lastra, 'IMF Conditionality' (2002) 4 Journal of International Banking Regulation 167, 171.

2. Conditionality procedures represent the essence of the 'adequate safeguards' prescribed in Article 1(v) of the Articles of Agreement. ('[T]o give confidence to members by making the general resources of the Fund temporarily available to them under adequate safeguards.') Conditionality is consistent with the nature of the IMF resources, which are finite and exist for the benefit of the entire membership. Conditionality protects the quality of the IMF asset portfolio, as Manuel Guitián emphasized.[178] Access limits, phasing of purchases, and repurchase policies[179] constitute important safeguards for the temporary use of such resources.

   In recent years, the Fund has developed other safeguards[180] both to protect outstanding credit (such as 'safeguards assessments of central banks', which aim at preventing the misuse of Fund resources and the misreporting of information[181]) as well as to assist members in clearing 'arrears' (ie, overdue financial obligations) to the Fund.

3. It is a tool to promote 'good policies'. Countries seeking IMF financial assistance know that only good policies will 'earn' them a programme. This knowledge makes the 'ownership' issue all the more difficult. This issue is addressed by the 2002 Guidelines (Principle 7), which aims to circumscribe the scope of conditionality:[182]

   > Program-related conditions governing the provision of Fund resources will be applied parsimoniously. . . . Conditions will normally consist of macro-economic variables and structural measures that are within the Fund's core areas of responsibility. Variables and measures that are outside the Fund's core areas of responsibility may also be established as conditions but may require more detailed explanation of their critical importance. The Fund's core areas of responsibility in this context comprise: macroeconomic stabilization; monetary, fiscal, and exchange rate policies, including the underlying institutional arrangements and closely related structural measures; and financial system issues related to the functioning of both domestic and international financial markets.

4. It serves as a substitute for collateral. Banks require collateral in commercial lending. Conditionality operates as a substitute for collateral in lending to sovereign borrowers.[183]

5. It signals policy credibility to the markets. The existence of an IMF programme encourages private investment into the country. This explains why countries are ready to tighten their belts (and the belts of their citizens) in order to get and maintain an IMF programme. The eagerness to get or

---

[178] See Manuel Guitián, 'Conditionality: Past, Present, Future', above note 170, 796.
[179] Above note 32, 30–8.   [180] Above note 32, 13. See also above note 34, 17.
[181] See Press Release No 02/19, 4 May 2002, 'IMF adopts safeguards assessments as a permanent policy'. See also above note 34, 14.
[182] <http://www.imf.org/external/pubs/ft/sd/index.asp?decision=12864-(02/102)>.
[183] See Ch 14.

maintain a programme may also help explain why, in some instances, specific measures in a programme have been proposed, without a full awareness or analysis of their potentially negative social implications. The importance attached by countries to IMF conditionality goes beyond the importance they attach to the fulfilment of other obligations undertaken as members of international organizations. In a tacit acknowledgement of the need to take into account the circumstances of members, Principle 4 of the 2002 Guidelines states:[184]

> In helping members to devise economic and financial programs, the Fund will pay due regard to the domestic social and political objectives, the economic priorities, and the circumstances of members, including the causes of their balance of payments problems and their administrative capacity to implement reforms.

6. It is an instrument to reduce moral hazard. In the words of Guitián:

> The availability of IMF financial assistance provides a measure of insurance against adverse shocks and the emergence of external imbalances. In common with all insurance activities, it raises the spectre of moral hazard in the form of *less determination on the part of the member countries toward the adoption or maintenance of appropriate policies.* By making its resources conditional on the implementation of adjustment measures, the risk of moral hazard is thus contained[185] (emphasis added).

The critique of conditionality

Conditionality has been the subject of fierce opposition and criticism through the years.[186] The Meltzer Report concluded that 'the use of IMF resources and conditionality to control the economies of developing nations often undermines the sovereignty and democratic processes of member governments receiving assistance.'[187] A report produced by an independent task force within the Council on Foreign Relations stated that 'The IMF should limit the scope of its conditionality to monetary, fiscal, exchange rate, and financial-sector policies.'[188]

In part in response to some of these criticisms, the IMF undertook its own review of conditionality (which led to the 2002 guidelines) in order to identify a number of issues that ought to be revised and that constituted an agenda for reform of conditionality.

---

[184] <http://www.imf.org/external/pubs/ft/sd/index.asp?decision=12864-(02/102)>.

[185] See Manuel Guitián, 'Conditionality: Past, Present, Future', above note 170, 796.

[186] A former IMF Executive Director once told me: 'To some people the word conditionality evokes memories of Gestapo knocking at the door at 4.00 am.'

[187] Report to the US Congress by the International Financial Institutions Advisory Commission (commonly known as the 'Meltzer Report' since Allan Meltzer chaired the Commission), March 2000, available at <http://www.house.gov/jec/imf/ifiac.htm>.

[188] Council on Foreign Relations, Report of an Independent Task Force, 'Safeguarding Prosperity In A Global Financial System, The Future International Financial Architecture', 1999, 116.

With regard to the policies that ought to be covered by conditionality, a considerable broadening in the scope of Fund programmes was identified as a problem. The expansion of conditionality into the 'structural' area has been the consequence of a number of factors. First, it reflects the increasing emphasis on growth as a policy objective, driven by the view that demand management alone is inadequate to address the pressing economic problems of member countries and, thus, that supply-side measures and institutional policies are necessary. Secondly, it is a result of the Fund's involvement with low-income countries (suffering from structural imbalances), with transitional economies (where structural reforms have been essential), and with countries experiencing financial crises, where 'structural weaknesses' in the financial sector have been at the root of the problem. Thirdly, the very success of macroeconomic policies depends on structural reforms (hence the name 'structural conditionality'), including the removal of market distortions and the establishment of the institutional underpinnings for effective policy making in a market economy. The broadening of conditionality into areas like legal reform is a recognition that durable capital flows these days take the form of equity investments and that those investors are at much greater risk of weaknesses in the local legal system.

The problem with the broadening scope of these programmes is that structural reforms in areas outside the Fund's core of expertise, such as public enterprise restructuring, privatization, and social security reform, have also grown, on the consideration that they are linked to fiscal adjustment. Against this broadening scope of conditionality, the Board rightly recommended the need to streamline and focus it. The Fund should not overstep its mandate and expertise.

Another area of streamlining identified by the Board referred to the monitoring of programmes. An excessive degree of detail in programme monitoring may create the impression that the Fund is trying to 'micro-manage' the authorities' policy programme. Performance criteria, programme reviews, prior actions, and structural benchmarks are the tools of monitoring subject to review.[189] While the first three techniques were mentioned in the 1979 Guidelines, structural benchmarks were not. Structural benchmarks, however, have become increasingly used in the last decade as a monitoring technique, owing to the fact that structural reforms are often difficult to characterize through quantifiable objective performance criteria. This proliferation in the use of structural benchmarks,[190] however, is one of the factors contributing to the excessive

---

[189] A definition of each of these four forms of programme monitoring is provided in the Staff Paper on 'Structural Conditionality in Fund-Supported Programs', above note 166.

[190] Examples of structural benchmarks are provided, for instance, with regard to a stand-by arrangement approved in July 1996 for Estonia, cited in the paper on 'Structural Conditionality in Fund-Supported Programs', above note 166, 44. Twenty-two structural benchmarks are mentioned, of which twelve are legal measures.

expansion of conditionality, and therefore has been criticized by the IMF Board. Interestingly, a great number of these structural benchmarks are legal measures, reflecting the demand by investors for a reliable local legal infrastructure. The Board also expressed a concern that excessively detailed conditionality may undermine the national ownership of a policy programme and strain the country's administrative capacity.

The Board recommended that letters of intent (LOIs) should make a clearer distinction between the authorities' overall policy programme and the part of that programme that is subject to the Fund's conditionality. Fund-supported programmes have sometimes 'short-circuited' national decision-making processes and failed to take adequate account of the authorities' ability to muster public support for the policies envisaged, as well as their administrative capacity to implement these policies. This was identified as a serious problem, one which undermined the nature of conditionality. Governments frequently outlined in LOIs their broader policy agenda—including reforms agreed with other institutions such as the World Bank—to reaffirm their agenda before domestic and international audiences. Such broad policy agendas often become untenable objectives both to carry out and to monitor. Hence the need to streamline the contents of the LOIs.

The 2002 guidelines on conditionality

The 2002 guidelines on conditionality replace the 1979 guidelines.[191] They comprise two decisions, which elaborate upon principles applied to the 'use of Fund's resources' under Article V, section 3(a), (b), and (c) of the Articles of Agreement.

The first decision[192] is divided into three sections: section (A) on 'principles' (paras 1–8), section (B) on 'modalities' (paras 9–13) and section (C) on 'evaluation and review'. This division is somewhat unclear in my opinion, since the section on principles comprises both some of the principles underlying conditionality (which are then spelt out in a staff statement attached to the guidelines) and some other definitional issues. Furthermore, the section on 'modalities' refers to the nature of the Fund arrangement and the member's programme on the one hand, and to the monitoring techniques the Fund uses to assess the performance of a member on the other hand.

---

[191] Above note 168. Paragraph No 16 of the 2002 Guidelines (Decision I) states: 'Decision No. 270–(53–95), adopted December 23, 1953, *Stand-by Arrangements* as amended, Decision No. 6056–(79–38), adopted March 2, 1979, *Guidelines on Conditionality*, and Decision No. C-3220–(01/24), adopted March 9, 2001, *Concluding Remarks by the Chairman—Conditionality in Fund-supported programs* are repealed.'

[192] See <http://www.imf.org/external/pubs/ft/sd/index.asp?decision=12864-(02/102)>.

So, how does conditionality work in practice? Along with the request for financial assistance, the member presents to the IMF a plan of reform (a 'programme') typically outlined in a Letter of Intent (LOI) or a Memorandum on Economic and Financial Policies (MEFP) that may be accompanied by a Technical Memorandum of Understanding (TMU).[193] In the programme documents, the member sets out some macroeconomic (fiscal, monetary, and exchange rate), financial, institutional, or closely related structural objectives or policies. The specifics of the programme are selected by the member, not by the Fund. Indeed, the primary responsibility for the design of the programme lies with a member's authorities. 'The letter of intent is a statement of intention, not the undertaking of obligations.'[194]

The issue of the national 'ownership' of the programme remains a thorny one. The truth is that in the past the Fund has exerted a very influential role in the design of these programmes. On the one hand, this is a result of its surveillance function, as the Fund identifies problems through its Article IV consultations. On the other hand, this is a result of the members' eagerness to get the assistance; countries know what the Fund likes and dislikes—often referred to as 'the Washington consensus'—and are unlikely to choose policies or objectives that run against that consensus. In addition, the countries know that the Executive Board will judge the sufficiency of the reform measures and whether the IMF can reasonably expect payment before giving the green light to the approval of the assistance.

A member's programme is the member's unilateral commitment to policies, as set forth in the LOI or MEPF. This unilateral character is important for legal purposes, because if it formed part of an 'agreement' between the Member and the Fund, then failure to fulfil the letter of intent could be seen as giving rise to a breach of an international obligation. It is important to make a distinction between a member's 'programme' and the 'Fund arrangement'.

A Fund arrangement is a decision by the Fund to provide financing to the member, subject to certain conditions. These conditions are merely elements of the member's programme that the Fund finds particularly important, but they are always derived from the member's programme. From a conditionality perspective, the programme sets forth the design of policies, while the arrangement provides the basis for monitoring the implementation of those policies.

> A Fund arrangement is a decision by the Executive Board by which a member is assured that it will be able to make purchases or receive disbursements from the

---

[193] ibid, para 10.
[194] See Gianviti, 'The Role of the Fund in the Financing of External Debt', above note 135, 253.

Fund in accordance with the terms of the decision during a specified period and up to a specified amount. *Fund arrangements are not international agreements and therefore language having a contractual connotation will be avoided in arrangements and in program documents.* Appropriate consultation clauses will be incorporated in all arrangements. (Emphasis added).[195]

The monitoring of performance, assessing the implementation of the member's understandings with the Fund (the programme), is carried out through prior actions, performance criteria, programme or other reviews, and other variables and measures established as structural benchmarks or indicative targets.[196]

A performance criterion is defined as a variable or measure whose observance or implementation is established as a formal condition that must be met for the Fund's financing to continue, unless the IMF Executive Board grants a waiver. The availability of further instalments or purchases under the arrangement (phasing out) is made conditional on the member's observance of those variables or measures. Non-observance leads to the interruption of the financing. The 'phasing out technique' is at the core of IMF conditionality and remains an essential component in the new guidelines. If the money were to be disbursed in one single lump instalment, members would not be motivated to continue reform, and, thus, the very logic of conditionality would be distorted. Though performance criteria are generally expected to be met by a specified date, the possibility of 'floating tranches' is foreseen in the new guidelines, when the Fund judges that introducing 'flexibility in timing would promote national ownership', in particular in the case of 'structural performance criteria'.[197]

Prior actions are measures that the Fund expects the member to adopt in some cases (eg, before approving an arrangement or completing a review).

Programme reviews are typically held every six months to provide a framework for assessing whether the programme is on track or whether modifications are necessary. In addition to programme reviews, the Fund also conducts 'financing assurances reviews' in the case of members that have 'outstanding sovereign external payments to private creditors, or that by virtue of the imposition of exchange controls, has outstanding non-sovereign external payments arrears' so as 'to determine whether adequate safeguards are in place'.[198]

Indicative targets are variables that 'cannot be established as performance criteria because of substantial uncertainty about economic trends' or quantitative indicators introduced in addition to performance criteria to assess the progress of the member in meeting the objectives of a programme.[199]

---

[195] Paragraph No 9 of the 2002 Guidelines (Decision I).   [196] ibid, para 11.
[197] ibid, para 13.   [198] ibid, para 11(c)(ii).   [199] ibid, para 11(d)(i).

Structural benchmarks are defined in rather vague terms and comprise a variety of measures not included in the other categories of monitoring techniques.[200] A structural benchmark is different from a performance criterion in that failing to achieve it would not by itself interrupt the Fund's financing.

The Executive Board reviews the performance of the member under programmes supported by use of the Fund's resources in connection with Article IV consultation and in connection with further requests for assistance.[201] This review by the Executive Board is typically informed by the staff's appraisal of such performance.

Principles underlying the guidelines on conditionality

A staff statement attached to the 2002 guidelines explains the key principles that should guide the Fund in designing and implementing conditionality.[202] Chief among these 'principles underlying the guidelines on conditionality' are: (i) national ownership of reform programmes, (ii) parsimony in the application of programme-related conditions; (iii) tailoring of programmes to the member's circumstances; (iv) effective coordination with other multilateral institutions; and (v) clarity in the specification of conditions.

National ownership refers to a willing assumption of responsibility for a programme of policies, by country officials who have the responsibility to formulate and carry out those policies. National ownership along with the member's administrative capacity to implement reforms is identified as the key element for the success of the reform programme. However, as I mentioned above, the issue of national ownership remains a thorny one. Indeed the operational guidance on the new conditionality guidelines[203] acknowledges the limitations of national ownership when it admits that 'the [national] authorities might have limited capacity or inclination to draft program documents.' In this respect, technical assistance might be needed to enable those authorities to make 'informed choices'.

Programme conditions should not be too numerous, hence the principle of parsimony. Tailoring of programmes is the recognition that each programme is different, since the specific circumstances (causes of balance of payment difficulties), priorities, and time framework in each country are different. Fund policies

---

[200] ibid, para 11(d)(ii).   [201] ibid, para 13.

[202] <http://www.imf.org/external/np/pdr/cond/2002/eng/guid/092302.pdf>. With regard to the legal value of this staff statement, para 14 states: 'In case of conflicts between this explanatory staff statement and the guidelines or other related Board decisions, the language in the relevant decision takes precedence.'

[203] Above note 169.

must be applied consistently though, so as to maintain the uniform treatment of members.

Coordination with other multilateral institutions, in particular with the World Bank (and I would also add interdepartmental coordination), addresses the need to avoid overlaps, unnecessary duplications, as well as the need to have a lead agency in terms of responsibility and accountability. The guidelines specify in principle 8 (Decision 1) that 'There will be no cross-conditionality.'

Clarity is related to transparency and also to the principles of parsimony and tailoring. The authorities must clearly distinguish what is the specific domain of conditionality (ie, the parts of the reform agenda upon which continued access to Fund resources depend) and what is the broader policy agenda which they wish to set out for national and international audiences (but which is not a condition for the use of Fund resources).[204]

The provision of information and consequences of 'misreporting'

The effectiveness of conditionality is also dependent upon the provision of accurate information by the member with regard to the design and implementation of the programme.[205] Article VIII, section V imposes a legal obligation upon members with regard to the reporting of information to the Fund.

There have been cases in recent years in which countries receiving financial assistance have 'misreported' economic data to the Fund.[206] Misreporting has major consequences under the Fund's policies on use of its resources and may constitute a breach of Article VIII, section 5. Failure to report at all or to do so in a timely manner, or to report inaccurate information, can lead to the imposition of the sanctions specified in Article XXVI (including, ultimately, the compulsory withdrawal from membership of the Fund if the member persistently fails to fulfil the obligation).[207]

In January 2004 the Executive Board adopted a decision to strengthen the effectiveness of Article VIII, section 5.[208]

---

[204] ibid.

[205] See François Gianviti, 'Provision of Information to the IMF' in *Current Developments in Monetary and Financial Law*, Vol 2 (Washington DC: IMF, 2003) 13–14.

[206] See Ross Leckow, 'The obligation of Members to Provide Information to the International Monetary Fund under Article VIII, Section 5: Recent Developments' in *Current Developments in Monetary and Financial Law*, Vol 4 (Washington DC: IMF, 2005) 42. Leckow cites the case of Ukraine, where the IMF found that the Ukrainian National Bank misreported international reserves (IMF News Brief No 00/77, 9 June 2000).

[207] ibid 48–9.

[208] See Decision No 13183–(04/0), 30 January 2004, 'Strengthening the Effectiveness of Article VIII, Section 5', available at <http://www.imf.org/external/pubs/ft/sd/index.asp? decision=13183-(04/10)>.

In 1984, the IMF put in place a separate framework of guidelines on misreporting to deal with cases in which members fail accurately to report information associated with the provision of IMF financial assistance, such as information regarding the observance of performance criteria.[209] The guidelines specify the corrective actions or remedies to be taken in the case of misreporting.[210]

A decision of the Executive Board of 27 July 2000 on the 'Establishment of General Policy to Condition Decisions in the General Resources Account on Accuracy of Information Regarding Implementation of Prior Actions', reads as follows:

> Any decision on the use of resources in the General Resources Account (including decisions approving an arrangement or an outright purchase, completing a review, or granting a waiver either of applicability or for the non-observance of a performance criterion) will be made conditional upon the accuracy of the information provided by the member regarding implementation of prior actions specified in the decision.[211]

'Hard conditionality' versus 'soft conditionality'

Since the interpretation of conditionality is not independent of the international economic regime in place,[212] and since there is no absolute standard in the Articles of Agreement concerning its understanding, it is possible to talk about different types of conditionality. Today, 'hard' or 'strict' conditionality coexists with 'milder' or 'softer' conditionality in some cases and with 'stricter' conditionality in some other cases.

The Fund has tried over the years to apply more lenient standards in special cases. The lower the conditionality, the higher the degree of automaticity.

The Second Amendment to the IMF Articles of Agreement introduced the word 'special' in Article V, section 3(a), to 'adopt special policies for special balance of payments problems'. This is the legal basis for the creation over the years of *special* policies.[213] Article V, section 3(a) thus enables the Fund to establish different terms, different facilities, different mechanisms to respond to

---

[209] See Decision No 7842–(84/165), 16 November 1984, as amended by Decision No 12249–(00/77), 27 July 2000, 'Misresporting and Noncomplying Purchase in the General Resources Account—Guidelines on Corrective Action', and the 'Summing Up by the Acting Chair Review of Side Letters and the Use of Fund Resources', Executive Board Meeting 02/59, 12 June 2002, published in Selected Decisions (29th issue), above note 3, 234–7.

[210] See Gianviti, above note 205, 15.

[211] See Decision No 12250–(00/77), 27 July 2000, above note 3, 237.

[212] Above note 171.

[213] As Sir Joseph Gold points out (above note 158, 11): 'The legal justification for a special policy is that it deals with a difficulty that is distinguishable from other difficulties according to *bona fide* economic criteria and that there are good reasons why a special policy should be created to take care of that difficulty.'

diverse needs. Special policies are often more attractive because they have more favourable terms, such as longer repurchase periods (eg, the Extended Fund Facility, EFF). However, in some cases the terms are more severe; for example the surcharge—higher rate of interest—that applies in the case of the Supplemental Reserve Facility, SRF.

The controversy that surrounds the relaxation of conditionality is not new. Sir Joseph Gold already pointed out in 1979 some of the problems of 'milder conditionality':

> The contention that conditionality should be milder creates a dilemma. . . . If the Fund's standards of conditionality were lowered, the change would become known and probably the Fund would have less influence on other potential lenders. . . . The dilemma would not be so grave for some members because they do not have access to other means of financing. . . . For these members, the provision of larger resources by the Fund on the basis of milder conditionality than at present would be a net financial benefit in the short run. Lower standards of conditionality, however, could be detrimental to all members in a difficult balance of payments or reserve position if this relaxation were to discourage some members from agreeing to increase the Fund's resources by the adjustment of quotas or by loans to it. Some members argue that milder conditionality would not result in the neglect of adjustment but would only extend it over a longer period.[214]

From a legal point of view, the coexistence of different types of conditionality can be justified through the principle of uniformity in combination with the legal objective of symmetry. The principle of uniformity, embodied in the IMF Articles of Agreement, provides that policies adopted by the Fund in the exercise of its functions must not discriminate against or in favour of a particular member.[215] It is reminiscent of the doctrine of the equality of states in international law.[216] However, the uniformity of rights and obligations and the uniform application of the policies of the Fund require that members be treated alike if they are in the same circumstances.

Symmetry focuses on the treatment of members in different circumstances. Unlike uniformity, the objective of symmetry does not aim at ensuring equality of treatment (of members in the same circumstances), but focuses instead on the comparability of the treatment of members in different circumstances, which involves in turn, a subjective judgement.[217] Circumstances create different types of countries: debtor and creditor countries, deficit and surplus countries,

---

[214] See Sir Joseph Gold, 'Conditionality', IMF Pamphlet Series No 31 (1979), 14–15.
[215] See Sir Joseph Gold, 'Uniformity as a Legal Principle of the International Monetary Fund' (1975) 7 Law and Policy in International Business 765, 767.
[216] ibid 768.
[217] See Sir Joseph Gold, 'Symmetry as a Legal Objective of the International Monetary System' (1980) 12 New York University Journal of International Law and Politics 423, 475.

developed and developing countries, reserve and non-reserve centres, countries that adopt the obligations of Article VIII and countries that operate under the transitional arrangements of Article XIV. The rights and obligations of different types of countries are not the same. Countries of the same type, however, must have the same rights and obligations. The symmetrical effects of rights and obligations on the different classes of members is an important consideration in the Fund's operations.[218]

(3) Technical Assistance

The third main function performed by the IMF is technical assistance (Art V, s 2(b) of the Articles of Agreement). This task has grown in importance in recent years. The IMF provides technical assistance to its members on their request. However, technical assistance is not a right of a member and requests are sometimes turned down or discouraged because of tight resources or for other reasons.[219]

The IMF began providing technical assistance in the mid 1960s when many newly independent countries sought the advice of the IMF to set up their central banks and ministries of finance.[220] Technical assistance and training in banking and monetary policy, foreign exchange, fiscal policy and statistics became a major function of the International Monetary Fund in the early 1990s, particularly in the transition from centrally planned economies to market economies in the formerly communist countries of Eastern Europe and the Former Soviet Union. More recently, as I further discuss in Chapter 14, the IMF's technical assistance function has focused on strengthening the international financial architecture.

The Legal Department of the IMF offers 'legal technical assistance' in the areas of banking and finance, central banking, taxation, foreign exchange, secured transactions, bankruptcy, and others.[221] This assistance includes drafting and reviewing legislation and implementing regulations and providing other legal advice.

Though the IMF 'competes' in the provision of technical assistance with other private institutions, members may often find it to their advantage to receive advice from the IMF, particularly if they have also requested conditional financial assistance from the Fund. In this sense, these two functions are

---

[218] ibid.

[219] The IMF's technical assistance work, with emphasis on 'legal technical assistance' is discussed in William E Holder, 'The IMF's Technical Assistance Activities' in Robert Effros (ed), *Current Legal Issues Affecting Central Banks*, Vol 3, (Washington DC: IMF, 1995).

[220] Above note 21.

[221] See Ch 5 regarding 'Monetary and Financial Law Reform in Emerging Economies'.

mutually reinforcing. Furthermore, through its surveillance function, the Fund can identify weaknesses in the economy and in the financial system, which can be corrected through adequate advice. The interplay between surveillance, conditionality, and technical assistance is a feature of the operations of the Fund.

In October 2005, the Fund approved a proposal establishing Policy Support Instruments to provide policy support to low-income countries that do not want—or do not need—financial assistance from the IMF, but still want the Fund to support, monitor, and endorse their policies.[222] This is in fact a form of technical assistance.

H. The Evolution of IMF Financial Facilities and Policies

This section surveys the various facilities, policies, and procedures that the Fund has devised over the years to channel financial resources to its members.

The term 'facilities' lacks conceptual precision in the Fund jargon (and in Fund publications), encompassing facilities, policies, instruments, procedures, and even accounts.

Though the Fund has been often criticized on the grounds that it prescribes the 'same medicine' no matter what the malaise may be, this criticism is not always justified, as the evolution of IMF facilities throughout its sixty years of existence evidences.

Taxonomy

IMF financial facilities and policies for the use of its resources can be classified according to different criteria. The first criterion is the concessional–non-concessional divide. Non-concessional financing is typically offered on a revolving basis, through the purchase and repurchase technique that characterizes standby arrangements, drawing on the Fund's general resources.[223] Concessional

---

[222] See Public Information Notice (PIN) No 05/145, 14 October 2005, 'IMF Executive Board Approves the Establishment of Policy Support Instruments for Aiding Low-Income Countries', at <http://www.imf.org/external/np/sec/pn/2005/pn05145.htm>. See also, International Monetary Fund, 'Policy Support Initiative. A Factsheet', December 2005, available at <http:www.imf.org/external/np/ext/facts/psi.htm>.

[223]

The borrowing member purchases from the Fund currencies of members in strong financial positions (which are reserve assets or currencies to be converted into reserve assets) in exchange for its own currency. The Fund has a claim on the borrowing member to repurchase its currency (represented by the use of Fund credit on the asset side of the balance) in exchange for reserve assets. The other member that provided the reserve assets has a claim on the Fund, called a reserve tranche position shown on the liability side of the

facilities are typically offered via loans. The resources available for concessional financing have been provided in part by members voluntarily and independently from their quota subscriptions and in part by the IMF itself. These resources are administered by trust funds (currently the PRGF and PRFG–HIPC Trusts) for which the IMF acts as a trustee (administered accounts).[224]

The mandatory policies referred to in Article V, section 3(a) are the credit tranche policies, including first credit tranche policies. The optional 'special policies' referred to in the same provision refer to those facilities that either (i) have a special repurchase period under Article V, section 7(d) or (ii) have a special rate of charge under Article V, section 8(d). These special policies include the Extended Fund Facility (EFF), the Compensatory Financing Facility (CFF), the Supplemental Reserve Facility (SRF), and the now defunct Currency Stabilization Funds and Contingent Credit Line (CCL, also defunct).[225]

The unduly complex structure of the facilities and policies adopted by the Fund with regard to the provision of financial assistance to members, the intricate and idiosyncratic terminology, and the lack of conceptual precision of the very term 'facilities' is acknowledged by the Fund in the review it conducted of its own (non-concessional) facilities. For the sake of 'presentational simplicity', the review states, that 'the paper refers collectively to the various policies on the use of Fund resources as *facilities*'.[226]

Concessional facilities: Financial assistance to low-income countries

The Fund is a monetary institution, not a development organization. However, the Fund has over the years addressed the 'special' needs of developing countries in various ways. As I mention below, the creation of the Extended Fund Facility in 1974 took account of the needs of these countries, since short-term balance of payments assistance is not the solution to remedy longer-term structural problems.

---

balance sheet. The currency that is provided in the financing is either a freely usable currency (U.S. dollar, euro, Japanese yen, and pound sterling) or the creditor member (if so requested by the borrowing member) exchanges its currency for a freely usable currency.

See International Monetary Fund, 'Financial Risk in the Fund and the Level of Precautionary Balances', Prepared by the Finance Department (in consultation with other departments), approved by Eduard Brau, 3 February 2004, 7, available at <http://www.imf.org/external/np/tre/risk/2004/020304.pdf>.

[224] Above note 52.

[225] I thank Sean Hagan for observations on this point. According to Gianviti, 'The Role of the Fund in the Financing of External Debt', above note 135, 251, 'All policies other than credit tranche policies are "special policies".'

[226] See International Monetary Fund, 'Review of Fund Facilities—Preliminary Considerations', prepared by the Policy Development and Review Department in consultation with other Departments, 2 March 2000, 5, <http://www.imf.org/external/np/pdr/fac/2000/faciliti.pdf>.

Low-income developing countries (which often lack access to private international capital markets) need a different set of responses to help them address their problems. They need lending over an extended period of time (or grants, with no expectation of repayment), and they need concessional terms regarding repayment, rate of charge, and access policy.

The Fund has created over the years several lending facilities to help the poorest countries in the world address their problems. In 1976 the IMF established the Trust Fund which drew upon the profits generated from the sale of part of the IMF's gold holdings and provided concessional loans to low-income developing countries.[227] In 1986 the Fund established the Structural Adjustment Facility to provide concessional loans by recycling resources lent under the Trust Fund. In 1987 the Fund established the Enhanced Structural Adjustment Facility. In October 1999 the ESAF was renamed as Poverty Reduction and Growth Facility (PRGF).[228]

Concessional facilities are made available via loans, and not through purchase and repurchase arrangements.

The resources used in concessional lending are separate from the IMF's general resources generated from quota subscriptions (GRA) and are typically provided through voluntary contributions by a large number of IMF members as well as by the IMF itself. These resources are administered under Trusts (currently the PRGF and PRGF–HIPC Trusts) for which the Fund acts as a Trustee.

Structural Adjustment Facility

The Fund established the Structural Adjustment Facility, SAF, within the Special Disbursement Account, in 1986 to provide all low-income developing countries eligible for IDA resources with concessional loans in support of medium-term macroeconomic adjustment policies and structural reforms. It is interesting to point out that 'structural benchmarks' were first introduced in the context of the SAF in 1986.

Under the SAF, the member, with the help of the Fund and the World Bank, developed a medium term policy framework for a three-year period, with loan disbursements made annually, an applicable rate of interest of 0.5 per cent, and repayment due in five and a half to ten years. In November 1993, the IMF's Executive Board agreed that no new commitments would be made under the SAF.

---

[227] Above note 32, 118.   [228] ibid.

Enhanced Structural Adjustment Facility

The ESAF was established in 1987[229] and enlarged in 1994. Under the ESAF, loans were disbursed semi-annually at an interest rate of 0.5 per cent and repayment was due in five and a half to ten years.

An eligible member (low-income) that sought to use ESAF resources developed, with the assistance of the IMF and World Bank, a policy-framework paper (PFP) for a three-year adjustment period. The resources available under the ESAF were provided primarily by bilateral contributions.

Poverty Reduction and Growth Facility

In 1999 the IMF transformed the ESAF and ESAF Trust into the more positively named Poverty Reduction and Growth Facility, PRGF, and the PRGF Trust[230] and expanded the facility's objectives to support programmes that substantially strengthen balance of payments positions and make them sustainable, while fostering durable growth, leading to a reduction of poverty. Uganda became the first recipient of the new facility on 10 December 1999.

To determine eligibility for PRGF loans the Fund has in practice relied upon the level of per capita income and eligibility under the International Development Association (the part of the World Bank that helps the earth's poorest countries).[231] However, there is no automatic link between PRGF and IDA eligibility and it is up to the IMF Executive Board to establish the list of PRGF-eligible countries. The PRGF Trust (which is administered by the Fund as a trustee) borrows resources from central banks, governments, and official institutions generally at market-related interest rates, and lends them on a pass-through basis to PRGF-eligible countries. The difference between the market-related interest rate paid to PRGF Trust lenders and the rate of interest of 0.5 per cent per year paid by the borrowing members is financed by contributions from bilateral donors and the IMF's own resources.[232] PRGF operations are conducted through three accounts within the PRGF Trust: the Loan Account, Reserve Account, and Subsidy Account.[233]

PRGF loans are provide under three-year PRGF arrangements (with the possibility of one-year extension), with annual programmes for each of the three

---

[229] Decision No 8759–(87/176), 18 December 1987, on the Establishment of the Enhanced Structural Adjustment Facility Trust.

[230] Decision No 12087–(99/118), 21 October 1999, on the Transformation of the Enhanced Structural Adjusted Facility.

[231] <http://web.worldbank.org/WBSITE/EXTERNAL/EXTABOUTUS/IDA/0,,menuPK: 83991-pagePK:118644-piPK:51236156-theSitePK:73154,00.html>.

[232] See 'The Poverty Reduction Growth Facility, PRGF. A fact-sheet', September 2005, at <http://www.imf.org/external/np/exr/facts/prgf.htm>.

[233] Above note 32, 125.

years. Disbursements under PRGF arrangements are typically tied to performance criteria and semi-annual reviews (conditionality). An eligible country may borrow up to 140 per cent of its quota under a three-year arrangement, although this limit may be increased to a maximum of 185 per cent.[234]

PRGF-supported programmes are framed around Poverty Reduction Strategy Papers (PRSP) which are prepared by the borrowing country.[235]

Other forms of financial assistance to low-income developing countries: Debt relief and the HIPC Initiative

In addition to concessional loans, financial assistance for low-income developing countries is also provided through grants and through debt relief. Debt relief under the Heavily Indebted Poor Countries Initiative,[236] which was jointly launched by the IMF and the World Bank in 1996, was linked to the PRGF in 1997,[237] with the setting up of an HIPC–PRGF Trust in February 1997 with resources administered by the IMF.

An increasing recognition by the international community that the external debt levels of a number of countries—mostly in Africa—have become unsustainable and that a concerted effort is needed (through debt relief, concessional financing, institutional reform, and pursuit of sound economic policies) to place those countries on the road to sustainable development culminated in an enhanced HIPC in September 1999. The objective of this enhanced HIPC initiative is to provide faster and deeper and broader debt relief to help countries reach and maintain a sustainable debt position.

The IMF provides its share of assistance under the HIPC Initiative to eligible members typically in the form of grants which are used to help meet debt service payments.[238]

The members that currently benefit from HIPC debt relief are: Benin, Bolivia, Burkina Faso, Burundi, Cameroon, Chad, Congo, Ivory Coast, Ethiopia, Gambia, Ghana, Guinea, Guinea-Bissau, Guyana, Honduras, Madagascar, Malawi, Mali, Mauritania, Mozambique, Nicaragua, Niger, Rwanda, São Tomé and Príncipe, Senegal, Sierra Leone, Tanzania, Uganda, and Zambia.[239]

---

[234] ibid 122.

[235] ibid. See also 'Poverty Reduction Strategy Papers, PRSPs. A fact-sheet', February 2005, at <http://www.imf.org/external/np/exr/facts/prsp.htm>.

[236] See 'Debt Relief under the Heavily Indebted Poor Countries (HIPC) Initiative. A Fact-sheet' at <http://www.imf.org/external/np/exr/facts/hipc.htm>.

[237] Instrument to establish—under Article V, Section 2(b)—the Poverty Reduction and Growth Facility Trust, Decision No 8759–(87/176) ESAF 18 December 1987, as amended.

[238] Above note 32, 131.

[239] See IMF Survey of 29 August 2005, 263 at <http://www.imf.org>.

The IMF and the World Bank introduced the Poverty Reduction Strategy approach in 1999 to strengthen their approach to providing assistance to low-income countries, including both new financial assistance and debt relief under the enhanced Heavily Indebted Poor Country (HIPC) Initiative.[240] Poverty Reduction Strategy Papers (PRSPs) describe the macroeconomic, structural, and social policies and programmes that a country will pursue over several years to promote broad-based growth and reduce poverty, as well as external financing needs and the associated sources of financing.[241]

The PRSPs aim to provide the crucial link between national public actions, donor support, and the development outcomes needed to meet the United Nations' Millenium Development Goals, centred on halving poverty between 1990 and 2015.[242]

New developments: the Multilateral Debt Relief Initiative and the Exogenous Shocks Facility

As I proceed to complete the revisions of this chapter, two new developments must be mentioned. The IMF Board has recently approved the Multilateral Debt Relief Initiative, that involves 100 per cent debt relief to a group of low income developing countries, and which is much more consequential than the HIPC Initiative.[243] The IMF Executive Board has also approved the so-called

---

[240] Independent Evaluation Office (IEO) of the International Monetary Fund, 'Report on the Evaluation of Poverty Reduction Strategy Papers (PRSPs) and The Poverty Reduction and Growth Facility (PRGF)', 6 July 2004, <http://www.imf.org/External/NP/ieo/2004/prspprgf/eng/index.htm>.

[241] International Monetary Fund, 'Poverty Reduction Strategy Papers (PRSP): A Factsheet', September 2004, <http://www.imf.org/external/np/exr/facts/prsp.htm>.

[242] On 8 September 2000, the eighth plenary meeting of the United Nations in General assembly adopted the Resolution No 55/2 also know as the 'Millennium Declaration', by which all its 191 members have pledged that by the year 2015 they would meet the following goals: (i) to eradicate extreme poverty and hunger by reducing by half the proportion of people living on less than a dollar a day and suffering from hunger; (ii) to achieve universal primary education by guaranteeing that everybody would be able to complete a full course of primary schooling; (iii) to promote gender equality by eliminating gender disparity in primary and secondary education; (iv) to reduce child mortality by two thirds in children under 5 years; (v) to improve maternal health by a three quarters reduction of the maternal mortality ratio; (vi) to halt and begin to reverse the spread of HIV/AIDS and the incidence of malaria and other major diseases; (vii) to ensure environmental sustainability by reversing the loss of environmental resources; and, (viii) to develop a global partnership for development. The outline of the so-called Millennium Development Goals is available at <http://www.un.org/millenniumgoals/>. The Resolution No 55/2 'Millennium Declaration', adopted by the General Assembly of the United Nations is available at <http://www.un.org/millennium/declaration/ares552e.htm>.

[243] See International Monetary Fund, 'The Multilateral Debt Relief Initiative (MDRI). A Factsheet', December 2005, available at <http://www.imf.org/external/np/exr/mdri/eng/index.htm>. See also Public Information Notice (PIN) No 05/164, 8 December 2005, 'IMF Agrees on Implementation Modalities for the Multilateral Debt Relief Initiative' at <http://www.imf.org/external/np/sec/pn/2005/pn05164.htm>, and Press Release No 05/286,

Exogenous Shocks Facility, which forms part of the PRGF Trust, to strengthen its support for low-income countries. This facility is to assist poor countries trying to deal with economic shocks (such as high oil prices, natural disasters, and spillovers from neighbouring countries suffering conflict or crisis). Loans from this facility will be on concessional terms.[244]

Special policies

Over the years the Fund has developed 'special policies' and facilities to address special balance of payments problems according to Article V, section 3(a). Some of those facilities have been allowed to lapse (since they were designed to address a particular problem, once the problem was solved the facility was no longer needed). Others still remain in operation.

Compensatory Financing Facility

The Compensatory Financing Facility (CFF) was established in 1963[245] to assist commodity exporter countries experiencing a sudden shortfall in export earnings arising from events beyond their control (fluctuating world commodity prices).

The CFF has been modified on a number of occasions: the coverage of export shortfalls eligible for compensation has been broadened, an element for excess costs of cereal imports introduced in 1981 (in response to humanitarian concerns), a contingency financing element was added and then dropped, an oil element with a sunset clause added and then allowed to expire, and access limits have been adjusted.[246]

Several important changes in the CFF were introduced in 2000 in the context of a broader review of the Fund's facilities. The Buffer Stock Financing Facility

---

21 December 2005, 'IMF to Extend 100 Percent Debt Relief for 19 Countries Under the Multilateral Debt Relief Initiative', at <http://www.imf.org/external/np/sec/pr/2005/pr05286.htm>. The 19 countries that have initially qualified are: Benin, Bolivia, Burkina Faso, Cambodia, Ethiopia, Ghana, Guyana, Honduras, Madagascar, Mali, Mozambique, Nicaragua, Niger, Rwanda, Senegal, Tajikistan, Tanzania, Uganda, and Zambia.

[244] See International Monetary Fund, 'The Exogenous Shocks Facility, A Factsheet', December 2005, available at <http://www.imf.org/external/np/exr/facts/esf.htm>. See also Public Information Notice (PIN) No 05/163, 8 December 2005, 'IMF Establishes an Exogenous Shocks Facility', at <http://www.imf.org/external/np/sec/pn/2005/pn05163.htm>.

[245] See Decision No 1477–(63/8), 27 February 1963.

[246] See International Monetary Fund, 'Review of the Compensatory Financing Facility', prepared by the Policy Development and Review Department in Consultation with other Departments, approved by Mark Allen, 18 February 2004, <http://www.imf.org/external/np/pdr/cff/eng/2004/021804.pdf>, 3.

(BSFF) and the External Contingency Mechanism (ECM) of the CFF were eliminated.[247]

Assistance under the CFF is typically provided via a standby arrangement (with conditionality applied), though outright purchases can also be used.[248]

Calls have been made to redesign the CFF in order to make it more useful to members, for instance, by reducing or eliminating the conditionality attached to CFF purchases or by establishing concessional funding within the CFF. A concessional CFF could help a large number of low-income countries reliant upon a narrow range of exports to deal with a sudden decline in the price or volume of such exports.[249]

Emergency assistance (natural disasters and post-conflict situations)

Emergency assistance was a concept introduced by the IMF in 1962 to help member countries with urgent balance of payments financing needs in the wake of natural disasters such as floods, earthquakes, hurricanes, or droughts. Its scope was expanded in 1995 to deal with post-conflict situations, that is, the aftermath of armed conflicts.[250]

The idea of quick disbursement which is inherent in the provision of emergency financial assistance is an element which has been adopted in the facilities that have been devised over the last decade to deal with crises stemming from international capital markets (in particular the Supplemental Reserve Facility, further analysed earlier, and the now defunct Contingent Credit Line) and with the accelerated procedures that were introduced following the Mexican crisis in 1995 (the so-called 'emergency financing mechanism').

While emergency assistance following natural disasters is aimed at meeting immediate foreign exchange financing needs arising from shortfalls in export earnings and/or increased imports, to avoid a serious depletion of a country's external reserves, in the case of post-conflict situations, the assistance is aimed at rebuilding the capacity for developing and implementing an economic programme, as a catalyst for support from other sources, as part of an international concerted effort to address the aftermath of an armed conflict.[251]

---

[247] See International Monetary Fund, 'Summing Up by the Acting Chairman, Review of the Compensatory and Contingency Financing Facility (CCFF) and Buffer Stock Financing Facility (BSFF)—Preliminary Considerations' (BUFF/00/9, Executive Board Meeting 00/5, 14 January 2000), available at <http://www.imf.org/external/np/sec/buff/2000/0009.htm>.

[248] Above note 246, 7.   [249] ibid 14.

[250] International Monetary Fund, 'IMF Emergency Assistance: Supporting Recovery from Natural Disasters and Armed Conflicts. A Factsheet', September 2004, available at <http://www.imf.org/external/np/exr/facts/conflict.htm>.

[251] ibid.

Emergency assistance was converted into a special policy in 2000.[252]

Extended Fund Facility

The Fund established the Extended Fund Facility (EFF) in 1974 to assist members (in particular, developing countries) to meet balance of payment difficulties that stem from structural problems and require a longer period of adjustment. The IMF Executive Board in its decision on the Extended Fund Facility explained that the purpose of 'extended arrangements' is to support 'comprehensive programs that include policies of the scope and character required to correct structural imbalances in production, trade and prices'.[253]

Thus, the EFF is a financing facility (window) under which the IMF supports economic programmes aimed at overcoming balance of payments difficulties which require a longer period of time for their resolution. Such medium-term assistance (under the EFF) is given through an 'extended arrangement' which can be defined as a decision of the IMF under the Extended Fund Facility that gives a member the assurance of being able to purchase (draw) resources from the General Resources Account (GRA) in accordance with the terms of the decision during a specified period, usually three years, and up to a particular amount.[254] Typically, the member's economic programme states the general objectives for the three-year period and the specific policies for the first year; policies for subsequent years are spelled out at the time of programme reviews.

Emergency Financing Mechanism

Following the Mexican crisis sparked by the devaluation of the peso at the beginning of the Zedillo administration and the 'bailout' package arranged by the IMF (and the US Treasury), the IMF introduced the Emergency Financing Mechanism in September 1995. The Emergency Financing Mechanism is a set of accelerated procedures to facilitate rapid Executive Board approval of IMF financial support in response to crises in a member's external account that require an immediate IMF response. This Emergency Financing Mechanism is not a new facility, but rather the adaptation of existing facilities (standby arrangements) to accelerated procedures so as to facilitate rapid Executive Board approval of IMF financial support in response to crises in a member's external

---

[252] See Decision No 12341–(00/17), 28 November 2000, 'Conversion of Emergency Assistance into a Special Policy', at <http://www.imf.org/external/pubs/ft/sd/index.asp?decision=12341-(00/117)>.

[253] Decision No 4377–(74/114) of 13 September 1974 as amended.

[254] <http://www.imf.org/external/np/exr/glossary/showTerm.asp?term_id=34>.

account that require an immediate response.[255] The Emergency Financing Mechanism was adopted in the approval of the standby arrangements for Korea (SDR 15.5 billion, about $21 billion), for Indonesia (SDR 7.3 billion, about $10.1 billion) and Thailand (SDR 2.9 billion, about $3.9 billion).[256] The Emergency Financing Mechanism as a procedure is reminiscent of the workings of the lender of last resort role of the central bank (LOLR) at the national level: it is the speed, the immediacy, of the availability of liquidity assistance that makes the LOLR particularly suited to confront emergency situations.

Supplemental Reserve Facility

The problems in Thailand, Indonesia, and South Korea in 1997 reignited the debate about the role that the Fund should play in the resolution of financial crises. It appeared that countries suffering 'sudden' problems arising from the capital account needed a quick solution involving also a massive injection of financial assistance (the arrangements were in the range of 490–690 per cent of the quota, compared with the cumulative access limit of 300 per cent of the quota).

In December 1997, the IMF adopted the Supplemental Reserve Facility (SRF)[257] as a new facility intended to provide financial assistance to a member country experiencing exceptional balance of payments difficulties due to a large short-term financing need resulting from a sudden and disruptive loss of market confidence reflected in the pressure on the capital account and member's reserves. The SRF is a clear step in the formalization of the role of the IMF as International Lender of Last Resort. The legal basis for the establishment of the SRF is Article V, section 3(a), (b), and (c), regarding use of Fund resources.

The Supplemental Reserve Facility (SRF) is intended 'to provide financial assistance to a member country experiencing exceptional balance of payments difficulties due to a large short-term financing need resulting from a sudden and disruptive loss of market confidence reflected in pressure on the capital account and the member's reserves'.[258] Assistance under the facility is available when there is a reasonable expectation that the implementation of strong adjustment policies and adequate financing will result, within a short period, in an early

---

[255] M. Guitián argues in 'Conditionality: Past, Present and Future', *Staff Papers*, Vol 42, No 4, International Monetary Fund, December 1995, that the interpretation of conditionality is not independent of the international economic regime in place.

[256] See *IMF Survey* of 15 December 1997 for the approval of the Korean arrangement, *IMF Survey* of 17 November 1997 for the approval of the Indonesian stand-by arrangement, and *IMF Survey* of 17 September 1997, for the approval of the Thai standby arrangement.

[257] Decision No 11627–(97/123), 17 December 1997 on the Supplemental Reserve Facility, available at <http://www.imf.org/external/pubs/ft/sd/index.asp?decision=11627-(97/123)>.

[258] ibid.

correction of the balance of payments difficulties. 'In order to minimise moral hazard, a member using resources under this decision is encouraged to seek to maintain participation of creditors, both official and private, until the pressure on the balance of payments ceases. All options should be considered to ensure appropriate burden sharing.'[259]

Financing under the SRF is made available in the form of additional resources under a standby or extended arrangement. The terms are 'special': no access limits apply, the repayment period is much shorter, and a surcharge above the GRA rate of charge applies. These features are reminiscent of the workings of the lender of last resort at the national level.

Access under the SRF is separate from the access limits under the credit tranches and the EFF, and the SRF is not subject to access limits of its own.[260] Financing under the SRF is generally available in two purchases. The first purchase is made available at the time of the approval of the financing and the subsequent purchase is available subject to the conditions of the corresponding arrangement.[261]

Countries borrowing under the SRF are expected to repay within one to one and a half years of the date of each disbursement; this period can be extended to a maximum repurchase period of two to two and a half years. During the first year from the date of approval of the SRF, borrowers pay a surcharge of 300 basis points above the basic 'rate of charge'. This surcharge increases by fifty basis points at the end of that period and every six months thereafter until the surcharge reaches 500 basis points.

Upon a member's request of an extension of the repurchase expectations (which could be up to one year), the IMF Executive Board may decide not to approve this request, and to turn unmet expectations into immediate obligations.[262]

Conditionality in an arrangement involving SRF resources is similar to that in a standby or extended arrangement,[263] though some terms are stricter.

Other facilities/policies

In 1989, the Fund designed policies to support Debt and Debt Service Reduction (DDSR) operations aiming to provide financing in conjunction with the World Bank and other official sources for the advance costs of members'

---

[259] ibid.

[260] International Monetary Fund, 'Review of Fund Facilities—Further Considerations', prepared by the Policy Development and Review and the Treasurer's Departments (in consultation with other Departments), 10 July 2000, <http://www.imf.org/external/np/pdr/roff/2000/eng/fc/index.htm#_ftn14>.

[261] Decision No 11627–(97/123), 17 December 1997 on the Supplemental Reserve Facility.

[262] ibid.   [263] ibid.

DDSR operations with commercial banks. Fund support for such operations is provided under a standby or extended arrangement or (since 1997) an ESAF–PRGF arrangement.[264]

In 1995 the Fund established the Currency Stabilization Funds as an element within a standby or extended arrangement to provide additional, precautionary balance of payments support in the initial stage of an exchange rate based stabilization. However, no member has made use of this policy yet.[265]

Though it is not a facility, a mention ought to be made of the Trade Integration Mechanism (TIM) established by the IMF Executive Board in April 2004.[266] The TIM allows the IMF to stand ready to provide resources, as necessary, to assist member countries in meeting balance of payments shortfalls that might result from multilateral trade liberalization. The TIM is not a new lending facility, but rather a policy aimed at making Fund resources more predictably available to qualifying member countries under existing IMF facilities. The establishment of a Trade Integration Mechanism within the Fund's existing lending facilities clarifies further how the Fund stands ready to help its members mitigate short-term balance of payments pressures stemming from trade liberalization. The TIM is designed to mitigate concerns among some developing countries that their balance of payments positions could suffer, albeit temporarily, as liberalization changes their competitive position in world markets.[267]

Defunct facilities

The Fund identified in the 2000 review of its own facilities a number of instruments that should be eliminated or allowed to lapse. The purpose of this so-called 'housecleaning' and 'renovation' was to facilitate the understanding of the financial assistance offered by the Fund to its members.[268] The following facilities (special policies, typically with less stringent conditionality) are now defunct:

(i) The Buffer Stock Financing Facility was created in 1969 and eliminated in 2000. It provided financing to members to help finance their contributions to approved commodity price stabilization funds.

(ii) The first Oil Facility was created in June 1974 in response to the oil price shock, and lapsed in December 1974. It was designed to help members finance deficits related to oil import price increases following OPEC's decision in 1973; only two conditions were required: (a) to consult with the IMF on balance of payments needs; (b) to avoid enacting restrictions on

---

[264] Above note 141, 13–14.   [265] ibid 14–15.
[266] See Press Release No 04/73, 13 April 2004, 'IMF Executive Board Approves Trade Integration Mechanism', available at <http://www.imf.org/external/np/sec/pr/2004/pr0473.htm>.
[267] ibid.   [268] Above note 202, 9.

international transactions. A second Oil Facility was created in April 1975 (through the establishment of a Subsidy Account) to provide additional financing, and lapsed in March 1976.

(iii) An oil import element was added to the Compensatory and Contingency Financing Facility in November 1990, when oil prices rose sharply during the Gulf War. It was allowed to lapse at the end of 1991.

(iv) The Systemic Transformation Facility was created in April 1993[269] and allowed to lapse in April 1995. It provided support for the early stages of transition from centrally planned to market economies, in relatively small amounts and with relatively low conditionality. Former communist countries in Eastern Europe and the former Soviet Union temporarily suffered sharp drops in exports and permanent increases in import costs, particularly for energy products, because of the shift to market prices, thus creating severe balance of payments problems. The STF was used by twenty countries from 1993 to 1995. It was designed to pave the way for these countries to move to regular IMF facilities.[270]

(v) The contingency element of the Compensatory and Contingency Financing Facility, created in 1988 and eliminated in 2000, which provided additional access under arrangements, according to pre-specified calculations, in the event of unanticipated adverse current account developments.

(vi) The Y2K Facility was created in September 1999, to deal with possible strains resulting from the Y2K computer bug. It has not been used, and lapsed at the end of March 2000.

(vii) The Contingent Credit Lines (CCL), created in 1999, was allowed to expire in November 2003, on its scheduled sunset date.[271] The CCL had been intended for members concerned with potential vulnerability to contagion, but not facing a crisis at the time of commitment. Financing under the CCL was to be provided if a member experienced exceptional payments difficulties resulting from unforeseen 'adverse developments in international capital markets'.[272] However, this precautionary line of defence

---

[269] Decision No 10348–(93–61), April 1993.

[270] Sir Joseph Gold already advanced in 1979 some of the issues at stake in the transformation of formerly communist countries from a command economy into a market economy: 'It is argued that the pace of adjustment may be a political as well as an economic problem. It is not necessarily easier, however, to pursue a slower pace. In some countries, adjustment may be more acceptable politically if pursued rapidly. In others, political determination may weaken if adjustment is a prolonged process.' Sir Joseph Gold, 'Conditionality', IMF Pamphlet Series No 31, 1979, 15.

[271] International Monetary Fund, 'The IMF's Contingent Credit Lines (CCL). A Factsheet', March 2004, available at <http://www.imf.org/external/np/exr/facts/ccl.htm>.

[272] Decision No 11627–(97/123) on the Supplemental Reserve Facility, as amended by Decision No 11492–(99/48), 23 April 1999, on the Supplemental Reserve Facility/Contingent Credit Line; further amended by Decision No 12340–(00/117) on the Supplemental Reserve Facility/Contingent Credit Line, 28 November 2000.

was never used for various reasons. For a start, 'potentially eligible countries may have lacked confidence that a CCL would be viewed as a sign of strength rather than weakness'; furthermore, 'there had been some uncertainty about whether Fund resources under a CCL would in fact be readily available in the event of need, as the release of funds would require Executive Board approval'. Finally, 'many potentially eligible countries had reduced their vulnerability to external shocks through . . . reforms, thus reducing the perceived demand for insurance in the form of a CCL'.

Terms applicable to the facilities and access limits

In this subsection I provide a brief summary of the access policy and the terms (repurchases terms and charges) applicable to the facilities currently in operation, drawing upon a table available from the IMF's website[273] (see Table 13.1).

The amount that a country can borrow from the Fund, referred to as 'access limit', is typically a multiple of the country's quota subscription.[274] In April 2005, the Fund approved a decision on access limits, establishing that access by a member to the Fund's general resources in the credit tranches and under the Extended Fund Facility shall be subject to an annual limit of 100 per cent of quota and a cumulative limit of 300 per cent of quota, net of scheduled repurchases, with common provisions governing exceptional access, that apply to any financing provided under the GRA exceeding these limits.[275] These limits shall not be regarded as targets. The Fund may approve access in excess of these limits only in exceptional circumstances

Access under a PRGP arrangement is subject to a limit of 140 per cent of quota and an exceptional maximum limit of 185 per cent of quota. There is no cumulative access limit.

Except for the PRGF, all facilities are subject to the IMF's market-related interest rate, known as the 'rate of charge', and some large loans carry an interest rate premium or 'surcharge'.[276] The rate of charge is based on the SDR interest rate, which is revised weekly to take account of changes in short-term interest rates in the major international money markets. The surcharge was introduced in the last few years with the advent of large financing packages to help members

---

[273] International Monetary Fund, 'IMF Lending: A Factsheet', December 2005, available at <http://www.imf.org/external/np/exr/facts/howlend.htm>.

[274] ibid.

[275] See Decision No 13642–(05/32), 1 April 2005, 'Access Policy and Limits in Credit Tranches and Under Extended Fund Facility—Exceptional Access to Fund General Resources—Review', at <http://www.imf.org/external/pubs/ft/sd/index.asp?decision=13462-(05/32)>.

[276] International Monetary Fund, 'IMF Lending: A Factsheet', December 2005, available at <http://www.imf.org/external/np/exr/facts/howlend.htm>.

Table 13.1 General Terms of IMF Financial Assistance

Facility or Policy	Charges	Repurchase Terms		
		Obligation Schedule (Years)	Expectation[1] Schedule (Years)	Instalments
Standby Arrangement	Basic rate[2] plus surcharge[3]	3¼–5	2½–4	Quarterly
Extended Fund Facility	Basic rate[2] plus surcharge[3]	4½–10	4½–7	Semi-annual
Compensatory Financing Facility	Basic rate[2]	3¼–5	2¼–4	Quarterly
Emergency Assistance	Basic rate[2,4]	3¼–5	N/A	Quarterly
Supplemental Reserve Facility	Basic rate[2] plus surcharge[5]	2½–3	2–2½	Semi-annual
Poverty Reduction and Growth Facility; and Exogenous Shocks Facility	0.5 percent per annum	5½–10	N/A	Semi-annual
Memorandum Items[6]				
Service Charge	50 basis points			
Commitment Charge[7]	25 basis points on committed amounts of up to 100 percent of quota, 10 basis points thereafter			

[1] Disbursements made after 28 November 2000—with the exception of disbursements of Emergency Assistance and loans from the Poverty Reduction and Growth Facility—are expected to be repaid on the expectation schedule. A member not in a position to meet an expected payment can request the Executive Board to approve an extension to the obligations schedule.

[2] The basic rate of charge is linked directly to the SDR interest rate by a fixed margin that is set each financial year. The basic rate of charge therefore fluctuates with the market rate of the SDR, which is calculated on a weekly basis. The basic rate of charge is adjusted upward for burden sharing to compensate for the overdue charges of other members.

[3] The surcharge on high levels of credit outstanding under Standby Arrangements (SBA) and the Extended Fund Facility (EFF) is 100 basis points for credit over 200 per cent of quota, and 200 basis points for credit over 300 per cent of quota. This surcharge is designed to discourage large use of IMF resources.

[4] For PRGF-eligible members, the rate of charge may be subsidized to 0.5 per cent per annum, subject to the availability to subsidy resources.

[5] The surcharge on the Supplemental Reserve Facility (SRF) is 300–500 basis points, with the initial surcharge of 300 basis points rising by 50 basis points after one year and each subsequent six months. The surcharge increases over time in order to provide an incentive for repurchases ahead of the obligation schedule.

[6] These charges do not apply to Poverty Reduction and Growth Facility and Exogenous Shocks Facility.

[7] Commitment charge does not apply to Compensatory Financing Facility and Emergency Assistance.

Source: International Monetary Fund, *IMF Lending: A Factsheet*, December 2005, available at <http://www.imf.org/external/np/exr/facts/howlend.htm>

weather capital account crises, supplementing the general policy on early repurchases.[277]

I. Conclusions

The study of the law of the IMF is a fascinating and complex subject which has appealed to me ever since I worked in the Legal Department of the IMF back at the beginning of the 1990s. The institution is at the centre of the international monetary system and at the centre of the so-called international financial architecture.

The interplay between law and economics is a constant in the history of the Fund, with economics taking a leading role. However, economists within the Fund (as well as outside it) have grown accustomed to the use of references to key provisions of the Articles of Agreement, in particular Article IV; Article VIII, section 2; and Article V, sections 2 and 3. Economists need to be conversant with the key legal principles that apply to the Fund. There are some official histories commissioned by the Fund, which include some legal citations,[278] and there are plenty of economic studies dealing with the various issues that fall within the mandate of the Fund's responsibilities. Lawyers have also produced a number of studies on the international monetary system, in particular two former General Counsels of the institution: the late Sir Joseph Gold and François Gianviti. The originality of this chapter is that it provides a comprehensive yet succinct legal analysis of the workings of the Fund that is accessible for both economists and legal practitioners.

A recurring feature in this chapter is the complexity of the Fund's operations and financial structure, 'shrouded in clouds of specialized terminology'.[279] Complexity and opacity tend to frustrate accountability and transparency. This is a challenge that IMF must confront. The Fund has over the last years made a conscious effort to become more transparent, and its website and publications are a valuable source of information. However, the language applicable to the Fund operations is often esoteric for those not familiar with the institution. In this chapter, I have endeavoured to explain the workings of the Fund in plain

---

[277] International Monetary Fund, 'Financial Risk in the Fund and the Level of Precautionary Balances', Prepared by the Finance Department (in consultation with other departments), approved by Eduard Brau, 3 February 2004, 9, available at <http://www.imf.org/external/np/tre/risk/2004/020304.pdf>.

[278] See James M Boughton, *Silent Revolution: the IMF 1979–1989* (Washington DC: IMF, 2001), for the latest title (the fourth one) in this series of 'official' histories of the Fund.

[279] Polak, above note 5, 1.

terms in the light of the law applicable to it. It is no easy task and only the reader can judge whether I have succeeded in my endeavour.

Despite the abandonment of the par value regime in the 1970s, the importance of the IMF has remained undiminished. Over the last three decades, the IMF's mandate has been broadened: from being primarily an international monetary institution to becoming an international financial institution, encompassing not only monetary issues but also other financial issues (capital markets, payments systems, etc). The IMF played a leading role in the sovereign debt restructuring of the less-developed countries in the 1980s, in the transition to a market economy of formerly communist countries in the early 1990s, and in the resolution of financial crises in Mexico and Asia in the mid- to late-1990s, though its handling of such crises has been the subject of much controversy. The domain of surveillance has extended beyond macroeconomic policies to encompass financial sector and structural issues.

From the Fund's point of view, surveillance is the key function. From the member countries' point of view, financial assistance is the key. Countries in need (of balance of payments support) subject themselves to conditionality, surveillance, and technical assistance as the 'price' that must be paid to obtain financial support. Members are not always keen to tighten their belts or the belts of their citizens to obtain the resources they need to address balance of payments difficulties, but they are well aware that non-observance of their financial obligations with the Fund will lead them into further trouble.

One feature of the international monetary system which is unsettled concerns the law governing international capital transfers. The extension of the Fund's jurisdiction from current account to capital account convertibility is a matter of great controversy. The wisdom of capital account liberalization remains contested in the aftermath of the financial crises in East Asia in the late 1990s (capital account driven crises). The economic literature on the issue is still divided, with some distinguished economists favouring such liberalization and some other equally distinguished economists opposing it. The experience with restrictions on current transactions (under the transitional arrangements of Art XIV) suggests that a revised code of conduct extending the mandate of the IMF to capital account convertibility would be problematic. As a result, no amendment to the IMF Articles of Agreement is foreseeable in the near future.

The evolution of the role of the Fund over the last three decades has affected the practice of conditionality, that is, the policies and procedures developed by the Fund to govern the access to, and the continuing use of, its resources by members. Though the institution continues to focus on macroeconomic management, growing emphasis has been placed over the last decade on efficiency issues, microeconomic measures, structural policies, and legal and institutional reform. This shift in emphasis has contributed to the broadening scope of conditionality, which has become increasingly attached to structural reforms including legal reforms. In response to these changes, the IMF Executive Board conducted a review of conditionality which ended in the adoption of new guidelines (replacing the 1979 decision) in September 2002. This chapter provided an extensive analysis of these guidelines in particular and of conditionality generally.

Two of the major challenges confronted by the Fund in the twenty-first century are the effective prevention and resolution of international financial crises on the one hand and the financial support to the poorest countries in the world on the other hand. The former is further analysed in Chapter 14. The latter, which would deserve another volume, has been the subject of some considerations in this chapter. And it is with reference to the goal of poverty reduction that I conclude this chapter.

The position and reputation of the IMF in the international financial community make it a particularly suitable actor in the process of financing development in the world's poorest countries. The Fund has the instruments that can make financial assistance through debt relief and concessional lending effective, in particular, technical assistance (fundamental for legal and institutional reform), surveillance, and conditionality, keeping a vigilant eye on the temptation of corruption. Poverty alleviation is a daunting task, but one that the international community 'cannot afford' to neglect.

445

14

INTERNATIONAL FINANCIAL ARCHITECTURE

At the beginning of the new millennium, the major challenge for the specialists of monetary law is no doubt the strengthening of the international financial architecture with a view to promoting international monetary stability.

Mario Giovanoli, *International Monetary Law* (Oxford: Oxford University Press, 2000) x

A. Introduction

This chapter presents a number of issues under the rubric of 'international financial architecture'. First, it provides a definition of this vague term, considering the various actors involved. Secondly, it critically examines the growth of soft international financial law and the role of the Financial Stability Forum, the Basel Committee on Banking Supervision, and other 'international financial standard setters' in this process. Thirdly, it analyses the framework for the prevention and resolution of international financial crises, and, in particular, the evolving role of the IMF and alternative (or complementary) market-based solutions.

At the national level, financial regulation and supervision and disclosure act as instruments of crisis prevention. At the international level, the proliferation of standards and codes (soft law rules), enhanced surveillance, and the compilation and dissemination of financial data (transparency) can also act as effective mechanisms for 'crisis prevention'.

National financial systems have at their disposal a set of institutional and legal arrangements—a national financial architecture—for the safeguard of financial stability (as I explained in Chapters 3 and 4). In contrast, the international financial system lacks a strong legal and institutional framework for the orderly resolution of regional and international financial crises. The objective of 'international financial stability' often appears as elusive as the pursuit of the 'holy grail'.

In recent years, the responses of the international community to 'crisis resolution' have ranged from replicating at the international level the domestic structures with regard to bankruptcy proceedings (including proposals to create a sovereign debt restructuring mechanism) and emergency liquidity assistance (international lender of last resort) to relying upon contractual mechanisms to allow for an orderly restructuring of debt instruments (eg, insertion in bond agreements of collective action clauses). The cooperation between the International Monetary Fund and private creditors with regard to sovereign debt crises remains a contentious issue, which I also survey in this chapter.

B. Definition of International Financial Architecture

The definition of international financial architecture lacks precise contours and refers to a variety of issues.[1] According to Giovanoli (drawing on Andrew Crockett): 'This concept is generally understood as encompassing the rules, guidelines and other arrangements governing international financial relations as well as the various institutions, entities and bodies through which such rules, guidelines and other arrangements are developed, monitored and enforced.'[2]

While this definition focuses on the rule-making aspects of the international financial architecture, other definitions emphasize instead the framework for the prevention and resolution of international financial crises:

> While there is no agreed definition of what constitutes international financial architecture, it refers broadly to the framework and set of measures that can help prevent crises and manage them better in the more integrated international financial environment. Several aspects of the agenda for crisis prevention and crisis resolution deal with weaknesses in the international financial system that potentially contribute to the propensity and magnitude of global instability, hence requiring collective action at the international level. But there is widespread recognition that global financial stability also rests on robust national systems and hence requires enhanced measures at the country level as well.[3]

This chapter considers both aspects of the definition: rule making and international financial soft law, on the one hand, and the framework for the management of financial crises on the other hand. The common element of these two aspects is that they are aimed at ensuring financial stability.[4] 'The objective

---

[1] In 1999, I edited a book on *The Reform of the International Financial Architecture*, which was published by Kluwer Law International in 2001. The contributions by distinguished scholars and international public servants are a testimony of the multifaceted aspects included under the rubric 'international financial architecture'. Some contributions, like those by Loukas Mistelis, Joseph Norton, and Jeswald Saluacuse, focused on law reform and soft law. Some other contributions, like those by Thomas Baxter and Lee Buchheit, focused on financial crises and their resolution. Finally some other contributions, like those by Huw Evans, Francois Gianviti, Antonio Sainz de Vicuña, George Walker, the preface by Peter Cooke, and my own contribution focused on the institutional framework. With regard to the definition of the 'new international financial architecture' (NIFA), Norton points out (ch 1, 45): '[T]he NIFA terminology, while vague, serves as a critical "code word" or point of reference for the ongoing search for coherence, meaning, effectiveness and some semblance of structure within what essentially has become a highly fragmented, volatile, yet interconnected network of financial market systems.' According to Buchheit (ch 10, 237), 'The new international financial architecture is the name that has been given to a rather vague set of official policy incentives designed to make the international capital markets more efficient, more stable and more transparent.'

[2] See Mario Giovanoli, 'A New Architecture for the Global Financial Markets: Legal Aspects of International Financial Standard Setting' in Mario Giovanoli (ed), *International Monetary Law. Issues for the New Millenium* (Oxford: Oxford University Press, 2000) 9.

[3] See <http://www.worldbank.org/ifa/ifa_more.html>.

[4] For a definition of financial stability, see Ch 3.

of the various norms governing international financial relations is . . . to ensure international financial stability, which has two fundamental aspects, crisis prevention . . . and crisis resolution.'[5]

The actors in the international financial architecture

The actors in the international financial architecture are 'formal' international financial institutions, regional financial institutions, international fora meeting under the auspices of a formal international organization (such as the Financial Stability Forum, and the Basel Committee on Banking Supervision), other international fora (such as the International Organization of Securities Commissions), 'informal' international groupings where international financial issues are discussed (such as the Group of Seven, G7 and Group of Ten, G10 countries), national central banks and ministries of finance or treasuries (which can play a role individually or collectively meeting in an international forum of a formal or informal character), and private financial institutions acting on a global scale. This multiplicity of actors and the mushrooming of international fora create a very complex structure. As Cooke explains, 'Outside the supervisors' window there is a kaleidoscope of financial markets and institutions and range of services—all interlinked to a greater or lesser degree. Each regulator, national or sectoral, only sees a part of this kaleidoscope and cannot be sure he controls all that he can see.'[6]

'Formal' international financial institutions

Under the genus of 'formal' international financial institutions, whose existence is formally recognized by a treaty, there are multilateral organizations and regional institutions. The main multilateral organizations (international financial institutions) are the International Monetary Fund, the World Bank Group (comprising the International Bank for Reconstruction and Development, IBRD; the International Development Association, IDA; the Multilateral Investment Guarantee Agency, MIGA; and the International Centre for the Resolution of Investment Disputes), the Bank for International Settlements (BIS), the Organization for Economic Cooperation and Development, and the World Trade Organization (with regard to trade in financial services). The regional institutions are a broad category that includes the European Bank for Reconstruction and Development and other regional development banks (Inter-American Development Bank, African Development Bank, Asian Development Bank), other supranational organizations at the European level,

---

[5] Above note 2, 9.
[6] See Peter Cooke, above note 1 (Preface, 'The Future of Global Financial Regulation and Supervision') xxiv.

such as the European System of Central Banks and the European Investment Bank, and supranational institutions in other 'regions' of the World.

Having examined the role and functions of the IMF in detail in Chapter 13, in this chapter I will only discuss briefly the role of the BIS (the oldest international financial institution in the world) and I will not enter into the detail of the working of other 'formal' international organizations such as the World Bank (the sister institution of the IMF, whose origins also stem from the Bretton Woods conference in 1944), the Organisation for Economic Cooperation and Development, OECD (whose predecessor was the OEEC, Organisation for Economic Cooperation and Development), or the WTO, whose formal existence was finally sanctioned in 1994, and whose agenda for trade liberalization is a very broad one, covering all goods and services. (It is with regard to trade in financial services, where the work of the WTO must be considered by financial lawyers.[7] In particular, the competing or conflicting character of the goals of prudential supervision and financial liberalization is a fascinating subject,[8] whose analysis, however, exceeds the scope of this book.)

The Bank for International Settlements   The Bank for International Settlements (BIS) is an international organization which fosters cooperation among central banks and other agencies in pursuit of monetary and financial stability and which provides banking services to central banks (a bank for central banks) and international organizations.[9]

As I mentioned in Chapter 12, the BIS was set up in 1930 in Basel, Switzerland (in the context of the Young Plan) by a decision of the Hague Conference that dealt with the German reparations payments imposed by the Treaty of Versailles after the First World War. From a legal point of view, the BIS has a defined, albeit complex, legal personality. On the one hand, it is a company limited by

---

[7] A recent study of the subject is provided by Apostolos Gkoutzinis, 'International Trade in Banking Services and the Role of the WTO: Discussing the Legal Framework and Policy Objectives of the General Agreement on Trade in Services (GATS) and the Current State of Play in the Doha Round of Trade Negotiations' 39 (4) International Lawyer. (Winter 2005), 877–914,

[8] For a brief analysis of this issue, see Rosa M Lastra, 'Cross-Border Trade in Financial Services' in Ian Fletcher, Loukas Mistelis, and Marise Cremona (eds), *Foundations and Perspectives of International Trade Law* (London: Sweet & Maxwell, 2001) 428–36.

[9] See generally <http://www.bis.org>. See also Gianni Toniolo, *Central Banking Co-operation at the Bank for International Settlements, 1930–1973* (Cambridge: Cambridge University Press, 2005). Toniolo's book—which constitutes an in-depth study of central bank cooperation during the period covered—explores the foundation of the BIS, its role in the financial crisis of 1931, the London financial conference of 1933, the much criticized activity of the BIS during the Second World War, the Bretton Woods system, the creation of the European payments union in the 1950s, and the support of the Bretton Woods system in the 1960s. The last chapter is devoted to the first steps towards monetary union in Europe and financial stability. Toniolo surveys the legal basis of the BIS in ch 2 (48–52).

shares;[10] on the other, it is an international organization which was established pursuant to the Hague Agreements of 20 January 1930 and, as such, is governed by international law.[11] The BIS was also created as a forum for the cooperation of central banks and this feature has remained a constant in the history of the BIS.

The BIS fulfils its mandate by promoting discussion and facilitating decision-making processes among central banks and within the international financial community, by providing a centre for economic and monetary research, by acting as a prime counterparty for central banks in their financial transactions, and by performing agent or trustee functions with regard to various international financial arrangements.

Throughout its history the BIS has carried out important monetary and banking functions. The BIS was the agent for the European Payments Union (EPU, 1950–8), helping the European currencies restore convertibility after the Second World War. Similarly, the BIS has acted as the agent for the Exchange Rate Mechanisms of the European Monetary System before the adoption of the euro.

The BIS has also provided financial assistance to support the international monetary system in various instances. During the 1931–3 financial crisis, the BIS organized support credits for both the Austrian and German central banks. In the 1960s, the BIS arranged special support credits for the Italian lira (1964) and the French franc (1968), and two so-called Group Arrangements (1966 and

---

[10] The BIS is owned by fifty-five central banks and monetary authorities and its Board of Directors consists of the eleven Governors of the G10 central banks, and of six representatives of finance, industry, or commerce each appointed by the Governors of the central banks of Belgium, France, Germany, Great Britain, Italy, and the United States. On 8 January 2001, an Extraordinary General Meeting of the BIS decided to restrict the right to hold shares in the BIS exclusively to central banks and approved the mandatory repurchase of all 72,648 BIS shares held by private shareholders as of that date against payment of compensation of CHF 16,000 per share. The former private shareholders were informed by means of the Notes to Private Shareholders dated 15 September 2000 and 10 January 2001, which described the transaction in more detail; a further Note was sent on 27/28 November 2002 following the Tribunal's 22 November 2002 decision. Pursuant to Article 54 of the BIS Statutes, disputes concerning the interpretation or application of the Statutes, in particular between the Bank and its shareholders, must be referred for final decision to the Hague Arbitral Tribunal. In 2001, three former private shareholders challenged the shares withdrawal by initiating proceedings before the Tribunal. On 13 October 2003, the Hague Arbitral Tribunal published its final determination regarding the amount of additional compensation to be paid by the BIS to former private shareholders for the shares withdrawn on 8 January 2000. See <http://www.bis.org/about/shareswd.htm>.

[11] The Convention respecting the Bank for International Settlements (of 20 January 1930), the Constituent Charter of the Bank for International Settlements (of 20 January 1930), and the Statutes of the Bank for International Settlements (of 20 January 1930, as amended in 1937, 1950, 1961, 1969, 1974, 1975, 1993, 1994, 1999, 2001, and 2005) are available at <http://www.bis.org/about/legal.htm>. (Switzerland issued the Charter and the annexed Statutes.)

1968) to support sterling. More recently, the BIS has provided finance in the context of IMF-led programmes of financial assistance (eg, Brazil in 1998).[12]

Since the BIS provides an institutional framework for cooperation in the monetary and financial area and serves as a meeting place mainly for central banks and other financial and regulatory authorities (centre for economic research), the BIS has played an important role in the development of international financial standards through the various experts' committees that meet under its auspices and to which the BIS provides secretariats. Special mention ought to be made of the Basel Committee of Banking Supervision and of the Committee on Payment and Settlement Systems (CPSS) and the Committee on the Global Financial System. By providing the secretariat to these committees, and a physical location, the BIS contributes to their work. I further discuss below the work of the Financial Stability Forum, which also has a secretariat at the BIS.

In addition to the FSF, the work of the Joint Forum on Financial Conglomerates (created in 1996 under the aegis of the Basel Committee on Banking Supervision, the International Organization of Securities Commissions, IOSCO, and the International Association of Insurance Supervisors, IAIS) is also noteworthy.

The Financial Stability Institute, created by the Bank for International Settlements and the Basel Committee on Banking Supervision in 1999 to assist supervisors around the world in improving and strengthening their financial systems,[13] is an internal department of the BIS, which draws upon the resources of the BIS and of the Basel Committee to organize its training for supervisors.

C. 'Soft Law' and International Financial Standard Setting

The growth in 'soft law' is one of the most relevant developments in the field of international monetary and financial law in recent years. As Gionavoli points out in his excellent study on this issue, with a few exceptions (notably, the Articles of Agreement of the IMF), most of the international standards, rules, principles, guidelines, codes of conduct, best practices, and other arrangements governing cross-border financial relations can be characterized as 'soft law'.[14]

The international legal system has long been described as a system comprised of equal and sovereign states whose actions are limited only by rules freely accepted as legally binding. In the well-known Lotus Case, the Permanent Court of International Justice described this system: 'International law governs relations between independent states. The rules of law binding upon states therefore

---

[12] ibid.   [13] <http://www.bis.org/fsi/aboutfsi.htm>.
[14] See Giovanoli, above note 2, 33.

emanate from their own free will as expressed in conventions or by usages generally accepted as expressing principles of law and established in order to regulate the relations between these coexisting independent communities or with a view to the achievement of common aims.'[15]

However, globalization has challenged the traditional law-making process. The international financial standard-setting process is only one aspect of a wider trend towards the development of a variety of international commitments, which are often described as 'soft law'.[16]

In this section,[17] I provide first a definition of soft law. Secondly, I survey the actors in the process of international financial standard setting, with emphasis upon the role of the Basel Committee of Banking Supervision (a de facto international banking regulator) and the Financial Stability Forum (which could still play a central coordinating role among the plethora of standard setters). Thirdly, I provide a taxonomy of soft law rules. Then, I examine advantages and disadvantages of soft law and the crucial issues of implementation and monitoring observance of the rules. Finally, I consider the process of formalization of law over time and how this process affects soft law and its evolution.

Definition of soft law

According to Goode, soft law can be defined as rules that are not legally binding, but which in practice are adhered to by those to whom they are addressed or by those who subscribe to them, for a variety of reasons (moral suasion, fear of adverse action, and other 'incentives' to observe the rules).[18]

While 'hard' law is characterized by formality, 'soft' law is characterized by informality. Soft law is observed in a voluntary, self-imposed way. Hard law is binding in a coercive, externally imposed way. Enforcement is the key element for distinguishing between hard and soft law.[19]

The concept of 'soft law' remains unsettled. Abbott and Snidal[20] argue that one

---

[15] See the Case of the SS 'Lotus', 1927 PCIJ, Series A, No 10, 18, available at <http://www.worldcourts.com/pcij/eng/decisions/1927.09.07_lotus.

[16] See generally Hiram Chodosh, 'Neither Treaty nor Custom: The Emergence of Declarative International Law' (1991) 26 Texas International Law Journal 88; Prosper Weil, 'Toward Relative Normativity in International Law' (1983) 77 American Journal of International Law 413.

[17] I draw substantially in this section on Giovanoli's study (above note 2), since it provides—in my opinion—a seminal contribution to the analysis of international financial soft law.

[18] See Roy Goode, *Commercial Law*, 2nd edn (London: Penguin Books,1995) 20–1.

[19] Above note 2, 35. Giovanoli points out (ibid n 83) that 'from the legal point of view, no remedies are available if the rules are not followed. This does not, of course, preclude the existence of factual "sanctions", either from the market or from other bodies, which can be very effective.'

[20] See Kenneth W Abbott & Duncan Snidal, 'Hard and Soft Law in International Governance' (2000) 54 International Organization 421, 422.

approach to defining soft law is to identify what soft law is not. It is not 'hard law', nor is it a purely political understanding without a legal component. Rather, soft law is what lies between these two alternatives.[21] Some commentators use the term to define rules of international law which are imprecise or weak. 'It would seem better to reserve the term "soft law" for rules that are imprecise and not really compelling, since sub-legal obligations are neither "soft law" nor "hard law": They are simply not law at all.'[22] According to Goldsmith and Posner, 'The legal literature usually labels non-legal international agreements as "soft law". We avoid this label here for two reasons. First, non-legal agreements are not binding under international (or any other) law, so it seems inappropriate to call them "law", soft or otherwise. Second, "soft law" typically includes not only non-legal agreements, but also legally binding agreements that are vague or indeterminate.'[23]

Under another view, soft law 'tends to blur the line between the law and the non-law, be that because merely aspirational norms are accorded legal status, albeit of a secondary nature; be that because the intended effect of its usage may be to undermine the status of established legal norms'.[24]

Perhaps the most traditional position views agreements other than treaties as nothing more than evidence of custom.[25] '[M]ost public international lawyers, realists, and positivists consider soft law to be inconsequential.'[26] Hence, 'it seems inappropriate and unhelpful to use the term soft law to describe norms and normative instruments which are clearly not in legal form, not intended to be legally binding, and thus not, in any of the usual senses in which we use the word, law at all.'[27]

According to Sir Joseph Gold, 'soft law expresses a preference and not an obligation that states should act, or should refrain from acting, in a specified manner.'[28]

---

[21] For more about 'soft law' see generally Gunther F Handl et al, 'A Hard Look at Soft Law' in 82 (1998) American Society of International Law Proceedings 371.

[22] See generally Weil, above note 16, n 7.

[23] See Jack L Goldsmith and Eric A Posner, 'International Agreements: A Rational Choice Approach' (2003) 44 Virginia Journal of International Law 113, n 2.

[24] See Handl et al, above note 21.

[25] See Pierre-Marie Dupuy, 'Soft Law and the International Law of the Environment' (1991) 12 Michigan Journal of International Law 420, 432.

[26] See Richard H Steinberg, 'In the Shadow of Law or Power? Consensus-Based Bargaining and Outcomes in the GATT/WTO' (2002) 56 International Organization 339, 340.

[27] See Richard Bilder, 'Beyond Compliance: Helping Nations Cooperate' in Dinah Shelton (ed), *Commitment and Compliance: The Role of Non-Binding Norms in the International Legal System* (Oxford: Oxford University Press, 2000) 72.

[28] See Joseph Gold, *Interpretation: The IMF and International Law* (The Hague: Kluwer Law International, 1996) 31.

The contribution of non-sovereign entities to the formulation of non-binding rules which are nevertheless expected or designed to be implemented and observed in national legal systems marks a sharp departure from the standard law-making process in the international legal system.[29]

Who is involved in the process of setting international standards for financial markets?

Many of the actors in the international financial architecture that I mentioned above participate in the process of international financial standard setting.[30] The entities and bodies which are directly or indirectly involved in this process encompass formal international financial organizations (most prominently the International Monetary Fund); regional organizations (such as the European Bank for Reconstruction and Development, EBRD); de facto groupings created at the initiative of governments (such as the G7, G10, or G20 and other Gs);[31] financial sector-specific international groupings of supervisors and regulators; central bank experts' committees (Basel Committee on Banking Supervision, International Organization of Securities Committees, International Association of Insurance Supervisors, International Association of Deposit Insurers, and others); the Financial Stability Forum; market entities and professional associations (the International Accounting Standards Committee, the Emerging Markets Trade Association, the International Chamber of Commerce, ICC, and its various commissions and working groups,[32] and others); think tanks with a contribution to international financial stability such as the Group of Thirty, and so on.

From a 'private law' perspective, the work of the organizations concerned with the harmonization of transnational commercial law, such as UNCITRAL

---

[29] See generally Dinah Shelton, 'The Impact of Globalization on the International Legal System', (paper presented in the conference of the University of Sydney 'Globalisation and its Challenges', Sydney, 12–14 December 2001) available at <http://www.econ.usyd.edu.au/global/images/papers.pdf> (5 March 2004).

[30] See Giovanoli, above note 2, 11–33. See also Financial Stability Forum, 'Who Are the Standard-Setting Bodies?' <http://www.fsforum.org/compendium/who_are_the_standard_setting_bodies.html> and International Monetary Fund, 'Standard Setting Agencies', at <http://www.imf.org/external/standards/agency.htm>.

[31] See Giovanoli, above note 2, 17–20.

[32] The ICC has 16 commissions of experts which cover every specialized field of concern to international business. Subjects range from banking techniques and financial services to taxation, trade policy, competition policy, telecommunications, intellectual property, information technology, and others. *Self-regulation is a common thread running through the work of the commissions.* The ICC has direct access to national governments all over the world through its national committees. The ICC's Paris-based international secretariat feeds business views into intergovernmental organizations on issues that directly affect business operations. See <http://www.iccwbo.org/id93/index.html>.

(United Nations Commission on International Trade Law),[33] the UNIDROIT (the International Institute for the Unification of Private Law),[34] and the Hague Conference on International Private Law,[35] must also be mentioned.

While most of the entities involved in the process of international financial standard setting are intergovernmental or official entities, and their principles or recommendations can be characterized as 'top down' rules (typically 'public law'), the work done by professional associations and market entities (uniform rules and standards, voluntary 'codes of conduct', 'codes of practice', etc) can be characterized as 'bottom up' rules, an exercise in self-regulation.[36] With regard to the harmonization of international commercial law ('private law' governing cross-border transactions), the work of UNIDROIT and similar efforts offer a 'set of rules produced and agreed by scholars representative of the main legal families of the world which, though deriving their inspiration from many legal systems, are not the rules of any one system and in various instances offer new solutions'.[37]

The issuing and the oversight of implementation of the international financial standards are currently the responsibility of a growing number of bodies. Despite the plethora of 'international financial standard setters', there is no formal legal framework for the allocation of responsibilities and the division of labour among them. Though the creation of the Financial Stability Forum (FSF) aimed to improve the way in which existing institutions function, the reality is that problems of coordination remain.

The streamlining of the 'international standard setters' and of the standards themselves is not only desirable, but necessary, given the 'mushrooming' of bodies with standard-setting responsibilities over the last few years, the potential for overlap and duplication, and the multiplicity of principles financial institutions must take into account.[38]

In the following paragraphs I elaborate first on the work of the Basel Committee

---

[33] <http://www.uncitral.org>.   [34] <http://www.unidroit.org>.

[35] <http://www.hcch.net/index_en.php>.

[36] See also Giovanoli, above note 2, 10 and n 20. See also Mistelis, above note 1, 163–5.

[37] See Roy Goode, 'Rule, Practice and Pragmatism in Commercial Law' (2005) 54 International Comparative Law Quarterly 539, 553. Goode refers to the UNIDROIT Principles of International Commercial Contracts. Goode points out (ibid 539) that transnational commercial law is the product of various means: 'international conventions, model laws, contractually incorporated uniform rules, international restatements and conscious or unconscious legislative or judicial parallelism, which lead to the harmonization of commercial law at the international level'. He also points out (ibid) that his concern 'is primarily with the private law governing cross-border transactions, not with international economic law or regulatory law'. My approach, on the other hand, is with international economic law and with regulatory law.

[38] Above note 2, 32–3. Perhaps the role of the FSF should be revamped so that it could provide that necessary coordinating function, ibid 56–8.

on Banking Supervision, given the significance of its work in the field of banking regulation, and, then, I provide a brief note on the work of the Financial Stability Forum.[39]

The Basel Committee on Banking Supervision

The Basel Committee on Banking Supervision comprises representatives of the central banks and supervisory authorities of the Group of Ten countries, which in fact are eleven (Belgium, Canada, France, Germany, Italy, Japan, the Netherlands, Sweden, Switzerland, United Kingdom, and United States), plus Luxembourg, and meets in Basel under the auspices of the Bank for International Settlements (BIS). The Committee, whose original name was Committee on Banking Regulations and Supervisory Practices, was established at the end of 1974 to encourage cooperation in the prudential supervision of international banks.[40] Though the Committee acts as an informal forum (a club of central banks and other supervisory agencies), and its decisions do not have direct legal binding force upon the member countries of the expanded Group of Ten (G10), it has become a de facto international regulatory body. A wide array of countries have adopted many of the Committee's resolutions and recommendations, incorporating them into national legislation and regulations. In this respect, the powers and influence of the Committee extend well beyond its founding mandate. The Committee currently has a number of technical working groups and task forces which meet regularly.

According to its own website,

> The Committee does not possess any formal supranational supervisory authority, and its conclusions do not, and were never intended to, have legal force. Rather, it formulates broad supervisory standards and guidelines and recommends statements of best practice in the expectation that individual authorities will take steps to implement them through detailed arrangements—statutory or otherwise—which are best suited to their own national systems. In this way, the Committee encourages convergence towards common approaches and common standards without attempting detailed harmonisation of member countries' supervisory techniques.[41]

Arguably, the informality and independence of the Committee have served well in the design of international banking rules, as it has acted with a fair degree of depoliticization and a considerable amount of technical expertise and competence in banking and monetary affairs. However, such an informal character

---

[39] For an analysis of other institutions and bodies involved in international financial standard setting, see generally Giovanoli, 11–33.

[40] See Joseph Norton, *Bank Regulation and Supervision in the 1990s* (London, Lloyd's of London Press, 1991), 83–5.

[41] <http://www.bis.org/bcbs/aboutbcbs.htm>.

is likely to change in years to come. While cooperation and coordination can be reached within a framework of informal rapprochement between bank supervisors and regulators, convergence and harmonization of rules require a formal mandate.

For the first two decades of its existence, the Committee focused on the effective supervision of cross-border establishments and on the establishment of a framework for the measurement and adequacy of bank capital. Over the past few years, the Committee has moved more aggressively to promote sound supervisory standards worldwide. In close collaboration with many non-G10 supervisory authorities, the Committee in 1997 developed a set of Core Principles for Effective Banking Supervision. To facilitate implementation and assessment, the Committee in October 1999 developed the so-called Core Principles Methodology.[42]

In order to enable a wider group of countries to be associated with the work being pursued in Basel, the Committee has always encouraged contacts and cooperation between its members and other banking supervisory authorities. It circulates to supervisors throughout the world published and unpublished papers. In many cases, supervisory authorities in non-G10 countries have seen fit publicly to associate themselves with the Committee's initiatives. Contacts have been further strengthened by an International Conference of Banking Supervisors which takes place every two years.

The Committee's Secretariat is provided by the Bank for International Settlements in Basel. The twelve-person Secretariat is mainly staffed by professional supervisors on temporary secondment from member institutions. In addition to undertaking the secretarial work for the Committee and its many expert sub-committees, it stands ready to give advice to supervisory authorities in all countries.

The Financial Stability Forum

The Financial Stability Forum was set up in 1999 by the Group of Seven (G7) Ministers and Governors to promote international financial stability through information exchange and international cooperation in banking supervision and surveillance.[43] The Forum brings together twenty-five representatives of national authorities (central banks, ministries of finance, supervisory authorities) from Australia, Canada, France, Germany, Hong Kong, Italy, Japan, the Netherlands, Singapore, United Kingdom and, United States, six representatives from four international financial institutions (International Monetary

---

[42] ibid.   [43] See the FSF's website, <http://www.fsforum.org>.

Fund, World Bank, Bank for International Settlements, and the Organization for Economic Cooperation and Development), seven representatives from four international standard-setting, regulatory, and supervisory groupings (Basel Committee on Banking Supervision, International Accounting Standards Board, International Association of Insurance Supervisors, and International Organization of Securities Commissions), one representative from the BIS Committee on Payment and Settlement System, one representative from the BIS Committee on the Global Financial System, and one from the European Central Bank. The FSF is serviced by a small secretariat located at the Bank for International Settlements in Basel, Switzerland. The current Chairman is Roger W Ferguson, Vice Chairman of the Board of Governors of the US Federal Reserve System (the first Chairman was Andrew Crockett).

The Forum seeks to coordinate the efforts of these various bodies in order to promote international financial stability and to reduce systemic risk. The Forum, as before the Basel Committee on Banking Supervision, fills a legal need, a legal vacuum. In the absence of legal mechanisms for setting rules at the international level, informal mechanisms have emerged. The informal legal nature of the Forum and the lack of a clear mandate suggest a degree of flexibility in its operations that may be appropriate for responding to some of the needs of the international financial community, but that falls short of the legal certainty that characterizes 'formal law'. The lack of effective enforcement is the 'eternal' problem of international financial soft law.

The Compendium of Standards   As part of its efforts to coordinate the work of the various international standard setters the Forum publishes a Compendium of Standards which it regularly updates.[44]

The Compendium of Standards comprises twelve standard areas which have been designated by the Financial Stability Forum as Key Standards for Sound Financial Systems. Of those twelve standards, three refer to 'macroeconomic policy and data transparency', six refer to 'institutional and market infrastructure', and three to 'financial regulation and supervision'.

The first three, all issued by the IMF, are the Code of Good Practices on Transparency in Monetary and Fiscal Policies, the Code of Good Practices in Fiscal Transparency, and the Special Data Dissemination Standard/General Data Dissemination System. The 'institutional and market infrastructure standards' cover insolvency (with the World Bank coordinating a broad-based effort

---

[44] The Compendium of Standards compiled by the Financial Stability Forum is available at the FSF's website: <http://www.fsforum.org/compendium/key_standards_for_sound_financial_system.html>.

to develop a set of principles and guidelines on insolvency regimes[45]), corporate governance (issued by the OECD), accounting (issued by the International Accounting Standards Board), auditing (issued by the International Federation of Accountants), payment and settlement (issued by a Task Force comprising the Committee on Payment and Settlement Systems jointly with IOSCO), and market integrity (recommendations by the FATF or Financial Action Task Force on Money Laundering).

The latter three standards concerning 'financial regulation and supervision' are the Core Principles for Effective Banking Supervision issued by the Basel Committee on Banking Supervision in September 1997,[46] the Objectives and Principles of Securities Regulation issued by the International Organization of Securities Commissions (IOSCO) and fully updated in October 2003,[47] and the Insurance Core Principles and Methodology issued by the International Association of Insurance Supervisors (IAIS) and fully updated in October 2003.[48]

The standards regarding financial regulation and supervision (in particular the Basel Core Principles for Effective Banking Supervision) have become widely accepted in both developed and developing countries.

Taxonomy

'Soft law' rules are not a homogeneous group of rules. They can be classified according to various criteria: their effect, their scope, their degree of specificity, their source and nature, and the contents of the rules.

From the point of view of their effect, they range from professional practices at the lowest end of the legal scale (best practices, gentlemen's agreements) to uniform rules, codes and guidelines, and progressively more 'forceful' arrangements with various degrees of actions (sanctions) in the event of 'non-observance'.[49]

---

[45] Work is in progress between the World Bank and Uncitral (The United Nations Commission on International Trade Law), in consultation with the Fund, to develop standards on insolvency based upon the Bank's 'Principles for Effective Insolvency and Creditor Rights Systems' and UNCITRAL's Legislative Guide on Insolvency Law (UNCITRAL adopted a Model Law on Cross-Border Insolvency in 1997).

[46] See Basel Committee of Banking Supervision, *Core Principles for Effective Banking Supervision* (Basel: BIS, 1997), at <http://www.bis.org/publ/bcbs30a.pdf>.

[47] See International Organization of Securities Commission, *Objectives and Principles of Securities Regulation* (Madrid: IOSCO, 2003), at <http://www.iosco.org/pubdocs/pdf/IOSCOPD154.pdf>.

[48] See International Association of Insurance Supervisors, *Insurance Core Principles and Methodology* (Basel: IAIS, 2003), at <http://www.iaisweb.org/358icp03.pdf>.

[49] See Giovanoli, above note 2 35–6. Giovanoli also uses other criteria to classify soft-law rules. With regard to the 'gradation' of rules, see also Weil, above note 16. I use the term 'forceful' instead of binding (which denotes hard law) and the term 'non-observance' instead of non-compliance.

From the point of view of their scope they can be classified, according to the Compendium of Standards published by the FSF, into sectoral standards (eg, banking, securities, insurance) and functional standards (eg disclosure and transparency, governance, accounting, etc).

From the point of view of their 'degree of specificity', the FSF Compendium classifies standards into 'principles', 'practices', and 'methodologies/guidelines'.[50] This degree of specificity with regard to their implementation influences, in turn, the discretion afforded to the national authorities.[51] Principles are defined in the Compendium as fundamental tenets pertaining to a broad policy area, which offer a degree of flexibility in implementation to suit the country's circumstances. Practices spell out the practical applications of the principles within a more narrowly defined context. Methodologies/guidelines provide detailed guidance on steps to be taken or requirements to be met.

With regard to the contents of the rules, a distinction can be made between 'substantive rules' and rules that allocate regulatory jurisdiction. Most international financial 'soft law' instruments intend to regulate the substantive aspect of a given matter, for example, the Basel Capital Accord. Other international standards however are concerned with the allocation of regulatory responsibility—division of labour—among national authorities in cross-border financial transactions or activities, for example, the Basel Concordat of 1975.[52]

With regard to the sources of international soft law, a distinction can be made between 'top-down' rules and 'bottom-up' rules, as I pointed out above.[53] 'Top-down' rules emanate from official entities (formal intergovernmental institutions and groupings created at the initiative of governments). 'Bottom-up' rules typically constitute an exercise in self-regulation. The former rules are generally agreed among regulators, supervisors, or other national authorities and groups of experts. They are not addressed to the persons to whom the standards are ultimately intended to apply, but to national authorities who in turn undertake the obligation to implement them in the national jurisdiction. In that respect, they resemble European Directives that are addressed to Member States who must transpose them into national law and are not the final addressees of the relevant standards.[54]

Typically, the 'top-down' rules that I referred to in the previous paragraph can be characterized as 'public law' rules. The rules that emanate from professional

---

[50] See <http://www.fsforum.org/compendium/what_are_standards.html>.
[51] See generally Norton, above note 1, ch 1, 'Pondering the Parameters of the New International Financial Architecture: A Legal Perspective', 16–19.
[52] See Giovanoli, above note 2, 39–40.   [53] See also Mistelis, above note 1, 163.
[54] See Giovanoli, above note 2, 39 and 55–6.

associations (such as ICC) are typically 'private law' rules (an exercise in self-regulation). The rules of UNIDROIT, UNCITRAL, and other organizations involved in the harmonization of commercial law are also 'private law' rules governing cross-border transactions (albeit of a different character from those that emanate from professional associations).

Advantages and disadvantages of soft law

It is often argued that the advantages of soft law are its flexibility, informality, and pragmatism.[55] While international treaty making is a formal and time-consuming process, which lacks flexibility for the purposes of revision or amendment,[56] international standards provide flexibility and informality to the rule-making process.[57] 'The extreme length of international treaties' negotiations and approval compared with the speed of financial innovations in the market-place has made these traditional tools of international diplomacy ineffective in the financial domain.'[58]

It is also argued that the modus operandi of many 'international standard setters' (ie, the technical expertise of those involved, the commonality of knowledge and interests, and the relatively small size of the working groups) fosters pragmatism and mutual trust.[59]

Another advantage is that their conceptual definition as minimum standards, which are largely binding as to their effect but leave scope to national discretion (akin to EC Directives), enhance their prospects for national implementation without the anxiety of eroding (or appearing to erode) national sovereignty.

There are several drawbacks of relying upon soft law. First and foremost, there are concerns about legitimacy. Treaty-making is slow, but formal and legitimate. In a democratic system, this is a very important consideration.

Secondly, since implementation remains at the discretion of national authorities, problems of legal certainty, predictability, and consistency may arise. As Giovanoli points out, the lack of precise legal force until they are converted into national law may create problems of protection for the parties concerned in the absence of formal legal remedies if the rules are not followed.[60]

---

[55] ibid 41–4.

[56] See eg Anthony Aust, 'The Theory and Practice of Informal International Instruments' (1986) 35 ICLQ 787, 791–2.

[57] See Hartmut Hillgenberg, 'A Fresh Look at Soft Law' (1999) 10 European Journal of International Law 499; Charles Lipson, 'Why are Some International Agreements Informal?' (1991) 45 International Organization 495, 500.

[58] See Cally Jordan and Giovanni Majnoni, *Financial Regulatory Harmonization and the Globalization of Finance* (Washington DC: World Bank, 2002) 6–7.

[59] See Giovanoli, above note 2, 42.   [60] ibid 43.

Thirdly, the proliferation of standards may lead to complexity, inconsistency, overlaps, or gaps (though the work of the Financial Stability Forum could contribute to simplifying and providing consistency to the process of international standard setting).

Finally, there are concerns about 'country ownership', in particular with regard to developing countries, as I further explore in the following paragraphs.

The problems of country 'ownership'

The question of fair representation in international standard-setting bodies,[61] particularly with regard to emerging market countries, is a fundamental issue in the process of soft-law making, one that is directly related to the 'ownership of financial law reform' projects, an issue which is related to the legitimacy of the process of international financial standard setting.[62]

The implementation of international standards may not travel well to emerging or transition economies owing to incompatibility with the domestic legal culture (eg, the implementation of fiduciary duties towards investors and shareholders in civil law systems)[63] or the complexity or level of sophistication of some standards.

The Basel Committee of Banking Supervision, recognizing the need to include in its proposals the interests of emerging market economies, developed its 1997 Core Principles of Banking Supervision working in cooperation with non-G10 supervisory authorities from Chile, China, the Czech Republic, Hong Kong, Mexico, Russia, and Thailand. Nine other countries (Argentina, Brazil, Hungary, India, Indonesia, Korea, Malaysia, Poland, and Singapore) were also closely associated in the work.

However, the more recent work of the Basel Committee (regarding the revised capital framework) has often been perceived as inadequate for developing countries because of its complexity. For instance, the People's Republic of China (PRC) has made it clear that it will not adopt the Basel II proposals (in their current form).

---

[61] ibid 30.

[62] See Ch 5. See generally John J Kirton, 'The G20: Representativeness, Effectiveness and Leadership in Global Governance' in John J Kirton, Joseph P Daniels, and Andreas Freytag (eds), *Guiding Global Order: G8 Governance in the Twenty-First Century* (Aldershot: Ashgate, 2001) 143–72; Tony Porter, 'The G-7, the Financial Stability Forum, the G-20 and the Politics of International Financial Regulation' (Paper prepared for the International Studies Association Annual Meeting, Los Angeles, California, 15 March 2000).

[63] See Katharina Pistor et al, *Economic Development, Legality and the Transplant Effect* (Michigan: The Davidson Institute, 2000).

It is also questionable whether standards developed in and designed to fit large and developed economies fit equally well small, emerging countries which account for the majority of jurisdictions around the world. Even independent from the level of development, the size of an economy is by itself an important determinant of the desirable structure and size of its financial and regulatory system. The fixed costs in setting up a regulatory structure, a market, a bank, are such that not many countries around the world can be expected to have all financial intermediation services produced domestically and conversely to have all the regulatory structures currently considered by the standards and codes currently in circulation.[64]

The perceived under-inclusiveness of the process may create the impression that peculiarities and special conditions of countries not directly involved in the standard-setting process are not taken into account.[65] The non-binding character of most international standards indicates that the implementation of those standards relies on the cooperation between the countries that are supposed to implement them and the standard-setting organizations. It is therefore important that implementing countries assume 'ownership' of those rules (an important issue also with regard to IMF 'conditionality').[66]

Ownership of financial law reform matters because it provides safeguards of genuine compliance with the spirit of the international standards, because it generates political acceptance and streamlines the implementation process.[67]

The experience so far with Reports on the Observance of Standards and Codes (ROSCs), which I examine below is that country participation (in ROSCs) is higher in developed countries than in developing countries and that regional participation rates remain uneven, with Europe having the highest and Sub-Saharan Africa and East Asia the lowest.[68]

Implementation and monitoring observance of standards

Implementation of international financial standards is typically done at the national level, through appropriate legislation or regulation.[69] Once they

---

[64] See Jordan and Majnoni, above note 58, 19.

[65] ibid. 'Fair representation of all parties is crucial for the acceptance of standards with no legally binding character. On the other hand, it must be recognized that rules are much easier to draft in relatively small and manageable groups, as broad groups, especially if they are not homogeneous, move slowly and may fail to achieve the necessary degree of consensus. Reconciling at the international level the conflicting requirements of legitimacy and effectiveness is akin to squaring the circle.'

[66] See Ch 13 for a discussion on this issue.

[67] See Mohsin S Khan and Sunil Sharma, *Conditionality and Country Ownership of Programs* (Washington DC: IMF, 2001) 14.

[68] See International Monetary Fund and the World Bank, 'The Standards and Codes Initiative—Is it Effective? And How Can it be Improved?', 1 July 2005, available at <http://www.imf.org/external/np/pp/eng/2005/070105a.htm>.

[69] Above note 2, 45–50.

are incorporated into national law, standards become 'hard law' and thus enforceable.

As Giovanoli points out, it is important to differentiate between implementation and enforcement.[70] While enforcement is a legal concept, implementation is a 'factual' concept. The competent state authorities—such as administrative authorities or courts of justice—enforce the rules, that is, take the necessary measures to apply legally binding rules. It is the binding force of the rules that triggers the 'availability of measures of compulsory execution. Implementation, on the other hand, is a factual concept, meaning that a certain result has been achieved, through appropriate legislation or otherwise'.[71]

Soft law rules are not 'legally enforceable' and yet they have often proven to be effective in finding their way into national law or into EC law, as the success of the Basel process (ie, the work of the Basel Committee on Banking Supervision) clearly indicates.

Voluntary observance is often driven by regulatory competition which induces national jurisdictions to adopt and implement the latest 'must have' set of rules, lest they be frowned upon by the international community and international business.

The international bodies which issue international financial standards tend to provide assistance for implementation. For instance, with regard to the Basel Core Principles of Banking Supervision (1997), the Core Principles Methodology (of October 1999) sets out detailed guidelines for the assessment of compliance with the core principles. For each principle, there is a set of criteria (essential and additional) against which compliance can be assessed.[72]

The Financial Stability Forum (FSF) established, in 1999, an ad hoc Task Force on Implementation of Standards, chaired by Andrew Sheng, Chairman of the Securities and Futures Commission, Hong Kong. In 2000, the Task Force published a paper[73] identifying *inter alia* official and market incentives to promote standards implementation.

---

[70] Above note 2, 46.   [71] ibid.

[72] See Basel Committee on Banking Supervision, *The Core Principles Methodology* (Basel: BIS, 1999), at <http://www.bis.org/publ/bcbs61.pdf>.

[73] See Financial Stability Forum, *Issues Paper of the Task Force on Implementation of Standards Meeting of the Financial Stability Forum* (Basel: BIS, 2000) at <http://www.fsforum.org/publications/Issues_Paper_Standards00.pdf>. See also above note 2, 49.

Incentives to promote observance of soft law rules

In the absence of formal enforcement mechanisms, 'incentives' compel those to whom they are addressed to observe the rules.[74] These incentives function as a substitute for formal enforcement mechanisms.

The official sector has developed a number of policies and measures to promote observance of soft law rules.[75] For example, the 'name and shame' practice associated with the list prepared by the Financial Action Task Force on Money Laundering (FATF) regarding non-cooperating jurisdictions[76] or the OECD list of offshore financial centres responsible for harmful tax competition[77] act as deterrents against 'non observance'. Institutionalized peer review is another official incentive to promote observance, often as a complement to financial sector surveillance.

The use of IMF conditionality acts as a very powerful official incentive, when the country's adherence to a particular set of standards is made a 'condition' for the disbursement of IMF funds under a standby or extended arrangement.[78]

In the view of the Working Group on Strengthening Financial Systems, official oversight is another way in which implementation can be encouraged.[79] The Working Group recommends that financial sector surveillance be anchored in the IMF's surveillance process but that it benefit from expertise at the World Bank and elsewhere.[80]

In addition to official incentives, there are various instruments of market discipline, such as credit risk weightings, private ratings, borrowing spreads, differentiated interest rates, inter-bank exposure, and others that act as incentives to adhere to soft law rules.[81] These forms of market discipline are typically voluntary and require a developed framework of transparency or disclosure.

International investors often require that developing countries adopt the best

---

[74] Though the word 'compliance' is a term typically used in the case of hard law and 'observance' (or adherence to) in the case of soft law, sometimes the word compliance is also used in references to soft law.

[75] Above note 2, 46–7.

[76] See Financial Action Task Force on Money Laundering, *Non-Cooperative Countries and Territories* (Paris: OECD Financial Action Task Force, 2004), at <http://www1.oecd.org/fatf/NCCT_en.htm#List>.

[77] See Organisation for Economic Cooperation and Development, 'List of Uncooperative Tax Havens' at <http://www.oecd.org/document/57/0,2340,en_2649_33745_30578809_1_1_1_37427,00.html>.

[78] See Ch 13.

[79] Group of Ten, *Report of the Working Group on Strengthening Financial Systems* (Basel: BIS, 1998) 42–6.

[80] ibid.   [81] See Giovanoli, above note 2, 48.

available standards of best practice. This adoption enhances their credit standing and improves the attractiveness and reputation of their financial systems in the international marketplace.

The success of standardized clauses and model rules in private contracts developed by trade and financial industry associations (such as the rules developed by the International Swaps and Derivatives Association, ISDA,[82] governing derivative contracts) has demonstrated that markets are capable of spreading existing standards across jurisdictions and developing common rules (self-regulation).

Monitoring progress in standards implementation

The IMF and the World Bank have developed a framework for assessing member countries' observance of standards and codes, working in cooperation with national authorities, standard-setting agencies, and other international bodies.[83] The standards relate to policy transparency, financial sector regulation and supervision, and market integrity.[84] Assessments of the degree of implementation of these standards by countries result in the Reports on the Observance of Standards and Codes (ROSCs).

FSAP and ROSCs　The Financial Sector Assessment Programme (FSAP) was introduced in May 1999 in the wake of the financial crises of the late 1990s. The FSAP

> aims to increase the effectiveness of efforts to promote the soundness of financial systems in member countries. Supported by experts from a range of national agencies and standard-setting bodies, the program seeks to identify the strengths and vulnerabilities of national financial systems; to determine how key sources of risk are being managed; to ascertain the needs of development and technical assistance in particular financial sectors; and to help prioritize policy responses.[85]

---

[82] Above note 2, 28. See generally <http://www.isda.org>.

[83] See generally International Monetary Fund, 'Standards and Codes: The Role of the IMF', (Washington DC: IMF, 2003), at <http://www.imf.org/external/np/exr/facts/sc.htm>. The standards and codes initiative was launched in 1999 as a prominent component of efforts to strengthen the international financial architecture. The initiative was designed to promote greater financial stability through the development, dissemination, adoption, and implementation of international standards and codes. The initiative covers 12 standards which the Bank and Fund Boards recognized as relevant for their work with regard to policy transparency, financial sector regulation and supervision, and market integrity. Assessments of the degree of implementation of these standards by countries result in the Reports on the Observance of Standards and Codes (ROSCs).

[84] See International Monetary Fund and the World Bank, 'The Standards and Codes Initiative—Is it Effective? And How Can it be Improved?', 1 July 2005, available at <http://www.imf.org/external/np/pp/eng/2005/070105a.htm>.

[85] See International Monetary Fund, 'Financial Sector Assessment Program' at <http://www.imf.org/external/np/fsap/fsap.asp>.

The World Bank describes the FSAP in the following terms:

> The Financial Sector Assessment Program . . . provides more uniform advice in
> financial sector work. It helps to identify financial system strengths and vulner-
> abilities and to reduce the potential for crisis. The program, which fits within the
> context of the Fund's Article IV surveillance, is responsive to calls by the inter-
> national community for closer cooperation to assist countries willing to work to
> reduce the likelihood and/or severity of financial sector crises. The emphasis of
> the FSAP program is on prevention and mitigation rather than crisis resolution.
> Countries benefit from broader coverage and more consistent and rigorous analysis
> of their financial systems. The FSAP helps alert national authorities to likely
> vulnerabilities within their financial sectors while assisting the Bank and the Fund,
> and the international community more broadly, in designing appropriate assist-
> ance. Because each FSAP report identifies follow-up measures for the authorities, it
> also provides a foundation for financial sector technical assistance programs.[86]

The FSAP is a product of the Financial Sector and Poverty Reduction and
Economic Management Vice Presidencies in the Bank, and the Monetary and
Exchange Affairs Department in the Fund. The Bank–Fund Financial Sector
Liaison Committee coordinates the programme in consultation with the Bank's
regions and the Fund's area departments.[87]

An FSAP report is prepared at the request of a member country by the staff of
the Bank and the Fund. An FSAP report consists of three volumes.[88] The first
volume (Main Report) is an overall assessment of the member's financial sector.
It is confidential and made available only to the country's competent authorities. The second volume (Selected Financial Sector Issues) is a detailed technical
analysis, which is also confidential. These first two volumes are not published by
the member, the Fund, or the Bank. The third volume of the FSAP report
(Assessment of Observance of International Standards and Codes) contains a
detailed assessment of the observance of selected financial sector standards,
codes, and good practices. The authorities may publish these detailed assessments
but only with the consent of the Bank and the Fund.[89]

On the basis of the FSAP findings, the staffs of the Fund and the Bank prepare
two separate reports to their respective Executive Boards. The report to the
Fund's Board is a Financial System Stability Assessment (FSSA). The report to
the Bank's Board is Financial Sector Assessment (FSA). FSSAs focus on stability

---

[86] See The World Bank, 'The Financial Sector Assessment Program' at <http://www1.
worldbank.org/finance/html/fsap.html>.

[87] ibid.

[88] See François Gianviti, 'Legal Aspects of the Financial Sector Assessment Program', paper
presented at the IMF Seminar on Current Developments in Monetary and Financial Law in May
2002, available at <http://www.imf.org/external/np/leg/sem/2002cdmfl/eng/gianv2.pdf>.

[89] ibid.

issues of relevance to Fund surveillance. The FSSA, however, will not disclose information concerning the health or prospects of any particular financial institution.[90] The FSSA report can be published by the Fund with the consent of the member. While the FSAP report is for the member's own use, the FSSA report is for the exercise of Fund surveillance.[91]

The Reports on Observance of Standards and Codes (ROSCs), which are a key component of the FSAP, summarize the extent to which countries observe relevant internationally recognized standards and codes and are prepared and published at the request of the member country.[92] Participation by countries in standard assessment and ROSC publication are voluntary. The IMF has recognized twelve areas and associated standards as useful for the operational work of the Fund and the World Bank, as I explained in Chapter 13. These comprise accounting; auditing; anti-money laundering and countering the financing of terrorism (AML/CFT); banking supervision; corporate governance; data dissemination; fiscal transparency; insolvency and creditor rights; insurance supervision; monetary and financial policy transparency; payments systems; and securities regulation; AML/CFT was added in November 2002. They are used to help sharpen the institutions' policy discussions with national authorities, and in the private sector for risk assessment (by rating agencies and others).

FSAPs and ROSCs are related but separate concepts. The FSAP reports are joint reports of Bank and Fund staff on financial sector issues, while ROSCs can be prepared separately by Bank and Fund staff and are not limited to financial sector issues.[93] Countries voluntarily sign up for intensive reviews of their financial system under the FSAP and, although the results remain confidential, they serve as the basis for the country's compliance with the relevant standards—the ROSCs—which appear (if the country agrees to have them published) on the IMF's website and, thus, are available to private sector investors for use in their lending and investment decisions. The idea behind the ROSCs (ie, assessing the compliance with standards, which become a benchmark against which countries are measured) is gaining support among official and market participants. Gianviti cites the example of a US pension fund which has commissioned a consultancy firm to prepare a report on observance by certain countries of the Fund's codes on monetary and fiscal transparency.[94]

Both the ROSCs and the FSAP are an indication of a truly worldwide interest in aligning national legal and regulatory frameworks with international best

---

[90] ibid. According to Art VIII, s 5(b) of the Articles of Agreement, 'Members shall be under no obligation to furnish information in such detail that the affairs of individuals or corporations are disclosed.'

[91] ibid.   [92] <http://www.imf.org/external/np/rosc/rosc.asp>.

[93] See Gianviti, above note 88.   [94] ibid.

practices, ensuring consistency and comparability in the implementation of standards.

Though ideally the observance of standards should be assessed by the institution that has developed them, the Fund and the Bank have been urged to offer their services in cooperation with standards setters, to assess compliance with standards.[95] (The only other organization producing ROSCs, and solely in the area of anti-money laundering and combating the financing of terrorism, is the FATF, Financial Action Task Force, including its FATF-style Regional Bodies.)[96]

The 'good practices' identified through ROSCs can, in turn, generate more standards and codes. For instance, the IMF Statistics Department has proposed that the examples of good statistical practices identified through the ROSC process could be brought together in a Compendium of Good Statistical Practices to serve as a guide to countries in improving their statistical system.[97]

From informal law to formal law

The evolution of law provides evidence of the formalization of rules over time. Many legal rules that are today binding were at some point customs, usages, or practices. Since financial law and, in particular, international financial law is a rather novel field of law, its dynamic and evolving character is unsurprising. The process of law creation still continues.

> Historical experience with soft law in other fields suggest that sooner or later a process of consolidation and 'crystallisation' into legally binding rules occurs. . . . Soft law has proved to be a precursor of emerging hard law. . . . The relation between soft law and legally binding rules (statutory law in domestic jurisdictions, formal treaties at the international level) often appears to be an evolutionary process.[98]

Soft law, informal law, and the 'lex mercatoria'

Formal law has often been born out of the development of informal law. This is not a new phenomenon. It is a recurrent feature in the history of law. The evolution of international law and of commercial law, to cite two relevant examples, provides clear evidence in this regard.

The primary sources of international law are conventional law (treaty law), customary law, and the general principles of the law, as recognized by Article 38

---

[95] ibid.   [96] Above note 84, 10.

[97] See International Monetary Fund, 'Fifth Review of the Fund's Standards Initiative', paper prepared by the Statistics Department in consultation with other Departments (approved by Carols Carson), 18 June 2003, at <http://www.imf.org/external/np/sta/dsbb/2003/eng/061803.pdf>.

[98] See Giovanoli, above note 2, 52.

of the Statute of the International Court of Justice.[99] Customary international law results when states follow certain practices generally and consistently. Customary law, however, can evolve into conventional law. Indeed, important principles of customary international law have became codified in the Vienna Convention of the Law of the Treaties,[100] thus acquiring the characteristic of 'conventional law'.

The birth and development of formal commercial law was influenced by the medieval *lex mercatoria*, that is, by the mercantile codes and customs which reflected the usages of trade, the international maritime and commercial practice at the time. Goode recalls that the *lex mercatoria* or law merchant (which was international rather than English and which was administered by its own mercantile courts) was given full recognition by the common law courts (absorbed in the common law itself) not 'by way of judicial notice of a proposition of law but by receiving evidence of mercantile custom as a question of fact'.[101] Many of the uncodified usages of trade that constituted the *lex mercatoria* eventually became formal law. 'The fertility of the business mind and the fact that a practice which begins life by having no legal force acquires over time the sanctity of law are key factors to which the commercial lawyer must continually be responsive.'[102]

Interestingly, the increasing volume and complexity of international trade nowadays have led to a resurgence of interest in a new *lex mercatoria*.[103] The work of UNCITRAL (United Nations Commission on International Trade Law), Unidroit (International Institute for the Unification of Private Law), the ICC (International Chamber of Commerce), and other harmonizing measures indicate a revival of the spirit of internationalism that characterized the old *lex mercatoria*.[104] Roy Goode, in the 28th FA Mann Annual Lecture in November 2004, discusses the changing face of transnational commercial law, whose sources encompass 'the so-called lex mercatoria and a variety of forms of soft law, including model laws, legislative guides, contractually incorporated uniform rules, trade terms promulgated by international business organizations and

---

[99] See Art 38 Statute of the International Court of Justice (ICJ). As acknowledged, the Statute of the ICJ is a an integral part of the Charter of the United Nations, signed in San Francisco on 26 June 1945, and which came into force on 24 October 1945.

[100] The Convention was adopted on 22 May 1969 in Vienna and entered into force on 27 January 1980, in accordance with its Art 84(1).

[101] See Goode, above note 18, 3.   [102] ibid 14.   [103] ibid 1210–11.

[104] ibid 21. However, while uncodified international trade usages exist, they do not have legal force merely by virtue of their existence. Those principles are only given formal legal effect by the express or implied adoption of the parties entering a transaction (incorporation by contract) or by reception into the law of a national or supranational legal system (adoption by legislation or judicial reception).

international restatements prepared by scholars from different legal families and jurisdictions'.[105]

Relationship between soft law and hard law

Soft law sometimes complements or supplements hard law. For instance, in the context of the law of the IMF, a number of international guidelines, recommendations, codes of conduct, standards, and policies have been developed to interpret, supplement, or implement the Articles of Agreement.[106]

It is often argued that while lawyers express a preference for hard law (legally binding, legitimate, and enforceable treaties), economists support the opposite view, acknowledging the advantages of soft law rules (speed, flexibility, and pragmatism).[107] Giovanoli explores a third way, espousing the view that soft law and hard law can be combined in an optimal manner: 'Standards on which an international consensus has been established on an informal basis could be made the object of an international treaty, under which countries could sign up to specific standards, thus committing themselves to implement and enforce them within their national jurisdictions.'[108]

Lichtenstein[109] contends that an effort to embody international financial law standards into a treaty structure might focus on the enforcement model applicable to the violation of treaty obligations (based on a coercive approach and the imposition of sanctions for failure to comply) rather than a better 'compliance-based' or 'managerial model' which relies more upon a cooperative, problem-solving approach.[110]

My own view on the relationship between 'soft law' and 'hard law' can be summarized as follows. Law has progressed throughout time, both with regard

---

[105] See Roy Goode, above note 37, 541. Goode makes a case (ibid 547–8) for 'confining the *lex mercatoria* to international trade usage, which is surely the epitome of spontaneous law creation'. He clarifies (ibid 550) that 'Usages (in the sense of practices that have acquired normative force) are to be distinguished from rules set out in codes of practice promulgated by trade and professional organizations . . ., which take effect in the first instance by their express or implied incorporation into contracts'.

[106] See Joseph Gold, *Interpretation: The IMF and International Law* (London, the Hague, Boston: Kluwer Law International, 1996), 299–401. See also Joseph Gold, 'Strengthening the Soft International Law of Exchange Arrangements' (1983) 77 American Journal of International Law 443.

[107] See Giovanoli, above note 2, 51–2. See Tommaso Padoa-Schioppa and Fabrisio Saccomanni, 'Managing a Market-Led Global Financial System' in Petter K Kenen (ed), *Managing the World Economy Fifty Years After Bretton Woods* (Washington DC: Institute of International Economics, 1994) 266.

[108] See Giovanoli, above note 2, 53. ibid 38.

[109] See Cynthia C Lichtenstein, 'Hard Law v. Soft Law: Unnecessary Dichotomy?' (2001) 35 International Lawyer 1433.

[110] ibid 1441.

to its substance and with regard to the way it is created (the process or procedures). It is in this context that soft law—as an instrument of change and reform—ought to be understood. Soft law is indeed law (rules of an informal nature, but yet rules). International financial soft law is often well suited to the changing needs and rapidly evolving structures that characterize the workings of financial markets. It would be wrong to dismiss it because of its 'softness'. It is 'soft' from the perspective of traditional mechanisms of enforcement (international standards are not international obligations), but in many instances it is or it can become as compelling as 'hard law'.[111] Indeed, one can argue that there is hard 'soft law' (eg, the international standards on money laundering, ie, the Forty Recommendations on Money Laundering and the Nine Special Recommendations on Terrorist Financing by the Financial Action Task Force, with specific measures that countries should have in place covering their criminal justice, law enforcement, and financial regulatory systems) and soft 'hard law' (eg, treaties dealing with economic integration in West Africa, such as the 1975 and 1993 ECOWAS Treaties,[112] notorious for their lack of enforcement). Furthermore, soft law can turn into hard law and/or complement hard law, as exemplified by the case of the IMF mentioned above.

D. Sovereign Debt Crises and the Role of the IMF

In Chapter 4 I explained the recurrent feature of financial crises at the domestic level. By analogy, it can be said that sovereign debt crises are a recurrent feature in the international financial system. The history of sovereign debt is also the history of sovereign debt crises.

The literature on financial crises draws heavily on the distinction between illiquidity and insolvency. However, an insolvent country is more difficult to identify conceptually than an insolvent company (or bank). 'An insolvent country is one that cannot pay its debts, not because it has insufficient assets but because it cannot mobilize the revenues required to service its debt without imposing great pain on its citizens, jeopardizing the survival of its government and impairing the social and political stability of the country itself.'[113]

The IMF has developed a number of policies over the years to deal with debt crises and the problems of recalcitrant sovereign debtors. Debt crises are of two

---

[111] See Tommaso Padoa–Schioppa, *Regulating Finance* (Oxford: Oxford University Press, 2004) 41.

[112] ECOWAS stands for Economic Community of West African States.

[113] See Peter Kenen, 'The International Financial Architecture: Old Issues and New Initiatives' (2002) 5 International Finance 23, 31.

types: those arising in low income (and heavily indebted) countries with no access to international private capital markets (countries which fall under HIPC initiative which I discussed in the preceding chapter) and those arising in middle income countries with access to international private capital markets.

This chapter deals mostly with policies applied to the latter group of countries, where official financial assistance coexists with private financing (borrowing in international capital markets). Since the interests of private creditors are also at stake (private law), this final chapter shows the fluidity that exists between private law and public law.

According to Buchheit,[114] there have been three periods of intense intellectual activity in the field of sovereign debt management since Mexico's default on 22 August 1982. The first period lasted from 1982 to 1985. The issues of the day were the restructuring of billions of dollars of commercial bank loans in a way that would not threaten the stability of the domestic financial systems of the creditor countries.

The second period lasted from 1990 to 1993, following the adoption of the so-called 'Brady Initiative'. Commercial bank loans were no longer 'rolled over', but instead were transformed into freely tradable securities (Brady bonds) at a discount (ie, debt reduction). 'A new species of investor—the bond investor—was introduced to the rewards and to the risks of lending to sovereign borrowers.'[115] The myths held by these investors with regard to the alleged 'inviolability' of bonds were not disabused by the so-called official bailouts given to Mexico, Thailand, Indonesia, South Korea, and Brazil. However, after Russia it became clear that sovereign bonds were not 'inviolable' and that, therefore, restructuring was indeed possible. This brings us into the third period of intellectual activity, which commenced in 2000.

The big question at the beginning of the twenty-first century is how to restructure sovereign bonds in an orderly fashion.[116] The problems posed by the so-called 'hold-out' creditors in a sovereign debt restructuring are at the root of the Sovereign Debt Restructuring Mechanism (SDRM) proposed by the IMF and of the collective action clauses increasingly inserted in bond agreements.[117] The question, however, is far from answered. In this section I try to dissect some of the main issues at stake.

Creditor litigation against sovereign debtors has increased in recent years (as

---

[114] See Lee Buchheit, 'A Quarter Century of Sovereign Debt Management: An Overview' (2004) 35 Georgetown Journal of International Law 637.

[115] ibid.   [116] ibid.

[117] For an official view see Anne O Krueger and Sean Hagan, 'Sovereign Workouts: and IMF Perspective' (2005) 6 Chicago Journal of International Law 203.

I further explain below). The restrictive theory of sovereign immunity[118] now prevails in most jurisdictions, so that a sovereign state can be subject to civil proceedings in a foreign court with respect to its commercial activities. Sovereign immunity is now largely confined to *acta jure imperii* as opposed to *acta jure gestionis*.[119] Sovereign debt documentation typically provides—through a waiver of sovereign immunity—for the sovereign's consent to a foreign jurisdiction and judgment enforcement proceedings.[120]

Private capital flows to emerging economies and sovereign debt problems

The composition and volume of private capital flows to emerging economies has changed considerably over the last three decades. While in the 1970s, commercial bank loans (typically in the form of a syndicated loan agreement) were the primary financing instrument, following the debt crisis in the 1980s and the subsequent debt restructuring, the relative importance of bank lending has declined. Countries have turned increasingly from loans to bonds. This was in part a result of the Brady initiative (securitization) and in part a result of the damaged reputation of bank lending following the debt crisis and the perceived creditworthiness of bonds. Since countries defaulted on their bank loans but continued to service their bonds (though the outstanding amount of bonds was very small in the 1970s–80s), the bonds acquired an aura of de facto seniority that was a contributing factor to the growth of bond issues in the 1990s.[121]

Sovereign debt restructuring has evolved substantially in response to the change in financing patterns (from bank loans to bonds). In the 1980s the restructuring of sovereign debt brought bank creditors to the negotiating table. While bank creditors are easily identifiable, bond creditors are numerous, anonymous

---

[118] As acknowledged, the doctrine of sovereign immunity (precluding bringing suits against the government without its consent) is founded in the ancient principle that 'the King can do no wrong'. See Hal Scott, 'A Bankruptcy Procedure for Sovereign Debtors?' (2003) 37 The International Lawyer 103. 'Bond debt obligations are not normally protected in foreign courts by sovereign immunity as the issuance of such debt is regarded as a commercial activity, and commercial activities are outside the protection of sovereign immunity.'

[119] See Goode, above note 18, 21. 'When in 1981 the House of Lords decided to abandon the old rule and bring English law into line with that of other jurisdictions by removing sovereign immunity in relation to the trading activities of the state, it thereby received into English law a restrictive doctrine of sovereign immunity which had by that time become adopted by almost all influential trading nations.'

[120] See Report of the International Monetary Law Committee, International Law Association, Berlin Conference (2004), 6 at <http://www.ila-hq.org/pdf/monetary%20Law/2004%20 Berlin%20report.pdf>. Under US law, foreign state property enjoys immunity from prejudgment attachment unless the state has expressly waived that immunity, and from post-judgment attachment unless the sovereign has explicitly or implicitly waived that immunity or the property seized is the very property upon which the plaintiff's claim is based.

[121] I thank Lee Buchheit for explaining this point to me. See Buchheit, above note 114, 637–8.

(in the case of bearer bonds), and more difficult to coordinate. In addition, many investors who hold these bonds have no close links with the debtor countries and no commitment to repeat or further investments. The variety of bond instruments and the range of jurisdictions in which debt is issued further complicate the restructuring. Finally, the problems are exacerbated by the incentives that some private creditors have to 'hold out' from the restructuring in the hope of obtaining more favourable terms, or to sue in order to get better terms.[122]

The 'hold-out' problem and 'sovereign pirates'

The problems of recalcitrant creditors suing for better terms by 'holding out' can be illustrated by the Elliott case, though the case of the Dart family in Brazil[123] and the case of *Pravin Banker Associates v Banco Popular del Peru*[124] also constitute a relevant precedent.

Vulture funds ('sovereign pirates') and other private investors have a greater

---

[122] See IMF fact-sheet, 'Proposals for a Sovereign Debt Restructuring Mechanism', January 2003 at <http://www.imf.org/external/np/exr/facts/sdrm.htm>.

[123] See *CIBC Bank & Trust Co (Cayman) Ltd v Banco Central do Brasil*, 886 F Supp 1105, 1115–16 (SDNY 1995). The Dart family had been accumulating Brazilian debt from creditor banks in the secondary market at discounts of 60% or more since 1991. The Darts tendered the entirety of their claims in response to Brazil's restructuring proposal, but balked at Brazil's unilateral changes to the terms of the restructuring after tenders from creditors had been submitted. They were not the only ones that held out debt, though; the Banco Central do Brasil and Banco do Brasil also kept holdings of unrestructured debt in a coordinated response aimed at combating the Darts. The Darts sued (with the Canadian Imperial Bank of Commerce, CIBC, acting as the holder of record of the debt) the Central Bank of Brazil arguing that the defendants were subject to an implied covenant of good faith and fair dealing. (The defendant banks intentionally retained their debt to ensure that they were the majority holders, thus precluding the Dart family from accelerating the debt.) US government officials filed an *amicus curiae* brief urging the court to dismiss the Darts' suit because of the undermining effects that such litigation had on the sovereign debt restructuring process. The case was eventually settled in March 1994, with the Darts emerging as the victorious party. See John Nolan, 'Emerging Market Debt & Vulture Hedge Funds: Free-Ridership, Legal & Market Remedies', Financial Policy Forum, Derivatives Study Center, Special Policy Report 3, 29 September 2001, at <http://www.financialpolicy.org/DSCNolan.htm>.

[124] *Pravin Bankers Assocs Ltd v Banco Popular del Peru*, 109 F3d 850, 853 (2d Cir 1997). Pravin had bought a portion of Peruvian debt on the secondary market at a steeply discounted price (27cents on the dollar) from Mellon Bank. Banco Popular del Peru (a state-owned bank) made interest payments to Pravin until February 1992. In December 1992 Banco Popular was liquidated. Pravin did not participate in the liquidation process nor in the Brady debt restructuring. Pravin sued Banco Popular requesting full payment on principal of its debt and brought its claim to the Southern District of New York. In October 1996 the Court ruled in favour of Pravin, thus confirming the ability of debt-holders to enforce their demands individually upon default by the issuer. See Cynthia Mullock, 'Sovereign Debt Restructuring Proposals and Their Effects on Emerging Market Debt Instruments', The Chazen Web Journal of International Business, Columbia Business School, 2003 at <http://www2.gsb.columbia.edu/journals/files/chazen/SDR_proof.pdf>.

propensity to litigate than commercial banks. In the so-called Elliot case,[125] a distressed debt purchaser,[126] Elliott Associates LP (a hedge fund), acquired $20.7 million of Peruvian debt (commercial loans that had been guaranteed by Peru) at a discounted price and, unlike most other creditors, did not accept Brady bonds in exchange for Peruvian debt. Elliott did not participate in the restructuring ('hold out') and instead filed a suit in a New York court in 1996 for recovery of the full amount of the principal plus interest on the loans that it held. Elliott succeeded in its litigation strategy (on appeal) and obtained a favourable judgment against Banco Nacional del Peru and the Republic of Peru—who acted as guarantor—for $55.7 million. After obtaining this judgment, Elliott resorted to the Brussels courts, since it was not able to freeze any assets in the US. The Brussels Court of Appeals issued an order restraining Chase Manhattan and Euroclear to pay the interest due on Peru's Brady Plan bonds. One of the arguments espoused by Elliott was that Peru, by paying its Brady bond creditors rather than Elliott, was actually violating the *pari passu* clause inserted in the loan agreement, which provided that the loan in question would rank equally with all other indebtedness. With the judicial order not to make any payment, Peru was facing default on the restructured bonds. Confronted with this situation, the Republic of Peru was obliged to reach an agreement with Elliott Associates LP in order to avoid a new default in its restructured debt. By means of this agreement, Elliott obtained a substantial gain (worth 400% of the purchase value of the defaulted bonds)[127] and emboldened other maverick creditors to bring litigation to exact maximum profit.

This success of this litigation hinders creditor coordination and exacerbates the free-rider incentives, the problems of the dissenting minority.

Official and private sector solutions to sovereign debt crises

Having identified the problems with sovereign bond restructuring in general and the 'hold-out' problem in particular, I will proceed now to examine the official and private sector-based responses to them. There are at least three solutions that have been proposed in recent years: (1) a statutory solution, (2) a

---

[125] See *Elliott Associates, LP v Banco de la Nacion*, 194 F3d 363 (2d Cir 1999). For a doctrinal elaboration on the problems of the litigation by dissenting minorities, see G Mitu Gulati and Kenneth N Klee, 'Sovereign Piracy', UCLA, School of Law Research Paper No 01–7, at <http://www.law.ucla.edu/faculty/bios/klee/kleeeicfinal.htm#_edn3>. See also, Eduardo Luis López Sandoval, 'Sovereign Debt Restructuring: Should We Be Worried About Elliott?', Harvard Law School, at <http://www.law.harvard.edu/programs/pifs/pdfs/eduardo_sandoval.pdf> and Samuel Goldman, 'Mavericks in the Market: The Emerging Problem of Hold-Outs in Sovereign Debt Restructurings' (2000) 5 UCLA Journal of International Law and Foreign Affairs 159.

[126] 'Distressed debt' is debt that has been defaulted by the debtor to its creditors.

[127] See Gabrielle Lipworth and Jens Nystedt, 'Crisis Resolution and Private Sector Adaptation', IMF Working Paper, Washington DC, November 2000.

contractual solution, (3) a voluntary solution based on the adoption of a 'code of conduct'.[128] A dispute resolution forum would be established to resolve disputes that may arise during the voting process or when claims are being verified.

The SDRM (the statutory solution)

Domestic bankruptcy laws and bankruptcy courts provide a statutory solution at the national level to the problems of corporate insolvency (including bank insolvency). At the international level, there is no international bankruptcy court nor an international bankruptcy code.

The ad hoc resolution of international debt crises and the involvement of a variety of actors, including international organizations (notably the IMF), informal clubs (the Paris Club for official debt, the London Club for commercial bank debt), national authorities, and private financial institutions have sometimes been criticized as inefficient. A centralized statutory solution has been hailed in some official and academic circles as an improvement over the current piecemeal approach.

The 'statutory solution' to the problem of orderly resolution of sovereign debt crises refers to the possible adoption of what has been referred to as the Sovereign Debt Restructuring Mechanism or SDRM. This 'mandatory approach' would entail the creation at an international level of a bankruptcy procedure for countries, akin to Chapter 11 of the US bankruptcy code, and of an independent dispute resolution forum to verify claims.

Advocates of the SDRM claim that it would fill a gap in the international financial system by providing a framework to help resolve the problems of collective action and creditor coordination and to encourage a country with unsustainable debt and its creditors to restructure before it gets to the point where default is the only option.

The IMF started considering the SDRM in 2001,[129] though Jeffrey Sachs[130]

---

[128] Above note 120, Report of the International Monetary Law Committee, Berlin Conference, 6–8. This part of the report was written by François Gianviti.

[129] See Anne Krueger, 'International Financial Architecture for 2002: A New Approach to Sovereign Debt Restructuring', address at the National Economists' Club Annual Members' Dinner, American Enterprise Institute, Washington DC, 26 November 2001, at <http://www.imf.org/external/np/speeches/2001/112601.htm>.

[130] See Jeffrey Sachs, 'Do We Need an International Lender of Last Resort?', Frank D Graham Lecture, Princeton University, 1995, at <http://www.earthinstitute.columbia.edu/about/director/pubs/intllr.pdf>. Sachs argues that international bankruptcy procedures modelled upon Chapter 9 and Chapter 11 of the US Bankruptcy Code would be the best response to cope with crises of the Mexican type. Sachs's proposals included the reorganization of the IMF to act as a kind of international bankruptcy court rather than as a lender of last resort to member governments. Sachs emphasized the need to prevent a 'grab race' by creditors and the need to prevent a small

anticipated the concept in 1995 and the idea of an international bankruptcy procedure was also discussed in the 1980s.[131]

Since the so-called SDRM was first proposed by Anne Krueger (under the auspices of the IMF), it has gone through several modifications.[132] According to the latest proposal,[133] the design of a standstill on payments and the imposition of a stay on creditor litigation remain the most debated features of the SDRM.[134]

In 2002, the International Monetary and Financial Committee (IMFC) endorsed the Fund's work and encouraged the IMF to continue to examine the legal, institutional, and procedural aspects of two approaches, which could be complementary and self-reinforcing: a statutory approach, which would enable a sovereign debtor and a super-majority of its creditors to reach an agreement binding all creditors; and an approach, based on contract, which would incorporate comprehensive restructuring clauses in debt instruments.[135] However, the enthusiasm for the SDRM has waned since 2003 and reliance on market solutions (contractual mechanisms) has been the preferred approach. As expressly stated by an IMF officer, '[t]he debate on the Sovereign Debt restructuring

---

number of dissident creditors from blocking an agreement acceptable to the vast majority of creditors. See also Barry Eichengreen and Richard Portes, *Crisis? What Crisis? Orderly Workout for Sovereign Debtors* (London: Centre for Economic Policy Research, 1995), and Peter Kenen (ed), 'From Halifax to Lyons: What has been done about crises management?' Essays in International Finance No 200, Princeton University, October 1996.

[131] See eg Benjamin Cohen, 'A Global Chapter 11', (1989) 75 Foreign Policy 109.

[132] Anne Krueger, 'New Approaches to Sovereign Debt Restructuring: An Update on Our Thinking', Conference on 'Sovereign Debt Workouts: Hopes and Hazards', Institute for International Economics, Washington DC, 1 April 2002, at <http://www.imf.org/external/np/speeches/2002/040102.htm>.

[133] See PIN No 03/45, 3 April 2003, 'IMF Board discusses possible features of a Sovereign Debt Restructuring Mechanism' at <http://www.imf.org/external/np/sec/pn/2003/pn0345.htm>. On 24 March 2003, the Executive Board of the International Monetary Fund (IMF) continued its discussions on the possible features of a new Sovereign Debt Restructuring Mechanism (SDRM) based on the staff paper 'Proposed Features of a Sovereign Debt Restructuring Mechanism'. 'A number of Directors continued to be of the view, however, that a broad-based cessation of payments combined with a temporary, automatic stay on enforcement should be a feature of the mechanism.'

[134] The first SDRM proposal included an automatic stay on the enforcement of creditors' rights. The second SDRM proposal did not include an automatic stay. In US bankruptcy law, immediately upon the filing of a voluntary petition under the Bankruptcy Code, a stay arises which generally bars all debt collection efforts against the debtor. The court need not sign any order to give rise to the stay; the mere filing of the petition, with supporting documentation, with the clerk is sufficient.

[135] See International Monetary Fund, 'Communiqué of the International Monetary and Financial Committee of the Board of Governors of the International Monetary Fund', 20 April 2002, available at <http://www.imf.org/external/np/sec/pr/2002/pr0222.htm>.

Mechanism, SDRM, has been shelved for the time being.'[136] Political opposition in the US and resistance on the side of many market participants have contributed to the loss of momentum.

The adoption of the SDRM would imply an amendment to the IMF's Articles of Agreement. An alternative and much more modest proposal would be a creative interpretation of Article VIII, section 2(b) of the Articles of Agreement (the most debtor friendly provision in the Fund's Articles) which could be used as a means to impose a temporary stay on creditors' actions and, thus, could have a significant impact on litigation in this field.[137] One of the problems with this provision is the lack of uniformity of interpretation among the courts of countries that are members of the Fund, a problem which could be remedied if the Fund adopted an 'authoritative interpretation' of Article VIII, section 2(b) under Article XXIX(a).[138]

Collective Action Clauses and other contractual techniques

Reliance on contractual techniques is the approach that has been favoured over the last three years to confront the problems of sovereign debt workouts and in particular the hold-out problem. In 1996, a G10 Working Group issued a report (known as the Rey Report, after its Chairman, Jean-Jacques Rey of Belgium) recommending *inter alia* the inclusion of Collective Action Clauses in sovereign bonds and greater reliance on market discipline, following the Mexican 'bailout'.[139] This approach is consistent with the enforceability of contracts, which is at the heart of our trade and financial system. The US Government, the G7, the International Monetary and Financial Committee of the IMF, and others supported this solution, which also enjoyed considerable academic support.

Collective Action Clauses (CACs) are provisions contained in bonds that allow the holders of a specified majority (seventy-five per cent) to amend the terms (payment and non-payment terms) of the bonds and make them binding on the

---

[136] International Monetary Fund, 'Interview with Mark Allen: IMF needs to do far more to help countries learn from each other's successes and failures', IMF Survey, Volume 33, Number 7, 12 April 2004, 99, available at <http://www.imf.org/external/pubs/ft/survey/2004/041204.pdf>.

[137] See Pierre Francotte, Comment on 'The Fund Agreement in the Courts', in Robert Effros (ed), *Current Legal Issues Affecting Central Banks*, Volume 1 (Washington DC: IMF, 1992).

[138] See François Gianviti, 'The Reform of the International Monetary Fund' in Rosa M Lastra (ed), *The Reform of the International Financial Architecture* (London: Kluwer Law, 2001)102. Gianviti questions whether Art VIII, s 2(b) could be revitalized through interpretation or amendment, to make exchange controls on private creditors (and standstills on sovereign debt) more effective as the ultimate defence for the indebted country while negotiations with creditors are taking place. It could also be used, in cases where agreement is reached with a majority of creditors, to avoid litigation by rogue creditors.

[139] See <http://www.bis.org/publ/gten03.htm>. There was another G10 Report on CACs published in September 2002.

minority. CACs thus allow the debtor to restructure its debt by a resolution of a binding majority of bondholders. CACs can deal effectively with the 'hold-out' problem, that is, of creditors who use litigation and other means to extract preferential terms at the expense of the debtor and the other creditors, but such clauses can only bind the creditors in the specific instruments in which they appear.[140]

Under English law, the amendment clauses in bonds (sometimes called 'majority action' clauses) have typically permitted a change to the payment terms of the bond with the consent of seventy-five per cent of the bondholders who attend a bondholders' meeting (assuming the quorum requirement for the meeting has been met). CACs thus permit a form of contractual 'cram-down' of changes to payment terms on dissenting minorities, something that could not happen until recently in bonds governed by New York law (where unanimity was required to change the terms of payment of a bond issue).[141] However, since 2003 (with the bond issuances of Mexico and Brazil), the prevailing practice with regard to bonds governed by New York law is to include CACs.

The following countries have also adopted CACs in sovereign bonds, as advocated by Buchheit and others:[142] Belize, Chile, Colombia, Costa Rica, Guatemala, Indonesia, Israel, Korea, Mexico, Panama, Peru. Philippines, Poland, South Africa, Uruguay, and Venezuela.[143]

A special mention ought to be made to Uruguay's 2003 debt re-profiling, since it changed the international sovereign debt restructuring scenario.[144] Uruguay had nineteen series of bonds issued in the international markets (some of them rather small issues), which made the Uruguayan debt stock rather fragmented

---

[140] See Lee Buchheit and G Mitu Gulati, 'Sovereign Bonds and the Collective Will' (2002) 51 Emory Law Journal 1317, 1324.

[141] ibid. Restrictions on changing bond terms spring from a concern that a majority of creditors can abuse a minority. This fear was reflected in the enactment in the USA of the 1939 Trust Indenture Act (TIA) requiring unanimity for the change of payment terms in corporate bonds. Though the TIA did not apply to sovereign bonds, it became a contractual practice in the documentation of sovereign bonds governed by New York law to include such requirement. See also Scott, above note 118. In 2003, with the bond issuances of Mexico and Brazil, majority action clauses were incorporated in sovereign bonds used under New York law. See Alinna Arora and Rodrigo Olivares Caminal, 'Rethinking the Sovereign Debt Restructuring Approach' (2003) 9 Law and Business Review of the Americas 101, 135.

[142] See eg Barry Eichengreen and Richard Portes, above note 130, and Peter Kenen, above note 113. The US Treasury has also favoured CACs. See eg John B Taylor, 'Sovereign Debt Restructuring: A U.S. Perspective', remarks at the conference on Sovereign Debt Workouts: Hopes and Hazards? at the Institute for International Economics, April 2002, Washington DC, available at <http://www.ustreas.gov/press/releases/po2056.htm>.

[143] Above note 120, 7.

[144] Lee Buchheit and Jeremiah Pam, 'Uruguay's Innovations' (2004) 19 Journal of International Banking Law and Regulation 28.

and dispersed.[145] Uruguay made an offer (pre-emptive action, since Uruguay had not defaulted at the time) to all holders of its foreign currency denominated bonds (other than a Japanese yen samurai issue) to exchange those instruments for new bonds. Uruguay sought the consent of bond holders to amendments of their sovereign bonds prior to the completion of the exchange offer ('exit consents').[146] Uruguay elected to issue its new bonds through a trust indenture rather than a fiscal agency agreement.[147] Uruguay's debt re-profiling resulted in the inclusion of CACs in each series of new bonds issued as part of the exchange.[148]

A major innovation of Uruguay's version of the CAC was the 'aggregation mechanism', by which a proposed amendment to the payment terms of two or more series of bonds could be incorporated through aggregated voting to other series of bonds simultaneously by the approval of a double majority (of eighty-five per cent of the aggregate principal amount of all affected series and by $66\frac{2}{3}$ per cent of each specific series).[149] This aggregation feature was designed to address one of the perceived infirmities of conventional CACs (that they operate only to bind holders within the specific instrument containing the clause).

The Uruguay transaction challenged the widely held view that investors would refuse to take seriously a proposal to restructure sovereign bonds unless forced to confront an open payment default. The way the transaction was structured increased the participation of bondholders. It also challenged the view that CACs were of marginal importance for small issues of bonds.

The aggregation voting mechanism *à la* Uruguay also facilitates a more comprehensive approach to sovereign debt workouts than a single series Collective Action Clause, since it affects multiple series of bonds, rather than an individual bond issue. In this respect, the aggregation mechanism bridges the gap between

---

[145] ibid.

[146] On the use of exit consents, see Buchheit and Mitu Gulati, 'Exit Consents in Sovereign Bond Exchanges' (2000) 28 UCLA Law Review 59. Exit consents (exit amendments) were used in Ecuador's debt exchange in 2000. When holders tendered their old bonds, they agreed to certain amendments of those bonds (ie, exit amendments), which removed the cross-default, cross acceleration, and negative pledge clauses. The idea was to make the old bonds so unattractive that all of the creditors would tender them for the new bonds. The difference between the use of exit consents in Ecuador and in Uruguay is that in the latter case, the creditors could vote against the package of exit amendments (a consensual approach).

[147] Above note 144.

[148] ibid 30. 'This part of the clause followed the lead of the model collective action clause proposed by the G-10 working group in 2002, which in turn influenced the drafting of a clause used by Mexico in a Yankee bond offering in late February 2003.'

[149] ibid 31. I must thank Lee Buchheit for taking the time to explain to me the workings of this aggregation technique.

the SDRM proposals (dealing with the whole existing stock of debt, thus including different classes of creditors) and the single series CAC.[150]

What is interesting about CACs and other contractual techniques used in sovereign bond documentation is that they are increasingly becoming 'standard', a kind of new *lex mercatoria* in this field (creation of law *ex novo*).

A code of conduct

The adoption of a voluntary 'code of conduct' with principles that could guide the negotiations of sovereign debtors and their creditors has been discussed in several fora, such as INSOL International (an association of international insolvency practitioners).[151] The Council of Foreign Relations and the Institute of International Finance have also done work in this regard.[152] The G20 has held some meetings with representatives of the private sector to develop a voluntary code on debt restructuring.[153]

The idea of a code of conduct is in line with the process of standard setting that I discussed above. A code of conduct accepted by market participants should also be helpful to guide judges dealing with the problems of litigious dissenting minorities. 'The world of commerce functions largely on the principle that what are generally accepted by business people as the legal consequences of their actions will be recognised by the courts.'[154]

In the field of cross-border insolvency, the work of the World Bank, which is coordinating a broad-based effort to develop a set of principles and guidelines on insolvency regimes ('Global Bank Insolvency Initiative') must be taken into account.[155] The World Bank and UNCITRAL, in consultation with the Fund staff, are developing standards on insolvency, based upon the Bank's Principles for

---

[150] ibid.

[151] INSOL International, 'Statement of Principles for a Global Approach to Multi-Creditor Workouts', available at <http://www.insol.org/statement.htm>.

[152] Above note 120, 8.

[153] ibid. The members of the G20 are the finance ministries and central banks of 19 countries: Argentina, Australia, Brazil, Canada, China, France, Germany, India, Indonesia, Italy, Japan, Korea, Mexico, Russia, Saudi-Arabia, South Africa, Turkey, the United Kingdom, and the United States. Another member is the European Union, represented by the Council presidency and the European Central Bank. To ensure that the G20's activities are closely aligned with those of the Bretton-Woods institutions, the managing director of the IMF and the president of the World Bank, plus the chairpersons of the International Monetary and Financial Committee and Development Committee of the IMF and World Bank, also participate in the talks as ex-officio members. See <http://www.g20.org/Public/AboutG20/index.jsp>.

[154] Goode, above note 18, 22.

[155] <http://www4.worldbank.org/legal/insolvency_ini.html>.

Effective Insolvency and Creditor Rights Systems and UNCITRAL's Legislative Guide on Insolvency Law.[156]

The second and third solutions (the market approach and the adoption of a 'code of conduct') are clearly complementary and can be pursued in parallel, as evidenced by the 'standardization' of collective action clauses in sovereign bonds in recent years.

The role of the IMF in the safeguard of international financial stability

The approach favoured by the IMF in the resolution of financial crises has changed over time. However, two principles remain constant. First, the IMF provides financial assistance to remedy temporary balance of payments problems (whether they are general or special balance of payments problems) and is not geared to countries with unsustainable debts (nor to finance long-term development projects, the domain of the World Bank). This means that the IMF will in principle only lend itself when the problems are of 'liquidity', not when the problems are of 'prolonged and unsustainable debts' (insolvency). The debate below about the international lender of last resort further expands upon this point. Secondly, any financial assistance provided by the Fund must be consistent with the Articles of Agreement. This second principle, which is at the root of conditionality (as I explained in Chapter 13), is also at the root of the other policies and procedures adopted by the Fund over the years to safeguard the quality of the IMF asset portfolio (the 'adequate safeguards' of Art 1(v) of the Articles of Agreement) and, therefore, to safeguard repayment.

In the resolution of international debt crises, the IMF typically has a vested interest, since it is a creditor in its own right (it provides financial support to troubled countries). As I explained in Chapter 13, the IMF has developed a number of special facilities to deal with acute and sudden financial crises stemming from problems in the capital account. The problem is that 'these acute and sudden' financial crises (a terminology reminiscent of liquidity problems) can turn into something more prolonged, leading to a sovereign debt crisis, where the problems are no longer of illiquidity but of insolvency. The IMF has also developed over the years a number of policies to deal with these problems, in particular in its relationships with other creditors vis-à-vis the debtor country.

---

[156] Above note 45. As I mentioned above, the FSF lists 'insolvency standards' in its Compendium at <http://wwww/fsforum.org/compendium/key_standards_for_sound_financial_system.html>.

Private creditors and the IMF

The Fund has a unique position vis-à-vis private creditors in that it has ongoing relationships with both creditor and debtor countries. Private creditors in the 1970s and 1980s were mostly commercial banks. The situation has changed in the last two decades, with the change in financing patterns and the shift from loans to bonds.

In the relations between the IMF and commercial bank creditors in the 1970s, the commercial banks were often 'third party beneficiaries of the Fund's stabilization programmes'.[157] Commercial bankers typically applauded a country's acceptance of a stabilization programme, since they received the 'implicit protection of IMF conditionality'.[158] The de facto (unofficial) coordination of bank's private loans with IMF financing explains the influential role of the IMF in the debt restructuring proceedings and negotiations in the 1980s. The banks typically required that countries reach an arrangement with the Fund as a precondition for rescheduling, as an assurance that the policies pursued by the debtor in question would help restore external viability and would be subject to enhanced Fund surveillance.

The Fund's influential role in sovereign debt work-outs has been a characteristic feature of the international financial system since 1982 and one that has had a profound influence on private creditors' incentives on the one hand and on the design of certain IMF policies on the other hand.

The IMF's desire to safeguard is own assets provides an important rationale for the Fund's involvement in the debtor countries' dealings with private creditors.[159] It is in this context that the Fund's 'lending into arrears policy', the concept of 'burden sharing', and the defence of its de facto 'preferred creditor' status must be understood.

The IMF's preferred creditor status The Fund enjoys a de facto preferred creditor status and its claims are not subject to rescheduling. This practice has been recognized in the Paris Club and in other fora for sovereign debt

---

[157] This point is made by Lee Buchheit and Mark Walker, 'Legal Issues in the Restructuring of Commercial Bank Loans to Sovereign Borrowers' in Michael Gruson and Ralph Eisner (eds), *Sovereign Lending: Managing Legal Risk* (London: Euromoney Publications, 1984) 149.

[158] See Victoria E Marmorstein, 'Responding to the Call for Order in International Finance: Co-operation between the International Monetary Fund and Commercial Banks' (1978) 18 Virginia Journal of International Law 445, 453. Marmorstein (ibid 454) cites the example of Peru, where a consortium of banks syndicated a loan to the government trying to impose an economic stabilization programme 'patterned after an IMF stand-by [sic] as a condition of their commitment'. The banks failed and thus decided that 'it would be more prudent to leave the role of adjustor to the Fund.'

[159] See Lee Buchheit, 'The Role of the Official Sector in Sovereign Debt Workouts' (2005) 6 Chicago Journal of International Law Symposium 333, 341.

restructuring. However, creditors have not legally subordinated their claims to those of the Fund.

The Fund justifies this priority ranking on the grounds that the IMF is not a commercial organization seeking profitable lending opportunities. In fact, the Fund likes to remind its members that it often lends precisely at the point where other creditors are reluctant to do so, and at interest rates that are below those that would be charged at that juncture by the private sector.[160] In so doing, the IMF helps countries to catalyse private financing and to avoid disorderly adjustment and policies that would harm themselves, private creditors, and other countries. Putting IMF claims together with commercial claims in a workout would fundamentally undermine the Fund's capacity to play that vital role in future.

Therefore, from the IMF perspective, its preferred creditor status is fundamental to the Fund's financial responsibilities. 'If the Fund were no longer a preferred creditor, the risk on its lending would increase and the funds made available by creditor members could no longer be regarded as risk free. If reserve positions in the Fund are not regarded as fully liquid and of the highest quality, members cannot treat them as part of their international reserves, which is crucial for the Fund's financing mechanism to operate.'[161]

From the members' perspective, remaining current (ie, not being in arrears) with the Fund is considered essential to get access to additional financing or debt relief from other official creditors. Members thus give priority to repayment of their obligations to the Fund over their obligations to other creditors.

It is also argued that the Fund's preferred creditor status benefits not just Fund members but official and private creditors alike by allowing the Fund to assist member countries in regaining a sustainable financial path and helping to promote orderly resolutions to debt problems, when needed.[162]

'Burden sharing'   The concept of 'burden sharing' (ie, dividing the burden of financing or restructuring between the IMF and other creditors) has been an important component of the IMF strategy toward the resolution of debt crises. The concept of sharing is a very difficult one to enforce and implement. My

---

[160] International Monetary Fund, 'Proposals for a Sovereign Debt Restructuring Mechanism (SDRM). A Factsheet', January 2003, available at <http://www.imf.org/external/np/exr/facts/sdrm.htm>.

[161] See International Monetary Fund, *'Financial Risk in the Fund and the Level of Precautionary Balances'*, prepared by the Finance Department (in consultation with other departments), approved by Eduard Brau, 3 February 2004, Box 1, at <http://www.imf.org/external/np/tre/risk/2004/020304.pdf>.

[162] ibid.

three-year-old daughter often tells her brothers: 'Share, you have to share.' Her concept of sharing, though, is 'unilateral'. If she has something, she does not expect to share it. If the others have something, they should share it with her. In international finance, this 'selfish' behaviour of small children often gets replicated.

As Lee Buchheit reminds us: 'Creditors to the same borrower exist in a Hobbesian state of nature.'[163] He further points out that, while in corporate lending these Hobbesian tensions have a logical stopping point, which is bankruptcy, in the sovereign context, there is no neutral referee like a bankruptcy judge, which means that every class of creditor, and every creditor within every class, must look out for itself.[164]

In the absence of a formal bankruptcy procedure, sovereign creditors have developed some principles to manage their relationships. The first and foremost principle is parity of treatment among private creditors.[165] The principle of parity of treatment among private creditors has influenced a number of clauses that were inserted in international loan agreements, such as the negative pledge cause, the *pari passu* clause, and the sharing clause.[166] With regard to bond agreements, the adoption of majority action clauses or collective action clauses, CACs, is also influenced by this principle of parity of treatment. The insertion of CACs allows the holder or holders of a specified majority to amend all the terms (payment and non-payment terms) of the bonds and make them binding on the minority, as I explained above.

Coordination amongst creditors is always problematic. In the words of Buchheit and Gulati:

> Multi-creditor debt instruments such as bonds and syndicated bank loans are uncommon legal arrangements. In most contracts, the parties know each other's identity beforehand and they make a conscious effort to enter into a legal relationship. In multi-creditor debt instruments, the borrower's identity is of course

---

[163] Lee Buchheit, 'The Search for Inter-creditor Parity' (2002) 8 Law and Business Review of the Americas 73.

[164] ibid.

[165] Official creditors such as the IMF and the World Bank, however, enjoy a 'preferred creditor' status.

[166] The negative pledge clause is a restriction on the borrower's ability to grant security interests in its property to secure other lenders. The *pari passu* clause is a covenant on the part of the borrower that the debt will always rank equally in priority of payment with the borrower's other unsubordinated indebtedness. The sharing clause is a requirement in many syndicated loan agreements that any bank receiving a disproportionate payment share that payment rateably with its fellow lenders. See Lee Buchheit, *How to Negotiate Eurocurrency Loan Agreements*, 2nd edn (New York: Euromoney, 2000) 76, 82, and 86.

known by each investor, but what the investors don't know—what they often never know—is the identity of each other.[167]

By definition, the problems of inter-creditor coordination ('the tyranny of the minority') are greater in the case of bonds than in the case of loans.[168] 'One recalcitrant group of creditors can stop an entire debt restructuring program in its tracks.'[169] (Though from the creditors' perspective, one might also argue that there are 'recalcitrant sovereign debtors', too, such as Argentina.) The dissenting minority can be very forceful, as the case of Elliott evidences.

Contractual provisions in loan and bond agreements have limitations and sometimes fail to achieve parity of treatment.[170] This is where the IMF can step in and play a useful role: the role of a referee, someone 'above' the creditor and creditor groups, who can decide who should contribute and how much.[171] The IMF has inside information about the debtor countries through its surveillance function (Art IV consultation) and can help debtors sort out their problems through balance of payments assistance, and technical assistance. This IMF's unique set of responsibilities helps countries restore their creditworthiness through economic reform (we must remember here the 'logic' of conditionality: a country that overspends—ie, spends more than it takes in—will continue to overspend unless economic reform takes place).

'Lending into arrears policy' The Fund's policy regarding 'lending into arrears', that is, lending to members who have incurred payment arrears to private creditors, has undergone significant developments in that last two decades.[172]

In the early 1980s, the policy of the Fund was 'not to lend into arrears', that is, arrears to private creditors (mostly commercial banks at the time) were not tolerated. However, in 1989, the Fund changed its 'arrears policy', acknowledging the difficulties faced by some members with regard to the approval of their adjustments programmes. These difficulties arose from the fact that commercial bank creditors had a 'de facto veto' over the extension of IMF financial assistance

---

[167] Lee Buchheit and G Mitu Gulati, 'Sovereign Bonds and the Collective Will' (2002) 51 Emory Law Journal 1317, 1320.

[168] ibid 1336.   [169] See Buchheit, above note 163, 78.

[170] ibid 77. 'Words like "comparable" are too imprecise to be given a strict legal meaning. . . . If the clauses have any effect on a sovereign borrower's behaviour it is *in terrorem.*'

[171] ibid 78–9.

[172] International Monetary Fund, 'Fund Policy on Lending into Arrears to Private Creditors— Further Consideration of the Good Faith Criterion', prepared by the International Capital Markets, Policy Development and Review and Legal Departments (in consultation with the other Departments), approved by Gerd Häusler, Timothy Geithner, and François Gianviti, 30 July 2002, 3, at <http://www.imf.org/external/pubs/ft/privcred/073002.pdf>. This subsection, 'Lending into arrears policy' draws heavily on this document.

via a standby arrangement, since the provision of financial assistance by the Fund had become effectively linked to the existence of an agreement between the debtor country and its commercial bank creditors.[173] The Fund also established a policy to help members finance their debt-service reduction (DDSR) operations.[174]

According to the decision adopted in 1989, the Fund could provide financial support to a member before an agreement had been reached with its commercial bank creditors ('lending into arrears') if the following three criteria were met: (i) such support was considered essential for the success of the adjustment programme; (ii) negotiations between the debtor and its commercial bank creditors had begun, and (iii) agreement on a financial package was expected within a reasonable period.[175]

In 1998, as a result of the changes in the composition of capital flows to emerging market economies (shift from bank loans to bonds), the Fund's policy was generalized to encompass also sovereign bonds.[176] The revised policy replicated the first two criteria established in 1989 and introduced a third criterion specific to bondholders. According to this third criterion, 'lending into arrears' could take place if 'there were firm indications that the sovereign borrower and its private creditors would *negotiate in good faith* on a debt restructuring plan' (emphasis added).[177]

In 1999, in recognition of the fact that some creditors were inclined to delay negotiations, because of the perceived rewards of litigation or problems of intercreditor coordination, the Fund revised its policy again and replaced the 'negotiation in good faith' criterion with a 'good faith efforts' test.[178] Accordingly, if the member was consider to be making 'good faith efforts' to reach an agreement with its creditors, then the Fund could lend ('lend into arrears') to the member.[179]

The reaction of many private creditors to the changes in the Fund's policy of 'lending into arrears' was rather critical.[180] Some argue that 'there should be a presumption of close and timely consultations with creditors on steps to remedy the underlying problem and the development of restructuring proposals.'[181] Some others have advocated that 'recognition should be accorded to bondholders committees similar to that given to bank steering committees' in the 1980s.[182] Investors, in short, want clarity and predictability in the interpretation

---

[173] ibid 3.   [174] ibid 4–5.   [175] ibid 5. See EBM/89/61, 24 May 1989.
[176] ibid 5–6. See SM/98/8, 9 January 1998.   [177] ibid 6.   [178] ibid.
[179] ibid. See EBS/99/67, 30 April 1999.   [180] ibid 7.   [181] ibid 8.   [182] ibid 8.

of this 'good faith efforts' criterion. The debtor countries, on the other hand, want flexibility and continuing access to IMF financing.[183]

In an effort to align the contrasting interests of sovereign debtors and private creditors, a number of principles and procedures with regard to the Fund's 'lending into arrears' policy, as well as issues for discussion, have been suggested.[184] It is clear, however, that 'lending into arrears' does not resolve the member's problems. The country must endeavour to get to an agreement with its private creditors with regard to the rescheduling or restructuring of the debt, in order to enjoy access to international capital markets.[185]

Difference between arrears to private creditors and arrears to the Fund   The Fund's policy concerning arrears to private creditors must be clearly distinguished from its policy on arrears to the Fund. The latter are treated severely by the Fund, since they are a demonstrative non-cooperative action that imposes financial costs to the Fund and damages the member's reputation in the international community. As of June 2005, members with protracted arrears to the Fund (overdue financial obligations for six months or more) are Liberia, Somalia, Sudan, and Zimbabwe.[186]

International lender of last resort

The debate about the need for an international lender of last resort (ILOLR) is a consequence of the globalization and interdependency of financial markets across the world. The fear that a domestic crisis can expand—by contagion—to other countries has led to the emergence of the International Monetary Fund as a de facto international lender of last resort. Proposals to entrust the IMF with such a role were first debated in 1995 following the Mexican crisis sparked by the devaluation of the peso at the beginning of the Zedillo Administration.[187] The Emergency Financing Mechanism was a response by the Fund to the need for prompt support assistance, a typical feature of the operation of the lender of last resort at the domestic level.

---

[183] ibid 9.   [184] These are outlined in pages 9–21, ibid.

[185] See François Gianviti, 'The Reform of the International Monetary Fund' in Rosa M Lastra (ed), *The Reform of the International Financial Architecture* (London: Kluwer Law, 2001) 101—2.

[186] See International Monetary Fund, 'Review of the Fund's Strategy on Overdue Financial Obligations', 24 August 2005, at <http://www.imf.org/external/np/pp/eng/2005/082405.htm>. The Fund's Articles of Agreement, Schedule J, para 6, recognized the possibility of a loss only after the withdrawal of a member. A procedure on Zimbabwe's compulsory withdrawal from the Fund (under Art XXVI, s 29(c) of the Articles of Agreement) was initiated in February 2004, with the issuance of the Managing Director's complaint regarding Zimbabwe's persistent failure to fulfil its obligations under the Articles of Agreement. However, the Executive Board (See Release No 05/205 of 9 September 2005), to allow Zimbabwe a further chance to improve cooperation with the Fund, decided to postpone a recommendation to the IMF's Board of Governors with respect to Zimbabwe's compulsory withdrawal from the IMF.

[187] See Sachs, above note 130.

The crises in Thailand, Indonesia, and South Korea reignited the debate in 1997, as the International Monetary Fund provided—through stand-by arrangements—a rescue package to these countries. What became known in the jargon as a 'bailout' was deemed necessary at the time to restore confidence and to renew access to funding in the international capital markets. The creation of the Supplemental Reserve Facility, SRF, in 1997 was another step forward in the 'formalization' of the role of the Fund as ILOLR. The workings of the SRF are reminiscent of the workings of the domestic lender of last resort role of the central bank at the domestic level, in terms of access beyond the normal access limits, relatively high rate of charge (surcharge) and disbursements. Indeed, the 'special' policy—according to Article V, section 3(a)—in the case of the SRF entails the application of terms of conditionality more severe than the regular terms applied to general stand-by arrangements.

A distinctive feature of the crises at the end of the twentieth century and beginning of the twenty-first century—crises in Mexico, Thailand, Indonesia, South Korea, Russia, Brazil, Turkey, Argentina, and others—is that the acute balance of payments problems these countries suffered stemmed from the capital account instead of the current account.

As I explained in Chapter 13, the Fund also created another facility to deal with the contagion effects of a crisis, the Contingent Credit Line, CCL, established in 1999. However, the CCL was never used and was allowed to expire in 2003.

Stanley Fischer argues that although the IMF is not an international central bank, it acts in important respects as an international lender of last resort, a role which, in his opinion, is needed in the international monetary system.[188] The need for a lender of last resort can be rationalized by the fact that emerging countries' external debt is mostly denominated in foreign currency, which national lenders of last resort hold in insufficient quantity to repay all creditors at short notice.[189]

A few considerations ought to be made when comparing the lender of last resort role of the central bank at the national level and the role of the IMF as an international lender of last resort.[190]

---

[188] See generally Stanley Fischer, 'On the Need for an International Lender of Last Resort', Essays in International Economcis No 220, Princeton University, November 2000.

[189] See Olivier Jeanne, 'The IMF: An International Lender of Last Resort', September 2000, at <http://www.imf.org/external/pubs/ft/irb/2000/eng/02/index.htm>.

[190] See Ch 4 for a review of the theoretical foundations of the lender of last resort doctrine, in particular the contributions by Henry Thornton and Walter Bagehot. ('Lend freely at a higher interest rate and with good collateral.')

First, the IMF cannot create money, which limits its lending capacity.[191] However, Fischer argues that despite its inability to issue its own currency, the Fund has been able to assemble sizeable packages of financial assistance when needed.[192] Goodhart contends that the key factor determining the scope and scale of a domestic LOLR is its ability to absorb losses, an ability which rests ultimately with the government. Since governments are constrained by the domain of their domestic jurisdiction, they cannot create foreign currency. So, just as commercial banks will turn to their central bank when they cannot borrow at acceptable terms in the money markets, these national governments and central banks will turn to an ILOLR when then cannot borrow foreign currency on acceptable terms in the international money market.[193]

Secondly, the lender of last resort should generally address problems of illiquidity, not of insolvency. Problems of insolvency are best dealt with—nationally and internationally—by other legal and policy mechanisms of crisis management.

Thirdly, the risk of contagion is the key factor affecting the discretionary decision to provide (or not) lender of last resort assistance.[194]

Fourthly, any degree of protection justifies regulation and supervision, nationally and internationally. The greater the expected protection, the more justifiable regulation and supervision becomes. It then follows that any degree of international protection justifies strengthening international banking rules[195] and enhancing surveillance of domestic bank supervisory and regulatory policies. In fact, this increased surveillance and enhanced transparency in banking and financial matters is needed to preserve international financial stability. As I explained in Chapter 13, greater and closer surveillance over financial systems and their supervision and regulation has become an important component of an Article IV consultation. The FSAP programme is another step forward in the Fund's efforts to gather appropriate information to assess the stability and soundness of the financial systems of member countries.

---

[191] According to Forrest Capie and Geoffrey Wood, 'Unless the IMF . . . can issue any currency it wishes on demand and without limit, there can be no ILOLR.' See Forrest Capie and Geoffrey Wood, 'The IMF in a Changing World', a paper prepared for Essays in Honour of Sir Joseph Gold, mimeo, 7 November 2001.

[192] Fischer, above note 188, 28.

[193] See Charles Goodhart, 'Myths about the Lender of Last Resort' (1999) 2 International Finance 339, 348–52.

[194] See Charles Goodhart and Haizhou Huang, 'A Model of Lender of Last Resort', Financial Markets Group of the London School of Economics, Discussion Paper 313, January 1999. Goodhart and Huang's model suggests that contagion (and not moral hazard) is the main concern in providing LOLR.

[195] The Core Principles for Effective Banking Supervision, adopted by the Basle Committee on Banking Supervision in September 1997, are a step in this direction.

Drawbacks of official sector 'bailout' packages I have questioned elsewhere the wisdom of having an international lender of last resort, giving the finite nature of IMF resources and the magnitude of private capital flows nowadays.[196] As in a fair, the merry-go-round keeps on going until it stops. And after the relative success stories of Mexico, Thailand, Indonesia, and South Korea, came Russia (a 'managed' default) and Argentina (a 'chaotic' default, a failure). However, the idea of an official sector bailout has not been abandoned, and, indeed, it was used again in Turkey in 2001 (where geopolitical considerations played an important role).

The key to determining the success (or failure) of 'bailout' packages (indeed of any crisis resolution mechanism) is the ability to renew access to funding in the international capital markets and, thereby, help restore confidence in the country.

There are several problems and disadvantages with international bailouts. First, they give rise to moral hazard incentives: investors' folly, reckless bank lending, irresponsible policies, delays in policy change, and so on. Though the moral hazard is not created by the bailout per se, but by the precedent it constitutes and by the expectations it generates, particularly on creditors.

Secondly, other techniques to deal with crises may prove more efficient and less costly than bailouts; for instance, what appeared to settle the issue in South Korea in December 1997 was the agreement between Western banks and Korean banks as to the restructuring of the Korean debt (rolling it over).[197]

Thirdly, any commitment of funds in advance might not only give rise to moral hazard incentives but also be insufficient to contain a crisis when massive financial assistance is needed. Unlike domestic central banks, the IMF cannot print money and, thus, cannot lend freely. Neither in the Mexican nor in the Asian bailout package did the IMF provide the funds alone. The IMF acted as a leader or coordinator in the design of the packages (akin to the role of the lead bank in a syndicated loan), but the support of national governments—in particular of the US Government—was essential. Indeed, if what people want in a crisis is US dollars, one could argue that the Fed is also assuming a quasi-international LOLR role.

---

[196] I further discuss the role of the IMF as international lender of last resort in Rosa M Lastra, 'Lender of Last Resort, an International Perspective' (1999) 48 International and Comparative Law Quarterly 339.

[197] However, Kenen (above note 113, 30) claims that the banks agreed to roll over their claims on Korean banks because they were *told* to volunteer by their own countries' governments. He also points out that the Korean government guaranteed the claims of the Korean banks. He cites other authors (ibid n 10) who suggest that the IMF might have 'sought to engineer an earlier rollover of interbank claims not only in the Korean case, but also in the Thai case'.

Fourthly, bailouts may be inequitable if they allow investors to 'escape' when they should take a hit for their bad decisions.

Fifthly, financial crises are often a good stimulus for reform; the moral hazard of an international LOLR may allow bad policies to remain in effect much longer. Ultimately, the response must be at the domestic level: reforming the domestic financial sector and strengthening its institutional framework.

Sixthly, standby arrangements of the magnitude of those for Mexico and Korea stretch IMF resources which exist for the benefit of the entire membership, impeding the use of those resources for other purposes. (Indeed, following the Russian and Brazilian crises in 1998, access to borrowed funds was needed.)[198] The IMF can only engage at any given time in a limited number (very few) of 'bailout' packages, thus raising questions of possible asymmetrical treatment of members.

Finally, given the recurrent nature of financial crises,[199] and the difficulties in predicting and preventing the next crisis, one might wonder if today's solution (ie, a bailout package) might be a good response for tomorrow's crisis.

Final considerations on the role of the IMF in the international financial system

The IMF often acts as an honest broker, as a 'master-of-ceremonies', as an arbiter in sovereign debt negotiations (and debt restructuring) between debtor countries and creditors and creditor countries. The IMF can give or withhold its blessing on the member country's plan of reform. Creditors expect that the debtor country will address the structural economic problems that contributed to the crisis and they know that the IMF is the only player that can 'prescribe economic medicine' to the sovereign debtor with a certain degree of independence from their own interests and the interests of debtor countries.[200] (Even though the IMF also has an interest at stake since it itself lends, it has a de facto preferred creditor status and treats arrears in repayments to the Fund with severity.)

---

[198] In July 1998 the General Arrangements to Borrow (GAB) were activated for an amount of SDR 6.3 billion in connection with the financing of an Extended Arrangement for Russia. Of that amount, SDR 1.4 billion was used. The New Arrangements to Borrow (NAB), which came into effect in November 1998, were first activated in the extended arrangement offered to Brazil in December 1998, when the IMF called on funding of SDR 9.1 billion, of which SDR 2.9 billion was used. The activations for both Russia and Brazil were cancelled in March 1999, when the Fund repaid the outstanding amounts following payments of quota increases under the Eleventh General Review of Quotas.

[199] See Ch 4.

[200] See Buchheit, above note 163, 78. 'The IMF has more information than any other creditor, greater access to government decision-makers and a broader peripheral vision of the effects of measures on neighbouring countries. It also occupies a building that is infested with economists who profess sublime diagnostic and prognostic powers.'

In the words of Walter Robicheck, advisor to the IMF Managing Director from 1982 to 1984:

> The role of the IMF as an honest broker between debtor countries and their creditor banks consists of serving as ultimate judge of the appropriate mix between the magnitude of a heavily indebted developing country's adjustment effort and the commitment to it of new external finance for its remaining balance of payments deficit. This judgment calls for the performance of three major tasks. The first is to help a country frame an adjustment program that would qualify for a standby or extended arrangement with the IMF. This task involves the prudent exercise of conditionality. The second is to commit IMF resources in support of such an adjustment program, which involves setting the IMF's own contribution toward financing a country's balance of payments deficit. In setting its own contribution, the IMF takes into account the enhanced leverage which this commitment of its own resources affords the country with other foreign lenders and, more particularly, with the banks with exposures in the country. Third, the IMF intercedes directly in support of the country's efforts for raising external finance from third parties. This task is commonly referred to as its catalytic role.[201]

Buchheit contends that,

> If indeed the important decisions about inter-creditor relations are made at the time the IMF negotiates a stabilization program with the sovereign debtor, the obvious question is how the views of the soon-to-be-affected creditors can be brought into those discussions at a point when they may influence the outcome. . . . No one should expect bondholders to remain bovinely impassive as their fate in these restructurings is settled by economists employed by multilateral financial institutions.[202]

Buchheit elaborates upon the logic behind the need to involve private creditors. One cannot construct an economic recovery programme, he argues, without making assumptions about how much fresh money will come in and about how much each group of creditors should contribute to 'burden sharing'. Such judgements are forward-looking and must accurately predict the effect of any measures taken today upon the investors' willingness to finance the sovereign borrowers tomorrow.

I believe that the IMF should take a step forward in its assessment of the stability and soundness of countries' financial systems (an assessment which has

---

[201] See E Walter Robicheck, 'The International Monetary Fund: An Arbiter in the Debt Restructuring Process' (1984) 23 Columbia Journal of Transnational Law 143, 146. Buchheit (above note 163) points out that 'judgements about burden sharing among creditors are not just a function of arithmetic. Such judgements, the private sector would argue, must also be forward-looking; they must accurately predict the effect of any measures taken today on the market's willingness to finance the sovereign borrower tomorrow . . . Burden sharing decisions are best left to financiers, not economists or politicians.'

[202] See Buchheit, above note 163, 79–80.

been greatly improved via the FSAP programme and ROSCs) through the development of an internal rating system for countries' banking and financial systems akin to the CAMEL system in the USA.[203] CAMEL ratings are composite ratings that take into account capital adequacy, asset quality, management competence, earnings, and liquidity. CAMEL ratings are unpublished as opposed to the ratings prepared and published by private rating agencies. CAMEL ratings are a supervisory technique, which can act as an instrument of 'crisis prevention' by helping identify problems early on (effective supervision needs to be based upon the best possible information). The information (about banks) in the USA is provided to the authorities through on-site examinations and reporting requirements. Supervisors have the duty of alerting or warning institutions perceived to be in trouble, prompting in some cases early corrective action or restructuring.

The IMF ratings that I propose would also be composite ratings with regard to the safety and soundness of a country's banking and financial system and would be based upon the results of Article IV consultations, FSAP reports, FSSAs and ROSCs, and upon the data compiled by members in accordance with the Special Data Dissemination Standard or SDDS and the General Data Dissemination System or GDDS.[204] These ratings would help identify vulnerabilities (a function that is already performed to some extent by ROSCs and through the practice of surveillance) and, therefore, act as an instrument of 'crisis prevention'. Article VIII, section 5 imposes an obligation upon members with regard to the reporting of information to the Fund. However, the requirements of Article VIII, section 5(b), which place members 'under no obligation to furnish information in such detail about the affairs of individuals

---

[203] In the USA, following criticism of the General Accounting Office regarding the existent of divergent approaches and bearing in mind that the determination of the soundness of a financial institution is not an 'exact science', the federal regulatory agencies adopted the Uniform Financial Institutions Rating System in 1978–9. For banks the rating system is commonly known as the CAMEL system. With regard the CAMEL system, see Rosa M Lastra, *Central Banking and Banking Regulation* (London: Financial Markets Group of the London School of Economics, 1996) 113–14.

[204] See <http://www.imf.org/external/np/exr/facts/data.htm>. The need for data dissemination standards has been highlighted by financial crises in which information deficiencies played a role. The standards for data dissemination consist of two tiers. The first is the SDDS which was established in 1996 to guide countries that have access, or might seek access, to the international capital markets. The second tier, the GDDS was established in 1997 to help countries provide more reliable data. It is open to all IMF members. Importantly, the GDDS is focused on improving statistical systems, whereas the SDDS focuses on commitments to data dissemination standards in countries that already meet high data quality standards. Both are voluntary, but once a country subscribes to the SDDS, observance of the standard is mandatory. Countries also agree to post information about their data dissemination practices on the IMF's external website on an electronic bulletin board known as the Dissemination Standards Bulletin Board, DSBB. Further, they must establish an Internet site containing the actual data, called a National Summary Data Page (NSDP), to which the DSBB is linked.

or corporations' would certainly be a hurdle to surpass, since countries would only provide this information on a voluntary basis. Another legal requirement to take into account is Article XII, section 8.

The question of publication (on a voluntary basis) of these proposed IMF composite ratings is debatable. According to Article XII, section 8, which governs the communication of views to members, the Fund may—by a seventy per cent majority of the total voting power—decide to publish a report regarding its monetary or economic conditions and developments which directly tend to produce 'a serious disequilibrium in the international balance of payments of members'. The IMF would need to balance the incentives for members to remain open and candid in their relations with the Fund with the need to provide valuable information to investors. Since there is no collateral in international sovereign lending (conditionality serves as a substitute for collateral), the decision to support a troubled country or a country which appears to be heading for trouble needs to be based upon the best possible information.[205] The IMF can provide credible and reliable information on the health of the borrower country's economic and financial institution.

Arminio Fraga, former Central Bank Governor of Brazil, has suggested a different proposal. He wrote in 1996 that the IMF should act as 'the permanent auditor of countries, which should voluntarily submit themselves to examination in order to lower their borrowing costs. Annual Article IV consultations could be supplemented by quarterly reviews that would enhance the credibility of the data released under the IMF's recent initiative [he refers to the Special Data Dissemination Standard] and thus help to reduce the costs of adjustment programs'.[206]

In the absence of a 'formal' international bank regulator (or even, more broadly, of an international financial regulator), it is pertinent to ask whether the IMF should adopt such a regulatory role (which would require an amendment to the Articles of Agreement). The IMF is, to some extent, better suited than the Basel Committee to adopt that role, because it is a formal international organization (as opposed to the Basel Committee, whose existence is not formalized by an International Treaty), with a large membership comprising developing and

---

[205] The Fund should be commended for its recent efforts to collect and disseminate data with regard to the financial sector. In its 'Fifth Review of the Fund's Standards Initiative', above note 97, the inclusion of financial soundness indicators (FSIs) in the SDDS and the completion of a Compilation Guide on Financial Soundness Indicators are hailed as important proposed modifications to the SDDS.

[206] See Arminio Fraga, 'Crisis Prevention and Management: Lessons from Mexico' in Peter Kenen (ed), 'From Halifax to Lyons: What Has Been Done About Crisis Management', Essays in International Finance No 200, Princeton University, October 1996, 54–5.

developed countries (as opposed to the Basle Committee, which comprises only the expanded G10 countries), and with strong communication ties with ministries of finance, central banks, and other representative governments in countries all around the world (the members of the Basel Committee are central banks and supervisory agencies from the G10 countries). Indeed, the IMF, through its surveillance function (Art IV), already exercises a regulatory or jurisdictional function over its members. Another candidate for the position of 'international financial regulator' is the BIS. The role of the BIS as an umbrella organization for several international financial standard setters (though IOSCO is oddly placed in Madrid) and the BIS history and tradition as a forum for central bank cooperation makes the institution well suited for this position. This is the view espoused among others by William Peter Cooke, former Chairman of the Basel Committee.[207]

E. Conclusions

The IMF is not only the international monetary institution par excellence; the IMF is also at the centre of the international financial system. The IMF's unique set of responsibilities (in particular, surveillance and conditional financial assistance) and its singular role in sovereign debt negotiations explain its central position in the 'international financial architecture'.

The IMF plays different roles and wearing different 'hats': that of an 'honest broker' or arbiter between creditors and debtors, a primary lender (financial assistance to countries experiencing balance of payments needs), a preferred creditor (hence with an interest at stake), an international lender of last resort, a crisis manager, a standard setter, and others.

This chapter examined the evolving legal framework for the prevention and

---

[207] See Peter Cooke, above note 1, preface, xxiv:

My own view, not least because of an involvement with the organisation for over 40 years, is to believe that the BIS is likely to play a critical role in this whole area of work. There are a number of reasons for this. First and foremost, it is there. It also has a measure of independence (despite being subject to the ultimate authority of its central bank shareholders). It has, for many years, been a forum where the macro-economic, macro-prudential issues have been discussed. . . . The BIS has widened its membership over the past few years to embrace a much more representative group of countries around the world than its original shareholders. It has also become a little more comfortable in allowing Ministries of Finance to participate in bodies spawned by what has traditionally been a Central Bankers club. It already houses the secretariats of the major international bodies working on banking and insurance regulation. If the securities regulators could be persuaded to establish themselves in Basel [they were not!] . . ., then the ongoing capacity in and around the BIS to pursue a continuing regulatory and supervisory debate internationally would be unparalleled.

resolution of international financial crises (in the pursuit of international financial stability) and the process of law-making with regard to cross-border financial relations.

The change in financing patterns of capital flows to emerging economies over the last years (from loans to bonds) has signified a change in the legal framework to deal with sovereign debt crises. Problems of creditor coordination and collective action (the 'hold-out' incentive, in particular) are more acute in the case of bonds than in the case of loans. The need for an orderly workout for sovereign debtors has triggered a number of official and private-based responses. The solutions currently favoured by the international community are 'market-based', relying upon contractual mechanisms, such as the inclusion of CACs in bond agreements, coupled with the observance of a voluntary code of conduct.

While 'hard law' governs the IMF functions and activities, the IMF has developed—within the framework of its Articles of Agreement—a number of policies, practices, standards, and codes of good practice that can be characterized as soft law. The IMF, however, is not the only international financial standard setter, nor is it the most relevant one. That regulatory function is shared by a number of formal and informal groupings and fora of an international character, with the Basel Committee on Banking Supervision and other Committees that have grown under the auspices of the Bank for International Settlements playing a significant role. However, the IMF is uniquely placed to monitor the compliance with standards through its function of surveillance, through its assessment of the health of the financial sector (via the FSAP programme, ROSCs, and FSSAs), and to provide countries with the incentive to comply through the design of conditionality policies.

The process of international financial standard setting that I have critically examined in this chapter is a key feature of the evolving international financial architecture. Soft law is informal law. Its main problem is enforcement. Its main drawback is legitimacy. Its greatest advantage is flexibility. Hard law is formal law, enforceable and legitimate. It is also rigid and this rigidity can be problematic with regard to the regulation of money and financial markets. Soft law fills a need, a legal vacuum in the regulation of cross-border banking activities. It cannot therefore be dismissed.

International financial soft law is often a 'top-down' phenomenon with a two-layer implementation scheme. The rules are agreed by international financial standard setters and national authorities must implement them in their regulation of the financial industry. The financial intermediaries are the 'final' addressees of those rules. Standards and uniform rules, however, can also be designed by the financial industry itself. Self-regulation, by definition, has a 'bottom-up' character.

International law-making relies upon a variety of sources. It is in the confluence of 'hard law' (legally enforceable rules), soft law of a 'public law' nature (which can complement, coexist or turn into hard law), and soft law of a 'private law' nature (comprising rules of practice, standards, usages, and other forms of self-regulation as well as rules and principles agreed or proposed by scholars and experts) where the future of international financial and monetary law lies.

BIBLIOGRAPHY

Abbott, K W, and Snidal, D, 'Hard and Soft Law in International Governance' 54 *International Organization* (2000)

Abrams, R K, and Taylor, M W, *Issues in the Unification of Financial Sector Supervision*, Working Paper 213 (International Monetary Fund, 2000)

Aharony, J, and Izhak, S, 'Additional Evidence on the Information-Based Contagion Effects of Bank Failures' (20) *Journal of Banking and Finance* (1996)

Akinrinsola, I, 'Monetery Integration in West Africa' 5 *Journal of International Banking Regulation* (2003)

Alesina, A, and Summers, L, 'Central Bank Independence and Macro-economic Performance: Some Comparative Evidence' 25(2) *Journal of Money, Credit and Banking* (1992)

Amtenbrink, F, *The Democratic Accountability of Central Banks: A Comparative Study of the European Central Bank* (Hart Publishing, 1999)

—— and De Haan, J, 'Economic Governance in the European Union: Fiscal Policy Discipline versus Flexibility' 40 *Common Market Law Review* (2003)

Andenas, M, 'Liability for Supervisors and Depositors' Rights: the BCCI and the Bank of England in the House of Lords' *The Company Lawyer*, Vol 22, No 88, 2001

—— and Fairgrieve, D, 'To Supervise or to Compensate? A Comparative Study of State Liability for Negligent Banking Supervision' in Andenas, M, and Fairgrieve, D (eds), *Judicial Review in International Perspective, Liber Amicorum in Honour of Lord Slynn of Hadley* (Kluwer Law, 2000)

Arora, A, and Olivares Caminal, R, 'Rethinking the Sovereign Debt Restructuring Approach' 9 *Law and Business Review of the Americas* (2003)

Aslund, A, 'When a Banking Crisis is a Good Thing', Financial Times, 13 September 1995

Aust, A, 'The Theory and Practice of Informal International Instruments' 35 ICLQ (1986)

Bagehot, W, *Lombard Street. A Description of the Money Market* (Wiley, 1999, originally published in 1873)

Baliño Tomás, J T, and Cotarelli, C (eds), *Frameworks for Monetary Stability. Policy Issues and Country Experiences* (International Monetary Fund, 1994)

Barro, R J, and Gordon, D B, 'Rules, Discretion, and Reputations in a Model of Monetary Policy' 12 *Journal of Monetary Economics* (1983)

Basel Committee on Banking Supervision, 'Principles for the Supervision of Banks' Foreign Establishments' (BIS, 1983), available at <http://www.bis.org/publ/bcbsc312.pdf>

—— 'Information Flows between Banking Supervisory Authorities' (1990), available at <http://www.bis.org/publ/bcbsc004.htm>

—— 'Minimum Standards for the Supervision of International Banking Groups and Their Cross-border Establishments' (1992), available at <http://www.bis.org/publ/bcbsc004.htm>

Basel Committee on Banking Supervision, 'Risk Management Guidelines for Derivatives' (BIS, 1994)

—— 'The Supervision of Cross-Border Banking' (1996), available at <http://www.bis.org/publ/bcbsc004.htm>

—— 'Core Principles for Effective Banking Supervision' (BIS, 1997), available at <http://www.bis.org/publ/bcbs30a.pdf>

—— 'The Core Principles Methodology' (BIS, 1999), available at <http://www.bis.org/publ/bcbs61.pdf>

—— 'BCBS Compendium of documents Volume III: International Supervisory Issues' (BIS, 2000), available at <http://www.bis.org/publ/bcbsc004.htm>

Baxter, T, 'Cross-Border Challenges in Resolving Financial Groups', paper presented at the Federal Reserve Bank of Chicago Conference on Systemic Financial Crises: Resolving Large Bank Insolvencies, 30 September–1 October 2004

Begg, I, 'Future Fiscal Arrangements in the European Union' 41 *Common Market Law Review* (2004)

Benston, G J, Eisenbeis, R A, Horvitz, P M, Kane, E J, and Kaufman, G G, *Perspectives on Safe and Sound Banking: Past, Present and Future* (MIT Press, 1986)

Bergsten, F, 'How to Target Exchange Rates', Financial Times, 20 November 1998

—— 'Alternative Exchange Rate Systems and Reform of the International Financial Architecture' (Testimony before the Committee on Banking and Financial Services, United States House of Representatives, Washington DC 21 May 1999), at <http://www.iie.com/publications/papers/bergsten0599.htm>

Berkowitz, D, Pistor, K, and Richard, J-F, *Economic Development, Legality and the Transplant Effect* (The Davidson Institute, 2000)

Bickel, A M, *The Least Dangerous Branch, The Supreme Court at the Bar of Politics* (Bobbs-Merrill, 1962)

Bilder, R, 'Beyond Compliance: Helping Nations Cooperate' in Shelton, D (ed), *Commitment and Compliance: The Role of Non-Binding Norms in the International Legal System* (Oxford University Press, 2000)

Bini Smaghi, L, 'What Went Wrong with the Stability and Growth Pact' in Sørensen, P (ed), *Monetary Union in Europe. Essays in Honour of Niels Thygesen* (DJØF Publishing Copenhaguen, 2004)

Black, B S, 'The Legal and Institutional Preconditions for Strong Securities Markets' 48 *UCLA Law Review* (2001)

Board of Governors of the Federal Reserve System, 'The Federal Reserve System Purposes and Functions' (Washington DC, 1984)

—— 'Policy Statement on Payments System Risk' (Board of Governors of the FRS, 30 May 2001)

Bodin, J, *The Six Books of the Commonwealth* (Basil Blackwell, 1955), Book I ('The Final End of the Well-Ordered Commonwealth: Concerning Sovereignty') available at <http://www.constitution.org/bodin/bodin_.htm>

Bokros, L, 'A Perspective on Financial Sector Development in Central and Eastern Europe' in Fleming, A, Bokros, L, and Votava, C (eds), *Financial Transition in Europe and Central Asia—Challenges of the New Decade* (The World Bank, 2001)

Bordo, M, 'The Gold Standard: the Traditional Approach' in Bordo, M, and Schwartz, A (eds), *A Retrospective on the Classical Gold Standard 1821–1931* (Chicago University Press, 1984)

—— 'Alternative Views and Historical Experience' 76(1) *Federal Reserve Bank of Richmond Economic Review* (1990)

Boughton, J M, *Silent Revolution: the IMF 1979–1989* (International Monetary Fund, 2001)

Brand, R A, 'Sovereignty: The State, The Individual and the International Legal System in the Twenty First Century' 25 *Hastings International and Comparative Law Review* (2002)

Brittan, S, 'EMU in Perspective', in Andenas, M, Gormley, L W, Hadjiemmanuil, C, and Harden, I (eds), *European Economic and Monetary Union: The Institutional Framework* (Kluwer Law International, 1997)

Brok, E, Discussion Paper 111, CONV 325/2/02 REV 2, 27.01.2003, available at <http://register.consilium.eu.int/pdf/en/02/cv00/cv00325-re02en02.pdf>

Buchanan, J, *The Limits of Liberty: Between Anarchy and Leviathan* (University of Chicago Press, 1975)

Buchheit, L, *How to Negotiate Eurocurrency Loan Agreements* (2nd edn, Euromoney, 2000)

—— 'The Search for Inter-creditor Parity' 8 *Law and Business Review of the Americas* (2002)

—— 'A Quarter Century of Sovereign Debt Management: An Overview' 35 *Georgetown Journal of International Law* (2004)

—— 'The Role of the Official Sector in Sovereign Debt Workouts' 6 *Chicago Journal of International Law Symposium* (2005)

—— and Mitu Gulati, G, 'Exit Consents in Sovereign Bond Exchanges' 28 *UCLA Law Review* (2000)

—— and Mitu Gulati G, 'Sovereign Bonds and the Collective Will' 51 *Emory Law Journal* (2002)

—— and Pam, J, 'Uruguay's Innovations' 19 *Journal of International Banking Law and Regulation* (2004)

—— and Walker, M, 'Legal Issues in the Restructuring of Commercial Bank Loans to Sovereign Borrowers' in Gruson, M, and Eisner, R (eds), *Sovereign Lending: Managing Legal Risk* (Euromoney Publications, 1984)

Buira, A, 'Reflections on the International Monetary System', *Princeton Essays in International Finance*, No 195 (1995)

Burdeau, G, 'L'Exercice des Compétences Monétaires par les Etats' 212 *Recueil des Cours* (1988)

Callen, T, and Ostry, J D (eds), *Japan's Lost Decade. Policies for Economic Revival* (International Monetary Fund, 2003)

Calomiris, C W, 'Statement before the Joint Economic Committee' (United States Congress, Tuesday, 24 February 1998), at <http://www.house.gov/jec/hearings/imf/calomiri.htm> (visited 10 March 2004)

—— and Kahn, C, 'The Role of Demandable Debt in Structuring Optimal Banking Arrangements' 81 *American Economic Review* (1991)

—— Kahn, C, 'The Efficiency of Self-regulated Payments Systems: Learning from the Suffolk System' 28 *Journal of Money, Credit, and Banking* (1996)

Capie, F, and Wood, G, 'The IMF in a Changing World', paper prepared for Essays in Honour of Sir Joseph Gold, mimeo, 7 November 2001

Caprio, G, Folkerts-Landau, D, and Lane, T D (eds), *Building Sound Finance in Emerging Economies* (International Monetary Fund, 1994)

——, Dooley, M, Leipziger, D, and Walsh, C, *The Lender of Last Resort Function under a Currency Board. The Case of Argentina* (World Bank Policy Research Working Paper No 1648, 1996)

Carreau, D, *Souveraineté et Coopération Monétaire Internationale* (Cujas, 1970)

Carreau, D, and Juillard, P, *Droit International Economique* (Dalloz, 2003)

Chari, V, and Jagannathan, R, 'Banking Panics, Information, and Rational Expectations Equilibrium' 43 *Journal of Finance* (1988)

Chodosh, H, 'Neither Treaty nor Custom: The Emergence of Declarative International Law' 26 *Texas International Law Journal* (1991)

Chung, J, and Atkins, R, 'ECB sends powers signal on debt', Financial Times, 10 November 2005

Clifford Chance, 'European Monetary Union: the Legal Framework', October 1997

Coase, R H, *The Firm, the Market and the Law* (The University of Chicago Press, 1988)

Cohen, B, 'A Global Chapter 11' 75 *Foreign Policy* (1989)

—— 'Life at the Top: International Currencies in the Twenty-First Century', *Essays in International Economics* No 221 (Princeton University, December 2000)

—— 'EMU and the Developing Countries' in Wyplosz, C (ed), *The Impact of EMU on Europe and the Developing Countries* (OUP, 2001)

Colares Juscelino, F, 'Formal Legal Theory and the Surrender of Political Control over Monetary Policy: What Can Ulysses' Journey to Ithaca Teach Argentina about Appropriate Legal Form?' 36 *Cornell International Law Journal* (2003)

Comité Intergouvernemental Creé par la Conference de Messine, 'Rapport des chefs de delegation aux Ministres des Affaires Etrangeres' (Brussels, 21 April 1956), available at <http://aei.pitt.edu/archive/00000996/01/Spaak_report_french.pdf>

Commission of the European Communities, 'Completing the Internal Market', White Paper from the Commission to the European Council, 1985, COM (85) 310

—— 'One Market, One Money: An Evaluation of the Potential Benefits and Costs of Forming an Economic and Monetary Union' 44 *European Economy*, October 1990

—— 'Updating and Simplifying the Community Acquis', Communication to the Council, the European Parliament, the European Economic and Social Committee, and the Committee of the Regions of 11 February 2003, COM (2003) 71

Committee for the Study of Economic and Monetary Union, 'Report on Economic and Monetary Union in the European Community', 12 April 1989, available at <http://europa.eu.int/comm/economy_finance/euro/origins/delors_en.pdf>

Committee on Payment and Settlement Systems, 'Delivery versus Payment in Securities Settlement Systems', *CPSS Publications No 6* (1992)

—— 'Settlement Risk in Foreign Exchange Transactions', *CPSS Publications No 17* (1996)

Council on Foreign Relations Task Force, co-chaired by Hills, C, and Peterson, P, *Safeguarding Prosperity in a Global Financial System, The Future International Financial Architecture* (Institute for International Economics, 1999)

Cranston, R, *Principles of Banking Law* (Oxford University Press, 1997)

Crockett, A, 'Marrying the Micro- and Macro-Prudential Dimensions of Financial Stability' (Remarks before the Eleventh International Conference of Banking Supervisors, held in Basel, 20–21 September 2000)

Cross, S, 'Thoughts on the International Monetary System and the Future of the IMF', Background paper prepared for the Bretton Woods Commission, 'Bretton Woods: Looking into the Future' (1994)

Cukierman, A, *Central Bank Strategy, Credibility and Independence: Theory and Evidence* (MIT Press, 1994)

——, Webb, S, and Neyapti, B, 'Measuring the Independence of Central Banks and its Effects on Policy Outcomes' 6(3) *World Bank Economic Review* (1992)

Culp Davis, K, *Administrative Law and Government* (2nd edn, West Publishing Co, 1975)

Curtis, C T, 'The Status of Foreign Deposits under the Federal Deposit Preference Law,' 21(2) *University of Pennsylvania Journal of International Economic Law* (2000)

Dale, R S, 'Deposit Insurance, Policy Clash over EC and US Reforms' in Shadrack, F C, and Korobow, L (eds), *The Basic Elements of Bank Supervision* (Federal Reserve Bank of New York, 1993)

—— 'Risk Management and Public Policy in Payment, Clearing and Settlement Systems' 1(2) *International Finance* (1998)

—— 'Deposit Insurance in Theory and Practice' 8(1) *Journal of Financial Regulation and Compliance* (2000)

—— and Wolfe, S, 'The UK Financial Services Authority: Unified Regulation in the New Market Environment' 4(3) *Journal of International Banking Regulation* (2003)

Davies, H, 'Euro-regulation' 1(2) *Journal of International Banking Regulation* (1999)

Davis, P, *Debt, Financial Fragility and Systemic Risk* (Clarendon Press, 1992)

De Bandt, O, and Hartmann, P, *Systemic Risk: A Survey* (European Central Bank Working Paper No 35, 2000)

De Grauwe, P, *International Money: Post-War Trends and Theories* (Oxford University Press, 1990)

De Krivoy, R, 'An Agenda for Banking Crises Avoidance in Latin America' (Paper presented at the Inter-American Development Bank Group of Thirty Conference on Banking Crises in Latin America, Washington DC, October 1995)

—— *Collapse. The Venezuelan Banking Crisis of 1994* (The Group of Thirty, 2000)

Demirgüç-Kunt, A, and Detragiache, E, 'The Determinants of Bank Crisis in Developing and Developed Countries' 45(1) *International Monetary Fund Staff Papers* (1998)

—— and Kane, E, *Deposit Insurance Around the Globe, Where Does it Work?* (World Bank, World Bank Paper No 2679, 2001)

Dobson, J M, 'Treaty Developments in Latin America', in Fletcher, I (ed), *Cross-Border Insolvency: Comparative Dimensions, The Aberystwyth Insolvency Papers* (United Kingdom National Committee of Comparative Law, 1990), vol 12

Dornbusch, R, and Fischer, S, *Macroeconomics* (5th edn McGraw-Hill, 1990)

Dowd, K (ed), *The Experience of Free Banking* (Routledge, 1992)

—— *Competition and Finance* (Macmillan, 1996)

Dupuy, P-M, 'Soft Law and the International Law of the Environment' 12 *Michigan Journal of International Law* (1991)

Dziobek, C, and Van der Vossen, J W, 'Banking Sector Reform' in Knight, M, Petersen, A B, and Price, R T (eds), *Central Bank Reforms in the Baltics, Russia and the other Countries of the Former Soviet Union* (International Monetary Fund, 1997)

Edison, H, 'Testing the Links. How Strong are the Links between Institutional Quality and Economic Performance' 40 *Finance and Development* (2003), at <http://www.imf.org/external/pubs/ft/fandd/2003/06/pdf/edison.pdf>

Editorial Comments, 'Whither the Stability and Growth Pact?' 41 *Common Market Law Review* (2004)

Effros, R C (ed), *Payment Systems of the World* (Oceana Publications, 1994)

—— 'The Maastricht Treaty, Independence of the Central Bank and Implementing Legislation' in Baliño, T, and Cotarelli, C (eds), *Frameworks for Monetary Stability. Policy Issues and Country Experiences* (International Monetary Fund, 1994)

Eichengreen, B, *Golden Fetters: The Gold Standard and the Great Depression, 1919–1939* (Oxford University Press, 1992)

—— 'Central Bank Co-operation and Exchange Rate Commitments: the classical and inter-war gold standards compared' 2 *Financial History Review* (1995)

—— '*The Dollar and the New Bretton Woods System*', text of the Henry Thornton Lecture, delivered at the Cass School of Business, 15 December 2004, 5, available at <http://emlab.berkeley.edu/users/eichengr/policy/cityuniversitylecture2jan3–05.pdf>

—— and Portes, R, *Crisis? What Crisis? Orderly Workout for Sovereign Debtors* (Centre for Economic Policy Research, 1995)

Eijffinger, S, 'How can the Stability and Growth Pact be improved to achieve stronger discipline and higher flexibility', *European Parliament Briefing Paper*, November 2002

Elshtain, J B, 'Sovereign God, Sovereign State, Sovereign Self' 66 *Notre Dame Law Review* (1991)

Enoch, C, and Gulde, A-M, *Making a Currency Board Operational* (International Monetary Fund, 1997)

European Central Bank, 'European Central Bank Agreement of 1 September 1998, between the European Central Bank and the national central banks of the Member States outside the euro area laying down the operating procedures for an exchange rate mechanism in stage three of Economic and Monetary Union' (98/C 345/05)

—— 'Opinion 1999/06 [1999] OJ C127/5, (1999)

—— 'European Central Bank Agreement of 14 September 2000 between the European Central Bank and the national central banks of the Member States outside the euro area amending the Agreement of 1 September 1998 laying down the operating procedures for an exchange rate mechanism in stage III of economic and monetary union' (2000/C 362/10)

—— 'Opinion CON/2004/6' of 13 February 2004, at <http://www.ecb.int/ecb/legal/pdf/en_con_2004_6_f_sign.pdf>

—— 'European Central Bank Agreement of 29 April 2004 between the European Central Bank and the national central banks of the Member States outside the euro area on 1 May 2004 amending the Agreement of 1 September 1998 laying down the operating procedures for an exchange rate mechanism in stage three of economic and monetary union' (2004/C 135/03)

—— 'Opinion on Andorra', CON/2004/32, OJ C 256 16.10.2004, available at <http://www.ecb.int/ecb/legal/pdf/c_25620041016en00090009.pdf>

—— 'The Implementation of Monetary Policy in the Euro area', February 2005, available at <http://www.ecb.int/pub/pdf/other/gendoc2005en.pdf>

—— 'Memorandum of Understanding on Co-operation between the Banking Supervisors, Central Banks and Finance Ministries of the European Union in Financial Crisis situations', available at <http://www.eu2005.lu/en/actualites/documents_travail/2005/05/14ecofin_mou/index.html> (2005)

—— 'Press Release on the Memorandum of Understanding on Co-operation between the Banking Supervisors, Central Banks and Finance Ministries of the European Union in Financial Crisis situations', available at <http://www.ecb.int> (2005)

European Commission, 'The examination of stability and convergence programmes', at <http://europa.eu.int/comm/economy_finance/about/activities/sgp/scp_en.htm>

—— 'Tracking Financial Integration', Staff Working Paper, available at <http://europa/eu/int/comm/internal_market/en/finances/cross-sector/reporting/tracking-financial-integration_en.pdf>

—— 'Communication of 11 May 1999 entitled "Implementing the framework for financial markets: action plan" ', COM (1999) 232, available at <http://www.europa.eu.int/comm/internal_market/en/finances/general/action_en.pdf> (1999)

—— 'Report on Financial Stability prepared by the ad-hoc working group of the Economic and Financial Committee', Economic Papers No 143, FC/ECFIN/240/00, DG ECFIN, May 2000, Brussels

—— 'Report on Financial crisis management' (2nd Brouwer Report), EFC/ECFIN/251/01, DG ECFIN, Brussels, April 2001)

—— 'Note of the European Commission [Internal Market DG Financial Institutions] to the Ecofin Council', Brussels, 3 December 2002, available at <http://www.europa.eu.int/comm/internal_market/en/finances/cross-sector/consultation/ecofin-note_en.pdf>

—— Financial Services Tenth Report, 'Turning the Corner. Preparing for the Challenges of European Capital Market Integration', Brussels, 2 June 2004

—— 'Green Paper on Financial Services Policy (2005–2010)', COM (2005) 177, 1–13, available at <http://www.europa.eu.int/comm.internal_market/finances/docs/actionplan/index/green_en.pdf> (2005)

—— 'The Stability and Growth Pact' at <http://www.eu.int/comm/economy_finance/about/activities/sgp/sgp_en.htm> (2005)

European Community, 'Monetary Agreement between the Italian Republic, on behalf of the European Community and the Republic of San Marino' [2001] OJ C209/1 (2001)

—— 'Monetary Agreement between the State of the Vatican City, represented by the Holy See, and the Italian Republic on behalf of the European Community' [2001] OJ C299/1, (2001)

—— 'Monetary Agreement between the Government of the French Republic, on behalf of the European Community, and the Government of His Serene Highness the Prince of Monaco' [2002] OJ L142/59, (2002)

European Council, 'Presidency Conclusions of the Hanover European Council', DN DOC/88/8, 28 (1988)

—— 'Presidency Conclusions of the Madrid European Council', DN DOC/89/1, 27 (1989)

—— 'Presidency Conclusions of the Edinburgh European Council', OJ 1992, No C 348/2 (1992)

—— 'Presidency Conclusions of the Madrid European Council' (1995), available at <http://ue.eu.int/ueDocs/cms_Data/docs/pressData/en/ec/00400-C.EN5.htm>

—— 'Resolution on the Stability and Growth Pact', Amsterdam, 17 June 1997, OJ 1997 C236/1

—— 'Opinion of 21 January 2003 on the updated Stability Programme of France', 2004–2006, OJ C 026, 4 February 2003, 5–6

—— 'Recommendation of 26 June 2003 on the broad guidelines of the economic policies of the Member States and the Community (for the 2003–2005 period)' OJ 2003 L195/1, (2003)

European Court of Justice, 'Press Release No 57/04' of 13 July 2004 concerning Case C–27/04, (2004)

European Parliament, 'Resolution on the Implementation of Financial Services Legislation' (2001/2247(INI)) of 5 December 2002, (2002)

European Shadow Financial Regulatory Committee, 'Challenges to financial regulators in the accession countries', Statement No 18, Budapest, 17 May 2004, available at <http://www.ceps.be> and <http://www.aei.org>

European Union Economic and Financial Committee, 'Report on Financial Regulation, Supervision and Stability', Brussels, 9 October 2002, available at <http://www.europa.eu.int/comm/internal_market/en/finances/cross-sector/consultation/efc-report_en.pdf>

Feinberg, J, 'Autonomy, Sovereignty and Privacy: Moral Ideals in the Constitutions?' 58 *Notre Dame Law Review* (1983)

Ferran, E, *Building an EU Securities Market* (Cambridge University Press, 2004)

Fforde, J S, 'Setting Monetary Objectives', 23 *Bank of England Quarterly Bulletin* (1983)

Financial Services Committee (EU), 'Report to the Economic and Financial Committee/Council on Financial Integration', FSC 4156/04, Brussels, 17 May 2004, (2004)

Financial Stability Forum, 'Issues Paper of the Task Force on Implementation of Standards Meeting of the Financial Stability Forum' (Bank for International Settlements, 2000), available at <http://www.fsforum.org/publications/Issues_Paper_Standards00.pdf>

Financial Times, 1 October 1993, 'Bundesbank's record in standing up to Bonn Government'

—— 4 June 1997, 'Bonn backs down over gold reserve revaluation'

—— 11 November 2004, 'Italy raises the prospect of intervention on euro'

—— 20 November 2005, 'ECB shows its hand'

Firth, S, *Derivatives: Law and Practice* (Sweet & Maxwell, 2003)

Fischer, I, 'The Debt Deflation Theory of Great Depressions' 1 *Econometrica* (1933)

Fischer, S, 'Modern Central Banking', in Capie, F, Goodhart, C, Fischer, S, and Schnadt, N (eds), *The Future of Central Banking: The Tercentenary Symposium of the Bank of England* (Cambridge University Press, 1994)

—— 'Capital Account Liberalization and the Role of the IMF' in Fischer, S, Cooper, R, Dornbusch, R, Garber, P, Massad, C, Polak, J, Rodrik, D, and Tarapore, S, 'Should the IMF Pursue Capital Account Convertibility?', *Essays in International Finance* No 207 (Princeton University, May 1998)

—— 'On the Need for an International Lender of Last Resort', *Essays in International Economics* No 220 (Princeton University, November 2000)

Fitzpatrick, J, 'Sovereignty, Territoriality and the Rule of Law' 25 *Hastings International and Comparative Law Review* (2002)

Flandreau, M, 'Central Bank Co-operation in Historical Perspective: a Sceptical View' 4 *Economic History Review* (1997)

Folkerts-Landau, D, 'Systemic Financial Risk in Payment Systems' in International Monetary Fund, *Determinants and Systemic Consequences of International Capital Flows* (International Monetary Fund Occasional Paper No 77, 1991)

Fraga, A, 'German Reparations and Brazilian Debt: a Comparative Study' *Essays in International Finance* No 163 (Princeton University, July 1986)

—— 'Crisis Prevention and Management: Lessons from Mexico' in Kenen, P (ed), 'From Halifax to Lyons: What Has Been Done About Crisis Management', *Essays in International Finance* No 200 (Princeton University, October 1996)

Francotte, P, Comment on 'The Fund Agreement in the Courts', in Effros, R (ed), *Current Legal Issues Affecting Central Banks*, Vol 1 (International Monetary Fund, 1992)

Frattiani, M, von Hagen, J, and Waller, C, 'The Maastricht Way to EMU', *Essays in International Finance* No 187 (Princeton University, 1992)

Freedman, C, and Goodlet, C, 'Large-Value Clearing and Settlement Systems and Systemic Risk' 7(2) *North American Journal of Economics & Finance* (1996)

Freixas, X, 'Crisis Management in Europe' in Kremer, J, Schoenmaker, D, and Wierts, P (eds), *Financial Supervision in Europe* (Edward Elgar, 2003)

Frenkel, J, and Goldstein, M, 'A Guide to Target Zones', *International Monetary Fund Staff Papers* No 33 (1996)

Friedman, M, 'A Monetary and Fiscal Framework for Economic Stability' 38 *American Economic Review* (1948)

—— 'The Case for Flexible Exchange Rates', *Essays in Positive Economics* (University of Chicago Press, 1953)

—— *The Control of Money. A Program for Monetary Stability.* (Fordham University Press, 1959)

—— *Program for Monetary Stability* (Fordham University Press, 1960)

—— and Schwartz, A, *The Great Contraction 1929–1933* (Princeton University Press, 1965)

Fries S M, and Lane, T D, 'Financial and Enterprise Restructuring in Emerging Market Economies' in Caprio, G, Folkerts-Landau, D, and Lane, T D (eds), *Building Sound Finance in Emerging Market Economies* (International Monetary Fund/World Bank, 1993)

—— and Taci, A, *Banking Reform and Development in Transition Economies* (European Bank for Reconstruction and Development, 2002)

Garcia, G, *Deposit Insurance: A Survey of Actual and Best Practices* (International Monetary Fund Occasional Paper No 197, 2001)

—— and Nieto, M, 'Banking Crisis Management in The European Union: Multiple Regulators and Resolution Authorities' 6 *Journal of Banking Regulation* (2005)

Gardner, R, *Sterling-Dollar Diplomacy: The Origins and Prospects of Our International Economic Order* (McGraw-Hill, 1969)

George, E A J, 'The New Lady of Threadneedle Street' (Governor's Speech, Bank of England, London, 24 February 1998)

Geva, B, *Bank Collections and Payment Transactions—A Comparative Legal Analysis* (Oxford University Press, 2001)

Ghosh, A R, Gulde, A-M, and Wolf, H C, *Currency Boards: The Ultimate Fix?* (International Monetary Fund, 1998)

Gianviti, F, 'The Role of the Fund in the Financing of External Debt', *Recuil des Cours* III (1989)

—— 'The Fund Agreement in the Courts' in Robert Effros (ed), *Current Legal Issues Affecting Central Banks*, Vol 1 (International Monetary Fund, 1992)

—— 'Developments at the International Monetary Fund', in Robert Effros (ed), *Current Legal Issues Affecting Central Banks*, Vol 4 (International Monetary Fund, 1997)

—— 'Special Drawing Rights' in Robert Effros (ed), *Current Legal Issues Affecting Central Banks*, Vol 5 (International Monetary Fund, 1998)

—— 'The International Monetary Fund and the International Monetary System. Decision Making in the International Monetary Fund' in *Current Developments in Monetary and Financial Law* (International Monetary Fund, 1999)

—— 'The Reform of the International Monetary Fund (Conditionality and Surveillance)' in Lastra, R (ed), *The Reform of the International Financial Architecture* (Kluwer Law International, 2001)

—— 'Evolving Role and Challenges for the International Monetary Fund' in Andenas, M, and Norton, J (eds), *International Monetary and Financial Law Upon Entering the New Millenium. A Tribute to Sir Joseph and Ruth Gold* (The British Institute of International and Comparative Law, 2002)

Gianviti, F, 'Legal Aspects of the Financial Sector Assessment Program', paper presented at the International Monetary Fund Seminar on Current Developments in Monetary and Financial Law in May 2002, available at <http://www.imf.org/external/np/leg/sem/2002cdmfl/eng/gianv2.pdf>

—— 'Use of a Foreign Currency under the Fund's Articles of Agreement' (17 May 2002), at <http://www.imf.org/external/np/leg/sem/2002/cdmfl/eng/gianvi.pdf>

—— 'Provision of Information to the IMF' in *Current Developments in Monetary and Financial Law*, Vol 2 (International Monetary Fund, 2003)

Gillen, M, and Potter, P, 'The Convergence of Securities Laws and Implications for Developing Securities Markets' 24 *North Carolina Journal of International Law and Commercial Regulation* (1998)

Giovanoli, M, 'A New Architecture for the Global Financial Markets: Legal Aspects of International Financial Standard Setting' in Giovanoli, M (ed), *International Monetary Law. Issues for the New Millenium* (Oxford University Press, 2000)

GKoutzinis, A, 'International Trade in Banking Services and the Role of the WTO: Discussing the Legal Framework and Policy Objectives of the General Agreement on Trade in Services (GATS) and the Current State of Play in the Doha Round of Trade Negotiations' 39(4) *International Lawyer* (Winter 2005)

Gloyens, P, 'The Landesbanks: How Long Can They Retain Competitive Advantage' 17(3) *Journal of International Banking Law* (2002)

Goebel, R J, 'European Economic and Monetary Union: Will the EMU Ever Fly?' 4 *Columbia Journal of European Law* (1998)

Gold, J, 'The International Monetary Fund and International Law. An Introduction', *International Monetary Fund Pamphlet Series* No 4, 1965

—— 'The Legal Structure of the Par Value System' 5 *Law and Policy in International Business* (1973)

—— 'Law and Reform of the International Monetary System' 10 *The Journal of International Law and Economics* (1975)

—— 'Uniformity as a Legal Principle of the International Monetary Fund' 7 *Law and Policy in International Business* (1975)

—— *A Report on Certain Legal Developments in the International Monetary Fund* (World Association of Lawyers, Washington DC, 1976)

—— 'A Third Report on Some Recent Legal Developments in the International Monetary Fund' (World Association of Lawyers, Washington DC, 1978)

—— 'Trust Funds in International Law: The Contribution of the International Monetary Fund to a Code of Principles' 72 *The American Journal of International Law* (1978)

—— 'Conditionality', *International Monetary Fund Pamphlet Series* No 31 (1979)

—— 'Symmetry as a Legal Objective of the International Monetary System' 12 *New York University Journal of International Law and Politics* (1980)

—— 'The Fund Agreement in the Courts—XV', *International Monetary Fund Staff Papers*, Vol 27, No 3 (1980)

—— 'The Legal Character of the Fund's Stand-by Arrangements and Why it Matters', *International Monetary Fund Pamphlet Series* No 35 (1980)

—— 'Gold in International Monetary Law: Change, Uncertainty and Ambiguity' 15 *The Journal of International Law and Economics* (1981)

—— 'Strengthening the Soft International Law of Exchange Arrangements' 77 *American Journal of International Law* (1983)

—— 'Legal Models for the International Regulation of Exchange Rates' 82 *Michigan Law Review* (1984)

—— 'Borrowing by the IMF' in Frenkel, J A, and Goldstein, M (eds), *International Financial Policy: Essays in Honour of Jacques J Polak* (International Monetary Fund and De Nederlandsche Bank, 1991)

—— *Interpretation: The IMF and International Law* (Kluwer Law International, 1996)

Goldman, S, 'Mavericks in the Market: The Emerging Problem of Hold-outs in Sovereign Debt Restructurings' 5 *UCLA Journal of International Law and Foreign Affairs* (2000)

Goldsmith J L, and Posner, E A, 'International Agreements: A Rational Choice Approach' 44 *Virginia Journal of International Law* (2003)

Golove, D, 'The New Confederalism: Treaty Delegations of Legislative, Executive and Judicial Authority' 55 *Stanford Law Review* (2003)

Gómez Giglio, G, 'Emergency Law and Financial Entities in Argentina' 10 *Journal of International Banking Law and Regulation* (2003)

Goode, R, *Commercial Law* (2nd edn, Penguin Books, 1995)

—— 'Rule, Practice and Pragmatism in Commercial Law' 54 *International Comparative Law Quarterly* (2005)

Goodhart, C A E, *The Evolution of Central Banks* (The MIT Press, 1988)

—— *Money, Information and Uncertainty* (2nd edn Macmillan, 1989)

—— *The Central Bank and the Financial System* (MIT Press, 1995)

—— 'The Transition to EMU' in Andenas, M, Gormley, L, Hadjiemmanuil, C, and Harden, I (eds), *European Economic and Monetary Union: The Institutional Framework* (Kluwer Law International, 1997)

—— 'Myths about the Lender of Last Resort' 2(3) *International Finance* (1999)

—— 'Time, Inflation and Asset Prices' (Financial Markets Group, Special Paper 117, London School of Economics, 1999)

—— 'The Organizational Structure of Banking Supervision' (LSE Financial Markets Group Special Paper 127, 2000)

—— (ed), *Which Lender of Last Resort For Europe?* (Central Banking Publications, 2000)

—— 'The Political Economy of Financial Harmonisation in Europe' in Kremer, J, Schoenmaker, D, and Wierts, P (eds), *Financial Supervision in Europe* (Edward Elgar, 2003)

—— 'Multiple Regulators and Resolutions', Paper presented at the Federal Reserve Bank of Chicago Conference on Systemic Financial Crises: Resolving Large Bank Insolvencies, 30 September—1 October 2004

—— and Huang, H, 'A Model of Lender of Last Resort' (Financial Markets Group of the London School of Economics, Discussion Paper 313, 1999)

—— and Meade, E, 'Central Banks and Supreme Courts 218 *Moneda y Crédito* (2004)

—— and Schoenmaker, D, 'Institutional Separation between Supervisory and Monetary Agencies' (LSE Financial Markets Group, Special Paper No 52, 1993)

—— and Schoenmaker, D, 'Should the Functions of Monetary Policy and Banking Supervision be Separated?' 47 *Oxford University Papers* (1995)

——, Hartmann, P, Llewellyn, D, and Rojas-Suarez, L (eds), *Financial Regulation: Why, How and Where Now?* (Routledge, 1998)

Grande, M, 'Possible Decentralisation of State Aid Control in the Banking Sector' presented at the EU Competition Workshop on State Aids in Florence in June 1999

Greenspan, A, 'Financial Innovations and the Supervision of Financial Institutions', Paper presented in Proceedings of the 31st Annual Conference on Bank Structure and Competition, Federal Reserve Bank of Chicago, May 1995)

Greenspan, A, 'Remarks at a Conference on Risk Measurement and Systemic Risk' (Board of Governors of the Federal Reserve System, Washington DC, 1995)

—— 'Issues for Monetary Policy' (speech to the Economic Club of New York, December 2000), at <http://www.federalreserve.gov/boarddocs/speeches/2002/20021219/default. htm> (visited 14 October 2003)

Grilli, V, Mascianddaro, D, and Tabellini, G, 'Political and Monetary Institutions and Public Financial Policies in the Industrial Countries' 13 *Economic Policy* (1991)

Gros, D, Mayer, T, and Ubide, A, 'EMU at risk', Seventh Annual Report of the CEPS Macroeconomic Policy Group, Centre for European Policy Studies, June 2005, at <http://www.ceps.be>

Group of Ten, *Report of the Working Group on Strengthening Financial Systems* (Bank for International Settlement, 1998)

Group of Thirty, *Derivatives: Practices and Principles* (Group of Thirty Special Report, 1993)

—— *Global Institutions, National Supervision and Systemic Risk, A Study Group Report* (Group of Thirty, 1997)

Gruson, M, 'The Scope of *Lex Monetae* in International Transactions: a United States Perspective' in Giovanoli, M (ed), *International Monetary Law: Issues for the New Millennium* (Oxford University Press, 2000)

—— 'Dollarisation and Euroisation', in *Current Developments in Monetary and Financial Law*, Vol 2 (International Monetary Fund, 2003)

Guitián, M, 'Fund Conditionality: Evolution of Principles and Practices', *International Monetary Fund Pamphlet Series* No 38 (1981)

—— 'The Unique Nature of the Responsibilities of the International Monetary Fund', *International Monetary Fund Pamphlet Series* No 46 (1993)

—— 'The IMF as a Monetary Institution: The Challenge Ahead', *Finance and Development*, International Monetary Fund, September, Vol 31, No 3 (1994)

—— 'Conditionality: Past, Present and Future', *International Monetary Fund Staff Papers*, Vol 42, No 4 (1995)

Guzman, A T, 'Capital Market Regulation in Developing Countries: A Proposal' 39 *Virginia Journal of International Law* (1999)

Hadjiemmanuil, C, 'European Monetary Union, the European System of Central Banks and Banking Supervision: A Neglected Aspect of the Maastricht Treaty' 5 *Tulane Journal of International and Comparative Law* (1997)

—— and Andenas, M, 'Banking Supervision and European Monetary Union' 1(2) *Journal of International Banking Regulation* (1999)

Hamilton, A, Madison, J, and Jay, J, *The Federalist Papers* (Mentor, New American Library, 1961; a reprint of the original McLean Edition of 1788)

Handl, G F, Reisman, M, Simma, B, Dupuy, P M, and Chinkin, C, 'A Hard Look at Soft Law' 82 *American Society of International Law Proceedings* (1998)

Hanke, S H, 'On Dollarization and Currency Boards: Error and Deception' 5 *Policy Reform* (2002)

—— 'Statement, International Economic and Exchange Rate Policy Hearings, before the Banking, Housing and Urban Affairs Committee of the United States Senate' (2002)

—— and Schuler, K, 'Currency Boards and Currency Convertibility', 12(3) *Cato Journal* (1993)

Herrmann, C W, 'Monetary Sovereignty over the Euro and External Relations of the Euro Area: Competences, Procedures and Practice', 7 *European Foreign Affairs Review* (2002)

Hillgenberg, H, 'A Fresh Look at Soft Law' 10 *European Journal of International Law* (1999)

Ho, C, *A Survey of the Institutional and Operational Aspects of Modern-Day Currency Boards* (Bank for International Settlements Monetary and Economic Department, 2002)

Hobbes, T, *Leviathan* (Collier, 1962)

Hochreiter, E H, and Siklos, P L (eds), 'From Floating to Monetary Union: The Economic Distance between Exchange Rate Regimes', *SUERF Studies* (SUERF (The European Money and Finance Forum), (2004)

Hodson, D, Begg, I, and Maher, I, 'Economic Policy Coordination in the European Union', *National Institute Economic Review*, 183 No 1 (January 2003)

—— and Maher, I, 'Hard, Soft and Open Methods of Policy Coordination and the Reform of the Stability and Growth Pact', Paper prepared for the Conference *Building EU Economic Government: Revising the Rules?*, organized by NYU in London and UACES, London, 25/26 April 2003

Holder, W E, 'The IMF's Technical Assistance Activities' in Robert Effros (ed), *Current Legal Issues Affecting Central Banks*, Vol 3 (International Monetary Fund, 1995)

—— 'On Being a Lawyer in the International Monetary Fund' in Robert Effros (ed), *Current Legal Issues Affecting Central Banks*, Vol 5 (International Monetary Fund, 1998)

Honohan, P, and Lane, P, 'Will the Euro Trigger More Monetary Unions in Africa?' in Wyplosz, C (ed), *The Impact of EMU on Europe and the Developing Countries* (Oxford University Press, 2001)

Horsefield, K, *The International Monetary Fund 1945–1965*, Vol 1, 'Chronicle' (International Monetary Fund, 1969)

—— (ed), *The International Monetary Fund 1945–1965*, Vol 3, 'Documents' (International Monetary Fund, 1969)

Hudson, M O (ed), *World Court Reports*, vol II (Carnegie Endowment for International Peace, 1935)

Humphrey, D B, 'Payments Finality and Risk of Settlement Failure' in Saunders, A, and White, L J (eds), *Technology and the Regulation of Financial Markets: Securities, Futures, and Banking* (Lexington Books, 1986)

Humphrey, T M, and Keleher, R E, 'The Lender of Last Resort: A Historical Perspective' 4(1) *Cato Journal* (1984)

Humphreys, N, *Historical Dictionary of the International Monetary Fund* (2nd edn, The Scarecrow Press, 1999)

INSOL International, Statement of Principles for a Global Approach to Multi-Creditor Workouts, available at <http://www.insol.org/statement.htm> (2000)

International Association of Insurance Supervisors, 'Insurance Core Principles and Methodology' (IAIS, 2003), available at <http://www.iaisweb.org/358icp03.pdf> (2003)

International Law Association, 'Report of the International Monetary Law Committee', Berlin Conference (2004), available at <http://www.ila-hq.org/pdf/Monetary-%20Law/2004%20Berlin%20report.pdf> (2004)

International Monetary Fund, 'Reports on Observance of Standard and Codes', available at <http://www.imf.org/external/np/rosc/rosc.asp>

International Monetary Fund, 'Financial Organization and Operations of the IMF', *International Monetary Fund Pamphlet Series* No 45 (2nd edn International Monetary Fund, 1991)

—— 'The IMF & the European Economic and Monetary Union', March 1999, available at <http://www.imf.org/external/np/exr/facts/emu.htm>

—— 'Summing Up by the Acting Chairman, Review of the Compensatory and Contingency Financing Facility (CCFF) and Buffer Stock Financing Facility (BSFF)—Preliminary Considerations' (BUFF/00/9, Executive Board Meeting 00/5, 14 January 2000), available at <http://www.imf.org/external/np/sec/buff/2000/0009.htm> (2000)

—— 'Review of Fund Facilities—Preliminary Considerations', prepared by the Policy Development and Review Department in consultation with other Departments, 2 March 2000, available at <http://www.imf.org/external/np/pdr/fac/2000/faciliti.pdf> (2000)

—— 'Review of Fund Facilities—Further Considerations', prepared by the Policy Development and Review and the Treasurer's Departments (in consultation with other Departments), 10 July 2000, available at <http://www.imf.org/external/np/pdr/roff/2000/eng/fc/index.htm#_ftn14> (2000)

—— 'Financial Organization and Operations of the IMF', International Monetary Fund *Pamphlet Series* No 45 (6th edn International Monetary Fund, 2001), available at <http://www.imf.org/external/pubs/ft/pam/pa,45/contents.htm>

—— 'Structural Conditionality in Fund-Supported Programs', prepared by the Policy Development and Review Department 16 February 2001, available at <http://www.imf.org/external/np/pdr/cond/2001/eng/struct/> (2001)

—— 'Trade Policy Conditionality in Fund-Supported Programs', prepared by the Policy Development and Review Department, 16 February 2001, available at <http://www.imf.org/external/np/pdr/cond/2001/eng/trade/> (2001)

—— 'Conditionality in Fund-Supported Programs—Overview', prepared by the Policy Development and Review Department, 20 February 2001, available at <http://www.imf.org/external/np/pdr/cond/2001/eng/overview/> (2001)

—— 'Strengthening IMF–World Bank Collaboration on Country Programs and Conditionality', prepared by PDR (IMF) and OPCS and PREM (World Bank), 23 August 2001, available at <http://www.imf.org/external/np/pdr/cond/2001/eng/collab/coll.htm> (2001)

—— 'Managing Director's Report to the International Monetary and Financial Committee—Streamlining Conditionality and Enhancing Ownership', 6 November 2001, available at <http://www.imf.org/external/np/omd/2001/110601.htm> (2001)

—— 'Strengthening Country Ownership of Fund-Supported Programs', prepared by the Policy Development and Review Department in consultation with other departments, 5 December 2001, available at <http://www.imf.org/external/np/pdr/cond/2001/eng/strength/120501.htm> (2001)

—— 'Draft Report of Executive Directors to the Board of Governors on the Twelfth General Review of Quotas', available at <http://www.imf.org/external/np/tre/quota/2002/eng/111820.htm> (2002)

—— 'The Modalities of Conditionality—Further Considerations', prepared by the Policy Development and Review Department, 8 January 2002, available at <http://www.imf.org/External/np/pdr/cond/2002/eng/modal/010802.htm> (2002)

516

—— 'Communiqué of the International Monetary and Financial Committee of the Board of Governors of the International Monetary Fund', 20 April 2002, available at <http://www.imf.org/external/np/sec/pr/2002/pr0222.htm> (2002)

—— 'Fund Policy on Lending into Arrears to Private Creditors—Further Consideration of the Good Faith Criterion', prepared by the International Capital Markets, Policy Development and Review and Legal Departments (in consultation with the other Departments), approved by Gerd Häusler, Timothy Geithner, and François Gianviti, 30 July 2002, available at <http://www.imf.org/external/pubs/ft/privcred/073002.pdf> (2002)

—— 'Proposals for a Sovereign Debt Restructuring Mechanism. A fact-sheet', available at <http://www.imf.org/external/np/exr/facts/sdrm/htm> (2003)

—— 'Standards and Codes: The Role of the IMF' (International Monetary Fund, 2003), available at <http://www.imf.org/external/np/exr/facts/sc.htm> (2003)

—— 'Proposals for a Sovereign Debt Restructuring Mechanism (SDRM). A Factsheet', January 2003, available at <http://www.imf.org/external/np/exr/facts/sdrm.htm> (2003)

—— 'IMF Board discusses possible features of a Sovereign Debt Restructuring Mechanism', PIN No 03/45, 3 April 2003, available at <http://www.imf.org/external/np/sec/pn/2003/pn0345.htm> (2003)

—— 'Fifth Review of the Fund's Standards Initiative', Paper prepared by the Statistics Department in consultation with other Departments (approved by Carols Carson), 18 June 2003, available at <http://www.imf.org/external/np/sta/dsbb/2003/eng/061803.pdf> (2003)

—— 'Report on the Evaluation of Poverty Reduction Strategy Papers (PRSPs) and The Poverty Reduction and Growth Facility (PRGF)', available at <http://www.imf.org/External/NP/ieo/2004/prspprgf/eng/index.htm> (2004)

—— 'Financial Risk in the Fund and the Level of Precautionary Balances', prepared by the Finance Department (in consultation with other Departments), approved by Eduard Brau, 3 February 2004, available at <http://www.imf.org/external/np/tre/risk/2004/020304.pdf>

—— 'Review of the Compensatory Financing Facility', prepared by the Policy Development and Review Department in Consultation with other Departments, approved by Mark Allen, 18 February 2004, available at <http://www.imf.org/external/np/pdr/ccff/eng/2004/021804.pdf> (2004)

—— 'The IMF's Contingent Credit Lines (CCL). A Factsheet', March 2004, available at <http://www.imf.org/external/np/exr/facts/ccl.htm> (2004)

—— 'Interview with Mark Allen: IMF needs to do far more to help countries learn from each other's successes and failures', *International Monetary Fund Survey*, Vol 33, No 7, 12 April 2004, available at <http://www.imf.org/external/pubs/ft/survey/2004/041204.pdf> (2004)

—— 'IMF Executive Board Approves Trade Integration Mechanism', Press Release No 04/73', 13 April 2004, available at <http://www.imf.org/external/np/sec/pr/2004/pr0473.htm> (2004)

—— 'IMF Executive Board Discusses Euro Area Policies', PIN No 04/79, 3 August 2004

—— 'IMF Borrowing Arrangements: GAB and NAB: A Factsheet', September 2004, available at <http://www.imf.org/external/np/exr/facts/gabnab.htm>

—— 'IMF Emergency Assistance: Supporting Recovery from Natural Disasters and Armed Conflicts. A Factsheet', September 2004, available at <http://www.imf.org/external/np/exr/facts/conflict.htm> (2004)

International Monetary Fund, 'IMF Lending: A Factsheet', September 2004, available at <http://www.imf.org/external/np/exr/facts/howlend.htm> (2004)

—— 'Debt Relief under the Heavily Indebted Poor Countries (HIPC) Initiative. A Fact-sheet', available at <http://www.imf.org/external/np/exr/facts/hipc.htm> (2005)

—— 'Executive Board Review of the Experience with the Financial Sector Assessment Program', 6 April 2005, PIN No 05/47, available at <http://www.imf.org/external/np/sec/pn/2005/pn0547.htm> (2005)

—— 'Financial Sector Assessment Program (FSAP)', available at <http://www.imf.org/external/np/fsap/fsap.asp> (2005)

—— 'IMF Executive Board Approves the Establishment of Policy Support Instruments for Aiding Low-Income Countries', PIN No 05/145, 14 October 2005, available at <http://www.imf.org/external/np/sec/pn/2005/pn05145.htm> (2005)

—— 'Poverty Reduction Strategy Papers, PRSPs. A fact-sheet', February 2005, available at <http://www.imf.org/external/np/exr/facts/prsp.htm> (2005)

—— 'Review of the Fund's Strategy on Overdue Financial Obligations', 24 August 2005, available at <http://www.imf.org/external/np/pp/eng/2005/082405.htm> (2005)

—— *Selected Decisions of the International Monetary Fund* (29th edn, International Monetary Fund, 2005)

—— 'The Exogenous Shocks Facility (ESF). A fact-sheet', available at <http://www.imf.org/external/np/exr/facts/mdri.htm> (2005)

—— 'The Multilateral Debt Relief Initiative (MDRI). A fact-sheet', available at <http://www.imf.org/external/np/exr/facts/mdri.htm> (2005)

—— 'Financial Sector Assessment Program', available at <http://www.imf.org/external/np/fsap/fsap.asp> (2006)

—— and the World Bank, 'The Standards and Codes Initiative—Is it Effective? And How Can it be Improved?', 1 July 2005, available at <http://www.imf.org/external/np/pp/eng/2005/070105a.htm> (2005)

International Monetary Fund Independent Evaluation Office, 'Report on the Evaluation of the IMF's Approach to Capital Account Liberalization', 25 May 2005, available at <http://www.imf.org/ieo>

International Organization of Securities Commission, 'Objectives and Principles of Securities Regulation' (IOSCO, 2003), available at <http://www.iosco.org/pubdocs/pdf/IOSCOPD154.pdf> (2003)

Jacklin, C, and Bhattacharya, S, 'Distinguishing Panics and Information-based Bank Runs: Welfare and Policy Implications' 96 *Journal of Political Economy* (1988)

Jackson, J, Davey, W, and Sykes, A (eds), *Legal Problems of International Economic Relations* (3rd edn, West Publishing Co, 1995)

Jackson, H E, 'The Selective Incorporation of Foreign Legal Systems to Promote Nepal as an International Financial Services Centre' in McCrudden, C (ed), *Regulation and Deregulation—Policy and Practice in the Utilities and Financial Services Industries* (Oxford University Press, 1998)

—— and Symons, E L, *Regulation of Financial Institutions* (West Group, 1999)

Jackson, J, *The World Trade Organization: Constitution and Jurisprudence* (Royal Institute of International Affairs, 1998)

James, A, *Sovereign Statehood* (Allen & Unwin, 1986)

James, H, *International Monetary Cooperation since Bretton Woods* (International Monetary Fund and Oxford University Press, 1996)

Jeanne, O, 'The IMF: An International Lender of Last Resort', available at <http://www.imf.org/external/pubs/ft/irb/2000/eng/02/index.htm> (2000)

Jonk, A, Kremers, J, and Schoenmaker, D, 'A New Dutch Model' *Financial Regulator*, Vol 6, No 3, December 2001

Jordan, C, and Majnoni, G, *Financial Regulatory Harmonization and the Globalization of Finance* (World Bank, 2002)

Kahn-Freund, O, 'On Use and Misuse of Comparative Law' 37 *Modern Law Review* (1974)

Kaufman, G, 'Bank Contagion: A Review of the Theory and Evidence' 8 *Journal of Financial Services Research* (1994)

—— 'Bank Failures, Systemic Risk and Bank Regulation' 6(1) *Cato Journal* (1996), available at <http://www.cato.org/pubs/journal/cj16n1–2.html>

—— and Scott, K E, 'What is Systemic Risk and Do Bank Regulators Retard or Contribute to It?' 7 *The Independent Review* (2003)

Kenen, P, 'The Theory of Optimum Currency Areas: an Eclectic View' in Mundell, R, and Swoboda, A (eds), *Monetary Problems of the International Economy* (Chicago University Press, 1969)

—— 'The Role of the Dollar as an International Currency', *Occasional Papers* No 13, (Group of Thirty, 1983)

—— *Managing Exchange Rates* (Routledge, 1988)

—— *EMU and ESCB after Maastricht* (Financial Markets Group of the London School of Economics, 1992)

—— (ed), 'From Halifax to Lyons: What has been done about crises management?' *Essays in International Finance* No 200 (Princeton University, 1996)

—— 'The International Financial Architecture: Old Issues and New Initiatives' 5 *International Finance* (2002)

Keynes, J M, *The Economic Consequences of the Peace* (Macmillan, 1919)

Khan, M S, and Sharma, S, *Conditionality and Country Ownership of Programs* (International Monetary Fund, 2001)

Kindleberger, C P, *Manias, Panics and Crashes. A History of Financial Crises* (John Wiley & Sons, 1996; originally published in 1978)

King, M, and Wadhwani, S, 'Transmission of Volatility between Stock Markets' 3 *Review of Financial Studies* (1990)

Kirton, J J, 'The G20: Representativeness, Effectiveness and Leadership in Global Governance', in Kirton, J J, Daniels, J P, and Freytag, A (eds), *Guiding Global Order: G8 Governance in the Twenty-First Century* (Aldershot, 2001)

Knight, M, Petersen, A B, and Price, R T (eds), *Central Bank Reforms in the Baltics, Russia and the other Countries of the Former Soviet Union* (International Monetary Fund, 1997)

Kremers, J, Schoenmaker, D, and Wierts, P J (eds), *Financial Supervision in Europe* (Edward Elgar Publishing, 2001)

—— and Schoenmaker, D, and Wierts, P J, 'Cross Border Supervision: Which Model?' in Herring, R, and Litan, R (eds), *Brookings-Wharton Papers on Financial Services* (Brookings Institution, Washington DC, 2003)

Krueger, A, 'International Financial Architecture for 2002: A New Approach to Sovereign Debt Restructuring', address at the National Economists' Club Annual Members' Dinner, American Enterprise Institute, Washington DC, 26 November 2001, available at <http://www.imf.org/external/np/speeches/2001/112601.htm>

Krueger, A, 'New Approaches to Sovereign Debt Restructuring: An Update on Our Thinking', Conference on 'Sovereign Debt Workouts: Hopes and Hazards', Institute for International Economics, Washington DC, 1 April 2002, available at <http://www.imf.org/external/np/speeches/2002/040102.htm>

—— and Hagan, S, 'Sovereign Workouts: and IMF Perspective' 6 *Chicago Journal of International Law* (2005)

Krugman, P, 'Can Deflation be Prevented?' available at, <http://www.pkarchive.org/economy/deflator.html> (visited 23 February 2004)

Kumar, M S, Baig, T, Decressin, J, Faulkner-MacDonagh, C, and Feyzioğlu, T, 'Deflation: Determinants, Risks and Policies', *Occasional Paper* No 221 (International Monetary Fund, 2003)

—— 'Deflation, the New Threat?', *Finance and Development*, International Monetary Fund, June 2003, at p 16, available at <http://www.imf.org/external/pubs/ft/fandd/2003/06/pdf/kumar.pdf>

Kydland, F E, and Prescott, E C, 'Rules rather than Discretion: The Inconsistency of Optimal Plans' 86 *Journal of Political Economy* (1977)

Lamfalussy, A, 'Reflections on the Regulation of European Securities Markets', *SUERF Studies* (SUERF (The European Money and Finance Forum), 2001)

—— interview published in *The Guardian*, 16 August 2003

Lanno, K, *EU Securities Market Regulation. Adapting to the Needs of a Single Capital Market* (Centre for European Policy Studies Task Force, 2001)

—— *Supervising the European Financial System* (Centre for European Policy Studies, Policy Brief No 21, 2002)

—— and Casey, J P, 'Financial Regulation and Supervision Beyond 2005', *CEPS Task Force Report* No 54 (2005)

Lastra, R M, 'The Independence of the European System of Central Banks' 33 *Harvard International Law Journal* (1992)

—— *Central Banking and Banking Regulation* (Financial Markets Group, London School of Economics, 1996)

—— 'The Accountability of the Bank of England', ordered by the House of Commons to be printed, 23 October 1997, House of Commons, Session 1997–98, HC 282

—— 'The City's Troubleshooter: Interview with Howard Davies' 5(3) *Parliamentary Brief* (1998)

—— 'Lender of Last Resort, an International Perspective', *International and Comparative Law Quarterly*, Vol 48 (1999)

—— 'The Division of Responsibilities Between the European Central Bank and the National Central Banks Within the European System of Central Banks', *The Columbia Journal of European Law*, Vol 6, No 2, Spring 2000

—— 'The International Monetary Fund in Historical Perspective' 3 *Journal of International Economic Law* (2000)

—— 'Cross-Border Trade in Financial Services', in Fletcher, I, Mistelis, L, and Cremona, M (eds), *Foundations and Perspectives of International Trade Law* (Sweet & Maxwell, 2001)

—— 'How Much Accountability for Central Banks and Supervisors?' 12(2) *Central Banking* (2001)

—— (ed), *The Reform of the International Financial Architecture* (Kluwer Law International, 2001)

—— 'IMF Conditionality' 4(2) *Journal of International Banking Regulation* (2002)

—— 'Cross-Border Bank Insolvency: Legal Implications in the Case of Banks Operating in Different Jurisdictions in Latin America' 6(1) *Journal of International Economic Law* (2003)

—— 'Regulating European Securities Markets: Beyond the Lamfalussy Report' in Andenas, M, and Avreginos, Y (eds), *Financial Markets in Europe: Towards a Single Regulator?* (Kluwer Law International, 2003)

—— 'The Governance Structure for Financial Regulation and Supervision in Europe', *The Columbia Journal of European Law*, Vol 10, No 1, Fall 2003

—— and Arner, D W, 'Comparative Aspects of Depositor Protection Schemes:' in Arner, D W, and Lin, J-J (eds), *Financial Regulation, A Guide to Structural Reform* (Sweet & Maxwell Asia, 2003)

—— and Miller, G, 'Central Bank Independence in Ordinary and Extraordinary Times' in Kleineman, J (ed), *Central Bank Independence. The Economic Foundations, the Constitutional Implications and Democratic Accountability* (Kluwer Law International, 2001)

—— and Shams, H, 'Public Accountability in the Financial Sector' in Ferran, E, and Goodhart, C (eds), *Regulating Financial Services and Markets in the 21st century* (Hart Publishing, 2001)

Latin American Shadow Financial Regulatory Committee, Statement No 4, Montevideo, 18 October 2001, 'Central Bank Independence: the Right Choice for Latin America', available at <http://www.aei.org>

Lawson, G, 'The Rise and Rise of the Administrative State' 107 *Harvard Law Review* (1994)

Leckow, R, 'Conditionality in the International Monetary Fund' in *Current Developments in Monetary and Financial Law*, Vol 3 (International Monetary Fund, 2005)

—— 'The Obligation of Members to Provide Information to the International Monetary Fund under Article VIII, Section 5: Recent Developments' in *Current Developments in Monetary and Financial Law*, Vol 4 (International Monetary Fund, 2005)

Lefort, D, 'Central Bank Ownership Issues', a presentation given in the Central Banking Annual Training Course, organized by Central Banking Publications (Cambridge, 7 September 2005)

Lichtenstein, C, 'International Jurisdiction over International Capital Flows and the Role of the IMF: Plus ça Change?' in Giovanoli, M (ed), *International Monetary Law: Issues for the New Millennium* (Oxford University Press, 2000)

—— 'Hard Law v. Soft Law: Unnecessary Dichotomy?' 35 *International Lawyer* (2001)

Lipson, C, 'Why are Some International Agreements Informal?' 45 *International Organization* (1991)

Lipworth, G, and Nystedt, J, 'Crisis Resolution and Private Sector Adaptation', Paper presented at the IMF's First Annual Research Conference, held in Washington, November 2000

Litan, R, and Nordhaus, W, *Reforming Federal Regulation* (Yale University Press, 1983)

Llewellyn, D, *International Financial Integration: The Limits of Sovereignty* (John Wiley & Sons, 1980)

Locke, J, *Two Treatises of Government* (New American Library 1965)

López Escudero, M, *El Euro en el Sistema Monetario Internacional* (Tecnos, 2004)

López Sandoval, E L, *Sovereign Debt Restructuring: Should We Be Worried About Elliot?*, Harvard Law School, available at <http://www.law.harvard.edu/programs/pifs/pdfs/eduardo_sandoval.pdf>

Louis, J-V, 'The New Monetary Law of the European Union' in Giovanoli, M (ed), *International Monetary Law: Issues for the New Millennium* (Oxford University Press, 2000)

Louis, J-V, 'The Economic and Monetary Union: Law and Institutions' 41 *Common Market Law Review* (2004)

—— 'Monetary Policy and Central Banking in the Constitution', *Legal Aspects of the European System of Central Banks, Liber Amicorum Paolo Zamboni Garavelli* (European Central Bank, 2005)

Lowenfeld, A, *International Economic Law* (Oxford University Press, 2002)

—— 'The International Monetary System and the Erosion of Sovereignty. Essay in Honor of Cynthia Lichtenstein' 25 *Boston College International and Comparative Law Review* (2002)

Lucatelli, A, *Finance and World Order—Financial Fragility, Systemic Risk and Transnational Regimes* (Greenwood Press, 1997)

Ludwikowski, R R, 'Supreme Law or Basic Law? The Decline of the Concept of Constitutional Supremacy' 9 *Cardozo Journal of International and Comparative Law* (2001)

Macey, J R, and Miller, G P, *Banking Law and Regulation* (Boston: Little Brown and Company, 1992)

Macey, J R, Miller, G P, and Carnell, R S, *Banking Law and Regulation* (Aspen Law & Business, 2001)

Machiavelli, N, *The Prince* (Collier & Son 1909–14, The Harvard Classics, vol 36, pt I), available at <http://www.bartleby.com/36/1/>

Majone, G, *Independence versus Accountability? Non-Majoritarian Institutions and Democratic Government in Europe* (European University Institute, EUI Working Paper, 1994)

Mann, F A, *The Legal Aspect of Money* (5th edn, Clarendon Press, 1992)

Manuel, T A, 'Africa and the Washington Consensus. Finding the Right Path' 40(3) *Finance and Development* (2003), available at <http://www.imf.org/external/pubs/ft/fandd/2003/09/pdf/manuel.pdf>

Marmorstein, V E, 'Responding to the Call for Order in International Finance: Co-operation between the International Monetary Fund and Commercial Banks' 18 *Virginia Journal of International Law* (1978)

Marsh, D, *The Most Powerful Bank: Inside Germany's Bundesbank* (Times Books, 1992)

Mason, E S, and Asher, R E, *The World Bank since Bretton Woods* (The Brookings Institution, 1973)

Mathernová, K, 'The World Bank and Legal Technical Assistance: Initial Lessons', World Bank Policy Research Working Paper No 1414, Legal Department, World Bank January 1995, available at <http://ssrn.com/abstract=620591>

Mayes, D, and Liuksila, A (eds), *Who Pays for Bank Insolvency?* (Palgrave, MacMillan, 2004)

McKinnon, R, 'Optimum Currency Areas' 53 *American Economic Review* (1963)

—— 'Private and Official International Money: The Case for the Dollar', *Essays in International Finance*, No 74 (Princeton University, 1969)

—— 'Mundell, the Euro and Optimum Currency Areas', 22 May 2000, available at <http://www-econ.stanford.edu/faculty/works/swp00009pdf> (visited 17 May 2004)

McNamara, K R, and Meunier, S, 'Between National Sovereignty and International Power: What External Voice for the Euro' 78 *International Affairs* (2002)

Millán Pereira, J L, 'Economic Restructuring and the European Monetary Union' 9 *University of Miami International and Comparative Law Review* (2001)

Miller, G P, Independent Agencies', *Supreme Court Review* (1986)

—— 'Constitutional Moments, Pre-commitment, and Fundamental Reform. The Case of Argentina' 71 *Washington University Law Quarterly* (1993)

—— 'An Interest Group Theory of Central Bank Independence' 17 *Journal of Legal Studies* (1998)

Minksy, H P, *John Maynard Keynes* (Columbia University Press, 1975)

—— 'The Financial Stability Hypothesis: Capitalistic Processes and Behaviour of the Economy' in Kindleberger, C, and Laffargue, J P (eds), *Financial Crises: Theory, History and Policy* (Cambridge University Press, 1982)

Mishkin, F, 'Comment on Systemic Risk' in Kaufman, G (ed), *Research in Financial Services: Banking, Financial Markets and Systemic Risk* (JAI Press, 1995) vol 7

Mistelis, L, 'Regulatory Aspects: Globalization, Harmonisation, Legal Transplants and Law Reform—Preliminary Remarks' in Lastra, R (ed), *The Reform of the International Financial Architecture* (Kluwer Law International, 2001)

Mitu Gulati, G, and Klee, K N, 'Sovereign Piracy', UCLA, School of Law Research Paper No 01–7, available at <http://www.law.ucla.edu/faculty/bios/klee/kleeeicfinal.htm#_edn3>

Mohamed, S, *European Community Law on the Free Movement of Capital and the EMU* (Kluwer Law International, 1999)

Moloney, N, *EC Securities Regulation* (Oxford University Press, 2002)

Montesquieu, C de, *The Spirit of Laws* (2 vol: G Bell & Sons, 1878 and 1909)

Monti, M, *Toughen Up the Reform Agenda and Make it Count*, Financial Times, 22 March 2005

Morgenthau, H, Jr (US Treasury Secretary and Permanent Secretary of the Conference) at the Inaugural Plenary Session, 1 July 1944, *United Nations Monetary and Financial Conference, Bretton Woods, New Hampshire, July 1 to July 22, 1944: Final Act and Related Documents* (US Government Printing Office, 1944)

Mortelmans, K, 'The Common Market, the Internal Market and the Single Market, What's in a Market?' 35 CMLR (1998)

Mullock, C, 'Sovereign Debt Restructuring Proposals and Their Effects on Emerging Market Debt Instruments', *The Chazen Web Journal of International Business* (Columbia Business School, 2003), available at <http://www2.gsb.columbia.edu/journals/files/chazen/SDR_proof.pdf>

Munchau, W, 'Return to Keynes', Financial Times, 26 October 1998

—— 'Eurozone Faces Risks if Inflation Rates Stay Out of Line', Financial Times, 31 May 2004

—— 'Is the Euro forever? As the strains turn to pain, its foundations look far from secure', Financial Times, 8 June 2005

Mundell, R A, 'A Theory of Optimum Currency Areas' 51 *American Economic Review* (1961)

—— 'The European Monetary System 50 Years after Bretton Woods: A Comparison Between Two Systems', Paper presented at Project Europe 1985–95, the tenth edition of the 'Incontri di Rocca Salimbeni' meetings, in Siena, 25 November 1994 available at <http://www.columbia.edu/~ram15/ABrettwds.htm>

—— 'Optimum Currency Areas', extended version of a luncheon speech presented at a 'Conference on Optimum Currency Areas', Tel Aviv University, 5 December 1997, available at <http://www.columbia.edu/~ram15/eOCATAviv4.html>

—— 'Money and the Sovereignty of the State', in Leijonhufvud, A (ed), *Monetary Theory and Policy Experience* (Palgrave, 2001, in association with the International Economic Association)

—— 'Monetary Unions and the Problem of Sovereignty' 579 *The Annals of the American Academy of Political and Social Science* (2002)

Munzberg, R, 'Issues Regarding the Special Drawing Right of the International Monetary Fund' in Effros, R (ed), *Current Legal Issues Affecting Central Banks*, Vol 4 (International Monetary Fund, 1997)

Naím, M, 'Latin America: The Second Stage of Reform' in Diamond, L, and Plattner, M F (eds), *Economic Reform and Democracy* (Johns Hopkins University Press, 1995)

Newman, P, Milgate, M, and Eatwell, J, *New Palgrave Dictionary of Money and Finance* (Macmillan Press Ltd, 1992)

Nierop, E, and Stenström, M, 'Cross-Border Aspects of Insolvency Proceedings for Credit Institutions—A Legal Perspective', Paper presented at an International Seminar on Legal and Regulatory Aspects of Financial Stability, Basel, January 2002

Nieto, M, 'Comments on a paper presented by Kahn and Santos on "Allocating Bank Regulatory Powers: Lender of Last Resort, Deposit Insurance and Supervision" at the Bank of Finland Conference on "The Structure of Financial Regulation" ', September 2004, available at <http://www.bof.fi/eng/7_tutkimus/MariasWritten CommentsOnKahnSantos.pdf>

Nolan, J, 'Emerging Market Debt & Vulture Hedge Funds: Free-Ridership, Legal & Market Remedies', *Financial Policy Forum, Derivatives Study Center*, Special Policy Report 3, 29 September 2001, available at <http://www.financialpolicy.org/ DSCNolan.htm>

Norman, P, 'Finance Minister in Waiting', Financial Times, 4 October 1998

—— *The Accidental Constitution. The Story of the European Convention* (EuroComment, 2003)

North, D C, *Institutions, Institutional Change and Economic Performance* (Cambridge University Press, 1990)

Norton, J, *Bank Regulation and Supervision in the 1990s* (Lloyd's of London Press, 1991)

—— *Financial Sector Law Reform in Emerging Economies* (The British Institute of International and Comparative Law and the London Institute of International Banking, Finance and Development Law, 2000)

—— and Sarie-Eldin, H, 'Securities Law Models in Emerging Economies' in Norton, J J, and Andenas, A (eds), *Emerging Financial Markets and the Role of International Financial Organizations* (Kluwer Law International, 1996)

Ohmae, K, *The End of the Nation-State* (Simon & Schuster, 1996)

Oliver, D, 'Law, Politics and Public Accountability: The Search for a New Equilibrium', *Public Law* (1994)

Olsson, C, and Roman, J-C, *A Harmonized Price Index for Owner Occupied Housing. Experiences from the Eurostat Pilot Study*, Paper submitted by Eurostat at the joint UNECE/ILO Meeting on Consumer Price Indices in Geneva on 4–5 December 2003, available at <http://www.unece.org/stats/documents/ces/ac.49/2003/17.e.pdf> (visited 24 February 2004)

Oosterloo, S, and Schoenmaker, D, 'A Lead Supervisor Model for Europe', *The Financial Regulator*, Vol 9, No 3 (2004)

Organisation for Economic Cooperation and Development Financial Action Task Force on Money Laundering, 'Non-Cooperative Countries and Territories' (OECD Financial Action Task Force, 2004), available at <http://www1.oecd.org/fatf/ NCCT_en.htm#List> (2004)

—— 'List of Uncooperative Tax Havens', available at <http://www.oecd.org/ document/57/0,2340,en_2649_33745_30578809_1_1_1_37427,00.html>

Padoa-Schioppa, T, 'EMU and Banking Supervision', Lecture at the London School of Economics (24 February 1999), available in Goodhart, C (ed), *Which Lender of Last Resort for Europe?* (Central Banking Publications, 2000)

—— *The Road to Monetary Union in Europe: The Emperor, the Kings and the Genies* (Oxford University Press, 2000)

—— 'Central Banks and Financial Stability. Exploring a Land in Between', Speech delivered in the European Central Bank's Second Central Banking Conference 'The Transformation of the European Financial System', 24–25 October 2002, available at <http://www.ecb.int/home/conf/cbc2/tps.pdf>

—— *Regulating Finance* (Oxford University Press, 2004)

—— and Saccomanni, F, 'Managing a Market-Led Global Financial System' in Kenen, P K (ed), *Managing the World Economy Fifty Years After Bretton Woods* (Institute of International Economics, 1994)

Pardy, R, *Institutional Reform in Emerging Securities Markets* (The World Bank, 1992)

Parker, G, 'EU Agrees a Financial Crisis Plan', Financial Times, 16 May 2005

Parkin, M, and Bade, R, *Central Bank Laws and Monetary Policies: A Preliminary Investigation*, Research Report No 7804 (University of Western Ontario, November 1977)

Partnoy, F, 'Why Markets Crash and What Law Can Do About It' 61 *University of Pittsburgh Law Review* (2000)

Pohl, G, Jedrzejczak, G T, and Anderson, R E, *Creating Capital Markets in Central and Eastern Europe* (World Bank, 1995)

Polak, J, 'The Articles of Agreement of the IMF and the Liberalization of Capital Movements' in Fischer, S, Cooper, R, Dornbusch, R, Garber, P, Massad, C, Polak, J, Rodrik, D, and Tarapore, S, 'Should the IMF Pursue Capital Account Convertibility?', *Essays in International Finance* No 207 (Princeton University, 1998)

—— 'Streamlining the Financial Architecture of the International Monetary Fund', *Essays in International Finance* No 216 (Princeton University, 1999)

Porter, T, 'The G-7, the Financial Stability Forum, the G-20 and the Politics of International Financial Regulation' Paper prepared for the International Studies Association Annual Meeting, Los Angeles, California, 15 March 2000

Proctor, C, *The Euro and the Financial Markets, The Legal Impact of EMU* (Jordans, 1999)

—— *Mann on the Legal Aspect of Money* (6th edn, Oxford University Press, 2005)

Quinn, B, 'Rules v Discretion: The Case for Banking Supervision in the Light of the Debate on Monetary Policy' in Goodhart, C A E (ed), *The Emerging Framework of Financial Regulation* (Central Banking Publications, 1998)

Quintyn, M, and Taylor, M W, 'Regulatory and Supervisory Independence and Financial Stability' 49 *CESifo Economic Studies* (2003), available at <http://www.cesifo.de/pls/guestci/download/CESifo+Economic+Studies+2003./CESifo+Economic+Studies+2/2003./econstudies-2-03-S259.pdf>

Robicheck, W E, 'The International Monetary Fund: An Arbiter in the Debt Restructuring Process' 23 *Columbia Journal of Transnational Law* (1984)

Rochet, J-C, and Tirole, J, 'Interbank Lending and Systemic Risk' 28 *Journal of Money, Credit and Banking* (1996)

Rodrik, D, 'Who Needs Capital Account Convertibility?' in Fischer, S, Cooper, R, Dornbusch, R, Garber, P, Massad, C, Polak, J, Rodrik, D, and Tarapore, S, 'Should the IMF Pursue Capital Account Convertibility?', *Essays in International Finance* No 207 (Princeton University, 1998)

—— and Subramanian, A, 'The Primacy of Institutions' 40 *Finance and Development* (2003), available at <http://www.imf.org/external/pubs/ft/fandd/2003/06/pdf/rodrik.pdf>

Rodrik, D, Subramanian, A, and Trebbi, F, *Institutions Rule: The Primacy of Institutions and Integration in Economic Development*. NBER Working Paper No 9305 (NBER, 2002)

Rojas-Suárez, L, and Weisbrod, S R, 'Banking Crises in Latin America: Experience and Issues', Paper presented at the Inter-American Development Bank Group of Thirty Conference on Banking Crises in Latin America, Washington DC, 1995

Rolnick, A, and Weber, W, 'Inherent Instability in Banking: The Free Banking Experience' 5(3) *Cato Journal* (1986)

Rose, A, 'Explaing Exchange-Rate Volatility: An Empirical Analysis of the "Holy Trinity" of Monetary Independence, Fixed Exchange Rates and Capital Mobility' 15 *Journal of International Money and Finance* (2003)

Sachs, J, 'Do We Need an International Lender of Last Resort?', Frank D Graham Lecture, Princeton University, 1995, available at <http://www.earthinstitute. columbia.edu/about/director/pubs/intllr.pdf>

Sainz de Vicuña, A, 'The Concept of Money in the XXIst Century', Paper presented at the MOCOMILA meeting in Tokyo on 1 April 2004

Salacuse, J W, 'The Legal Architecture of Emerging Markets' in Lastra, R M (ed), *The Reform of the International Financial Architecture* (Kluwer Law International, 2001)

Salzberger, E M, and Voigt, S, 'On Constitutional Processes and the Delegation of Power, with Special Emphasis on Israel and Central and Eastern Europe' 3 *Theoretical Inquiries in Law* (2002)

Santiprabhob, V, *Bank Soundness and Currency Board Arrangements: Issues and Experience* International Monetary Fund Working Paper No PPAA/97/11 (International Monetary Fund, 1997)

Sarkar, R, *Development Law and International Finance* (Kluwer Law International, 1999)

Schiffman, H N, 'Legal Measures to Manage Bank Insolvency in Economies in Transition' in Lastra, R M, and Schiffman, H N (eds), *Bank Failures and Bank Insolvency Law in Economies in Transition* (Kluwer Law International, 1999)

Schinassi, G, *Safeguarding Financial Stability. Theory and Practice* (International Monetary Fund, 2006)

——, Craig, R S, Drees, B, and Kramer, C, *Modern Banking and OTC Derivatives Markets—The Transformation of Global Finance and its Implications for Systemic Risk*, International Monetary Fund Occasional Paper No 203 (International Monetary Fund, 2000)

Schoenmaker, D, *Contagion Risk in Banking*, LSE Financial Markets Group, Discussion Paper No 239 (Financial Markets Group, 1996)

—— 'What Kind of Financial Stability for Europe?' in Goodhart, C (ed), *Which Lender of Last Resort for Europe?* (Central Banking Publications, 2000)

—— 'Financial Supervision: from National to European?' *Financial and Monetary Studies*, Vol 22, No 1 (NIBE-SVV, 2003)

Schröder, G, 'A Framework for a Stable Europe', Financial Times, 17 January 2005

Schwartz, A J, 'Real and Pseudo-Financial Crises' in Capie, F and Wood, G E (eds), *Financial Crises and the World Banking System* (Macmillan, 1986)

—— 'The Misuse of the Fed's Discount Window' 75(4) *Federal Reserve Bank of St Louis Review* (1992)

Scott, H, 'A Bankruptcy Procedure for Sovereign Debtors?' 37 *The International Lawyer* (2003)

Servais, D, and Ruggeri, R, 'The EU Constitution: its Impact on Economic and Monetary Union and Economic Governance' in *Legal Aspects of the European System of Central Banks, Liber Amicorum Paolo Zamboni Garavelli* (European Central Bank, 2005)

Seyad, S M, 'Destabilisation of the European Stability and Growth Pact' 19 *Journal of International Banking Law and Regulation* (2004)

Sheldon, G, and Maurer, M, 'Inter-Bank Lending and Systemic Risk: An Empirical Analysis for Switzerland' 134 *Swiss Journal of Economics and Statistics* (1998)

Shelton, D, 'The Impact of Globalization on the International Legal System', Paper presented at the conference at the University of Sydney, 'Globalisation and its Challenges', Sydney, 12–14 December 2001, available at <http://www.econ.usyd.edu.au/global/images/papers.pdf> (2004)

Shuster, M R, *The Public International Law of Money* (Clarendon Press 1973)

Simmons, B A, 'Money and the Law: Why Comply with the Public International Law of Money?' 25 *Yale Journal of International Law* (2000)

Simons, H C, 'Rules versus Authorities in Monetary Policy' 44 *Journal of Political Economy* (1936)

Slot, P, 'The Institutional Provisions of the EMU' in Curtin, D, and Heukels, T (eds), *Institutional Dynamics of European Integration. Essays in honour of Henry G. Schemers*, Vol II (Martinus Nijhoff, 1994)

Smith, V C, *The Rationale of Central Banking and the Free Banking Alternative* (Liberty Press, 1990)

Smits, R, *The European Central Bank. Institutional Aspects* (Kluwer Law International, 1997)

—— *The European Central Bank in the European Constitutional Order* (Eleven International Publishing, 2003)

—— 'The European Constitution and EMU: an Appraisal' 42 *Common Market Law Review* (2005)

—— 'The Role of the ESCB in Banking Supervision', *Legal Aspects of the European System of Central Banks, Liber Amicorum Paolo Zamboni Garavelli* (European Central Bank, 2005)

Stacey, H, 'Relational Sovereignty' 55 *Stanford Law Review* (2003)

Stanford Encyclopedia of Philosophy, available at <http://www.plato.stanford.edu>

Steinberg, R H, 'In the Shadow of Law or Power? Consensus-based Bargaining and Outcomes in the GATT/WTO' 56 *International Organization* (2002)

Steinberger, H, 'Sovereignty' in *Encyclopedia of Public International Law*, vol 10 (North Holland, 1987)

Stern, K, 'Staatsorgane, Staatsfunktionen, Finanz- und Haushaltsverfassung, Notstandsverfassung' in *Das Staatsrecht der Bundesrepublik Deutschland*, vol II (C H Beck, 1980)

Stiglitz, J, 'Boats, planes and capital flows', Financial Times, 25 March 1998

—— 'Capital Market Liberalization, Globalization and the IMF' 20 *Oxford Review of Economic Policy* (2005)

Strange, S, *The Retreat of the State: The Diffusion of Power in the World Economy* (Cambridge University Press, 1996)

Strauss, P L, 'The Place of Agencies in Government: Separation of Powers and the Fourth Branch' 84 *Columbia Law Review* (1984)

Stumpf, C A, 'The Introduction of the Euro to States and Territories outside the European Union' 28 *European Law Review* (2003)

Summer, M, 'Banking Regulation and Systemic Risk' 14 *Open Economies Review* (2003)

Svensson, L E O, 'Inflation Forecast Targeting: Implementing and Monitoring Inflation Targets' 41 *European Economic Review* (1997)

Svensson, L E O, 'Inflation Targeting as a Monetary Policy Rule' 43 *Journal of Monetary Economics* (1999)

Symposium, 'Administering the Administrative State' 57 *University of Chicago Law Review* (1990)

Symposium on Administrative Law, 'The Uneasy Constitutional Status of Administrative Agencies' 36 *American University Law Review* (1987)

Taylor, J B, 'Sovereign Debt Restructuring: A U.S. Perspective', remarks at the conference on *Sovereign Debt Workouts: Hopes and Hazards?* at the Institute for International Economics, April 2002, Washington DC, available at <http://www.ustreas.gov/press/releases/po2056.htm> (2002)

Taylor, M, *Twin Peaks: A Regulatory Structure for the New Century* (Centre for the Study of Financial Innovation, 1995)

The World Bank, 'Judicial Reform' in *Legal and Judicial Reform*, available at <http://www4.worldbank.org/legal/leglr/>

—— 'The Financial Sector Assessment Program', available at <http://www1.worldbank.org/finance/html/fsap.html>

Thieffry, G, 'After the Lamfalussy Report: The First Steps Towards a European Securities Commission' in Andenas, M, and Avreginos, Y (eds), *Financial Markets in Europe. Towards a Single Regulator?* (Kluwer Law International, 2003)

Thornton, H, *An Enquiry into the Nature and Effects of the Paper Credit of Great Britain* (A M Kelley, 1991, originally published in 1802)

Thygesen, N, 'The Political Economy of Financial Harmonisation in Europe' in Kremer, J, Schoenmaker, D, and Wierts, P (eds), *Financial Supervision in Europe* (Edward Elgar, 2003)

Tocqueville, A de, *Democracy in America* (Vintage Classics, 1990)

Toniolo, G, *Central Bank Co-operation at the Bank for International Settlements: 1930–1973* (Cambridge University Press, 2005)

Torrent, R, 'Whom is the European Central Bank the Central Bank of? Reaction to Zilioli and Selmayr' 36 *Common Market Law Review* (1999)

Treves, T, 'Monetary Sovereignty Today' in Giovanoli, M (ed), *International Monetary Law: Issues for the New Millennium* (Oxford University Press, 2000)

Triffin, R, *Gold and the Dollar Crisis* (Yale University Press, 1960)

Tsoukalis, L, *The New European Economy Revisited* (Oxford University Press, 1997)

United Nations, 'Resolution No 55/2 "Millennium Declaration"', adopted by the General Assembly on 8 September 2000, available at <http://www.un.org/millennium/declaration/ares552e.htm> (2000)

US Congress Joint Economic Committee, 'Report to the US Congress by the International Financial Institutions Advisory Commission', March 2000, available at <http://www.house.gov/jec/imf/ifiac.htm> (2000)

Van den Bergh, R, 'Regulatory Competition or Harmonization of Laws? Guidelines for the European Regulator' in Marciano, A, and Josselin, J-M (eds), *The Economics of Harmonizing European Law* (Edward Elgar, 2002)

Verhoeven, A, *The European Union in Search of a Democratic and Constitutional Theory* (Kluwer Law International, 2002)

Vervaele, J A E, 'Counterfeiting the Single European Currency (Euro): Towards the Federalization of Enforcement in the European Union?' 8 *Columbia Journal of European Law* (2002)

Von Hayek, F A, *Monetary Nationalism and International Stability* (reprint, Augustus M Kelly, 1971)

—— *Denationalization of Money* (Institute of Economic Affairs, 1976)

Wahlig, B, 'European Monetary Law: the Transition to the Euro and the Scope of Lex Monetae' in Giovanoli, M (ed), *International Monetary Law: Issues for the New Millennium* (Oxford University Press, 2000)

Waldman, A R, 'OTC Derivatives and Systemic Risk: Innovative Finance or the Dance into the Abyss?' 43 *American University Law Review* (1994)

Walker, J L, 'Building the Legal and Regulatory Framework', Paper presented in the Conference of the Federal Reserve Bank of Boston, 'Building an Infrastructure for Financial Stability', June 2000, available at <http://www.bos.frb.org/economic/conf/conf44/cf44_3.pdf> (4 March 2004)

Walters, A, *Sterling in Danger: The Economic Consequences of Pegged Exchange Rates* (Fontana Collins, in association with the Institute of Economic Affairs, 1990)

Weenik, H, 'The Legal Nature of Euro Banknotes' 18 *Journal of International Banking Law and Regulation* (2003)

Weil, P, 'Toward Relative Normativity in International Law' 77 *American Journal of International Law* (1983)

Werner, P, Report to the Council and the Commission on the Realisation by Stages of Economic and Monetary Union in the Community ('Werner Report'), 8 October 1970, *Bulletin of the European Communities*, Supplement 11/1970, available at <http://aei.pitt.edu/archive/00001002>

White, L, *Free Banking in Britain: Theory, Experience, and Debate, 1800–1845* (Cambridge University Press, 1984)

Williams, M, 'Rethinking Sovereignty' in Kofman, E, and Youngs, G (eds), *Globalization: Theory and Practice* (Pinter 1996)

Williams, R C, and Johnson, G G, *International Capital Markets: Recent Developments and Short-term Prospects*, International Monetary Fund Occasional Paper No 7 (International Monetary Fund, 1981)

Williamson, J, 'What Washington Means by Policy Reform' in Williamson, J (ed), *Latin American Adjustment: How Much Has Happened?* (Institute for International Economics, 1990)

—— *What Role for Currency Boards?* (Policy Analyses No 40 in *International Economics*, Institute of International Economics, 1995)

—— 'From Reform Agenda to Damaged Brand Name' 40(3) *Finance and Development* (2003), available at <http://www.imf.org/external/pubs/ft/fandd/2003/09/pdf/williams.pdf>

—— and Kuczynski, P-P (eds), *After the Washington Consensus: Restarting Growth and Reform in Latin America* (Institute for International Economics, 2003)

Wolf, M, 'The Crushing Reality of Making the Eurozone Work', Financial Times, 8 June 2005

Wood, G E, 'Lender of Last Resort Reconsidered', *The Journal of Financial Services Research*, Vol 18, Nos 2/3, December 2000

Woolcock, S, 'Competition among Rules in the Single European Market' in Bratton, W W, McCahery, J, Picciotto, S, and Scott, C (eds), *International Regulatory Competition and Coordination : Perspectives on Economic Regulation in Europe and the United States* (Clarendon Press, 1996)

Wouters, I, 'Towards a European Securities Commission? Reflections in an International and Transatlantic Perspective' in Andenas, M, and Avreginos, Y (eds), *Financial Markets in Europe: Towards a Single Regulator?* (Kluwer Law International, 2003)

Zarazaga, C, 'Argentina, Mexico and Currency Boards: Another Case of Rules versus Discretion' *Federal Reserve Bank of Dallas Economic Review*, 4th Quarter (1995)

Zilioli, C, 'Accountability and Independence: Irreconcilable Values or Complementary Instruments for Democracy? The Specific Case of the European Central Bank' in Vandersanden, G, with de Walsche, A (eds), *Mélanges en Hommage à Jean-Victor Louis* (ULB, 2003)

—— 'The Constitution for Europe and its Impact on the Governance of the Euro' in Torres, F, Verdun, A, and Zimmerman, H (eds), *EMU and Democracy: Governance in the Eurozone* (Nomos, 2006)

—— and Selmayr, M, 'The External Relations of the Euro Area: Legal Aspects' 36 *Common Market Law Review* (1999)

—— and Selmayr, M, 'The European Central Bank: an Independent Specialized Organization of Community Law' 37 *Common Market Law Review* (2000)

—— and Selmayr, M, *The Law of the European Central Bank* (Hart Publishing, 2001)

Zuberbuhler, D, 'The Financial Industry in the 21st Century. Introduction', Speech in the Bank for International Settlements, Basel, 21 September 2000, available at <http://www.bis.org/review/rr000921c.pdf>

INDEX

531